THE

Statutes at Large;

BEING

A COLLECTION

OF ALL THE

LAWS OF VIRGINIA,

FROM THE

FIRST SESSION OF THE LEGISLATURE,

IN THE YEAR 1619.

PUBLISHED PURSUANT TO AN ACT OF THE GENERAL ASSEMBLY OF VIRGINIA, PASSED ON THE FIFTH DAY OF FEBRUARY, ONE THOUSAND EIGHT HUNDRED AND EIGHT.

VOLUME III.

BY WILLIAM WALLER HENING.

"The *Laws* of a country are necessarily connected with every thing belonging to the people of it; so that a thorough knowledge of *them*, and of their progress would inform us of every thing that was most useful to be known about them; and one of the greatest imperfections of historians in general, is owing to their ignorance of law."

Priestley's Lect. on Hist. vol. 1, pa. 149.

PHILADELPHIA:

PRINTED FOR THE EDITOR, BY THOMAS DESILVER, No. 253, MARKET STREET.

1823.

WE, Peter V. Daniel, William H. Roane, Robert G. Scott, and William Robertson, members of the executive council of Virginia, do hereby certify that the *laws* contained in the third volume of HENING's *Statutes at Large* have been, by us, examined and compared with a copy as corrected by the certificate of the examiners heretofore appointed, from which *they* were taken, by Robert G. Scott and William H. Roane, from page 1, to page 226 inclusive, by Robert G. Scott and William Robertson, from page 227 to page 481 inclusive, and by Robert G. Scott and Peter V. Daniel, from page 482 inclusive, to the end, and we have found the pages respectively examined by us, truly and accurately printed except as to the following list of errata, to the number of thirty-two.

P. V. DANIEL.
WM ROBERTSON.
ROBERT G. SCOTT.
W. H. ROANE.

ERRATA.

Page 17, line 11 from bottom, for "urniture" read "furniture" and in the same line for "fusual" read "usual"
23, line 2 from top, for "inhabitant" read "inhabitants"
30, top line, in title for "*and*" read "*an*"
35, line 10 from bottom, for "lgear" read "large"
" line 2 from bottom, for "baed" read "breed"
36, line 17 from bottom for "peson" read "persons"
" line 13 from bottom, for "this" read "his"
56, line 15 from top, insert "by" between "tobacco" and "the"
62, line 12 from bottom, for "*i*" read "*it*"
" line 11 from bottom, for "port" read "ports"
67, line 20 from top, for "aqually" read "equally"
" line 8 from bottom, for "diposed" read "disposed"
70, line 9 from bottom, for "iaken" read "taken"
77, line 12 from top, for "not" read "no"
113, line 22 from top, strike out "and" between "of" and "writs"
114, line 6 from bottom, after "ways" read "of" instead of "or"
124, line 3 from bottom, for "tithable" read "tithables"
129, line 13 from bottom, for "purposes" read "purpose"
144, line 9 from top, for "or" read "of"
155, line 12 figure from top, for "3" read "5"
180, line 22 from top, for "brought" read "bought"
184, line 8 from bottom, strike out "of" after "revisors"
186, line 17 from top, strike out "at"
187, line 21 from top, for "posts" read "ports"
188, line 18 from bottom, for "and" read "or" where it last occurs.
" bottom line, strike out "made"
189, line 10 from top, strike out "to" between "proceed" and "therein"
307, line 20 from bottom, for the second "person" read "persons"
323, line 16 from top, for "formendon" read "formedon"
456, line 18 and 19 from bottom, for "masters" read "master"
469, line 10 from bottom, for "Nansiaitico" read "Nansiattico"

PREFACE

TO THE

THIRD VOLUME OF THE STATUTES AT LARGE.

THE second volume terminated with the acts of 1682: this comprises the laws from that period, both printed and MS, to the year 1710.—In presenting this volume to the public, the Editor feels it incumbent on him to offer some apology, for the various *errata* which have appeared in this, and the preceding volume.* To those who have been in the habit of reading old MSS, no apology would be necessary:—it would be found in the labour of decyphering characters, so differently formed from those in use, at the present time; in the obliteration of many of the letters, and the difficulty of determining whether a character represented one letter or another.—Most of the *errata* noted, are merely *literals;* but even these will not hereafter appear, the Editor having gone almost entirely thro' the manuscripts.

In this volume, some very important laws will be found, which had hitherto existed only in MS. The act of 1705, prescribing the various modes of acquiring lands, under the colonial government, and which was in force to the period of the revolution, had been omitten in all our printed revisals. It will be found in this volume. (*a*) So, the first law authorising the assignment of bonds and obligations, and giving an action against the assignor, which had been omitted, is here inserted.(*b*) Many other laws, which are important in deducing the history of our Statutes, are comprised in this volume, which will be found in no other printed collection.

WILLIAM WALLER HENING.

---

* This remark was applicable to the first edition; in the present edition the errors have been corrected.

(*a*) See pa. 304.　　(*b*) See pa. 377.

LIST OF GOVERNORS

OF VIRGINIA, DURING THE PERIOD COMPRISED IN THIS VOLUME.

[*From a MS belonging to Thomas Jefferson, late President of the United States, and purchased by him from the executor of Richard Bland, decd.*]

(CONTINUED FROM VOL. 2, PAGE VIII.)

Nicholas Spencer, President.

NICHOLAS SPENCER continued President [from September, 1683,] 'till the 15th of April, 1684, on which day a commission to Francis lord Howard, dated 28th September, 35, Car. II, (1683) was read.

Lord Howard, of Effingham.

Lord Howard was not present in the General Court, after 22d April, 1687, and then Nathaniel Bacon was president: but lord Howard did not leave the country then, for he signed patents till 20th October, 1688.

Nathaniel Bacon, President.

Nathaniel Bacon continued president all April court 1690: and the 16th of October, 1690, Francis Nicholson, esq. Lieut. Governor was present.

Francis Nicholson, Lieut. Governor.

Nicholson continued Lieut. Governor till 15th October, 1692, and then he and sir Edmund Andros chief Governor, were both present, all the court. His commission dated 1st March, 4th William & Mary (169$\frac{2}{3}$.)

Sir Edmund Andros.

Sir Edmund Andros continued till 9th December, 1698, and then Francis Nicholson was chief Governor.

Francis Nicholson, Gov.

Nicholson continued till 15th August, 1705, when Edward Nott, esq. came governor.

Edward Nott.

Nott continued till August, 1706, and died; and Edmund Jenings, esq. was President.

Edmund Jennings, President.

Jennings continued president, till 23d June, 1710, and then Alexander Spotswood, esq. came in Lieut. Governor.

ATT A

Generall* Assembly,

BEGUN AT JAMES CITTY

THE SIXTEENTH DAY OF APRILL, IN THE SIX AND THIRTIETH YEARE OF THE RAIGN OF OUR SOVERAIGN LORD CHARLES THE SECOND, BY THE GRACE OF GOD OF ENGLAND, SCOTLAND, FRANCE AND IRELAND, KING, DEFENDER OF THE FAITH, &c. AND IN THE YEARE OF OUR LORD GOD, ONE THOUSAND SIX HUNDRED EIGHTY-FOUR.

Lord Howard of Effingham, governor.

ACT I.

An act for altering the time of houlding Generall Courts.

Edi. 1733 and 1752.

FOR as much as by experience, it is found very grievous and burthensome to the inhabitants of this country, that the two generall courts held for this country, in the months of September and November, are

Preamble.

☞ The preceding volume terminated with Purvis's printed collection of the laws of Virginia:—This volume commences with the laws which have been preserved in MS. and which were passed after the period embraced by Purvis.—Except Purvis, & Beverley's abridgment, the laws of Virginia existed entirely in MS. till the revisal of 1733.—Three MSS. will be used in this volume, the *Northumberland* MS. designated 'Northb MS.' the *Charles City* MS. designated 'Ch. Cit. MS.' and the *Peyton Randolph* MS. designated P. Rand. MS. The first was presented to the editor by the court of Northumberland county; for the two latter, he is indebted to the kindness of Thomas Jefferson, esqr. late President of the U. States.—In referring to the revivals of 1733, 1752 and 1769, where the title only is given: these editions will be noted opposite the title in this volume, where the act at large is inserted in either of these revisals, a similar reference will be made opposite the comment of the act.

* 'GRAND' in Northb. MS.

the one too early before tobacco comes in demand and ships arrivall into this country. And November court held in the depth of winter, and soe immediately following the other, as the suiters can scarce returne home before they are exposed, to the danger and charge of returning againe, to their great hazard and detriment, which might be prevented if the generall courts were appointed to be held but twice in one yeare, viz: The first generall court, according to a former act, made the fifth day of June, one thousand six hundred sixty six, to begin the fifteenth day of Aprill, and to hold eighteen dayes; and the second generall court to begin the fifteenth day of October, and to continue eighteen dayes and noe longer.

Terms of the general court, altered.

Bee it therefore enacted by the Governour, Councill and Burgesses of this generall assembly, and by the authority thereof, and it is hereby enacted and declared, That the first generall court in each yeare begin upon the fifteenth day of Aprill, if the same happen not upon a Sunday, and be held and continued eighteen dayes, not accounting Sundayes in the number; and the other generall court to begin upon the fifteenth day of October, if the same happen not to be on Sunday, and then on the day following, and to be held and continued eighteen dayes, not including Sundayes in the said number and noe longer, and that all and every act and acts constituteing the generall courts at any other time or times, be, and are from henceforth utterly (*a*) repealed and made voyd to all intents and purposes. Any law, custome or usage to the contrary thereof in any wise notwithstanding.

Two terms in a year.

Commencement and duration.

ACT II.

Edit. 1752.

An act for the better preservation of the Peace of Virginia, and preventing unlawfull and treasonable associations.

Edit. 1733.

Preamble, reciting an unlawful combi-

WHEREAS many evill and ill-disposed persons inhabitants of this his majesties collony and dominion of Virginia, contrary to their duty and alle-

---

Various Readings.

* The running title to the acts of this session, in the editions of 1733 and 1752 is, 'Anno tricessimo sexto Caroli secundi regis.'

(*a*) The word 'utterly,' omitted in Ch. Cit. and P. Rand MSS.

giance, on or about the first of May, in the thirty-fourth yeare of his majesties raigne, and divers other dayes, and times tumultuously and mutinously assembled and gathered together to cut up and destroy all tobacco plants, and to perpetrate the same in a trayterous and rebellious manner, with force and armes entered the plantations of many his majesties good subjects of this his collony, resolving by open force, a generall and totall destruction of all tobacco plants within this his majesties dominion, to the hazarding the subvertion of the whole government, and ruine and destruction of his majesties good subjects, if by Gods assistance, and the prudent care and conduct of the then lieutenant governour and councill, the mutineires had not been timely prevented, for which treasons and rebellions against his majesty and this his (*b*) government, some notorious actors have been indicted, convicted, and some of them executed, and suffered such paines and punishments as for their treasons and rebellions they justly deserved. Now to the end and purpose, that none of his majesties subjects may be at any time hereafter seduced by the specious pretenses of any persons, that such tumultuous and mutinous assemblyes, to cut up or destroy tobacco plants or any other the crop or labours of the inhabitants of the said collony, are but riotts and trespasses; and to the end, his majesties subjects of this his dominion, may be the better secured in their estates and possessions. The burgesses of this present generall assembly pray that it may be enacted, *And bee it enacted by the governour, councill and burgesses of this assembly*, That if any person or persons whatsoever, to the number of eight or above, being assembled together, shall at any time after the first day of June now next ensuing, intend, goe about, practice or put in use with force, unlawfully to cut, pull up or destroy any tobacco plants, either in bedds or hills, growing within the said collony, or to destroy the same, either cureing or cured, either before the same is in hogsheads or afterwards, or to pull downe, burne or destroy the houses or other places

nation to cut up and destroy all tobacco plants.

☞ This has reference to the *plant-cutting* mention'd among the historical documents at the end of the preceding volume, p. 562.

If any persons to the number of 8, or more, after the first of June, 1684, assemble together forcibly to destroy tobac. or plants, or houses;

Various Readings.

(*b*) 'The,' in Northb. MS. 'this his' in Ch. Cit. and P. Rand. MSS. and edit 1733.

where any such tobacco shall be, or to pull downe the fences or enclosures of any tobacco plants, with intent to cut up or destroy the same, (and such person or persons being commanded or required in his majesties name by the governour or other commander in chief, or any one of the councell, or one or more of the justices of the peace of the said collony, commanding and requireing such persons to disperse themselves, and peaceably to depart to their habitations) shall continue together by the space of four houres after such proclamation made, at or nigh the place where such persons shall be soe assembled; that then every such persons soe willingly assembled, in forceable manner, to doe any of the acts before mentioned (*a*) and soe continuing together as aforesaid, and being thereof lawfully convicted, shall be deemed, declared and adjudged to be traytors, and shall suffer paines of death, and alsoe loose and forfeite as in cases of high treason. *Provided always*, that noe person or persons whatsoever shall incurr the pains and penalties hereby inflicted, unlesse he or they be prosecuted and indicted thereupon, within twelve months after the offence committed, Any thing herein contained to the contrary notwithstanding.

and do not disperse within 4 hours after proclamation,

deemed traitors.

Proviso, that the prosecution be within 12 months.

ACT III.

Edi. 1733 and 1752.

An act repealing the act, concerning the pursuit of runawayes.

Act 8, of September, 1663, repealed.

WHEREAS the eighth act of assembly, made at James City the tenth day of September, one thousand six hundred sixty-three, intituled, an act concerning the pursuit of runawayes, is by experience found, very inconvenient; *Bee it therefore enacted by the governour, councill and burgesses of this general assembly, and it is hereby enacted*, That the said act and every clause, and article therein contained be, and is here repealed, to all intents and purposes, whatever.

Various Readings.

(*a*) 'Aforementioned' in Ch. Cit. and P. Rand. MSS. and edit. 1733.

ACT IV.

An act for the better supply of the country with armes and ammunition.

Edi. 1733 and 1752.

FOR the encouragement of the inhabitants of this his majesties collony and dominion of Virginia, to provide themselves with arms and ammunition, for the defence of this his majesties country, and that they may appear well and compleatly furnished when commanded to musters and other the king's service, which many persons have hitherto delayed to do, for that their arms have been imprest and taken from them.—*Be it (a) enacted by the governour, councill and burgesses of this present general assembly, and the authority thereof, and it is hereby enacted,* That all such swords, musketts, (b) pistolls, carbines, guns, and other armes and furniture, as the inhabitants of this country are already provided, or shall provide and furnish themselves with, for their necessary use and service, shall from henceforth be free and exempted from being imprest or taken from him or them, that already are provided or shall soe provide or furnish himselfe, neither shall the same be lyable to be taken by any distresse, seizure, attachment or execution, Any law, usage or custom to the contrary thereof notwithstanding.

Encouragement to provide arms and ammunition.

Arms and ammunition exempted from impressment, distress or execution.

And be it further enacted, That between this and the five and twentieth day of March, which shall be in the yeare of our Lord one thousand six hundred eighty six, every trooper of the respective counties of this country, shall furnish and supply himself with a good able horse, saddle, and all arms and (c) furniture, fitt and compleat for a trooper, and that every foot soldier, shall furnish and supply himselfe, with a sword, musquet and other furniture fitt for a soldier, and that each trooper and foot souldier, be provided with two pounds of powder, and eight pounds of shott, and shall conti-

What arms, &c. the militia to supply themselves with.

Various Readings.

(a) The word 'therefore' after 'it' in Ch. Cit. and P. Rand. MSS.

(b) The word 'musketts' omitted in Northb. MS. but inserted in Ch. Cit. and P. Rand. MSS.

(c) The words 'all arms and' omitted in Northb. MS. but inserted in Ch. Cit. and P. Rand. MS.

nually keep their armes well fixt, cleane and fitt for the king's service.

Penalty for failure.

And be it further enacted, That every trooper, failing to supply himselfe within the time aforesaid, with such arms and furniture, and not afterwards keeping the same well fixt, shall forfeite four hundred pounds of tobacco, to his majesty, for the use of the county in which the (*a*) delinquent shall live, towards the provideing of colours, drums and trumpetts therein, and every foot souldier soe failing to provide himselfe, within the time aforesaid, and not keeping the same well fixt, shall forfeit two hundred pounds of tobacco to his majesty, for the use aforesaid, and that all the militia officers of this country, take care to see the execution and due observation of this act, in their several and respective regiments, troops and companies.

Musters, when to be.

And be it further enacted by the authority aforesaid, That every collonell of a regiment within this country, shall once every yeare, upon the first Thursday in October, yearly, cause a generall muster, and exercise of the regiment under his command, or oftner if occasion shall require.

And that every captain or commander of any troop of horse or foot company, within this country, shall once at the least in every three months, muster, traine and exercise, the troop or company under his command, to the end, they may be the better fitted and enabled, for his majesties and the countryes service, when they shall be commanded thereunto.

ACT V.

Edi. 1733, 1752.

An act repealing the forty-second and forty-third act of the printed laws and for building prisons in each county, and for ascertaining rules to each prison.*

Acts 42 & 43, of the printed laws, (vol. 2, p. 76 77,) repealed.

BEE it enacted by the governour, councell and burgesses of this present general assembly, and by the authority of the same, That the forty-second act of the

Various Readings.

(*a*) 'Such' in Ch. Cit. and P. Rand. MS.

* It is not probable that Purvis's collection was printed at this time. Had it been the case, there certainly would have been some reference more distinct, than merely to the *printed* laws. This fur-

printed laws, intituled, prisons to be built in each county, And the forty-third act of the said printed laws, intituled, dwellers within the rules of any prison, not to have the benefit thereof, bee and shall be repealed, and the same and every clause and article therein, and in each of them contained, is and are hereby repealed and made null and voyd to all intents and purposes whatsoever *And be it further enacted*, That a good strong and substantiall prison, after the forme of Virginia houseing be built, and continued in each county sometime before the first of January next, by the justices of the peace in their sessions, and at the charge of each county, under penalty of being fined five thousand pounds of tobacco, and of being answerable for any escape which shall be made for want of such sufficient prison. *And bee it further enacted*, that the justices of the peace in each county be, and are hereby empowered, sometime before the said first of January to appoint, set and lay out a certaine space distance or parcell of land adjoyning or circumjacent to each prison, not exceeding eighty poles square to be a place of liberty and priviledge for each prisoner (*a*) (not committed for treason or fellony) giving bond with good security to the sherriff of the county for his true imprisonment, to walke and abide in for their health and refreshment, within which compasse, soe long as such prisoner (not committed for treason or fellony) shall remaine and continue; he shall not be adjudged to have made an escape, Any law, usage or custome to the contrary thereof notwithstanding. And for the better notifieing and makeing known the bounds of the rules, or places of liberty or priviledges to each prison belonging, *Bee it further enacted*, That the justices of each county doe sometime before the first of January next aforesaid, goe round the bounds of such rules and places of liberty and priviledges, and by some means mark out, notifie and describe the said bounds and the same bounds soe notified and described, to enter into

Prisons to be built in each county, after the form of Virginia houses.

Justices failing to be fin'd and liable for escapes.

Prison rules or bounds to be laid out

Privilege of prisoners, not committed for treason or felony.

Bond to be given.

Bounds to be marked out & recorded.

Various Readings.

nishes additional evidence that the revisal of 1661-2 was printed long before Purvis, and is the collection so often referred to, by the 'printed laws,' See note to vol 2. pa. 164, 165.

(*a*) 'Prison' in Ch. Cit. and P. Rand, MSS.

Where prisons already built, counties excused from build'g others.

and amongst the records of the county court. *Provided alwayes neverthelesse*, that all counties where such prisons are already built and standing shall be excused from building others. Any thing herein contained to the contrary notwithstanding.

ACT VI.

Edi. 1733 and 1752.

An act to repeale the act giving encouragement for Linnen and Woolen manufactuaries.

Act giv'g premiums for linen and woolen cloths repealed. (See vol. 2, p. 503.)

FOR as much as by an act, entituled, an act for encouragement of the manufacture of linnen and woollen cloth, there are certaine encouragements allowed and payable to such person and persons, as shall by due proof made according to the prescriptions and method in the said law appointed of his, her or their haveing performed the conditions therein lymitted, and soe by the said law, justly intituled to the reward therein mentioned, which said encouragements, in such manner payable, are found to be rather a charge and inconvenience, then any benefitt to the publique; the charge thereby accumulated likely to be great, and the effect a transposition of tobacco, through officers hands, and much thereof thereby exhausted; and the persons themselves to whome the encouragements are thereby due, desiring to relinquish all their claimes; and the same being soe represented to this assembly, finding sufficient encouragement by the benefitt received of their labours to promote and propagate soe beneficiall manufactures; *Bee it enacted by the governour, councell and burgesses of this present generall assembly and it is enacted by the authority aforesaid*, That the act aforesaid, with all incouragements therein allowed with all fines and penalties therein mentioned, and every clause, article and thing therein contained, giving any allowance for such lynnen and woollen manufactures and other encouragements whatsoever therein allowed, and every penalty thereby imposed, are, and shall be hereby utterly repealed and made null and voyd to all intents and purposes, The said act, or any other act or acts to the contrary thereof in any case notwithstanding.

ACT VII.

An Act for the better defence of the Country.

Edi. 1773 and 1752.

FOR the better safeguard and defence of the country then by any former act or law hath been hitherto provided, *Bee it enacted by the governour, councell and burgesses of this present generall assembly, and by the authority thereof, and it is hereby enacted,* That one act of assembly made at James Citty the 25th of Aprill, 1679, intituled, an act for defence of the country against the incurtions of the Indians, and one other act made at James Citty aforesaid, the 8th day of June, 1680, intituled, an act for the continuation of the severall fortifications and garrisons at the heads of the four great rivers, and one other act made at James Citty aforesaid, the 10th day of November, 1682, intituled, an act disbanding the present souldiers in garrison in the forts of the severall rivers, as alsoe, for the raiseing of other forces in their stead, and every of them, and every clause, article and provisoe in them, each and either of them, bee, and are hereby repealed and made null and voyd to all intents and purposes whatsoever, as if the said acts had never been made. And for the forming of a standing force for the more sure and safe guarding the frontiers, and preventing the murthers, depredations, incurtions and spoiles by the Indians, *Bee it enacted by the authority aforesaid, and it is hereby enacted,* That four troops of horsemen (each troop to contain thirty able men) be raised for the purposes aforesaid, every way well horsed and armed: viz. [Every man to have a good able horse for service, a case of pistolls, a carbine, sword and all other urniture fusuall and necessary for horse-souldiers or troopers,] one of the four troops to be raised on the upper parts of James river, one troop thereof on the upper parts of York river, one troop thereof on the upper parts of Rappahannock river, and the other troop on the upper parts of Potomack river out of such as shall voluntarily offer themselves in each river for that service; but in case the full number of thirty men compleatly mounted, armed and provided as aforesaid, cannot be raised by such as shall voluntarily offer themselves for that service, that then his ex-

Certain enumerated acts for defence of the country repealed; and a regular army provid'd

4 troops of volunteer cavalry to be raised.

How equipped.

Where to be raised.

If a sufficient number of volunteers, do not offer, the deficiency to be drafted.

cellency the governour, aud in his absence, the commander in chief for the time being, is desired (upon applycation to him made by the captain or chiefe commander of each troop) to issue forth his warrant for the raiseing soe many men (armed and appointed as aforesaid) as shall be wanting to compleat the number of thirty men by this act appointed.

Officers to nominate those under degree of captain.

And bee it enacted, That the chief officers of the militia for the upper counties, on the aforesaid rivers, out of the thirty men raised or to be raised as aforesaid, may present to his excellency the fittest and most able person to command under the captain as lieutenant of each troop, who, in the absence of the captain (occasioned by sicknesse or otherwise) is to command, lead, train and exercise the troope.

Pay of officers and privates.

And be it enacted, That the pay of each captain finding himselfe provision, ammunition, horse, armes and all other necessaries for one whole yeare, shall be ten thousand pounds of tobacco and cask, and so after that rate for a longer or shorter time, and the pay for the leiutenant for one whole yeare, finding himselfe horse, armes, ammunition, provision and all other necessaries, shall be five thousand pounds of tobacco and caske, and soe after that rate for a longer or shorter time, and the pay for every private souldier mounted, armed and provided as aforesaid, shall be three thousand pounds of tobacco and cask for one whole yeare, nd soe after that rate for a louger or shorter time, all which summes shall be paid by the country.

Troops to be muster'd every month.

And bee it further enacted, That each captain of the troops (to be appointed or commissionated by the governour) or in his absence the leiutenant shall once every month, at the least, muster, traine, exercise, instruct and discipline the troope under his command, on paine or forfeiture of being abated out of his pay for every time he shall omit the same, the summe of one thousand pounds of tobacco, unlesse occationed by sicknesse And further, that every captain, or in his absence, the leiutenant, shall once every weeke (and oftner if occasion shall require) range and scout about the heads of the rivers, for which they serve (that is to say) the forces appointed for the head of Potomack doe scout and range from the head of Potomack aforesaid, above the frontier plantations, to the head of Rap-

Penalty for neglect.

To range and scout every week.

At what places.

pahannock river; and the forces appointed for the head of Rappahannock to range from the head of Rappahannock (*a*) above the frontiere plantations to the north side of Mattapany river; the forces appointed for the heads of York river, to range from the south side of Mattapany river* (*b*) above the frontiere plantations, to Chiccahominie swamp; and the forces for the heads of James river doe range from Chiccahominie swamp, above the frontiere plantations, to the heads of Apomatack river, and in such other places as shall be most likely for the discovery of the enemy, and further observe such rules, commands and directions as from time to time, he or they shall receive from the governour, or in his absence from the chiefe commander, or other theire superior officers, under paine of looseing or being abated out of his pay for every time he shall omitt such scouting and ranging, one thousand pounds of tobacco for their disobedience, contempt or neglect, and that every souldier that shall neglect to appeare at any muster well mounted and prepared as aforesaid, shall forfeite for each time he shall soe neglect the same, the summe of (*c*) one hundred pounds of tobacco to be abated out of his pay, and for every time he shall fayle to arrange or scout, two hundred pounds of tobacco to be abated out of his pay, the one halfe of all and every which forfeitures shall be paid by the country to him or them that will informe and make due proofe thereof, before the collonel or chiefe officer of the militia next adjoyning, such informer produceing a certifficate from the collonell or chiefe officer of haveing made such proofe, which certifficate the said collonell or chiefe officer is hereby required and authorized to give. *And be it further enacted*, that upon discovery, notice or advice of the approach or attempt of an enemy, the said captain or leiutenant of the troope is hereby required to give speedy advice thereof to the governour, or in his absence to the commander in

Penalty for neglect.

Duty of offi'rs on approach of the enemy

Various Readings.

(*a*) The words 'to range from the head of Rappannock' omitted in Northb. MS. but inserted in Ch. City MS.

(*b*) The word 'river' omitted in Ch. City MS. but inserted in Northumberland MS.

(*c*) The words 'the sume of,' omitted in Ch. City MS. but serted in Northumberland MS.

chiefe for the time being, and in the mean time to attend the motion of the enemie, only unless the enemie dureing that time shall first committ some act of hostility, either in burning or in forcible entering into our houses, or by killing, maiming or carrying away any of the inhabitants, and then in such case to engage and destroy them, if he see cause, and in all things to observe and execute such orders and commands, as he shall from time to time receive from the governour, or in his absence from the commander in chiefe for the time being. And that for the better manageing and ordering their horses and makeing them fitt for service, noe souldier presume to use or bring to service any other horse than that which shall be first mustered and approved of, of which the captain is to take such perticuler notice, that he may know the same horse againe. Except where such horse as first past muster, be, by some accident or disease, made unfitt for service, in which case such souldier, shall provide himselfe of another able horse, in his stead, which he is likewise not to part with, unless for his first horse againe. And to the end that the said troopes may att all times be the more speedily got together the captain of each troop is to take especiall care that his troop be quartered, neare the frontieres and heads of each river, and as near together as possible they may. And for encouragement of officers and souldiers in each troop. *Bee it enacted*, that in case any souldier shall loose his horse or armes, or any part thereof, in any actual engagement against the enemie, he shall be allowed the vallue thereof by the country, he makeing proofe of the reall vallue before the county court next adjoining. And farther, that each such souldier dureing the time of his service, be exempted and excused from the payment of publique levies.

Horses not to be changed, except in cases of accident.

Troops to be quartered near the frontiers.

Horses lost in actual service to be paid for.

And bee it further enacted, That upon the approach or first discovery of an enemie the officers of the militia next adjoyning, shall imediately put the militia under their comand, in a posture of defence and readinesse, for such further service as shall be commanded them by the governour as the emergencys shall require, which said auxillaries (if at any time of imminent danger they are drawne out for the aiding or reinforcing of the troopes of thirty men by this act provided) and

Militia, when to be called out.

shall continue in such service above (a) the space of six dayes, (which six dayes they shall serve at their owne charge) That then and in such cases, each person, if a horseman, well mounted, armed and furnished, and finding himselfe ammunition and provision as aforesaid, shall have the like allowance, for such further time he shall serve as a trooper or horseman, hereby this act appointed have for the like time, and every foot souldier well armed, and finding himselfe armes, ammunition and provision after the rate of two thousand pounds of tobacco and cask per annum.

Pay of militia continued in service over 6 days.

And for the more easy and expeditious performing of any services hereby injoyned, or to be injoyned to the officers and souldiers aforesaid, *Bee it enacted*, that there be deposited into the hands of collonell George Mason, collonell John West, collonel John ffarrar and captain George Taylor, the summe of twelve hundred pounds of tobacco each. To the end the said collonell Mason, collonel West, collonell ffarrar and captain George Taylor, shall each of them buy (b) build or provide an able boate for the transporting the souldiers and horses over the severall rivers and places hereafter mentioned, vizt: One boat for James river to be placed and kept at such places as the chief officers of the militia for the county of Henrico shall appoint, one other boate to be placed and kept at such place on Pamonkey river as the chiefe officers for the militia, for the county of New-Kent shall appoint, and one other boate to be kept at such place on Ocquan (c) river as the chiefe officers of the militia for the county of Stafford shall appoint, and one other boate to be kept at such place on Rappahannock river, as the chiefe officers of the militia for the county of Rappahannock shall appoint.

Boats to be provided by certain persons.

Where deposited.

Provided alwayes, and it is the true intent and meaning of this act, that the twenty troopers by the former act appointed, and at present in service at the heads of each river, shall continue and be in pay, and be paid as formerly, untill such time as the troopers

Troops raised by a former act to be continued in service.

Various Readings.

(a) The word 'above' omitted in North. MS. but inserted in Ch. City MS.
(b) The word 'buy' omitted in Northb. MS. but inserted in Ch. City MS.
(c) This world is spelt 'Ocquan' in all the MSS.

and to be preferred in new enlistments.

by this act appointed to be raised, be fully formed and compleated; and *Provided alsoe*, that such and soe many of the said twenty troopers, now in service, as shall be willing (and against whome there is noe just exceptions) to be lysted in the new troopes, by this act to be raised, shall be lysted, preferred and accepted of before any other as part of such troop and troops, and to be paid rateably, according to the allowance in and by this act specified

Militia officers in Accomack and Northb. to provide for security of those counties.

And. be it further enacted, That upon the incursion, invasion or inroad of any Indian enemie, into either of the counties of Accomack or Northampton, or into any other county or counties in this country, it shall and may be lawfull to and for the militia officers of both; or either, or any of the said counties (as the emergency or occasion shall require) to put the souldiers under their command, into a posture of war and defence for the safeguard of the counties, and if they shall happen to continue in such service, above the space if six dayes (which six dayes they shall serve at their owne charge) that then, and in such case, each person (if a horseman, well mounted, armed and furnished, and finding himselfe ammunition and provision as aforesaid, shall have the like allowances for such further time as he shall serve as a trooper or horseman by this act appointed, shall have for the like time, and every foot souldier, well armed, and finding himselfe armes, ammunition and provision as aforesaid, after the rate of two thousand pounds of tobacco and caske per annum as aforesaid This act to continue in force three yeares and noe longer.

Pay of militia over 6 days.

Pensions allowed wounded soldiers.

And bee it further enacted by the authoritie aforesaid, That if it shall happen that any of the souldiers by this act appointed shall be wounded, maimed or disabled in his majesties and the countryes service, that then the person or persons soe wounded, shall be carefully provided for, and his cure endeavoured at the charge of the country, and the person or persons continueing maimed or disabled, shall have an annuall pension from the country for and towards his or theire maintenance.

ACT VIII.

Edi. 1733 and 1752.

An act for lessening the levies by poll, and laying an imposition upon Liquors.

Duty of three pence a gallon imposed on wine, brandy, rum & spirits imported.

FOR the abateing and takeing of the greateness of the leavies and taxes laid by the poll on the inhabitant of this his majesties dominion of Virginia as formerly & at present is used, and for the raiseing of money for building a Courthouse and place of judicature for the sitting of the generall court and meeting of the generall assembly, and to and for such other uses, intents and purposes as shall hereafter be appointed by the governour, councell, and burgesses of the generall assembly, and to noe other use, intent or purpose whatsoever, *Bee it enacted* by the governour, councell and burgesses of this present generall assembly and the authority thereof, and it is hereby enacted, that for every gallon of wine of all sorts whatsoever, brandy, rum or any other spirits imported into this collony (except what shall come directly from England) from and after the twenty-ninth day of September now next ensueing, there shall be paid, or well and sufficiently secured to his majesty, his heires and successors for the defraying of the publique charge and expences of this his majesties dominion, by the owner or importer thereof, before the same and any part thereof be exposed to sale, the summe of three pence upon every gallon, of all or any the said liquors. And for the better and more true collecting the said duty or imposition. *Bee it enacted*, that all masters of any ship, barque or vessell, shall at his or their first arrivall, or before he breake bulk, or sell or dispose of any of the wine, brandy, rum, or other spirits by him imported, make entry with the collector or collectors, by this act, for that purpose to be appointed, of all such wine, brandy, rum and spirits as shall be on board his shipp or vessell, or by him imported, and pay the duty, or secure the same, as aforesaid, on paine of forfeiting his ship or vessell, with all her gunns, tackle, ammunition, furniture and apparell; the one third part thereof to his majestie for the publique use of the country, one third part thereof to the governour, and the other third part thereof to him or them that will informe, to be recovered by action of

Masters of vessels to report to collectors.

Penalty, forfeiture of vessel and furniture.

debt, bill, plaint, or information in any court of judicature of this country, in which noe essoigne or wager of law shall be allowed.

Gov'r & council to appoint collectors.

And bee it further enacted, That the governour for the time being, with the advice of the councill, shall be, and hereby is empowered, from time to time, and at all times to order, direct and appoint such, and soe many collectors and other officers, as allsoe such wayes, methods, courses and orders for the collecting of the said duty as to them shall seem best. *Provided* that this act shall not extend to charge any the inhabitants of this dominion, tradeing and importing any the liquors aforesaid, that doe bona fide properly and solely belong to them, into this country in their owne shipps and vessells, built in, or properly belonging to Virginia, with the imposition aforesaid, but that they are, and shall be exempted and free of the said imposition, or any claim or demand for the same. And for prevention of frauds that may be used in colouring and concealing of wine, rum, brandy and other liquors in this act mentioned, imported in vessells belonging to Virginia, upon pretence the same doth belong to the inhabitants, proprietors and owners of this country,

Not to extend to inhabitants import'g their own liquors, in their own vessels.

Report to be made on oath.

Bee it enacted by the autherity aforesaid, That every person and persons to whome any of the wine, rum, brandy, or any of the liquors in this act mentioned shall be consigned, or who shall receive the same, shall upon his or their oath (if thereunto required) before the collector, truely declare the quantity of any the said liquors imported, or any part thereof that doth bona fide, really and solely belong to him or them.

Collectors to account to auditors of Virginia.

Provided alsoe, that all and every summe and summes of mony raised, or to be raised, by vertue of the imposition aforesaid be constantly accompted for by the collector thereof to the auditor of Virginia for the time being, and by him to the governour, councell and burgesses of the generall assembly, and converted to the uses by them directed according to the true intent and meaning of this act, and to or for noe other use, intent and purpose whatsoever. This act to continue in force for three yeares from the twenty ninth day of September aforesaid, and noe longer.

ACT IX.

An act for the Publique Leavie.

Edi. 1733 & 1752

Taxes for the year 1684

BEE it enacted by the Governour, Councell and Burgesses of this present generall assembly, and the authority thereof, That the summe of forty and seaven pounds of tobacco be paid by every tythable person within this his majesties collony and dominion of Virginia for the defraying and payment of the publique charge of the country, being the publique leavy for this present yeare, and that it be paid by the collectors of the severall counties, to the severall persons to whome it is proportioned by this present generall assembly; and if it shall happen that there shall be more tithables in any county than the present leavy is layd on, then such county to have creditt for soe much to the ease of the county, and if there shall happen to be lesse, then such county shall beare the losse.

Signed by Lord EFFINGHAM, *Governor.*
EDWARD HILL, *Speaker.*

Copia,
THO. MILNER, Cl. Assembly.

☞ The signature of governor and speaker from note to edit. of 1733 and 1752.

NORTHUMBERLAND COUNTY*

To 624 tythables at 47 per poll - -	29328
To Sallary - - - - - - -	02666
To Mr. Secretary Atourney of the Lord Culpepper	09601
To Capt. George Brent, in part - -	17061
	29328
To the Clerk of the Assembly for the acts Copies and petitions assigned to Mr. Knight for the vallue received.	500

THO. MILNER, Cl. Assembly.

May the 16th, 1684.

* This account raised against the county of Northumberland, for its proportion of the levies or taxes, and the apportionment of them among the several creditors, is to be found only in the Northumb. MS. and is conclusive proof that the laws were furnished in MS. to that county, at the date of their passage.

BY THE HOUSE OF BURGESSES

Upon reading a Report from the Committee of Propositions and Greivances, viz:

Persons holding lands for life of themselves, wives, or others, entitled to vote for burgesses in the county where the lands lie.

RESOLVED, That it is the undoubted right of every person who holds lands, tenements or hereditaments for his owne life, for the life of his wife, or for the life of any other person or persons to vote in Election of Burgesses for the county where such lands, tenements, &c. doe lye

Test,

THO MILNER, Cl. Assembly.

APRILL THE 26TH, 1684.

His Excellency, amongst other things was thus addrest by the House of Burgesses:

Memorial of the inhabit'ts of the Northern Neck to the governor, praying that they may have their lands secured to them by patent, as the rest of the inhabitants of Virginia.

☞ The evils here comp'nd of arose from the grant to lord Culpeper; concerning which, see 'Historical Documents' at the end of this & the preceding volume.

AND whereas the inhabitants of Northumberland county, and other the inhabitants of Potomack neck, within this his majesties dominion, have taken up divers tracts of land, and have been at great charge to seate, save and defend the same, and have possessed the same many yeares, and have since their takeing up the same, made their applycation at divers times, according to the usuall custome in such cases used by the rest of the inhabitants of this dominion for the obteigning pattents for the said land, and yett have not obteined any, whereby the said lands might be secured to them the said inhabitants, their heires and assignes. The house of burgesses therefore in behalfe of the said inhabitants of Northumberland county, and the other aforementioned, doe humbly pray your excellency that they may have their severall parcells of land by them taken up, seated, held and possessed as aforesaid, and what lands shall be by them, or any of them hereafter taken up, granted and confirmed to them and their posteritie by pattent under the same conditions as his most sacred majesties subjects of the other parts of this his dominion doe enjoy their lands from his majestie.

To which his excellency was pleased to returne this answer Aprill the 29th.

The governers answer.

Whereas it is presented as a grieviance to the Northerne neck that they are under uncertaine conditions as to their lands, pattents not issuing to them as to other inhabitants of this dominion. His majestie out of his great goodnesse, grace and favour, has bin pleased to take the same under his royall consideration, in which I doe dayly expect to receive from England, and by the arrivall of the next ship, doe hope, shall receive such directions as may assure the inhabitants of the Northerne neck, that their lands will be confirmed unto them under the same tenures as the rest of his majesties subjects of this collony held their lands, therefore, cannot take this to be a suitable time to make any representation of it to his majestie, least we should seem to anticipate the intentions of his majesties goodnesse to us, but in case matters should soe intervene, that this concerne between this and the meeting of the next generall assembly bee not commoded, myselfe and the councill will then readily joyne with the house of burgesses in a fitt representation of the same to his majestie.

THO. MILNER, Cl. Assembly.

ATT A

Generall Assembly,

Begun at James Citty

Lord Effingham gov'nor.

THE FIRST DAY OF OCTOBER, 1685, AND IN THE FIRST YEARE OF THE RAIGN OF OUR SOVERAIGN LORD KING JAMES THE SECOND, OF ENGLAND, SCOTLAND, FRANCE & IRELAND, DEFENDER OF THE FAITH, &c AND THENCE PROROGUED BY SEVERALL PROROGATIONS TO THE 20TH DAY OF OCTOBER, 1686.*

These following acts and lawes were made, viz:

ACT I.

An additionall Act about runawayes.

Edi. 1733 and 1752. Act 1, of Oct. 1670, contin'd with amendments.

BEE *it enacted by the governour, councell and burgesses of this generall assembly, and the authority thereof, and it is hereby enacted,* That the 1st act of assembly made at James Citty the 3d of October, 1670, entituled an act concerning runawayes be continued and confirmed with these following alterations and

---

* The commencement of the acts of this session precisely agrees in all the MSS. of this period.—In the editions of 1733 and 1752, it is, 'At a General Assembly, begun at James City, (a) the first 'day of October, in the first year of the reign of our sovereign 'lord James II. by the grace of God, of England, Scotland, France 'and Ireland, king, defender of the faith, &c. and prorogued to 'the second day of November following, and thence continued by 'several prorogations, to the twentieth day of October, 1686.'

(a) The assembly met at this time, and being the same day prorogued to the 2d day of November following, William Kendal was chosen speaker; and after sitting some time, several bills were prepared and offered to the governor, but none passed.

[*Note to Edi.* 1733 & 1752.]

amendments. That every certificate for takeing up any one or more servant or servants runaway from his or her master or mistress before the same be admitted into the assembly for allowance shall make mention of their (*a*) master or mistriss, their proper name and sir name, the county where they dwell, time of takeing up the said servant and distance of place where taken up from the dwelling plantation of such servants master or mistriss, together with the proper name and sirname of such servant, and at the same sessions of assembly when such certificate shall be allowed, the like sum be assest upon the master or mistrisss of such runaway servant or servants for which he or she shall be reimbursed by the service of such delinquent servant, according as by the aforesaid act is provided for reimbursement of the publique; and that all such certificates come proved from the county courts, as all other claimes are enjoyned to be brought to the assembly for allowance.

Certificates for apprehending runaways, what to specify.

Expences reimbursed by servants.

ACT II.

An Act declaring Maryland and North Carolina debts pleadable.

Edi. 1733 and 1752.

BEE *it enacted by the governour, councell and burgesses of this generall assembly, and the authoritie thereof, and it is hereby enacted,* That all debts contracted, or to be contracted in Maryland or North Carolina are, and shall be recoverable in Virginia in equall manner and by the same lawfull wayes and meanes, as though the same were or had been contracted in Virginia, Any law, statute or usage heretofore to the contrary notwithstanding.

Debts contracted in Maryl'd or N Carolina recoverable in Virginia.

☞See ante volume 1, pa. 189, foreign debts not recoverable, unless contracted for goods imported.

Various Readings.

*. The running title to the acts of this session, in edition 1733 is, 'Anno secundo Jacobi secundi regis.'

(*a*) 'The' Ch. City MS. 'their' in Northb. MS.

ACT III.

Edi.1733 and 1752.

An act reviveing the act entituled, and act for the advancement of manufactures of the growth of this country, &c.

Act 12, of November, 1682, for encouragement of manufactures, revived.

BEE *it enacted by the governour, councell and burgesses of this general assembly, and the authoritie thereof, and it is hereby enacted,* That the 12th act of assembly made at James Citty the 10th day of November, 1682, entituled an act for the advancement of manufactures of the growth of this country, and for the better and more speedy payment of debts and levies be revived, and that the same doe continue in force three yeares from the end of this session, and after that to the end of the next session of assembly.

ACT IV.

Edi.1733 and 1752.

An act repealing the 17th act of assembly, made the 8th day of June 1680.

Act of 8th of June, 1680, restraining the striking of fish at certain periods, repealed.

BEE *it enacted by the Governour, Councill and Burgesses of this generall assembly, and the authoritie thereof, and it is hereby enacted,* That the act entituled, an act restraining strikeing and killing fish at unusual times, made at James City the 8th day of June 1680, be from henceforth repealed, and the same is hereby repealed to all intents and purposes.

ACT V.

Edi.1733 and 1752.

An act ascertaining days for Courts in Accomack County.

Court days of Accomack county.

BEE *it enacted by the governour, councell and burgesses of this general assembly, and the authoritie thereof, and it is hereby enacted,* That the court dayes for Accomack County for the time to come, be annually as hereafter followeth, viz: The 3d Tuesday in June, the 3d Tuesday in September, the 3d Tuesday in November, the 3d Tuesday in December, the 3d Tuesday in ffebruary, and the 3d Tuesday in March, and that the said dayes be constantly observed, held and kept as court dayes annually for the time to come, Any former law, usage or custome to the contrary hereof notwithstanding.

ACT VI.

An act regulateing the tare of Tobacco Hogsheads.

Edi. 1733 and 1752.

Preamble.

WHEREAS great abuses, frauds and deceits are dayly practiced by coveteous persons for their own singular lucre and gaine in the unreasonable weights of tobacco hogsheads, commonly past away at a much lighter, and more moderate tare then they really weigh, *Bee it enacted by the governour, councell and burgesses of this generall assembly and the authority thereof, and it is hereby enacted*, That for the prevention of the like unjust practices in time to come, noe planter or planters, or other persons whatsoever, being and abideing in this country, from and after the 10th day of September next, shall pack, pay away, or put to sale any tobacco or tobaccoes whatsoever, in any sort of caske whatsoever but what shall be marked or branded, according as hereafter shall be exprest by such cooper or coopers, artificer or artificers as shall sett up and make the same.

All tobacco hogsheads to be branded by the maker.

How to be branded

And be it alsoe enacted by the authoritie aforesaid, and it is hereby enacted, That all and every cooper or coopers, or other persons whatsoever that will either by himselfe or his owne servants to his use, exercise and practice the makeing and setting up of all or any sort of tobacco casques from and after the said 10th day of September next, shall and doe procure and provide certaine marks or brands for his or their proper and (*a*) peculiar use, that is to say the two first letters of his or their proper name and sirname, and figures sufficient to mark or brand the weight of every respective tobacco caske made and sett up, to be provided by all and every such cooper or coopers, planter or plan-

---

Various Readings.

(*a*) 'Or' in Ch. City MS. 'and' in Northb. MS.

ters that will either by themselves or their owne servants make and sett up such caske as aforesaid, and with the said marks or brands as is aforesaid upon the head and bulge of every tobacco caske put the two first letters of their proper name and sirname, together with the exact and just (*a*) weight or tare of every such tobacco caske, as either they or any of them shall afterwards undertake to sett up, to the intent the true weight of every tobacco caskue may be knowne. And that every such cooper, planter or other person or persons as is aforesaid, that after the said 10th day of September next, shall either voluntarily neglect to put his proper mark on every respective tobacco caske at the makeing thereof, or willfully place an unjust weight or tare thereupon, whereby any person afterwards buying or receiving the same, shall or may be defrauded and wronged contrary to the form and intent of this act, shall for every such offence, and for every tobacco caske wanting such marks, or any of them as this act requires, forfeite and pay five hundred pounds of tobacco and cask, one moyety thereof to our Soveraign Lord the King, his heires and successors, for and towards the better support of this government and the contingent charges thereof, and the other moyety to him or them that shall informe and sue for the same in any court of record within this his majesties dominion of Virginia, by bill, information, plaint or other action, wherein noe essoign, protection or wager in law shall be allowed.

Penalty for not branding or putting a false weight on.

Penalty for packing tobacco in casks not truly branded.

And be it alsoe further enacted by the authoritie aforesaid, and it is hereby enacted, That all and every planter or planters or other persons whatsoever which shall either pack with intent to pay away or put to sale, or shall directly pay away or put to sale any tobacco or tobaccoes whatsoever, from and after the said 10th day of September next, in any other caske whatsoever but what are really marked according to the forme and intent of this act, shall for every such offence, and for every tobacco caske wanting the same forfeit and pay five hundred pounds of tobacco and caske to and for the uses aforesaid and to be recovered in manner aforesaid.

Various Readings.

(*a*) The words 'and just' omitted in Northb. MS. but inserted in Ch. City MS.

And be it further enacted by the authoritie aforesaid, and it is hereby enacted, That all and every purchaser and (*a*) receiver of any tobacco or tobaccoes in caske soe marked as aforesaid, shall and doe receive and accept the same at the particular tares thereon placed and putt. And that for every hogshead soe purchased or received, the buyer or receiver shall pay and allow to the respective seller or payer away as a consideration in vallue thereof thirty pounds of tobacco and no more. Any law, usage, statute heretofore to the contrary notwithstanding. Purchasers to take tobac. at the tares marked on the casks.

Provided alwayes, and it is the true intent and meaning of this act, That all sherriffes or other collectors of the publique dues, shall pay and allow to the planter for caske, after the rate of eight per cent, according as by law is already established. Allowance.

Provided alsoe, and it is the true intent and meaning of this act, that all and every court of judicature within this his majesties dominion, before whom any information of the breach of this law shall be brought, shall and are hereby impowered to consider what any tobacco hogshead after it hath lain (*b*) sometime packt, may by the moisture of the weather, or the tobacco therein packt increase in waight and give judgment accordingly. Any thing in this act to the contrary hereof notwithstanding. This act to continue in force three yeares from and after the 10th day of September next, and noe longer. Courts to allow for variation in weights.

ACT VII.

An act declareing the 107th act of Assembly, made the 23d day of March 1661-2, to be in force.

Edi. 1733 & 1752.

WHEREAS severall doubts have arisen, and doe dayly arise whether the 107th act made at James Citty the 23d day of March, 1661-2, entituled, noe seconds or slips, be not repealed by a later act of assembly made at James City the 29th of September, Preamble.

Various Readings.

(*a*) 'And' in Northb. MS. 'or' in Ch. City MS.
(*b*) 'Lain' in Northb. MS. 'bin' in Ch. City MS.

1664, entituled, an act for liberty to plant and divers persons, doe thereupon endeavour to excuse as well their tending such seconds and slips as their packing, selling and sending away ground leaves and other trash with the notion and colour of being suffered to make the benefitt of their labour, when indeed noe such trash was thereby ever intended to be permitted and allowed.

Act 107, of March 1661-2 revived and continued.

Bee it enacted by the governour, councell and burgesses of this general assembly, and the authority thereof, and it is hereby enacted, That the said 107th act of assembly made at James Citty the 23d day of March, 1661-2, entituled, noe seconds or slips, be now continued in full force, power and vertue, with this alteration and amendment, that from and after this session of assembly every person or persons that shall be found guilty of breach of the said law, or any branch thereof, shall for such offence forfeit, suffer and pay such forfeitures, penalties and fines, as is therein mentioned and ordained to be forfeited, payd and suffered; one moyety to our Soveraigne Lord the King, his heires and successors for and towards the better support of the government of this his majesties dominion of Virginia and the contingent charges thereof, the other moyety to him or them that shall informe or sue for the same in any court of record within this his majesties dominion of Virginia, by byll, information, plaint or other action, wherein noe essoigne, protection or wager in law shall be allowed

Penalties for breach of that law.

Provision against making trash tobacco.

And for the better prevention of makeing such trash tobaccoes, whereby his majestie is much injured in his customes, and many frauds are put upon merchants and others in England, by reason that such seconds, slips and late planted tobaccoes, not having sufficient time to come to full growth and maturity, the same proves in generall to be damaged by the greenness, thinness and other ill qualities thereof, although noe other wett or moisture then what it hath in its owne naturall case come to the same, and by reason of such damage the importer thereof payes little or noe custome for it. And yett the said tobacco being cutt and mixed with stalks is commonly put to sale at underrates, and thereby the commoditie in general much undervalued and reduced to soe low a price in this country, that many planters are, and will be by reason thereof compelled to leave of planting tobacco, and to employ themselves about husbandry, and in makeing and improveing severall manufactures, with which this country hath been alwayes heretofore furnished from England.

Bee it therefore further enacted by the authority aforesaid, and it is hereby enacted, That noe tobaccoes be planted or re-planted after the last day of June annually, for the time to come, and that whoever shall, directly or indirectly plant or re-plant, or cause to be planted or re-planted any tobacco after the said last day of June, shall for such offence forfeit and pay ten thousand pounds of tobacco to the uses aforesaid, to be recovered in manner aforesaid. No tobacco to be planted or re-plant'd after last of June.

And for as much as severall persons strip the stalkes out of the leafe of theire tobaccoes in this country, and then afterwards ship the said tobacco stalkes for England, with intention to defraud his majesty of his duty here and customs there, when it doth arrive, and the price of tobacco by that practice alsoe further leasened and diminished.

Be it therefore further enacted by the authority aforesaid, and it is hereby enacted, That whosoever shall ship any tobacco stalks, from which the leafe has been stript and taken away for exportation out of this country, shall for every pound of such tobacco stalkes, forfeit and pay fifty pounds of tobacco to the uses aforesaid, to be recovered in manner aforesaid. Penalty for shipp'g tobacco stalks from which the leaf has been stript.

ACT VIII.

An act for the better improveing the breed of Horses.

Edi. 1733 and 1752.

FOR as much as the breed of lgear and strong horses in this country, will not only extend to the great help and defence of the same, but alsoe prove of great use and advantage to the inhabitants thereof, which now is much decayed and impair'd by reason that small ston'd horses, of low stature and value, be not only suffered to pasture and feed in our woods and other waste grounds, but alsoe to cover and leap mares feeding there, whereof cometh a numerous beed to the little profit but great damage of this country, and will Preamble.

farther encrease to the detriment thereof, unlesse some effectuall remedy be speedily provided to prevent the same. ffor prevention therefore of soe great an evill, and for the encrease and breed of better and stronger horses hereafter to be had in this collony.

Pen'ty for suffering *stoned* horses, of two years of age, and under 13 *handfulls* high to run at large

Bee it enacted by the Governour, Councell and Burgesses of the General Assembly and by the authoritie thereof, and it is hereby enacted, That noe person or persons whatsoever after the last day of July, which shall be in the yeare of our Lord 1687, shall have or put to feed into or upon any woodland grounds, marshes or other waste grounds, not haveing a sufficient fenee about the same, any ston'd horse or horses, being of the age of two yeares, and not being of the height of therteen hand full and an halfe, to be measured from the lowest part of the hoofe of the forefoot, unto the highest part of the wither, and every hand full to contain four inches of the standard, upon the penalty and forfeiture of such horse or horses, or four hundred pounds of tobacco and cask for every such horse which shall be soe found in or upon any such woodland, ground, marshes or other waste grounds at any time after the said last day of July, which shall be in the said year of our Lord, 1687, contrary to the true intent and meaning of this act; and it shall be lawfull to every person or persons that shall find any such horse or horses, contrary to the form of this act to seize the same in manner and form following, that is to say: the said person or pesons soe finding any horse or horses contrary to this act, in any woodland, grounds, marshes or other waste grounds, not having a sufficient fence about the same, shall forthwith, after this or their takeing up such horse or horses soe found, goe unto some one or other of his majesties justices for the peace for that county, haveing also with him or them such horse or horses as he or they shall take up, and before him make proof by his or their own corporall oathes, and another single testimony at the least, that he or they did find and take up such ston'd horse or horses as is aforesaid, running in such woodland, grounds, marshes or other waste grounds as is aforesaid. And that after such sufficient proof made, the said justice of the peace is hereby desired and required, then and there before him to cause the said horse or horses to be measured, and if it be soe found

How such *stoned* horses may be seized and disposed of.

that the said horse or horses be contrary to this act, and the said justice grant his certificate thereof, that then it shall be lawful to every such person or persons to chalenge and seize the said horse or horses, and every of them to his own use, as his owne proper goods and chattles for ever, without interruption, vexation, suit or trouble of the owner or owners of them, or of any other persons.

Notice of such seizure, how to be given.

Provided alwayes, and it is the true intent and meaning of this act, That every person or persons that shall soe find and take up such horse or horses as is aforesaid, and shall receive certificate thereof in manner and form as is aforesaid, shall and do forthwith give open notice and knowledge thereof, by setting up his or their note or notes, and therein expressing the mark, colour and brand of such horse or horses as he or they shall soe find and take up, at the court-house door of that county, and parrish churche of that place. *Provided alsoe*, that whatsoever owner or owners of such horse or horses soe found in any wood land, grounds, marshes or other wast grounds as aforesaid, shall or doth within two months after such sufficient and open publication, as is above required and recited, come to the person or persons who have according to this act, soe found and took up his or their horse or horses, and for every particular horse of his or theires soe taken up, shall tender to such person or persons four hundred pounds of tobacco and caske to be immediately payd, or well secured to be payd at the next succeeding crop, such owner or owners shall thereby ipso facto recover and redeem all and every such horse or horses from the penalties and forfeitures, that every such like horse or horses, are otherwaies lyable to by vertue of this act. Any thing in this act heretofore contained to the contrary thereof notwithstanding. This act to continue in force 7 yeares from and after the last day of July 1687, and noe longer.

How such horse may be regained by the owner.

ACT IX.

Edi. 1733 and 1752.

An act repealing the 7th act of assembly made at James Cittie the 16th day of Aprill, 1684.

Act 7 of April 1684, repealed.

BEE *it enacted by the Governour, Councell and Burgesses of this generall assembly, and the authority thereof, and it is hereby enacted,* That the 7th act of assembly made at James Citty the 16th day of Aprill, 1684, entituled, an act for the better defence of the country, be, and stand repealed from and after the last day of November next, to all intents and purposes. And that his excellency the governour be desired forthwith to disband the officers and souldiers settled by the said law at the heads of the four great rivers.

Soldiers to be disbanded.

ACT X.

Edi. 1733 and 1752.

An act continueing the Imposition upon Liquors.

Act 8 of April 1684, imposing a duty on liquors, continued.

BEE *it enacted by the Governour, Councell and Burgesses of this General Assembly and the authoritie thereof, and it is hereby enacted,* That the 8th act of assembly, made at James Citty the 16th day of Aprill 1684, entituled, an act for lessening the levies by the pole, and laying an imposition on liquors be, and is hereby continued in force for three yeares from and after the 29th day of September, which shall be in the year 1687.

ACT XI.

Edi. 1733 and 1752.

An act for raiseing a public leavy.

Pnblic taxes.

BE *it enacted by the governour, councell and burgesses of this generall assembly, and the authority thereof, and it is hereby enacted,* That the sume of one hundred and four pounds of tobacco he paid by every tithable person within this his majesties colonie and dominion of Virginia, for the defraying and payment of the publique charge of the country, being the publique levie from Aprill 1684, to this present time, and that it be paid by the collectors of the severall counties to the severall persons to whom it is proportioned by this present generall assemble.* To be paid to county creditors.

A true copie, Test,

ROBERT BEVERLY, Cl. Assm.

Anno 1686—*Northumberland County Dr.* *Tob.* Northumberland county's proportion of the levies or taxes. How appropriated.

By 702 tythables at 104lbs per pole	73008
To be paid, viz.	
To John Bridgman	00200
To sallary	06637
To capt George Brent for himselfe and souldiers . . .	66170
	73008

Test, ROBERT BEVERLEY, Cl. Assem'ly.

Ditto, Dr. To Robert Beverley, Cl. Ass.

Clerk's fee, for a copy of the laws.

To copie of the lawes	00300
To copie of proportion of levy	00050
	00350

Various Readings.

* This act is omitted in the Northumberland MS. but is inserted in the Ch. City MS. where it is thus subscribed:

'From folio 120 vera copia
'Test FRANCIS PAGE, Cl. of the 'House of Burgesses.'

In the Northumberland MS. the laws of this session are attested, as above, by 'Robert Beverley, Clk. Assembly.' Now it is evident that, in this instance, the Northb. MS. is most correct; because we not only find from the letter of the king, subjoined to the acts of this session, that the removal of Robert Beverley, as clerk, was not required till August, 1686, a period too late to have had its effect at this session, but it appears from another MS. in the possession of the editor, that Francis Page was not appointed clerk of the house of burgesses by the governor and council, under the new arrangement of king, till the 25th of April, 1668, [See *Bland* MS. pa. 507] so that it was impossible for Francis Page to have attested the acts of the session of 1686, as of the time when they passed.

NOVEMBER THE 15th, 1686.

Gentlemene,

Governor's letter to the county of Northumberland.

☞ In the margin of the MS. it is, 'His excellency's letter to this co'ty court.'

THIS letter of mine to you, is to wait upon his majesties command to mee, relateing to the extraordinary proceedings of the house of burgesses, in the yeare sixteen hundred eighty and five, how his majestie resents those proceedings, his majesties letter of which you have here the copie will plainly demonstrate, which you are to cause to be openly and publiquely read at your county court, that the inhabitants, as well as yourselves and burgesses may be made sencible how displeasing such obstinate proceedings are to his majestie. And alsoe how his majestie hath approved the measures, I then tooke to moderate them.

I am,

Your affectionate ffriend,

EFFINGHAM.

JAMES R.

Locus Sigili—Right trusty and well-beloved, we greet you well.

King James II's letter to the governor, complain'g of the conduct of assembly which met in 1685: in spending their time in frivolous debates: and in contesting the negative power of the governor in the passing of laws.

WHEREAS wee have been informed of the irregular and tumultuous proceedings of the house of burgesses in the late meeting of the assembly of Virginia, the members whereof have not only spent their time in frivolous aud unnecessary debates, but likewise have presumed soe far as to raise contests, touching the power of the negative voice, wherewith our governour of that our collony is intrusted by us, which we cannott attribute to any other cause then to the disaffected and unquiett dispositions of those members, and their sinister intentions to protract the time of their sitting to the great oppression of our good subjects, from whome they receive their wages for their attendance in the assembly, wherefore wee doe very much approve of what you have done in putting an end to that session by proroguing the assembly. Wee have thought fitt hereby, as a mark of our displeasure towards the said members, to charge and command you to dissolve your present assembly, to the end the inhabitants of that our collony may at such time as you shall think fitt have opportunitie of electing such other members as may have a more carefull regard to our service and the good of our collony

And whereas Robert Beverley, clerk of the house of burgesses appeares to have cheifly occasioned and promoted those disputes and contests, Our will and pleasure is that he be declared uncapable of any office or public imployment within our collony of Virginia, and that he be prosecuted according to the utmost severity of the law for altering the records of the assembly if you shall see cause; and wee doe further hereby charge and require you and your commander in cheife of our said collony for the time being, to appoint a fitt person to execute the office of clerk of the house of burgesses, and not to permitt upon any pretence whatsoever any other person to execute the said office then such as shall be soe chosen by you, to whome wee expect the usuall allowance shall be made by the assembly for his service and attendance, as hath been formerly given to others in his place, and soe wee bid you heartily farewell.

Governor instructed to appoint a clerk of the house of burgesses for the future.

Given at our court at Windsor, the first of August 1686, in the second yeare of our raigne.

By his majesties command.

SUNDERLAND.

To our right trusty and well beloved ffrancis Lord Howard, of Effingham, our leiut. and gov'r. genll. of our collony and dominion of Virginia in America.

Vera copia of his majesties letter to his excellency.

NICHO. SPENCER, *Sec'ry.*

Signed by LORD EFFINGHAM, *Gov'r.*
ARTHUR ALLEN, *Speaker.*

(*Note to editions of* 1733 & 1752.)

AT A

Generall Assembly,

BEGUN AT JAMES CITTY

Francis Nicholson, esq. lieut. governor.

THE 16th DAY OF APRIL, ANNO 1691, AND IN THE THIRD YEARE OF THE REIGN OF OUR SOVERAIGN LORD & LADY WILLIAM AND MARY BY THE GRACE OF GOD, KING & QUEEN OF ENGLAND, SCOTLAND, FRANCE & IRELAND, DEFENDERS OF THE FAITH, &c.*

ACT I.

Edi. 1733 and 1752.

An act giveing reward for killing of Woolves.

Preamble.

☞ In the margin, opposite the titles of the acts of this session, and many others, it is said in the editions of 1733 and 1752, that the act was repealed, generally by some act of 1705. But it is a mistake; as the acts of 1705 were a revisal, and, in most cases, a mere repetition of former acts.

WHEREAS it is found by frequent experience since the severall former acts of this country giveing a reward for killing of wolves have been repealed, and the encouragement which incited many people to use their best endeavours and industery to distroy them wholly taken away, that wolves have and do greatly increase in number, and that frequent spoyle and distruction, in every part of this country, is by them made upon hogs, sheep and cattle, to the great injury, damage and loss of the inhabitants, *Bee it therefore enacted by their majesties leiutenant governour, councill and the burgesses of this Generall Assembly and the authority thereof, and it is hereby*

Various Readings.

* The commencement of the acts of this session is alike in all the MSS.—In the editions of 1733 and 1752, it is, 'At a General 'Assembly, begun at James City, the sixteenth day of April, in the 'third year of the reign of our sovereign lord and lady William 'and Mary, by the grace of God, of England, Scotland, France, 'and Ireland, king and queen, defenders of the faith, &c. and in 'the year of our Lord 1691.'

enacted, That whosoever hereafter shall kill and destroy wolves, either by gun, pitt, trapp, or other meanes or waies whatsoever, shall, for every wolfe soe killed and destroyed, be paid in the county where the same is done, by pit or trapp, three hundred pounds of tobacco and casque, and for a wolfe killed by gun or otherwaise two hundred pounds of tobacco and casque for his encouragement and reward. Any law, usage, or custome to the contrary notwithstanding. *Provided alwaies, and it is hereby intended*, That whosoever shall kill a wolfe, shall make proofe before the next justice of the peace of that county, at least by his own corporall oath or other sufficient proofe, at the discretion of the justice, how, when, and where hee killed the said wolfe, and alsoe bring in his head, and take from the said justice of the peace a certificate thereof, which being produced to the county court, (*a*) at the proportioning of the levy, shall be sufficient to cause the said court to raise upon the county the severall summes and rewards before mentioned, to be paid unto such person as by such service shall deserve the same.

Reward for killing wolves

What proof necessary to entitle to rewards.

ACT II.

An act directing how publique claimes shall be certified for allowance.

Edi. 1733 and 1752.

BEE it enacted by the right honourable their majesties leiutenant governour, the councill and burgesses of this present generall assembly, and the authority thereof, and it is hereby enacted, That for the time to come there be constant courts held by (*a*) the justices in each county, at some convenient time before every assembly, for proofe of such debts as shall be due by law from the country, and that certificates, together with a full account of all perticulers, claimed, and by what authority, and for what service the same became

Co't of claims to be held in every county.

Various Readings.

* The running title to the acts of this session, in the editions of 1733 and 1752 is 'Anno regni Gulielmi & Mariæ tertio.'

(*a*) The word 'court' omitted in Northb. MS. but inserted in Ch. City and P. Rand. MSS.

(*b*) 'For' in Northb. MS. 'by' in Ch. City and P. Rand. MSS.

How accounts against the public to be passed.

due, be issued by the clerk of each court, endorsed upon the account claimed, and be delivered unto the burgesses of that county in order to their allowance in the assembly, which proofe shall be made at the least by the oath of the party claiming and produceing the warrant or certificate by which he claimes, or otherwise sufficient proofe, and that the court do, and are hereby enjoyned strictly to inspect and seriously to consider every article of the account so exhibited, and regulate the same according to law, and that the clerke in full of all fees due to him for every person that claimes, and hath certificates granted be allowed twenty pounds of tobacco from the county (a) where the claime amounts to one hundred pounds of tobacco or more, and if under, to be done exofficio, *Provided alwaies*, that all claimers intending to receive benefit by this act do and shall make proof of their claimes as aforesaid, and returne the same to the first or second succeeding assembly after the said claime becomes due, otherwise to be excluded and barred forever, and also that every sherrif in this their majesties dominion of Virginia shall not for the future have, or receive from the country any satisfaction for publique services by him or them done more than what is already set down, exprest and ascertained in the law, nominating and appointing sherriffes fees. *And be it further enacted by the authority aforesaid, and it is hereby enacted*, that this act shall be read and published at every parish church in each countie by the sherrif of the county or the deputy on the Sunday next preceeding such court, and likewise that this act be constantly read by the clerks at the first opening of every such court.

Fee to clerk for certificate.

When claimants to present their claims to assembly.

Sheriffs to receive no other fees than those prescribed by law.

When and where this act to be read.

ACT III.

Edi. 1733 and 1752.

An act prohibiting ordinary keepers to give credit to seamen and others.

Preamble.

FORASMUCH as the unlimited credit given by the ordinaries and tipling houses, within this their majesties country and dominion of Virginia, to the sea-

---

Various Readings.

(a) 'County' in Northb. MS. 'country' in Ch. City & P. Randolph MSS.

men and others, where they spend not only their ready money, but their wages and other goods, which should be for the support of themselves and families, is found very prejudiciall, and occations many persons newly free to run away to the neighbouring plantations, to the great disadvantage of this country, *Bee it therefore enacted* (a) *by the right honourable their majesties leiut. governour, the councill and burgesses of this present generall assembly, and the authority thereof, and it is hereby enacted*, that if any ordinary keepers or master of a tipling house shall, after publication of this act, trust or sell drinke to any person or persons, who are not master of two servants, or being visiably worth fifty pounds sterling at least, more then the vallue of three hundred pounds of tobacco, such ordinary keeper, or master of a tipling house, shall loose all such overplus tobacco or money, for which they shall give such credit; and in case any such ordinary keeper or master of a tipling house shall take or get from any person, trusted as oforesaid, any obligation, bill, or other security, for any sum above three hundred pounds of tobacco spent in one year, under pretence that it is for other goods, where any such fraud shall be discovered and proved, the said ordinary keeper shall, upon conviction, be made uncapable of keeping ordinary, and shall forfeit double the sum of such obligation, so covenously taken, one halfe to their majesties their heires and succossors, for and towards the better support of the government, and the contingent charges thereof, and the other halfe to him or them that shall informe and sue for the same, in any court of record of this country, by action of debt, bill, plaint or information, wherein noe essoign, protection or wager of law shall be allowed.

Ord'y keepers selling drink to any person not owner of 2 servants, or worth 50*l.* sterling more than to the amount of 300 lbs. tobacco in one year, shall lose the overplus;

and taking any obligation, bill &c. for such overplus, rendered incapable of keeping ordinary, and forfeits double the amount

How recoverable.

And bee it further enacted by the authority aforesaid, and it is hereby enacted, That if any ordinary keeper or master of a tipling house, shall, after prohibition, or being forewarned by the master of any ship or vessell trading to this country, entertaine any of the seamen

Keepers of ordinaries or masters of tipling houses, entertaining sailors after being forwarned by their masters, liable as for entertaining runaway servants.

Various Readings.

(a) The word 'enacted' omitted in P. Rand. MS. but inserted in Northb. and Ch. City MSS.

belonging to any such ship or vessell, such ordinary keeper or master of a tipling house shall be, for such offence lyable to the masters complaint, wherein upon sufficient proofe made, such damages shall be allowed as is provided in the act against entertainment of other mens servants. *Provided* that this act or any thing therein contained shall not extend to the ordinary keepers of James Citty giveing credit to any person whatsoever, in the time of the generall court or dureing this setting of a generall assembly; any thing aforesaid to the contrary notwithstanding.

This act not to extend to James's City, during general courts or assemblies.

ACT IV.

Edi. 1733 and 1752.

An act to prevent the casting of ballast into Rivers and Creekes.

Preamble.

FORASMUCH as the throwing and casting of stones, gravell, and other ballast out of the ships and vessells, arriveing into the rivers, creeks, and ports of this their majesties country and dominion of Virginia, is found very distructive and dangerous to the passage of vessells, sloops, and boats, and a stopping to the chanels of the said creeks; for prevention of which mischief, *be it enacted by their majesties leiutenant Governour and Councill and the Burgesses of this Generall Assembly, and the authority thereof, and it is hereby enacted*, that from and after the 24th day of June now next comeing, no master or masters, owner or owners, of any ship, sloop, boat, or other vessell or any other person or persons whatsoever, do cast or unload their gravel or ballast, at or in any of the rivers, creeks, ports, havens, or harbours of this country, but on the land only, above high water marke, upon paine that every such owner, master of a ship, sloop, boat, or other vessell, casting and laying the gravell, stones, or other ballast, or permitting the same to be so cast or laid, into any of the rivers, creeks, or harbours of this country, shall forfeit for every time so offending, the summ of ten pounds sterling, one halfe thereof to be to their majesties, their heirs and successors, for and towards the better support of the government of this their majesties dominion of Virginia, and the contingent

Ballast to be unloaded on the land only above high water mark, under penalty of 10*l.* sterling for every offence.

How recoverable.

charges thereof, and the other halfe to him or them that will sue for the same in any court of record, within this their majesties dominion, by action of debt, bill, plaint, or information wherein no essoign, protection, or wager of law, shall be allowed; *Provided alwaies nevertheles,* that if it shall hereafter appeare to the justices of the court of any county within this dominion, in which any ship or vessell shall happen to ride, that the throwing or casting of ballast into the roads or rivers (*a*) within such county, shall be of advantage to such road or river, for the better moreing and secureing of ships and vessells there, it shall and may be lawfull, in such case, for the justices of the peace of such county, upon the request of the masters of such ships, as usually ride and moore in such roads and rivers as aforesaid, to permit, suffer, and give liberty, by warrant out of court to such masters as, in manner aforesaid, shall request the same, to throw and cast over their ballast into such road or river, any thing aforesaid in this act contained to the contrary notwithstanding.

Provided, that where it shall appear that the throwing of ballast into a river or creek, will improve the navigation, the justices of the county may give permission to do so.

ACT V.

An act directing how Sherriffes and Collectors shall account for Publique dues.

Edi. 1733 and 1752.

WHEREAS severall persons have been, and still are lyable to be prejudiced by remisness of sherriffs and collectors of the publique, county, and parish levies, who often take their own advantagious times to demand and receive the publique dues, and other collections, for which they may, in severall cases, make seisure and distress; for prevention whereof for the future, *Bee it enacted by the right honourable their majesties leiutenant Governour, the Councill and Burgesses of this present generall assembly and the authority thereof, and it is hereby enacted,* that the 80th act of assembly in the printed booke of acts, limitting a certaine time when creditors shall demand their debts, shall be

Preamble.

Act 80, in the printed book, (ante vol 2. p. 104) extended to public dues, and sheriffs and clerks' fees.

Various Readings.

(*a*) 'River' in P. Rand. MS. 'rivers' in Northb. & Ch. Cit. MSS.

interpreted and holden to extend to sherriffs, and other collectors, of the publique, county and parish levies, and of all sherriffs, and clerks fees; and also that all publique, county, and parish debtors, and all debtors of or for sherriffs, or clerks fees, may have the benefit and liberty of the second act of assembly in the yeare 1666, which admits of tenders of tobaccoes to the creditors, according to the full intent, meaning or purport thereof. *And bee it further enacted by the authority aforesaid, and it is hereby enacted*, that in case of collecting the publique, county, or parish dues, or other fees, as aforesaid, any sherriffe or collector shall at any time make seisure or distress of more tobaccoes then are at that time due from the debtor, that in all such cases, the persons seiseing shall make imediate satisfaction to the party from whome they shall make such seisure, or otherwaies that he be allowed to take his overplus tobaccoes out of the hogshead so seized, and that no sherrife or publique collector shall and may from and after the publication of this act, presume to make seisure of any hogshead of tobacco before that time paid away and marked, if there be at that time other merchantable tobaccoes ready in such plantation, where such seisure is made, and which shall be offered and tendered by the debtor. *And bee it further enacted by the authority aforesaid, and it is hereby enacted*, That all sherrifes and collectors of publique, county, and parish dues, shall on or before the 31st day of January yearly produce and present to the justices of the peace of that county, of which he is sherrif or collector, at such convenient time as the said justices shall appoint, his the said sherrifs or collectors booke, kept by him, of his whole collection, as well of all publique dues as aforesaid, as also of all sherrifes, or clerks fees, or private debts put into his hands to collect, and collected together with publique dues, together with a true, full and perfect account of the quantity, quallity and weight of all tobaccoes received by him, as well for the publique, county and parish, as for sherriffs fees, clerks fees, and private debts, with a true account from whome the same was received, and where the same lies, which said account is to be delivered upon the oath of each respective sherrif or collector; and to the end that the publique credit of this country may be

and debtors, on those accounts entitled to the benefit of the 2d act of June 1666, ante vol. 2, p. 226.

Sheriff or collector seizing more tobacco than is due to make immediate payment for the overplus.

Not to seize tobacco paid away & marked, if other merchantable tobacco be offered.

Sheriffs and collectors, annually to lay an acc'nt of their collections before the court specifying the quantity and quality of the tobacco received, and of whom.

well answered and discharged, the justices of each county be, and are hereby empowred and required, thoroughly to examine the accounts, in presence of the severall creditors, who are to have notice of the time of examination of such accounts, at the preceding court held for the said county, and that the said justices order and appoint to each of the said creditors, and to other persons concerned, in sherrifs and clerks fees, and private debts, intermixt in the said sherriffs and collectors booke of accounts, their and every their due part and proportion of the tobaccoes, received and accounted for as aforesaid; haveing due regard to the quallity and convenience of the said tobaccoe, to the end each person concerned may have equall right therein; and that it shall not be lawfull for any sherrif or sherrifes, publique collector, or publique collectors, to convert to his or their owne use directly or indirectly, any part or parcell of the tobaccoes so received or collected, or to be received or collected by him or them, untill the account thereof be presented, examined and ordered as aforesaid, under the penalty of forfeiting four times the value of such tobaccoes, so converted to his own use, one third part of which said forfeiture shall be to their majesties their heires and successors towards the better support of the government of this their majesties dominion of Virginia, and the contingent charges thereof, one third part to the governor of this their majesties dominion of Virginia, and the other third part to him or them that shall sue for the same in any court of record within this their majesties dominion by bill, information, plaint or other action, wherein no essoign, protection or wager of law shall be allowed. *Provided alwaies*, that it shall and may be lawfull to and for every such sherrife and collector, and they and every of them are hereby required, to discount with all and every the creditor or creditors of the countie, publique and parish levies, the full sum and quantity due to them of the said levies out of his, her or their levies due from them to the publique, county and parish without any allowance for the same; *and provided* that all and every the sherrifs and collectors aforesaid shall be lyable to make good all tobaccoes to be received by them as aforesaid if it shall appear that the same or any part thereof shall be rotten, unsound,

Court to examine the ac'ts in presence of the several creditors, and apportion the tobacco among them.

Penalty on sheriffs or collectors for converting any tobaccoes collected by them to their own use.

Provided that sheriffs and collectors may discount with the creditors, for the amount of their public dues;

and that they shall be liable for all tobaccos paid to creditors, which appear to be rotten, within ten days thereafter. insufficient or not merchantable, within ten daies after the same shall be ordered and appointed to the creditors as before is directed, after which time all the said tobaccoes shall lie and be on the creditors account and hazard; *Provided also* that nothing herein shall be construed, deemed or taken, to extend to their majesties quitrents, or other dues, but that the same be excepted out of this act.

This act not to extend to quitrents.

ACT VI.

Edi. 1733 and 1752.

An act reviveing the act for advancement of manufactures of the growth of this country.

Preamble.

WHEREAS an act of assembly was made in the year 1682, entituled an act for the advancement of manufactures of the growth of this country and for the better and more speedy payment of debts and levies, to continue in force untill the 10th day of November 1685, (*a*) and no longer, and the same act was on the 20th day of October, anno 1686, revived and enacted to continue in force three yeares from the end of that session of assembly, and after that to the end of the then next session of assembly (*b*) now for as much as it hath since, by experience appeared, that the same is a good and wholesome law, and very beneficiall to the people of this dominion, *Bee it enacted by their majesties leiutenant Governour, Councill and burgesses of this present generall assembly, and the authority thereof, and*

Various Readings.

(*a*) The figures '1685' omitted in P. Rand. MS.—In the Ch. City MS. the words '9 ber 1685' are omitted.—It may not be amiss to observe, that before the alteration of the style, in 1752, when the 25th of March was the beginning of the year, or the first month, it was usual to write the names of the months terminating in 'er' thus: *September*, '7 ber' or seventh month; *October*, '8 ber' or eighth month; *November*, '9 ber' or ninth month; *December*, '10 ber' or tenth month.

(*b*) The words 'of assembly' omitted in P. Rand. MS. but inserted in Northb. MS.—In the Ch. City MS. it is 'to the end of 'that then session, and after that to the end of the then next session of assembly,' which latter words from the word 'and' are omitted in Northumberland MS.

it is hereby enacted, that the said act shall remaine, continue, and be, and every branch, article, and provisoe therein contained, revived and from henceforth continue, stand, and endure in force and strength, to all intents, constructions, and purposes, and shall be observed and kept, in all things, according to the tenor, effect and true meaning of the same. This act to continue for the space of three yeares, and so from thence to the end of the next session of assembly.

Act 12 of 1682 (ante vol. 2, p. 506) revived: and to continue in force for 3 years.

ACT VII.

An act reviveing the 6th act of assembly made at James Citty the 20th of October 1686, regulateing the tares of tobacco hogsheads.

Edi. 1733 and 1752.

FOR the prevention of abuses, frauds, and deceits, daly practised in the passing away of tobacco hogsheads, at a much higher tare then they really weigh, and for remedy of the great damages done and suffered by tobaccoes being packt in hogsheads made of green and unseasoned timber, or such thin and slight staves and hoops as will not endure rowling to the water, *Bee it enacted by their majesties leiutenant governour, councell and burgesses of this present generall assembly and the authority thereof, and it is hereby enacted,* That the 6th act of assembly made at James Citty the 20th day of October 1686, entituled, an act regulating the tare of tobacco hogsheads be now revived and put in force, with the severall explynations, clauses, and additions as hereafter shall be exprest, that is to say, that all and every tobaccoe casque in the said act directed to be marked or branded with the first letter of the proper name, and the first letter of the sirname of the person or persons that shall set up the same, be, and shall be, for time to come, respectively branded with an iron brand, and noe other, in such places, and in such manner, as in the said act is exprest and set downe, and that the true intent, meaning and sense of the said act, for the future, be soe deemed, taken, and held, by and in all and every court of judicature within this their majesties dominion of Virginia, which shall hereafter have occasion to give judgment in the same.

Preamble.

Act 6, of Oct. 1686, revived, with amendments.

Tobacc. casks how to be branded.

To be made of dry & seasoned timber.

And be it further enacted by the authority aforesaid, That all and every tobaccoe hogshead made and set up from and after the publication of this act, be made of dry and well seasoned timber, and set up in strong and substanciall hoopes, according to the size, demension and seasoning hereafter mentioned and set down, that is to say, all and every stave belonging to any tobaccoe hogshead or other tobaccoe casque, in which tobaccoes are paid away, or put to sayle, shall be at least the thickness of one third of an inch, on the thinest edge thereof, and be made of such dry and seasoned timber as hath been fallen and hewed three months at least before the makeing and setting up thereof, and that all and every cooper or coopers or other persons whatsoever, who, from and after the publication of this act, shall presume to work up unseasoned timber not being fallen and hewed three months at least, and thereof make use in the staves or heading of any tobacco casque whatsoever, shall for every tobacco caske so made and set up forfeit and pay five hundred pounds of tobaccoe, and also all and every planter, or planters, or other persons whatsoever, that from and after the publication of this act, shall pay away or put to sale any tobaccoes whatsoever in any hogshead or caske whatsoever, but such as shall be made according to the directions and true intent and meaning of this act, shall for every such caske, forfeit and pay five hundred pounds of tobacco, one moyety of the said fines and forfeitures to be to their majesties, their heires and successors for and towards the better support of the government and the contingent charges thereof, and the other moyety to him or them that shall sue for the same in any court of record within this their majesties dominion of Virginia by bill, information, plaint or other action wherein no essoign, protection or wager of law shall be allowed.

Thickness of staves.

Penalty on coopers for working timber not fallen & hew'd three months.

Pen'ty for paying away tobacco in casks not made according to the directions of this act.

An allowance to be made for the hogshead, altho' the specialty be for *tobacco and caske.*

And forasmuch as divers differences and disputes have arisen, and may hereafter arise, about the allowance of thirty pounds of tobacco for every tobacco hogshead (*a*) where the specialty of the debtor or

---

Various Readings.

(*a*) 'Caske' in Ch. City and P. Randolph MSS. 'hogshead' in Northumberland MS.

agreement of the contractor, of or for tobaccoes, doth or shall express tobacco and caske, and thereupon advantage may be taken of the planter to the utter loss of his caske, contrary to the intent and meaning of this act, *Bee it enacted and declared by the authoritie aforesaid*, that all and every creditor, buyer, receiver, or other person whatsoever, that receiveth tobaccoes in caske for and in satisfaction of any bill, bond, purchase, contract or other account whatsoever, (whether the same express tobacco and caske or not) shall refuse or denie to abate, deduct, or otherwise satisfie and make payment of thirty pounds of tobacco for every hogshead unto the person or persons of whome he shall receive the same, and at the time he doth receive it of the debtor, seller or payer away, shall for every such offence forfeit and pay the party injured the sume of five hundred pounds of tobaccoe, to be recovered by action of debt in any court of record within this their majesties dominion of Virginia, any law, statute, usage or custome to the contrary notwithstanding. This act, or any thing herein contained not to be construed or taken to extend or relate to any bill, bond, or obligation already taken, for any debt contracted before the publication of this act.

Not to be extended to debts previously contracted.

This act to continue in force three yeares and noe longer.

ACT VIII.

An act for Ports, &c.

Edi. 1733 and 1752.

Preamble.

WHEREAS their majesties customes and revenues of this their dominion of Virginia, by the present waies and practices of landing and shipping of all sorts of merchandiseing goods inward, and all tobaccoes and other goods outwards, whether for England or elsewhere, are rendered impossible to be secured, to be duly paid into the hand of their majesties respective collectors, and other officers thereto appointed, and commissionated to receive and secure the same, great oppertunity being thereby given to such as attempt to import or export goods and merchandises, without entering or paying the duties and customes due thereupon, much practised by greedy and covetous persons, respecting more their private gaines and commodities, then their duty and allegiance, or the common profitt of their majesties good subjects, to the apparent diminution of their majesties revenues and great discouragement of such who duly pay the same, which abuses cannot be better prevented then by appointing certaine limited ports, Wharfes, keyes, and places for laying on shoar and loading on board all goods, tobaccoes and other merchandises, to be exported out of, and imported into, this their majesties dominion of Virginia; for prevention of which frauds and abuses for the time to come, (a) *Bee it enacted by their majesties leiutenant Governor, Councill and Burgesses of this present general assembly, and the authority thereof, and it is hereby enacted,* That from and after the first day of October, which shall be in the year of our Lord one thousand six hundred ninety and two, all shipps, barques, and other vessells whatsoever, arriveing into, or sayling out from this country for trayd, shall unload and put on shoare, and take from shoar to load on board, all tobaccoes, goods and merchantdises, at some one or other of the poarts, Wharfes, keyes, or places hereafter mentioned in this act, and at none other place or places whatsoever, under the penalty and forfeiture of such ship, barque, or other vessell, with all her gunns, tackle, (b) ammunition, furniture and apparell.

Ves'ls to load and unload at certain ports only.

And bee it enacted by the authoritie aforesaid, and it is hereby enacted, That all goods, wares and merchandises of whatsoever nature, kind or condition which shall be imported into or exported out of this their majesties dominion of Virginia, after the said first day of October, anno 1692, shall be landed and laid on shoar at some one of the ports or places herein after mentioned, and there and at none other place or places whatsoever sould and bought, and whosoever shall presume to buy, sell, land, or lay on shoar (unless in case of wreck to

Goods to be bought and sold at those places only.

Various Readings.

(a) The words 'time to come' omitted in Northb. MS. but inserted in Ch. City and P. Rand MSS.

(b) The word 'takle' omitted in Northb. MS. but inserted in Ch. City and P. Rand MSS.

preserve the same) any goods, or merchantdises whatsoever to be imported or exported as aforesaid at any other place or places, then some one of the ports, wharfes, keyes, or other place or playces hereafter named in this act, shall forfeit and loose all such goods, wares, and merchandises, as shall in other manner then is by this law directed, be landed or laid on shoar, bought, sold, shipped of, received or taken on board any ship, barque, or other vessell whatsoever, as aforesaid.

Penalty, forfeiture of the goods.

And bee it further enacted by the authority aforesaid, and it is hereby enacted, That for the better secureing all tobaccoes, goods, wares, and merchantdises, which shall be brought to and landed at the ports, wharfes, keyes and places, by this act named, for reception and landing thereof, the justices of each county are hereby authorized, commanded, and impowered, within three months after publication of this act, to appoint and command the surveyor of each county to lay out and survey fifty acres of land, at such place and places as are hereafter in this act named, appointed, and set down for the ports, wharfes, keyes, and places for receiveing on shoar, and shipping, all goods, tobaccoes, wares, and merchantdises as aforesaid; and for the erecting ware houses, or any other houses, for the better secureing all such good, tobaccoes, wares and merchantdises to be imported or exported as aforesaid.

Justices to lay out 50 acres of land, at certain places whereon to erect warehouses, stores, &c. for the reception of tobaccoes, goods, &c.

And bee it further enacted by the authority aforesaid, and it is hereby enacted, That if any owner or owners or other present possessor, where the owner is absent, of such lands as are by this act hereafter appointed for a port, wharfe, keye, or place as aforesaid shall not be willing to agree for and sell such land at such price as shall be, by the justices aforesaid, thought reasonable, that then and in such case at the request of the said justices, their majesties governour for the time being is hereby desired and impowered to issue forth his warrant or warrants, directed to the sherrife of some neighbouring county thereby commanding him to impannell twelve of the most able and discreet freeholders of his bayliwicke, in convenient time, to goe upon the land appointed by this law for a towne, port, wharfe, key, or place of landing goods, wares or merchantdises to be imported or exported, and upon their corporall oaths

How land acquired, for a town, if owner refuses to sell, or be absent.

How the value of the land, to be paid.

to value the same at the true worth, haveing regard to the inconveniency that may happen to the owner by reason of the (a) sale thereof. in the best of their judgments, which worth or value by them so made and found shall be paid and satisfied, or well secured to be paid and satisfied, the next succeeding croppe to the owner or owners, guardian, attorney, present possessor, or possessors by the inhabitants of the county where such lands lie, to be by vertue of this act levied by the justices of that county or any four or more of them (whereof one to be of the quorum) upon the inhabitants of the county, by the pole, on every tytheable, in manner as other county charges are or have been heretofore usually laid and levied, that in consideration of such summe or summes of tobacco the jury assessed, or of so much as the jury aforesaid shall vallue the said lands to be worth, such owner or owners, guardian, attorney, present possessor, or possessors shall well and sufficiently convey and assure unto such person and persons as the county court shall appoint feofees in trust a good and absolute estate in fee, of and in the said fifty acres of land, in trust and confidence, and to and for the uses, intents and purposes herein after mentioned, that is to say, to the uses, intents and purposes, that the said feofees shall out of the said fifty acres of land, convey and assure to any person requesting the same, and paying and reimburseing the county pro rata what the same at first cost, the like good and sufficient conveyance and assurance in the law, unto such person or persons, their heires and assignes for ever one or more half acre or halfe acres, but under such consideration that such grantee, his heires or assignes shall within the space of four months next ensueing such grant begin and without delay proceed to build and finish on each halfe acre granted to him one good house, to containe twenty foot square at the least, wherein if he failes to performe then such grant to be void in law, and the lands therein granted lyable to the choyce and purchase of any other person.

Owner or possessor to convey to certain feoffees, in trust.

How they are to convey.

Conditions of sale.

Various Readings.

(a) 'His' in P. Rand. MS. 'the' in Ch. City & Northb. MSS.

And bee it further enacted by the authoritie aforesaid, and it is hereby enacted, That in case where the owner, proprietor or his their or her guardian or guardians or known attorney or attornies, where such owner or owners proprietor or proprietors shall be under full age, or out of this countrey, or county where the land lies, appointed by this act to the uses aforesaid, shall upon tender of payment or security of payment the next succeeding cropp of the value or consideration for the purchase of the said lands so assessed as aforesaid, refuse to make such assurance and conveyance as by this act is directed, such denyall or refuseall shall *ipso facto* be taken for a forfeiture of the said lands to the feoffees or trustees appointed or intrusted by the court as aforesaid, proofe thereof being first made (*b*) in the county court where the lands lie, and that imediately from and after such refusall as aforesaid, it shall and may be lawfull to and for the said feoffees or trustees in and upon the said fifty acres of land to enter, and the same to have, hold, occupy and enjoy as of an estate in fee to and for the uses, intents and purposes aforesaid.

A refusal by the owners of the land, to convey, ipso facto, a forfeiture to the feoffees.

And they may enter.

And bee it enacted by the authoritie aforesaid, and it is hereby enacted, That imediately upon such entery the said feofees, and every of them are and shall be seized of and in a pure, absolute, perfect and indefeasible estate of inheritance in fee, in trust, and to and for the intents, uses and purposes aforesaid, and such conveyances or grants as shall be made by them of any of the said lands according to the power and trust in them by this act reposed and given shall be adjudged, deemed and taken to be good, valid and effectuall in law to all intents and purposes whatsoever as if the said grants were made by the true and rightfull owner, proprietor or possessor of the same; any law, statute, usage or custom to the contrary hereof notwithstanding. *And bee it further enacted by the authoritie aforesaid, and it is hereby enacted,* That the surveyors appointed to lay out the said fifty acres of land shall have for the same and for delivering unto the county court a fair plot

On the entry of the feoffee they seized of an absolute estate in fee in trust for the purposes of this act.

Fees of surveyors.

Various Readings.

(a) The words 'first made' omitted in Northb. MS. but inserted in Ch. City and P. Rand. MSS.

thereof five hundred pounds of tobaccoe and caske to be paid by each county, and for every halfe acre and giving a plot thereof twenty pounds of tobacco to be paid by him that shall imploy him, and that such surveyor appointed to lay out the whole fifty acres of land as shall refuse or neglect upon timely notice thereof given to him to surv~y or lay out any one or more halfe acre or half acres of land for the respective purchasers thereof, or demand more pay or allowance for his soe doeing and giving a plot thereof sufficient to ground the conveyance upon, in the bounding and expressing the lines of the said one or more half acre or halfe acres of land then what is by this act allowed shall upon proofe made pay to the party so aggrieved five hundred pounds of tobacco and caske to be recovered by action of debt, bill or plaint in any court of record within this their majesties dominion of Virginia. *And bee it enacted by the authority aforesaid* That these severall nominated ports, wharfes, keyes, and places hereafter named and set downe, be and shall be the severall and respective ports, wharfes, keyes, and places constituted and appointed by this act for the uses, intents and purposes before named, that is to say,

Penalty for exacting more.

At what places towns to be built.

In Charles City county. ffor Charles Citty County at flower de hundred over against Swyneards, (*a*) where it was by a former law appointed and accordingly layd out and payd for and severall d elling houses and warehouses built.

James City co. ffor James Citty County, James Citty.

Nantzemond. ffor ^antzemond (*b*) County at Huffes (*c*) Poynt where formerly by law appointed and accordingly laid out and paid for and built upon pursuant to the said law.

Various Readings.

(*a*) 'Swynards' in P. Rand. MS.—In the Ch. City MS. the description of the places for ports or towns, is remarkably defective. After the words 'flour de hundred' there is an '&c.' in that MS. and the description there ends. The same is observable with respect to other places.

(*b*) 'Nancemond' in Ch. City MS. 'Nantzemund' in P Rand. MS—No word has, perhaps, undergone more variations in the spelling than this: It was originally called 'Nansimum.' See vol. 1, pa 321.

(*c*) 'Huss' in Ch. City MS. 'Huffes' in Northumberland and P. Rand. MSS.

ffor Elizabeth Citty County, on the west side of Hampton river, on the land of Mr. William Wilson, lately belonging unto Mr. Tho. Jarvis deceased, the plantation where he late lived, and the place appointed by a former law and severall dwelling houses and warehouses already built. Elizabeth City county.

ffor Lower Norfolke County on Nicholas Wise his land on the entrance of the Eastern Branch of Elizabeth River being the land appointed by a former law, and accordingly laid out and paid for and severall dwelling houses and ware houses already built. Lower Norfolk county.

ffor Yorke County upon Mr. Benjamin Reads land begining at the lower side of Smiths Creeke, and so runing downward by the river towards the fferrey. York county.

ffor the upper parts of Yorke River at West Point to be paid for by the county in which it lies. Upper parts of York river.

ffor Gloster County at Tyndall's Point, part on the land of Coll Lawrence Smyth, and part on the land of Mrs. Rebecca Rhoydes. Glo'ster co'y.

ffor Midlesix County, on the land belonging to Ralph Wormeley, Esqr. on the West side of Nimco k Creeke, and over against the plantation where he now liveth formerly laid out by the surveyor of the county according to the directions of the act made in anno 1680, intituled, an act for cohabitation and incouragement of trayd and manufacture, and fully paid for to the said Ralph Wormley Esqr at the price sett by the said act, and a good sufficient warehouse built thereon. Middlesex county.

ffor Rappahanock County at Hobs his hole, the said land laid out by a former law and paid for where the Court house, severall dwelling houses, and ware houses already built. Rappahannock county.

ffor Stafford County on the land where Capt. Mallachy Peale now liveth called Potomack neck. Stafford co'y.

ffor Accomacke county at Anancock, in Calvert ne ck formerly laid out pursuant to a former law made in anno 1680, where the Court house, severall dwelling houses, and ware houses are already built. Accomack co.

ffor Northampton County upon one of the branches of Cherry Stone Creek, on the land of Mrs. Anna Lee the daughter of Capt. Hancock Lee, now in the tenure of the widow of Andrew Small. Northampton county.

Lancaster co. ffor Lancaster county on the land where (a) Mrs Hannah Ball now liveth scituate on the Westerne side (b) of the mouth of Corotoman River.

Northumberland county. ffor Northumberland county on Chicacone river, being the land of Mr Spencer Mottrom, formerly laid out for a towne according to a former act.

The following places appointed for buying and selling of goods, but not to be ports for entry & clearing. And that the places hereafter nominated may be, and are hereby appointed to be places for buying and selling of all manner of goods, wares, and merchantdises under the same limitations and conditions as are mentioned to be observed and performed in settling and appointing the ports aforesaid, but shall not have liberty to land from on board any ship or vessell at (c) the first importation, or shipp of in order to the imediate exportation any goods wares or merchandises but only to and from some one of the ports in this act beforementioned, that is to say,

In Henrico county. ffor Henrico County at Bermuda hundred poynt, on the land belonging to the wife of John Woodson.

Isle of Wight. ffor the Isle of Wight County, at the mouth of Pagan Creeke, formerly laid out for a towne, by the name of Paitesfield and payd for, and houses built upon it

Warwick co. ffor Warwick County at the mouth of Deep Creek as by a former law appointed and laid out by the name of Warwick Town, and paid for, by directions of the said law, and severall houses there built, together with a brick Court house and prison.

Surry county. ffor Surry County at the mouth of Grays Creeke on the lower side thereof.

Westmorel'd county. ffor Westmorland County on the land of capt. William Hardidge, where he now liveth on the mouth of Nominy, a place formerly appointed by law.

How and from what places, tobaccoes and goods to be exported. *And be it enacted by the authority aforesaid, and it is hereby enacted,* That from and after the said first day of October 1692, no tobacco, goods, wares or merchantdises shall be taken on board any shipp, barque, or vessell whatsoever, from any part of this their majesties dominion, in order to be exported in the said shipp, barque, or vessell, but what shall come directly

---

Various Readings.

(a) 'Of' in Northb. MS. 'where' in P. Ran. MS.
(b) The word 'side' omitted in Northb. MS. but inserted in P. Rand. MS.
(c) 'Of' in Northb. MS. 'at' in P. Rand MS.

from some one or other of the ports, wharfes, keyes, or places mentioned in this act, nor unless the same tobaccoes or other goods so taken on board from such place or places allowed of by this act be first entered with the collector or officer duly appointed to collect, receive and secure the customes, and a cocquit or certificate thereof produce from him of such entry made together with the marke and number of such tobaccoes or other goods, wares and merchantdises so entered for exportation, in such ship, barke or other vessell as the same is entered to be put on board, under the paine and penalty of forfeiting all such tobaccoes, goods wares and merchantdises as shall be put on board any ship, barque or other vessell, and not comeing directly from such port, wharfe, key or other place mentioned and allowed in this act, and due entry made thereof with the lawfull officer according to the directions and true intent and meaning of this act. And for the better preventing and discovering of frauds and abuses; *Bee it further enacted by the authority aforesaid, and it is hereby enacted,* That all tobaccoes, skins, furrs, goods, wares, or merchantdises, that shall be found on board any, shipp, sloop, boat or other vessell, that hath passed by any of the ports mentioned in this act, after the takeing on board any such goods, wares or merchantdises, and hath not a permit from the collector or other officer of the customes, of that district for the same, declaring to what port or place they are to be carryed, shall be wholly forfeited, one third part of all which fines, forfeitures and penalties before mentioned to be to their majesties, their heires and successors towards the better support of the government of this their majesties dominion of Virginia, and the contingent charges thereof, one third part to the governour here, and the other third part to him or them that shall informe or sue for the same in any court of record within this their majesties dominion of Virginia, by byll, information, plaint, or other action wherein no essoign, protection, or wager of law shall be allowed. *Provided allwaise, and it is the true intent and meaning of this act* that any place already laid out and appointed by any former law, and now by this act againe appointed and confirmed to be one of the ports, wharfes, keyes and places of trayd and landing of goods and merchant-

Penalty for breach of this law.

Frauds, how prevented.

Tobaccos and goods found on board, without a permit, forfeited.

Fines, how appropriated.

Privilege of places formerly laid out for towns.

dises to be imported and for shipping tobaccoes and other goods and merchantdises to be exported wherein any thing hath been heretofore done and acted persuant to such law, the same shall be, and is hereby deemed, held good and valid in law, any thing herein or by any other law, order, usage or custome to the contrary thereof in any wise notwithstauding.

Vacancies in feoffees, how supplied.

Provided alwaise, that in case of death or departure out of this dominion of any one or more, who shall be appointed by virtue of this act as feofee or feofees in trust as aforesaid that then it shall and may be lawfull to and for the justices of that court where such death or departure shall happen, and the aforesaid justices are hereby impowered to constitute and appoint in the place or roome of such feofee or feofees so dead or departed, one or more feofee or feofees for the uses, intents and purposes aforesaid.

Provision, in cases where the possessor of the land is tenant by curtesy.

How the price apportioned.

Provided also, that in case any land to be laid out by force of this act for a port, wharfe, key, &c. shall be in the tenure and occupation of a tenant by the curtesy, that in all such cases the fourth part of the consideration for which the aforesaid land shall be purchased, shall be paid and satisfied to the said tenante by the curtesy, the other three fourth parts paid or secured to be paid to him who hath the fee therein, any thing herein, or by any other law, order, usage or custom to the contrary thereof in any case notwithstanding.

And bee it enacted by the authority aforesaid, and it i hereby enacted, That for the better securety of the port aforesaid, and their majesties customes there ariseing and towards the better mainetenance and encouragement (*a*) of a learned and pious ministry and advancement of learning and towards the lessening the levy by the pole, there shall be answer'd and paid to our soveraign Lord and Lady King William and Queen Mary for and dureing their naturall lifes, and the life of the survivor of them, to and for the uses, intents and purposes in this act mentioned and declared, and to and for no other uses, intents or purposes whatsoever to

---

Various Readings.

(*a*) The words 'and encouragement,' omitted in P. Rand. MS. but inserted in Northb. & Ch. Cit. MSS.

be received by such collector or collectors, officer and officers as shall be thereto appointed, and in such manner as is herein appointed, and no otherwaise, such duties, customes, and imposts, upon the following goods, wares and merchantdises as shall be exported and carryed out of this their majesties dominion, either by land or water, from and after the first day of June next ensueing, as followeth, that is to say; for every raw hide one shilling, for every tann'd hide two shillings, for every buck skin drest or undrest eight pence, every doe skin drest or undrest five pence, every pound of beaver eight pence, every otter skin six pence, every wild Catt skin three pence, every Minx skin two pence, every fox skin three pence, every Raccoon skin one penny, every dosen of muskrat skins six pence, for every Elk skin one shilling, for every pound of wool six pence, for every pound of iron one penny, which said duties, customes, and imposts are to be satisfied and paid by the person or persons exporting or carrying out the same either by land or water to the collector or collectors appointed to receive the said duties, customes or imposts, before the said goods, wares or merchantdises shall be shipped off, exported or carryed out of and from this dominion, either by land or water, and a certificate thereof obtained from the collector or collectors of that port or precinct where such goods, wares or merchantdises shall be so exported or carryed away, signifying the payment and satisfaction of the duties, customes and imposts aforesaid under the penalty of forfeiting all such goods, wares and merchantdises which shall be shipped of or loaded on board any boate, sloop, shipp or other vessell in order to exportation by water, or endeavoured to be carryed out of this country by land, and the full vallue thereof. *And bee it further enacted by the authority aforesaid and it is hereby enacted*, That if it shall at any time happen that any of the said goods, wares or merchantdises shall from and after the said first day of June be transported, conveyed or shipped out of this their majesties dominion of Virginia (*a*) by any person or persons before the

Duties, customs and imposts, on certain enumerated articles, exported.

On hides.
Buck skins.
Doe skins.
Beaver pr. lb.
Otter skins.
Wild cat skins.
Minx skins.
Raccoon sk's.
Muskrat, per dozen.
Elk skins.
Wool, per lb.
Iron, per lb.

How paid.

Certificate thereof.

Forfeiture, on non payment.

Penalty for ship'g goods, &c. without paying the duties, double the value of the goods.

Various Readings.

(*a*) 'The words 'of Virginia' omitted in Ch. City and P. Rand. MSS. but inserted in Northumberland MS.

said duties, customes or imposts are duly paid and satisfied, and certificates obtained for the same as aforesaid, and that the said person or persons who shall be thereof lawfully convicted either by their owne confession, or by other good sufficient evidence, shall forfeit and pay double the true vallue of all such goods, wares and merchantdises; and if any master, marriner, seaman, boatman, carryer, or other person whatsoever, shall be privy to such fraud and assist therein, he, they and every of them upon due conviction thereof, shall forfeit and pay for every such offence forty pounds sterling money, one third part of all which penalties and forfeitures shall be to their majesties their heires and successors to be imployed towards the better defence of the said ports and supplying the countrey with armes and ammunition, one other third part towards the better maintenance of the ministers of this country. and one other third part to him or them that shall sue for the same in any court of record within this country, by bill, plaint, information or other action, wherein no essoygn, protection or wager of law shall be allowed; and for the better collecting, secureing and receiveing all and every the duties, customes and imposts aforesaid, *Bee it further enacted by the authority aforesaid, and it is hereby enacted*, That the right honourable the leiutenant governour for the time being, or the governour or commander in cheife of this their majesties dominion for the time being, may be impowered and desired to nominate, constitute and appoint such and so many collector or collectors in all and every the ports, places and districts of this countrie for the receiveing, secureing and collecting all and every part of the said duties, customes aud imposts upon all and every the goods, wares and merchantdises aforesaid, as he with the advice of the honourable councill shall think fit and convenient, which said collector or collectors are hereby impowered to demand, secure, and receive all and every the duties, customes and imposts before mentioned with full power to go on board any boat, ship or other vessell, or into any house, in the day time, where he shall have just cause to suspect any fraud to be commited or done, contrary to the true intent and meaning of this act, and for the better discovery thereof to search such house, ship, or vessell, or other place, and upon

On masters of vessels being privy to the fraud.

Fines, how appropriated.

How recovered.

Governor to appoint collectors.

Power & duty of collector.

How he may search and make seizures.

oath or information made to a justice of the peace of a fraud suspected to be commited, and his warrant obtained for detecting the same, in the presence of a sherrif or constable, in the day time, upon refusall of the owner or possessor, the door or doors of all and every such house, and houses, to break, and open, and to break open any chest, trunke, casque, or other thing whatsoever, in which any of the goods, wares or merchantdises aforesaid are suspected to be packed and concealed, and upon finding and discovering any such fraud or deceit as aforesaid, all and every such goods, wares and merchantdises to seize, and take into his or their possession and secure to and for the uses, intents and purposes before mentioned. And all manner of persons are hereby required to be aiding and assisting to the collector and collectors, his and their officers the informer, discoverer and seizer of such goods, wares and merchantdises exported or endeavoured to be exported contrary to the true intent and meaning of this act. And that all and every collector and collectors aforesaid shall and are hereby required some time in Aprill and October generall courts yearly to render a true and just account upon oath, and make payment of all and every such summ and summes of money as they and every of them shall receive and collect for the duties and penalties by this act imposed as aforesaid to such person and persons as shall be named, impower'd and appointed by this generall assembly, who is hereby impower'd to account with every such collector and collectors, and to demand, receive and take of and from, and every of them, all and every the sum and sumes of money ariseing due upon the said collector and collectors account, and to give him or them the allowance of six per cent out of the same for his trouble and paines taken therein, and for so much to give him and them sufficient discharges, and that the person or persons who shall be appointed to receive the monies ariseing by the said duties and penalties as aforesaid from the collectors thereof as aforesaid, shall, and is hereby authorised and required to keep and retaine the same in his own custody and possession untill he shall be ordered and required to pay and dispose of the same in manner and by such warrant and direction as is hereafter mentioned, which shall be sufficient to discharge

All persons required to aid and assist the collectors.

Collectors when to acc't.

Their allowance.

him of so much as he shall from time to time issue and pay as aforesaid, and shall be allowed upon his account which he shall and must make of the same to the next succeeding assembly, and so to every assembly successively, for which the said person or treasurer shall be allowed four per cent for his trouble and paines therein, and that in case the person or persons to be named to receive the said duties, customes and imposts from the said collector or collectors shall dureing the intervall of assemblies (*a*) die or depart out of this country, that in such case, the governour or commander in cheife for the time being, with the advice of the councell shall be impowered, and are hereby desired to nominate, constitute and appoint another sufficient person to supply his or their said places with the like power untill the next succeeding assembly, who shall have power to call to account and receive of the heires, executors, administrators and estate of the person or persons who shall (*b*) die or depart the countrey as aforesaid haveing any of the monies ariseing by force of this act in his or their custody or possession all and every such sum and summs of money to and for the uses aforesaid. *And bee it enacted by the authority aforesaid, and it is hereby enacted,* That all sum and summes of money and every part and parcell ariseing by virtue of this act shall be divided into three equall parts, one part whereof shall be to our Soveraign Lord and Lady the King and Queens Majesties, their heires and successors, and to and for the better support of the government in provideing armes and ammunition for the better defence thereof and building and maintaining convenient fortifications for the defence of (*c*) ships ariveing into the said ports, to be paid by the treasurer or treasurers to be appointed by vertue of this act to such person or persons, and in such order and

Allowance to treasurer.

Vacancies in office of collectors, how supplied.

Monies arising from duties, how appropriated.

One third for procuring arms and ammunition and building fortifications.

Various Readings.

(*a*) The words 'of assemblies' omitted in Northb. MS. but inserted in Ch. City and P. Rand. MSS.

(*b*) The word 'shall' omitted in Northb. MS. but inserted in Ch. City and P. Rand. MSS.

(*c*) The words 'the defence of' omitted in Northb. MS. but inserted in Ch. City and P. Rand. MSS.

manner as by the generall assembly shall be from time to time ordered and appointed and no other waies; another third part thereof towards the maintenance and incouragement of a pious and learned ministry to be equally distributed amongst the ministers of Gods word being the incumbents of the severall parishes in this countrey, in equall proportions, and that all and every church warden and church wardens with the major part of every vestry and vestries of every respective parish and parishes within this dominion do annually, some time in March, call and hold a vestry, and at the same make a certificate of the name of the present incumbent, and how long he hath continued in that cure, to the treasurer appointed to receive and keep the duety ariseing by vertue of this act, who together with two of the honourable councell not being collectors and two of the clergy, such as shall be appointed by the governour or commander in chiefe are yearly in Aprill to divide the said part of the duety ariseing by force of this act, aqually amongst the severall ministers, whose names are certifyed as aforesaid which summes so paid and allowed, shall be certified by the persons who proportion the same amongst the said ministers to the severall vestries of the parishes where they are resident, to the end the same may be discounted and allowed out of the salary of the said minister, and that he may be paid the remainder of the yearly allowance appointed by law to each minister in this country, at the usuall time of laying the levy by the vestry of the said parish and that the person or persons who shall be appointed to receive the monies ariseing by the duties upon the goods mentioned in this act from the severall collector and collectors of the same, do keep and reserve in his and their hands and possession the other third part of the said money to be hereafter diposed of by order of the generall assembly of this their majesties dominion towards the encouragement of learning in case the good designe of building a free schoole and colledge shall take its desired effect, or otherwise to be disposed of for the defraying of the publique charge of this country, and lessening the levy by the pole, and to and for no other use, intent and purpose whatsoever.

One-third to the clergy, in part of their annual salary.

How to be obtained.

And the remaining third, for the encouragement of learning.

Collectors and treasurer to give bond.

Provided alwaies that all and every treasurer and treasurers, collector and collectors to be appointed by vertue of this act do before their entries into their respective offices give bond with good and sufficient security for their due performance of their severall offices, according to the true intent and meaning of this act; and for the further prevention of frauds and discovery thereof in the impost duties and customes laid upon the severall commodities mentioned in this act, *Bee it enacted by the authority aforesaid, and it is hereby enacted,* That whatsoever person or persons shall from and after the said first day of June next export or carry out, or cause to be exported or carryed out of this government by land or water into an other government for the purchase of skins, furrs, or other Indian traffique, any goods, wares or other merchantdises whatsoever, and shall not first have the lycense or permit of the collector or other officer of the customs of that district, from whence he carryes the same, who is hereby required and commanded before the granting any such permit or lycense to take bond with good and sufficient security, that the full and whole produce of the said goods, wares and merchantdises in skins, furrs, or what other Indian traffique soever it shall happen to be, shall be brought into this countrey, and at the importation entered with him or some other lawfull appointed collector or officer, shall forfeit such goods, wares and merchantdises, or the vallue thereof, to be recovered in such manner, and to such uses as is in this act before exprest.

None to carry out goods to trade with Indians, without first giving bond to bring the proceeds into this country.

And bee it enacted by the authority aforesaid and it is hereby enacted, That the leiutenant governour or commander in cheife for the time being, with the advice of the councill be empowered at any time hereafter, as it shall be found convenient and necessary, any one or more of the above nominated five places, or townes quallifyed by this act for the buying and selling all manner of goods, wares, and merchantdises, to constitute, appoint and make a port or place for laying on shoar, or loading on board, all goods, tobaccoes and other merchantdises to be exported out of and imported into this their majesties dominion of Virginia, and that the same being so appointed be ever after equally quallifyed, priviledged and admited, and be so deemed, held and taken with any of the other ports already

Governor and council authorised to assign other places, for ports, &c.

nominated and appointed by this act for ports and places of landing goods, tobaccoes, wares and merchantdises to be imported into or exported out of this countrey; any thing heretofore contained to the contrary notwithstanding.

ACT IX.

*An act for a free trade with Indians.**

Edi. 1733 and 1752.

BEE *it enacted by their majesties leiutenant governour, councill and burgesses of this present generall assembly, and the authority thereof, and it is hereby enacted,* That all former clauses of former acts of assembly limiting, restraineing, and prohibitting trade with Indians be, and stand hereby repealed, and they are hereby repealed, and that from henceforth there be a free and open trade for all persons at all times, and at all (*a*) places with all indians whatsoever And for the future prevention of such mischeifes as have frequently happened at huntings, commonly called fire huntings and other huntings remote from the plantations, *Bee it enacted by the authority aforesaid, and it is hereby enacted,* That no person or persons whatsoever shall hereafter presume to goe an hunting remote from the English plantations without first having obtained the lycense and permission of their majesties leiutenant govervour or commander in cheife for the time being and the councell of state under such restrictions, limitations and conditions as at the time of giveing such permission shall be by them thought fit to be enjoyned and appointed.

All former laws, limiting and restraining trade with Indians repealed.

Henceforth, a free and open trade with all Indians, at all times & places whatever.

No person to go a hunting remote from the settlements, without a license.

Various Readings.

* This act was re-enacted in the revisal of 1705, and again in the edition of 1733, in which last it forms sect. 12, of chap. 52.—This is the same law, on which the old general court first founded their decision, that the right of making slaves of Indians was taken away; though at that time it had not been discovered that the act existed as far back as 1691. The supreme court of appeals have since, extended the principle to cases where Indians were brought in between 1691 and 1705. See 2 Hen. & Munf. 149, *Pallas & others* v. *Hill & others*.

(*a*) The words 'at all' not in Northb. MS. but inserted in Ch. City and P. Rand. MSS.

ACT X.

Edi. 1733 and 1752.

An act to prevent Horses running at large and barkeing fruit trees.

Preamble.

FORASMUCH as sundry horses, mares, and colts runeing in the woods at large do often prove very injurious to the inhabitants of this countrey by breakeing into orchards, and barkeing and distroying fruit trees, and committing sundry other mischeifes; for prevention whereof for the future, *Bee it enacted by their majesties leiutenant governour, councell and burgesses of this present* (a) *Generall Assembly and by the authority thereof, and it is hereby enacted*, that from and after the first day of October next, all and every owner and owners of such horse or horses, mares or colts shall well and sufficiently keep and secure him or them within their owne fenced grounds, and in case that any time after the said first day of October, any such horse or horses shall be found running at large and without such fenced grounds, and shall be taken up and delivered to the owner or owners thereof, such owner or owners shall pay to the person delivering the same, and makeing good proofe by his owne corporall oath and one other evidence, before some one of their majesties justices of the peace for the county where such owner shall dwel, of his so takeing up the said horse or horses, without any means by him any other person to his knowledge used, for the letting at liberty such horses so iaken up, one hundred pounds of tobacco and casquê for each horse.

Owners of horses, notorious for barking fruit trees to keep them in their inclosures.

If taken when running at large, the owner to pay the taker up 100 lbs. of tobacco.

And bee it further enacted by the authority aforesaid, That if at any time after the said first day of October, any such horse or horses shall breake into any orchard or garden and spoyle, barke, or (b) distroy any fruit tree or trees, the owner or owners of such horse or horses, shall pay to the party injuryed as aforesaid, and that shall make sufficient proofe of the same, the sum

---

Various Readings.

(a) The word 'present' omitted in Ch. City & P. Rand. MSS. but inserted in Northb. MS.

(b) 'Or' in Ch. City and P. Rand. MSS. 'and' in Northb. MS.

of two hundred pounds of tobacco and casque, for the first trespass, and for such horse or horses second trespass proved as aforeaid, four hundred pounds of tobacco and casque, to be recovered by action of debt in any court of judicature within this colonie; and if any horse or horses shall (c) the third time commit any mischeife, it shall and may be lawfull for any person or persons injured thereby as aforesaid, and haveing sufficient proofe thereof, to kill and distroy any such horse or horses, either by gunn or other waies; *alwaise provided* that every owner or owners of any orchard or fruit trees intending to take the benefitt of this act shall from time to time, and at all times, after the said first day of October next, well and sufficiently fence and enclose such orchard or fruit trees with a good strong and substantiall ffence four foot and an halfe high at the least.

For the 1st offence of breaking into orchards and breaking fruit trees the owner to pay 200 lbs. of tobacco: and 400 lbs. of tobacco for 2d offence; and for 3d offence may kill the horse. Provided that the orchards be well inclosed with a fence 4 and ½ feet high.

Provided alwaies, and it is the true intent and meaning of this act, that the penalty of one hundred pounds of tobacco imposed upon the owners of such horses, mares, colts &c. as shall be found running at large and without fenced grounds shall be understood, deemed and taken to extend to the owners of such horses, mares and colts only as are notoriously known to be barkers and destroyers of fruite trees intended to be prevented by this act, and which may be proved such by sufficient witnesses, altho' not taken in the actuall doing thereof and to noe other, any thing in this act heretofore contained to the contrary notwithstanding.

And provided that the horse be notoriously a barker of fruit trees.

ACT XI.

An act for the more effectuall suppressing the severall sins and offences of swaring, cursing, profaineing Gods holy name, Sabbath abuseing, drunkenness, ffornication, and adultery.

Edi. 1733 and 1752.

WHEREAS notwithstanding the many good laws before this time made and still in force prohibiting swearing, curseing, prophaneing Gods holy name,

Preamble, reciting former laws against swearing, cursing and profaneness.

Various Readings.

(c) The word 'be' inserted in P. Rand. MS. but not in Northb. or Ch. City MSS.

Sabbath abuseing, drunkenness, fornication and adultery, perticularly the 13th act of assembly, entituled, Church wardens to make presentments, the 9th act of assembly entituled, Sundays not to be prophained, with severall other acts against (*a*) the aforesaid crimes and vices, partly for want of due observation of the same laws, have not produced the desired effect, and partly for the imperfection that is found and doth appeare in them in not directing what method shall be followed to bring the offenders to condign punishment, and for want of sufficient penalties being appointed in the said lawes; and as the said acts and statutes were at the time of makeing them, thought to be very good and beneficiall to the commonwealth (as all of them yet are) so as (*b*) if the substance of as many of the said lawes as are necessary to be continued, shall be digested and reduced into one sole law and statute, and in the same a method prescribed for the punishment of offenders with an account of what penalties the offenders therein shall incur, there is good hope that it will come to pass that the same law, being duly executed, will suppress the aforementioned vices, reforme our lives, and be a means that the blessings of Almighty God be showred down upon us; forasmuch therefore as all swareing, curseing and prophaining Gods holy name, is forbidden by the word of God, *Bee it enacted by their majesties leiutenant governour, councell and burgesses of this present general assembly, and the authority thereof, and it is hereby enacted* That no person or persons whatsoever shall from henceforth swear, curse, or prophaine Gods holy name, and if any person or persons shall offend herein, and shall thereof be convicted by the oath of two witnesses, or by confession of the party, then every such offender shall for every time soe offending, forfeit and pay the summ of one shilling; and forasmuch as nothing is more acceptable to God then the true and sincere service and worship of him according

Fine of 1 shilling imposed for every offence of swearing, cursing, or profaning God's holy name.

Various Readings.

(*a*) The word 'against' omitted in P. Rand. MS. but inserted in Ch. City and Northb. MSS.

(*b*) The word 'as' omitted in Ch. City and P. Rand. MSS. but inserted in Northb. MS.

to his holy will, and that the holy keeping of the Lords day is a principall part of the true service of God, which in very many places of this dominion hath been, and is now prophained and neglected, by a disorderly sort of people, *Bee it enacted by their majesties leiutenant Governour, Councell and Burgesses of this present General Assembly, and the authority thereof, and it is hereby enacted*, That there shall be no meetings, assemblies, or concourse of people out of their own parishes on the Lords day; and that no person or persons whatsoever shall travell upon the said day, and that no other thing or matter whatsoever be done on that day which tends to the prophanation of the same, but that the same be kept holy in all respects, upon pain that every person and persons so offending and being convicted as aforesaid shall loose and forfeit twenty shillings.

Lord's day to be kept holy; no meetings, assemblies, or concourse of people out of their own parishes, or travelling permitted on the Sabbath, under penalty of 20 shillings.

And whereas that loathsom and odious sin of drunkenness is of too common use within this dominion, being the root and foundation of many other enormous sins, as blood shed, stobbing, murther, swearing, fornication, adultery and such like, to the great dishonour of God and of this dominion, the overthrow of many good acts and manuall trades, the disableing of divers workmen, and the generall impoverishing of many of their majesties good subjects, abusively wasting the good creatures of God *Bee it enacted by their majesties leiutenant governour, councell and burgesses of this generall assembly, and the authority thereof, and it is hereby enacted*, That all and every person and persons who shall from henceforth be drunk, and of the same offence of drunkenness be lawfully convicted as aforesaid shall for every such offence forfeit and pay ten shillings, and if the offender or offenders of any, or of all the aforesaid vices or crimes be not able to pay the said fines and forfeitures aforementioned, then every offender or offenders therein, shall be committed to the stocks for every offence, there to be and remaine for the space of three full hours; and whereas fornication and adultery are two filthy and greivous sins and offences as well against the law of God, as of the law of man; *Bee it enacted by their majesties leiutenant governour, councill and burgesses of this generall assembly and the authority hereof, and it is hereby enacted*, That

Fine of 10 shillings for gett'g drunk.

Persons unable to pay the above fines, to be committed to the stocks 3 hours.

Person committing fornication, to pay a fine of 10*l* sterling; and adultery, 20*l*. sterling; and if the offenders be unable to pay, to receive thirty lashes, or be imprisoned 3 months.

every person and persons committing fornication, and being convicted as aforesaid, shall for every time so offending forfeit and pay the summ of ten pounds sterling, and that every person and persons committing adultery, and being convicted as aforesaid, shall for every time so offending forfeit and pay the sume of twenty pounds sterling, and if the offender or offenders of any of the aforesaid two sins and offences of fornication and adultery be not able to pay the fines and forfeitures for the said offences mentioned, then every offender and offenders therein shall for every time so offending receive on his, her, or their, bare backs, thirty lashes well laid on, or three moneths imprisonment without bail or maineprise; and whereas many inhabitants of this countrey of dissolute and ill lives and conversations entertain many times in their houses women of ill names and reputation, suspected of incontenency or by other indirect meanes provide for the maintenance of such women whose company they frequent,

Persons frequenting the company of a lewd woman, or entertaining her in his house after being admonished by the minister and church wardens with the consent of the vestry, to be punished as for adultery.

Bee it enacted by their majesties leiutenant governour, councell and burgesses of this generall assembly and the authority thereof, and it is hereby enacted, That every person and persons who shall so harbour, entertaine or provide for the maintenance of such woman or women, or frequent her or their company, or the company of any other lewd,* after publique admonition to avoid the same, given by the minister and Church wardens, by and with the consent of the vestrey and vestryes of the parish or parishes wherein such person or persons shall dwel, and in case there be no minister then the Church wardens of the same, by the consent aforesaid, shall forfeit and pay for every time it shall be proved, that he or they have been in company of such woman or women after such admonition as aforesaid, as if he or they had really been convicted of adultery, and every woman or women guilty of the same offence shall receive the like punishment.

Grand juries to present offences under this law.

And be it enacted by the authority aforesaid, and it is hereby enacted, That the grand juries of every respective county within this dominion do twice yearly make presentments against the offenders of this law, to the court of the county where the offence shall be committed, and that the justices of

* The word 'woman' seems to be wanting in the MSS.

the same punish the offenders according to this act, all which said forfeiture shall be divided into three equall parts, one third thereof towards the building aud repairing the Church or Chappel of ease in the parish where the said offence shall be committed one third towards the mainterance of the minister of the same, and the other third for him or them that will sue or informe for the same by bill, plaint, or information, or action of debt in any court of record within this dominion, in which no essoign, protection or wager of law shall be allowed. Fines how appropriated.

ACT XII.

An act declareing the dutie of Tanners, Curriers (a) and Shoemakers. Edit. 1752.

FORASMUCH as divers and sundry deceits and abuses have been hitherto committed, and daily are committed and practised by the Tanners, curriers, and workers of leather of this their majesties colony and dominion of Virginia, to the great injury and damage of the inhabitants thereof, for prevention of which for the future, *Bee it enacted by the lieutenant governour, councell and burgesses of this present generall assembly, and by the authority thereof, and it is hereby enacted,* That from and after the 29th day of March next comeing, no person or persons whatsoever, which shall after the said 29th of March, occupy or use by him or themselves, or by any other person or persons, the craft or mistery of tanning of leather, shall suffer any hyde or skin to lie in the limes till the same be over limed, nor shall put any hide or skins into any tanfattes before the lime be well and perfectly sokened and wrought out of them, and every of them, nor shall after the said 29th day of March, put to sale any tann'd hydes or skins but such as shall be first viewed, approved, and sealed by the viewers hereafter in this act appointed, upon forfeiture of such hydes, skin, or leather so offered or put to sale. Edit. 1733, Preamble. Duty of tan'rs in liming their hides.

Various Readings.

(a) The word '*curriers*' omitted in P. Rad. MS. but inserted in Northb. MS.

Duty of curriers prescribed.

And forasmuch as no leather can be so well tann'd but it may be marred and spoyled in the curring. *Bee it therefore enacted by the authority aforesaid, and it is hereby enacted*, that from and after the said 29th day of March next comeing, no person or persons shall curry any kind of leather except it be well and perfectly tann'd, nor shall after the said 29th day of March next, curry any hyde or skin being not thoroughly dry, after his wett season, with any other than good stuff, nor with less of that, then the leather will receive, nor shall curry any kind of leather meet for overleather and inner soales but with good and sufficient stuffe, being fresh and not salt, upon pain of forfeiture for every such offence ten shillings to the owner of each hyde or skin so damnified. *And be it further enacted by the authority aforesaid, and it is hereby enacted*, that the court of each respective county for the time being shall appoint one or more fitt person or persons, from time to time, to search and try all such curryed leather, and shall with a seale therefore to be prepaired with convenient speed, after currying, and request made, scale such leather as they shall find sufficiently curryed, takeing for every hyde so sealed after the rate of two shillings and six pence for the dicker of tenn hides, and for every six dosen of calves skins, two shillings and six pence and no more, to be paid by the owner of the said hyde or skins; and forasmuch as leather well tann'd and curryed may by the negligence, deceit, or evill workmanship of the cordwainer or shoemaker be used deceitfully to the hurt of the occupier or wearer thereof, *Bee it therefore enacted by the authority aforesaid, and it is hereby enacted*, That no person or persons which after the said 29th day of March next comeing shall occupy the mistry or occupation of a cordwainer or shoemaker, shall make, or cause to be made, any boots, shoes, slippers, or any part of them of Virginia leather not curryed other than deere skins, calfe skins, or goat skins made and dressed, or to be made and dressed like unto Spanish leather, but of leather well and truly tann'd and curryed in manner and form aforesaid, or of leather well and truly tann'd only, and well and substantially sewed with good thread well twisted and made and sufficiently waxed with wax well rosined, and the stitches hard drawn with handleathers.

Persons to be appointed by every court to examine and seal leather after it is curried.

Their fees for a *dicker* or ten hides;

for six dozen calves skins.

Cordwainers or shoemakers not to work up any leather but such as is well curried and dressed;

and shall use good thread well twisted and waxed.

And bee it further enacted by the authority aforesaid, and it is hereby enacted, That the justices of each respective county within this colony shall appoint and swear yearly one or more person of the most honest and skilfull men within their counties to search and view within the precincts of their said offices, which shall as often as they shall think good, or need shall be, make like search within their limits, and shall have a mark or seale prepaired for that purpose, and that the said searchers or one of them shall keep the same seale, or marke, and with the same shall seal and marke such leather as they shall find sufficient, and not other.

Searchers to be appointed to seal leather well tanned.

And if the said searchers, or any of them do find any leather sold or offered to be sold which shall be tann'd, wrought, converted, or used, contrary to the true intent and meaning of this act, or any leather insufficiently curryed, or any boots, shoes, bridles, or any other thing made of tann'd or curryed leather, insufficiently tann'd, curryed, or wrought, contrary to any provision in this present act, it shall be lawfull to the said searchers or any of them to seize all such leather, shoes, or other ware made of leather, and to retaine the same in their custody untill such time as the same shall be tryed by such tryers and in such manner and forme as is hereafter in this act appointed.

Their duty to seize all leather not well tanned or curried, or boots, shoes, &c. made of such.

And bee it further enacted by the authority aforesaid, and it is hereby enacted, That the justices of each respective county within whose precincts any such seisure of any kind of tann'd leather, red or curryed, or of any shoes, boots, or other wares, made of tann'd leather shall happen to be, shall with all convenient speed, after notice unto them given, of any such seisure appoint six honest and expert men to try whether the same leather, boots, shoes, or other wares, so seized be sufficient and according to the true intent of this act or not, the same tryall to be made openly upon the next court day after such seisure.

Six persons to be appointed, by the justices to examine the leather, boots, &c. seized.

Examination to be made openly on next court day.

And bee it further enacted, by the authority aforesaid, and it is hereby enacted, That each of the said persons so elected and appointed for the tryall of the said leather, shoes, boots, and other wares, made of tann'd leather, so to be seised as aforesaid, shall proceed and doe their duties therein without delay, according to the true intent and meaning of this present act, upon paine

Examiners liable to fines for failing to do their duty.

that every of them makeing default therein, shall be fined at the discretion ot the court of the said county.

Penalty, on searchers and sealers, failing to do their duty.

And be it fu 'her enacted by the authority aforesaid, and it is hereby enacted, That if any searcher or sealer of leather shall refuse with convenient speed to seale any leather sufficiently tann'd, wrought or used according to the true intent and (a) meaning of this present act, that then every such searcher or sealer shall forfeit for every such offence forty shillings; and further that if any searcher of leather shall receive any bribe, or exact any other fee for the execution of his said office, then is by this present law limited for the searching and sealing of leather, then every such searcher or sealer, so offending, shall forfeit for every such offence twenty pounds sterling, and that if any person or persons duly elected according to the true meaning of this present act, to and for the execution of the said office of searching or sealeing of leather, refuse to execute the said office, that then the person or persons so refuseing shall forfeit and pay five pounds sterling.

For receiving a bribe or exacting more than legal fees.

Penalty for resisting searchers and sealers in the execution of their office.

And bee it futher enacted by the authority aforesaid, and it is hereby enacted, That if any person will, after the said 29th of March next comeing, wilfully withstand any such search to be made according to the tenor of this act, as is aforesaid, or will not suffer the said tryers and searchers so appointed to enter into his or their house, or houses, or other places, to view and search, at their will and pleasure, all manner of tann'd leather, and all manner of shoes, boots, males saddles, and all manner of wares wrought and made, or to be wrought and made of leather, and to seize and carry away all such leather, shoes and ware as they shall find insufficiently tanned, curried or wrought, or (b) made of ill stuffe, that then all and every such person and persons so denying and withstanding, and not suffering the

---

Various Readings.

(a) The words 'intent and' omitted in P. Rand. MS. but inserted in Ch. City and Northb. MSS.

(b) The words 'or to be wrought and made of leather, and to 'seize and carry away all such leather, shoes and ware as they 'shall find insufficiently tanned, curried, or wrought, or' omitted in Northb. MS. but inserted in Ch. City and P. Rand. MSS.

said tryers and searches, or any of them so appointed for the time being, to enter and make search and seise as is aforesaid, shall loose and forfeit for every time so denying and withstanding five pounds sterling.

For selling or exchanging tan'd leather before it is searched and sealed.

And bee it further enacted by the authority aforesaid, (a) *and it is hereby enacted,* That it shall not be lawfull for any person or persons to buy, sell, or exchange any tann'd leather, before the same shall be searched and sealed, upon pain to forfeit the said leather and the value thereof so bought, sold or exchanged and not searched and sealed.

Penalties on curriers, cord wainers or shoemakers and cobblers, for violations of this act.

And be it further enacted by the authority aforesaid, and it is hereby enacted, That if any curryer after the said 29th day of March next comeing, doe curry any leather insufficiently tann'd, or after the said 29th day of March, do not curry such leather as he doth substantially and well, according to the meaning and purport of this act, or if any shoe maker, cordwainer or cobler, after the said 29th day of March, put any tann'd leather into any shoes, boots, slippers, or other things made of tan'd leather, which shall not be well and perfectly tann'd according to the purport and true meaning of this act, or after the said 29th day of March, doe put any curred leather into any boots, shoes or slippers, or other things, made of leather which shall not be well and sufficiently tann'd and curryed, and also sealed as is aforesaid, or doe make boots, shoes, slippers, or other things, made of tann'd leather, in any other manner then is above specified and ordained, or if any shoemaker, sadler, or other artificer useing, cutting or workeing of leather, doe make any wares of any tann'd leather insufficiently tann'd and of tann'd and curryed leather being not sufficiently tann'd and curryed as is aforesaid, or do not make their wares belonging to their severall occupations sufficiently and substantially, that then every person so offending shall forfeit for every such severall offence or default, the said wares and just vallue thereof, all which paines, penalties and forfeitures aforesaid of sums of money aforesaid shall be di-

Fines, how appropriated.

Various Readings.

(a) The word 'aforesaid' omitted in P. Rand. MS. but inserted in Ch. City and Northb. MSS.

vided into three equall parts, one part whereof shall be to our Soveraign Lord and Lady the King and Queen, their heires and successors towards the better support of the government of this their majesties colony and dominion of Virginia, and the contingent charges thereof, and another part to him or them that shall first sue for the same in any court of the record within this colony, by action of debt, bill, plaint, or information, or otherwise, in which suit no essoigne, protection or wager of law shall be admitted or allowed, and the other third part thereof shall be disposed by the court of such county where the offence shall be committed towards the building, erecting and supporting an house of correction, and all such leather, shoes, boots, slippers, wares, stuffe or other thing whatsoever made of tann'd leather or curryed leather, which shall be seized by virtue of this act, and shall be found by the tryers to be appointed as aforesaid to be insufficient, shall be forfeited and distributed as hereafter followeth, that is to say, such leather or stuffe so seised to be brought to the court house of the county, where such seizure shall be made, there to be appraized by indifferent persons, and the value thereof to be divided into three parts, whereof one to be to their majesties, their heires and successors towards the better support of the government and the contingent charges thereof, and another part to the first seizor or seizors of the said unlawfull stuffe, and another part to be disposed of by the court of such county where such seisure shall be made, towards the building, erecting and supporting an house of correction.

Such leather, shoes, &c. to be seized, and carried to the court-house.

How distributed.

What shall be deemed leather.

And for the avoyding of all ambiguities and doubts, which may and doe grow and arise upon the difinition and interpretation of this word leather, *Be it enacted and declared*, that the hydes and skinns of oxe, steer, bull, cow, calfe, deer, goats and sheep being tann'd shall be, and ever hath been reputed and taken leather.

ACT XIII.

And act enjoyning the planting and dressing of Flax and Hemp.

Edi. 1733 and 1752.

Preamble.

FORASMUCH as for some time past the inhabitants of this country have suffered great want of lynnen by reason of the warrs, and to the end the same may be endeavoured to be prevented, *Be it enacted by their majesties leiutenant governor, councill and burgesses of this general assembly, and the authority thereof, and it is hereby enacted,* That every tytheable person within this countrey, doe make or cause to be made, one pound of drest flax and one pound of drest hemp, or two pounds of either, by the last day of October, which shall be in the yeare 1692, and so yearely and every year after the said last day of October, upon penalty of forfeiting for every pound of flax or hemp neglected to be made as aforesaid, the sum of sixty pounds of tobaccoe to be paid by the master, owner or overseer of any family or company of servants, or by any free tytheable deficient as aforesaid; and for the better discovery of any such deficiency, *Be it enacted by their majesties leiutenant governour, councell and burgesses of this present generall assembly and the awhority thereof, and it is hereby enacted,* That all and every master, owner or overseer, or free tytheable as aforesaid makeing such quantity, as by this act is enjoyned, shall carry the same to the next justice of the peace of the county where he resides, and make oath or other sufficient proofe, that the same is of his or their owne growth, of which the said justice is hereby enjoyned to grant such person certificate, which he shall produce to the next court held for that county, and that all persons neglecting to obtaine such certificate as aforesaid, shall be adjudged, deemed and held to have made breach of this law, and to be proceeded against accordingly, the one third parte of such fines and forfeitures to be to our Soveraign Lord and Lady the King and Queen, their heires and successors for and towards the better support of this their majesties dominion of Virginia and the contingent charges thereof, one other third part to him or them that will informe of and sue for the same in any court of record within

Proportion of dressed flax and hemp to be made by each tythable

Penalty for neglect.

Certificate of the making, how to be obtained.

Fines, how appropriated.

his colony by action of debt, byll, plaint or information, and the other third part to the use of that county wherein the same shall be forfeited.

This act to continue in force for three yeares from and after the said last day of October, anno 1692.

ACT XIV.

Edi. 1733 and 1752.

An act for the alteration of the time for processioning of Lands.

Act 78 of printed laws (vol. 2, p. 101) amended.

WHEREAS in the act of assembly relateing to processioning land, being the 78th act of the printed lawes, it is directed that the said act be put in effectuall execution between Easter (*a*) and Whitsuntide, which time of the year being found inconvenient in many respects, *Bee it therefore enacted by their majesties leiutenant Governour, Councill and Burgesses of this present generall assembly, and the authority thereof, and it is hereby enacted,* That soe much of the said act as appoints the time of processioning be, and is hereby repealed. *And be it enacted by the authority aforesaid, and it is hereby enacted,* That the time for processioning lands hereafter be between the last day of 7ber (*b*) and the last day of March.

Lands, when to be processioned.

ACT XV.

Edi. 1733 and 1752.

An act for the better defence of the country.

Preamble.

WHEREAS great and many are the dangers which surround and threaten this dominion, being a defenceless and open countrey, subject either to invasions and incursions of our inveterate enemies, most neighbouring countries haveing already been in-

Various Readings.

(*a*) The word 'Easter' omitted in P. Rand. MS. but inserted in Ch. City and Northbb. MSS.

(*b*) 'September' in P. Rand. MS. '7ber' in Ch. City and Northumberland MSS.

volved in such difficulties and troubles that wee be not wholy surprised in case wee should be visited by such afflictions, but be capable of makeing as vigorous a defence as possible, and for the better and more effectuall preventing murthers, depredations, incursions and other spoyles that may be committed by our Indian and other enemies, *Bee it enacted by their majesties lieutenant governour, councell and burgesses of this present generall assembly, and the authority thereof and it is hereby enacted*, That whereas the right honourable the lieutenant governour by and with the advice of the councell out of their great (*a*) care for the preservasion and security of the peace of the countrey have already raised, listed and appointed one lieutenant, eleaven souldiers, and two Indians on the head of each great river, well furnished with horses and other accoutrements to range and scout about the heads of the said great rivers for which they serve, and in such other places as shall be most likely to discover our enemies, that the said soldiers be, and are hereby continued as already setled for so long time (not exceeding the last day of Aprill, which shall be in anno 1692) as the governour with the advice of the councell shall think convenient and necessary, and that the pay of each officer and soldier be as followeth: The lieutenant or commander of each party of souldiers finding himselfe horse, armes, ammunition and provision, shall have and receive five thousand pounds of tobacco and casque out of the publique levie for one whole year, and so after that rate for a longer or shorter time, and each soldier finding himselfe horse, armes, furniture, ammunition and other necessaries, three thousand pounds of tobacco and casque, and so after that rate for a longer or shorter time; and whereas it is impossible at present so to provide, that the countrey be effectually defended with the least trouble and charge to the inhabitants thereof, *Be it enacted by their majesties lieutenant governour, councell and burgesses of this present generall assembly, and the authority thereof, and it is hereby enacted*, That

A lieutenant, 11 soldiers & 2 Indians appointed by the gov'r to range & scout at the heads of each great river, continued in service.

Their pay.

Various Readings.

(*a*) 'Owne' in P. Rand. MS. 'great' in Ch. City and Northumberland MSS.

Gov'r authorised to raise men in cases of emergency; the lieutenant governour or commander in cheife for the time being with the advice of the councell have power upon all occasions between this time and the last day of Aprill 1692, to raise, levy and muster so many and such a number of men, horses, armes and ammunition for the better defence of the same, and such forces already raised, or to be raised at all times to disband and discharge, as to them sholl seem most conduceing to the advantage of this dominion, which said souldiers already settled or to be raised by force of this act, are upon all occasions to observe, performe and keepe all such directions, orders and commands as shall be appointed by the lieutenant governour, or commander in cheife for the time being, with the advice of the councell, and shall receive pay and be satisfyed proportionable to the time they shall be in service after these rates, vizt. each captain finding himselfe horse, armes, ammunition, provision and all other necessaries, tenn thousand pounds of tobacco and casque for one yeare, and so proportionably for a longer or shorter time, each lieutenant finding and provideing himselfe as aforesaid after the rate, as in this act is before exprest, and every private soldier mounted, armed and provided as aforesaid after the rate as in this act is before mentioned.

who are to obey the orders of the governor.

Their pay.

Pay of the two Indians. *And be it enacted by the authority aforesaid, and it is hereby enacted,* That the two Indians by this act appointed shall each of them have and receive from the lieutenant of the Rangers to whome he belongs, eight yards of duffills and two barrells of Indian corne for the service for one year, and so proportionably for a longer or shorter time, and the said lieutenant shall be reimburst by the publique, and that the said lieutenant doe take care to provide by warrant from the commander in cheife of the county where he resides, for each of the said Indians, one able horse, bridle and sadle, for which the owner or owners of the said horse or horses furnished as aforesaid, shall have and receive from the country in the next publique levie after the rate of eighty pounds of tobacco and casque for one moneth, and so proportionably for a longer or shorter time.

And forasmuch as by a clause of the 8th act of assembly, made at James Citty, October the tenth, 1665, it is enacted that the bounds of the Indians on the south side James river, be from the heads of the Southern branches of the Black water to the Appomatuck Indians, and thence to the Manokin Town, for the better explaining and ascertaining the bounds betwixt the English and Indians on the south side of James River, *Be it enacted by their majesties lieutenant governour, councell and burgesses of this present Generall Assembly and the authority thereof, and it is hereby enacted,* That a line from the head of the cheife or principle branch of the black water, to the upper part of the old Appamattocks Indian Town feild, and thence to the upper end of the Manokin Town be judged, deemed, held and taken, to be the said bounds, and that the right honourable the lieutenant governour, with the advice of the councell bee requested to appoint some surveyor or surveyors to lay out, ascertain and plainly marke the said lines, and that all pattents or other grants of any lands laying without the said bounds be, and hereby are declared void and null to all intents and purposes as if the same had never been granted. *And be it enacted by the authoritie aforesaid, and it is hereby enacted,* That the right honourable the lieutenant governour with the advice of the councill be, and is hereby requested and impowered to appoint surveyors to lay out and marke a road from such convenient place above the inhabitants on the north side James River as he shall think fit, to some place above the inhabitants on Rappahanoc river, and likewise to appoint persons to cleer the same at least twenty five foot wide, for which service the said surveyor or surveyors and other persons imployed shall be allowed in the next publique levie. *And be it further enacted by the authority aforesaid and it is hereby enacted,* That no surveyor or surveyors doe within three yeares next after the laying out and cleering of the said road presume to lay out or survey any land or lands without the same for any person whatsoever, and also that no person which already hath taken up or pattented any land which may happen to be without the said road, do adventure to seat thereon untill the said three yeares after such laying out be expired. *Alwaise provided,* that the said time of restraint shall not be accounted, deemed or taken to be any part of the time limited for seating or planting of lands.

Boundaries of Indians on the south side of James river explained.

Surveyor to mark the said lines.

Patents for lands, without those bounds, declared void.

A road from above the inhabitants on the north side of James river to a place above the inhabitants on Rappahannock river to be laid out and cleared.

No surveys of lands without that road to be made for three years.

Proviso.

ACT XVI.

Edi. 1733 and 1752.

An act for suppressing outlying Slaves.

WHEREAS many times negroes, mulattoes, and other slaves unlawfully absent themselves from their masters and mistresses service, and lie hid and lurk in obscure places killing hoggs and committing other injuries to the inhabitants of this dominion, for remedy whereof for the future, *Be it enacted by their majesties lieutenant governour, councell and burgesses of this present generall assembly, and the authoritie thereof, and it is hereby enacted*, that in all such cases upon intelligence of any such negroes, mulattoes, or other slaves lying out, two of their majesties justices of the peace of that county, whereof one to be of the quorum, where such negroes, mulattoes or other slave shall be, shall be impowered and commanded, and are hereby impowered and commanded to issue out their warrants directed to the sherrife of the same county to apprehend such negroes, mulattoes, and other slaves, which said sherriffe is hereby likewise required upon all such occasions to raise such and soe many forces from time to time as he shall think convenient and necessary for the effectual apprehending such negroes, mulattoes and other slaves, and in case any negroes, mulattoes or other slave or slaves lying out as aforesaid shall resist, runaway, or refuse to deliver and surrender him or themselves to any person or persons that shall be by lawfull authority employed to apprehend and take such negroes, mulattoes or other slaves that in such cases it shall and may be lawfull for such person and persons to kill and distroy such negroes, mulattoes, and other slave or slaves by gunn or any otherwaise whatsoever.

Outlying negroes, mulattoes or slaves, how to be apprehended.

Sheriff may raise forces to apprehend them.

Such negroes, mulattoes, or slaves, resisting, running away, or refusing to surrender may be killed and destroyed.

Compensation to master for slave killed.

Provided that where any negroe or mulattoe slave or slaves shall be killed in pursuance of this act, the owner or owners of such negro or mulatto slave shall be paid for such negro or mulatto slave four thousand pounds of tobacco by the publique. And for prevention of that abominable mixture and spurious issue which hereafter may encrease in this dominion, as well by negroes, mulattoes, and Indians intermarrying with English, or other white women, as by their unlawfull accompanying with one another, *Be it enacted by the authoritie aforesaid, and it is hereby enacted*, that for the time to come, whatsoever English or other white man or woman being free shall intermarry with a negroe, mulatto, or Indian man or woman bond or free shall within three months after such marriage be banished and removed from this dominion forever, and that the justices of each respective countie within this dominion make it their perticular care, that this act be put in effectuall execution. *And be it further enacted by the authoritie aforesaid, and it is hereby enacted*, That if any English woman being free shall have a bastard child by any negro or mulatto, she pay the sume of fifteen pounds sterling, within one moneth after such bastard child shall be born, to the Church wardens of the parish where she shall be delivered of such child, and in default of such payment she shall be taken into the possession of the said Church wardens and disposed of for five yeares, and the said fine of fifteen pounds, or whatever the woman shall be disposed of for, shall be paid, one third part to their majesties for and towards the support of the government and the contingent charges thereof, and one other third part to the use of the parish where the offence is committed, and the other third part to the informer, and that such bastard child be bound out as a servant by the said Church wardens untill he or she shall attaine the age of thirty yeares, and in case such English woman that shall have such bastard child be a servant, she shall be sold by the said church wardens, (after her time is expired that she ought by law to serve her master) for five yeares, and the money she shall be sold for divided as is before appointed, and the child to serve as aforesaid.

White man or woman, bond or free, intermarrying with a negro, mulatto or Indian, to be banished for ever.

White women having a bastard by a negro or mulatto to pay 15*l.* sterling; in default of payment to be sold for 5 years.

Such bastard to be bound by church wardens till 30 years of age.

Servant women offending to be likewise sold; after the expiration of their term of service.

And forasmuch as great inconveniences may happen to this country by the setting of negroes and mulattoes free, by their either entertaining negro slaves from their masters service, or receiveing stolen goods, or being grown old bringing a charge upon the country; for prevention thereof, *Be it enacted by the authority aforesaid, and it is hereby enacted*, That no negro or mulatto be after the end of this present session of assembly set free by any person or persons whatsoever, unless such person or persons, their heires, executors or administrators pay for the transportation of such negro or

No negro or mulatto to be set free, unless the person freeing them pay for their transportation out of the country within six months.

Penalty; applied towards paying the expenses of transportation.

negroes out of the countrey within six moneths after such setting them free, upon penalty of paying of tenn pounds sterling to the Church wardens of the parish where such person shall dwell with, which money, or so much thereof as shall be necessary, the said Church wardens are to cause the said negro or mulatto to be transported out of the countrey, and the remainder of the said money to imploy to the use of the poor of the parish.

ACT XVII.

Edi. 1733 and 1752.

An act for lessening the Levy by the Pole and laying an imposition on Liquors.

Preamble.

FORASMUCH as a more suitable expedient cannot be found to lessen the levy by the pole on the inhabitants of this their majesties dominion of Virginia, and to defray other contingent charges of the government then to lay an imposition on all liquors imported into this country, *Bee it therefore enacted by their majesties leiutenant governour. councell and burgesses of this present Generall Assembly and the authority thereof, and it is hereby enacted,* That the severall rates, duties, and imposts hereby set and imposed upon all and every the hereafter named foreign liquors which shall be imported or brought into all or any the ports of this dominion from and after the 31st day of May, anno 1691, shall be from time to time satisfied and paid to their majesties, their heires and successors, and to and for the uses, intents and purposes hereafter mentioned, and to and for no other use, intent or purpose whatsoever, by the merchant and merchants, owner and owners, importer or importers of the same. vizt. for every gallon of wine of all sorts whatsoever, brandy, rum. syder, or any other spirits or liquors imported into this dominion, except alwaise what shall come directly from England, the sum of foure pence, being imported in forreign built ships, and not belonging to the inhabitants of this countrey, and that for all and every the afore specified liquors imported in ships or other vessells wholely and solely belonging to the inhabitants of this dominion, and in which the importer hath an inte-

Duty of four pence a gallon on all foreign wines or spirits imported, not direct from England.

If imported in vessels wholly belonging to inhabitants, two pence a gallon duty;

reest or part, there shall be paid and satisfyed in full satisfaction of all rates, duties and imposts ariseing by virtue of this act two pence for every gallon only, and that all liquors imported into this dominion in ships and other vessells really and bona fide built within this dominion, and wholely and solely belonging to the inhabitants thereof, and in which the importer hath an interest and part shall be fully and cleerly exempted and freed from the rates, duties and imposts ariseing by this act. And for the better levying and collecting the rates, duties and imposts upon all furreign or imported liquors, *Bee it enacted by their majesties leiutenant Governour, Councell and Burgesses of this present General Assembly and the authority thereof, and it is hereby enacted,* That no such foreigne or imported liquors shall be landed or put on shoar out of any ship or other vessell from beyond the seas, before due entery be first made hereof, with the officer or collector appointed for the customes in the port or place where the same shall be imported, or before the duetie due and payable for the same be fully satisfyed, and that every warrant for the landing and delivering of any such forreign liquors shall be signed by the hand of the said officer or collectour in the said port or place respectively, upon pain that all such furreign liquors as shall be landed, put on shoar or delivered contrary (a) to the true intent and meaning of this act and the value thereof, shall be forfeited and lost, and to be recovered of the importer or proprietor of the same, and that no person or persons whatsoever bringing any the before recited liquors into any port or place of this dominion, nor any person or persons to whome the same or any of them shall be consigned, shall land or cause any such liquors to be landed or put on shoar, without makeing or causeing due entery to be made of the same, and giveing a true account of the gallons every casque did containe upon oath, with the officer or officers for the time being appointed to

& if such vessel be built here, free from duty.

Foreign liquors not to be landed till duties paid or secured.

Penalty.

Entry of liquors imported, how to be made.

Various Readings.

(a) The word 'contrary' omitted in Northb. MS. but inserted in Ch. City and P. Rand. MSS.

receive and take such enteries within the port or place where the same shall be landed, upon pain in every such case as aforesaid to forfeit double the value of the said liquors landed and put on shoar contrary to the true intent and meaning of this act, and that the master or purser of every ship, barque or other vessell, shall make a just and true entery upon oath, which the collector or other officer is hereby required to administer, of the burthen, contents, and ladeing of every such ship, barque, or other vessell with the perticular markes, numbers, quallities and contents of every casque therein laden with liquors to the best of his knowledge, also where and in what port she took in her ladeing, of what countrey built, how manned, who was master dureing the voyage, and who are owners thereof, upon penalty of forfeiting of one hundred pounds sterling.

Allowance for leakage.

And for the better encouragement of all masters, merchants, owners, and other persons whatsoever to make due entery and payment of the duties, rates, and imposts raised by virtue of this act, and in consideration for filling and leakeage, there shall be abated and allowed twenty gallons in every hundred, which said allowance and abatement, the said collectors to be appointed to receive the said dueties are hereby authorised to allow and make accordingly, *Provided alwaies*, that where any master, merchant, owner or other person whatsoever, shall wittingly or willingly make a false entery, and be convicted for the same, in that case such master, merchant, owner or other person shall forfeit and pay one hundred pounds sterling, and the said person or persons which are or shall be appointed to receive the duties and imposts ariseing by virtue of this act, and their deputies are hereby authorised and enabled to goe and enter on board any ship or other vessell, and from thence to bring on shoar all the before specified liquors for which the duties are not paid or compounded for within ten daies after the first entery of the said ship or other vessell, and that the officers of the customes and their deputies may freely stay and remain on board untill all the goods are delivered and discharged out of the said ship or other vessell; and

Penalty for false entry.

Collectors may go on board and seize liquors, not duly entered.

(a) if any officer or officers to be appointed to receive the dueties by this act ariseing, or other person or persons deputed and appointed by or under them (b) or any of them, or any other authority whatsoever, shall directly or indirectly take or receive any bribe, recompence or reward in any kind whatsoever, or connive at any false entery of any wines or other liquors, &c. whereby the duety be defrauded, the person or persons therein offending, shall forfeit the sum of one hundred pounds sterling, and be for ever afterwards incapable of any office or imployment within this dominion, as also the master, merchant, marriner or other person whatsoever who shall give or pay any such bribe, reward or recompence, shall forfeit the sum of fifty pounds sterling.

Penalty on officer receiving a bribe or conniving at a false entry.

And that all officers, captains and commanders of ships, as also all justices of the peace, sherriffs, constables, head boroughs, and all other their majesties officers, ministers, and subjects whatsoever, whome it may concerne, shall be aiding and assisting to all and every person and persons which are or shall be appointed by the governour to receive and collect the dueties, &c. and the collector and collectors, and their respective deputies in the due execution of all and every act and thing in and by this present act required and enjoyned, and all such who shall be aiding and assisting unto them in the due execution hereof shall be defended and saved harmeless by virtue of this act; and for the greater encouragement of masters, mariners and other seafareing men to settle themselves and inhabit with their families in this dominion, *Be it enacted by their majesties lieutenant governour, councell and burgesses of this present generall assembly, and the authoritie thereof, and it is hereby enacted*, That such masters, mariners and other seafareing men, who shall settle themselves and inhabit with their families in this dominion for the space of one full year, shall pay and satisfye in lieu and full satisfaction of all dueties ariseing by this

All capt'ns ships, and all civil officers and others to assist in the execution of this law.

Encouragement to masters of vessels and mariners to settle in this country;

Various Readings.

(a) The words 'and' omitted in Northb. MS. but inserted in Ch. City and P. Rand. MSS.

(b) The word 'them' omitted in P. Rand. MS. but inserted in Ch. Cit. and Northb. MSS.

duty, as to them reduced. act for every gallon of the before recited liquors, imported into this countrey, in any ship, barque, or other vessell, whereof he or they be master or mariner, upon their owne proper account, two pence only, altho' he or they have no interest or part in the same vessell, all

Forfeitures, how appropriated. which said forfeitures shall be divided into three equall parts, one third part thereof to their majesties, their heires and successors towards the better support of the government and defraying other contingent charges

Governor and council to appoint collectors. thereof, one other third part to the governour for the time being, and the other third part to him or them that will sue or informe for the same, by bill, plaint, information or action of debt in any court of record within this dominion in which no essoigne, protection or wager of law shall be allowed.

And be it enacted by the authority aforesaid, and it is hereby enacted, That the governour for the time being, with the advice of the councell shall be, and is hereby impowered from time to time, and at all times hereafter, to nominate, constitute and appoint such and soe many collectors and other officers, as also such sallaries, methods and orders not exceeding ten in the hundred for collecting the said duty as to them shall seem best. *And be it enacted by the authoritie aforesaid, and it is hereby enacted*, That all and every sum and sums of money rais-

Monies arising from duties imposed by this act, to be paid to the treasurer. ed or to be raised by virtue of this imposition aforesaid be constantly accounted for by the collector thereof to the treasurer of this dominion for the time being, and by him to the governour, councell and burgesses of the generall assembly, and converted to the uses by them directed according to the true intent and meaning of this act, and to and for no other use, intent and purpose whatsoever.

And this act to continue in force for three yeares, from the 31st day of May, anno 1691, and no longer.

ACT XVIII.

Edi. 1733 and 1752.

An act appointing a Treasurer.

Preamble. WHEREAS it is by this present generall assembly enacted, that all and every sum and sums of money raised or to be raised by force (*a*) and virtue of one act of assembly at this present session of assembly made and enacted, entituled, an act for ports, for better secureing their majesties customs, raising a revenue for securety thereof, and encouragement of learning and piety, and also all and every sum and sums of money raised, or to be raised by force and vertue of one other act of assembly of this present session of assembly, likewise made and enacted, entituled, an act for lessening the levy by the pole, and laying an imposition on liquors shall be constantly accounted for and paid by the collectors thereof to the treasurer of this dominion for the time being, and forasmuch as in the two before mentioned acts, there is no express nomination of any person in certain to be treasurer, *Be it therefore enacted by their majesties leiutenant governor, councill and burgesses of this present general assembly, and the authoritie thereof, and it is hereby enacted*, That Coll. Edward Hill be, and is hereby nominated, constituted and appointed (*b*) treasurer of the revenue ariseing by the two before specified acts, and is hereby authorised, impowered and required to demand, receive and take of and from every collector and collectors, all and every sum and sums of money ariseing by force of the two before specified acts of assembly, and the said Coll. Edward Hill is hereby authorised, required and commanded to keep and retain all such monies in his own custody and possession untill he shall be ordered and required to dispose of the same in such manner and by such warrant and for such uses, intents and purposes, and no other as are limited, appointed and directed in the said acts. *And be it enacted by the authority aforesaid, and it is hereby enacted*, That the said Coll. Edward Hill, before his entry and admission into the aforesaid office, and before his takeing upon him to execute and manage the same, do give bond in the secretaries office with good sufficient security in the sum of five thousand pounds sterling, payable to their majesties, their heires and successors

☞ This was the first act for appointing a treasurer; the reason and necessity whereof is explained in the preamble

Coll. Edward Hill appointed treasurer.

His power and duties.

To give bond and security.

(*a*) The word 'force' omitted in P. Rand. MS. but inserted in Ch. City and Northb. MSS.

(*b*) The words 'and appointed' omitted in P. Rand. MS. but inserted in Ch. City and Northumberland MSS.

for the true and just performance and discharge of the aforesaid office and place of treasurer, according to the true intent and meaning of the two said acts of assembly

And forasmuch as by the before recited act, entituled, an act for lessening the levy by the pole and laying an imposition on liquors, there is no provision made of salery to the treasurer of the said imposition, *Be it enacted by the authority aforesaid, and it is hereby* His salary. *enacted*, That the salary of six per cent be, and shall be allowed and paid unto the treasurer of this dominion, out of all and every sum and sums of money ariseing by vertue of the said imposition upon liquors and accounted for to the governour, councell and burgesses of the general assembly by the said treasurer according to the directions of the said act.

ACT XIX.

Edi. 1733 and 1752.

An act for dividing New Kent Countie.

WHEREAS sundry and divers inconveniences attend the inhabitants of New Kent county and all others who have occation to prosecute suites there, by reason of the difficulty in passing the river. *Be it therefore enacted by their majesties lieutenant governour, councell and burgesses of this present generall assembly, and the authority thereof, and it is hereby enact-* NewKent county divided. *ed*, That the aforesaid county of New Kent be divided into two distinct counties, so that Pomunkey river de- Boundaries. vide the same, and so down York river to the extent of the county, and that the part which is now on the south side of Yorke and Pomunkey river be called New Kent, and that the North side with Pomunkey Neck be called and known by the name of King and King and Queen county formd. Queen county. *And be it further enacted by the authoritie aforesaid, and it is hereby enacted*, That the inhabitants of Pomunkey Necke, that now belong to Parishes of St. Peter's & St. John's, boundaries of. St. Peters parish be restored and added to St. Johns parish, from which they formerly were taken, and that Pomunkey river be the bounds betwixt the two parishes, any law usage or custome to the contrary notwithstanding.

And for the due administration of justice, *Be it further enacted by the authority aforesaid, and it is hereby enacted,* That a court for the said King and Queen county be constantly held by the justices thereof upon the 12th day of the moneth in such manner as by the laws of this country is provided and shall be by their commission directed. Court days of King and Queen county.

ACT XX.

An act for deviding Lower Norfolk County. Edi. 1733 and 1752.

FORASMUCH as by the largness of the county of lower Norfolke, many inconveniences are found by the inhabitants of the lower part of the said county bounding on the main ocean and the parts of North Carolina, which have been by the said inhabitants much complained of, and now from the said inhabitants of the Eastern parts remonstrated to this generall assembly as a grievance, wherein they pray to be redressed, *Be it therefore enacted by their majesties leiutenant Governour, Councill and Burgesses of this present generall assembly and the authority thereof, and it is hereby enacted,* That the said county of lower Norfolke shall be divided and made two counties in manner following, that is to say, beginning at the new inlet of Little Creeke, and so up the said Creeke to the dams between Jacob Johnson and Richard Drout, and so out of the said dams up a branch, the head of which branch lyeth between the dwelling house of William Moseley, senr. and the new dwelling house of Edward Webb, and so to run from the head of the said branch on a direct line to the dams at the head of the Eastern branch of Elizabeth river, the which dams lie between James Kemp and Thomas Ivy, and so down the said branch to the mouth of a small branch or gutt that divides the land which Mr. John Porter now lives on, from the land he formerly lived on, and so up the said small branch according to the bounds of the said plantation, where the said Porter now liveth, and from thence to the great swamp, that lyeth on the East side of John Showlands, and so along the said great swamp to the North river of Corotucke, and down the said North

Preamble. Lower Norfolk county divided. Boundaries.

river to the mouth of Simpsons creeke, and so up the said creeke to the head thereof, and from thence by a south line to the bounds of Carolina, and that this devision shall be, and remaine the bounds between the said two counties, which shall hereafter be, and be held, deemed and taken as and for two intire and distinct counties, each of which shall have, use, and enjoy all the liberties, priviledges and advantages of any other county of this colony to all intents and purposes whatsoever, and that the uppermost of the said two counties, in which Elizabeth river and the branches thereof are included, doe retain and be ever hereafter called and known by the name of Norfolk countie, and that the other of the said two counties be called and known by the name of Princess Ann County; and for the due administration of justice, *Be it enacted by the authority aforesaid, and it is hereby enacted*, That a court for the said Princess Ann county be constantly held by the justices thereof upon the second Wednesday of the moneth in such manner as by the law of this countrey is provided, and shall be by their commission directed.

The upper part to retain the name of Norfolk county.

Princess Ann county formed of the lower part.

ACT XXI.

Edi. 1733 and 1752.

*An act for raiseing a Publique Levy.**

BE *it enacted by their majesties leiutenant governour, councell and burgesses of this present generall assembly and the authority thereof, and it is hereby enacted*, That the sum of eighteen pounds and one halfe of tobacco be paid by every titheable person within this their majesties colonie and dominion of Virginia for the defraying and payment of the publique charge of the country, being the publique levy from October 1686, to this present time, and that it be paid by the collectors of the severall counties to the severall persons to whome it is proportioned by this present generall assembly, and if it shall happen that there shall be

Taxes or public levy.

---

* The title of this act is given in the Ch. City MS. Then follows the words 'Be it enacted, &c. that 18 lb. tobacco be paid by 'every tythable person, &c.' and there the act ends.

more tytheables in any county then the present levy is laid on, then such county to have credit for so much to the use of county, and if there shall happen to be less in any county, then such county shall bear the loss.

Vera Copia,

Test, PETER BEVERLEY,
Clerk of the House of Burgesses.

Signed by FRANCIS NICHOLSON, Esq. *Gov'r.*
THOMAS MILNER, *Speaker.*
(*Note to editions 1733 & 1752.*)

AT A

General Assembly,

BEGUN AT JAMES CITTY

Francis Nicholson, Esq. Govr.

THE 16th DAY OF APRIL, 1691, IN THE THIRD YEARE OF THE REIGNE OF OUR SOVERAIGNE LORD AND LADY WILLIAM AND MARY BY THE GRACE OF GOD, KING AND QUEEN OF ENGLAND, SCOTLAND, FRANCE AND IRELAND, DEFENDERS OF THE FAITH, &c.

And thence continued by prorogation to the first day of Aprill, 1692, *in the fourth yeare of their Majesties Raigne.**

ACT I.

Edit.1733 and 1752.

An act for the better defence of the Countrey.

BE *it enacted by their majesties lieutenant Governour, Councell and Burgesses of this present Generall Assembly, and the authoritie thereof, and it is hereby enacted,* That one act of assembly made at James City, the 16th day of Aprill last, entituled an act for the better defence of the Countrey, and all clauses therein be, stand, and are from henceforth repealed and voyd, to all intents and purposes whatsoever.

Act XV. of last session repealed.

And be it further enacted, by the authority aforesaid, that whereas one lieutenant, eleaven soldiers, and two Indians well furnished with horses aud other accoutre-

---

Various Readings.

* The commencement of the acts of this session, precisely agrees in all the MSS.—In the editions of 1733 and 1752 it is, "At a General Assembly, begun at James City, the sixteenth day of April, in "the third year of the reign of our sovereign lord and lady William and Mary, by the grace of God, of England, Scotland, "France and Ireland, king and queen, defenders of the faith, &c.; "and in the year of our Lord 1691: And thence continued, by prorogation to first day of April 1692, in the fourth year of their "majesties reign, being the second session of this present General "Assembly."

ments, are already listed on the head of each river to range and scout at the heads of the said great rivers, for which they serve, and in such other places, as shall be most likely to discover our enemics, that the said soldiers be, and are hereby continued as already setled, for soe long time not exceeding the last day of Aprill 1693, as the governour with the advice of the councell shall think convenient and necessary, and that the pay of each officer and soldier shall be as followeth, the lieutenant or commander of each party of soldiers finding himself horse, arms, amunition and provision, shall have and receive five thousand pounds of tobacco and casque out of the publique Levy, for one whole (a) year, and soe after that rate for a longer or shorter time, and each soldier finding himself horse, armes, furniture, amunition and other necessaries, three thousand pounds of tobacco and casque, and so after that rate for a longer or shorter time. And whereas it is impossible at present soe to provide that the countrey be effectually defended with the least trouble and charge to the inhabitants thereof,

Rangers and scouts already in service to be contiued.

Pay of officers and soldiers.

Be it enacted by their Majesties Lieutenant Governour, Councell and Burgesses of this present generall assembly and the authority thereof, and it is hereby enacted, That the Lieutenant Governour or Commander in Chiefe for the time being, with the advice of the Councell, have power upon all occations between this time and the last day of Aprill, which shall be in the year 1693, to raise, levy and muster soe many and such a number of men, horses, arms and amunition, for the better defence of the same, and such forces already raised or to be raised, at all times to disband and discharge, as to them shall seem most conducing to the advantage of this dominion, which said soldiers already setled or to be raised by force of this act, are upon all occations to observe, performe, and keepe all such directions, orders and commands, as shall be appointed by the Lieutenant Governour or Commander in Chiefe for the time being, with the advice of the Councell, and

Governor and council authorised to raise additional forces;

who are to obey the orders of the governor.

Various Readings.

(a) The word "whole" omitted in Ch. Cit. MS. but inserted in Northb. and P. Rand. MSS.

and receive pay in proportion to their time of service.

shall receive pay and be satisfyed proportionably to the time they shall be in service and after these rates, viz.

Rates of pay, of officers and soldiers;

Each Captain finding himselfe horse, arms, amunition, provision, and all other necessaries, ten thousand pounds of tobaccoe and casque for one whole year, and so proportionably for a longer or shorter time, each Lieutenant finding and providing himselfe as aforesaid, after the rate as is in this act before exprest, and every private soldier mounted, armed and provided as aforesaid, after the rate in this act before exprest and mentioned.

of the two Indians.

And be it further enacted by the authority aforesaid, and it is hereby enacted, That the two Indians by this act appointed shall each of them have and receive from the Lieutenant of the Raingers to whom he belongs, eight yards of duffils and two barrels of Indian corn for his service for one yeare, and so proportionably for a longer or shorter time, and the said lieutenant shall be reimburst by the publique, and that the said lieutenant doe take care and provide by warrant from the Commander in Chiefe of the county where hee resides for each of the said Indians, one able horse, bridle and saddle, for which the owner or owners of the said horse or horses furnished as aforesaid shall have and receive from the countrey in the next publique levy, after the rate of eighty pounds of tobacco and casque for one month, and so proportionably for a longer or shorter time.

English or Indians bringing in any news, or giving intelligence, how to be dealt with.

And be it further enacted by the authority aforesaid, and it is hereby enacted, That for the future if any English or Indians shall bring any news or give any intelligence to any of their majesties officers civil or military, that he or they bringing the same (*a*) be kept in custody till it may reasonably be known whether what they report be true or not, and if it prove true and be of use and service to the government he or they shall be well rewarded, but if false, punished as the crime shall deserve, and the court of the county where such intelligence shall be given together with the militia officers

---

Various Readings.

* The running title to the acts of this session in edi. 1733 and 1752 is "Anno regni Gulielmi et Mariæ quarto."

(*a*) The words "the same" omitted in Northb. MSS. but inserted in Ch. Cit. and P. Rand. MSS.

are hereby impowered to consider what reward any person shall deserve, and certifie the same to the next generall assemble for allowance, as also to cause to be inflicted such punishments as any persons crime shall deserve.

ACT II.

An act for Confirmation of Lands.

Edi. 1733, & 1752

Preamble.

WHEREAS severall doubts and controversies have arisen and daly doe arise upon the fifth act of assembly made in anno 1677, entituled an act ascertaining the price of double pattents, the same having been variously expounded, for the clearing therefore of all doubts and ambiguities as may be therein,

Lands added to a patent already create ed, not to be forfeited for want of seating, provided it be seated within three years, from the passing of this act.

Be it enacted by their Majesties Lieutenant Governeur, Councell and Burgesses of this present generall assembly, and the authoritie thereof, and it is hereby enacted, That where one or more tract or tracts of land have been taken up and added to a pattent already seated, that no such tract or tracts of land shall henceforth be deemed forfeited for want of due seating, *Provided* such tract or tracts, be duly seated within three years from the publication of this law, as is by law required, but that the same be and are hereby confirmed to such person or persons as are the present owner or possessor thereof, as fully as if such tract or tracts had been actually seated as the law enjoyned, this law nor any thing herein contained not prejudiceing the grants already made of any lands, which were joyned with former seated dividents, and were not themselves seated, but that the present proprietors enjoy the same according to the grants made them, *Provided* they have or shall within the time limited by the said grants comply with the condition of them.

All such confirmed to the present possessors.

But such lands hereafter to be adjudged forfeited, unless seated within the time prescribed by law.

Provided nevertheless, That all lands hereafter to be taken up and pattented as aforesaid, shall be adjudged forfeited for want of due seating unless, according to the time by pattent limited, they shall be duly seated as the law requires: *Provided alwaies,* that no land found by a survey of any seated tract to be within the bounds of the said tract or any not habitable marshes or sunken grounds taken up or to be taken up as afore-

Not to extend to surplus.

lands, within the bounds of a patent, or marshes or sunken grounds.

said, shall be liable to the penalties thereof, any law, usage or custome to the contrary notwithstanding, *Provided* the said marshes or sunken grounds be exactly surveyed and their majesties quitt rents paid for the same.

ACT III.

Edit. 1733, & 1752.

An act for the more speedy prosecution of slaves committing Capitall Crimes.

☞ This is the *first law* constituting a tribunal expressly for the trial of slaves.

WHEREAS a speedy prosecution of negroes and other slaves for capital offences is absolutely necessarie, that others being detered by the condign punishment inflicted on such offenders, may vigorously proceed in their labours and be affrighted to commit the like crimes and offences, and whereas such prosecution has been hitherto obstructed by reason of the charge and delay attending the same,

Slave committing a capital offence, to be committed to the jail of the county.

Sheriff to give notice to the governor;

who is to issue a commission of *oyer and terminer*, to such persons as he shall think fit.

Be it therefore enacted by their Majesties Lieutenant Governour, Councell and Burgesses of this present Generall Assembly and the authority thereof, and it is hereby enacted, That every negro or other slave which shall after this present session of Assembly commit or perpetrate any cappitall offence which the law of England requires to be satisfyed with the death of the offender or loss of member, after his commiting of the said offence, shall be forthwith committed to the common gaol of the county within which (*a*) such offence shall be committed, there to be safely continued, well laden with irons, and that the sheriff of the said county doe forthwith signifie the same to the governour for the time being, who is desired and impowered to issue out a commission of *oyer* and *terminer* directed to such persons of the said county as he shall think fitt, which persons forthwith after the receipt of the said commission are required and commanded publicly at the courthouse

---

Various Readings.

(*a*) The word "which" omitted in Ch. Cit. MS. but inserted in Northb. and P. Rand. MSS.

of the said county to cause the offender to be arraigned and indicted, and to take for evidence the confession of the party or the oaths of two witnesses or of one with pregnant circumstances, without the sollemnitie of jury, and the offender being found guilty as aforesaid, to pass judgment as the law of England provides in the like case, and on such judgment to award execution.

Offender to be arraigned and indicted. Evidence. No jury. Judgment.

And be it enacted by the authority aforesaid, and it is hereby enacted, That all horses, cattle and hoggs marked of any negro or other slaves marke, or by any slave kept, and which shall not by the last day of December next, be converted by the owner of such slave to the use and marke of the said owner, shall be forfeited to the use of the poore of the parish wherein such horse, beast, or hogg shall be kept, seizable by the church wardens thereof.

Horses, cattle and hogs, marked with the mark of a slave to be converted by the owner of the slave to the uses and marks of the owner, otherwise forfeited to the parish.

And be it enacted by the authority aforesaid, and it is hereby enacted, That where it shall happen that any damage shall be hereafter commited by any negro or other slave living at a quarter, where there is noe christian overseer, the same damage shall be recompenced by the owner of such slave to the party injured.

Damage done by slaves, at a quarter, where no white overseer, to be paid by the owner of the slaves.

ACT IIII.

An act about Physicians and Chyrurgeons accounts.

Edit. 1733, & 1752.

WHEREAS it is expressed and declared in the 92 act of assembly entituled Chyrurgeons accounts regulated, that it shall be lawfull for any person or persons conceiving the accounts of Physician or Chyrurgeon unreasonable, to arrest the said Physician or Chyrurgeon to the generall or county court,

Act 92, of March 1661-2 amended. (See vol. 2, pa. 109.)

Be it enacted by their Majesties Lieutenant Governour, Councell and Burgesses of this present Generall Assembly and the authority thereof, and it is hereby enacted, That the same clause be henceforth repealed, and it is hereby repealed, the same being in itselfe unreasonable.

And be it enacted by the authority aforesaid, and it is hereby enacted, That every Physician or Chyrurgeon be allowed the true vallue of his druggs and means, with cent per cent upon the first cost, he making oath to the same, and that where the Physician and Chyrur-

Physicians and surgeons hereafter allowed, one hundred per cent on the value of their drugs and medicines.

To declare on oath he value of their medicines. Otherwise the court to decide according to their best judgments.

geon cannot declare upon his oath the first cost of his medicines the court wherein any controversey shall depend about the same, shall and are hereby empowered to give judgment therein according to the best of their knowledge, allowing the physician or chyrurgeon for his care, visitts, and attendance, a recompence suitable to his deserts.

ACT V.

Edit. 1733, & 1752.

An act for dividing Rappahanoc county.

WHEREAS sundry inconveniences attend the inhabitants of Rapahanoc county and all others who have occations to prosecute law suits there, by reason of the difficulty in passing the river.

Rappahannock county formed into two distinct counties. That part lying on north side of the river, to be called *Richmond;* and that on the south, *Essex.*

Be it therefore enacted by their Majesties Lieutenant Governour, Councell and Burgesses of this present generall assembly and the authority thereof, and it is hereby enacted, That the aforesaid county of Rappahanoc be divided into two distinct counties, soe that Rappahanoc river divide the same, and that that part which is now on the north side thereof be called and known by the name of *Richmond* county, and that that part which is now on the south side thereof be called and known by the name of *Essex* county; and for the due administration of justice,

Court days of Richmond county.

Be it enacted by the authority aforesaid, and it is hereby enacted, That the court of the said county of Richmond be constantly held by the justices thereof on the first Wednesday of the month, in such manner as by the laws of this countrey is provided, and shall be by their commission directed.

Of Essex.

And the court for the said county of Essex be constantly held by the justices thereof on the 10th day of the month, in such manner as by the laws of this countrey is provided, and shall be by their commission directed.

And be it enacted by the authority aforesaid, and it is hereby enacted, That whereas the town land lying at

Hobs hole (*a*) on the south side of the said county was purchased by the intire county as now it is, the charge thereof being equally defrayed by the whole number of the tytheables of the said county, that the moyety of the tobacco arising from the sales thereof, to the severall takers up of the aforesaid lands, be repaid unto the inhabitants of the north side thereof, upon the takeing up of the said land at the town aforesaid. Town land, at Hobs hole how appropriated.

And be it enacted by the authority aforesaid, and it is hereby enacted, That the records belonging to the county court of Rappahanoc before this division be kept in Essex county, that belonging wholly to their majesties and the other to the proprietors of the Northern Neck. Records of Rappahanock county, to be transferred to Essex.

ACT VI.

An act for the altering the day for Princess Ann county court.

Edi. 1733 and 1752.

FORASMUCH as it is by experience found that the day appointed for holding courts in Princess Ann county, according to the 20th act of the last session of assembly, entituled an act for dividing lower Norfolke county, is very inconvenient for the inhabitants of that and adjacent counties, whose affaires frequently require their attendance at that court, and forasmuch as is desired that the said day may be altered, and another day appointed by an act of assembly. Preamble.

Be it therefore enacted by their Majesties Lieutenant Governour, Councell and Burgesses of this present Generall Assembly and the authority thereof, and it is hereby enacted, That so much of the said act as appoints the day for holding courts in Princess Ann county be, and is hereby repealed.

And be it enacted by the authority aforesaid, and it is hereby enacted, That for the future the court for the said Princess Ann county be constantly held by the justices thereof on the first Wednesday of the month in such manner as by the laws of this country is provided Court days of Princess Ann county altered.

Various Readings.

(*a*) "Hops" hole in Chs. Cit. MS. "Hobs hole" in Nothb. and P. Rand. MSS.

and shall be by their comissions directed, any law usage or custome to the contrary notwithstanding.

ACT VII.

Edi. 1733 and 1752.

An act for raiseing a publique levy. (a)

BE *it enacted by their Majesties Lieutenant Governour, Councell and Burgesses of this present Generall Assembly and the authoritie thereof, and it is hereby enacted*, That the sum of 17lb and one quarter of tobaccoe be paid by every tythable person within this their majesties colony and dominion of Virginia, for the defraying and payment of the publique charge of the countrey being the publique levy from the 16th day of Aprill 1691 to the first day of this present Aprill (b) being in the year of our Lord 1692, and that (c) it be paid by the collectors of the severall counties to the severall persons to whome it is apportioned by this present generall assembly, and if it shall happen that there shall be more tytheables in any county, then this present levy is laid on, then such county to have credit for so much to the use of the county, and if their shall happen to be less in any county, then such county shall beare the loss.

Taxes, or public levy for 1692.

How appropriated.

Vera Copia,

Teste, PETER BERVERLY,
Clerke of the House of Burgesses.

Various Readings.

(a) The title of this act omitted in Northb. MS. but it is inserted, as above, in Ch. Cit. and P. Rand. MSS.

(b) The word "Aprill" omitted in Northb. MS. but inserted in Ch. Cit. and P. Rand. MSS.

(c) The words "and that" omitted in Northb. MS. but inserted in Ch. Cit and P. Rand. MSS.

Att a Generall Assembly begun at James Citty the 16th day of Aprill 1691, *and thence continued by prorogation to the first day of Aprill* 1692.

Northumberland countie, Dr.		Contra Cr.	
To salary	1536	By 980 titheables at 17 1-4 per pole,	16935
To the Lieut. on Potomac river over the Rangers	2169		
To the 11 soldiers at Ditto	13200		
	16905		

Vera Copia,
Teste,
PETER BEVERLY,
Clerke of the House of Burgesses.

Ditto Dr.	
To Peter Beverley for a copy of the laws	300
To a copy of the proportion	050
	350

P. B. cl. H. B

Signed by FRANCIS NICHOLSON, Esq. *Gov'r.*
THOMAS MILNER, *Speaker.*

(*Note to editions* 1733 *and* 1752.)

ATT A

Generall Assembly,

BEGUN AT JAMES CITTY

Sir Edmund Andros, Governor.

THE 2nd DAY OF MARCH, 1692-3, AND IN THE 5th YEARE OF THE REIGNE OF OUR SOVEREIGNE LORD AND LADY WILLIAM AND MARY BY THE GRACE OF GOD OF ENGLAND, SCOTLAND, FRANCE AND IRELAND, KING AND QUEEN, DEFENDERS OF THE FAITH, &c.*

ACT I.

Edi. 1733, and 1752.

An act for suspending the execution of the act for ports, &c.

WHEREAS at a Generall Assembly begun and holden at James Citty the 16th day of Aprill in the 3d yeare of the reign of our Sovereigne Lord and Lady William and Mary of England, Scotland, France and Ireland, King and Queen, an act was made and established entituled an act for portes, &c. to be of full force and effect from and after the first day of October last past, and whereas the said act is of great moment, weight and consequence and the said act lying before their majesties, and their majesties pleasure relating thereto not yet signified,

---

Various Readings.

* The commencement of the acts of this session precisely agrees in all the MSS.—In the editions of 1733 and 1752, it is different, thus, 'At a General Assembly, begun at James City, the second 'day of March, in the fifth year of the reign of our sovereign lord 'and lady William and Mary, by the grace of God, of England, 'Scotland, France and Ireland, king and queen, defenders of the 'faith, &c. and in the year of our Lord 1692.'—The omission, in the editions of 1733 and 1752, to annex the figure "3" to the date of the year, as in the MSS. thus, 1692-3, exhibits this strange appearance, that the acts of the *preceding* session, of *April* 1692, are inserted before those of *March* 1692; but, by annexing the figure "3" according to the custom, of that day, no such impropriety appears.

Be it therefore enacted by the Governour, Councell and Burgesses of this Generall Assembly and the authority thereof and it is hereby enacted, That the execution of the said law and all and every article, clause, branch and provision therein contained shall be and is hereby to all intents, constructions and purposes, suspended till their majesties pleasure shall be known therein or till the next assembly.

Act of 1691, for ports, &c. suspended, till the pleasure of the king and queen should be known, or until the next assembly.

ACT II.

An act concerning Indian hoggs.

Edi.1733 and 1752.

WHEREAS the 6th act of assembly made in the yeare 1674, entituled an act comanding such Indians who keepe hoggs, to marke the same, injoynes all Indians that keepe hoggs to have a particular marke for their towne, and forasmuch as it hath been represented to this assembly that the *Notoway* Indians and others keeping hoggs have divers markes and more especially the markes of sundry English adjacent to them and under colour thereof doe kill and dispose of the hoggs belonging to the English and it seeming disputable what county courts shall assign the marke of the *Notoway* and *Weyonock* Indians,

Preamble.

Be it therefore enacted by the Governour, Councell and Burgesses of this Generall Assembly and the authority thereof, and it is hereby enacted, That *Surry* county court be appoynted and is hereby authorised and impowered within this six months after the publication hereof to assign a particular marke to each of the townes of the *Notowayes* and *Weyonock* Indians, and that for the future if any English whatsoever shall buy or receive from any Indian whatsoever any porke, and is not able to prove such porke soe bought or received as aforesaid to be of the proper marke belonging to the towne of Indians to which the said Indian or Indians that sell the same doe belong, shall forfeit and pay one thousand pounds of tobacco one halfe to their majesties their heires and successors for and towards the better supporte of this government and defraying the contingent charge thereof; and the other halfe to him or them that will sue for the same to be recovered by action of debt, by bill, plaint or information in any courte of judicature in this country.

Surry county court authorised to assign a mark for the Nottoway and Weyonock Indians.

Penalty for buying or receiving pork of an Indian, without being able to prove it to have been of the proper Indian mark.

ACT III.

Edi. 1733 and 1751.

An act for giveing encouragement to erect Fulling Mills.

Preamble.

WHEREAS by the third act of assembly made at James Citty the 23d of September 1667 entituled an act for encouragement for erecting of mills, it is enacted that if any person willing to erect one or more mills upon convenient places hath land only on one side the said place and the owner of the land on the other side refuse to lett him have an acre of land to the use aforesaid, that then the county courte upon the request of the party soe refused shall order and impower two of their commissioners or such other credible persons as they shall thinke fitt to view the said land, and if it take not away howsing orchards and other immediate conveniences then to value the said quantity of land and put the same in the possession of the party building the said mill or mills, he paying the consideration the land is valued at; for the encouragement therefore erecting fulling mills in this countrie,

Provisions of act of 1677, for erecting grist mills, extended.

Be it enacted by the governour, councell and burgesses of this present generall assembly and the authority thereof, and it is hereby enacted, That the same priviledge, advantage and benefitt be hereafter deemed construed held and taken to extend and be accordingly given and allowed unto all and every person or persons who shall be minded to erect and sett up one or more thereof.

ACT IV.

Edi. 1733 and 1752.

An act for ascertaining the price of coasting coquitts and requiring officers attendance.

Preamble.

WHEREAS complaint hath been made to this assembly that collectors for the time past have usually taken and received divers and distinct sums of money from the inhabitants of, and traders into this collony for coasting permitts, let passes and cocquitts although there be noe fee ascertained or established for the same by law.

Be it therefore enacted by the governour, councell and burgesses of this present generall assembly and the authority thereof, and it is hereby enacted, That for the time to come nothing shall be demanded received or taken by any collector, sub-collector or any other manner of person or persons whatsoever they be, which now have or which at any time hereafter shall have power and authority to enter and cleare shipes, sloopes or other vessells by himselfe or themselves or by any other of his or their ministers for a coasting permitt, let pass and cocquet above one shilling current money except for the enumerated comodities according to law, and that every collector, sub-collector, and other person and persons having or which hereafter shall have power and authority to enter and cleare shipes, sloopes, or other vessels and all other their ministers whatsoever they be, that shall doe or attempt or cause to be done or attempted against this act in any thing shall forfitt and loose for every time soe offending to the party grieved in that behalfe soe much money as any such person aforesaid shall take contrary to this present act, and over that shall loose and forfitt ten pounds sterling, whereof one moyety shall be to theire majesties theire heires and successors to and for the better suport of this government and other the contingent charges thereof, the other moyety to the party grieved in that behalfe, that will sue by action of debt by bill information or otherwayes, in any court of record within this country for recovery of the same in which action by bill or information noe essoigne protection nor wager of law shall be allowed or admitted; and whereas many of the inhabitants of and traders into this colony are divers times exposed to great charge and trouble in coming to collectors to make entry of and cleare theire shipes, sloopes or other vessells when the said collectors are absent from home and none their attend that are qualified to enter and cleare ships sloopes or other vessells, for the removeing such inconveniences, for the future,

Price of coasting permit, let pass, and cocquet ascertained.

Penalty for exceeding legal rates.

Be it enacted by the authority aforesaid, and it is hereby enacted, That every collector and collectors and every other manner of person or persons they be which now have or which at any time hereafter shall have power and authority to enter and cleare shipes, sloopes or other vessels shall by himselfe and themselves or by sume other his or theire ministers or substitutes be constantly resident at and abide at the place he holds his office, to be ready at all lawfull times to make entry of and cleare shipes, sloopes or other vessells.

Officers authorised to clear ships or vessels, to reside at the place where the clearance is to be granted.

ACT V.

Edi. 1733 and 1752.

An act for encourageing the erecting of a Post Office in this country.

Preamble, reciting an act of parliament, which authorises Thos. Neale, esq. to establish a post office, in the several islands and American colonies.

WHEREAS the erection and establishment of a post office within this collony is conceived to be of generall concernement and of great advantage for the increase and preservation of trade and comerce therein for thereby speedy and safe dispatch may be had, and whereas theire majesties by theire letters pattents under the greate seale of England bearing date the 17th day of February in the 4th yeare of theire reigne have given unto Thomas Neale esq his executors administrators and assignes full power and authority to errect, settle and establish within the chiefe portes of theire severall islands colonyes and plantations in America, an office or offices for the receiving and dispatching away of letters and pacquetts, and to receive, send and deliver the same under such rates and sumes of money as the planter or inhabitants should agree to give or should be proportionable to the rates for the carriage of letters ascertained in the act of parliament for the erecting and establishing a post office to hold and enjoy the same for the terme of one and twenty yeares under the yearely rent of six shillings and eight pence as by the said letters patents relation thereunto being had will more fully appeare.

General post office establishment;

and a post office in each county.

Be it therefore enacted by the governour, councell and burgesses of this present Generall Assembly and the authority thereof, and it is hereby enacted, That if the said Tho. Neale his substitutes substitute or deputy shall by virtue of the said letters patents erect settle and establish in some convenient place within this colony and dominion one generall post office from whence all letters and pacquetts whatsoever may with expedition be sent unto any part of this colony and to every other place whatsoever and at which said office all returnes and answers may be received and shall alsoe in each county within this colony, setle and establish one or more post office or post offices as is in this act hereinafter provided, then it shall and may be lawfull to and for the said Tho. Neale Esqr. his substitutes and deputyes by him thereunto sufficiently authorised to demand, have, receive and take for the postage and conveyancy for all such letters which he or they shall soe conveye, carry or send post, according to the severall rates and sumes of current money hereafter mentioned, not to exceed the same, that is to say, for the post of every letter not exceeding one sheet to or from any place not exceeding fourscore English miles distance from the place where such letter shall be received three pence, and for the like post of every letter not exceeding two sheets six pence, and for the like post of every pacquet of letters proportionable unto the said rates, that is to say, for every sheet not exceeding two sheets, to advance five pence and noe more, and for the like post of every pacquet of writs, deeds and other things after the rate of twelve pence for every ounce weight, and for the post of every letter not exceeding one sheet above the distance of fourscore English miles from the place where the same shall be received four pence half penny, and for the like post of a letter not exceeding two sheets nine pence, and proportionable to rates for the like post of all pacquets of letters, that is to say, for every sheet exceeding two sheets to advance four pence half penny and noe more, and for the like post of every pacquet of and writs, deeds and other things after the rates of eighteen pence for every ounce weight; *Provided alwaies*, that all merchants accounts and bills of exchange, invoyces and bills of loading are and shall be understood to be allowed at the rate and price of double letters, and shall be understood to be allowed to pass at the same rate and payment.

Rates of postage.

Proviso as to merchants accounts and bills of exchange, &c.

Provided alwaies, That nothing in this present act contained shall extend or construed to extend to restraine any marchants masters or others from sending any letters or pacquetts to or from this collony by any masters of ships or other vessells or by any other person or persons which such merchants masters or others will specially imploy or intrust for the carriage of the same according to the respective derections, *provided likewise*, that all letters superscribed for theire majesties and countries service comonly called state letters which are usually carried postage free in England shall pass free throughout this collony; *provided likewise*, that the said Thomas Neale his executors administrators or assignes or such person or persons as he or they shall nominate shall and will from time to time

This act not to prevent merchants from sending letters by masters of vessels, or others.

Not to extend to public letters.

Duty of postmaster in relation to letters received from England, and to be sent there, and to other foreign parts;

upon his or theire receipt of any letters or pacquets which shall be directed into this collony from England or any other parts, or from any parts or places within this collony, to any other parts or places within the same, cause the said letters or pacquetts to be forthwith dispersed caried and delivered in the severall parts of this collony as they shall be directed, and from time to time as he or they or any of them shall collect or receive any letters or pacquets to be sent from this collony to England shall dispatch and send away the same by the first ship that shall be bound for any part of England, to be there delivered to the next deputy postmaster and where any letters or pacquetts shall be derected from this collony to some other foreigne parts that he or they shall dispatch and send away the same according to theire respective derections by the first conveniancy of carriage or conveyance thereof, and that those services shall be performed with care and without any neglect or delay at the rates and prices before mentioned.

and, in relation to public orders from the governor and council.

Provided likewise, That all publique orders which the governour councell and other theire majesties officers for the time being shall issue out from time to time for the imediate service of theire majesties and this countrie shall be dispatched and distributed by the respective post officers within this collony without any charge, *provided likewise*, that the said Tho. Neale Esqr. his substitutes or deputies shall at theire owne proper costs and charges errect setle and establish or cause to be errected setled or established one or more post office or post offices in every respective county of this collony at the most convenient places of the same; except alwaies out of this act letters of masters and merchants which shall be sent by any masters of any shipes barques or other vessells of merchandise or by any other person imployed by them for the carriage of such letters aforesaid according to the respective derections, and alsoe except letters to be sent by any private friend or friends in theire wayes or joyrneye or travell or by any messenger or messengers sent on purpose for or concerning the private offices of any person or persons whatsoever.

To establish a post office, in each county.

Exceptions, out of this act.

Limitation of act.

Provided alwaies, That this act shall continue in force for and during the terme granted by theire majesties letters pattents before receited unto Tho. Neale

Esqr. his executors administrators and assignes under the greate seale of England bearing date the 17th day of February in the 4th yeare of theire reigne and noe longer.

ACT VI.

An act for continuing the Rangers at the head of the four great Rivers.

Edi.1733, and 1752.

Preamble.

WHEREAS it is verry necessary and beneficiall for the defence of this theire majesties dominion and the inhabitants thereof that the rangers at the heads of the four grate rivers be continued,

Rangers continued at the heads of the four great rivers.

Be it therefore enacted by the governour, councell and burgesses of this present generall assembly, and the authority thereof, and it is hereby enacted, That from and after the last day of Aprill, one lieutenant, eleaven soldiers and two Indians well furnished with horses and other accoutrements be continued leived armed and mustered to range and scout about the great rivers and in such other places as shall be most likely to discover our enemies and that the pay of each officer or soldier leived or to be leived armed and mustered shall be as followes, viz. the leiutenant or comander of each party of soldiers finding himselfe horse, accoutrements, furniture, amunition and provision, shall have and receive five thousand pounds of tobacco and casque out of the publique levie for one whole yeare, and soe after that rate for a shorter time, and each souldier finding himselfe horse, armes, furniture, ammunition and other necessaries, three thousand pounds of tobacco and casque for one yeare, and soe after that rate for a shorter time.

Their pay.

And be it further enacted by the authority aforesaid, and it is hereby enacted, That the two Indians by this act appointed shall each of them have and receive from the lieutenant of the rangers to whom he belongs eight yeards of duffils and two barrels of Indian corne for his service for one yeare, and soe proportionable for a shorter time, and the said lieutenant shall be reimbursted by the publique, and that the said lieutenant doe take care and provide by warrant from the commander in chiefe of the county wherein he resides, for each of the said Indians an able horse bridle and sadle for which the owner or owners of said horse or horses furnished

Pay of Indians.

Horses to be provided.

as aforesaid shall have and receive from the county in the next publique levie after the rates of eighty pounds of tobacco and casque for one month, and soe proportionable for a longer or shorter time and that the said comander in chiefe of the respective counties take care that the said officers and souldiers be duly mustered and an account thereof sent from time to time to the secretaries office, and forasmuch as there is no certainty of future events and therefore uncertaine how to provide for the effectual defence of the country, and to the end it may be provided for with the least charge,

Duty of commanders in chief of the several counties.

Soldiers to be raised by governor and council, in cases of emergency.

Be it enacted by the authority aforesaid, and it is hereby enacted, That upon any emergency all such souldiers which the governour with the advice and consent of the councell shall levei arme and muster for the better defence of this country shall be paid out of the publique levie and that the governour may from time to time and at all times by and with the advice and consent of the said councell disband and discharge all forces raised or to be raised by virtue of this act, as to the said governour with the advice and consent of the said councell shall seeme most conduceable to the advantage of this theire majesties dominion, which said souldiers shall receive pay and be satisfied proportionably to the time they shall be in service and after these rates: viz.

How paid.

Each captain finding himselfe horse, armes, ammunition, provision and all other necessaries ten thousand pounds of tobacco and casque for one year and soe proportionable for a shorter time, each lieutenant finding and providing himselfe with horse, armes, ammunition, provision and all other necessaries, five thousand pounds of tobacco and casque for one year and soe proportionable for a shorter time, and every private souldier finding and providing himselfe with horse, armes, amunition, provision and all other necessaries three thousand pounds of tobacco and casque for one yeare and soe proportionable for a shorter time.

And be it further enacted by the authority aforesaid, and it is hereby enacted, That for the future if any English other christians or Indians shall bring any newes or give any inteligence to any of theire majesties officers civill or military such officer to whom the same shall be brought shall diligently inquire into and examine the grounds thereof, and if such newse prove true, and be of use and service to the government, that then he or they bringing the same shall be rewarded, but if false punished as the crime shall deserve, and the county court when such inteligence shall be given are hereby impowered to consider what reward such person bringing newes and giveing inteligence shall deserve, and certifie the same to the next generall assembly for allowance, and if the newes and intilegence be false cause such punishment to be inflicted on the person telling the same as his crime shall deserve.

Divulgers of news, to be rewarded, or punished according to the fact.

This act to continue in force untill the last day of Aprill, which shall be in the year 1694 and no longer.

ACT VII.

An act for raising the publique Levie.

Edi. 1733, and 1752.

Be it enacted by the governour, councell and burgesses of this present generall assembly and the authority thereof, and it is hereby enacted, That the sume of thirteen pounds and three quarters of tobacco be paide by every tithable person within this their majesties collony and dominion of Virginia for the defraying and payment of the publique charge of the countrey being the publique levie from the first day of Aprill 1692 to this present time, and that it be paide by the collectors of the severall countys to the severall persons to whome it is proportioned by this present generall assembly and if it shall happen that there shall be more tithables in any county then the present levy is laid on then such county to have credit for soe much to the use of the county, and if there shall happen to be less in any county then such county shall bear the loss.

Public taxes for 1692.

Vera Copia,

Teste, Peter Beverley,
Clerks of the House of Burgesses.

At a Generall Assembly begun at James Citty the 2nd day of May 1692.

	Northumberland county, Dr.		Contra Credr.	
Northumberland county.	To sallary	1224	By 980 tithables at 13 3-4 per pole	13475
	To Col. Samll. Griffin,	0157		
	To James Crawley,	3240		
Public taxes.	To the Lieut. and 11 souldiers for Patomack River	8853		
		13475		
	Ditto Dr.			
For a copy of the laws.	To Peter Beverley for a coppy of the lawes,	300		
	For a coppy of the proportion,	050		

Teste, Peter Beverly,
Clerke of the House of Burgesses.

ATT A

Generall Assembly,

BEGUN ATT JAMES CITTY.

THE 10th DAY OF OCTOBER IN THE FIFTH YEARE OF THE REIGN OF OUR SOVEREIGNE LORD AND LADY WILLIAM AND MARY, BY THE GRACE OF GOD OF ENGLAND, SCOTLAND, FRANCE, AND IRELAND, KING AND QUEEN, DEFENDERS OF THE FAITH, &c. ANNOQUE. DOMINI 1693.

Sir Edmund Andros, governor.

ACT I.

An act appointing Rangers on the frontiers of the four great rivers.

Edi. 1733, & 1752.

Preamble.

WHEREAS it is very necessary and beneficiall for the defence of this theire majesties dominion and the inhabitants thereof, that rangers be levied on the frontiers of the four great rivers,

Rangers and scouts continued.

Be it therefore enacted by the governour, councell and burgesses of this present generall assembly and the authority thereof, and it is hereby enacted, That from and after the last day of Aprill next, one lieutenant, eleaven soldiers and two Indians well furnished with horses and other accoutrements be levied, armed and mustered to range and scout about the heads of the great rivers and in such other places as shall be most likely to discover our enemies and that the pay of each officer and soldier levied or to be levied, armed and mustered, shall be as follows, viz the lieutenant or commander of each party of soldiers finding himselfe horse, furniture, armes, amunition and provision shall have and receive out of the publique levie five thousand pounds of tobacco and casque for one whole yeare, and soe after that rate for a shorter time, and each soldier finding himselfe horse, armes, furniture amunition and other necessaries three thousand pounds of tobacco and casque for one whole yeare and soe after that rate for a shorter time.

Their pay.

And be it further enacted by the authority aforesaid, and it is hereby enacted, That the two Indians by this act appointed shall each of them have and receive from the lieutenant of the rangers to whome he belongs eight yards of duffils and two barrells of Indian corne for his service for one yeare and soe proportionably for a shorter time, and the said lieutenant shall be reimbursed by the publique and that the said lieutenant doe take care and provide by warrant from the commander in chiefe of the county where he resides for each of the said Indians an able horse, bridle and saddle for which the owner or owners of the said horse or horses furnished as aforesaid shall have and receive from the country in the next publique levie after the rate of eighty pounds of tobacco and casque for one month and soe proportionably for a longer or shorter time and that the comander in chiefe of theire respective counties take care that the said officers and soldiers be duely mustered and an account thereof sent from time to time to the secretaryes office, and forasmuch as there is noe certainty of future events and therefore incertaine how to provide for the effectual defence of the country and to the end it may be provided for with the least charge,

Pay of the two Indians.

Horse, &c. to be provided for each.

Duty of commander in chief, in each county.

Be it enacted by the authority aforesaid, and it is hereby enacted, That upon any emergencye all such soldieres which the governour with the advice and consent of the councell shall levie, arme and muster for the better defence of this country, shall be paide out of the publique levie and that the governour may from time to time and att all times by and with the advice and consent of the councell disband and discharge all forces raised or to be raised by virtue of this act as to the said governour with the advice and consent of the councell shall seem most conducible to the advantage of this theire majesties dominion, which said soldiers shall receive pay and be satisfyed proportionably to the time they shall be in service, and after these rates (viz.) Each captain finding himselfe horse, armes, amunition and provision and all other necessaryes, ten thousand pounds of tobacco and casque for one yeare and soe proportionably for a shorter time, each lieutenant finding

Governor with advice of council, may raise soldiers in cases of emergency.

Pay of such officers and soldiers.

---

* The running title to the acts of this session in the editions of 1733 and 1752, is, "Anno regni Gulielmi and Mariæ quinto."

and providing himselfe with horse, armes, amunition and provision and all other necessaries five thousand pounds of tobacco and casque for one yeare and soe proportionably for a shorter time, and every private soldier finding and providing himselfe with horse, armes, amunition and provisions and all other necessaries, three thousand pounds of tobacco and casque for one yeare and soe proportionably for a shorter time

And be it further enacted by the authority aforesaid, and it is hereby enacted, That for the ffuture if any English or other christians or Indians shall bring any news or give any intelligence to any of there majesties officers civill or military such officers to whome the same shall be brought shall diligently inquire into and examine the grounds thereof, and if such news prove true and be of use and service to the government that then he or they bringing the same shall be rewarded, but if false punished as the crime shall deserve, and the county courts where such inteligence shall be given are hereby impowered to consider what rewards such person bringing news and giving inteligence shall deserve, and certifie the same to the next generall assembly for allowance, and if the news and inteligence be false to cause such punishment to be inflicted on the person telling the same as his crime shall deserve. This act to continue in force until the last day of Aprill, which shall be in the yeare 1695 and noe longer.

Divulgers of news, to be rewarded or punished, as the same may be true or false.

Limitation of this act.

ACT II.

An act for the encouragement of the manufacture of Linen Cloth.

Edi. 1733, and 1752.

Be it enacted by the Governour, Councell and Burgesses of this present generall assembly and the authority thereof, and it is hereby enacted, That the justices of the peace of every respective county within this colony doe annually in November or December meet at theire usuall places of holding courts, and then and there set, appoint, and establish three severall and distinct rewards to be levied on the inhabitants of their severall countyes and to be disposed by the said justices as an incouragement to such person or persons who shall produce to the justices at the next court ffor laying the le-

Rewards, for the encouragement of linen, to be established, by the justices.

vie the three best peices of lining of their own makeing to containe in length ffifteen ells at the least three quarters of a yard wide: *provided*, the reward exceed not eight hundred pounds of tobacco and casque for the first peice six hundred pounds of tobacco and casque for the second piece and ffour hundred pounds of tobacco and casque for the third piece. This act to continue in force six years and noe longer.

Rewards.

ACT III.

Edi.1733, and 1752.

An act ascertaining the place for erecting the College of William and Mary in Virginia.

Preamble, reciting the charter, for founding the college of Wm. and Mary.

WHEREAS their majesties have been most graciously pleased upon the humble supplication of the generall assembly of this country by their charter bearing date the 8th day of Ffebruary in the fourth yeare of theire reign to grant their royall lycence to certaine trustees to make, found, erect and establish a college named the college of William and Mary in Virginia at a certaine place within this government known by the name of *Townsends Land*, and heretofore appointed by the generall assembly, or if the same should be found inconvenient at such other place as the generall assembly should think fitt, and whereas the said fformer designed place for divers causes is found to be very unsuitable for such an use and severall other places have been nominated in the room thereof upon consideration of which and a full enquirie into the conveniences of each one of the said places the *Middle Plantation* situate between York and James Rivers appearing to be the most convenient and proper for that designe,

To be erected at Middle Plantation, (now Williamsburg.)

Be it therefore enacted by the governour, councell and burgesses of this present generall assembly and the authority thereof, and it is hereby enacted That *Middle Plantation* be the place for erecting the said college of *William and Mary* in Virginia and that the said college be at that place erected and built as neare the church now standing in *Middle Plantation* old ffields as convenience will permitt.

ACT IV.

An act laying an imposition upon skins and ffurrs for the better support of the Colledge of William and Mary in Virginia. Edi. 1733 and 1752.

BE *it enacted by the governour, councell and burgesses of this present generall assembly and the authority thereof, and it is hereby enacted,* That from and after the first day of January next, there shall be sattisfyed and paid to theire majesties theire heires and successors for and towards the better support and maintenance of the colledge of *William and Mary* in Virginia speedily intended by Gods grace to be erected at *Middle Plantation* within this government. The following dutyes, customes and impost for the following goods, wares and merchandises which shall be exported, carryed out of this theire majesties dominion either by land or water (that is to say) for every rawhide three pence for every tan'd hyde six pence, for every dressed buckskin one peney three ffarthings, for every undrest buckskin one peney, for every doe skin dressed one peney and halfe peney, for every undrest doe skin three farthings, for every pound of beaver three pence, for every otter skin two pence, for every wild catt skin one peney halfe peney, for every minx skin one peney, for every fox skin one peney halfe peney, for every dozen of racoon skins three pence, and soe proportionably for a greater or lesser quantity, for every dozen muskrat skins two pence, and soe proportionably for a lesser or greater quantity, and for every elke skin four pence halfe peney.

Duties, customs, and imposts, for the support of the college.

On raw hides, Tanned hides Buckskins dressed and undressed. Doe skins, Otter skins. Wildcat skins Minx skins. Fox skins. Raccon skins. Muskrat skins Elk skins.

And be it enacted by the authority aforesaid, and it is hereby enacted, That the said dutyes, customes and impost shall be paid and satisfyed by the person or persons exporting or carrying out the same either by land or water to the collector or collectors which shall be appointed by the governour or commander in chiefe for the time being to receive the said dutyes, customes and impost before the said goods, wares or merchandises shall be shipped off exported or carryed out of and from this dominion either by land or water and a certificate thereof obtained from the collector or collectors of the district where such goods wares and merchandises shall be soe exported or carryed away signifying the payment and sattisfaction of such dutyes, customes and

Duties to be paid by exporter.

Certificate of payment of duties, how obtained.

Penalty for a breach of this law.

impost as aforesaid, under the penallty of fforfeiting such of the said goods, wares and merchandizes which shall be shiped off or loaden on board of any boat, sloop, shipp or other vessell, in order to the exportation thereof by water or endeavoured to be carryed out of this countrey by land, the one moyety thereof to their majesties, theire heires and successors to and for the better support of the government and the contingent charges thereof the other moyety to him or them that shall sue or prosecute for the same in any court of record within this colony by action of debt, bill, plaint or information wherein noe essoyn protection or wager of law shall be allowed.

Collectors to account to governors of the college.

And be it further enacted, That the severall collectors or officers appoynted to collect and receive the said duties, customes and imposts shall from time to time be accountable and pay the same to the governour of the said colledge of William and Mary, or such other person or persons as shall be by them lawfully deputed, and that for the receiving and paying thereof the said collector or collectors shall be allowed ten per cent.

Commission for collection.

ACT V.

Edit 1733, and 1752.

An act for raising a publique levy to be paid in the yeare 1694.

Taxes, or public levy, for 1694.

BE it enacted by the Governour, Councell and Burgesses of this present generall assembly and the authority thereof, and it is hereby enacted, That the sum of one and twenty pounds of tobacco be paid by every titheable person within this theire majesties colony and dominion of Virginia in the yeare 1694 ffor the defraying and payment of the charge of keeping and maintaining one lieutenant, eleaven soldiers and two Indians at the heads of each of the four great rivers ffor the terme of seaventeen months from the first day of December next, and for the sattisfaction of all such other claimes and allowances as have been made by this generall assembly, and that the same be paid by the collectors of the severall countyes in the said yeare to the severall persons to whome it is now proportioned, and if it shall happen that there shall be more tithable in any county, then the said levie of one and twenty pounds of tobacco is now layed on, then such county to have credit for soe much to the use of the county and if there shall happen to be less in any county then such county shall beare the loss.

Vera Copia,

Teste, PETER BEVERLEY,
Clerke of the House of Burgesses.

Att a Generall Assembly begun at James Citty the 10th *day of October* 1693.

Northumberland county, Dr.		Contra Cr.	
To sallary	1871	By 980 tithables at 21 lbs. tobacco per pole,	20580
To Capt. Wm Lee	0200		
To Coll. Samll. Griffin	0675		
To the lieut. and rangers at the head of Potomac River	17834		
	20580		
Ditto Dr.			
To Peter Beverley ffor a copy of the laws	300		
Ffor a copy of the proportion	050		
	350		

Test, PETER BEVERLEY,
Clerke of the House of Burgesses,

Signed by SIR EDMUND ANDROS, *Govr.*
THOMAS MILNER, *Speaker.*

(*Note to editions* 1733 *and* 1752.)

ATT A

Generall Assembly,

BEGUN ATT JAMES CITTY

Sir Edmund Andros. Gov. THE 18TH DAY OF APRIL, IN THE SEVENTH YEAR OF THE REIGNE OF OUR SOVERAIGNE LORD AND LADY WILLIAM AND MARY BY THE GRACE OF GOD, OF ENGLAND, SCOTLAND, FRANCH AND IRELAND, KING AND QUEEN, DEFENDERS OF THE FAITH, &c. ANNOQUE DOM. 1695.

ACT I.

Edit. 1733, & 1752.

An act appoynting Rangers att the heads of the four great rivers.

WHEREAS it is verry necessary and beneficiall for the defence of this their majesties dominion and the inhabitants thereof that rangers be levied on the frontiers of the fower great rivers,

Rangers continued, at the heads of the four great rivers.

Be it therefore enacted by the governour, councell and burgesses of this present generall assembly and the authority thereof, and it is hereby enacted, That from and after the first day of May next one lieutenant, eleaven soldiers and two Indians well furnished with horses and other accoutrements be levied, armed and mustered, to range and scout about the heads of the great rivers and in such places as shall be most like to discover our enemies, and that the pay of each officer and soldier levied or to be levied armed and mustered shall be as followeth, viz. the lieutenant or commander of each party of soldiers finding himselfe horse, furniture, armes amunition and provision shall have and receive five thousand pounds of tobacco and casque out of the publick levy for one whole year, and soe after that rate for a longer or shorter time, and each soldier finding himself horse, armes, furniture, amunition and other necessaries, three thousand pounds of tobacco and cask for one yeare and soe after that rate for a longe ror shorter time.

Their pay.

And be it further enacted by the authority aforesaid, and it is herby enacted, That the two Indians by this act appoynted shall each of them have and receive from the Lieutenant of the Raingers to whome he belongs, eight yards of duffils and two barrels of Indian corn for his service for one yeare, and so proportionable for a longer or shorter time, and the said lieutenant shall be reimbursed by the publique. and that the said lieutenant doe take care and provide by warrant from the Commander in Chiefe of the county where he resides for each of the said Indians, an able horse, bridle and saddle, for which the said owner or owners of the said horse or horses furnished as aforesaid shall have and receive from the county in the next publique levy, after the rate of eighty pounds of tobacco and casque for one month, and so proportionably for a longer or shorter time, and that the commander in chiefe of their respective counties take care that the said officers and soldiers be truly mustered and an account thereof sent from time to time to the secretaries office, and forasmuch as there is noe certainty of future events and therefore uncertaine how to provide for the effectuall defence of the country. and to the end it may be provided for with the least charge,

Pay of the two Indians.

Bee it enacted by the authority aforesaid, and it is hereby enacted, That upon any emergency all such soldiers which the governour with the consent and advice of the councill shall levy, arme and muster for the better defence of this country shall be paid out of the publick levy, and that the governour may from time to time and att all times by and with the advice and consent of the councill disband and discharge all forces raised or to be raised by virtue of this act, as to the said governour with the advice and consent of the said councill shall seem most conducible to the advantage of this theire majesties dominion, which said soldiers shall receive pay and be satisfied proportionably to the time they shall be in service and after these rates viz Each Captain finding himselfe horse, armes, amunition, and provision, and all other necessaries, ten thousand pounds of tobaccoe and casque for one year, and so proportionably for a longer or shorter time, each Lieutenant finding and providing himselfe with horse, armes, amunition and provision and all other necessaries five thousand

Soldiers may be raised by Govr. & Council, in cases of emergency.

Their pay.

pounds of tobacco and casque for one year, and so proportionably for a longer or shorter time.

Divulgers of news how to be dealt with.

And be it further enacted by the authority aforesaid, and it is hereby enacted, That for the future if any English or other christians or Indians shall bring any news or give any intelligence to any of their majesties officers civil or military, such officers to whome the same shall be brought, shall diligently inquire into and examine the grounds thereof, and if such news prove true and be of use and service to the government, that then he or they bringing the same shall be rewarded, but if false punished as the crime shall deserve, and the county courts where such intelligence shall be given are hereby empowered to consider what reward such person bringing news and giving intelligence shall deserve and certifie the same to the next generall assembly for allowance, and if the news and intelligence be false to cause such punishment to be inflicted on the person telling the same, as his crime shall deserve.—This act to continue in force untill the last day of October, which shall be in the year 1696 and noe longer.

ACT II.

Edi. 1733 and 1752.

An act for inlargeing the bounds of Princess Ann County.

Preamble.

FORASMUCH as the division of Lower Norfolk county into Norfolk county and Princess Ann county by reason of misrepresentation to the assembly, begun att James Citty the 16th day of April 1691, appears to be unequally assigned and made, of which the inhabitants of Princess Ann county and that part of Norfolk county which belongs to Lynn Haven Parish have made complaint to this assembly and desired therein to be redressed

Bounds of P. Anne county.

Be it therefore enacted by the Governour, Councell and burgesses of this present generall assembly and the authority thereof, and it is hereby enacted, That the limitts and bounds of Princess Ann county be inlarged and extended unto the utmost bounds of Lynn Haven Parish, and that the respective inhabitants dwelling in that part of Lynn Haven parish which by the xxth act of assembly 1691 entituled an act for dividing Lower Norfolk county, is taken within the bounds of Norfolk be hereafter deemed accounted taken and held for inhabitants of Princess Ann county and as such be constantly reckoned the tithables of the said county and make their payments accordingly, any law, usage or custome to the contrary notwithstanding.

ACT III.

An act for lessening the levy by the pole and laying imposition upon Liquors.

Edi 1733, and 1752.

Preamble.

FORASMUCH as a more suitable expedient cannot be found to lessen the levy by the pole on the inhabitants of this their majesties dominion of Virginia than to lay an imposition on all liquors to be imported into this country,

Impost duty on wine, brandy, rum, cyder, or other spirits or liquors.

Except imported directly from England, Wales, or Berwick, upon Tweed.

Duties, how secured.

Be it therefore enacted by the governour, councell and burgesses of this present generall assembly, and the authority thereof, and it is hereby enacted, That for every gallon of wine of any sort whatsoever, brandy, rum, cyder or any other spirits or liquors imported into this dominion (except allways what shall come directly from England, Wales, or the towne of Berwick upon Tweed) from and after the first day of June in the year 1695 and before the last of October in the year 1696, the imposition or custome of fower pence shall be paid by the merchant or merchants, owner or owners, importer or importers of the same to their majesties their heirs and successors to and for the uses intents and purposes hereafter mentioned and to no other use intent or purposes whatsoever. And for the better levying and collecting the imposition or custome by this act laid on all liquors to be imported (except as before excepted,)

Entry, how to be made.

Be it enacted by the Governour, Councill and Burgesses of this present generall assembly, and the authority thereof, and it is hereby enacted, That noe liquors to be imported within the time before limitted (except as before excepted) shall be landed or putt on shoar out of any shipp or other vessell from beyond the seas, before due entry be made thereof with the officer or collector appointed for the customes in the port or place where the same shall be imported, or before the duty due and payable for the same be fully satisfied, and that every warrant for the landing and delivering of any such liquor shall be signed by the hand of the said officer or collector in the said port or place respectively upon pain that all such forreign liquors as shall be landed, putt on shoar or delivered contrary to the true intent and meaning of this act, and the value thereof shall be forfeited and lost and to be recovered of the importer or proprietor of the same, and that noe person or persons whatsoever bringing any of the before recited liquors (except as before excepted) into any port or place of this country, or any person or persons to whome the same or any of them shall be consigned shall land, or cause any such liquors to be landed or putt on shoare without makeing or causing due entry to be made of the same and giveing a true account of the gallons every casque did containe upon oath with the officer or officers for the time being appoynted to receive and take such entries within the port or place where the same shall be landed or putt on shoar upon pain in every such case as aforesaid to forfeit double the value of the said liquors landed or putt on shoar contrary to the true intent and meaning of this act. And that the master or purser of every shipp barque or other vessel, shall make a true and just entry upon oath, which the collector or other officer is hereby impowered and required to administer, of the burden, contents and ladeing of such shipp, barque or other vessell with the particular marks numbers qualities and contents of every cask therein laden with liquors to the best of his knowledge and also where and in what port she took in her ladeing, how named, who was master dureing the voyage, and who are owners thereof upon penalty of forfeiture of one hundred pounds sterling, and for the better encouragement of all masters, merchants, owners and other persons whatsoever to make due entry and payment of the imposition or duty laid by virtue of this act, and in consideration of filling and leakage there shall be abated and allowed twenty gallons in every hundred, which said allowance and abatement the said collectors to be appoynted to receive the said duties are hereby authorised to allow and make accordingly *Provided always*, That where any master, merchant, owner or other person whatsoever shall wittingly or willingly make a false

Entry of vessel, and cargo, captains name, and from what port to be made.

Abatement for leakage.

entry and be convicted for the same, in that case such master, merchant owner or other person shall forfitt and pay one hundred pounds sterling, and that the said person or persons which are or shall be appoynted shall receive the duties or imposts arising by virtue of this act, and their deputies are hereby authorised and impowered to goe and enter on board any shipp or other vessell and from thence to bring on shoare all the before specified liquors (except as before excepted) for which the duties are not paid or compounded for within ten dayes of the first entry of the said shipp or other vessell, and that the officers of the customes and their deputies may freely stay and remaine on board untill all the goods are delivered and discharged out of the said shipp or other vessell and if any officer or officers be appointed to receive the duties by this act ariseing or any other person or persons deputed and appointed by or under them or any of them or any other authority whatsoever shall directly or indirectly take or receive any bribe, recompence or reward, in any kind whatsoever, or shall connive att any false entry of any wines or other liquors aforementioned, whereby the duties be defrauded the person or persons therein offending shall forfitt the sum of one hundred pounds sterling and be forever afterwards uncapable of any office or imployment within the dominion as also the master, merchant, marriner or other person whatsoever who shall give or pay any such bribe, reward or recompence, shall forfitt the sum of fifty pounds sterling, and that all officers, captains, commanders of shipps, as also all justices of the peace, sheriffs, constables, headboroughs and all other their majesties officers, ministers and subjects whatsoever whome it may concerne, shall be aiding and assisting unto all and every person or persons which are or shall be appointed by the governour to receive and collect the dute by this act laid, and the collector or collectors and their respective deputies in the due execution of all and every act and thing in and by this persent act required and injoyned, and all such who shall bee aiding and assiting unto them in the due execution hereof shall be defended and saved harmless by virtue of this act, and forasmuch as severall forfeitures and penalties may by virtue of this act arise,

Penalty, for false entry.

Collectors, and their deputies authorised to make searches and seizures.

Penalty on officer for receiving a bribe.

On master or owner for giving it.

All civil officers to aid in the execution of this law.

Forfeitures, how appropriated.

Bee it therefore enacted by the authority aforesaid, and it is hereby enacted, That all such forfeitures shall be divided into three equall parts, one third part thereof shall be paid to their majesties their heires and successors towards the better support of the government and defraying the contingent charges thereof, one third part shall be paid to the governour for the time being to and for his own proper use and behoof, and the other third part to him or them that will sue for the same by byll playnt information or action of debt in any court of record in this dominion in which no essoigne protection or wager of law shall be allowed.

Governor with advice of council may appoint collectors.

And be it enacted by the authority aforesaid, and it is hereby enacted, That the governour for the time being with the advise of the counsell shall be and is hereby impowered from time to time and att all times hereafter (dureing the time in this act before limitted) to nominate, constitute and appoint such and soe many collectors and other officers as also such sallaries methods and orders (not exceeding ten in the hundred) for the collecting the said duty as to them shall seem best.

Monies collected by this act, to be accounted for to the treasurer, and by him to the general assembly.

And be it enacted by the authority aforesaid, and it is hereby enacted, That all and every sum and sums of money raised or to be raised by vertue of the imposition aforesaid be constantly accounted for by the collector or collectors thereof to the treasurer of Virginia for the time being upon his or their oath, and by him to the governour, councell and burgesses of the generall assembly upon oath also, and convirted to the uses by them directed according to the true intent and meaning of this act and to and for noe other use intent or purpose whathsoever. any thing in this act contained or any other matter or things to the contrary in any wise notwithstanding. This act to continue in force from the first day of June 1695 untill the last day of October 1696 and noe longer.

Limitation of this act.

ACT IV.

Edi. 1733, and 1752.

An act impowering the governour with the advice of the councell to apply five hundred pounds sterling out of the imposition of liquors raised this assembly to the assistance and preservation of New-York, if found necessary.

Preamble.

THIS Assembly taking into their most serious consideration their majesties comands signified to their governour here relating to a quota of men or other assistance to be given to their majesties province of New York, as application should be made from that government for the same in proportion with their majesties other collonies, plantations and provinces adjacent, and being willing to manifest their readiness on all occations to give such supply for the defence and preservation of their majesties provinces as the circumstances of this needy and poor country will admitt have with due regard to their majesties royall commands and care for the peace, safety and preservation of this their dominion, inquired into the present state of this countrey, and notwithstanding they find the same verry needy and poor, haveing for a long time been and still continuing to be attended with great charge of keeping and maintaining soldiers att the heads of the rivers, and under daily feares of haveing too great occasion for raising more without any fund or other supply for the same then a levy from time to time raised upon the poll, yet to show their loyall and dutifull inclinations to the verry uttmost of their abilities and rather beyond, in hopes that nothing but such supply as shall be directed by this act be required either of men or money, and that for the future their majesties will be graciously pleased to take the low circumstances of this their country into their princely consideration, and thereupon to excuse their loyall subjects here;

The councill and burgesses now assembled pray your excellency that it may be enacted, And be it enacted by the governour, councell and burgesses of this present Generall assembly and the authority thereof, and it is hereby enacted, That whereas by one act intituled an act for lessening the levy by the poll and laying an imposition upon liquors made this session of assembly, an imposition of four pence per gallon is raised upon certain liquors to be imported from and after the first day of June next, untill the last day of October 1696, the governour for the time being, by and with the advice of the councill be empowered to take and apply such a sum of money not exceeding the sum of five hundred pounds sterling as it shall arrise from the imposition upon liquors in and by vertue of the said act and noe otherwayes, and by the said governour with the advice of the councill shall from time to time be found neces-

Governor authorised to apply a sum, not exceeding 500 pounds sterling, to be raised from the imposition on liquors to the releif of the province of New York.

sary and convenient for the immediate preservation of their majesties province of New-York, upon application of their majesties governour or commander in chiefe of their said province, any thing in their said act laying an imposition upon liquors as aforesaid notwithstanding. *Provided alwayes, and it is hereby intended*, that if between the end of this session of assembly and the expiration of the said act intituled an act for lessening the levy by the poll and laying an imposition upon liquors noe application be made from the governour or commander in chiefe of the province of New York for assistance or supply in and by vertue of their majesties comands relating thereto, or that upon such application it shall be found necessary and convenient by the governour and councill of this their majesties dominion to forbear the imploying useing or remitting the said sum of five hundred pounds sterling, or any part thereof, as it may be required. that then the said intire sum of five hundred pounds sterling or such par thereof as shall not be imployed made use of or remitted to their majesties said province of New-York for the intents and purposes aforesaid, shall be accounted for to the generall assembly and thereby applyed to such uses intents and purposes as by the governour councell and burgesses of the said general assembly shall be thought fitt for lessening the levy by the poll, according to the first intent purport and meaning of the said act made this assembly, by vertue of which the same was levyed and raised, any thing in this act to the contrary or seeming to the contrary notwithstanding.

ACT V.

Edi. 1733 and 1752.

An act for reviving the 7th act of assembly made att James Citty the 16th day of Aprill 1691, and for the ascertaining the size of tobacco hogsheads

Preamble.

FORASMUCH as the seventh act of assembly made att James Citty the 16th day of Aprill 1691, intituled an act reviveing the 6th act of assembly made att James Citty the 20th October 1686, regulateing the tares of tobacco hogsheads hath been found verry advantageous and usefull for the prevention of frauds and abuses in the tares of tobacco hogsheads and damages that accrue from unseasoned timber and slight staves.

Bee it therefore enacted by the Governour, Councell and Burgesses of this present generall assembly and the authority thereof, and it is hereby enacted, That the said seventh act of assembly in all its parts and clauses as well such as relate to the said 6th act of assembly made att James Citty the 20th October 1686 as otherwayes be from henceforth revived and putt in force, and for the future ascertaining the size of tobacco hogsheads. 7th act of 1791 revived.

Bee it further enacted by the authority aforesaid, that the certain size of every tobacco hogshead be as followeth, that is to say in the length of the stave forty-eight inches and noe more, and in the diameter of the head thirty inches and no more, and whatsoever cooper or coopers shall make tobacco casque contrary to this act if he be a freeman and in case he be not his master or mistress, or whatsoever planter or other person shall pay away or putt to sale, or putt on board any boate, sloope, shipp or other vessell in order to exportation any tobacco whatsoever packed in cask of a greater size than is herein expressed and sett downe, such cooper, planter or other person shall for every tobacco hoggshead soe made paid away, putt to sale or shipped forfeit and pay the sum of five hundred pounds of tobacco one moyety thereof to be to our sovereigne lord and lady the king and queen, their heirs and successors for and towards the better support of this government and the contingent charges thereof and the other moyety to him or them that shall sue for the same in any court of record within this collony by bill, information, plaint or other action, wherein noe essoign protection or wager of law shall be allowed, *And be it enacted,* that this act continue in force seaven years and noe longer. Size of tobacco hogsheads. Penalty.

ACT VI.

An act for raiseing a publique levy. Edi. 1733 and 1752.

Be it enacted by the governour, councell and Burgesses of this present generall assembly, and the authority thereof, and it is hereby enacted, That the sum of twenty two pounds and three quarters of tobacco be paid by every tithable person within their majesties collony and dominion of Virginia in this present year 1695 for the Taxes, or public levy, for 1695.

defraying and payment of the charge of keeping and maintaining one lieutenant, eleaven soldiers and two Indians att the heads of each of the four great rivers for the terme of twelve months from the last day of this instant month of April and for the satisfaction of all such other claims and allowances as have been made this generall assembly, and that the same be paid by the collector of the severall counties in the said year to the severall persons to whome it is now proportioned, and if it shall happen that there shall be more tithables in any county than the said levy of twenty-two pounds and three quarters of tobacco is now laid on, then such county to have credit for soe much to the use of the county and if there shall happen to be less in any county then such county shall bear the loss.

A true copy,

Teste, PETER BERVERLY,
Clerke of the House of Burgesses.

[Here follows in the MS. an appropriation of the taxes of Northumberland county, among sundry public creditors, which it is unnecessary to insert.]

Signed by SIR EDMUND ANDROS, *Gov'r.*
PHILIP LUDWELL, *Speaker.*
(*Note to editions* 1733 *and* 1752.)

ATT A

Generall Assembly,

BEGUN ATT JAMES CITTY

THE 24th DAY OF SEPTEMBER IN THE EIGHTH YEAR OF THE REIGN OF OUR SOVEREIGN LORD, WILLIAM THE THIRD, BY THE GRACE OF GOD OF ENGLAND, SCOTLAND, FRANCE AND IRELAND, KING, DEFENDER OF THE FAITH, &c. ANNOQUE DOM. 1696.* Sir Edmund Andros, Govr.

ACT I.

An act for punishment of ffornication and seaverall other sins and offences. Edi. 1733 and 1752.

WHEREAS there are severall and many laws now in force for the suppression of the sins of swear- Preamble.

Various Readings.

* In all the MSS. of this period, the commencement of this session is stated to be on the 24th of *September*, in the eighth year of the reign of *William* the third; but in the revisals of 1733 and 1752, the session is said to commence on the 24th of *April*, in the eighth year of the reign of *William and Mary*. How a session of the assembly, in 1696, could be held in the reign of William and *Mary*, when it is a well established historical fact that Mary died, on the 28th of December 1694, it is difficult to conceive.—William and Mary reigned jointly, from the 13th of February 1688-9, till her death on the 28th of December 1694, in the 7th year of their reign. William then assumed the title of William the third, and reigned alone till his death, on the 8th of March 1701-2; but in the computation of the time of *his* reign, the period in which he reigned jointly with Mary, is calculated. Thus, the year 1696, is said to be in the *eighth* year of the reign of William the third, as that of 1695 was the *seventh* of William and Mary. At the end of the acts of 1695, there is the following note, in the editions of 1733, and 1752. "N. B. There was another session of this assembly, held the 23rd of April 1696, in the 8th year of king William's reign, but no laws passed."—This is another proof of the want of correctness in the printed copies;—for it is impossible to suppose that an assembly should be held on the *twenty-third* of April, at which no laws passed, and on the very next day, the *twenty-fourth*, that another assembly should be held, at which were passed the number of laws which we see were enacted at this session. The fact must have been, that the word *April* was introduced in the commencement of the acts of this session, in the edition of 1733, by mistake, and was copied in the revisal of 1752, without reference to the MSS. William and Mary, account of their reign.

S

ing, cursing, profaining God's holy name, sabbath abuseing, drunkenness, fornication and adultery, which have not had their desired effect by reason that some of the same lawes seem to be contradictory to the other, for the better regulation whereof for the future, and the better to prevent and deter all offenders from the said offences and sins,

Certain enumerated laws repealed.

Be it enacted by the Governour, Councell and Burgesses of this present Generall Assembly and the authority thereof, and it is hereby enacted, That the ninth act of assembly in the printed book intituled Sundayes not to be prophained, and the thirteenth act of assembly in the printed book entituled, Church-wardens to make presentments, and the hundredth act of assembly in the printed book, entituled an act against ffornication, and the twelfth act of assembly made the 23d of December 1662, entituled an act for molatto children being bond or free, according to the condition of the mother, and the 11th act of assembly made att James Citty 1691 entituled an act for the more effectuall suppressing the severall sins and offences of swearing, cursing, prophaining God's holy name, sabbath abuseing, dunkeness, fornication and adultery and every clause and article in the said acts contained, shall bee and are hereby repealed, made void, null and of noe effect, to all intent, constructions and purposes as if the said acts had never been made.

Penalty for swearing, cursing, or profaning God's name;

And be it further enacted by the authority aforesaid, and it is hereby enacted, That noe person or persons shall from henceforth swear, curse or prophaine God's holy name, and that if any person or persons shall hereafter offend therein and shall thereof be lawfully covicted by the oath of two witnesses or by confession of the party then every such offender shall forfeit and pay for every such offence the sum of one shilling, And for the prevention of sabbath breaking,

for not keeping holy, the sabbath;

Bee it further enacted by the authority aforesaid, that there shall be noe unlawfull meetings or assemblies of people on the Lord's day, and that noe person or persons whatsoever shall travell upon the said day, and that noe other thing or matter whatsoever shall be done upon that day tending to the breach of the sabbath but that the same in all respect be kept holy, upon pain that every person or persons soe offending and being convicted as aforesaid, shall forfeit and pay for every such offence, the sume of twenty shillings or two hundred pounds of tobacco att the election of such offender or offenders. And for the suppression of drunkenness,

Be it further enacted by the authority aforesaid, That all and every person or persons who shall from henceforth be drunk and of the same offence of drunkenness shall be lawfully convicted as aforesaid, shall forfeit and pay the sume of ten shillings or one hundred pounds of tobacco att the election aforesaid, and if the offender or offenders in any of the aforesaid vices be not able to pay the fines and forfeitures aforementioned then every such offender or offenders therein, shall be committed to the stocks for every such offence there to remaine the space of two full howers. And for the more effectual suppression and prevention of the sins of fornication and adultery, for drunkenness;

Bee it further enacted by the authority aforesaid, that every person or persons comitting fornication and being therein lawfully convicted by the oath of two witnesses or confession of the party shall forfeit and pay the sume of five hundred pounds of tobacco and casque for every time soe offending and that every person or persons comitting adultery and being thereof lawfully convicted as aforesaid, shall forfeit and pay for every such offence the sume of one thousand pounds of tobacco and casque, and if the offender or offenders in any or both the aforeasid two sins or offences, be not able to pay theire fines and forfeitures for the said offences mentioned then every offender or offenders therein, shall for every time soe offending receive on his her or their bare backs twenty-five lashes well laid on, or two monthes imprisonment without bayle or mainprize, and if they or either of them comiting fornication as aforesaid be servants, then if the master or mistress of such servant or servants so offending or any other person doe pay the aforesaid five hundred pounds of tobacco the said servant in compensation thereof, shall serve halfe a year after the time by indenture or custome is expired, and if the master or any other person doe not pay the said fine the said servant shall receive upon his or her bare back twenty-five lashes well layed on, and if it happen that a bastard child be gotten in such fornication, then the servant if a woman in regard of the for fornication; for adultery. Fornication and adultery, by servants. Bastards by servants.

less or trouble her master or mistress sustained by her haveing a bastard shall serve one year after her time by indenture or custome is expired or pay one thousand pounds of tobacco to her master or mistress besides the fine or punishment for committing the offence and the reputed father to putt in security to kepp the parrish harmless.

Grand juries, & church-wardens to present offences against this act. *And be it further enacted by the authority aforesaid,* That the grand jures and church-wardens and each of them in every respective county or parrish within this dominion, doe twice every year make due presentments of all the sins and offences comitted and perpetrated contrary to this act, and that the justices of the said court, are by vertue of this act impowered to punish the offender or offenders accordingly, all which fines and forfeitures shall be appropriated to the use of the parrish for their ease towards the maintenance of the minister, where such offence or offences shall be committed which fines or forfeitures shall or may be recovered by the church-warden or church-wardens of any parrish or parrishes by action of debt, byll, plaint or information in any court of record in this dominion, in which no essoign protection or wager of law shall be allowed.

Justices empowered to punish offenders.

Penalties, how recovered.

All children to be bond or free according to the condition of the mother. *And be it enacted and declared by the authority aforesaid, and it is hereby enacted and declared,* That all children born in this country be bond or free, according to the condition of their mother.

ACT II.

Edi. 1733 and 1752.

An act for altering the court dayes in Accomack county.

Preamble. WHEREAS the fifth act of assembly made the 20th of October 1686, entituled an act for ascertaining dayes for courts in Accomack county is found verry inconvenient and injurious to the inhabitants of the said county of Accomack, who desire that the said law may be repealed, and that another law may be made more suitable to their conveniency,

Be it therefore enacted by the Governour, Councell and Burgesses of this present Generall Assembly and the authority thereof, and it is hereby enacted, That the said act and every clause and article therein contained be repealed and they and every of them are hereby repealed and made null and void.

Court day of Accomack county changed.

And it is further enacted by the authority aforesaid, That for the future the court of the said county of Accomack, be constantly held by the justices thereof on the first Tuesday of the month in such manner as by the law of this country is provided, and shall be by their comissions directed, any law, usage or custome to the contrary notwithstanding.

ACT III.

An act for giveing a reward to Indians for killing of Wolves.

Edi. 1733, and 1752.

Preamble.

WHEREAS the first act of assembly, made att James Citty the 16th day of April 1691, entituled an act for giveing reward for killing of Wolves hath been variously construed, some county courts haveing allowed the reward therein mentioned, and other county courts noe rewards att all unto Indians which have killed Wolves, for the prevention of the like mistakes for the future, and to the end Indians may be also encouraged to use their endeavours to destroy those injurious creatures,

Rewards to Indians to kill Wolves.

Bee it enacted by the Governour, Councell and Burgesses of this present Generall Assembly and the authority thereof, and it is hereby enacted, That every Indian that shall hereafter destroy and kill Wolves by any way or means whatsoever, shall for every Wolfe he kills be paid in the county where the same is done, one hundred pounds of tobacco and casque for his encouragement and reward and no more, any law, usage or custome to the contrary notwithstanding. *Provided alwayes.* and it is the true intent and meaning of this act, that whatsoever Indian shall kill a Wolfe shall bring in the head of the said Wolfe, to a justice of the peace, and by some proofe or circumstance att the discretion of the justice, make it probably appear how, when and where he killed the said Wolfe, and also take from the said justice of the peace a certificate thereof, which being produced to the county court att proportioning the levy, shall be sufficient to cause the said

What proof necessary.

court to raise upon the county the said reward, to be paid to such Indian as by such service shall deserve it, and to the end noe cheat may be putt upon the county by means of an Indian killing a Wolfe in one county and bringing his head to another county for allowance,

Wolfe to be killed in the county where the claim is made.

Bee it enacted by the authority aforesaid, and it is hereby enacted, That it shall and may bee lawfull for every justice of the peace to whome such Indian shall make application for a certificate upon the least suspicion he hath of a fraud to forbear giveing the same, untill the Indian can bring him sufficient testimony to convince him that he killed the Wolfe in the county where he makes his claime.

ACT. IV.

Edi. 1733 and 1752.

An act for repealing the prohibition of planting tobacco after the last day of June, annually.

Preamble.

FORASMUCH as the prohibition of planting or replanting tobacco after the last day of June in every year, as is provided by a clause or section of the 7th act of assembly made att James Citty the 20th of October 1686, entituled an act declareing the 107th act of assembly made the 23d day of March 1661-2 to be in force, hath been found to bring great hardshipps upon some part of this his majesties dominion, and not to have those good effects which were generally expected from it,

Acts prohibiting the planting, or replanting of tobacco, after the last day of June repealed; and liberty given to plant, at any time.

Be it therefore enacted by the governour, councell and burgesses of this present generall assembly and the authority thereof, and it is hereby enacted, That the said clause or section of the said act which prohibits the planting or replanting of tobacco directly or indirectly after the last day of June annually under the pain and penalty of forfeiting and paying ten thousand pounds of tobacco for soe doeing be from henceforth repealed, annulled and made utterly voyd, and that it bee lawfull for all and every person or persons within this his majesties collony and dominion, to plant or replant tobacco att any time, as if no such restraint or prohibition of planting or replanting tobacco had ever been made.

ACT V.

An act for ascertaining damages upon Appeales.

Edi. 1733 and 1752.

Preamble.

WHEREAS the acts already made giveing damages upon appeales doe admitt of divers constructions, for ascertaining of which and for remedy whereof for the future,

Bee it enacted by the Governour, Councell and Burgesses of this present generall assembly and the authority thereof, and it is hereby enacted, That the 26th act of assembly in the printed book entituled appeales how to be made, and the third act of assembly made att James Citty the 17th September 1668, entituled an act concerning damages in Appeals and every clause and article in the said acts contained be from henceforth repealed and made void, to all intents constructions and purposes as if the said act had never been made, any thing in the said act to the contrary notwithstanding.

Certain acts repealed, see vol. 2. pa. 65 & 266.

And be it further enacted by the authority aforesaid, and it is hereby enacted, That in all appeales to the generall court from the judgement of any county court or courts where the appellant shall be cast in such appeale, and the county courts judgment by the generall court shall be affirmed, the appellant soe cast for his vexatious appeall and suit, shall pay to the appellee fifteen per cent damages upon the principall debt, damages and costs of the county court, which shall be taxed in the bill of costs and levyed by execution in the principall debt, damages and costs of suite.

15 per cent damages on appeals from county courts to genel. court, on principal debt, damages & costs.

And be it further enacted by the authority aforesaid, and it is hereby enacted, That the county courts in their respective counties shall not admitt of any appealle to the generall court, without the party appealing doe enter into bond with good and sufficient security to the appellee to appear and prosecute his said appeale at the said gennerall court and to stand and abide the award and judgment of the said court and pay the said damages of ffifteen per cent upon the principall debt, damages and cost, if cast in the appeale.

No appeal to be allowed, without bond and security given by the appellant.

And be it further enacted by the authority aforesaid, and it is hereby enacted, That no person or persons shall commence any action or suit against any person or persons whatsoever to the generall court for any sum or sums for debt or damages under the value of two

Jurisdiction of general court.

thousand pounds of tobacco or ten pounds current money upon the penalty of paying the non-suit and such damages as are imposed by the 7th act of assembly made att James City the 3d of October 1670 entituled an act concerning litigious suits.

ACT VI.

Edit. 1733, & 1752.

An act for imposeing penalties upon the non appearance of Evidences.

Preamble.

WHEREAS many causes of great consequence depending in courts or judicature between parties and parties are utterly lost for want of appearance of evidences, and the king's process of subpœna contemned,

Former act repealed—See vol. 2. pa. 69.

Bee it enacted by the governour, councell and burgesses of this present generall assembly, and the authority thereof, and it is hereby enacted, That the clause of the 30th act of assembly in the printed book entituled penalties for non-appearance of evidences, relateing to the penalties for the non-appearance of evidences, be from henceforth repealed, made null and void, as if the said clause had never been made.

And be it further enacted by the authority aforesaid, and it is hereby enacted and declared, That if any wittness or witnesses being lawfully summoned by writ of subpœna to any gennerall court doe not make his or their personall appearance att the genneral court att the time in the writ mentioned to give his or their evidence, and likewise give his or their attendance as the said court shall think fitt in the tryall of the said cause or causes, he or they soe offending shall be fined and amerced to our sovereign lord the king, the sume of one thousand pounds of tobacco for the contempt of such process (unless the said offender shall appear att the next gennerall court and shew good cause for his said non-appearance) and shall be liable to pay all such demages as by the common law is given to the party injured for want of such evidence. And if any wittness or wittnesses lawfully sumoned by subpœna to any county court or courts doe not make his or their personall appearance att the time to which they were summoned to give his or their evidense, and likewise to

Fine to the king, and damages to the party, for non-appearance of witnesses; at the general court.

at the county courts.

give his or their attendance, as the said court or courts shall think fitt in the tryall of the said cause or causes, he or they soe offending shall be fined and amerced to our sovereign lord the king the sume of three hundred and fifty pounds of tobacco, for the contempt of such process (unless he shall appear att the next county court or courts and shew good cause for his non-appearance) and shall be liable to pay all such damages as by the comon law is given to the party injured, for the want of such evidence.

And be it further enacted by the authority aforesaid, and it is hereby enacted, That if any witness or witnesses lawfully sumoned by subpœna to give in his or their evidence upon any dedimus potestatem do not appear att the time and place in the subpœna mentioned, he or they so offending, if the cause for which the said dedimus potestatum is issued be depending in the generall court, shall be fined and amerced to our sovereign lord the king the sume of one thousand pounds of tobacco for the contempt of such process (unless he shall appear att the next generall court and shew good cause for his said non-appearance) and if in the county court, the sume of three hundred and fifty pounds of tobacco for the contempt of such process (unless th esaid offender shall appear att the next county court, and shew good cause for his said non-appeasance) and shall be liable to pay all such damages, as by the comon law is given to the party injured for want of such evidence. Penalty on witnesses, sumoned by subpœna to give their depositions, failing to attend.

ACT VII.

An act declareing how long judgements and specialties shall be pleadable. Edi. 1733 and 1752.

WHEREAS the law now in force for the limitation of actions and suits upon bills and bonds doth admitt of many doubts and ambiguities in the construction thereof, for the better explanation whereof for the future, Preamble.

Be it enacted by the Governour, Councill and Burgesses of this present Generall Assembly, and the authority thereof, and it is hereby enacted, That the eighty first act of assembly in the printed book, intituled, judgements and specialties how long pleadable and every See vol. 2, pa. 104.

T

clause and article thereof be from henceforth repealed and made void to all intents constructions and purposes as if the said act had never been made.

Limitation in the recovery, on bills and bonds,—five years.

And be it therefore enacted by the authority aforesaid, and it is hereby enacted, That noe bills or bonds shall be of force or recoverable by any action or actions above the space of five years after the date of the said bills or bonds, if noe time of payment be therein expressed, but if any time or times of payment be therein expressed then the said bills or bonds shall be in force five years after the last time of payment in the said bills or bonds expressed and mentioned, and noe longer.

On judgments; seven years.

And be it further enacted by the authority aforesaid, and it is hereby enacted, That noe judgement or judgements obtained in any court shall be of force any further or longer time then seaven years after the date of the said judgment or after that the same has been renewed by writ of sciere facias. *Provided alwaies,* and it is the true intent and meaning of this act. that this act nor any thing therein contained, shall bee deemed or taken to extend to the limitting or annulling any bonds or obligations for the performance of covenants, but that the said bonds and obligations shall be in force, and recoverable, five years after the breach of the covenants in the conditions of the said bonds or obligations contained, any thing in this act to the contrary notwithstanding.

on bonds, for performance of covenants.

Proviso, where the debtor removes, from the county.

Provided likewise, That if the debtor or obligor doe privately depart this country or the county where he resided and dwelt or contracted such debt or debts and have not a sufficient estate in the county where he so resided or contracted such debt or debts, or where such judgment or judgments were obtained against him, to satisfie the same, the said bill bond or judgment shall remaine and be in force and recoverable notwithstanding the said five yeares or seaven yeares be expired and past, any thing in this act to the contrary notwithstanding.

ACT VIII.

Edi. 1933 and 1652.

An act for ascertaining the place where the court of York county shall bee kept.

Preamble.

FORASMUCH as upon the complaint of divers inhabitants of York county it hath been made appear to this assembly, that the place where the court for the said county hath usually been held and kept is verry inconvenient and remote to a great part of the inhabitants of the said county and may bee appointed elsewhere to the greater ease and advantage of the people in generall,

Court of York county, to be held at York town.

Bee it therefore enacted by the governour, councell and burgesses of this present generall assembly, and the authority thereof, and it is hereby enacted, That from and after the last day of October which shall be in the year of our Lord 1697, the court for York county be constantly held and kept by the justices upon those dayes and in such manner as the lawes of this countrey and the governours comission shall from time to time provide and direct, within the limitts and bounds of a certain parcell or tract of land, which by vertue of the eighth act of assembly made att James Citty the 16th day of April 1691, entituled an act for ports &c. was designed and laid out for and is now comonly called York Towne, and att noe other place or places whatsoever, any law, usage or custome to the contrary notwithstanding, and to the end due provision may be made for keeping the said court according to this act,

Court house to be built.

Bee it enacted by the authority aforesaid, and it is hereby enacted, That the justices or members of the said court take care that an house suitable and fitt to hold courts in and as bigg in dimension att least as the present court house now is, be errected built and finished att the charge of the county upon some certain place within the said limitts of York Towne between the end of this session of assembly and the said last day of October 1697, upon pain that each respective justice or member of the said court for his default shall forfeit the sume of fifty pounds sterling, one moyety thereof to our sovereign lord the king, his heirs and successors for and towards the better support of the government and the contingent charges thereof, and the other moyety to the informer to be recovered by action of debt, byll, plaint or information in any court of judicature within this collony.

ACT IX.

Edit. 1733, and 1752.

An act for ascertaining the gage of Pork, Tarr and other Barrells.

Preamble.

WHEREAS many frauds and abuses have been committed and done verry injuriously to the trade of this dominion by reason that pork, beef and tarr barrells have not a gage ascertained by law, for the prevention whereof for the future,

Size of barrels for beef, pork, and tar.

Bee it enacted by the Governour, Councell and Burgesses of this present generall assembly and the authority thereof, and it is hereby enacted, That from and after the 29th day of September next every beef, pork and tarr barrell that shall or may hereafter be shipped off for exportation or that shall be putt to sale by any person or persons in this dominion shall hold and contain att least the quantity of thirty gallons.

Penalty for making, exposing to sale, or exporting barrels, of less dimensions.

And be it further enacted by the authority aforesaid, and it is hereby enacted, That if any cooper or coopers or any other person or persons after the 29th day of September next, shall make or sett upp any barrell or barrells for pork or tarr or any other thing of a less gage or dimension, then to hold and containe the quantity of thirty gallons per barrell, and if any person shall export or put to sale any barrell or barrells other then of the gage and dimension aforesaid, he or they makeing or putting up or exporting or putting to sale any such barrell or barrells shall forfeit and pay for every barrell so made or put up, exported or putt to sale the sume of five pounds current money, one moyety to our sovereign lord the king, his heirs and successors towards the better support of this government and the contingent charges thereof, the other moyety to him or them that shall sue for the same by action of debt, byll, plaint or information in any court of record in this dominion, in which noe essoign protection or wager of law shall be allowed.

How appropriated, and recoverable.

Packers of beef and pork to be appointed, in counties, where deemed necessary by the justices.

And be it enacted by the authority aforesaid, and it is hereby enacted, That the justices of every county court shall be and are hereby impowered in their respective counties, wherein their discretion shall be thought necessary to appoint one or more packers to pack pork and beef barrells, and that every packer shall and may by vertue of this act take and demand the sume of six pence for every pork or beef barrell soe by him packed, and if any packer or packers shall pack any unwholesome meat or trash in any barrell or barrells or shall pack any meat in other barrell or barrells then of the gage as aforesaid, he or they for every barrell so packt shall forfeit and pay the sume of five pounds currant money to be recovered and divided as aforesaid.

Penalty for filling up barrels, with unmerchantable pitch and tar.

And be it further enacted by the authority aforesaid, and it is hereby enacted, That if any person or persons shall fill up or putt to sale in any barrell or barrells as aforesaid any pitch or tarr not true made and merchantable or which shall be mingled with any trash or other thing then true made pitch, if it be pitch in the barrell, or clean tarr, if it bee tarr in the barrell and being thereof lawfully convicted, he or they soe offending shall forfeit and loose the said pitch and tarr, and twenty shillings for every barrell of pitch and ten shillings for every barrell of tarr soe falsely made filled or putt to sale to be recovered with costs and divided as aforesaid.

Justices to appoint a mark to be put on the barrels.

And be it further enacted by the authority aforesaid, and it is hereby enacted, That the county courts in their respective counties are hereby likewise impowered where they think it necesary to appoint a mark which shall be putt by the said packers upon every barrell soe by them packed to marke the said barrells therewith, as likewise to marke upon the said barrell or barrells the just quantity and contents of the said barrell or barrells upon the paines or penalties as aforesaid to be recovered and divided as aforesaid.

ACT X.

An act for prevention of clandestine Marriages.

Edi. 1733 and 1752.

Preamble.

WHEREAS many great and grievous mischeifes have arisen and dayly doe arise by clandestine and secrett marriages to the utter ruin of many heirs and heiresses and to the great greif of all their relations, and whereas the lawes now in force for the prevention of such marriages do inflict too small a punishment for so heinous and great an offence,

Bee it enacted by the governour, councell and burgesses of this generall assembly and the authority

Former act repealed.

See vol. 2, pa. 49.

thereof, and it is hereby enacted, That the twelfth act of assembly in the printed book entituled none to be married but by ministers nor by them but by lycense or publishing the banes and every clause or article therein contained be from and after the tenth day of November next repealed and made void to all intents constructions and purposes, as if the said act had never been made, any thing in the said act to the contrary notwithstanding.

None to be mrried, except as the rubrick in the common prayer book prescribes.

And be it further enacted by the authority aforesaid, and it is hereby enacted, That noe minister or ministers shall from henceforth marry any person or persons togeather as man and wife without lawfull lycense, or without their publication of banns, according to the rubrick in the common prayer book prescribes which enjoynes, that if the persons to be married dwell in seaverall parishes, the banes must be asked in both parishes, and that the curate of the one parish shall not solemnise the matrimony, untill he have a certificate from the curate of the other parish, that the banes hath been thrice published and noe objection made against the parties joyned together. And if any minister or ministers shall contrary to this act without such lycence or publication marry any person or persons, he or they soe offending shall for every such offence be imprisoned for one whole year without bayle or mainprize and shall forfeitt and pay the sume of five hundred pounds current money, one moyety thereof to our sovereign lord the king, his heirs and successors towards the better support of the government and the contingent charges thereof and the other moyety to him or them that shall sue or informe for the same by action of debt, byll, plaint or information in any court of record in this dominion in which noe essoign nor protection or wager of law shall be allowed.

Penalty on ministers for marrying otherwise.

How licences to be granted by clerks.

And be it enacted by the authority aforesaid, and it is hereby enacted, That if the clerk of any county court doe grant any certificate or certificates to any person or persons for any lycence or lycences for any marriage or marriages without the personall consent of the parent or guardian or signified under the hands and seales of the said guardian or parent and attested by two wittnesses or if any person or persons doe grant any lycence or lycenses for any marriage or marriages without such certificate or certificates, he or they soe offending shall for every such offence forfeit and pay the sume of five hundred pounds current money, to be recovered and divided as aforesaid, and be imprisoned the space of one whole yeare, without bayle or mainprise.

Penalty for granting them otherwise.

And be it enacted by the authority aforesaid, and it is hereby enacted, That if any woeman child or maiden being above the age of twelve and under the age of sixteen years doe att any time consent or agree to such person, that so shall make any contract of matrimony without the consent of the parent or guardian or without the publication of the banes as aforesaid, that then the next of kin to the said woman, child or maid to whome the inheritance should descend, fall or come after the death of the said woman, child or maiden, shall from the time of such agreement and assent hold, have and enjoy all such lands, tenements and hereditaments as the said woman, child or maiden had in possession, reversion or remainder att the time of such assent and agreement and dureing such coverture and after the decease of the husband of the said woman, child or maiden haveing so contracted matrimony that then the said lands, tenements and hereditaments shall descend revert and remain to such woman, child or maiden, or such person or persons as they should have done in case this act had never been made.

Females, between 12 and 16 years of age contracting marriage forfeit their inheritance to the next of their kin.

How it shall descend after their death.

ACT XI.

An act for the better supply and mentainance of the Clergy.

Edi. 1733, and 1752.

WHEREAS a competent and sufficient provision for the clergy will be the only means to supply this dominion with able faithfull and orthodox ministers whereby the glory of God may be advanced, the church propagated and the people edified, and whereas the law now in force entituled glebes to be laid out, in makeing such provision, doth seem verry deficient and uncertain.

Preamble.

Bee it enacted by the Governour, Councell and Burgesses of this present generall assembly and the authority thereof, and it is hereby enacted, That the said act of assembly in the printed book entituled glebes to be laid out, and every clause and article thereof be from henceforth repealed and made void, to all intents constructions and purposes as if the said act had never been made, any thing in the said act or in any other act to the contrary in any wise notwithstanding

Salary of ministers fixed at sixteen thousand pounds of tobacco a year, besides perquisites.

And be it enacted by the authority aforesaid, and it is hereby enacted, That all and every minister or ministers in all and every parish and parishes in this dominion incumbent in the said parish or parishes and therein officiateing as minister or ministers shall have and receive for his or their meantenance the sume of sixteen thousand pounds of tobacco* besides their lawfull perquisites, and that it shall and may be lawfull for the vestry or vestryes of any parish or parishes and they are by vertue of this act authorised and impowered to raise and levy the same in their respective parish or parishes, as also to levy five per cent for collecting and paying the said tobacco convenient.

Vestry of each parish to appoint collectors; who may make distress

And be it further enacted by the authority aforesaid, That it shall and may be lawfull for the vestry and vestries of all and every parish and parishes to appoint the church-wardens or whome they think fitt to collect and receive the ministers or other parish dues. and the said person or persons soe qualified as aforesaid, shall bee and are hereby impowered in case of non-payment to make distress for the same.

Vestry empowered to purchase a glebe at the charge of the parish, and build a house for the minister.

And be it further enacted by the authority aforesaid, That all and every vestry and vestryes in this dominion shall bee and are hereby authorised and impowered where the same is not allready done to purchase and lay out a tract of land for the glebe att their discretion and att the charge of their respective parishes. And likewise to build and errect a convenient dwelling house for the reception and aboad of the minister of such parish or parishes att the discretion of such vestry or vestryes. *Provided allwayes,* and it is the true intent and meaning of this act. that if any vestry or vestryes of any parish or parishes shall find their parishes to be so small and poor and not to be able to allow and main-

---

* This was the first law which fixed the salary of the clergy of the Church of England at 16,000 lbs. of tobacco a year; and it so continued till the revolution.

taine a minister as aforesaid, that then application of the vestry or vestries to the governour of the time being, that their respective parishes may be united and consolidated to the next adjacent parrish or parishes. And whereas the clerk of the registers fee seems to be so small an incouragement for an office of soe much trust, When small parishes may be consoli-dated.

Bee it enacted by the authority aforesaid, and it is hereby enacted, That every clerk of the register shall and may lawfully by vertue of this act take and demand the sume of five pounds of tobacco or sixpence for recording and registring every birth, buriall or marriage and the church wardens of the said parish or parishes or any other person or persons appointed by the vestry or vestryes are hereby authorised and impowered to collect the same, or in case of non-payment to make distress. Fee of clerk of registers, for births, marriages, and deaths.

ACT XII.

An act for regulating and ascertaining county court clerk fees. Edi. 1733 and 1752.

WHEREAS the fees of county court clerkes are att present scattered and dispersed in the body of the lawa of this country for the true knowledge whereof as there hath been occation from time to time all and every person or persons therein concerned have been necessitated not only to search and look into the seaverall acts of assembly relateing thereto in particular, but also into many clauses and branches of other acts, wherein some particular fee or fees are appointed, and whereas through a misconstruction of what the lawes relateing to county court clerks fees do really intend, or an avaritious humor, them thereunto moveing, diverse clerks of county courts have for some time past charged, demanded and taken and do still continue to charge demand and take sundry unreasonable fees, for prevention of the like exactions for the future and for regulateing and ascertaining fees to county court clerks, Preamble.

Bee it enacted by the Governour, Councell and Burgesses of this present Generall Assembly, and the authority thereof, and it is hereby enacted, That so much and such

All former laws relating to fees of clerks of county courts, repealed.

a part of all and every act and acts, law and laws heretofore made, and of every clause, article and parragraph of any act or acts, law or lawes, whereby any fee or fees are appointed, given and allowed to clerks of county courts for any matter, business or thing by them or any of them done, be from and after the last day of November next repealed and made void, and that they and every of them and every clause, article and paragraph therein contained, so farr as the same any way relate to or concerne such fee or fees, do from the last of November stand repealed null and voyd to all intents and purposes, as if such law or lawes, act or acts, clauses, articles and paragraphs had never been made constituted and ordained.

What fees may be demanded, after the last day of November 1696.

And be it enacted by the authority aforesaid, and it is hereby enacted, That from and after the said last day of November next it shall and may be lawfull for all and every county court clerk or clerks of this his majesties collony and dominion to charge, demand and take for any business matter or thing by the said county court clerk or clerks or any of them done and performed, after the said last day of November all and every such fee and fees, as by this act are hereafter mentioned declared and sett down to the fee or fees for such business, matter or thing, and that no other or greater fee or fees bee by any county court clerk or clerks after the said last day of November next, upon any pretence whatsoever charged, demanded or taken, for any business matter or thing by them or any of them done and performed as clerk of a county court, then whatt in this act are specially declared, mentioned and sett down and to be the fee or fees for such business matter or thing, under the paine of forfeiting and paying for the same such penalty and forfeiture as hereafter in this act is made and provided. And for the good encouragement of good and able clerks,

For the encouragement of good and able clerks.

Bee it enacted by the authority aforesaid, and it is hereby enacted, That the clerke of the county courts fees be as in the following table:

Table of fees.

	Tob.
For an action and proseedings thereupon: Action	8
If no further proceeding in the said action, then for entry order for dismissment	4
Butt if the action be further proceeded in, then for action	8

Ffor declaration or petition if it be written by the clerk	10
If not written by the clerk	5
Ffor entry of the petition or declaration	3
For endorsing and fileing of the petition or declaration both	3
Ffor entry of the order	8
And if the action be continued to another court, then for returning refference upon the docquett	5
For entring the order of that court	8
Ffor endorsing the courts order upon the declaration or plea as the case is	3
And for every court the said action shall be continued called and an order made therein ffor returning upon the docquett	5
For entring the order	8
Ffor endorsing the order upon the declaration or plea	3
And if in tryall of the action any evidences made use of, then ffor every oath taken in court viva voce or for the oath of plaintiff or defendant	3
Ffor entring the subpœna of every evidence	10
And if a deposition be taken in writing if the clerk write it for that deposition no more than	10
And if the clerk do not write it, then	5
For endorsing and fileing that deposition both	3
And if the party require the deposition to be recorded, ffor recording the said deposition but not otherwayes	10
And if any pleas, replications, rejoynders, surrejoynders, rebutters, surrebutters, be made in writing for every such plea, replication, rejoynder and surrejoynder, rebutter and surrebutter if the same be writt by the clerke	10
If not writ by the clerke	5
For entring each of the same	3
For endoring and filing each of the same (a)	3
And if a jury be made use of in the action ffor recording the pannell of the jury and their oath no more butt	10

Various Readings.

(a) The words "for endorsing and filing each of the same," omitted in Northb. MS. but inserted in Ch. Cit. and P. Rand. MSS.

For recording the verdict of the jury 10
And if in the action there be a survey of land, for recording the report of the surveyor and for endorsing and fileing the same 20
Ffor recording the report of the jury endorsing and fileing 20
And if in the action there be a report of auditors for recording the report of the auditors and for endorsing and fileing the same 20
And for all papers made use of in tryall of the action, as bill, bond, account &c. which are filed with the declaration for endorseing and fileing each paper 3
And if upon a judgement given there bee an appeall to gennerall court for order and copy of the appeall 16
For order and coppy of the security 16
For the bond 10
For recording the bond where it is desired and not otherwayes 10
For recording acknowledgement of the bond if desired and not othewayes 10
For returning the appeale and security to the secretaries office 30
And if upon an appeale any clerk returne to the secretaries office any more of the proceedings of the county court, as coppies of orders declarations or pleadings, then the judgment from which the appeale is made he shall dema*d noe fee for the same, but if plaintiff or defendant demand any coppies for their particular use the elerk shall have for them according as is sett down in this act And if either plaintiff or defendant in the tryall of an action imploy one or more atturney or atturneys, then ffor entering every such atturney upon the dockett once for one cause and noe more 5
And if a warrant of an atturney be in writing, then for the said warrant recording 10
For endorseing and fileing the warrant both 3
And if an execution had upon a judgement for execution 15
For entring the time of issuing the execution in the margent of the record 3

For recording the returne on the execution 10
Although not returned because it is the sheriffs or parties duty to make returne.
Ffor an attachment and proceedings therein more then there is in an action If upon an action brought on attachment be granted the fees of the action to bee in all points as is before sett down for the action and besides that, If the order for an attachment bee proceeded in, ffor a coppy of the order 8
For the attachment thereupon 15
And if the next court the attachment be returned executed but not else for returning the attachment 5
For recording the returne 20
For endorsing and fileing the attachment both 3
And if an apprisement be ordered for order and coppy appoynting appraisers and justices to swear them 16
For recording the appraisers report 20
For endorsing and fileing the same both 3
And if an attachment be granted by a justice of the peace and is returned executed to court, ffor entring the attachment upon the dockett 5
Ffor the petition or declaration if writ by the clerk 10
If not writ by the clerk 5
For endorsing and fileing the petition both 3
For entring the petition 3
For recording the returne of the attachment 20
Ffor endorsing and fileing the attachment both 3
For entering judgement 8
And so on as in other attachments for appraisments &c. if any, and for continuance from court to court as for like continuance upon actions ffor a suit in chancery the fees to bee in all points as is sett down for the action except that for a bill in chancery writt as ordinary declarations and on one side of the sheet 20
And if otherwayes every side of a sheet except the first which is twenty 10
Ffor petitions complaints in writing or informations except of cunstables, surveyors of the highwayes, grand jury men and others which relate to the county service, if a petition, complaint or

information for or concerning any matter or thing, ffor a petition if writ by the clerk 10
If not writ by the clerk 5
Entry of the petition (a) 3
Endorsing and if fileing the petition both 3
For entring order thereuppon 8
And if the said petition be referred to another court then the charge for returning and other proceedings thereupon from court to court as for the action, ffor a scire facias 10
And all other proceedings thereupon as for an action.

Deeds and Conveyances.

And if a deed be acknowledged for lands, for the order 8
For recording the deed 30
For acknowledgment, recording the acknowledgment (b) and endorsing the same upon the deed 25
And if the deeds be lease and release acknowledged, for the order for recording deeds 8
For recording a lease 30
For acknowledgment, recording acknowledgment and endorsing the acknowledgment upon lease 25
For recording release 30
For acknowledgment. and recording acknowledgment and endorsing acknowledgment upon release 25
And if a bond be for performance of covenants acknowledged, for order for recording bond 8
For recording bond 20
For recording acknowledgment bond and endorseing acknowledgment upon bond 10
And if a deed be for a personall matter acknowledged, for order 8
For recording the deed 20
For acknowledgment recording acknowledgment and endorsing the acknowledgment upon the deed 10

Various Readings.

(a) The words "Entry of the petition 3" omitted in P. Rand. MS. but inserted in Ch. Cit. and Northb MSS.

(b) The words "recording the acknowledgment" omitted in Northb. MS. but inserted in Ch. Cit. MS.

And for relinquishment of dower, order	8
Recording of relinquishment of dower	20

Letters of Atturney and other Deeds proved.

Ffor proveing and recording letter of Atturney or deed whether the same be done by one, two or any more witnesses and for all fees incident thereunto	40

Probates

Ffor probate of a Will and for all fees incident thereunto if the estate exceed not five pounds (*a*) or one thousand pounds of tobacco upon lawfull appraisment	50
For such probate and all fees incident thereunto if the estate exceed (*b*) five pounds or one thousand pounds of tobacco and be not above fifty pounds or ten thousand pounds of tobacco upon lawfull appraisment	150
For such probate and all fees incident thereunto, if the estate exceed fifty pounds, or ten thousand pounds of tobacco, upon lawfull appraisement	250 (*c*)
And for every probate and all fees incident thereunto, where the executor doth not within fower monthes after the probate bring in an inventory and valuation of his testators estate	250

Administrations

For a comission of administration upon an estate not exceeding the value of five pounds or one thousand pounds of tobacco upon a lawfull appraisment and for all fees incident thereunto	50
Ffor a comission of administration and for all fees incident thereunto, if the estate exceed five pounds or one thousand pounds of tobacco upon lawfull appraisment and do not exceed fifty pounds or ten thousand pounds of tobacco	150
Ffor a comission of administration and for all fees incident thereunto if the estate exceed fifty	

Various Readings.

(*a*) The word "pounds" omitted in Northb. MS. but inserted in Ch. Cit. and P. Rand. MSS.

(*b*) The word "exceed" omitted in Northb. MS. but inserted in Ch. Cit. and P. Rand. MSS.

(*c*) This clause omitted in Northb. MS. but inserted in Ch. Cit. and P. Rand. MSS.

pounds or ten thousand pounds of tobacco upon lawfull appraisment 250

Administrations with the Will annexed.

Ffor a comission of administration with the Will anexed, and for all fees incident thereunto, if the estate exceed not five pounds or one thousand pounds of tobacco upon lawfull appraisment 50

Ffor such comission of administration with the Will anexed, and for all fees incident thereunto, if the estate exceed five pounds or one thousand pounds of tobacco and doe not exceed fifty pounds or ten thousand pounds of tobacco, upon lawfull appraisment 200

Ffor a codicill proveing recording and all other fees relateing to it upon any estate 50

Ffor such comission of administration with Will anexed, and for all fees incident thereunto, if the estate exceed fifty pounds or ten thousand pounds of tobacco upon lawfull appraisment 300

Ffor a marriage lycense and all fees incident to it 50

Ffor proveing of rights for land certificate issuing certificate and all fees incident, if under the number of ten 13

If above the number of ten and under twenty 23

If above the number of twenty 33

For a bill of costs 3

Ffor a coppy of the laws of every assembly if required by the justices or any other person 150

Ffor a coppy of an inventory, or inventory and appraisment 30

Ffor a coppy of a Will and certificate of probate thereupon 30

Ffor a coppy of an order of court 8

Ffor a coppy of a deed for land and certificate of the acknowledgement 30

Ffor a coppy of a petition, plea, replication &c. each 10

And for all other coppies not in this table enumerated so much as is given by this act for entring or recording the thing

And if a coppy be required of any thing above a year old, ffor the search besides paying for the coppy 5

And if noe coppy be had or the thing be not to be found, then onely for the search	
If a servant be brought to bee judged, for recording his age and the order of court	18
And for a coppy of the same	5
For recording acknowledgment, satisfaction of a judgment	15
For a caveatt	5
Ffor a didimus	25
Ffor attendance att a didimus and all fees incident as subpœnas, takeing depositions, &c. if required to attend	100
Ffor attending att appraisment, outcryes, or in takeing inventory if the clerk be required to give his attendance but not else for every dayes attendance	100
Ffor a certificate of a publick claime above the value of one hundred pounds of tobacco, except for takeing up a runnaway to be paid by the country	20
And if it bee a runnaway certificate, the party to pay	20
Ffor a certificate of any other nature	10
If upon the motion of any other person any paper or papérs be desired to be recorded, order for recording	8
And for each paper recorded	20
Ffor publishing any persons departure att the court-house door giveing a certificate to the secretary as usuall for a pass and all other fees incident	18
Ffor a private courts attendance, except orphanes courts	200

And because the clerk of every county court annually makes entries and issues coppies for surveyors of the highwayes, constables and grand jurymen, and for takeing lyst of tithables for binding out of poor orphanes and chuseing guardians, and does extraordinary service for the county whereof he is clerke for which it is impossible for a law to ascertain the true fees being more or less as occation is,

Bee it therefore enacted by the authority aforesaid, and it is hereby enacted, That in consideration of all such services the severall county courts bee and they are hereby respectively impowered and required att

Allowance to clerks for public services.

the laying of the county levy in each year, to raise assess and proportion in the said levy to the clerke of their respective court the sume of one thousand pounds of tobacco and casque, and noe more, any law, usage or custome to the contrary notwithstanding.

Clerks not to charge for copies, unless required & had.

And be it further enacted by the authority aforesaid, and it is hereby enacted, That noe county court clerke or clerks charge or demand any fee for the coppy of any order of court or other record, unless such coppy be required and had of him, and also that it shall and may be lawfull for the clerk of the county court, if he be in court required by any person to shew forth an order of court or other record in the bookes which such person for his advantage and benefitt in the tryall of his cause desires may be read, to charge and demand for the same as much as the same fee, as if the said clerk had really given a written coppy of the said order or record.

The same fee for shewing an order or record, upon a trial, as for a copy.

And be it further enacted by the authority aforesaid, and it is hereby enacted, That if any business, matter or thing be from and after the last day of November next done and performed by any county court clerk as clerk of the county courts for which there is no fee ascertained, mentioned or declared in the before recited tables of fees such county court clerke or clerkes shall charge and demand no fee or fees for the same. And if any county court clerke or clerks shall after the said last day of November next, charge or exact, demand or take any fee or fees for any business, matter or thing by him or them done and performed as clerke of the county court, for which there is noe fee ascertained, expressed or declared in the abovesaid table of fees in this act, or shall charge, demand, or take any more or greater fee or fees, for any business matter, or any thing by him or them done, after the said last of November next then by this act is appointed, allowed and given, or shall in makeing up the costs of an action, suit in chancery, attachment or any thing else, in the aforesaid table of fees, mentioned and expressed, advance, multiply and augment, the bill of costs in or after any other method or way, then is in this act prescribed, directed and laid downe, such county court clerke or clerkes shall for every offence in all or any of the premissed cases, forfeit and pay the sume of two

No fees to be taken, unless specified in the foregoing table.

Penalty for breach of this law.

thousand pounds of tobacco, one moyety to the kings most excellent majesty, his heirs and successors, towards the better support of this government and the contingent charges thereof, and the other moyety to the party injured to be recovered by action of debt, byll, plaint or information in any court of record in this dominion, in which noe essoign protection or wager of law shall bee allowed. *Provided allwayes*, and it is the true intent and meaning of this act that all and every person and persons claiming the forfeiture or penalty of this act against any county court clerke or clerkes for exorbitant, unjust and wrongfull fee or fees, shall bring his suit or information for the same within eighteen monthes, after cause of action doth arrise or bee totally barred.

Limitation of prosecution.

And be it further enacted by the authority aforesaid, and it is hereby enacted, That all and every county court clerkes account or accounts of clerkes fees shall be pleadable three yeares from and after the time the said account or accounts are made and bear date but noe longer, and that if within the said three years any account or accounts of a county court clerkes fees, be exhibited for payment by the sheriff of the county or his deputy may lawfully demand and make distress for levies, and the person or persons to whome such account or accounts are exhibited for payment, doe refuse to pay and satisfie the same and shall and may be lawfull for the said sherriffe or his deputy and either of them to make distress for the same. And in case the said sherriff or his deputy doe not accordingly make distress, where such account or accounts are refused to be paid and satisfied and the person or persons from whome the said account or accounts are due and owing doe pay their quittrents and levies, and have besides a visible estate att the time of paying their quittrents and levies, which will satisfie the clerks account or accounts such sheriff or his deputy shall be answerable unto the clerke of the county court, for all and every such account or accounts, as if he had really received the same. *Provided allwayes*, that if the sheriff or his deputy doe make distress for want of tobacco to pay the clerkes fees in specie the clerke shall take such goods so distrained, and the sherriff not be otherwayes liable to pay the clerkes fees. And to the end the table of fees in

Clerk's fees may be distrained for, within three years, and not after.

When sheriff liable for.

Clerk bound to take the property distrained.

this act prescribed may be made publick and known as much as may bee to all persons,

Table of fees, to be set up, in office.

It is further enacted by the authority aforesaid, That every county court clerk doe write or cause to be written a fair coppy of the aforesaid table of fees and sett up or cause the same to be set up within two months after the publication of this act, in the court house of the county to which he is clerk, and that if any county court clerke faile therein, such county court clerke shall for such his failure and neglect forfeit and pay the sume of one thousand pounds of tobacco and casque, one moyety to the kings most excellent majesty, his heirs and successors for and towards the better support of this government and the contingent charges thereof, and the other moyety to him or them that shall sue for the same by action of debt, byll, plaint or information, in any court of record in this dominion, wherein noe essoign protection or wager of law shall bee allowed.

Penalty for neglect.

Limitation of this act.

And be it enacted, That this continue in force five yeares from and after the last day of November next, and from thence to the next session of assembly.

ACT XIII.

Edi. 1733 and 1752.

An act appointing Rangers att the heads of the fower great rivers.

[☞ This act agrees verbatim, in all the MSS. with those which had been passed at each session, for several years, in succession, except that it contains no provision for the employment of Indians. It was limited in its operation to the last day of October, 1698.]

ACT XIV.

Edi. 1733, and 1752.

An act for raising a Publick Levy.

BE *it enacted by the governour, councell and burgesses of this present generall assembly and the authority thereof, and it is hereby enacted*, That the sume of sixteen pounds of tobacco be paid by every tithable person within his majesties collony and dominion of Virginia, for the defraying and payment of the publick charge of the country being the publick levy from the eigh-

Public levy, or taxes for 1696.

teenth day of Aprill 1695 to this present time, and that it be paid by the collectors of the seaverall counties to the seaverall persons to whome it is proportioned by this present generall assembly, and if it shall happen that there shall be any more tithables in any county then the present is laid on then such county to have credit for so much to the use of the county, and if there shall happen to be less in any county then such county shall bear the loss.

A true copy,

Test, PETER BEVERLEY,
Clerke of the House of Burgesses.

Signed by SIR EDMUND ANDROS, *Govr.*
ROBERT CARTER, *Speaker.*

(*Note to editions* 1733 *and* 1752.)

ATT A

Generall Assembly,

BEGUN ATT JAMES CITTY

Sir Edmund Andros, Govr. THE 24th DAY OF SEPTEMBER IN THE EIGHTH YEAR OF THE REIGN OF OUR SOVEREIGN LORD, WILLIAM THE THIRD, BY THE GRACE OF GOD OF ENGLAND, SCOTLAND, FRANCE AND IRELAND, KING DEFENDER OF THE FAITH, &c. ANNO. DOM. 1696,

And thence continued by adjournment till the. 21st day of October in the ninth year of his majesties reigne Annoque Dom. 1697.*

ACT I.

Edi. 1733 and 1752.

An act for raising a Publick Levy.

BEE it enacted by the governour, councell and burgesses of this present generall assembly and the authority thereof, and it is hereby enacted, That the sume

Public levy, or taxes for 1697.

of sixteen pounds of tobacco be paid by every tithable person within this his majesties collony and dominion of Virginia for the defraying and payment of the public charge of the country being the publick levy from the 25th day of September 1696 to this present time, and that it be paid by the collectors of the seaverall coun-

* At the end of the acts of the last session, there are the following notes, in the editions of 1733, and 1752.—MEMORANDUM, That this assembly was continued by several adjournments, to the 21st day of October 1697; and then met and passed only one act for raising a public levy, and was dissolved.

MEMORANDUM, That a general assembly was begun and held at James City, the 28th day of September, in the tenth year of the reign of King *William*, anno. 1698; and continued to the 6th day of October following, *William Randolph* being speaker. And then the governor sent for the House of Burgesses, and told them he was concerned, upon the occasion of an act of parliament, to dissolve the assembly; and it was dissolved accordingly, without doing any business. *Quere,* What act of parliament was this?

ties to the seaverall persons to whome it is proportioned by this generall assembly, and if it shall happen that there shall bee more tithables in any county then the present levy is laid on, then such county to have credit for so much to the use of the county, and if there shall happen to be less in any county, then such county to beare the loss. [☞ Here the P. Rand. Rand. MS. ends.]

A true coppy,

Teste, PETER BEVERLEY,
Clerke of the House of Burgesses.

Att a Generall Assembly begun at James Citty the 24th day of September 1696, and thence continued by adjournment till the 21st day of October 1697.

Northumberland county's public account.

Northumberland county, Dr.		Contra Cr.	
To sallary	1425	By 980 tithables at 16 per poll	15680
To 11 soldiers on Rappahannock river	12079	By capt Rod. Kenner for paid Nath. Carpinter for takeing up his servant Eliz Wilcocks	200
To 11 soldiers on Potomack river	1576	By ditto Kenner and paid John Letham for taking up ditto Wilcocks	200
	15080		
Ditto Dr.			
To Peter Beverly for a coppy of the law and proportion	350		

Copy of the law.

A true Copy,

Teste, PETER BEVERLEY,
Clerke of the House of Burgesses.

AT A

Generall Assembly,

BEGUN AT JAMES CITTY

Francis Nicolson, esq. governor.

THE 27th DAY OF APRIL, IN THE ELEAVENTH YEARE OF THE REIGNE OF OUR SOVERAIGNE LORD WILLIAM THE THIRD, BY THE GRACE OF GOD OF ENGLAND, SCOTLAND, FRANCE AND IRELAND, KING DEFENDER OF THE FAITH, &c. ANNOQUE DOMINI 1699.

ACT I.

Edi. 1733, and 1752.

An act for the more effectuall suppressing of Blasphemy, Swearing, Cursing, Drunkenness and Sabbath breaking.

Preamble.

WHEREAS notwithstanding many good and wholesome laws already made for the punishment and restraining of vice, many wicked blasphemus, dissolute and vitious persons doe still continue theire unpious and abominable practices and avow theire horrid and Atheisticall principles greatly tending to the dishonour of Almighty God, and may prove destructive to the peace and wellfaire of this his majesties collony and dominion, for the more effectuall suppression of the said detestable crimes,

To deny the being of a God or the trinity, or to assert that there are more Gods than one, or to deny the christian religion to be true, or the scriptures to be of divine authority, subjects the

Be it enacted by the Governour, Councell and Burgesses of this present Generall Assembly and the authority thereof, and it is hereby enacted, That if any person or persons brought upp in the christian religion shall by writeing printing, teaching or advisedly speakeing, deny the being of a God or the holy Trinity or shall assert or maintaine there are more Gods then one or shall deny the christian religion to be true, or the holy scriptures of Old and New Testament to be of divine authority, and be thereof lawfully convicted upon indictment or information in the generall court of this his majesties collony and dominion by the oathes of two or more credible witnesses such person or persons for the first offence shall bee adjudged incapable or disabled in law to all intents and purposes what soe ever to hold and enjoy any office or imployment ecclesiasticall civill or military or any part in them, or any profitt or advantage to them appertaining or any of them. And if any person or persons soe convicted as aforesaid shall at the time of his or theire conviction enjoy or possess any office place or imployment, such office place or imployment shall be voyd and is hereby declared voyd. And if such person or persons shall be a second time lawfully convicted as aforesaid of all or any the crime or crimes aforesaid that then hee or they shall from thenceforth bee disabled to sue, prosecute, plead or use any action or information in any court of law or equity or to be guardian to any child or to be executor of any person or capable of any deed of gift or legacy or to beare any office ecclesiasticall, civill or military forever within this his majesties collony and dominion, and shall alsoe suffer from the time of such conviction, three years imprisonment without baile or mainprize.

offender for the first offence to incapacity to hold any office.

and for the second offence, to disability to sue, and disqualification to be guardian or executor, or to take any gift or legacy; & moreover shall be incapable of bearing any office, and shall suffer 3 years imprisonment.

Provided alwayes, And be it enacted by the authority aforesaid, and it is hereby enacted, That noe person shall be proseuted by virtue of this act for any word spoken, unless information upon oath be given in of the words before one or more justice or justices of the peace within one month after such words spoken and the prosecution of such offence be within twelve monthes after such information.

Provided that information be made within three months.

Provided alsoe, And be it enacted by the authority aforesaid, and it is hereby enacted, That any person or persons convicted of all or any the aforesaid crime or crimes in manner aforesaid, shall for the first offence upon his or theire acknowledgment and renunciation of such offence or erronious opinions in the same court where such person or persous was or were convicted within the space of six monthes after his, her or theire conviction be discharged from all penalties and disabilityes incurred by such conviction, any thing in this act to the contrary in any wise notwithstanding. And for

A person convicted, may be discharged from the penalties, by renouncing opinions, within six months.

* The running title to the acts of this session in the editions of 1733 and 1752, is, " Anno andecimo; Gulielmi III Regis.

the more effectual prevention and punishment of drunkeness, sweareing and curseing,

For cursing, swearing or getting drunk, the offender to pay a fine of five shillings.

Be it further enacted by the authority aforesaid, and it is hereby enacted, That if any person or persons shall profanely sweare or curse or shall be drunk, he or they soe offending for every such offence being thereof convicted by the oath of one or more witnesses (which oath any justice of the peace is hereby impowered and required to administer) or by confession before one or more justice or justices of the peace in the county where such offence shall bee committed shall forfitt and pay the sume of five shillings or ffifty pounds of tobacco for every such offence, or if the said offence or offences bee committed in the presence and hearing of one or more justice or justices of the peace or in any court of record in this his majesties collony and dominion the same shall be sufficient conviction without any other evidence. And the said offender shall upon such conviction forfitt and pay the sume of five shillings or fifty pounds of tobacco for every such offence which said sume or sumes shall be payd to the church-wardens of that parrish where the offence shall be committed who shall be accountable for the same to the vestry of such parrish to the use of the poor of the parrish. And if any person or persons shall refuse to make present payment or give sufficient caution for the payment of the same att the laying of the next parrish levy after the said offence committed, then the said fines and penalties shall be levyed upon the goods of such person or persons by warrant or precept from any justice of peace before whome the same conviction shall be, which warrant may be directed to the sheriffe of the county or to the constable in his respective precincts to be appraised and vallued as another distress. And if the offender or offenders bee not able to pay the said sume or sumes then he, shee or they, shall have and receive ten lashes upon his, her or theire beare back well laid on for every such offence. And for prevention of sabbath breakeing,

What shall be sufficient evidence to convict.

Fines how collected.

In case of inability to pay, the offender to receive 10 lashes.

Be it enacted by the authority aforesaid. and it is hereby enacted, That if any person or persons of the age of twenty one yeares or more doe neglect or refuse to resort to their parrish church or chapell once in two monthes to heare devine service upon the sabbath day,

For neglecting to attend church;

every person or persons soe neglecting or refuseing and being thereof lawfully convicted by confession or otherwise before one or more justice or justices of the peace where such offence shall be committed shall forfitt and pay for every such offence the sume of five shillings or fifty pounds of tobacco to be payd to the church-wardens of that parrish wherein the said offence shall be committed, who shall be accountable for the same to the vestry for the use of the said parrrish. ☞ *Provided alwayes*, that if any person or persons can shew or make known to any justice or justices such cause or causes of his her or their absence from church at any time or times as the said justice or justices shall adjudge true and reasonable that then the said paines and penalties shall be remitted to such person or persons for such time and times and noe longer, any thing in this act to the contrary notwithstanding. *Provided alwayes*, that if any person or persons dissenting from the church of England being every way qualified according to one act of parliament made in the first year of the reigne of our sovereigne lord the king that now is, and the late queen Mary of blessed memory, entituled an act for exempting their majesties protestant subjects dissenting from the church of England from the penaltyes of certaine laws, shall resort and meet at any congregation or place of religious worship permitted and allowed by the said act of Parliament once in two months that then the said penaltyes and forfeitures imposed by the act for neglecting or refuseing to resort to their parrish church or chappel as aforesaid shall not be taken to extend to such person or persons, any thing in this act to the contrary notwithstanding.*

five shillings penalty.

Protestant dissenters, qualified according to the toleration act of 1 Wm. & Mary, shall be exempted from penalties, for not repairing to the parish church—See 4 Bl. Com. pa. 52, 53.

☞ A leaf is torn out of the Northb. MS. commencing at this place; and the subject matter is supplied from the Ch. Cit. MS.

* This is the first notice taken by the laws of Virginia of the *toleration* act, as it is called in England, of 1 Wm. & Mary. It is surely an abuse of terms to call a law a *toleration-act*, which imposes a religious test, on the conscience, in order to avoid the penalties of another law, equally violating every principle of religious freedom.—The provisions of this act may be seen in the 4th volume of Blackstone's Commentaries, page 53.—Nothing could be more intolerant than to impose the penalties, by this act prescribed, for not repairing to church, and then to hold out the idea of exemption by a compliance with the provisions of such a law, as the statute of 1 Wm. & Mary, adopted by a mere *general reference*, when not one person in a thousand could possibly know its contents.

ACT II.

Edi. 1733 and 1752.

An act for prevention of undue election of Burgeses.

FOR the prevention of undue election of Burgeses to serve in the generall assembly in this his majestyes colony and dominion,

None to vote for burgesses, but freeholders in a county or town.

Be it enacted by the Governour, Councill and Burgesses of this present generall assembly and the authority thereof, and it is hereby enacted, That no person or persons shall be enabled to give a vote for the election of a burgess or burgeses to serve in the generall assembly hereafter to be caled but those who are freeholders in the respective county or towne for which the said burgess or burgesses shall be elected and chosen, and if any person shall presume to give his vote for the election of a burgess or burgesses in any county or towne who is not a freeholder in such county or towne he shall forfeit and pay the sume of five hundred pounds of tobacco for every such offence. *Provided alwayes*, and it is the true intent and meaning of this act that no woman sole or covert, infants under the age of twenty-one years, or recusant convict being freeholders shall be enabled to give a vote or have a voice in the election of burgeses any thing in this act to the contrary notwithstanding.

Penalty for voting, not being qualified.

No woman sole, or covert, infant, Popish recusant entitled to vote.

How poll to be taken, if the election cannot be determined on view.

And be it further enacted by the authority aforesaid, and it is hereby enacted, That if the election of any burgess cannot be determined upon the veiw by the consent of the freeholders then present but that a poll shall be required for determination thereof, that then the sheriff of such county or in his absence his under sheriff shall proceed to take the poll and shall appoint such number of persons for the takeing thereof as to him shall seem convenient who shall sett downe the names in writeing of each freeholder and for whome he shall poll and every freeholder before he is admited to poll at the same election shall if required by the candidates freeholders or any of them first take the oath hereinafter mentioned or if such person being a Quaquer shall make the declaration prescribed in an act made in the seventh and eighth yeares of the reigne of his present majesty in these words: *I, A. B. do declare in the presence of Almighty God, the witness of the truth of what I say*— which oath or declaration the said sheriff or in his ab-

Oath or affirmation to be taken by freeholder, if required by a candidate.

sence his under sheriff is hereby impowered and requir-ed to administer to witt, *You shall swear that you are bona fide a freeholder in this county, or towne of to the best of your knowledge.* And if any of the candidates require a copy of such pole the sheriff or his under sheriff shall as soon as conveniently may be deliver to him or them a true and perfect copy thereof.

If any money, meat, drink, or provision be given, or promised to a voter, in order to be elected, the election declared void.

And be it further enacted by the authority aforesaid, and it is hereby enacted, That no person or persons hereafter to be elected as a burgess shall directly or indirectly by any ways or means at his or their proper charge before his or their election give, present or allow, to any person or persons haveing voice or vote in such election any money, meat, drink or provision, or make any present, gift, reward or entertainment or any promise, ingagement or obligation to give or allow any money, meat, drink or provision, present, reward or entertainment in order to procure the vote or votes of such person or persons for his or their election to be a burgess or burgesses, and every person or persons soe giveing, presenting or allowing, makeing, promising or engageing any money, meat, drink or provision in order to procure such election being elected shall be disabled and incapable to sit and act as a burgess in that assembly, but that such election* shall be void to all intents and purposes as if the said returne or election had never been made.

* Here the Northb. MS. again commences.

Form of return.

And be it further enacted by the authority aforesaid, and it is hereby enacted, That the sherrife or his under sherrife in his respective county shall returne for burgess such as shall be elected and chosen by the majority of the freeholders in manner aforesaid which returne he shall endorse and make in these words, viz: *By vertue of this writt I have caused to be legally summoned the freeholders of my county to meet this day being the day of at the courthouse of this county being the usuall place for election of burgesses and have given them in charge to make election of two of the most able and discreet persons of the said county for theire burgesses who accordingly have elected and chosen A B and C D burgesses for the said county for the next generall assembly to be held at the day of*

Elections, to supply vacancies, how to be conducted.

And be it further enacted by the authority aforesaid, and it is hereby enacted, That if it shall soe happen that by the death or disability of any burgesses so elected, a new writt do issue to any county dureing the sessions of an assembly for the election of a burgesse to serve in the said assembly that then it shall and may be lawffull for the sherrife of such county or his deputy who is hereby authorised and required so to do, immediately to cause so many persons as he shall think fitt to give notice to every ffreeholder of the time and place of election which shall be as soon as possible after the receipt of the writt and upon such election so made to make returne thereof upon the back of the writt in manner and forme aforesaid.

Penalty on sheriff refusing to hold a poll, or to give a copy; or to give notice of the election; or to make a false return, or in a different form.

And be it further enacted by the authority aforesaid, and it is hereby enacted, That if any sheriffe or his officer before the returne be endorsed upon the writt shall deny and refuse to take the poll in writeing as aforesaid if it be demanded by any candidate or ffreeholder or shall refuse to give copyes of the poll to such candidate or candidates, if by them required, or shall neglect to give legall notice of the election time and place of election, or shall make a false or duble returne of those who are not duly elected for burgesses as aforesaid or shall not make any returne or shall make returne in any other forme then is herein expressed he or they so offending in any of the premises and being thereof lawfully convicted, shall for every such offence forfeit and pay the sum of fforty pounds sterling money, all which paines and forfeitures in this act expressed shall be devided into two equall parts, one moyety thereof to our sovereigne lord the king, his heires and successors towards the better support of the government and the contingent charges thereof and the other moyety to the party agrieved, or if their be no party agrieved to the informer to be recovered with full costs of suit by action of debt, byll, plaint, or information in any court of record in this his majesties collony and dominion wherein noe essoigne protection or wager of law priveledge or imparlance shall be admitted or allowed.

Fines how appropriated.

How recoverable.

Provided alwayes, And be it further enacted by the authority aforesaid, and it is hereby enacted, That noe person hereafter shall be capable of being elected a member to serve in any assembly who is not of the age

No person eligible who is

of twenty-one yeares, and every election and returne of any person under that age is hereby declared to be null and voyd, any thing in this act to the contrary in any wise notwithstanding. under the age of 21 years.

ACT III.

An act to prevent the discontinuance of courts and process. Edi. 1733 and 1752.

WHEREAS many justices that constitute the county courts of this his majesties collony and dominion are oftentimes hindered from being at court by the difficulty of crossing of rivers, badness of wether, sickness or other accidents incident to those who live remote by reason of which it often happens that by the not meeting of a sufficient number of justices to hold the said courts at the days appoynted the processe is discontinued, justice delayed and many people putt to the great charge and expence of renewing there suits, for remedy whereof, Preamble.

Be it enacted by the Governour, Councell and Burgesses of this present generall assembly and the authority thereof, and it is hereby enacted, That if it shall hereafter happen that upon a court day there shall not be a sufficient number of justices to hold the said court that then all processe to the said court be continued to the next court in course without discontinuance, and that if it shall hereafter happen that if any of the justices be disabled from sitting to give judgment in any cause or causes by being concerned therein without whom there cannot be a court, that then such causes shall stand referred to the next court without any discontinuance as if the said cause had been actually referred by the said court or courts. No discontinuance, on account of failure to hold court.

ACT IV.

An act for regulateing of Juryes. Edi. 1733, and 1752.

FOR the better regulation of juryes to serve in the generall and county courts of this his majesties collony and dominion,

Qualification of jurers.

Be it enacted by the Governour, Councell and Burgesses of this present generall assembly and the authority thereof, and it is hereby enacted, Thatt no person or persons shall be enabled or capable to serve as jurymen in and upon any jury or juryes in the generall court of this his majesties collony and dominion, but those who are ffreeholders, and whose lands and goods, that is to say reall and personall estate are visibly of the reputed value of one hundred pounds sterling and not under and that noe person or persons shall be inable or capable to serve as jurymen in and upon any jury or juryes in any county court of this his majesties collony and dominion, but those whose land and goods, that is to say reall and personall estate are visible of the reputed value of fifty pounds sterling and not under.

And be it further enacted by the authority aforesaid, and it is hereby enacted, That noe sheriffe or sheriffes shall impannell or returne for jurymen any person or persons in or to the generall courts of this his majesties collony and dominion, but those who are ffreeholders and whose lands and goods, that is to say reall and personall estate, are visibly of the reputed value of one hundred pounds sterling, nor in or to any county court of this his majesties collony and dominion but those whose lands and goods, (that is to say) reall and personall estate are visibly of the reputed value of fifty pounds sterling any former law, statute or usage to the contrary in any wise notwithstanding. [☞ Here the Northb. MS. ends.]

ACT V.

Edi. 1733, and 1752.

An act for restraining and punishing of Pirates and Privateers. (a)

Preamble.

WHEREAS nothing can more conduce to the honour of his most sacred majesty then that such articles of peace as are concluded in all treaties should

(*a*) After the making of this act, at a session of parliament held the 16th of November 1699 in the 11th year of the reign of William 3, an act passed for the more effectual suppression of piracy which was to be in force for 7 years, and from thence to the end of the next session of parliament. And by 5th of Queen Ann chap. 34 was continued for 7 years longer: and from thence to the end of the next

be kept and preserved inviolable by his majestyes subjects in and over all his majestyes territories and dominions and forasmuch as great mischief and depredations are dayly done upon the high seas by pyrates privateers and sea robers in not onely takeing and pillageing severall ships and vessels belonging to his majestyes subjects but also in takeing, destroying and robing severall ships belonging to the subjects of fforeigne princes in leage and amity with his majesty—

Pirates, privateers, or sea-robbers putting on shore, may be apprehended, by any officer civil or military.

Be it therefore enacted by the Governour, Councell and Burgesses of this present Generall Assembly, and the authority thereof, and it is hereby enacted, That if any pirates, privateers or sea robers, or any other persons suspected to be such shall land and put on shoar in any port or place in this his majestyes collony and dominion upon notice given or knowledge thereof, all officers civill and military are hereby required and impowered to raise and levy such a number of well armed men as he or they shall judge necessary for the seizing, apprehending and carrying to goal of all and every such person or persons, and in case of any resistance or refusall to yield obedience to his majestyes authority it shall be lawfull to kill or destroy such person or persons and all and every person or persons that shall oppose or resist the said authority by strikeing or fireing upon any person in execution of this act, shall be deemed taken and adjudged as fellons without benefitt of clergy, and every such officer that shall omitt or neglect his duty therein and being lawfully convicted shall for every such offence forfeit fifty pounds sterling, one moyety to our sovereigne Lord the king, his heirs and successors for and towards the better support of the government and the contingent charges thereof, and the other moyety to him that shall sue or informe for the same in

In case of resistance, may be killed.

Penalty on officers, neglecting their duty.

---

session of Parliament, and by the 1st of George 1, chap. 25, was revived and to be in force during the continuance of that act, which was for 5 years and to the end of the next session of Parliament: and was made perpetual by the 6th of George 1, chap. 19, whereby a new method was established for trial of pirates in the Plantation. And by the same act the 4th of George 1, chap. 2, and the 8th of George 1, chap. 24, the law as to pirates is fully settled and declared, therefore this act of assembly is either of no use or become null.

(*Note to editions* 1733 *and* 1752.)

any court of record in this his majestyes collony and dominion, in which no essoigne protection or wager of law shall be allowed. And for the better and more speedy execution of justice upon such who haveing committed treasons, piricyes, felloneyes or other offences upon the sea, and shall be apprehended or brought prisoners to this his majestyes collony and dominion,

Crimes committed, at sea to be enquired into and punished, in the same manner as if committed on land.

Be it further enacted by the authority aforesaid, and it is hereby enacted, That all treasons, fellonyes, piracyes, robberies, murders or other capitall offences that shall be committed upon the high seas or in any river, haven, creek or bay where the admirall hath jurisdiction, shall be enquired, tryed, heared, determined, judged and execution awarded and done within this his majestyes collony and dominion in such forme as if such offence had been comited in and upon the land of this his majestyes collony and dominion. And to that end and purpose the governor or commander in chief of this his majestyes colony and dominion for the time being, is hereby desired and impowered to issue out commissions of oyer and terminer under his hand, and his majestyes seal of this his colony and dominion directed to the judge or judges of the admiralty of this his majestys colony and dominion for the time being and to such other substanciall persons as he shall think fitt to nominate and appoint, which said commissioners or such a quorum of them as by such commission shall be thereunto authorised shall have as full ample power and authority to hear and determine, adjudge and punish all and any the crimes and offences aforesaid as any commisioners under the great scale of England by virtue of a statute made in the twenty-eighth year of the reigne of King Henry the eighth might or could do and execute within the kingdom of England, and that such offenders which are or shall be apprehended in or brought prisoners to this his majestyes colony and dominion shall be lyable to such order, process, judgments and execution by virtue of such commission to be grounded upon this act as might be awarded or given against them if they were proceeded against within the realm of England by virtue of any commision grounded upon the said statute.

Commission of *oyer* and *terminer*, how to issue.

And be it further enacted by the authority aforesaid, and it is hereby enacted, That all and every person or persons that shall knowingly or wilfully conceal, entertaine, harbor trade or hold any correspondence by letter or otherwise with any person or persons that shall be deemed or adjudged to be pirates, privateers or other offenders within the construction of this act and shall not readily endeavour to the best of his or their power to apprehend or cause to be apprehended such offender or offenders shall be lyable to be prosecuted as accessaryes to the said offences and confederates with the said offenders and to suffer such pains and penalties as in such cases by law is provided.

Penalty for concealing pirates.

ACT VI.

An act for the punishment of slaves for the first and second offence of Hog stealing.

Exp. 1733 and 1752.

WHEREAS the third act of assembly made at James Citty the 16th day of Aprill. 1691, entituled an act for the more speedy prosecution of slaves commiting capitall crimes hath been found inconvenient by makeing the first offence of hog stealing felony, which is not so by the former laws of this his majestyes colony and dominion,

Preamble.

Be it therefore enacted by the Governour, Councell and Burgesses of this present Generall Assembly, and the authority thereof, and it is hereby enacted, That for the first offence of hog stealing commited by a negro or slave he shall be carried before a justice of the peace of the county where the fact was commited before whome being convicted of the said offence by one evidence or by his owne confession he shall by order of the said justice receive on his bare back thirty nine lashes well laid on, and for the second offence such negro or slave upon conviction before a court of record shall stand two hours in the pillory and have both his eares nailed thereto and at the expiration of the said two hours have his ears cutt off close by the nailes, any thing in the aforesaid act or in any other law to the contrary in any wise notwithstanding.

Punishment of slave for hog stealing; for the first offence; for the second offence.

ACT VII.

Edi 1733 and 1752.

An act prohibiting the unseasonable killing of Deer.

Preamble.

WHEREAS the Deer of this his majestyes colony and dominion is very much destroyed and diminished by the unseasonable kiling them when poor and of Does bigg with young to the great detriment of the inhabitants of this his majestyes colony and dominion without bringing any considerable benefitt to those that kill them, for remedy whereof,

Penalty for killing wild deer between the 1st of February and first of July, or buying or receiving such from Indians.

Be it enacted by the Governour, Councell and Burgesses of this present Generall Assembly and the authority thereof, and it is hereby enacted, That from and after the first day of February next ensuing no person or persons shall shoot or kill any Deer runing wild in the woods or unfenced grounds on this his majestyes colony and dominion at any time or times between the first day of February and last day of July that shall happen in every year, and if any person or persons shall contrary to the true intent and meaning of this act kill or destroy any Deer or cause any Deer to be killed or destroyed or shall buy or receive of any Indian or other person whatsoever any Deer kiled within the time before limited, he or they soe offending and being thereof lawfully convicted, shall for every Deer so kiled brought, destroyed or received as aforesaid, forfeit and pay the sume of five hundred pounds of tobacco one moyety to the kings most excellent majesty, his heirs and successors, to be applyed to the use of the parish where every such offence shall be commited respectively, and the other moyety with full costs of suit to him or them that will sue or informe for the same, by action of debt, bill, plaint or information in any court of record within this his majestyes colony and dominion, in which no essoigne protection or wager at law shall be allowed:

Servants and slaves, how punished.

Provided alwayes, that if any slave or other servant who is uncapable of paying the penaltyes provided by this act shall of his or their owne accord without the privity of his or their master, mistress or overseer kill or destroy any deer contrary to the true intent and meaning of this act he or they so offending shall for every such offence have and receive on his or their bare back or backs thirty lashes well laid on to be inflicted by order of such justice to whome information of the same shall be made upon oath.

ACT VIII.

An act appointing a committee for the revisall of the whole body of the laws of this his majesties colony and dominion. Edi. 1733 and 1752.

WHEREAS the whole body of the laws of this his majesties ancient and great colony and dominion of Virginia do lye in great disorder and confusion by reason that many of them are repealed, others obsolet and out of use some expired and many made in the infancy of this country inconsistent and hardly intelligible And forasmuch as a work so good and necessary for the service of his majesty and the interest of this his majesties colony and dominion cannot be conveniently effected dureing the session of an assembly without bringing a great and extraordinary charge upon the inhabitants of this his majesties colony and dominion, and whereas a more proper and easie method to effect the same cannot be prescribed then by appointing a joint comitee of the councill and house of burgesses to begin and compleat the said revisall, Preamble.

Be it enacted by the governour, councell and burgesses of this generall assembly and the authority thereof, and it is hereby enacted, That Edwd. Hill, Mathew Page and Benja Harison, Esqrs. members of the honorable councill, and that Miles Cary, Jno. Taylor, Robt. Beverly, Antho. Armstead, Henry Duke and Wm. Buckner, gentlemen, members of the house of burgeses or any six of them whereof two to be of the councill and four of the house of burgesses, shall be and are hereby appointed and declared a commitee for the revisall of the whole body of the laws of this his majesties colony and dominion, and that Peter Beverly gentleman, be clerk of the said comitee which commitee by virtue of this act shall have full power and authority to revise, alter, add to, diminish, repeal, amend or revive all or any of the said laws and reduce the same into bills in such manner and forme as they shall think fitt and necessary, which said bills so revised, altered, added to, diminished repealed, amended or revived, shall by the said comitee be reported to the next meeting of the assembly and so from time to time till all the said laws be fully and absolutely revised, and that the said commitee may be the better enabled to per- Joint committee of the council and house of burgesses, appointed to revise the laws. Names of revisors. Number to act. Their clerk. Powers of committee. Revisal to be reported to assembly.

Assistants. forme and accomplish the said revisall, Benja. Harrison, junr. and Bartho. Fowler, gentlemen, are hereby nominated and appointed assistants to the said committee from time to time to attend and give such advice and assistance therein as shall be required of them by the said commitee, and to prevent any deficiency or delay which may otherwise happen in the proceedings of the said commitee by reason of the departure from the country or any other disability of any member or members thereof,

Be it further enacted by the authority aforesaid, and it is hereby enacted, That the number of three councellors and six burgesses to constitute the said commitee shall from time to time be kept full and entire and if any member of the councill appointed to be of the said commitee be so disabled another member of the councill shall and may be appointed in his stead and place by his excellency the governor or by the governor and commander in chief of this his majesties colony and dominion of Virginia for the time being or if any member of the house of burgesses appointed to be of the said commitee shall be so disabled then the speaker of the house of burgesses or in case of his death or disability the major part of the burgeses of the said committee which shall be present at the next meeting after such disability, shall be, and are hereby impowered to elect and choose a burgess or burgesses out of the house of burgeses to supply the place and stead of the said burgess or burgesses so disabled, which said councellor or councellors, burgess or burgesses so elected and chosen shall be and are hereby declared members of the said committee as if he or they had been by this act particularly nominated and appointed, and in case of the death or disability of either of the said assistants or clerk the major part of the said commitee who shall be present at the next meeting after such disability shall have power to choose and appoint others in their stead.

Vacancies, how supplied.

Provided alwayes, And be it further enacted by the authority aforesaid, and it is hereby enacted, That no person whatsoever either councellor or burgess shall be enabled or admitted to give any vote or have any voice at any of the meetings of the said commitee other then those persons who are or shall from time to time hereafter by virtue of this act be appointed to attend as members of the said comitee.—*And be it further enacted by the authority aforesaid, and it is hereby enacted,* That the said comitee shall meet at James City or any other place where the publick records of this government shall be placed upon the first Wednesday in July next ensuing and afterwards monthly and shall sit de die in diem as long as they shall think necessary at any of their meetings, and all adjournments other than to the next day not being Sunday shall be made to the first Wednesday of every succeeding month and if the revisall of the whole body of the laws be not compleated by the end of the meeting of the said committee in November next then they shall have full power and authority by virtue of this act to adjourne themselves to the first Wednesday in Aprill following and then afterwards shall proceed from month to month in manner as is before expressed. *Provided always,* that if by badness of weather, sickness or other accidents it should so happen that a full number of the said comittee should not meet sufficient to act as a comitee or to adjourne at any of the time or times before expressed, the said comitee shall not be thereby discontinued but they shall and may meet and act the next day following or at any time or times before exprest in this act, as if the said comitee had really and actually adjourned themselves to any of the said time or times and also if any member or members of the said comitee either councellor or burgess shall be disabled in manner aforesaid the said comitee or the major part of them next present after such disability shall judge of the said disability and if they find it necessary shall make application to the governor or commander in chief for the time being, or to the speaker for the filling up of such a member in manner aforesaid, and until such application made, the governor or commander in chief for the time being, or the speaker may not appoint any such member or members in manner aforesaid, any thing in this act to the contrary in any wise notwithstanding.

Revisors when and where to

Power of adjournment.

And be it further enacted by the authority aforesaid, and it is hereby enacted, That if this present generall assembly should be hereafter prorogued or dissolved before the whole body of the laws of this his majesties colony and dominion be revised the said comitee shall not be thereby discontinued but the governor or com-

Committee not discontinued by prorogation or dissolution of assembly.

mander in cheife of this his majesties colony and dominion for the time being, and the speaker of the present house of burgesses or in case of his disability the major part of the committee then setting shall and may appoint any member or members of the councill or any burgess or burgesses of the present house of burgesses in case of any disability as aforesaid in manner aforesaid as if the said assembly had never been prorogued or desolved

Power of committee to send for MSS. and records relating to the first settlement of the country.

And be it further enacted by the authority aforesaid, and it is hereby enacted, That the said comitee shall be and is hereby authorised and impowered to send for any persons, papers, records or coppies of records by warrant under the hand of any one of the councill and two of the burgesses of the said comitee and all persons haveing any manuscripts papers or old records relateing to the first settlement of this country shall be and are hereby required to lay the same before the said committee if they require it by warrant as aforesaid, and also the said comitee is hereby impowered to receive all propositions of what nature soever offered them by any person or persons and if any officer or other person or persons shall neglect or refuse to obey any such warrant as aforesaid, he or they so offending and being thereof lawfully convicted shall for every such offence forfeit and pay the sume of twenty pounds to the kings most excellent majestie, his heirs and successors for and towards the defraying the charge of the said revisall and to no other use intent or purpose whatsoever, to be recovered by action of debt, bill, plaint or information in any court of record in this his majesties colony and dominion, in which no essoigne protection, wager of law, priviledge or imparlance shall be admitted or allowed

Penalty for refusing obedience to warrant of committee.

Provided alwayes, and it is the true intent and meaning of this act that notwithstanding the powers given by this act to the said revisors of the laws of Virginia shall stand, remaine and be in force as now they are untill they shall be repealed, abrogated, made void, amended or altered by act of assembly, and that all bills of what nature soever that shall be reported by the said comitee of revisors as aforesaid, shall be construed and deemed not to have any force or authority untill they have had their formall readings and are made laws by an assembly,

Present laws to remain in force till altered by act of assembly.

Bills reported by revisors, not to be of force, till they hav. had their formal readings, in assembly.

and that the assembly shall be fully at liberty to add to, alter, make void, amend or reject all or any of the bills that shall be reported as aforesaid, and shall proceed in order to have the laws of this his majesties colony and dominion assented to by his majestie, in such method and manner as to the assembly shall seem meet, any thing in this act to the contrary in any wise notwithstanding, and that the services of the said comitee clerk and assistants, with all reasonable and incident charges, be at the next assembly considered, rewarded and allowed, and so from time to time as they shall report to the succeeding assembly or assemblyes till all the laws be revised as aforesaid.

Assembly may alter or reject bills, reported by revisors.

Compensation to revisors.

ACT IX.

An act prohibiting the exportation of Indian Corne till the 25th day of December 1700.

Edi. 1733, and 1752.

FORASMUCH as the unseasonableness of the last two summers have caused a generall scarcity of Indian corne in all the parts of this his majestyes colony and dominion, to the end that corne may be kept in this his majesties colony and dominion, and that the same in this time of scarcity be not exported,

Preamble.

Be it enacted by the Governour, Councill and Burgesses of this present generall assembly, and the authority thereof, and it is hereby enacted, That from and after the fifteenth day of June 1699 no Indian corne of the produce of this his majesties colony and dominion shall be exported out of this country or laden or put on board any shipp or vessell in order to such exportation upon pain that the master of such shipp or vessell who shall export the same or suffer to be laden or taken on board his shipp or vessell any Indian corne in order to such exportation shall forfeit and pay for every barrell of corne so exported or so laden or putt on board the sume of five pounds sterling money, one moyety thereof to our sovereigne lord the king, his heirs and successors for and towards the better support of the government and the contingent charges thereof, and the other moyety to him or them that will sue or informe for the same by action of debt, bill, plaint or information in any court of record in this his majesties colony and do-

Exportation of Indian corn prohibited.

minion, in which no essoign protection or wager of law shall be allowed.

Provided alwayes, And be it enacted by the authoity aforesaid, and it is hereby enactea, That this act shall not be deemed or taken to extend or prohibit any master of shipp or vessell or any passenger from ladeing or takeing on board such shipp or vessell for exportation any corne for the use and necessary provision of the shipp dureing her voyage, any thing in this act to the contrary notwithstanding.

Proviso.

Provided likewise, that every such master of shipp or vessell shall make oath to the collector and naval officer with whome he clears his shipp or vessell who is hereby impowered and required to administer the same of the true quantity to the best of his knowledge of Indian corne laden and put on board his said ship or vessell and at that the same is truely and bona fide for the use and necessary provision of the said shipp or vessell and neither directly or indirectly, for any other use intent or purpose whatsoever.

Provided, that this act shall continue in force till the 25th day of December anno domini 1700, and no longer.

ACT X.

Edi. 1733 and 1752.

An act for confirming titles to towne Lands. (b)

Preamble.

WHEREAS the execution of the eighth act of assembly made the 16th day of Aprill 1691, entituled an act for ports, &c. stands suspended by the first act of assembly made the second day of March 1692-3 entituled an act for suspending the execution of the act for ports, &c. and forasmuch as pursuant to the said act for ports divers tracts of land have been purchased and laid out for ports and towns in the respective places appointed by the said act and vested in trustees many of

(*b*) This act was re-enacted almost verbatim, in the 44th chapter, Anno 1705, only two provisoes in this act for vesting lands purchased, pursuant to the act for ports, in the trustees, altho' the same had not been conveyed by the proprietors; and for giving twelve months time to build upon lots, are omitted.

(*Note to editions* 1733 *and* 1752.)

which have conveyed lots or halfe acres therein to severall persons who have built thereon and have made considerable improvements and severall others haveing accepted lots of halfe acres for which they have no conveyances and by reason of the aforesaid act for suspention they cannot obtaine also some of the trustees being dead and others departed the country, so that the remaining lands cannot be conveyed to such persons as desire to build thereon—For remedy of all which,

Lands heretofore vested in trustees, for ports, &c. confirmed.

Bee it enacted by the Governour, Councell and Burgesses of this present generall assembly and the authority thereof, and it is hereby enacted, That where any county or countyes have purchased, laid out and paid for any lands for ports or townes pursuant to the said acts for ports, &c. or to any other act of assembly and have vested the same in feofees or trustees according to the said act or acts such feofees or trustees so invested are hereby declared to have a good, absolute and indefeasible estate in fee in such lands respectively which have not been disposed of by former trustees in trust and confidence to and for the uses in the said act for posts, &c. mentioned, and for no other use or purpose whatsoever and the said land or lands are hereby confirmed to the said feofees or trustees in fee to such use or uses—any thing in the said suspention or any other law, statute, usage or custome to the contrary in any wise notwithstanding.

Where lands purchased, by counties, and not conveyed, how title to be acquired.

And be it further enacted by the authority aforesaid, and it is hereby enacted, That where any county or countyes pursuant to the said act for ports or any other act of assembly have purchased, laid out and paid for fifty acres of land and the same by the death or refusall of the proprietor or other accident hath not been conveyed to trustees according to the said law or laws such land or lands shall be and are hereby confirmed to such feofees or trustees as hereafter by virtue of this act shall be appointed by the county courts to and for the uses aforesaid, in as full and ample manner as if the said land or lands had been really and actually conveyed in law by such proprietor or proprietors to such feofees or trustees in manner as by the said act for ports is expressed.

And be it further enacted by the authority aforesaid, and it is hereby enacted, That if in any county the feo-

Vacancies, in trustees, how supplied.

fees or trustees already appointed by virtue of the said act for ports be dead or departed out of this country the county courts of such respective county is hereby impowered and required to appoint other feofees or trustees who are hereby invested and confirmed in the fee of all such land or lands not by the former trustees disposed of to the use or uses aforementioned, and to no other use or purpose whatsoever, and all feofees or trustees by virtue of the said act for ports, &c. already made or by virtue of this act hereafter to be made are hereby impowered and required in their respective countyes to convey and make over any lot or lots, halfe acre or half acres of land to such person or persons as shall desire to take up the same according to the said act for ports, and upon the conditions therein specified as if the said act for ports had never been suspended, any thing in the said act for suspention or any other law statute or custome to the contrary notwithstanding.

Purchasers, who have paid for their lots, confirmed in their titles,

And be it further enacted by the authority aforesaid, and it is hereby enacted, That if any person or persons have purchased and paid for any lott or lotts, half acre or halfe acres of land in any of the said places of any feofees or trustees pursuant to the said law and have fully complyed with the conditions in the said law mentioned and sett downe, such person and persons are hereby invested with and declared to have a good, absolute and indefeasible estate in fee to such lott or lotts, halfe acre or halfe acres of land, and the same is hereby confirmed to such person and persons and to his and their heirs forever.

and trustees to convey to them.

Provided alwayes, And be it further enacted by the authoity aforesaid, and it is hereby enacted, That if any person or persons have taken up and paid for any lott or lotts, halfe acre or halfe acres in any land laid out for ports or townes, &c. as aforesaid, and have yet received no conveyance for the same, the respective feofees or trustees already made or by virtue of this law hereafter shall be made are hereby impowered and required to give and make a firm and absolute estate in fee to such person or persons for such lott or lotts, halfe acre or halfe acres, as if the said suspention had never been made.

Provided alwayes, And be it further enacted by the authority aforesaid, and it is hereby enacted, That if any person or persons have taken up and paid for any lott or lotts, halfe acre or halfe acres in any such lands for ports and townes, &c. pursuant to the said law and have laid timbers upon the same or any wayes proceeded in order to comply with the conditions of building upon such lott or lotts, halfe acre or half acres according to the said act for ports, &c. but upon suspention thereof have neglected to proceed to therein, such person or persons are allowed and permitted twelve months time for the same after the publication of this act. Further time allowed for completing buildings.

ACT XI.

An act for lessening the levy by the pole, and laying an imposition upon lyquors for and towards the building a Capitoll and other publick uses. Edi. 1733, and 1752.

FORASMUCH as a more suitable expedient cannot be found to lesen the levy by the pole on the inhabitants of this his majesties colony and dominion of Virginia then to lay an imposition on all lyquors to be imported into this country, Preamble.

Be it therefore enacted by the Governour, Councell and burgesses of this present generall assembly and the authority thereof, and it is hereby enacted, That for every gallon of wine of any sort whatsoever, brandy, rum, syder or any other spirits imported into this his majesties colony and dominion, except alwayes what shall come directly from England, Wales or the towne of Berwick upon Tweed, from and after the publication of this act the imposition or custome of four pence shall be paid by the merchant or merchants, owner or owners, importer or importers of the same to his majestie, his heirs and successors to and for the uses, intents and purposes hereafter mentioned, and to no other use, intent or purpose whatsoever, and for every gallon of beer or ale imported as aforesaid, except what shall come directly from England, Wales or the towne of Berwick upon Tweed, the imposition or custome of one penny shall be paid as aforesaid, to the uses aforesaid, and for the better levying and collecting the imposition or custome by this act laid on all lyquors to be imported, except as before excepted, Duty of four pence a gallon on wines and spirituous liquors. One penny on beer and ale.

No liquors to be landed, till due entry be made, and duties paid.

Bee it enacted by the authority aforesaid, and it is hereby enacted, That no liquors to be imported within the time herein limited (except as before excepted) shall be landed or putt on shoar out of any shipp or other vessell from beyond the seas before due entry be made thereof with the officer or collector appointed for the customes in the port or place where the same shall be imported or before the duty due and payable for the same be fully satisfied, and that every warrant for the landing and delivering of any such liquors shall be signed by the hand of the said officer or collector in the said port or place respectively, upon paine that all such lyquors as shall be landed, put on shoar or delivered contrary to the true intent and meaning of this act or the value thereof, shall be forfeited and lost and to be recovered of the importer or proprietor of the same and that no person or persons whatsoever bringing any of the before recited lyquors (except as before excepted) into any port or place of this his majesties colony and dominion or any person or persons to whome the same or any of them shall be consigned, shall land or cause any such liquors to be landed or put on shoar without makeing or causeing due entry to be made of the same and giveing a true account of the gallons every caske did containe upon oath which the officer or officers for the time being appointed to receive and take such entrys within the port or place where the same shall be landed or put on shoar upon paine in every such case as aforesaid to forfeit double the value of the said liquors landed and put on shoar contrary to the true intent and meaning of this act, and that the master or purser of every shipp, barque or other vessell shall make a true and just entry upon oath which the collector or other officer is hereby impowered and required to administer of the burthen, contents and ladeing of such shipp, bark or other vessell with the particular marks, numbers, quantityes and contents of every caske therein laden with liquors to the best of his knowledge, and also where and in what port shee took in her laden, how maned, who was master dureing the voyage and who are owners thereof upon penalty of forfeiting one hundred pounds sterling. And for the better encouragement of all masters, merchants owners and other persons whatsoever to make due entry

Penalty.

How entry to be made.

and payment of the imposition or duty laid by virtue of this act, and in consideration of filing and leakage there shall be abated and allowed twenty gallons in every hundred which said allowance and abatement the said collectors to be appointed to receive the said duties are hereby authorised to allow and make accordingly: *Provided*, that where any master, merchant, owner or other person whatsoever shall witingly or willingly make a false entry and be convicted for the same, in that case such master, merchant, owner or other person shall forfeit and pay one hundred pounds sterling, and that the said person or persons which are or shall be appointed to receive the dutyes and impost ariseing by virtue of this act and their deputyes are hereby authorised and impowered to go and enter on board any ship or other vessell and from thence to bring on shoar all the before specified lyquors (except as before excepted) for which the duties are not paid or compounded for within tenn dayes after the first entry of the said shipp or other vessell and that the officers of the customes and their deputyes may freely stay and remaine on board untill all the goods are delivered and discharged out of the said shipp or other vessell, and if any officer or officers be appointed to receive the dutyes by this act ariseing or any other person or persons deputed and appointed by or under them or any of them or any other authority whatsoever shall directly or indirectly take or receive any bribe, recompence or reward in any kind whatsoever, or shall connive at any false entry of any wines or other liquors aforementioned, whereby the dutyes be defrauded the person or persons therein offending shall forfeit the sume of one hundred pounds sterling, and be forever afterwards disabled and made incapable of any office or imployment within this his majesties colony and dominion, as also the master, merchant, marriner or other person whatsoever, who shall give or pay any such bribe, reward or recompence shall forfeit the sume of fifty pounds sterling, and that all officers, captains and commanders of ships or other vessells, as also all justices of the peace, sheriffs, constables, headboroughes and all other his majesties officers, ministers and subjects whatsoever whome it may concerne shall be aiding and assisting unto all and every person and persons which are or shall be appointed by

Allowance for leakage.

Penalty for false entry.

Power of search.

Penalty for bribery.

All officers to assist in the execution of the laws

the governor to receive and collect the dutyes by this act laid, and the collector and collectors and their respective deputyes in the due execution of all and every act and thing in and by this present act required and enjoyned, and all such who shall be aiding and assisting unto them in the due execution hereof shall be defended and saved harmeless by virtue of this act. And forasmuch as severall forfeitures and penaltyes may by virtue of this act arise,

Forfeitures, how appropriated.

Be it therefore enacted by the authority aforesaid, and it is hereby enacted, That all such forfeitures and penaltyes shall be divided into three equall parts, one third part whereof shall be paid to his majestie, his heirs and successors towards the better support of the government and defraying the contingent charges thereof, one third part shall be paid to the governor for the time being to and for his owne proper use and behoofe, and the other third part to him or them that will sue for the same by action of debt, bill, plaint or information in any court of record within this his majesties colony and dominion, in which no essoigne protection or wager of law shall be admitted or allowed.

Collectors, how appointed.

And be it further enacted by the authority aforesaid, and it is hereby enacted, That the governor for the time being with the advice of the councill shall be and is hereby impowered from time to time and att all times, hereafter during the time in this act before limited, to nominate, constitute and appoint such and so many collectors and other officers as also such salleryes, methods and orders (not exceeding six in the hundred) for the collecting the said duty as to them shall seem best.

To account and pay to the treasurer

And be it further enacted by the authority aforesaid, and it is hereby enacted, That all and every sume and sumes of money raised or to be raised by virtue of this act shall be constantly accounted for by the collector or collectors thereof to the treasurer of Virginia for the time being upon his or their oath and by him to the governor, councill and burgesses of the generall assembly upon oath also and converted to the uses by them directed according to the true intent and meaning of this act, and to and for no other use, intent or purpose whatsoever, any thing in this act contained, or any other matter or thing to the contrary in anywise notwithstanding.

This act to continue in force three years from the day of publication thereof, and no longer. Limitation of this act.

ACT XII.

An act for laying an imposition upon servants and slaves imported into this country, towards building the Capitoll. Edi. 1733 and 1752.

WHEREAS the state house of this his majesties colony and dominion in which the generall assemblyes and general courts have been kept and held hath been unhappily destroyed and burnt downe, and it being absolutely necessary that a capitoll should be built with all expedition, and forasmuch as a more suitable expedient cannot be found for avoiding the laying a levy upon the poll for the building the same than by laying an imposition upon servants and slaves imported into this his majesties colony and dominion, Preamble.

Be it enacted by the Governour, Councell and Burgesses of this present generall assembly and the authority thereof, and it is hereby enacted, That from and after the publication of this act the sume of fifteen shillings per poll for every servant not born in England or Wales and twenty shillings for every negro or other slave which shall be imported into this his majesties colony and dominion shall be from time to time paid and satisfyed to his majestie, his heirs and successors for and towards the erecting and building a convenient capitoll for this his majesties colony and dominion and for no nother use, intent or purpose whatsoever, which said sume or sumes shall be paid by the importer or importers of such and for the better levying and collecting the said duty and impost, Duty on servants and slaves imported.

Be it enacted by the authority aforesaid, and it is hereby enacted, That from and after the publication thereof no servant or servants, negro or negroes imported into this country shall be landed or put on shoar out of any shipp or vessell before due entry first made with the officer or collector appointed for the customes in such port or place where the same shall be imported, nor before the master of the said shipp or vessell hath made oath to such officer or collector who is hereby impowered and required to administer the same of the No servant, or negro to be put on shore till due entry made, and duty paid.

number of servants or slaves imported in such shipp or vessell and of the reputed place of the birth of such servant or servants, nor before the duty due and payable for the same shall be fully paid and satisfyed to such officer or collector, and that every warrant for the landing of such servants or slaves shall be under the hand and seale of the said officer or collector respectively upon paine that all such servants or slaves as shall be landed or putt on shore contrary to this act or the vallue thereof shall be forfeited and lost and shall be recovered of the importer or proprietor of the same.

Penalty.

And be it further enacted by the authority aforesaid, and it is hereby enacted, That if any master of shipp or vessell shall witingly or willingly make a false entry of any such servants or slaves and be thereof convicted he shall forfeit and pay for every such offence the sume of one hundred pounds sterling, and if any collector or officer shall directly or indirectly take or receive any bribe, recompence or reward to connive at any false entry of any such servants or slaves, or if any person or persons shall give or pay any such bribe or reward, he or they so offending shall forfeit and pay the sume of one hundred pounds sterling, all which penaltyes and forfeitures in this act expressed shall be divided into three equall parts, one third part thereof to his majestie, his heirs and successors towards the better support of the government and the contingent charges thereof, one other third part to the governor for the time being, and the other third part to him or them that will sue or informe for the same by action of debt, bill, plaint or information in any court of record within this his majesties colony and dominion, in which no essoigne protection or wager of law shall be allowed.

Penalty for false entry.

For bribery.

Forfeitures, how appropriated.

And be it further enacted by the authority aforesaid, and it is hereby enacted, That the governor for the time being with the advice of the councill, shall be and is hereby impowered from time to time and at all times hereafter to nominate, constitute and appoint such and so many collectors or other officers, as also such salleryes not exceeding six in the hundred, for the collecting the said dutyes as to him shall seem best.

Collectors, how appointed.

And be it enacted by the authority aforesaid, and it is hereby enacted, That all and every sume and sumes of money raised or to be raised by virtue of this act be constantly accounted for by the collectors thereof to the treasurer of this his majesties colony and dominion for the time being, and by him to the governor, councill and burgesses of the generall assembly and converted to the uses by them directed according to the true intent and meaning of this act, and to and for no other use, intent or purpose whatsoever. Duties, how accounted for.

And be it therefore further enacted by the authority aforesaid, and it is hereby enacted, That this act shall continue in force for three years from the publication thereof, and no longer. Limitation of this act.

ACT XIII.

An act ascertaining Collectors and Navall Officers fees.

Edit 1733, and 1752.

WHEREAS the offices of the collectors and navall officers was formerly executed by one and the same person, and being now divided into two distinct offices, and forasmuch as the laws already made relateing thereto do not sufficiently provide for the same, and to the end that to each officer may be ascertained proper fees, Preamble.

BE it enacted by the Governour, Councell and Burgesses of this present generall assembly and the authority thereof, and it is hereby enacted, That one act of assembly made at James City the 5th of June 1676 entituled an act ascertaining the price of cocquets and one other act made at James City the 25th of Aprill 1679, entituled an act ascertaining collectors fees for entry and clearing ships, &c. another act of assembly made at James City the 2d day of March 1692, entituled an act for ascertaining the price of coasting cocquets and requireing officers attendance, and all and every clauses and articles in all and every the said acts contained, shall be and are hereby repealed and made void, null and of no effect to all intents, constructions and purposes as if the said acts had never been made, any thing in the said acts or any of them to the contrary in any wise notwithstanding. Certain acts repealed.

And be it further enacted by the authority aforesaid, and it is hereby enacted, That no collector or navall officer shall from and after the publication of this act

Fees of naval officers.

charge, demand, exact and take any more or greater fee or fees for any business, matter or thing by such collector or navall officer to be done or performed than what is hereafter particularly enumerated, sett downe and expressed in the following tables (to witt) that the navall officers fees shall be as followeth: first, for entring and clearing any vessell if under fifty tuns, seven shillings and six pence; for taking a bond 2s. 6d.; for a permit to trade 2s. 6d.; for every loading cocquet here 1s.; for a permit to sale 5s.; for a certificate for all imported goods that shall be removed out of one district into another after they are once landed 2s. 6.; for entring and clearing any shipp or vessell if above fifty tuns and under one hundred tuns, tenn shillings; for entring and clearing any ship or vessell if above one hundred tuns, one pound five shillings—

That the collectors fees shall be,

Fees of collectors.

For entring and clearing any ship or vessell under fifty tunn and all fees whatsoever incident thereunto, tenn shillings; for entring and clearing any shipp or vessell if above fifty tunn and under one hundred tunn, and all fees incident thereunto, fifteen shillings; for entring and clearing any shipp or vessell if above one hundred tunn and all fees incident thereunto one pound five shillings: and if any collector or navall officer shall charge, exact, demand and take any other fee or fees than what is by this act particularly sett downe and

Penalty for exceeding legal fees.

exprest and shall exact and take any larger or greater fee or fees for any matter or thing than is by this act allowed and given, he or they so offending and being thereof lawfully convicted shall for the first offence forfeit and pay the sume of one hundred pounds sterling, one moyety to the kings most excellent majestie, his heirs and successors for and towards the better support of the government, and the contingent charges thereof, and the other moyety to the party injured to be recovered in any of his majesties courts of record in this colony and dominion by action of debt, bill, plaint or information, in which no essoigne protection, wager of law, privilege or more than one imparlance shall be admitted or allowed, and for the second offence, being lawfully convicted as aforesaid, shall be utterly incapable and disabled in law to hold, execute and enjoy the place and office of collector or navall officer or any profits or advantage arising therefrom for ever, and the said place or office shall imediately after such conviction be void to such person or persons to all intents and purposes as if he or they had been naturally dead. *Provided alwayes*, the sute be commenced within twelve months after the breach of the said act by any officer aforesaid. Within what time prosecution to be commenced.

And be it further enacted by the authority aforesaid, and it is hereby enacted, That every navall officer and collector shall and is by this act enjoyned within months after the publication hereof to sett up or cause to be sett up fairly written in his respective office a table or copy of the fees in this said act before recited, which being so sett up shall be from time to time so continued by each navall officer and collector. Table of fees to be set up.

ACT XIV.

An act directing the building the Capitoll and the City of Williamsburg. Edi.1733, and 1752.

[☞ This act, together with the title, is repeated verbatim in the revisall of 1705, chap XLIII. and declared to be in force; and several clauses added for the better execution thereof.—It is therefore unnecessary to print it here.]

ACT XV.

An act appointing a Treasurer. Edi. 1733 and 1752.

WHEREAS by one act of assembly made this present sessions, intituled an act for laying an imposition upon servants and slaves imported into this country towards the building a capitoll, and by one other act of assembly made this present sessions entituled an act for lesening the levy by the pole and laying an imposition upon liquors towards the building a capitoll and for other public uses, Preamble.

It is enacted by the Governour, Councell and Burgesses of this present Generall Assembly and the authority thereof, and it is hereby enacted, That all and every sume and sumes of money raised or to be raised by virtue of the said acts shall be constantly accounted for and paid by the collectors thereof to the treasurer of this his majestyes colony and dominion for the time being. And forasmuch as there is no express nomination of any person in certaine to be treasurer,

Robert Carter appointed treasurer.

Be it therefore enacted by the authority aforesaid, and it is hereby enacted, That Coll Robert Carter shall be, and is hereby nominated, constituted and appointed treasurer of the revenues ariseing by the two before specified acts and is hereby authorised, impowered and required to demand, receive and take of and from every collector and collectors all and every sume and sumes of money ariseing by force of the two before specified acts of assembly. And the said coll. Robert Carter is authorised and required to keep and retaine all such money in his owne custody and possession untill he shall be ordered and required to dispose of the same in such manner and by such warrant, and for such uses, intents and purposes, and no other as are limited appointed and directed in the said acts, and in one other act made this assembly, entituled an act directing the building of the capitoll, &c. And forasmuch as by the before recited acts there is no provision made of sallery to the treasurer of the said impositions,

His duties.

Salary.

Be it enacted by the authority aforesaid, and it is hereby enacted, That the sallery of four per cent. shall be allowed and paid unto the treasurer of this his majestyes colony and dominion for the revenues aforesaid, out of all and every sume and sumes of money ariseing by virtue of the said acts and accounted for to the governor, councill and burgeses of the generall assembly by the said treasurer, according to the directions of the said acts.

And be it further enacted by the authority aforesaid, and it is hereby enacted, That the said Coll Robert Carter before his entry and admission into the aforesaid office and before his takeing upon him to execute and manage the same shall give bond in the secretaryes office with good and sufficient security in the sume of five thousand pounds sterling, payable to his majesty his heirs and successors for the true and faithful performance and discharge of the aforesaid office and place of treasurer according to the true intent and meaning of the aforesaid three acts of assembly. *Provided alwayes*, that in case of the death, departure out of the country or other disability of the treasurer hereby appointed before the next sessions of assembly, then it

Treasurer to give bond.

shall and may be lawfull for his excelency the governor and the governor or commander in chiefe for the time being, with the advice of the councill to appoint and constitute such other person as he shall think fitt to execute the said office of treasurer according to the severall rules and directions in this act expressed, who shall have, hold and enjoy the said office with all and singular its rights and profits, untill the next session of assembly, giveing such bond and security as is herein before directed, any thing in this or any other act to the contrary in any wise notwithstanding.

Vacancy in the office of treasurer to be supplied by governor with the advice of council.

ACT XVI.

An act for raising a Publick Levy.

Edi. 1733 and 1752.

BE *it enacted by the governour, councell and burgesses of this present generall assembly and the authority thereof, and it is hereby enacted,* That the sume of nineteen pounds of tobacco be paid by every tythable person within this his majestyes colony and dominion of Virginia for the defraying and payment of the publick charge of the country being the publick levy from the 24th day of September 1697 to this present time, and that it be paid by the collectors of the severall countyes to the severall persons to whome it is proportioned by this generall assembly, and if it shall happen that there shall be more tythables in any county then the present levy is laid on, then such county to have creditt for so much to the use of the county, and if there shall happen to be less in any county then such county shall bear the loss.

Taxes, or public levy, from 1697 to the present time.

Signed by FRANCIS NICHOLSON, Esq *Govr.*
ROBERT CARTER, *Speaker.*

(*Note to editions* 1733 *and* 1752.)

AT A

Generall Assembly,

BEGUN AT

Francis Nicholson, Esq. Gov.

HIS MAJESTYES ROYALL COLLEDGE OF WILLIAM AND MARY, ADJOYNING TO THE CITY OF WILLIAMSBURGH, THE 5th DAY OF DECEMBER, 1700, IN THE 12th YEAR OF HIS MAJESTYES REIGN.*

ACT I.

Edit. 1733, & 1752.

An act continuing the act prohibiting the exportation of Indian Corne.

WHEREAS the continuance of the law prohibiting the exportation of Indian corne is found very necessary and convenient,

Act prohibiting the exportation of Indian corn further continued.

Be it enacted by the Governour, Councill and Burgesses of this present generall assembly, and the authority thereof, and it is hereby enacted, That the 9th act of assembly made at a generall assembly begun at James City the 27th day of Aprill 1699, entituled an act prohibiting the exportation of Indian corne till the 25th day of December 1700, shall be and is hereby continued in full force to all intents and purposes from the 25th day of December next, till the 25th day of December that shall be in the year 1705.

---

* The commencement of the acts of this session in the edition of 1733, is, "At a General Assembly begun at his majesty's roial college of *William* and *Mary*, adjoining to the city of Williamsburg, the fifth day of *December Anno Domini* 1700.

ACT II.

An act makeing the French refugees inhabiting at the Manakin towne and the parts adjacent a distinct parrish by themselves, and exempting them from the payment of publick and county levyes for seaven years.

Edi. 1733, and 1752.

Preamble.

WHEREAS a considerable number of French protestant refugees have been lately imported into this his majestys colony and dominion severall of which refugees have seated themselves above the falls of James River at or near to a place comonly caled and known by the name of the Manakin towne, for the encouragment of the said refugees to settle and remaine together as near as may be to the said Manakin towne,

Lands, held by French refugees, at Manakin town & adjacent, to be a distinct parish by the name of King William parish in the county of Henrico.

Bee it enacted by the governour, councell and burgesses of this present generall assembly, and it is hereby enacted, That the said refugees inhabiting at the said Manakin towne and the parts adjacent, shall be accounted and taken for inhabitants of a distinct parrish by themselves and the land which they now do or shall hereafter poses at or adjacent to the said Manakin towne, shall be and is hereby declared to be a parish of itselfe, distinct from any other parish to be caled and knowne by the name of King Williams parish in the county of Henrico, and not lyable to the payment of parish levies in any other parish whatsoever.

Refugees exempted from payment of taxes and levies.

And be it further enacted by the authority aforesaid, That such and so many of the said refugees as are already settled or shall hereafter settle themselves as inhabitants of the said parish at the Manakin towne and the parts adjacent shall themselves and their familyes and every of them be free and exempted from the payment of publick and county levies for the space of seven years next ensuing from the publication of this act, any law, statute, custome, or usage, to the contrary in any wise notwithstanding.

ACT. III.

An act for the more effectuall and speedy carrying on the revisall of the laws.

Edi. 1733, and 1752.

Preamble.

WHEREAS by one act of assembly made att a generall assembly begun at James City the 27th day of Aprill 1699, entituled an act appointing a comitee for the revisall of the whole body of the laws of this his majestyes colony and dominion, it is enacted, that Edward Hill, Mathew Page and Benjamin Harrison, Esqrs. members of the honorable councill, and that Miles Cary, John Taylor, Robert Beverly, Anthoney Armsted, Henry Duke and William Buckner, gentlemen, then members of the house of burgesses, or any six of them, whereof two to be of the council and four of the house of burgesses, should be and were thereby appointed and declared to be a comitee for the revisall of the whole body of the laws of this his majestyes colony and dominion. And forasmuch as it is found necessary and convenient that the said clause of the aforesaid law should be altered,

Any one member of the council, with two of the burgesses, sufficient to carry on the revisal of the laws.

Be it therefore enacted by the Governour, Councell and burgesses of this present generall assembly and the authority thereof, and it is hereby enacted, That any one of the members of the honorable councill with any two of the burgeses appointed and to be appointed and impowered by virtue of the said act of assembly to revise the laws shall be and are hereby appointed and declared to be a comitee to revise the laws of this his majestyes colony and dominion at such times and places and with such powers and under such rules and limitations as by the aforesaid act of assembly is directed and laid downe and the proceedings of such comitee shall to all intents and purposes be accounted as good and valid as if they were done by any greater number or by the number appointed by the said act, any thing in the said act to the contrary notwithstanding.

ACT IV.

Edi. 1733, and 1752.

An act for raising a Publick Levy.

Taxes or public levy from 27th of April 1699, to the present time.

BEE it enacted by the governour, councell and burgesses of this present generall assembly and the authority thereof, and it is hereby enacted, That the sume of nine pounds of tobacco be paid by every tythable person within this his majesties collony and dominion of Virginia for the defraying and payment of the publick charge of the country being the publick levy from the 27th day of Aprill 1699 to this present time, and that it be paid by the collectors of the severall countyes to the several persons to whome it is proportioned by this generall assembly, and if it shall happen that there shall be more tythables in any county than the present levy is laid on, then such county to have creditt for so much to the use of the county, and if there shall happen to be less in any county, then such county shall bear the loss.

Signed by FRANCIS NICHOLSON, Esqr. *Govr.*
PETER BEVERLEY, *Speaker.*

(Note to editions 1733 *and* 1752.*)*

AT A

Generall Assembly,

BEGUN AT

Francis Nicholson, Esqr. Gov.

HIS MAJESTYES ROYALL COLLEDGE OF WILLIAM & MARY ADJOYNING TO THE CITY OF WILLIAMSBURGH, THE 5th DAY OF DECEMBER IN THE TWELFTH YEAR OF THE REIGNE OF OUR SOVEREIGNE LORD, WILLIAM THE THIRD, OF ENGLAND, SCOTLAND, FRANCE AND IRELAND, KING DEFENDER OF THE FAITH, &c. ANNOQ. DOMINI 1700,

And thence continued by severall prorogations to the 6th day of August 1701 *in the 13th year of his majestyes reigne.**

ACT I.

Edi. 1733, and 1752.

An act for the better strengthening the frontiers and discovering the approaches of an enemy.

Preamble.

WHEREAS the most proper wayes and means for the strengthening the frontiers of this his majesties most ancient colony and dominion against the invasions and incursions of an enemy by land, and for the better prevention of murthers, robberyes and other spoiles from being comited thereon is thought to be by setling in cohabitations upon the said land frontiers within this go-

* The commencement of the acts of this session, in the editions of 1733 and 1752, is, "At a general assembly, begun at his majesty's roial college of *William* and *Mary*, adjoining to the City of Williamsburg, the fifth day of December; in the twelfth year of the reign of our sovereign lord William III. of England, Scotland, France, and Ireland, king, defender of the faith, &c. *annoq;* Dom. 1700. And thence continued by several prorogations to the 6th day of August 1701; and in the thirteenth year of his majestyes reign; being the second session of this present General Assembly."

vernment, and that the best method to effect the same will be by encouragements to induce societyes of men to undertake the same, and whereas a less number than twenty able fighting men is not thought a sufficient defence in such cohabitations,

Be it therefore enacted by the Governour, Councell, and Burgesses of this present Generall Assembly and the authority thereof, and it is hereby enacted, That these following encouragements shall be given for such cohabitations under the conditions, rules and directions hereafter following, that is to say, that there shall be granted to every certaine number of men who shall enter into societyes and agree to undertake such cohabitations any quantity of land not under the quantity of tenn thousand acres, nor exceeding the quantity of thirty thousand acres upon any of the frontiers within this government wherever it shall be found not legally taken up or possessed by any of his majestyes leige people, which land shall be held by such societyes or companies of men in common as tenants in comon and undivided to them and each of them, their and each of their heirs for ever as to their severall respective interests and propertyes in the said land and every part thereof, so that at the death of any of them the right of such person may descend to his heirs and so from heir to heir and not go to the survivor. *Provided alwayes,* that the power of ordering and manageing the said land and the planting and setling thereof, still be and remaine in the said societyes of men or undertakers and such of the heirs and purchasers thereof as shall be of age or the major part of them. And whereas the easing the charge usually accrewing in the first surveying and takeing up of land in this his majestyes colony and dominion and in the payment of quitrents would be a very great inducement and encouragment for the makeing the said cohabitations and defensive settlements, this present generall assembly haveing taken the same into their serious considerations and the inability of the country at this time by any other wayes or means to make any forts and such like defences.

Encouragement to settlers on the frontiers.

A certain quantity of land, granted to societies, as tenants in common;

with power to make rules for the ordering thereof.

Be it therefore enacted by the authority aforesaid, and it is hereby enacted, That when any grant and settlement shall be made in pursuance of this act, the charges of the surveying thereof and laying out the two hun-

Surveys to be made, & quit-rents paid, at public expense for the first 20 years.

dred acres for the cohabitations and the land for the forts shall be defrayed by the country together with the quitrents due to his majesty for the first twenty years as they shall become due. And for a further encouragment,

Settlers exempted from taxes or levies for 20 years:

Be it also enacted by the authority aforesaid, and it is hereby enacted, That all persons that shall go or be sent to settle and remaine in any of the settlements or cohabitations to be made by virtue of this act shall for the first twenty years after such settlement made wherein they reside be free and exempted from paying any public, county or parish levyes within this government.— And also for their further encouragment,

and from military service, except for their own defence.

Be it enacted by the authority aforesaid, and it is hereby enacted, That all such persons as shall be seated in cohabitations by virtue of this act shall be also exempted from all military comands but what shall be setled by public authority among themselves and shall tend to their owne defence and security, and for the encouragment of all such persons able and well fited to serve in warr as shall join such undertakeing for cohabitations and be under the rules and directions herein and this act appointed and to be appointed where and so long as the quantity of land undertaken for shall be less than thirty thousand acres.

Settlement rights.

Conditions.

Be it also further enacted by the authority aforesaid, and it is hereby enacted, That there shall be granted to every such person untill the said quantity of thirty thousand acres shall be compleatly taken up a right to two hundred acres of land next adjacent at his choise together with halfe an acre to seat upon and live in not before seated upon within the said two hundred acres to be laid out for the cohabitation as shall be directed to be held and enjoyed by him, his heirs and assignes under the libertyes, freedoms, exemptions and franchises herein by this act given to such societyes and undertakers so long as the said person so joining himselfe his heirs or assignes shall continue and keep the conditions of the said settlements and cohabitation and no longer. *Provided alwayes,* and it is the true intent and meaning of this act that for every five hundred acres of land to be granted in pursuance of this act there shall be and shall continually be kept upon the said land one christian man between sixteen and sixty years of age perfect of limb, able and fitt for service who shall alsoe be continually provided with a well fixt musquett or fuzee, a good pistoll, sharp simeter, tomahauk and five pounds of good clean pistoll powder and twenty pounds of sizable leaden bulletts or swan or goose shott to be kept within the fort directed by this act besides the powder and shott for his necessary or usefull shooting at game. *Provided also*, that the said warlike christian man shall have his dwelling and continuall abode within the space of two hundred acres of land to be laid out in a geomitricall square or neare that figure as conveniency will admitt for the same to be laid out within the said quantityes of land first mentioned by this act to be granted. *Provided also*, that because the constitution of this country does not enable us to make such a settlement at once, and that it is not likely to be done among ourselves or from any other place without some reasonable time be given, it is the true intent and meaning of this act that if within two years from the obtaining any grant upon this act the grantees or undertakers shall seat or cause to be seated upon the said land and within the two hundred acres before mentioned to be laid out for cohabitation tenn able warlike christian men, armed and provided as aforesaid, and so for every two years, after tenn more such able, warlike christian men so armed and provided, untill the whole number shall be compleated of one such man so fixed for every five hundred acres such grant shall contain, and from time to time keep up such settlement it shall be taken for a full complyance and settlement within this act and to take and hold by virtue of such grant any thing in this act contained to the contrary notwithstanding. *Provided also*, that by the expiration of the two first years after the grant as aforesaid the said society or undertakers, and such as shall joine with them shall palesado in or cause to be pallisadoed in for a fort one half acre of land to be laid out in the middle of the said two hundred acres appointed for the cohabitation with good sound pallisadoes at least thirteen foot long and six inches diameter in the middle of the length thereof, and set double and at least three foot within the ground. And for further encouragement,

For every 500 acres of land, one able man; completely armed and equipt, to be constantly kept.

Where stationed.

Further encouragement to settlers.

Forts to be built.

Be it also enacted by the authority aforesaid, and it is hereby enacted, That when such fort shall be made

Part of the expence, to be paid by the public.

there shall be paid by the country tenn pounds sterling towards a publick store house and other necessary houses within the said fort: *Provided also*, that when any person or persons shall joine themselves to the said cohabitation after the first undertakeing as afore is said and shall desert the same or not keep up his or their part or parts of the conditions in this act mentioned, the said two hundred acres of land by this act appointed to be granted him or them shall revert to the king without any inquest or further inquiry, and be lyable to be taken up under the conditions he or they took up the same by the next that will and the halfe acre to the society of undertakers, any thing in this act to the contrary in any wise notwithstanding. *Provided alwayes*, that the governor or commander in chiefe of this his majestyes most ancient collony and dominion of Virginia may and he is hereby desired to nominate, choose and appoint one or more as to him shall seem meet that shall be resident in each of the cohabitations or townes to be made by virtue of this act to reside and lodge in the fort and to command and rule the rest in all military affaires according to such orders and directions as he or they shall from time to time receive from the governor or commander in chief for the time being, and also to give directions in what shall be needfull or convenient in raising, maintaining and keeping their fort in repaire and strengthening the same. And for the further security of the frontiers as well towards the sea as land dureing these times of danger and for discovering the approaches of an enemy by sea,

On failure of conditions, the land to revert to the king, without inquest.

Governor may appoint commander of fort.

Be it enacted by the authority aforesaid, and it is hereby enacted, That the colonels or commanders in chiefe of the militia in the severall countyes of Elizabeth City, Accomack and Northampton, order and appoint two men in each of the said countyes at such times and places as the governor for the time being shall appoint, which said men shall keep a constant looke out to seaward by night and by day, and if they or any of them shall hapen to see any ship or vessell upon the sea they shall dilligently observe the courses and motions of the said shipp or vessell, and if upon the same the look outs who shall spye them have any suspition of their being enemyes they shall imediately give notice thereof to the next commision officer of the militia who is hereby re-

Two men to be appointed, as look-outs, in the counties of Accomack and Northumberland.

Their duty.

quired forthwith to signify the same to the cheife commander for the time being of the militia of that county.

And be it further enacted by the authority aforesaid, and it is hereby enacted, That when any notice shall be given to the chief officer of the militia for the time being in any frontier county either by land or sea of the approach of an enemy, such cheife officer is hereby authorised, impowered and required imediately to issue his warrants for the impressing horse and man and boat and hands as the occasion shall require to carry the said notice to the governor or commander in cheife of this his majestyes colony and dominion for the time being and to the cheife officers of the militia in the next adjacent frontier county with what orders and directions he designes therein and is also hereby further authorized and impowered to call together such number of the militia as he shall think fitt and together with the advice of the commission officers who shall meet him to march the said militia against the enemyes and to imbattle, repell, subdue, take, kill or destroy them untill further order to be given by the governor or commander in cheif for the time being.

Power and duty of commanding officers of militia.

And it is further enacted by the authority aforesaid, That the look outs by this act appointed shall for what time they serve be paid by the public after the rate of two hundred pounds of tobacco per month.

And be it further enacted by the authority aforesaid, That the militia raised or to be raised by force and virtue of this act if they be out above four dayes they and every of them shall receive pay and be satisfyed by the publick for every day they shall be in service after these rates, vizt: each captaine finding himselfe horse, armes, ammunition, provisions and all other necessaryes tenn thousand pounds of tobacco and caske for one year, and so proportionably for a shorter or longer time, each lieutenant finding and providing himselfe with horse, armes, ammunition and all other necessaryes five thousand pounds of tobacco and caske for one year and so proportionable for a shorter or longer time, and every private souldier finding himselfe horse, armes and amunition and all other necessaryes three thousand pounds of tobacco and caske for one year and so proportionable for a shorter or longer time.

Pay of militia called into service.

ACT II.

Edi. 1733, and 1752.

An act for the more effectuall apprehending an outlying negro who hath commited divers robberyes and offences.

Preamble.

WHEREAS one negro man named Billy, slave to John Tillit, but lately the slave of Thomas Middleton, and formerly of James Bray, gentlemen, of James City county, has severall years unlawfully absented himselfe from his masters services, lying out and lurking in obscure places suposed within the countys of James City, York and New-Kent, devouring and destroying the stocks and crops, robing the houses of and committing and threatening other injuryes to severall of his majestyes good and leige people within this his colony and dominion of Virginia in contempt of the good laws thereof,

Act of attainder, against Billy, a slave.

Be it therefore enacted by the governour, councell and burgesses of this present generall assembly, and the authority thereof, and it is hereby enacted, That the said negro slave Billy stand and be adjudged by the authority of this present act convicted of unlawfully lying out, lurking and destroying the stocks and crops and comiting robberyes as aforesaid, and that he suffer the paines of death. And for a further encouragment in a more speedy and effectual apprehending or destroying the said negro and discovering and punishing his accomplices,

Reward, for killing him.

Be it enacted by the authority aforesaid, and it is hereby enacted, That whosoever shall kill or destroy the said negro slave Billy and apprehend and deliver him to justice in this colony and dominion, he, she or they shall be paid and allowed for the same by the publick one thousand pounds of tobacco: and that all persons whatsoever within this his majestyes colony and dominion that from and after the publication of this act shall witingly and wilingly entertaine, assist, harbour, conceale, truck or trade with the said negroe Billy, and every of them, shall be and by authority of this present act be adjudged guilty of felony and incur the paines, penaltyes and forfeitures lyable by law to be inflicted for felony, any thing in this act or any other act contained to the contrary in any wise notwithstanding. *Provided alwayes,* that if the said negro Billy shall be

Penalty for harboring, concealing or dealing with him.

kiled in pursuance of this act, his master or owner shall be paid by the publick four thousand pounds of tobacco, as is provided by a former act in the like cases. Allowance to his master, if killed.

ACT III.

An act giveing power to the sherifs attending the generall courts to summon jurors and evidences within the City of Williamsburgh, and halfe a mile round the same. Edi. 1733, and 1752.

WHEREAS it is found necessary that the sheriff and his officers which shall attend the generall courts have power beyond the bounds of his county to summon grand jurors and evidences to attend the said courts, Preamble.

Be it therefore enacted by the Governour, Councell and Burgesses of this present generall assembly and the authority thereof, and it is hereby enacted, That the sheriff and his deputyes and baylifs which shall attend the generall court and every of them over and above the power they have in their county be impowered and they and every of them are hereby impowered to summon grand jurors, jurors and evidences in all and every part of the City of Williamsburgh and halfe a mile compass from the same and to make returne thereof to the generall court, which returne so made shall be and be adjudged sufficient for the generall court to ground their judgment upon to fine as the law directs the delinquents in not appearing according to the said summonses. Sheriffs attending generall court empowered to summon jurors and witnesses, in Williamsburg, and half a mile around.

ACT IV.

An act for divideing King and Queen county. Edi. 1733, and 1752.

WHEREAS sundry and divers inconveniencies attend the inhabitants of that part of King and Queen county which lies within Pamunkey neck when they have occasion to prosecute law suits at the   or to go to any other publick meeting by reason of the difficulty in passing Matapiny river, Preamble.

Be it therefore enacted by the Governour, Councell and Burgesses of this present Generall Assembly and the authority thereof, and it is hereby enacted, That from and

King & Queen county divided.

after the 11th day of April which shall be in the year of our Lord God 1702 the said county of King & Queen be divided into two distinct countyes so that Matapiny river divide the same and that that part of the said county which is and lyes on the north side the said Matapiny river and York river remaine and shall for ever thereafter be called and knowne by the name of King and Queen county, and that that part of the said county which is and lyes on the south side of the said river within Pamunkey neck shall be called and knowne by the name of King William county. And for the due administration of justice,

Boundaries.

King William county formed.

Be it further enacted by the authority aforesaid, and it is hereby enacted, That after the time aforesaid a court for the said King William county be constantly held by the justices thereof upon the 20th day of every month in such manner as by the laws of this country is provided and shall be by their commission directed. And whereas the towne land lying at West Point in Pamunkey neck was purchased by the intire county of King and Queen as then it was all the charges about the same being equally levied upon the whole number of tythables of the said county.

Court days.

Be it enacted by the authority aforesaid, and it is hereby enacted, That two thirds of the tobacco ariseing from the sailes of the said towne lands to the severall takers up thereof be repaid to the inhabitants that shall be for the time being on the north side of the said Matapany and York rivers in King and Queen county upon the takeing up of the said towne land.

Proceeds of sale of town land, at West Point, to be equally divided between inhabitants of each county.

ACT V.

Edi. 1733, and 1752.

An act continuing the acts laying impositions on lyquors, servants and slaves untill the 25th of December, 1703.

BE it enacted by the governour, councell and burgesses of this present generall assembly and the authority thereof, and it is hereby enacted, That the 11th act of assembly made at James City the 27th day of Aprill 1699, intituled an act for lesening the levy by the pole and laying an imposition upon liquors for and towards the building the Capitoll and other publick uses as also

Certain former laws continued.

the 12th act of assembly made at James City the said 27th day of Aprill 1699 intituled an act for laying an imposition upon servants and slaves imported into this country towards building the Capitoll be and are hereby continued in full force untill the 25th day of December which shall be in the year of our lord 1703. And whereas for the encouragment of trade it is thought suitable that in case any liquors, servants or slaves chargeable by the said recited acts shall after the publication of this act be imported into this his majestyes colony and dominion, and that the importer of the said liquors slaves, shall within six weeks after such importation desire to transport the same out of this dominion in such case the said importer shall give a particular account of the contents, caske, markes and numbers of the said lyquors as also a particular account of the servants and slaves and subscribe the same to the officer with whom at their importation they were entered, and shall declare upon oath, which oath the said officer is hereby impowered to administer that the duty for the said lyquors, servants and slaves according to the said entry were duly answered and paid according to the said recited acts, and that the said lyquors, servants and slaves shall be directly carryed out of this dominion and not sold, delivered or put on shoar within the same, that then it shall be lawfull for the said officer and he is hereby required and enjoined to allow to the said importer three-fourths of the duty of the said lyquors, servants and slaves by him imported as aforesaid, any law, custome or useage to the contrary in any wise notwithstanding.

Draw back, allowed on exportation, within six weeks.

ACT VI.

An act giveing further directions in building the Capitoll and for building a Public Prison.

Edit. 1733, & 1752.

WHEREAS it is concluded to be more suitable and comodius for the uniforme carrying on and finishing the Capitoll now erecting in the City of Williamsburgh that some alterations be made in the modell of the said Capitoll laid downe and expresed in an act of assembly made at James City the 27th day of Aprill Anno Domini 1699,

☞ See act XLIII. of revisal of 1705, where the former law, (act XIV. of 1699,) is literally recited.

Be it therefore enacted by the governour, councell and burgesses of this present generall assembly and the authority thereof, and it is hereby enacted, That the following directions be observed, vizt.

Further directions, as to building the capitol.

That the porches of the said Capitoll be built circular fifteen foot in breadth from outside to outside, and that they stand upon cedar columns (if to be had) if not the same to be sett upon other good, lasting and substanciall wood; that the cross building betwixt the two main buildings be of the same breadth with the maine buildings that all the great doors be arched, and that it be left to the comitee which now is or hereafter shall be appointed to oversee the building of the capitoll to direct what other doors shall be made therein, that the placeing the four galleryes be left to the commitee that now is or hereafter shall be appointed to oversee the building of the Capitoll, and that they have liberty to take so much room out of the adjacent rooms as in their discretion they shall think fit for the carrying up a suitable pair of staires.

That the windows in the lower story be arched, and that the lower floors be raised two foot from the ground and that the comittee appointed to oversee the building of the said Capitoll have power and they are hereby impowered to send to England for all such materialls as are yet wanting to finish the said worke.

And whereas it is absolutely necessary that a publick prison be built near and convenient to the siting of the generall court for the reception of criminals of both sexes,

Public prison to be built;

its materials & dimensions.

Be it enacted by the authority aforesaid, and it is hereby enacted, That there be forthwith built convenient to the Capitoll and substantiall Brick Prison, thirty foot long in the clear and twenty foot wide in the clear three rooms on the lower floor, vizt. one with the Chambers above for the goalers or prison keepers owne use and for confinement of small offenders, and the other two smaler on the lower floor for goals for the criminals of both sexes, to be underlaid with timbers under ground to the foundations to prevent undermining and that at one end thereof there be walled in with a substantiall wall tenn foot high, twenty foot square of ground for the prisoners to be let into to aire them as occasion shall require for preservation of their life and health till tryall whereby it will be a convenient reception for all criminals upon their commitments and save the charge which necessarily accrews in each county by keeping continuall guards upon them, and that the comitee for overseeing the building the capitoll have power, and they are hereby impowered to send to England for iron barrs, bolts and all such materialls as shall be thought necessary for the same and direct the building thereof both in these and in all other things necessary thereunto.

And whereas the former law for building the capitoll gave power to the comitee to make use only of two thousand pounds sterling, which sume is well nigh expended,

Be it therefore enacted by the authority aforesaid, and it is hereby enacted, That the said comitee as often as they shall have occasion for money for the uses of the capitoll or prison, shall from time to time apply themselves to the governor or commander in chiefe for the time being, to issue out his warrant to the treasurer of this his majestyes colony and dominion, requireing him to pay so much money as they shall have occasion for; any former law to the contrary in any wise notwithstanding.

Signed by FRANCIS NICHOLSON, Esq. *Govr.*
PETER BEVERLEY, *Speaker.*

(Note to editions 1733 *and* 1752.*)*

AT A

Generall Assembly,

Begun at

Francis Nicholson, Esq. Gov.

HIS MAJESTYES ROIAL* COLLEDGE OF WILLIAM AND MARY, ADJOINING TO THE CITY OF WILLIAMSBURG, THE FIFTH DAY OF DECEMBER; IN THE 12TH YEAR OF THE REIGN OF OUR SOVEREIGN LORD WILLIAM III. OF ENGLAND, SCOTLAND, FRANCE, & IRELAND, KING, DEFENDER OF THE FAITH, &c. ANNOQ; DOM. 1700,

And thence continued, by several prorogations, to the thirtieth day of May, 1702: *in the fourteenth year of his majesty's reign; being the third session of this present General Assembly.*

[☞ The acts of this session are omitted in the MS. and only the titles are printed in the editions of 1733, and 1752. The numbering the acts by *Chapters*, was probably first introduced, in the revisal of 1733; it was not the case in the revisal of 1705. See a note prefixed to chap. II. of the next session.]

CHAP. I.

Re-enacted, Ch. 28, 1705.

AN ACT for the continuing, meeting, and sitting of General Assemblies, in case of the death or demise of his Majesty, his heirs and successors.

NOTE.

* The orthography in this place, and in the subsequent acts taken from the revisal of 1733, is according to the usage of that period; but it is very evident, from a view of the MSS. that it is different from that in use, at the date of the acts.

CHAP. II.

AN ACT to prevent Masters of Ships or Vessels running away, after Embargos are laid. Repealed, Ch. 47, 1705.

An ORDINANCE of Assembly for settling the dividing lines between the counties of Isle of Wight, Charles-City, and Nansemond, on the south side the Black Water Swamp.

[See chap. 57, of October 1705, "An act for settling the dividing lines between the counties of Prince George, Surry, Isle of Wight and Nansemond, on the south side Black Water Swamp."—*Note*, That act passed, after Prince George county was formed from Charles City, which was at the session of August 1702, and accounts for the name of Prince George being substituted, in the act of 1705; for Charles City, which occurs, in this Ordinance.]

Signed by Francis Nicholson, Esqr. *Govr.*
Peter Beverley, *Speaker.*

AT A

Generall Assembly,

BEGUN AT

Francis Nicholson, Esqr. Gov.

HER MAJESTYES ROIAL COLLEDGE OF WILLIAM AND MARY, ADJOINING TO THE CITY OF WILLIAMSBURG, THE FIFTH DAY OF DECEMBER; AND IN THE TWELFTH YEAR OF THE REIGN OF HIS LATE MAJESTY, KING WILLIAM III. OF BLESSED MEMORY:

And thence continued, by several prorogations, to the fourteenth day of August; in the first year of the reign of our sovereign Lady Anne, by the grace of God, of England, Scotland, France and Ireland, Queen, Defender of the Faith, &c. Annoq; Dom. 1702; being the fourth session of this present General Assembly.

ACT I.

Edi. 1733, and 1752.

An act for the regulation and settlement of ferryes and for dispatch of public Expresses, and for the speedy transporting of forces over rivers and creeks in time of danger.

Preamble.

WHEREAS a good regulation of ferryes in this her majestyes colony and dominion prove very useful for the dispatch of publick affaires and for the ease and benefitt of travellers and in business,

Be it therefore enacted by the Governour, Councell and burgesses of this present generall assembly and the authority thereof, and it is hereby enacted, That ferryes be constantly kept at the places hereafter named, and that the rates for passing the said feryes, be as followeth, vizt:

On James River.

In Henrico county at Varina, the price for a man six pence, for a man and horse a shilling. In Charles City county at Westopher, the price for a man a shilling, for a man and horse eighteen pence. In Appomatock river at the usuall place near coll. Byrd's store, the price for a man halfe a royall, for a man and horse one royall.

Ferries established; and rates of Ferriage.

On the south side in Charles City county at Cogan's point, the price the same as at Westopher. In Surrey county from Hog Island maine to Archershope, the price for a man two ryals, for a man and horse two shillings six pence.

At the mouth of upper Chipokes creek over to the Row or Martins Brandon, the price for a man six pence for a man and horse one shilling.

From Swans point to Jamestown, the price for a man a royall, for a man and horse two royalls.

From Crouches creek to James towne the price for a man one royall and a halfe, for a man and horse three royalls. In James City county at James town the price to Swans point for a man one royall, for a man and horse two royalls. To Crouches creek for a man one royal and a halfe, for a man and horse three royalls. At Chickahominy at Freemans point at the usual place the price for man six pence, for a man and horse one shilling. In Nanzemond county from Cofeild point to Robert Peals near Sleepy hole, the price for a man six pence, for a man and horse one shiling.

In Elizabeth City county at Hampton towne from the town point to Brooks point, the price for a man three pence, for a man and horse six pence.

In Norfolk county from Norfolke towne to Sawyers point or Lovets plantation, the price for a man six pence for a man and horse one shiling.

Upon York River.

In Newkent county from Robt. Peaslyes to Phill Williams's, the price for a man six pence, for a man and horse one shilling.

From the Brick house to West Point, the price for a man one shiling, for a man and horse eighteen pence.

From the Brick house to Gutteryes the price for a man one shiling, for a In King William county from Spencers over to the usuall landing place, the price for a man for a man and horse one shiling.

From Phill Williamses to Peaslyes point, the price for a man six pence, for a man and horse one shiling.

From West Point to the Brick house, the price for a man one shiling, for a man and horse eighteen pence.

From West Point to Gutteryes, the price for a man six pence, for a man and horse one shilling. In York county from York towne to Tindals point, the price for a man one royall, for a man and horse two ryals. In Glocester county from Tindalls point to York towne, the price for a man one royall, for a man and horse two royalls.

From Baylyes over Piankatank, the price for a man six pence, for a man and horse one shiling. In King and Queen county, from Gutteryes to West Point, the price for a man six pence, for a man and horse one shiling.

From Gutteryes to the Brick house, the price for a man one shiling, for a man and horse two shilings.—From Burfords to old Talbots, the price for a man six pence, for a man and horse one shiling.

In Middlesex county, over Pyankatank at Turks ferry the usuall place, the price for a man six pence, for a man and horse one shiling.

On Rapahanock River.

In Middlesex county from Dudly's plantation to Chewnings point and Martram Wrights plantation, the price for a man fifteen pence, for a man and horse two shilings and six pence.

In Essex county, over Rappahanock to Southings ferry, the price for a man six pence, for a man and horse one shiling. From Bowlers to Willowbys, the price for a man one shilling, for a man and horse two shillings. In Richmond county, from Sowthings over Rappahanock river, the price for a man six pence, for man and horse one From Willowbys to Bowlers, the price for a man one shilling, for a man and horse two shillings.

And from Martrum Wrights to Dudlys, the price for man fifteen pence, for a man and horse two shillings six pence.

And for the more orderly and better keeping thereof,

County courts empowered to license ferry-keepers and prescribe the number of boats & hands.

Be it enacted by the authority aforesaid, and it is hereby enacted, That the court of each county wherein any ferry is appointed by virtue of this act shall have and hereby hath full power and authority of lycencing allowing and appointing the ferry keeper, and of ordering and directing what boat or boats and hands shall be kept there, and also upon neglect or omision in the good and orderly keeping thereof of discharging and turning out that   in the place. *Provided alwayes*, that the said court upon appointing   to keep ferry do take bond with one sufficient surety in the sume of twenty pounds sterling payable to her majesty for the constant and well keeping of the same with boates and hands according to the direction of the said court, and alsoe for the giveing pasages without delay to such publick messengers and expreses as shall be mentioned by this act to be ferry free. And for encouragement of the said ferry keepers in the better keeping of the same, and in consideration of seting over the publick meseages and expresses,

Proviso.

Be it enacted by the authority aforesaid, and it is hereby enacted, That all the men attending on the said ferry boates shall be free of publick and county levyes and from all other publick services as musters, constables, clearing high wayes, being impresed and other things of the like nature, and shall have their lycence without any fee or reward paid for obtaining the same, or for the petition, bond or other matter or thing whatsoever relateing thereto, and also if the said county court shall find it requisite or usefull that an ordinary be kept at such ferry, then and in such case they are hereby authorised and impowered to lycence such ferry keeper to keep ordinary without any fee either for the lycence or for obtaining the same notwithstanding there be otherwise a sufficient number of ordinaryes in the same county, and moreover that in such case no other person be admited to keep ordinary within five miles of such ferry keeper so lycenced to keep ordinary unless it shall so happen that the place of a county court or land laid out for a towne shall require it. *Provided alwayes*, and it is the true intent and meaning of this act that when any ferry keeper shall be so lycenced to keep ordinary, the person so lycenced shall notwithstanding the imunityes aforesaid be lyable to such like bonds, securityes and penaltyes as other ordinary keepers are and shall be lyable unto.

Privileges, and exemptions of ferry-keepers.

Proviso.

And also be it enacted by the authority aforesaid, and it is hereby enacted, That if any other person whatsoever for reward shall set any person or persons over any of the rivers whereon ferryes are appointed by this act except necessity of a parrish require it for going to

Penalty on others for setting persons over a river or creek, where a ferry is established, except to go to church.

church, he or they so offending shall forfeit and pay for every such offence five pounds current money of Virginia, one halfe thereof to be to the nearest ferryman to the place where such offence shall be committed, and the other halfe to the informer, and if the ferry keeper be the informer, then to have the whole to be recovered with costs by action of debt, bill, plaint or information in any court of record in this her majestyes colony and dominion, wherein no essoigne protection or wager of law shall be allowed. And for explanation of what shall be accounted publick meseageses or expresses within the meaning of this act,

Public expresses.

Be it enacted by the authority aforesaid, and it is hereby enacted, That all expresses which shall be directed for her majestyes service, and signed upon the superscription by the governor or commander in chiefe of this her majestyes colony and dominion for the time being, or by the clerke of the councill for the time being, or that shall be directed for her majestyes service to the governor or commander in chiefe.

[☞ Here the Charles City MS. ends.]

☞ The editor has to regret, that, notwithstanding every possible exertion on his part, he has found it impracticable to supply a chasm in the MSS. from this place, to the commencement of the revisal of 1705, of which he has three MS. copies. He will therefore be compelled to print the title from the edition of 1733, and will give such notes selected from former and subsequent laws, as will shew the subject matter of the act itself, the title of which only is given.

From this period, the division of the acts into *sections,* and the numbering of them by *chapters,* will be pursued, according to the arrangement in the printed revisal of 1733, in which it was probably first introduced; for nothing of the kind appears in any of the MSS. or in Purvis, or the MS. revisal of 1705, or in Beverley's abridgment, printed so late as 1728. Until the year 1690, the acts, in the MSS. were generally numbered, and the references were invariably to such an *act* of a session. After that period, they were not even numbered, but the references to the *acts* still continued.]

CHAP. II.

AN ACT for dividing Charles-City county.

[Prince George county was formed, by this division. See Mercer's Abr. tit. "COUNTIES."—Charles City was one of the original counties established in 1634; and for many years, rather than submit to a division, the legislature established two courts, the one on the north, the other on the south side of James river. See vol. 1, pa. 224, 426, 497.]

CHAP. III.

AN ACT prohibiting seamen being harboured or entertained on shore.

Provided for, Ch. 53, 1705, and chap. 17, 1738.

CHAP. IV.

AN ACT for raising a Public Levy.

AN ORDINANCE for the defence of the Country, in Times of Danger.

Signed by FRANCIS NICHOLSON, Esq. *Govr.*
PETER BEVERLEY, *Speaker.*

AT A

Generall Assembly,

SUMMONED TO MEET AT

Francis Nicholson, Esq. Gov.

HER MAJESTY'S ROIAL COLLEGE OF WILLIAM & MARY ADJOINING TO THE CITY OF WILLIAMSBURGH, (a) THE SEVENTEENTH DAY OF MARCH; IN THE SECOND YEAR OF THE REIGN OF OUR SOVEREIGN LADY ANNE, QUEEN OF ENGLAND, SCOTLAND, FRANCE, AND IRELAND, &c.

And by prorogation, begun on the nineteenth day of the said month of March, 1702: *And thence continued by several prorogations, to the twentieth day of April,* 1704; *in the third year of her majesty's reign; and thence, by a prorogation, to meet at her majesty queen Anne's roial Capitol, the day following; being the Second Session of this present General Assembly.*

CHAP. I.

AN ACT to repeal the second act of assembly, made in the year 1664, intituled, An act for the frontiers to be seated with four able hands.

CHAP. II.

Repealed, Ch. 25, 1705.

AN ACT to prevent Indians hunting and ranging upon patented Lands.

(a) N. B. The first session of this Assembly, begun the 19th day of *March*, 1702, and continued to the 10th day of *April*, 1703, during which Time they were emploied in debating upon her Majesty's Letter for contributing Men and Money for *New-York*; which was refused, and no act passed.

CHAP. III.

AN ACT for taring and ascertaining the size of Tobacco Hogsheads. Repealed, Ch. 46, 1705.

CHAP. IV.

AN ACT reviving the Impositions on liquors, servants, and slaves, for one year, and no longer.

CHAP. V.

AN ACT appointing a Treasurer.

CHAP. VI.

AN ACT for removing Criminals from the Goals of the counties where they shall be apprehended, to the Public Goal at Williamsburg. Repealed, Ch. 38, 1705.

CHAP. VII.

AN ACT for allowing a greater number of Ordinaries. Repealed, Ch. 40, 1705.

CHAP. VIII.

AN ACT reviving the act for the better improving the breed of Horses, and for restraining unruly Horses. Part repealed, by Ch. 15, 1705, and the rest provided for by Ch. 8, 1713.

CHAP. IX.

AN ACT for raising a Public Levy.

CHAP. X.

AN ACT for dividing Sittenburn Parish.

CHAP. XI.

AN ACT for dividing St. Peter's Parish, in New-Kent county.

An ORDINANCE of Assembly for defence of the country in Time of Danger.

An ORDINANCE impowering Mr. Henry Cary to make sale of the Country Houses in the City of Williamsburg.

Signed by FRANCIS NICHOLSON, Esqr. *Govr.*
PETER BEVERLEY, *Speaker.*

AT A

Generall Assembly,

SUMMONED TO MEET AT

HER MAJESTY'S ROIAL COLLEGE OF WILLIAM & MARY ADJOINING TO THE CITY OF WILLIAMSBURGH, THE SEVENTEENTH, AND BEGUN THE NINETEENTH OF MARCH 1702; IN THE SECOND YEAR OF THE REIGN OF OUR SOVEREIGN LADY ANNE, BY THE GRACE OF GOD, OF ENGLAND, SCOTLAND, FRANCE, AND IRELAND, QUEEN, DEFENDER OF THE FAITH, &c.

Francis Nicholson, Esq. Gov.

And thence by several prorogations, continued and held at Her Majesty's Roial Capitol, the Eighteenth Day of April, 1705; *in the Fourth Year of Her Majestys Reign; being the Third Session of this Assembly.*

CHAP. I.

AN ACT permitting the exporting and disposing of Tobacco in old Casks. (a)

CHAP. II.

AN ACT for raising a Public Levy.

CHAP. III.

AN ACT impowering the Court of King and Queen county, to purchase land for a Town.

(a) This act had relation to an act passed the last session, *for taring and ascertaining the size of tobacco hogsheads.*

CHAP. IV.

AN ACT for the Naturalization of Claude Philip de Richbourg, Francis Ribot, Peter Faurr, John Joanny, James Champaine, and others.

AN ORDINANCE of assembly for defence of the country in Times of Danger.

Signed by FRANCIS NICHOLSON, Esq. *Govr.*
PETER BEVERLEY, *Speaker.*

AT A

General Assembly,

BEGUN AT

THE CAPITOL, IN THE CITY OF WILLIAMSBURG, THE TWENTY-THIRD DAY OF OCTOBER; IN THE 4TH YEAR OF THE REIGN OF OUR SOVEREIGN LADY ANNE, BY THE GRACE OF GOD, OF ENGLAND, SCOTLAND, FRANCE, AND IRELAND, QUEEN, DEFENDER OF THE FAITH, &c. ANNOQ; DOM. 1705.☞

Edward Nott, esq. gov.

*An act for laying an Imposition upon Liquors and Slaves.**

Edi. 1733, and 1752.

(From MS. Revisal of 1705.)

FORASMUCH as the late Impositions upon liquors and upon servants and slaves imported into this colony and dominion have proved very usefull and advantageous, and that no better expedient can be found to lessen the levy by the poll or to defray the charge of any publick design than impositions of that nature,

Be it therefore enacted by the Governour, Councill and Burgesses of this present generall assembly, and it is

---

☞This was the fifth revisal of our laws, since the settlement of the colony: the first was in September 1632; the second, in March 1642-3; the third in March 1657-8, during the existence of the commonwealth of England; the fourth in March 1661-2, after the revolution; and, for the present revisal, provision was made by an act of April 1699, (see ante pa. 181,) by which very ample powers were given to the committee. This revisal has remained till the present time, in MS. Three copies are in the possession of the editor; two were furnished by Thomas Jefferson, esq. late president of the United States, which are incomplete; and a third by William Nelson, esqr. one of the judges of the general court, which contains every act of that revisal. In the present collection, such of the acts of this session as are printed in the revisal of 1733, will be taken from the printed volume, but where the title only is given in that revisal, the act itself will be printed from MS.

* This act is from a MS. revisal of 1705, furnished the editor by William Nelson, esqr. one of the judges of the General Court.

Duty on spirituous liquors brought from any place except the West Indies.

hereby enacted by the authority of the same, That for every gallon of rum, brandy or other distilled spirits which after the five and twentyeth day of May in the year of our Lord God 1706, shall be imported or brought into this colony and dominion from any port or place whatsoever, except from the islands in the West Indies directly the duty or custome of six pence shall be paid by the owner or importer of the same.

On those bro't from the West Indies.

And be it further enacted, That for every gallon of rum, brandy or other distilled spirits which after the said five and twentieth day of May shall be imported or brought into this colony and dominion from any the islands in the West Indies the duty or custom of four pence shall be paid by the owner or importer of the same.

On wines.

And be it further enacted, That for every gallon of wine of any sort whatsoever which after the said five and twentieth day of May shall be imported or brought into this colony and dominion from any port or place whatsoever, the duty or custom of four pence shall be paid by the owner or importer of the same.

On cyder, beer and ale.

And be it further enacted, That for every gallon of cyder, beer or ale, which after the said five and twentieth day of May shall be imported or brought into this colony and dominion from any port or place whatsoever the duty or custom of one penny shall be paid by the owner or importer of the same.

Proviso, as to spirits, wines, &c. imported directly from England.

Provided nevertheless, and it is hereby enacted and declared, That no duty or custom whatsoever shall be required or paid for any of the liquors before enumerated which shall come directly from England, Wales or the town of Berwick upon Tweed, but that all such liquors shall remain and continue exempt and free from any imposition, duty or custome levyed or raised by this act as if this act had never been made.

Further proviso, in favor of Virginian owners of vessels.

Provided also, and it is hereby further enacted and declared, That no greater duty or custom shall be required or paid for any rum imported directly from the islands in the West Indies in any ship or other vessel wholy and solely belonging to the inhabitants of this country then a duty or custom of two pence per gallon in case the said rum do properly belong to an owner of the said ship or vessell, and such owner shall upon his corporall oath declare that the said rum and every part thereof was imported and came upon his proper account and risque, any thing in this act before contained to the contrary thereof in any wise notwithstanding.

And be it further enacted, That no liquors whatsoever lyable to a duty or custom by virtue of this act shall be landed, put on shoar, or any other way delivered out of the ship or vessell importing the same, before due entry be made thereof with the collector of the dutys upon liquors in the port or place where the same shall be imported or before the duty due and payable for the same by virtue of this act shall be fully sattisfyed and a warrant had under the hand of the said collector for landing or delivery thereof, and that all liquors landed, put on shoar or delivered contrary to the directions and true intent and meaning of this act as aforesaid or the value thereof, shall be forfeited and lost and shall or may be recovered of the importers or owners of the same.

No liquors to be landed, until due entry made.

Forfeiture.

And be it further enacted, That no person or pursons whatsoever, bringing liquors lyable to a duty or custom by virtue of this act into any port or place within this colony and dominion, or having such liquors consigned, shall land or cause the same to be landed or put on shore without making or causing due entry to be made thereof with the collector of the dutys upon liquors in such port or place and giving to him a true account of the gallons every cask did contain upon oath upon pain of forfeiting duble the value of the liquors so landed or put on shore.

Further penalties.

And be it further enacted, That the master or purser of every ship, barque or other vessell importing liquors lyable to a duty or custom by virtue of this act to any port or place within this colony and dominion shall make a true and just entry upon oath with the collector of the dutys upon liquors in the said port or place of the burthen, contents and lading of such ship, barque or other vessell with the particular marks and numbers of every cask therein laden with liquors to the best of his knowledge, and also where and in what port she took in her lading, upon penalty of forfeiting one hundred pounds sterling.

Entry, how to be made.

* The running title to the acts of this session in edi. 1733 & 1752, is, "Anno regni quarto Annæ reginæ."

Wines, how to be entered.

Provided always, and it is hereby enacted and declared, That no person or persons whatsoever shall be required to give an account upon oath of the true contents of any pipe or other cask of wine imported directly from the island where the same was made but that upon every such importation of wine the owners or importers thereof shall have liberty to enter a pipe at one hundred and ten gallons and all lesser cask after the same proportion, any thing in this act contained to the contrary or seeming to the contrary notwithstanding. And for the better encouragement of all persons whatsoever to make due entry and payment of the severall impositions, dutys or customs laid upon liquors by virtue of this act.

Allowance, for leakage.

Be it further enacted, That in consideration of filling and leakeage, every collector of the said impositions, dutys or customs shall be and hereby is authorised and required to abate and allow to such person or persons as shall enter liquors and pay the dutys for the same twenty gallons in every hundred. And if any person or persons whatsoever shall wittingly or willingly make a false entry and be convicted for the same, such person or persons shall forfeit and pay one hundred pounds sterling.

Power of collectors, in making searches, and seizures.

And be it further enacted, That the collectors of the dutys or customs upon liquors and their deputys be authorised and impowered, and they and every of them are hereby authorised and impowered to go and enter on board any ship or other vessell and from thence to bring on shore any liquors lyable to a duty or custom by virtue of this act, if the duty or custom be not paid or compounded for within ten days after the first entry of the said ship or vessell, and likewise to stay and remain on board the said ship or vessell untill all such liquors be discharged and delivered out of the same.

Penalty, for bribery.

And be it further enacted, That if any collector or collectors of the dutys upon liquors or any other person or persons deputed and appointed by or under them or any of them, or any other authority whatsoever, shall directly or indirectly, take or receive any bribe, recompence or reward in any kind whatsoever, or shall connive at any false entry of any liquors lyable to a duty or custom, by virtue of this act, by means whereof the dutys or customs shall be defrauded, the person or persons therein offending, shall forfeit and pay the sum of one hundred pounds sterling and be forever afterwards disabled in his said office and rendered uncapable of holding any office or employment relating to the customs in this colony and dominion and the person or persons giving or paying such bribe, reward or recompence, shall forfeit and pay the sum of one hundred pounds sterling.

Duty on negroes, or other slaves.

And be it further enacted, That the sum of twenty shillings shall be paid for every negro or other slave which after the said five and twentieth day of May shall be imported or brought into this colony and dominion from any port or place whatsoever by the importer or importers of the same.

No negroes, or other slaves to be landed, until due entry made.

And be it further enacted, That no negroes or other slaves which shall be imported into this colony and dominion after the publication of this act shall be landed or put on shore out of any ship or vessell importing the same before due entry be made with the collector of the dutys upon slaves in the port or place where the said negroes or slaves shall be imported or before the master of the said ship or vessell hath made oath of the number of slaves imported in such ship or vessell or before the duty due and payable for the said negroes or slaves shall be fully sattisfyed and paid and a warrant had for the landing of the same under the hand of the said collector, and that all negroes or other slaves which shall be landed or put on shore contrary to this act or the value thereof shall be forfeited and lost and shall be recovered of the importers or proprietors of the same.

Draw-back, on exportation of liquors, or slaves, within six weeks.

Provided always, and it is hereby further enacted, That if the importer of any liquors or slaves for which the dutys and customs according to this act shall be paid shall within six weeks after the importation thereof into this colony and dominion be desirous to export the same or part thereof in such case the said importer shall give a particular account of the contents, cask, marks and numbers of the liquors, and a particular account of the slaves he intends to export to the collectors with whom at their importation they were entered and shall subscribe the same and declare upon oath that the duty or custom for the liquors and slaves he desires to export were at the entry duly answered and paid according to this act, and that the said liquors and slaves shall be directly carried out of this dominion and not sold, delivered or put on shore within the same and then it shall be lawfull for the said collector and he is hereby required and enjoyned to allow to the said importer three-fourths of the duty or custom paid for the said liquors and slaves so to be exported, any thing in this act contained to the contrary in any wise notwithstanding.

Penalty, for false entry of negroes, or other slaves.

And be it further enacted, That if the master of any ship or vessell importing slaves after the publication of this act shall wittingly or willingly make a false entry of any of the slaves so imported and be thereof convicted he shall forfeit and pay for every such offence the sum of one hundred pounds sterling, and if any collector of the dutys upon slaves shall directly or indirectly take or receive any bribe, recompence or reward to connive at any false entry of any negroes or slaves imported as aforesaid, he shall forfeit and pay the sum of one hundred pounds sterling and be forever afterward disabled in his said office and rendered uncapable of holding any office or imployment relating to the customs in this colony and dominion, and the person or persons giving or paying such bribe or reward shall forfeit and pay the sum of one hundred pounds sterling.

And for an encouragement to import mony into this colony and dominion,

Abatement, where duties are paid in money imported.

Be it further enacted, That whatsoever person or persons shall pay any of the impositions, dutys or customs accruing due by virtue of this act in good and lawfull mony of his or their own importation into this colony and dominion to be proved by the oath of the party paying the same such person or persons shall have an abatement and allowance of ten per cent in all dutys so paid and sattisfyed, and every collector of the duties so paid is hereby authorised and required to make allowance accordingly.

Collectors, empowered to administer oaths.

And be it further enacted, That upon any entry payment or draw-back where an oath is directed and injoyned by this act, the collector of the dutys where such entry or payment shall be made or drawback allowed be impowered and required and such collector is hereby impowered and required to administer the oath.

And be it further enacted, That the several impositions, dutys or customs by this act laid upon liquors and slaves be from time to time paid and sattisfyed to our sovereign lady the Queen, her heirs and successors to and for the uses, intents and purposes hereafter mentioned, and to and for no other use, intent or purpose whatsoever.

Duties, how appropriated.

And be it further enacted, That the severall forfeitures and penaltyes which shall or may arise by virtue of this act shall be divided into three equall parts, one third part whereof shall be to our sovereign lady the Queen, her heirs and successors for and towards the better support of this government and the contingent charges thereof, one third part to the governor of this colony and dominion for the time being, to and for his own proper use and behoof, and the other third part to him or them that will informe or sue for the same, to be recovered with costs in any court of record within this colony and dominion, wherein no essoin, protection, or wager of law shall be allowed.

Forfeitures, how apportioned.

And be it further enacted, That the governor or commander in chief of this colony for the time being with the advice of the councill shall be and is hereby impowered from time to time and at all times hereafter to nominate, constitute and appoint such and so many collectors of the dutys laid by this act upon liquors and slaves, as also such sallarys not exceeding six in the hundred for collecting the said dutys, as to him shall seem best.

Governor, with advice of council, to appoint collectors.

And be it further enacted, That all and every sum and sums of money raised or to be raised by virtue of this act shall be constantly accounted for by the collector or collectors thereof to the treasurer of Virginia for the time being upon oath, and by him to the governor, councill and burgesses of the generall assembly upon oath also, and converted to such use or uses as from time to time they shall think fitt to direct for lessening the levy by the pol and defraying any publick charge whatsoever, according to the true intent and meaning of this act, and to and for no other use, intent or purpose whatsoever.

Duties, how accounted for.

And be it further enacted, That this act shall continue in force for two years from the said five and twentieth day of May and no longer.

Limitation of this act.

CHAP. II.

An act for regulating the Elections of Burgesses; for settling their Privileges; and for ascertaining their allowances.

(From edit. 1733.)

The freeholders of every county to elect two burgesses.

I. *BE it enacted and declared, by the governor, council and burgesses of this present generall assembly and it is hereby enacted and declared by the authority of the same,* That the Freeholders of every county that now is, or hereafter shall be in this dominion, now have, and hereafter shall have the privilege and liberty of electing and choosing two of the most fit and able men of such county respectively, to be present, and to act and vote in all General Assemblies, which, from time to time, and at any time hereafter, shall be held within this dominion; and also, that the freeholders of *James* City shall have the liberty of electing and choosing one Burgess, to be present, act, and vote in the General Assembly, as aforesaid.

James City, one burgess.

Method of issuing and executing the writs for elections.

II. And for the more regular and legal electing of the said Burgesses in all time coming, *Be it enacted, by the authority aforesaid,* That the following rules and methods shall be observed, (to wit,) That the writs for electing the said Burgesses shall be signed by the Governor, or Commander in Chief of this dominion for the time being, with the seal of the Colony affixed to them, and shall be delivered to the Secretary, at least forty days before the day appointed for the General Assembly to begin, to be by him transmitted to the sheriffs of the respective counties: That the Secretary shall cause the said writs to be safely conveyed and delivered to the several sheriffs of each respective county, within ten days after the date of such writs: That every sheriff in three days after he receives any such writ, shall cause one copy thereof to be delivered to every minister and reader of the several parishes in his county; upon every one of which said copies, shall be indorsed by the sheriff, the time and place by him appointed for the election of Burgesses, which shall always be made at the place where the county court is accustomed to be held, at least twenty days after the sheriff shall have received the writ: That after the receipt of such copy and indorsement, the minister or reader as aforesaid, shall publish the same after Divine

Service, in the Church or Chapel where they, or either of them officiate, upon every *Sunday* that shall be between the receipt of such copy, and the day appointed for the Election of Burgesses; and after such publication, the minister or reader shall return the said copy to the sheriff, with a certificate of the publication thereof, and of the time and place of the election. And if at any time hereafter, the secretary of this dominion for the time being, shall fail to cause the writs for electing of Burgesses, to be safely conveyed and delivered to the several sheriffs as aforesaid, he shall forfeit and pay the sum of forty pounds current money; one moiety thereof to our sovereign Lady the Queen, her heirs and successors, for and towards the better support of the government of this her majesty's dominion, and the contingent charges thereof; and the other moiety thereof to such person or persons as will inform and sue for the same: To be recovered, with costs, in any court of record within this dominion, by information, bill, plaint, or action of debt, wherein no essoin, protection, or wager of law, privilege, or any more than one imparlance shall be allowed. And if at any time hereafter, the sheriff of any county within this dominion, shall fail to cause to be delivered one fair copy of any writ for election of Burgesses, with an indorsement thereupon as aforesaid, unto every minister and reader as aforesaid, within his county respectively, in such time as is before directed, such sheriff shall forfeit and pay the sum of two thousand pounds of tobacco; one moiety thereof to our sovereign lady the Queen, her heirs and successors, for and towards the better support of the government of this her majesty's dominion, and the contingent charges thereof; and the other moiety thereof to such person or persons as will inform and sue for the same: To be recovered, with costs, in any court of record within this dominion, by information, bill, plaint, or action of debt, wherein no essoin, protection, or wager of law, privilege, or any more than one imparlance shall be allowed. And if any minister or reader, who shall hereafter receive from the sheriff of his county, the copy of a writ for election of burgesses in the said county, shall, after the receipt thereof, fail to make publication and return, according to the directions of this act, such minister or

Penalties on failure.

reader shall forfeit and pay the sum of one thousand pounds of tobacco; one moiety thereof to our sovereign lady the Queen, her heirs and successors, for and towards the better support of the government of this her majesty's dominion, and the contingent charges thereof; and the other moiety thereof to such person or persons as will inform and sue for the same: To be recovered, with costs, in any court of record within this dominion, by information, bill, plaint, or action of debt, wherein no essoin, protection, or wager of law, privilege, or any more than one imparlance shall be allowed.

Every resident freeholder to appear & vote at the election.

III. *And be it further enacted,* That after publication of writs, and time and place for election of burgesses as aforesaid, every freeholder, actually resident within the county where the election is to be made, respectively shall appear accordingly, and give his vote at such election, upon penalty of forfeiting two hundred pounds of tobacco to such person or persons as will inform and sue for the same: To be recovered, with costs, in any court of record within this dominion, by information, bill, plaint or action of debt, wherein no essoin, protection, or wager of law, privilege, or any more than one imparlance shall be allowed.

Penalty 200 lb. tobacco.

Proviso, persons disabled to vote.

IV. *Provided always,* That no freeholder being a feme-sole, or feme-covert, infant, under age, or recusant convict, shall be obliged to appear, and give his or her vote in any of the said elections; neither, if they do appear, shall they have liberty to vote, but shall be excluded therefrom, as though they were not freeholders. And if any person shall presume to give his vote for election of any burgess or burgesses, not being a freeholder in the county or town respectively where he shall give his vote, such person shall forfeit and pay five hundred pounds of tobacco; one moiety thereof to our sovereign lady the Queen, her heirs and successors, for and towards the better support of the government of this her majesty's dominion, and the contingent charges thereof; and the other moiety thereof to such person or persons as will inform and sue for the same: To be recovered, with costs, in any court of record within this dominion, by information, bill, plaint, or action of debt, wherein no essoin, protection, or wager of law, privilege, or any more than one imparlance shall be al-

Any person not being a freeholder, presuming to vote, forfeits 500 lbs tobacco.

lowed. And if, upon any suit brought, the question shall arise, whether any person be a freeholder, or not? In such case, the *Onus Probandi* shall lie upon the defendant. And if the election of any burgess or burgesses cannot be determined, upon the view, by consent of the freeholders, the sheriff, or, in his absence, the under-sheriff shall proceed to take the poll in manner following; *to wit,* he shall appoint such and so many person or persons, as to him shall seem fit, to take in writing, the name of every freeholder who gives his vote, and the person or persons he votes for; which person or persons so appointed, shall first take an oath for his true and impartial taking the poll; which oath the sheriff, or, in his absence, the under-sheriff, is hereby impowered and required to administer; and then (the sheriff, or under-sheriff, as aforesaid, having provided one or more book or books for that purpose, as occasion shall require) in the court-house of the county, in presence of the several candidates nominated, if they will be present, or such other persons, as (if they think fit) they may appoint to see the poll fairly taken, the person or persons so appointed and sworn as aforesaid, shall take the poll as followeth; *to wit,* first he or they shall write down the names of all the candidates, every one in a several page of the book, or in a particular column; and then the name of every freeholder coming to give his vote, shall be fairly written in the several pages or columns respectively, under the name or names of such person or persons as he shall vote for: Provided, that no freeholder, who, at such election, shall have given his vote for two persons, shall be permitted to vote or poll for any more. And when every freeholder present, shall have given his vote in manner as aforesaid, (or upon proclamation three times made at the court-house door, if no more freeholders will give their votes) the sheriff, or under-sheriff as aforesaid, shall conclude the poll; and afterwards, upon examination thereof whatsoever person or persons of the candidates shall appear to have the most votes, the sheriff, or under-sheriff as aforesaid, shall return him or them burgess or burgesses; and if two or more candidates shall have an equal number of votes, the sheriff, or under-sheriff as aforesaid, being a freeholder, shall and may return which of them he thinks fit: And every free-

Method of taking the poll.

And returning the burgesses. See ch. 2, 1736.

Freeholders, if required, shall be sworn.

holder, before he is admitted to a poll at any election, if it be required by the candidates, or any of them, or any other freeholder in their behalf, shall take the following oath; which oath the sheriff, or under-sheriff as aforesaid, is hereby impowered and required to administer; *to wit,*

The oath.

YOU shall swear, that you are a freeholder of the county of   and that you have not been before polled at this election.

Punishment of perjury, or subornation; See ch. 2, 1736, Sect. 7.

And in case any freeholder, or other person, taking the said oath, shall thereby commit wilful and corrupt perjury, and be thereof convicted; or if any person do unlawfully and corruptly procure or suborn any freeholder, or other person, to take the said oath, in order to be polled, whereby he shall commit such wilful and corrupt perjury, and shall be thereof convicted, he or they, for every such offence, shall forfeit and pay the sum of ten pounds current money; one moiety thereof to our sovereign lady the Queen, her heirs and successors, for and towards the better support of the government of this her majesty's dominion, and the contingent charges thereof; and the other moiety thereof to him or them that will inform or sue for the same: To be recovered, with costs, in any court of record within this dominion, by action of debt, bill, plaint, or information, in which no essoin, protection, or wager of law, shall be allowed.

V. And for prevention of disputes which may hereafter arise in elections of burgesses, who shall be accounted and pass for freeholders,

Who shall be accounted freeholders; See as before, sect. 2, 4, 5, 6.

VI. *Be it enacted, by the authority aforesaid, and it is hereby enacted and declared,* That every person who hath an estate real for his own life, or the life of another, or any estate of any greater dignity, shall be accounted a freeholder, within the meaning of this act.

Form of the returns.

VII. And after the election shall be made, in manner as herein is before directed, the sheriff, or under-sheriff as aforesaid, shall make return thereof in manner following; *to wit,* upon the writ shall be indorsed thus;

The execution of this writ appears in a certain schedule hereto annexed.

And in the Schedule to the writ annexed, the execution thereof shall be certified as followeth, *mutatis mutandis*, viz.

BY virtue of this writ to me directed, in my full county, held at the court-house for my said county, upon the day of in the year of the reign of by the grace of God, of England, Scotland, France, and Ireland, Queen, defender of the faith, &c. by the assent of my said county, I have caused to be chosen (two Burgesses) of my said county, to wit, A. B. and C. D. to act and do, as in the said writ is directed and required. For a county.

And for the College of William and Mary, or for any town, the form of the return shall be thus; For William & Mary College, or, a town.

BY virtue of this writ to me directed, I did make lawful publication thereof; and afterwards, to wit, upon the day of in the year of the reign of by the grace of God, of England, Scotland, France, and Ireland, Queen, defender of the faith, (at the said town of) or (at the said College) by the assent of the (freeholders) or (President and Masters, or Professors) thereof, I have caused to be chosen one Burgess for the said (town) or (College) to wit, A. B. of to act and do, as in the said writ is directed and required.

And if at any time, any candidate, or other person, in his behalf, shall desire a copy of the poll, the sheriff, or under-sheriff, who manages the election, as soon as may be, shall cause a fair copy thereof to be made, and shall deliver it, attested with his own hand, unto such candidate, or other person, as shall require the same as aforesaid. Sheriff shall deliver a copy of the poll, upon request.

VIII. And if, upon the death or incapacity of any member or members of the house of burgesses, the sheriff of any county shall receive a writ for the election of one or more burgess or burgesses, during the session of the general assembly; in such case, he is hereby required to appoint such and so many persons as to him shall seem fit, to give notice thereof, and of the time and place of election, unto every particular And shall execute new writs in the room of Burgesses dead or disabled.

freeholder residing within the county or town for which such election is to be made; which election shall be made as soon as possible, in manner as is herein before directed, and the person or persons so elected, shall be returned in form aforesaid. And if the sheriff of any county, or in his absence, the under-sheriff, (being thereunto required, before the return be made, by any candidate or freeholder) shall refuse to take the poll, or shall take it in other manner than is herein directed, or shall refuse to give a copy of the poll as aforesaid, or shall make any false return, or insufficient return, or shall fail to make any return, or shall make any return in any other form than is herein before directed, every such sheriff or under-sheriff as aforesaid, offending herein or in any of these cases respectively, shall forfeit and pay the sum of forty pounds sterling; one moiety thereof to our sovereign lady the Queen, her heirs and successors, for and towards the better support of the government of this her majesty's dominion, and the contingent charges thereof; and the other moiety thereof to him or them that will inform or sue for the same: To be recovered, with costs, in any court of record within this dominion, by action of debt, bill, plaint, or information, in which no essoin, protection, or wager of law, shall be allowed.

Penalty on sheriffs & under-sheriffs refusal or neglect.

Returns shall be to the secretary's office.

IX. *And be it further enacted,* That the sheriff of every county shall return every writ to him directed for the election of one or more burgess or burgesses, and shall cause the same to be safely delivered to the clerk of the secretary's office for the time being, or to such other person as shall attend in the said office, to receive the same, at least the day before the day mentioned in any such writ for the return thereof: And if any sheriff shall neglect or fail performing his duty herein, he shall forfeit and pay the sum of two thousand pounds of tobacco; one moiety thereof to our sovereign lady the Queen, her heirs and successors, for and towards the better support of the government of this her majesty's dominion, and the contingent charges thereof; and the other moiety thereof to him or them that will inform or sue for the same: To be recovered, with costs, in any court of record within this dominion, by action of debt, bill, plaint, or information, in which no essoin, protection, or wager of law, shall be allowed.

Penalty.

No candidate shall give or promise, &c. any money, treat, present, preferment, &c. to any freeholder, county or corporation.

X. *And be it further enacted by the authority aforesaid,* That no person or persons hereafter to be elected to serve in the General Assembly for any county, town, or corporation, within this dominion, after the test, or issuing out or ordering of the writ or writs of election, upon the calling, or summoning of any General Assembly hereafter, or after any place becomes vacant hereafter, in the time of this present, or any succeeding General Assembly, shall or do by himself or themselves, or by any other ways or means, on his or their behalf, or at his or their charge, before his or their election, to serve in the General Assembly for any county, town, or corporation, within this dominion, directly or indirectly, give, present, or allow to any person or persons having voice or vote in such election, any money, meat, drink, entertainment, or provision; or make any present, gift, reward, or entertainment; or shall at any time hereafter make any promise, agreement, obligation or engagement, to give or allow any money, meat, drink, provision, present, reward, or entertainment, to or for any such person or persons in particular, or to any such county, town, or corporation in general, or to or for the use, advantage, benefit, emploiment, profit, or preferment of any such person or persons, county, town, or corporation, in order to be elected, or for being elected to serve in the General Assembly for any such county, town, or corporation.

Persons making or promising presents, &c. disabled to sit in the house of burgesses.

XI. *And be it further enacted and declared,* That every person or persons so giving, presenting or allowing, making, promising or engaging, doing, acting or proceeding, shall be, and are hereby declared and enacted to be disabled and incapacitated, upon such election, to serve in the General Assembly for such county, town, or corporation; and that such person or persons shall be deemed and taken, and are hereby declared and enacted to be deemed and taken no members of the General Assembly, and shall not act, sit, or have any vote or place in the General Assembly; but shall be, and are hereby declared and enacted to be, to all intents, constructions, and purposes, incapacitated, as if they had never been returned or elected members for the General Assembly.

XII. *And be it further enacted and declared,* That no person under the age of one and twenty years, shall be ca-

Election of infants, or persons not freeholders, void. See ch. 10, 1730.

pable of being elected to serve in the General Assembly; neither shall any person be capable to be a burgess for any county, unless, at the time of such election, he shall be a freeholder in the same county; but every such election shall be, and is hereby declared to be, illegal and void.

Privilege of the members of the General Assembly.

XIII. *And be it further enacted and declared,* That all and every member and members of the General Assembly are, and ought to be, and for ever hereafter shall be, in their persons, servants, and estates, both real and personal, free, exempted, and privileged, from all arrests, attachments, executions, and all other process whatsoever, (save only for treason, felony, or breach of the peace,) during his or their attendance upon the General Assembly, by the space of ten days before the beginning, and ten days after the conclusion of every session of assembly: And if any process shall be depending against any such member or members before his or their election, such process shall be staied, and shall not be proceeded upon against such member or members, by the space of ten days before and after every session as aforesaid, and shall then be again revived, and may be prosecuted, as otherwise it might have been, without any discontinuance or abatement thereof, by reason of such being staied as aforesaid. And if at any time hereafter, the General Assembly shall be prorogued or adjourned for any longer time than twenty days; in such case it shall be lawful to commence any process against any member or members of the General Assembly: Provided always, that such process be staied as aforesaid, by the space of ten days before and after every session or meeting, by prorogation or adjournment as aforesaid.

Burgesses allowances; see ch. 7, 1730.

XIV. *And be it further enacted by the authority aforesaid,* That the allowances for burgesses attending at the General Assembly, shall be as followeth; that is to say, for every burgess coming by land, shall be allowed and paid by the county for which he serves, one hundred and thirty pounds of tobacco and cask, a day, besides the necessary charge of ferriage. And for every burgess which cannot come to the General Assembly, otherwise than by water, there shall be allowed and paid as aforesaid, one hundred and twenty pounds of tobacco and cask, a day. And over and above the said daily allowances, there shall be paid and allowed, for going and returning to and from the General Assembly, as followeth; *to wit*, To every burgess for the counties of *James-City, York, Warwick, Elizabeth-City, New-Kent, Gloucester, Charles-City, Surry*, and *Isle of Wight*, the allowance of one day for coming, and one day for returning. And to every burgess for the counties of *Henrico, Nansemond, Norfolk, Princess-Anne, King-William, Prince-George, King and Queen, Middlesex*, and *Essex*, the allowance of two days for coming, and two days for returning. And to every burgess for the counties of *Lancaster* and *Richmond*, the allowance of three days for coming, and three days for returning. And to every burgess for the counties of *Stafford, Northumberland, Westmoreland, Northampton*, and *Accomack*, the allowance of four days for coming, and four days for returning. And where the burgesses come by water, the sheriff is hereby required and impowered, by impressing, or otherwise, to provide a boat and two men, to carry the burgesses of his county respectively, to and from the General Assembly; for which boat, men, and their necessary provision, shall be allowed and paid as aforesaid, thirty-six pounds of tobacco for every day, during the time they are performing that service. But forasmuch as the burgesses for the counties of *Accomack* and *Northampton* cannot come in a boat to attend the General Assembly, therefore the sheriff of each of those two counties is hereby required and impowered, by impressing, or otherwise, to provide a sloop and men, to carry the burgesses of his county respectively, to and from the General Assembly; for which sloop, men, and their necessary provisions, shall be allowed and paid as aforesaid, sixty pounds of tobacco for every day, during the time they are performing that service.

This part repealed and altered by Ch. 14, 1736, sect. 2.

Propositions & grievances.

XV. *And be it further enacted, by the authority aforesaid*, That at the time and place of election of burgesses for any county within this dominion, the sheriff, or in his absence, the under-sheriff of such county respectively, at the door of the court-house, by proclamation to be there three times made, between the hours of one and three of the clock in the afternoon, shall give public notice of the time appointed for a court to be held, for receiving and certifying to the next session of the

And public claims.

General Assembly the propositions and grievances, and the public claims of all and every person and persons within his county; which propositions and grievances shall be signed by the person or persons presenting the same to the court; and thereupon the chief magistrate then present, or the clerk, by the direction of the court, shall certify the same to the General Assembly, and shall deliver the same to the burgesses for the county, to be by them presented accordingly. And in like manner, a court for receiving and certifying propositions and grievances, and public Claims as aforesaid, shall be appointed and held in each county respectively, before every session of the General Assembly: And the sheriff of the county is hereby required to cause public notice to be given of the time appointed for the holding such court at every respective church and chapel within his county.

To be certified to the Assembly. See ch. 8, 1705.

Notice.

Repealing clause.

XVI. *And be it further enacted,* That all and every other act and acts, and every clause and article thereof heretofore made, for so much thereof as relates to regulating the elections of burgesses, or settling their privileges, or ascertaining their allowances, is, and are hereby repealed, and made void, to all intents and purposes, as if the same had never been made.

CHAP. III.

An act prescribing the method of appointing sheriffs; and for limiting the time of their continuance in office, and directing their duty therein.

Sheriffs, when and how to be recommended & commissioned.

I. FOR the more regular nomination and appointment of sheriffs, *Be it enacted by the Governor, Council and Burgesses of this present general assembly, and it is hereby enacted, by the authority of the same,* That the court of every county within this dominion, at some convenient time between the last day of January, and the last day of March, yearly, shall present to the governor, or commander in chief of this dominion for the time being, a list or recommendation of three such persons (being justices) in the same county court respectively, as they shall think most fit and able to execute the office of sheriff for their respective counties, for the year then next ensuing; of which three persons so recommended, the said governor, or commander in chief shall accordingly commissionate such one as to him shall seem meet, for the executing the said office for the year then next coming.

II. *Provided always,* That it shall and may be lawful for the governor, or commander in chief of this dominion, for the time being, to continue any person, as to him shall seem fit, in the office of sheriff of any county, by the space of two years, next immediately succeeding each other; any thing herein contained to the contrary, notwithstanding.

How long continued in office.

III. *And be it further enacted, by the authority aforesaid,* That no person shall at any time hereafter be capable to execute or enjoy the office of sheriff of any county within this dominion, unless such person, at the time of his entring into and upon the said office, shall be a justice of the peace in the same county respectively; neither shall it be lawful for any person to execute or enjoy the said office for any longer than two years next succeeding each other.

None but justices to be sheriffs; and not more than two years.

IV. *And be it further enacted, by the authority aforesaid,* That when any person shall have obtained a commission for the office of sheriff of any county, before he shall be admitted to take the oath of a sheriff, or shall enter upon the execution of his said office, he shall, at the court of his county, enter into bond to our sovereign lady the Queen, her heirs and successors, with two good and sufficient sureties at the least, in the sum of one thousand pounds sterling, for his true and faithful performance of his office: Which bond the said county court is hereby impowered and required to take, and cause to be acknowledged before them in open court, and recorded in the records of their county.

Sheriff to give bond and security.

V. *And be it further enacted, by the authority aforesaid,* That every sheriff by himself, or his lawful officers, or deputies, shall execute all such writs and precepts, as from time to time shall be directed, according to the demand thereof; and also shall make due return thereof, in manner following; that is to say, all writs returnable in any county court, shall be executed, and returns thereof made, at the least two days, excluding Sunday, before the day therein mentioned for the return: And all writs returnable in the General court, shall be executed as is directed in the act for es-

Sheriff, by himself or deputy, to execute, and return process.

Return days.

tablishing the general court, and return thereof shall be made, at the least three days, excluding Sunday, before the day therein mentioned for the return. And every sheriff failing to make sufficient return of all writs and precepts to him directed as aforesaid, and according to the several times herein before limited, shall, for every such offence, forfeit and pay the sum of one thousand pounds of tobacco; one moiety thereof to our sovereign lady the Queen, her heirs and successors, for and towards the support of the government of this her majesty's colony and dominion, and the contingent charges thereof; and the other moiety to the party grieved: To be recovered by action of debt, bill, plaint or information, in any court of record within this dominion, in which no essoin, protection, or wager of law shall be allowed. And moreover, such sheriff so failing as aforesaid, shall be liable to an action at the common law, at the suit of the party grieved, for any damage which shall be sustained by such failure. And if any sheriff, by himself, officer or deputy, having executed any writ or precept to him directed, shall, by himself, officer, or deputy, make a false return thereof, every such sheriff so offending, shall forfeit and pay the sum of three thousand pounds of tobacco: To be recovered and divided as aforesaid; and also shall be liable to an action at the common law, at the suit of the party grieved, for any damage which shall be sustained by such false return.

Penalty for failure.

How appropriated.

Penalty for false return.

Process executed on Sunday, or at musters, or elections void.

VI. *Provided always*, That it shall not be lawful for any sheriff, or his officer, or deputy, to execute any writ or precept upon the Lord's Day, commonly called Sunday, nor upon any person attending or doing his duty at any muster of the militia, or at any election of burgesses: And the execution of any writ or precept, contrary to the true meaning hereof, is hereby declared to be null and void; any thing herein contained, or any law, custom, or usage to the contrary, notwithstanding.

But, for treason, felony, breaches of the peace, or escapes, may be executed at any time.

VII. *Provided nevertheless*, That it shall and may be lawful for the sheriff, his officer, and deputy, at any time and place whatsoever, to arrest and apprehend any person for treason, or felony, or suspicion of felony, or being accessory thereto; or for any riot, or breach of the peace; or upon any escape out of prison;

any thing herein contained to the contrary thereof, notwithstanding.

VIII. *And be it further enacted, by the authority aforesaid,* That no sheriff, or any of his officers, or deputies, shall take, or cause to be taken, or made, any obligation, for any cause whatsoever, by colour of their office, but only to themselves, of any person, nor by any person, which shall be in their ward, by the course of the law, but by the name of their office, and upon condition written, that the prisoner or prisoners shall appear at the day contained in the writ, bill, or warrant, and in such places as the said writs, bills, or warrants shall require. And if any sheriff, or other officer, take an obligation in other form, by colour of their offices, it shall be void. Obligations, how to be taken by sheriffs.

IX. *Provided always,* That it shall and may be lawful to and for any sheriff, or other officer, to take such other obligation of any person or persons in their ward, as is, or shall be particularly and expressly directed by any other act, upon any special case therein mentioned; any thing herein contained to the contrary, notwithstanding. Proviso.

X. *And be it further enacted,* That if any writ or precept in any civil action, shall be delivered to any sheriff, or other officer, to attach the body of any person which is not to be found within the county where such sheriff, or other officer resides; in such case, return of the same writ or precept, within the time herein before limited, shall be made, according to the truth of the case: And if the person, against whom such writ or precept issued, shall not appear, being thereto lawfully called by proclamation in open court, at the return thereof, an attachment shall be awarded against his estate, returnable to the next court; at which time, if the defendant shall fail to appear, the estate so attached, or so much thereof, as shall be sufficient to pay what shall appear to be due to the plaintiff, with the costs of suit, shall, by rule of court, be ordered to be appraised and delivered to the plaintiff for his satisfaction therein: But if, at the return of the attachment as aforesaid, the defendant shall appear, then the attachment shall cease and become void, and the trial shall proceed, as in other like cases, if the defendant had appeared at the return of the first writ or precept. Returns to be according to the truth of the case. Attachment, for nonappearance.

Non est inventus, when to be returned.

XI. *Provided always,* That no sheriff, or other officer shall make return upon any writ or precept, that the person against whom the same issued, is not to be found, until he shall actually have been at the dwelling-house, or place of residence of such person, and not finding him, shall have there left an attested copy of the same writ or precept.

Writ against a non-resident of the county to abate by return.

XII. *Provided also,* That if any writ or precept shall be delivered to any sheriff, or other officer, to attach the body of any person being a known inhabitant of another county, and not of the county where the said sheriff, or officer resides; in such case, the sheriff, or officer shall make return, according to the truth of the case; and not that the person is not to be found in his county, and thereupon the process shall abate and be dismissed.

Repealing clause.

XIII. *And be it further enacted,* That all and every other act and acts, and every clause and article thereof heretofore made, for so much thereof as relates to prescribing the method of appointing sheriffs, or limiting the time of their continuance in office, or directing them in the execution thereof, in or concerning any matters or things within the purview of this act, is, and are hereby repealed and made void, to all intents and purposes, as if the same had never been made.

CHAP. IV.

Edi. 1733, and 1752.

An act declaring who shall not bear office in this country.

Persons convicted of treason, murder, felony, blasphemy, perjury, forgery, or other crime punishable with loss of life and member, declared incapable of holding any office.

BE it enacted by the governor, council and burgesses, of this present general assembly, and it is hereby enacted by the authority of the same, That no person whatsoever, already convicted, or which hereafter shall be convicted in her majestys kingdom of England in this or in any other her majestys dominion, colonies, islands, territorys or plantations, or in any other kingdom, dominion or place, belonging to any foreign prince or state whatsoever, of treason, murther, fellony, blasphemy, perjury, forgery or any other crime whatsoever, punishable by the laws of England, this country, or other place wherein he was convicted with the loss of life or member, nor any negro, mulatto or Indian, shall, from and after the publication of this act, bear any office, ecclesiasticall, civill or military, or be in any place of public trust or power, within this her majestys colony and dominion of Virginia, and that if any person convicted as aforesaid, or negro, mulatto or Indian shall presume to take upon him, act in, or exercise any office, ecclesiasticall, civill or military, or any place of publick trust or power, within this colony and dominion, notwithstanding he be thereunto in any manner whatsoever comissionated, appointed, chosen or impowered, and have a pardon for his crime, he shall for such his offence, forfeit and pay five hundred pounds current money, and twenty pounds of like money for every month he continues to act in or exercise such office or place after a recovery made of the said five hundred pounds, one moiety thereof to our sovereign lady the queen, her heirs and successors for and towards the better support of this government and the contingent charges thereof, and the other moiety to him or them that will inform or sue for the same, in any court of record within this her majestys colony and dominion, by action of debt, bill, plaint or information, wherein no essoin, protection, or wager of law, shall be allowed.

Penalty, on such, or on any negro, mulatto, or Indian, for exercising an office.

How recovered, and appropriated.

Provided nevertheless, and it is hereby meant and intended, That nothing in this act contained, shall extend to disable any person who before the making of this act hath been convicted as aforesaid in this her majestys colony and dominion, and hath obtained the king's or queen's pardon, from taking and bearing any office, ecclesiasticall, civill or military, or from accepting and exercising any place of public trust or power, whereunto he hath been heretofore, or shall be hereafter comissionated, appointed, chosen or impowered, but that it shall be lawfull for every such person to take and bear any such office, and accept and exercise any such place without being lyable to any fine or penalty for the same, as if this act had never been made.

Not to extend to persons, heretofore convicted, and pardoned.

And be it further enacted, by the authority aforesaid, and it is hereby enacted, That no person whatsoever, shall, from and after the publication of this act, bear any office, civill or military, or be in any place of publick trust or power, within this her majestys colony and

No person to bear office, until after a residence of three years in this country.

dominion of Virginia, untill he hath been a personal resident in the same the full term of three years, and that if any person whatsoever do presume contrary to this act to take upon him, act in, or exercise any office, civill or military, or any place of trust or power within this colony and dominion, notwithstanding he be thereunto in any manner whatsoever comisionated, appointed or chosen before he hath personally resided therein three years as aforesaid, he shall for such his offence, forfeit and pay five hundred pounds current money, and twenty pounds of like money for every month he continues to act in, or exercise such office or place after a recovery made of the said five hundred pounds, untill he hath been three years in this country according to the tenor of this act, to be recovered and divided as aforesaid.

Penalty.

How recovered and appropriated.

Provided always, and it is the true intent and meaning of this act, That all natives of this her majestys colony and dominion, and such persons as have comissions from her majesty, her heirs or successors, be excepted, and that it be lawfull for every such native and person to bear any office, civill or military, or to be in any place of trust or power before hath resided three years according to the directions of this act, without being lyable to any fine or penalty for it, any thing in this act before contained, to the contrary notwithstanding.

Not to extend to natives, or those having commissions from the crown.

And for clearing all manner of doubts which hereafter may happen to arise upon the construction of this act, or any other act, who shall be accounted a mulatto,

Be it enacted and declared, and it is hereby enacted and declared, That the child of an Indian and the child, grand child, or great grand child, of a negro shall be deemed, accounted, held and taken to be a mulatto.

Who shall be deemed mulattoes.

And be it further enacted, That all and every other act and acts, and every clause and article heretofore made for so much thereof as relates to declaring who shall not bear office in this country, is, and are hereby repealed and made void, to all intents and purposes as if the same had never been made.

Repealing clause.

CHAP. V.

An act against importing Tobacco from Carolina, and other parts without the Capes of Virginia.

I. FOR prevention of such inconveniencies and disadvantages as reasonably may be expected in a short time to fall upon the inhabitants of this colony and dominion, in the sale or shipping of their tobacco, in case like provision be not now made, as hath been heretofore, against importing or bringing tobacco hither from parts without the Capes, (Preamble.)

II. *Be it enacted, by the Governor, Council and Burgesses of this present General Assembly, and it is hereby enacted, by the authority of the same,* That such importation from henceforth be, and by virtue of this act remain, prohibited and forbidden; and that if any tobacco hereafter, in any-wise whatsoever, shall be imported or brought from Carolina, or other parts without the Capes, into this colony and dominion, in order to be here laid on shore, sold, or shipped, the same shall be thereby forfeited and lost; one moiety to our sovereign lady the Queen, her heirs and successors, for and towards the better support of this government, and the contingent charges thereof; and the other moiety to him, her, or them, that shall inform or sue for the same in any court of record within this her majesty's colony and dominion, by action of debt, bill, plaint, or information, wherein no essoin, protection, or wager of law, shall be allowed. (Tobacco imported from Carolina, or other parts without the Capes, forfeited.) (Penalties, how appropriated.)

III. *Provided always,* That nothing aforesaid shall be construed to hinder the inhabitants of this colony and dominion, merchants, or others, to bring their tobacco round the Capes, for the purposes aforesaid, if it be of the growth of this colony, but that such importation shall be lawful, and shall be so accounted, deemed, and taken; any thing in this act before contained to the contrary, notwithstanding. (Not to extend to inhabitants, bringing tobacco of the growth of the colony.)

IV. *Provided nevertheless, and it is enacted, by the authority aforesaid,* That no such tobacco shall be laden or put on board any boat, sloop, or other vessel, in order to be brought round the Capes as aforesaid, before the owner thereof (by his own oath at least) make it appear to the collector of the two shillings per hogs- (But such tobacco, not to be brought without a certificate of the collector, &c.)

head for the district where such tobacco is to be taken in, that the said tobacco is all of the growth of this colony, and obtain his certificate or permit concerning the same: And that if any tobacco, though of the growth of this colony, be brought round the Capes without such certificate or permit, the said tobacco shall be thereby forfeited and lost, and shall also be divided, as other tobacco imported or brought into this colony, from parts without the Capes; any thing in the aforesaid proviso of this act to the contrary, notwithstanding.

Repealing clause.

V. *And be it further enacted, by the authority aforesaid*, That all and every other act and acts, and every clause and article thereof heretofore made, for so much thereof as relates to importing Tobacco from Carolina, and other parts without the Capes of Virginia, is, and are hereby repealed and made void, to all intents and purposes, as if the same had never been made.

CHAP. VI.

An act for ascertaining the gauge of barrels for pork, beef, tar, and pitch.

Preamble.

I. FOR prevention of frauds and abuses frequently practised by greedy and avaricious traders in pork, beef, tar and pitch, who, for their own private lucre and gain, not only make and set up, or cause to be made and set up, small barrels, but also slightly pack, and deceitfully fill the same, to the great prejudice of the trade of this her majestys colony and dominion, in the said commodities and merchandizes,

Size of barrels for pork, beef, tar or pitch.

II. *Be it enacted, by the Governor, Council and Burgesses, of this present General Assembly, and it is hereby enacted, by the authority of the same*, That from and after the nine and twentieth day of September next, all and every barrel or barrels, which shall be made and set up, to put pork, beef, tar, or pitch into; and also all and every barrel or barrels, wherein pork or beef shall be packed, or wherein tar or pitch shall be filled, either for exportation out of, or for sale within, this her majesty's colony and dominion, shall be of a size, gauge and dimension, large enough to hold and contain, at least, the quantity of thirty-one gallons and an half of Winchester measure; and that the contents of

Quantity of pork or beef, in a barrel.

every pork barrel, at exportation or sale, shall be at least two hundred and twenty pounds of neat pork, and of every beef barrel the like quantity of neat beef; and that every tar barrel shall be filled with clean tar, and every pitch barrel with true made pitch, without the least mixture of any sort of trash whatsoever.

Quality of tar and pitch.

III. And to the end, all and every barrel or barrels to be hereafter made use of, for any the purposes aforesaid, may from time to time be set up, or packed, and filled, according to the directions of this act,

IV. *Be it enacted, by the authority aforesaid, and it is hereby enacted,* That whatsoever person or persons professing or using the craft, mistery, or occupation of a cooper; or whatsoever other person or persons, which, without pretending to the profession of a cooper, make and set up cask for his or their own proper use only, shall, after the said nine and twentieth day of September, make or set up, any barrel or barrels for pork, beef, tar, or pitch, of a less size, gauge, and dimension, then is directed by this act; all and every such person or persons shall, for every barrell so made and set up, forfeit and pay the sum of five pounds current money.

Penalty for making smaller barrels.

V. *And be it further enacted, by the authority aforesaid,* That whatsoever person or persons, from and after the said nine and twentieth day of September, shall pack pork or beef, for sale, in any barrel or barrels made and set up, contrary to this act, in size, gauge, and dimension; or shall, in any barrel or barrels, pack less pork or beef, than this act requires, that is to say, sufficient to make each barrel hold out, at exportation or sale, the quantity directed by this act, to be the quantity and contents of a barrel of pork, or a barrel of beef; all and every such person or persons shall, for every such barrel, forfeit and pay the sum of five pounds current money.

For packing a less quantity of pork or beef.

VI. *And be it further enacted, by the authority aforesaid,* That whatsoever person or persons, from and after the said nine and twentieth day of September, shall put or fill tar or pitch, for sale, in any barrel or barrels made and set up, contrary to this act, in size, gauge, or dimension; or shall fill up or mingle any barrel or barrels of tar with any trash or mixture of any other matter or thing than clean tar; or any bar-

For tar or pitch, of less gauge, or mixed with other matter.

rel or barrels of pitch, with any trash or mixture of any other matter or thing than true made pitch; all and every such person or persons shall forfeit and lose all and every such barrel or barrels of tar or pitch, and besides that, ten shillings for every such barrel of tar, and twenty shillings for every such barrel of pitch.

On exporter of beef or pork.

VII. *And be it further enacted, by the authority aforesaid,* That whatsoever person or persons, from and after the said nine and twentieth day of September, shall export out of this her majesty's colony and dominion, to any other port or place, or put on board any ship, bark, sloop, or other vessel, in order to be exported as aforesaid, pork or beef, in any barrel or barrels made and set up, contrary to this act, in size, gauge, and dimension; or shall export, or put on board any ship, bark, sloop, or other vessel, in order to be exported as aforesaid, any barrel or barrels of pork, of less neat contents in pork, or any barrel or barrels of beef, of less neat contents in beef, than this act directs; all and every such person or persons shall, for every such barrel, forfeit and pay the sum of five pounds current money.

Of tar and pitch.

VIII. *And be it further enacted, by the authority aforesaid,* That whatsoever person or persons, from and after the said nine and twentieth day of September, shall export out of this her majesty's colony and dominion, unto any other port or place, or put on board any ship, bark, sloop or other vessel, in order to be exported as aforesaid, any tar or pitch, in any barrel or barrels made and set up, contrary to this act, in size, gauge, and dimension; or shall export, or put on board any ship, bark, sloop, or other vessel, in order to be exported as aforesaid, any barrel or barrels of tar, filled up, or mingled with any trash, or mixture of any other matter or thing than clean tar, or any barrel or barrels of pitch, filled up, or mingled with any trash, or mixture of any other matter or thing than true made pitch, all and every such person or persons shall forfeit and lose all and every such barrel or barrels of tar or pitch; and besides that, ten shillings for every such barrel of tar, and twenty shillings for every such barrel of pitch.

IX. *And be it further enacted, by the authority aforesaid,* That whatsoever person or persons, from and after the said nine and twentieth day of September, shall barter away, bargain for, or sell, or expose or offer to sale, in any way whatsoever, within this her majesty's colony and dominion, any pork or beef, in any barrel or barrels made and set up, contrary to this act, in size, gauge, and dimension; or shall barter away, bargain, or sell, or expose or offer to sale, in any way whatsoever as aforesaid, any barrel or barrels of pork, of less neat contents in pork, or any barrel or barrels of beef of less neat contents in beef, than this act directs, all and every such person or persons shall, for every such barrel, forfeit and pay the sum of five pounds current money.

For bartering or selling pork or beef, in barrels, contrary to law.

X. *And be it further enacted, by the authority aforesaid,* That whatsoever person or persons, from and after the said nine and twentieth day of September, shall barter away, bargain, or sell, or expose or offer to sale, in any way whatsoever, within this her majesty's colony and dominion, any tar or pitch, in any barrel or barrels made and set up, contrary to this act, in size, gauge, or dimension; or shall barter away, bargain, or sell, or expose or offer to sale, in any way whatsoever as aforesaid, any barrel or barrels of tar, filled up, or mingled with any trash, or mixture of any other matter or thing than clean tar, or any barrel or barrels of pitch, filled up, or mingled with any trash, or mixture of any other matter or thing, than true made pitch, all and every such person or persons shall forfeit and lose all and every such barrel or barrels of tar or pitch; and besides that, ten shillings for every such barrel of tar, and twenty shillings for every such barrel of pitch.

And tar and pitch.

XI. And forasmuch as pork, beef, tar, and pitch, are often in barrels, imported and brought hither from Carolina, and other parts and places, to be sold: For prevention of frauds and abuses therein,

XII. *Be it enacted, by the authority aforesaid, and it is hereby enacted,* That whatsoever person or persons, from and after the said nine and twentieth day of September, shall import or bring into this her majesty's colony and dominion, from Carolina, or any other port or place whatsoever, by land or water, any pork, beef, tar, or pitch, in barrel or barrels of less size, gauge, and dimension, than this act directs, or any barrel or barrels of pork, of less neat contents in pork, or any

The like penalties, for pork, &c. imported in barrels, contrary to law.

barrel or barrels of beef, of less neat contents in beef, than this act directs, or any barrel or barrels of tar, filled up, or mingled with any trash, or mixture of any other matter or thing than clean tar, or any barrel or barrels of pitch, filled up, or mingled with any trash, or mixture of any other matter or thing than true made pitch; and shall here bargain away, barter, or sell, or expose or offer to sale, in any way whatsoever, to any person or persons whatsoever, such barrel or barrels of pork, beef, tar, or pitch, or any of them; all and every such person or persons shall be liable to, and pay the forfeitures and penalties mentioned in this act, for every barrel bartered away, bargained, or sold, or exposed or offered to sale, contrary to this act: All which forfeitures and penalties aforesaid, shall be divided into two equal parts; *to wit*, one moiety to our sovereign lady the queen, her heirs and successors, for and towards the better support of this government, and the contingent charges thereof; and the other moiety to him or them that will inform or sue for the same: To be recovered, with costs, by action of debt, bill, plaint, or information, in any court of record within this her majesty's colony and dominion, in which no essoin, protection, or wager of law, shall be allowed.

How appropriated.

XII. *And be it further enacted*, That all and every other act and acts, and every clause and article thereof, heretofore made, for so much thereof as relates to ascertaining the gauge of barrels for pork, beef, tar, and pitch, or to any other matter or thing within the purview of this act, is, and are hereby repealed, and made void, to all intents and purposes, as if the same had never been made.

Repealing clause.

CHAP. VII.

An act concerning Tithables.

Who shall be deemed tithables.

I. *BE it enacted, by the Governor, Council, and Burgesses of this present general assembly, and it is hereby enacted, by the authority of the same*, That all male persons, of the age of sixteen years, and upwards, and all negro, mulatto, and Indian women, of the age of sixteen years, and upwards, not being free, shall be, and are hereby declared to be tithable, or chargeable, for defraying the public, county, and parish charges, in this her majesty's colony and dominion; excepting such only, as the county court, and vestry, for reasons, in charity, made appear to them, shall think fit to excuse.

II. And to the end, that the age of all children imported, or that shall be imported, who are, or shall be in a capacity of becoming tithable, within the intent and meaning of this act may be ascertained,

Ages of children imported to be adjudged,

III. *Be it further enacted by the authority aforesaid, and it is hereby enacted*, That the owner or purchaser of every child, being a servant, and the parent or importer of every child, being free, at the first, second, or third court, held for the county where such child shall be, after the arrival of the said child in this country, shall bring the said child before the county court, to have its age adjudged by the court; otherwise the said child to be accounted, and thereafter immediately become tithable as aforesaid, although not of the age of sixteen years: And the age of such child being adjudged by the court, shall be entered upon the records of the said court; and be accounted, deemed, and taken, for the true age of the said child, in order to its becoming thithable, within the intent and meaning of this act.

or deemed immediately tithable.

IV. And for the regular and exact taking account of the tithable persons in this her majesty's colony and dominion,

Lists of tithables, how taken and returned.

V. *Be it further enacted, by the authority aforesaid, and it is hereby enacted*, That the court of each county, divide the same into convenient precincts, and annually appoint one of the justices for each of the said precincts, to take a list of the tithables; every which justice, in convenient time, before the tenth of June then next following, shall give notice of his being appointed thereto, and of the place he designs to take the same at, by setting up a note thereof, at the church or chapel door of the precinct he is appointed for; and shall attend the same, on the said tenth day of June, if it happen not to be of a Sunday, and then on the next day following. And also in August court then next following, shall deliver the list so by him taken, together with the subscriptions of the tithables, to the clerk of the county court; who shall, the next court day, set fair lists thereof, up in the court-house, there to remain during the sitting of the court, for the view and inspection of all that please, and for the discovery of such as shall be concealed.

When and by whom to be delivered.

VI. And for the greater certainty therein, *Be it also enacted, by the authority aforesaid, and it is hereby enacted,* That every master or mistress of a family, or in his or her absence, or non-residence at the plantation, his or her attorney, or overseer, shall, on the said tenth day of June, by a list under his or her hand, deliver, or cause to be delivered, to the justice appointed to take the same, the names and number of all the tithable persons abiding in, or belonging to, his or her family, the ninth of June, or the master or owner thereof, shall be adjudged a concealer, and be liable as a concealer of such and so many tithables as shall not be listed and given in; and for every tithable person so concealed, or not given in, and listed, as afore is directed, shall forfeit and pay one thousand pounds of tobacco to the informer: To be recovered, with costs, by action of debt, bill, plaint, or information, in any court of record in this her majesty's colony and dominion, wherein no essoin, protection, or wager of law shall be allowed. And if any justice appointed to take the lists of tithables, shall not truly enter and list the names and number of his own tithables in that district, in the list he gives in, he shall be adjudged a concealer; and for every tithable person so by him concealed, and not listed, shall forfeit and pay one thousand pounds of tobacco, to the use aforesaid; and to be recovered, with costs as aforesaid, in manner and form aforesaid.

Penalty on person taken for concealing his own.

VII. *Provided nevertheless,* That if it shall happen, that any master or mistress, or overseer of a family, shall, by sickness, absence, ignorance of the person or place, or other accident, omit to carry, or send, their list of tithables the said appointed tenth day of June, to the place and justice appointed, it shall be lawful to the person or persons so failing, to carry or send their lists to the said justice's house, at any time between the said tenth day of June, and the last day of the said month; and so doing, shall be free and acquit from the penalty and prosecution aforesaid; any thing in this act to the contrary, notwithstanding.

Further time allowed.

VIII. *Provided also*, That nothing herein contained, shall be construed to extend to the governor, or commander in chief of this her majesty's colony and dominion, for the time being, and his family; or to the person of any beneficed minister within this colony, so as to charge them, or either of them, as tithables, within the meaning of this act.

Who exempted from.

IX. *And be it further enacted*, That all and every other act and acts, and every clause and article thereof, heretofore made, for so much thereof as relates to tithables, or any other matter or thing whatsoever, within the purview of this act, is, and are hereby repealed and made void, to all intents and purposes, as if the same had never been made.

Repealing clause.

CHAP. VIII.

An act concerning Public Claims.

I. *BE it enacted, by the governor, council and burgesses of this present generall assembly, and it is hereby enacted, by the authority of the same*, That a particular court shall be held in every county within this her majesty's colony and dominion, by the justices of the respective counties, at the court-house, before every session of assembly, for proof of all such debts as are to be paid by the public, which shall be none other than what are, or shall be so directed, by some particular act of assembly; and the said court shall be called a court for proof of public claims: And for holding the same, the sheriff of every county is hereby strictly required and enjoined to appoint a convenient day; upon which day, the justices of the county are hereby impowered and required to meet, for the purposes aforesaid; and the sheriff, and county court clerk, are hereby also required to attend them.

Court of claims when to be held.

II. *And be it further enacted*, That if the sheriff, or county court clerk, shall fail to give their respective attendance at the court appointed for proof of public claims, the sheriff, or clerk, for such failure, shall be fined one thousand pounds of tobacco: And if any justice of the peace for the county where such court is appointed to be held, shall be absent from the said court, and a sufficient number of justices be not there to make

Penalty on sheriff, clerk, and justices, failing to attend.

a court, then every justice so absent, without reasonable cause, shall be fined the sum of five hundred pounds of tobacco; the one half of which fines shall be to our sovereign lady the queen, her heirs and successors, for the use of the county; and the other half to the informer: To be recovered by action of debt, bill, plaint, or information, in any court of record within this colony and dominion, wherein no essoin, protection, or wager of law, or more than one imparlance, shall be admitted or allowed.

III. And to the end it may be ascertained, what proof the said courts shall take and allow,

Proof of public claims.

IV. *Be it further enacted, by the authority aforesaid, and it is hereby enacted,* That every person that hath any public claim to make, shall produce to the said court, the warrant or certificate upon which the claim is grounded, and shall exhibit a particular account of the services or disbursements claimed for; and shall make oath, or give some other sufficient proof before the court, that all and every the services, things, or disbursements, for and concerning which such claim is preferred and exhibited, are really, and *bona fide,* made, done, and performed, and that no satisfaction hath been received for the same.

How certified.

V. *And be it further enacted, by the authority aforesaid,* That proof of public claims being made as aforesaid, the clerk of the county court, in order to their allowance in the assembly, shall, by the burgesses of the county, transmit the said claims, and every of them, to the assembly, with the warrants or certificates, upon which they, and every of them, are grounded; and also indorse, upon every particular person's claim, that proof is made before the court, concerning the same; or shall thereunto annex a certificate thereof: All which, the said clerk shall do, *ex officio,* where it so happens, that any particular person's allowed claim, shall be under one hundred pounds of tobacco; and for every certificate upon an allowed claim, amounting to that sum, or more, the said clerk (in full of all fees for his trouble and certificate) shall be allowed twenty pounds of tobacco, by the country.

Fees of clerk.

Proviso.

VI. *Provided,* The claim be admitted in the assembly, upon examination there, to be a charge which ought to be paid by the country.

VII. And for prevention of such frauds as may be imposed upon the assembly, by two certificates for one and the same thing, and avoiding all occasion of looking far back to find out what public claims have been once allowed by the assembly,

VIII. *Be it enacted, by the authority aforesaid, and it is hereby enacted,* That no public claim whatsoever, shall be hereafter allowed by the assembly, which is not proved as aforesaid, and returned to the first or second session of assembly, next after the same becomes due: And that every person concerned in such public claims, shall ever afterwards be excluded and barred from the benefit of this act.

Limitation of public claims.

IX. *And be it also further enacted, by the authority aforesaid,* That no sheriff whatsoever, within this her majesty's colony and dominion, shall, for the future, have from the country, any allowance, reward, or satisfaction, for public services, more than the laws appointing sheriffs fees do direct, and give for such service; and that all such services of the sheriff, as the said laws are silent about, or provide no reward or allowance for, shall be done, *ex officio.*

Fees of sheriffs for public services.

X. And for the better direction of the courts, appointed by this act, to pursue and follow the same in every respect,

XI. *Be it enacted, by the authority aforesaid, and it is hereby enacted,* That all such courts shall, and they, and every of them, are hereby strictly required and enjoined, to cause this act to be duly read by their clerk, at the first opening of every such court.

This act to be read.

XII. *And be it further enacted,* That all and every other act and acts, and every clause and article thereof, heretofore made, for so much thereof as relates to public claims, or to any other matter or thing whatsoever, within the purview of this act, is, and are hereby repealed and made void, to all intents and purposes, as if the same had never been made.

Repealing clause.

CHAP. IX.

An act concerning the collection of public and county levies; and for the better paiment of the same, to the respective creditors therein concerned.

Sheriffs to be collectors of levies.

I. *BE it enacted, by the Governor, Council, and Burgesses of this present General Assembly, and it is hereby enacted, by the authority of the same,* That the several county courts within this her majesty's colony and dominion, shall, in the first place, admit, and they, and every of them, are hereby required, in the first place, to admit the sheriff of their respective counties, for the time being, to be collector of the public and county levies raised therein.

Must give bond.

II. *Provided always, and it is the true intent and meaning of this act,* That every sheriff, before such his admittance, shall, at the court held for laying the county levy, enter into bond to our sovereign lady the queen, her heirs and successors, with two sufficient sureties, in double the sum which the public and county levies shall amount to, that he will honestly and faithfully collect, and duly pay and answer all the said public and county levies, unto the respective country and county creditors, for whom they shall be raised, in such parts and proportion to every creditor, as the same shall be ordered and directed to be paid.

On refusal, court may appoint another.

III. *Provided also,* That if the sheriff of any county shall, at the laying of the county levy, refuse, or fail to give bond, with sureties as aforesaid, then it shall be lawful for the court of such county, and such county court is hereby impowered, to put the collection of the public and county levies into the hands of any other person such court shall think fit, which will give bond and security for his performance in collecting and paying the said levies, according to the aforesaid directions of this act.

Allowance for cash.

IV. *And be it enacted, by the authority aforesaid, and it is hereby enacted,* That every sheriff, or other collector, of the public and county levies, or of secretary's, clerks, and sheriffs fees, shall, for every hundred pounds of tobacco he receives in an hogshead, for such levies or fees, allow to the payer of the same, eight pounds of tobacco, as a consideration and satisfaction for the cask, and so proportionable for a less sum than one hundred pounds of tobacco: And that if any sheriff, or other collector as aforesaid, shall refuse or deny to make the said allowance of eight per cent. as aforesaid, for all or any of the tobaccos which shall be paid him in an hogshead, on account of levies and fees as aforesaid, such sheriff, or collector, shall forfeit and pay to the party grieved, one hundred pounds of tobacco, for every eight pounds of tobacco due for the cask, which he refuses to pay for as aforesaid, and so proportionably for a less sum than eight pounds of tobacco: To be recovered, with costs, (if the forfeiture exceed not two hundred pounds of tobacco,) upon a complaint before any justice of the peace of the county, wherein such refusal shall be made; and if it do exceed that sum, by action of debt, in any court of record within this dominion, wherein no essoin, protection, or wager of law, shall be allowed.

Penalty for refusal.

How recoverable.

V. *And be it further enacted, by the authority aforesaid, and it is hereby enacted,* That it shall not be lawful for any sheriff, or other collector as aforesaid, to make seizure of any hogshead of tobacco paid away and marked, for any levies or fees put into his hands to collect, although the said levies or fees may be levied by distress, if the person owing such levies or fees, shall, at the same time, and on the same plantation, where the seizure is made, offer and tender other good and merchantable tobaccos for satisfaction of the same.

When tobacco paid away and marked, not to be seized.

VI. *And be it further enacted, by the authority aforesaid, and it is hereby enacted,* That if any sheriff, or other collector as aforesaid, shall, for any levies or fees put into his hands to collect, and which may be levied by distress, make seizure of an hogshead of tobacco, containing neat more tobaccos, than is at that time due to him, for such levies or fees, such sheriff, or collector, shall suffer the debtor for such levies or fees, to take out of the hogshead all such surplus tobaccos, or make the said debtor immediate satisfaction for it.

Surplus of hogshead seized, to be immediately accounted for.

VII. *And be it further enacted, by the authority aforesaid, and it is hereby enacted,* That every sheriff, or other collector as aforesaid, having any public or county levies to demand of any person, who hath public or county levies in his hands, shall discount with such creditor, the tobaccos due for the said levies out of the

Discounts to be allowed.

said credit, or so much thereof as the credit in his hands shall amount to, without requiring or expecting any allowance from the creditor for the same.

VIII. And to the end, no public or county creditor may be delaied or kept from receiving his just dues in convenient time, or exposed to a tedious law suit in recovering the same,

When collectors to pay creditors.

IX. *Be it enacted, by the authority aforesaid, and it is hereby enacted,* That every sheriff, or other collector as aforesaid, shall take care to pay and satisfy all the public and county creditors concerned in the public or county levies put into his hands to collect, the respective sum or sums of tobacco due to every of them, out of the same, some time before the court held for that county whereof he is sheriff or collector as aforesaid, in the month of March, next after the collection is put into his hands: And that every public or county creditor, which shall be then unpaid by any sheriff or other collector as aforesaid, upon a complaint to that, or any succeeding court, shall have a judgment granted, with costs, against such sheriff, or other collector as aforesaid, and his sureties, for what shall be then due and owing, without any other process or farther delay; any former law, usage, or custom, to the contrary, notwithstanding.

Judgment on failure.

Proviso, if the sheriff be absent.

X. *Provided nevertheless,* That if such complaint be made to any court succeeding March court, and the sheriff be then absent, he shall, by rule of court, be ordered to answer the complaint, at the next court; wherein if he fail, judgment shall be granted to the complainant against him and his sureties, for what shall then appear to be due, with costs.

XI. And forasmuch as sheriffs, or other collectors as aforesaid, may be prejudiced, if the public or county creditors, to whom they are to make paiments, neglect to receive the tobaccos due to them when ready: For remedy in such cases,

How sheriff may tender payment.

XII. *Be it enacted, by the authority aforesaid, and it is hereby enacted,* Then when any public or county creditor, after ten days notice given by the sheriff, or other collector as aforesaid, that the tobacco due to such creditor, out of the public or county levy is ready, shall refuse or neglect to go or send to receive the same, then the sheriff, or other collector as aforesaid, shall at any time afterwards have liberty to make a tender of the said tobaccos to such creditor, in manner as is directed by an act of this present General Assembly, intituled, An act for improving the staple of tobacco, and for regulating the size and tare of tobacco hogsheads; and upon such tender made and executed as aforesaid, shall have and receive the same benefit and advantage, that debtors, in other cases do, by virtue of the said act.

XIII. *And be it further enacted,* That all and every other act and acts, and every clause and article thereof heretofore made, for so much thereof as relates to the collection of the public and county levies; and the paiment of the same to the respective creditors therein mentioned, or to any other matter or thing whatsoever, within the purview of this act, is, and are hereby repealed and made void, to all intents and purposes, as if the same had never been made. Repealing clause.

CHAP. X.

An act directing the building and maintaining of prisons, pillories, whipping-posts, stocks, and ducking-stools, in every county; and for settling the rules of prisons.

I. *BE it enacted, by the governor, council, and burgesses, of this general assembly, and it is hereby enacted, by the authority of the same,* That the court of every county within this dominion, at the charge of their respective county, shall cause to be built, and from time to time, for ever hereafter, shall maintain and keep in good repair, within their said county, one common goal, or county prison, to be built of brick, or timber, after the manner of Virginia housing; the chimnies and windows to be strongly grated with iron bars, and the doors to be well and strongly made secure with good locks and bars of iron; and also the court of every county shall cause to be built and maintained as aforesaid, within their county, (near the court-house) one pillory, whipping-post, and a pair of stocks: And if the court of any county within this dominion shall, at any time hereafter, fail to perform their duty herein, every magistrate

Prison, pillory, whipping-post and stocks, to be erected in each county.

Penalty for failure.

of such court so failing, shall forfeit and pay the sum of five hundred pounds of tobacco; one moiety thereof to the queen, her heirs and successors, for and towards the better support of the government, and the contingent charges thereof; and the other moiety to him or them that will inform or sue for the same: To be recovered, with costs, by action of debt, bill, plaint, or information, in any court of record within this dominion, in which no essoin, protection, or wager of law shall be allowed. And over and above the said forfeiture, such court so failing, shall be liable to pay all such sums as shall, from time to time, be recovered against the sheriff of their county, upon any escape which shall happen for or by reason of such failure to cause a prison to be built as aforesaid: which sum shall be recovered by the sheriff, (against whom any judgment for an escape as aforesaid shall be obtained,) his executors, and administrators, together with all costs and damages thereby sustained, in the general court, by action of debt, bill, plaint, or information, to be brought against them, or the survivors of them: And upon recovery in any such action, bill, plaint, or information, the general court is hereby impowered and required to ascertain how much every particular magistrate then living, (and the heirs, executors, and administrators of such as shall be deceased,) shall pay respectively; and accordingly, one or more executions shall and may be issued thereupon: And if the court of any county shall, at any time hereafter think fit, they are hereby authorised and impowered, at the charge of their county, to cause a ducking-stool to be built in such convenient place as they shall direct.

How recovered, and appropriated.

Ducking-stools.

II. And for the preservation of the health of such persons, as shall, at any time hereafter, be committed to the said county prisons, the county court shall have power to mark out, by meets and bounds, such a parcel of land as they shall think fit, (not exceeding ten acres) adjoining to the prison, for the rules thereof: And every prisoner (not committed for treason, or felony) giving good security to keep within the said rules, shall have liberty to walk therein, out of the prison, for the preservation of his or her health: And every prisoner giving security as aforesaid, and keeping continually within the said rules, shall be, and is hereby adjudged and declared to be in law, a true prisoner:

Prison bounds.

Who may have the benefit of.

And that every person therewith concerned, may know the true bounds of the said rules, the same shall be recorded in the county records, and the marks thereof, shall, from time to time, be renewed, as occasion shall require.

III. *And be it further enacted,* That all and every other act and acts, and every clause and article thereof, heretofore made, for so much thereof, as relates to directing the building and maintaining the prisons, pillories, whipping-posts, stocks, and ducking-stools, in every county, and settling the rules of prisons, is, and are hereby repealed and made void, to all intents and purposes, as if the same had never been made. Repealing clause.

CHAP. XI.

An act for the speedy and easy prosecution of Slaves, committing Capitall Crimes. Edi. 1733, and 1752.

WHEREAS a speedy prosecution of slaves for capitall crimes is absolutely necessary, and that the same be done without the extraordinary charge usually attending the tryalls of criminalls in the generall court, Preamble.

Be it enacted, by the Governor, Council and Burgesses of this present General Assembly, and it is hereby enacted, by the authority of the same, That every slave comitting such offence as by the law ought to be sattisfyed by the death of the offender, or loss of member, shall be forthwith comitted to the comon goal of the county within which such offence shall be comitted, there to be safely kept, and that the sheriff of such county, upon such commitment, shall forthwith certify such comitment with the cause thereof to the governor or comander in chief of this her majestys colony and dominion for the time being, who is thereupon desired and impowered to issue out a comission of oyer and terminer, directed to such persons of the county as he shall think fitt, which persons forthwith after the receipt of such comission, are impowered and required to cause the offender to be publickly indicted and arraigned at the court-house of the said county, and to take for evidence the confession of the party or the oath of two credible witnesses, or of one with pregnant circum- Slaves committing capital crimes to be committed to prison. Commission of oyer and terminer. Indictment & arraignment. Proof.

stances without the solemnity of a jury, and the offender being by them found guilty to pass such judgment upon such offender as the law provides in the like crimes, and on such judgment to award execution.

Judgment.

Provided always, and it is hereby intended, That the master or owner of any slave to be indicted or arraigned by virtue of this act, may appear at the tryall and make what just defence he can for such slave, so that such defence do only relate to matters of fact, and not to any formality in the indictment or other proceedings of the court.

Defence, in matters of fact, not to form of proceedings.

And be it further enacted, by the authority aforesaid, and it is hereby enacted, That when any slave shall be convicted and condemned upon any tryall to be had by virtue of this act, the justices that shall sitt in tryall shall put a valuation in money upon such slave so condemned, and certify such valuation to the next assembly, that the said assembly may be enabled to make a suitable allowance thereupon, to the master or owner of such slave.

Value of slave condemned, to be certified to assembly.

Allowance for.

And be it further enacted, That all and every other act and acts, and every clause and article thereof heretofore made for so much thereof as relates to the speedy and easy prosecution of slaves comitting capitall crimes, or to any other matter or thing whatsoever, within the purview of this act, is, and are hereby repealed and made void, to all intents and purposes, as if the same had never been made.

Repealing clause.

CHAP. XII.

An act to prevent the clandestine transportation or carrying of persons in debt, servants, and slaves, out of this colony.

I. *BE it enacted, by the Governor, Council, and Burgesses, of this present General Assembly, and it is hereby enacted, by the authority of the same*, That no master of a ship, sloop, boat, or other vessel, shall transport or carry any person whatsoever, out of this colony and dominion, without a license or pass for the same, signed by the secretary of this dominion for the time being, or such other person as he shall depute and authorize for that purpose, upon penalty of answering

Masters of ships, &c. not to carry any persons out of the country, without a pass, on penalty of paying all their debts.

and paying every debt and duty the said person, at going out of this colony, shall owe, or stand obliged for, to the queen's majesty, her heirs and successors, or to any of the inhabitants, merchants, or traders here, by judgment on record, bill, bond, covenant, account, or any other ways or means whatsoever: To be recovered against the said master, by action of debt, in any court of record within this colony and dominion.

Penalty for carrying servants or slaves.

II. *And be it also enacted, by the authority aforesaid, and it is hereby enacted,* That after publication of this act, no master of a ship, sloop, boat or other vessel, shall transport or carry any servant whatsoever, or any negro, mulatto, Indian, or other slave, out of this colony and dominion, without a licence, or pass as aforesaid, or the consent, leave, or permission of the person or persons to whom such servant or slave doth of right belong, upon penalty of forfeiting and paying, in current money, the sum of fifty pounds for every servant, and the sum of one hundred pounds for every slave transported or carried hence, contrary to this act; one moiety to our sovereign lady the Queen, her heirs and successors, for and towards the better support of this government, and the contingent charges thereof; and the other moiety to the party grieved: To be recovered, with costs, in any court of record within this colony and dominion, by action of debt, bill, plaint, or information, wherein no essoin, protection, or wager of law, shall be allowed.

III. And that the transporting or carrying debtors, servants or slaves, out of this colony, contrary to this act, may be the more effectually prevented,

No limitation to bar such actions.

IV. *Be it also further enacted, by the authority aforesaid, and it is hereby enacted,* That any master of a ship, sloop, boat, or other vessel, offending therein, shall be liable to be sued at any time for any debt due and owing as aforesaid, from the person he shall transport or carry hence, contrary to this act, and for any forfeiture accruing, due from himself, by virtue of this act: And that whensoever any action, plaint, information, or other suit, shall be brought against the said master, for or concerning the premises, or any of them, the court wherein the said action, plaint, information, or suit, shall be depending, shall not admit him to plead in bar, or give in evidence any act for limitation of actions;

any law, usage, or custom to the contrary, notwithstanding.

Pass, how obtained.

V. *And be it enacted, by the authority aforesaid, and it is hereby enacted,* That it shall not be lawful for the secretary, or any deputy appointed by him, to grant a licence or pass, for transporting or carrying any person whatsoever out of this colony, unless sufficient bond, with two sureties, be given to the secretary of this dominion, to the value of two thousand pounds sterling, with condition to answer and pay every debt and duty, the said person, at going out of this colony, shall owe, or stand obliged for, by any ways or means whatsoever; or unless the said person have a certificate from a county court clerk, in the form following:

I, A. B. clerk of Y county court, do hereby certify, that C. D. is, and for some time past hath been, an inhabitant of this county, and hath published his intentions of going out of this colony, according to law. Dated this day of

Rules, in granting certificates.

VI. *And be it further enacted, by the authority aforesaid, and it is hereby enacted,* That it shall not be lawful for any county court clerk to issue such certificate for any person whatsoever, 'till ten days after publication hath been made in his county, of the said person's intentions to go out of this colony, by a note thereof set up at the county court-house, on a court-day.

Caveats against granting passes, how awarded.

VII. *And be it further enacted, by the authority aforesaid, and it is hereby enacted,* That notwithstanding a certificate from a county court clerk as aforesaid, if a caveat be entered to hinder a licence or pass thereupon, and sufficient bond given, with one surety, paiable to the secretary of this dominion, for the sum of five hundred pounds, by the person entring the said caveat, with condition to answer and pay all damages, which the party stopped by the caveat, shall recover, it shall not then be lawful for the secretary, if the said caveat be entered with him, or any of his deputies, with whom the said caveat shall be entered, to grant a licence or pass upon the said certificate, unless the party so stopped, shall give sufficient bond, with one surety also, to the secretary of this dominion, for double the sum claimed by the person entring the caveat, with condition to answer and pay whatever the said person shall recover of his pretended claim.

Proviso.

VIII. *Provided always, and it is hereby enacted and declared,* That the said surety, or any other sureties for persons going out of this colony, after the expiration of two years, shall be discharged and acquitted from all claims and demands whatsoever, which may or can be brought against them, by virtue of their being sureties as aforesaid, except such, for which suit shall be then depending, or for which, suit hath been commenced within that time; any law, usage, or custom, to the contrary notwithstanding.

IX. And for the greater ease of the inhabitants of this colony and dominion, in procuring a licence or pass, when need shall be,

Secretary to appoint deputies, for granting passes.

X. *Be it enacted, by the authority aforesaid, and it is hereby enacted,* That the secretary of this dominion for the time being, shall appoint, have, and keep, in each district of the colony, at least, one deputy, for granting licences or passes, according to this act, to any person within the district: And that if for the space of two months after publication of this act, he shall fail to appoint deputies, according to this act; or having appointed the said deputies, shall fail to signify to the several county court clerks in each district, what person he hath appointed for the district; or shall fail, when a vacancy happens in a district, within two months after the vacancy, to appoint another deputy for the said district; or to signify his said appointment to the several county court clerks within the district as aforesaid, he shall forfeit and pay fifty pounds current money, for every such failure; one moiety to our sovereign lady the queen, her heirs and successors, for and towards the better support of this government, and the contingent charges thereof; and the other moiety to him, her, or them that shall inform or sue for the same, in any court of record within this colony and dominion, by action of debt, bill, plaint, or information, wherein no essoin, protection, privilege, or wager of law, or any more than one imparlance, shall be allowed.

XI. *And be it further enacted, by the authority aforesaid, and it is hereby enacted,* That if any person, desirous to go out of this colony and dominion, in order to

Penalty for refusing a pass.

obtain a licence or pass for it, shall offer to give bond, with sureties, or produce a county court clerk's certificate, according to this act; and the secretary, or his deputy, to whom such bond shall be offered, or certificate produced, shall refuse to grant a licence or pass thereupon, unless caveat be entered, according to this act, to hinder the same, the secretary, or his deputy, offending therein, shall forfeit and pay five hundred pounds current money; one moiety to our sovereign lady the queen, her heirs and successors, for and towards the better support of this government, and the contingent charges thereof; and the other moiety to the party grieved, prosecuting within six months next ensuing the offence committed; and afterwards, to the said party, or any other informer: To be recovered, with costs, in any court of record within this colony and dominion, by action of debt, bill, plaint, or information, wherein no essoin, protection, or wager of law, or any more than one imparlance shall be allowed.

XII. And to the end, every master of a ship, sloop, boat, or other vessel, which shall lawfully transport or carry any person out of this colony, may be the better enabled to manifest the same, if questioned, after he hath lost his licence or pass,

Duty of county court clerks and secretary, and returning certificates, & registering passes.

XIII. *Be it enacted, by the authority aforesaid, and it is hereby enacted,* That the county court clerks shall register, in their respective offices, all certificates by them issued, in pursuance of this act; that the secretary's deputies shall, in October general court, annually return certificates of all the licences or passes by them respectively granted the year before, to the secretary's office; that the clerk of the said office shall there register all the said certificates, as they come to his hands, or within a reasonable time after; and that if the secretary shall grant any licence or pass himself, he shall take care a certificate thereof be registered in the secretary's office within a year after the granting it: And if any of the persons aforesaid, shall at any time fail to perform the respective duty of his office as aforesaid, in any particular, for every such failure, he shall forfeit and pay the sum of five pounds current money; one moiety to our sovereign lady the queen, her heirs and successors, for and towards the better support of this government, and the contingent charges thereof; and the other moiety to the informer: To be recovered, with costs, in any court of record within this colony and dominion, by action of debt, bill, plaint or information, wherein no essoin, protection, or wager of law, shall be allowed.

XIV. *And be it further enacted,* That all and every other act and acts, and every clause and article thereof, heretofore made, for so much thereof as relates to the clandestine transportation, or carrying of persons in debt, servants, and slaves, out of this colony, is, and are hereby repealed and made void, to all intents and purposes, as if the same had never been made.

Repealing clause.

CHAP. XIII.

An act concerning Waifts and Strays.

I. *BE it enacted, by the governor, council and burgesses of this present general assembly, and it is hereby enacted, by the authority of the same,* That every person that shall take up any stray horse, mare, or cattle, or boat adrift, shall cause the same with the description thereof, viz. the mark, stature, and colour of the horses, mares, and cattle, and the burthen and built of the boat, to be published, by setting up a note or advertisement thereof, at each church or chapel in the county, two Sundays, or sermon days successively, within one month after the taking up such horses, mares, cattle, or boat; and if no owner appear upon such public notice given, shall then publish the same at the next county court, and set up, in writing, at the said court door, one whole court day: And for a reward of taking up the same, shall be paid, by the owner, five shillings for every such horse, mare, and boat; and every person making default herein, or making use of any such stray horses, mares, or cattle, or drift boat, shall forfeit and pay, for every such horse, mare, and head of cattle so taken up astray, and every boat so taken up adrift, the sum of fifteen shillings current money, to the informer: To be recovered, with costs, before a justice of the peace of the county where the offence is committed; and moreover, shall pay double damages to the owner.

Strays, and boats adrift, how advertised.

Reward.

Penalty for failing to advertise.

When the property shall vest in the taker up.

II. *Provided always, and be it enacted,* That when any horses, mares, and cattle, being above two years old, shall be taken up astray, or boat adrift, and so published, and no owner appear, to make his or her claim, within one year after such taking up, the taker up shall, by warrant from a justice of the peace of that county, have such horses, mares, cattle, and boat appraised; and shall then have the property of such horses, mares, cattle, and boat, and shall only be answerable to the owner, for the valuation thereof, after the abatement of the reward for taking up the same.

Repealing clause.

III. *And be it further enacted,* That all and every other act and acts, and every clause and article thereof, heretofore made, for so much thereof as relates to waifts and strays; or any other matter or thing whatsoever, within the purview of this act, is, and are hereby repealed, and made void, to all intents and purposes, as if the same had never been made.

CHAP. XIV.

An act against stealing Hogs.

Hog-stealing, penalty for,

I. *BE it enacted, by the Governor, Council, and Burgesses of this present general assembly, and it is hereby enacted, by the authority of the same,* That if any person or persons shall, from and after the publication of this act, steal any hog, shoat, or pig, every person so offending, shall, for the first offence, receive on his or

first offence;

her bare back, twenty-five lashes, or pay down ten pounds current money of Virginia; and if a negro, mulatto, or Indian, thirty-nine lashes well laid on, at the common whipping-post of the county wherein such offence shall be committed, or the party offending, arrested; and moreover, shall pay and satisfy four hundred pounds of tobacco, for every such hog, shoat, and pig; one half of the afore-mentioned fine to be to the owner

and how appropriated.

of such hog, shoat, or pig; and the other half to the informer: To be recovered, with costs, at the suit of the informer, by action of debt, bill, plaint, or information, in any court of record in this her majesty's colony and dominion, wherein no essoin, protection, or wager of law, shall be allowed. And if any person or persons, shall the second time offend, by stealing any hog,

2nd offence.

shoat, or pig, he or she so offending, and being thereof the second time convicted, shall stand two hours in the pillory, on a court day, and have both ears nailed thereto, and at the end of the said two hours, have the ears cut loose from the nails: which judgment, the county courts in this colony, are hereby impowered to give respectively, and to award execution thereon accordingly: Saving always and reserving to each party concerned, liberty of appealing to the general court; provided they give bond, with good security, in the sum of twenty pounds sterling, for his or her personal appearance in the general court, according to the appeal, and to perform and abide what they shall award therein; and moreover, each party offending as aforesaid, shall pay and satisfy four hundred pounds of tobacco for every such hog, shoat, and pig: To be recovered and divided as aforesaid.

Right of appeal.

Further penalty.

II. And if in either of the said cases, to wit, the first or second offence of hog-stealing, the person offending, be a servant by indenture, or custom, &c. then the master or owner of such servant shall pay and satisfy the said four hundred pounds of tobacco, and shall be satisfyed for the same again, by service of the said servant, after the rate of one hundred and fifty pounds of tobacco for one month's service; and judgment shall go accordingly.

Masters of servants, hog-stealers, to pay the fine, & be reimbursed by the servant.

III. And if such person so offending, be a slave, then the owner of such slave shall pay and satisfy two hundred pounds of tobacco to the owner of the hog; and judgment shall go accordingly.

Of slaves.

IV. And if there be more actors than one in the same offence of hog stealing, though it be but for one hog, shoat, or pig, *It is hereby enacted and declared*, That each person shall be adjudged to the punishment and whole fine, and may be particularly prosecuted.

Several offenders.

V. *Provided always*, That this clause shall not be construed to extend to owners of slaves paying more than once for one hog; but that having paid once two hundred pounds of tobacco for each hog so stolen, shall be acquit: And if slaves of several masters be concerned together in one offence of hog stealing, then the pay for such hog or hogs, shall be paid by the owners of such slaves, in proportion.

Proviso.

3d offence, felony.

VI. And if any person or persons shall the third time offend, by stealing a hog, shoat, or pig, he or she so offending, shall be adjudged a felon, and shall suffer death, as in the case of felony.

Persons, receiving hogs, without ears, deemed hog-stealers.

VII. And for the more effectual prevention of hog stealing, *Be it also enacted, by the authority aforesaid, and it is hereby enacted,* That if any person or persons shall bring, or cause to be brought, to his or her own house, or any other house of reception, any hog, shoat, or pig, without ears, or shall receive any such, and shall not immediately discover the same to a justice of the peace of the county, he, she, and they so offending, shall, by virtue of this act, be adjudged a hog stealer, and shall suffer the pains, penalties, and forfeitures accordingly.

Proviso.

VIII. *Provided nevertheless,* That if any person or persons so bringing, causing to be brought, or receiving such hog without ears, shall be able to prove the lawful propriety of the said hog, to be in him, her, or themselves, he, she, and they, shall not then, in such case, be liable to any pains, penalties, or forfeitures mentioned in this act; any thing therein contained to the contrary thereof, in any-wise, notwithstanding.

IX. And whereas many of the tributary Indians keep hogs, and are suspected, on pretence thereof, to steal and destroy the stocks of the English,

Indians' hogs, how to be marked.

Penalty for buying pork, of an Indian, where proof of the hogs mark cannot be made.

X. *Be it therefore further enacted,* That all Indians whatsoever, keeping any hogs, shall give them the same mark, which hath been, or by the next adjacent county court, shall be allowed to their town: And if any person, not being an Indian, shall buy or receive from any Indian, any pork, and cannot prove such pork to be of the proper mark of the town of Indians to which such Indian shall belong, he or she so offending, shall forfeit and pay one thousand pounds of tobacco; one half thereof to be to the queen, her heirs and successors, for and towards the support of this government, and the contingent charges thereof; and the other half to the informer: To be recovered, with costs, by action of debt, bill, plaint, or information, in any court of record in this her majesty's colony and dominion, wherein no essoin, protection, or wager of law, shall be allowed.

XI. *And be it further enacted and declared,* That it shall not be lawful for any person to hunt, shoot, or kill, any unmarked hog, shoat, or pig, if the same shall be found, either in company of the hogs, or ranging upon the land of any other person, on pain of being fined one thousand pounds of tobacco for every such offence: To be recovered, with costs, at the suit of the informer, by action of debt, bill, plaint, or information, in any court of record within this colony and dominion. And if any person kills any unmarked hog or shoat, ranging upon his or her land, or upon any unpatented lands, and being either alone or in company of his or her own hogs, or of other unmarked hogs, (in all which cases it is lawful to hunt or kill unmarked hogs or shoats) such person shall, within three months then next coming, give an account thereof, upon oath, to some justice of the peace of the county, and shall take a certificate thereof accordingly, for his or her justification: And every person failing to do what is enjoyned in this case, is hereby declared to be a hog stealer, and shall suffer the pains, penalties, and forfeitures accordingly.

Penalty for hunting, shooting, &c. unmarked hogs, on others land.

If killed on his own, or unpatented, notice to be given to a justice.

XII. *And be it further enacted*, That all and every other act and acts, and every clause and article thereof, heretofore made, for so much thereof as relates to stealing hogs, or to any other matter or thing whatsoever, within the purview of this act, is, and are hereby repealed and made void, to all intents and purposes, as if the same had never been made.

Repealing clause.

CHAP. XV.

An act for prevention of trespasses by unruly horses, cattle, hogs, sheep, and goats; and by taking away boats and canoes.

I. *BE it enacted, by the Governor, Council, and Burgesses of this present General Assembly, and it is hereby enacted, by the authority of the same,* That if any horses, mares, cattle, hogs, sheep, or goats, shall break into any grounds, being inclosed with a strong and sound fence, four foot and half high, and so close that the beasts or kine breaking into the same, could not creep through; or with an hedge two foot high, upon a ditch of three foot deep, and three foot broad, or instead of such hedge, a rail fence of two foot and half high, the hedge or fence being so close that none of the

What deemed a lawful fence.

creatures aforesaid can creep through, (which shall be accounted a lawful fence,) the owner of the said horses, mares, cattle, hogs, sheep, or goats, and of any one of them, shall, for the first trespass by any of them committed, make reparation to the party injured, for the true value of the damage he shall sustain, with costs of suit; and for every trespass afterwards, double damages, and costs of suit: To be recovered in any court of record in this her majesty's colony and dominion, in such manner as the law, in the like cases, directs.

1st trespass, how compensated.

Other trespass.

II. *Provided always, and it is hereby intended,* That for a third offence of any one or more horses, mares, cattle, hogs, sheep, or goats, breaking into inclosures as aforesaid, and barking fruit-trees, it shall be at the election of the party injured, to sue for his damages, or to kill and destroy the beasts or kine so trespassing, without being answerable to any one for the same.

3rd trespass.

III. And to the end, that the condition of the fence, at the time of the trespass committed, may be proved to a jury, upon trial, *Be it enacted, by the authority aforesaid, and it is hereby enacted,* That upon complaint made by the party injured, before any justice of the peace for that county wherein the trespass shall be committed, the said justice of peace is hereby impowered and required to issue his order, without delay, to three honest house-keepers of the neighbourhood, who are no ways related to the party injured, nor interested concerning the trespass, reciting the complaint, and requiring them to view the fence where the trespass is complained of, and to take memorandums of the same; and their depositions, in such case, shall be good evidence to the jury, as touching the lawfulness of the fence.

Fence, how viewed.

IV. *And be it further enacted, by the authority aforesaid, and it is hereby enacted,* That if any person damnified, for want of such sufficient fence, shall hurt, wound, lame, kill, or destroy, or cause to be hurted, wounded, lamed, killed, or destroied, by shooting, hunting with dogs, or otherwise, any of the kind or breed of horses, cattle, sheep, goats, or hogs, he, she, or they so offending, shall pay and satisfy to the owner of the creature so hurt, wounded, lamed, killed, or destroied, double damages, with costs; recoverable as aforesaid: Except the damage alledged, be under twenty shillings;

Penalty, for injuring beasts, if the fence be unlawful.

and then recoverable before any two justices of the county, *quorum unus*. How recoverable.

V. *And be it also further enacted, by the authority aforesaid, and it is hereby enacted*, That all persons whatsoever, owners of horses, mares, cattle, or other beasts, which are known to have barked fruit-trees, shall be and are hereby obliged to keep the said horses, mares, cattle, and other beasts, within their own fenced ground. Horses, known to have barked fruit-trees how to be kept.

VI. *And be it also enacted, by the authority aforesaid, and it is hereby enacted*, That if any person shall take up any horse, mare, kine, or other beast, that hath been known barking fruit-trees, and shall deliver the same to the owner thereof, the said owner shall pay to the taker-up, one hundred pounds of tobacco, for every beast so taken up and delivered: Recoverable, with costs, before any justice of the county wherein the beast was taken up, or the owner lives. Reward for taking up such.

VII. *Provided always*, That if it be required, the said taker-up of such horse, mare, or other beast, shall make oath before the said justice, of his taking up the same; and that no means were, by himself, or any other person that he knows of, used, to set the same at large; otherwise shall lose the said reward of one hundred pounds of tobacco. Proviso.

VIII. *And be it also enacted, by the authority aforesaid, and it is hereby enacted*, That every person whatsoever, that shall, without the leave of the owner, take away any boat, or canoe, shall pay to the said owner of such boat, or canoe, for every such offence, five hundred pounds of tobacco, over and above the damage the said boat, or canoe, shall sustain, and over and above the charge of regaining and bringing her back again: Penalty, for taking boat, or canoe, without leave. And if such person trespassing, be a servant, he or she shall make the like satisfaction, by his or her service, when the time due to his or her master shall be expired: In case of servants. And if there be several actors in one trespassing or taking away the boat, or canoe, at one time, it is hereby declared, that every person shall pay the whole fine. Several offenders.

IX. *And be it further enacted*, That all and every other act and acts, and every clause and article thereof heretofore made, for so much thereof as relates to trespasses by unruly horses, cattle, hogs, sheep, and Repealing clause.

goats; or to taking away boats and canoes; or to any other matter or thing within the purview of this act, is, and are hereby repealed and made void, to all intents and purposes, as if the same had never been made.

CHAP. XVI.

Edi. 1733, and 1752.

An act giving a reward for killing of Wolves.

[From MS.]

FOR an encouragement to all manner of persons to endeavour the destruction and killing of wolves, which in all parts of this her majestys colony and dominion very much obstruct the raising and increase of cattle, sheep and hogs,

Rewards for wolves killed, except by Indians.

Be it enacted, by the Governor, Council and Burgesses of this present General Assembly, and it is hereby enacted, by the authority of the same, That whatsoever person or persons (the tributary and all foreign Indians excepted) shall after the publication of this act, kill or destroy wolves old or young, such person or persons for every wolf taken and destroyed by means of a pitt or trap, made and kept for that purpose, shall have a reward of three hundred pounds of tobacco, and of two hundred pounds of tobacco for every wolf killed or destroyed by any other way.

Rewards to Indians.

That whatsoever Indian or Indians tributary to this dominion, shall kill or destroy wolves, such Indian or Indians for every wolf killed or destroyed by any means whatsoever, shall have a reward of one hundred pounds of tobacco and no more, and that the said severall rewards shall be paid to the respective person or persons meriting the same in the county where the fact happens to be done.

County courts to levy rewards.

And to that end, *Be it further enacted, by the authority aforesaid,* That the severall county courts within this her majestys colony and dominion, be impowered, and every of them is hereby impowered, authorised and required, at the laying of the county levy, annually to allow and order to all and every person or persons claiming or demanding any of the rewards aforesaid, the respective sum or sums of tobacco accruing, due to such person or persons by virtue of this act, and to assess, raise or levy, the same upon the tithable persons within their respective countys by a poll tax.

Provided always, and it is the true intent and meaning of this act, That whatsoever person or persons shall kill or destroy wolves for sake of the rewards given by this act, or any of them, such person or persons shall carry the head of every wolf so killed or destroyed, to a justice of the peace of the county where the fact happens to be done, shall before him make due proof how, when and where every wolf was killed or destroyed, and shall take from the said justice a certificate thereof, to the county court, and shall produce, or cause the same to be produced, when the county levy is laid, otherways it shall not be lawfull for the county court to grant or allow any claim or demand whatsoever, concerning the same.

Proof, how made.

And be it enacted, by the authority aforesaid, That every justice of peace within this her majestys colony and dominion, be impowered, and every of them is hereby impowered and required, within his respective county, to receive the heads of wolves killed or destroyed, in pursuance of this act, and upon due proof made to grant and issue certificates to the county court as aforesaid, how, when and where, such wolves were killed or destroyed, concerning which it shall and may be lawfull for every justice to whom application shall be made for certificate, to admit as good and due proof, either the oath or oaths of the person or persons making application, or such being refused or unfit to be taken, any other evidence, testimony or circumstance in his discretion, probable and convincing.

Justices authorised to grant certificates.

Mode of proof.

And forasmuch as frauds may happen frequently by means of Indians killing of wolves in one county and bringing the heads of them to another county, for sake of the reward in point of payment, in case great care be not taken to prevent the same,

Be it therefore enacted, by the authority aforesaid, That it shall and may be lawfull for every justice of peace to whom any Indian or Indians shall make application for a certificate upon the least suspition he hath of a fraud to forbear and delay giving the certificate untill such Indian or Indians shall bring him convincing and sattisfactory testimony that the wolf or wolves concerning which certificate is desired, were killed in that county to which such justice belongs.

Frauds, how declared.

Repealing clause.

And be it further enacted, That all and every other act and acts, and every clause and article thereof, heretofore made for so much thereof as relates to giving a reward for killing of wolves, or any other matter or thing within the purview of this act, is, and are hereby repealed and made void, to all intents and purposes, as if the same had never been made.

CHAP. XVII.

An act for encouragement of the Land Frontiers.

Preamble.

I. WHEREAS the counties on the land frontiers in this colony, are exposed to many dangers, from the incursions of Indian enemies, whereby the trouble and charge of the inhabitants of those counties are far greater than others of the inland parts of the country; and whereas the augmenting and enlarging the said frontier counties will very much add to their strength and safety, by increasing their militia, and thereby render the duty they are often obliged unto, less burthensome to the inhabitants in general: Therefore, as an encouragement to the aforesaid frontier plantations,

Conditions on which frontier counties may be divided.

II. *Be it enacted, by the governor, council, and burgesses, of this present general assembly, and it is hereby enacted, by the authority of the same,* That no county on the land frontiers, shall hereafter be divided, unless there shall be left in the upper county, at least eight hundred tithable persons; and unless the whole county, as it stood before the division, be obliged equally to contribute to the building a decent church, court-house, and prison, in such frontier county, after the form and manner now generally used within this colony.

Proviso.

III. *Provided always,* That if the upper inhabitants of any county, shall seek the division of themselves, they shall not then be intituled to any privilege, by virtue of this act.

CHAP. XVIII.

An act directing the building an house for the Governor of this colony and dominion.

Edi. 1733, and 1752.

[From MS.]

Preamble.

WE, her majestys most dutifull and loyall subjects, the burgesses now assembled, having taken into our serious consideration her majesty's commands concerning the building of an house for the governor of this her majestys colony and dominion, and how necessary it is that such an house be built without any further delay, have cheerfully and unanimously given and granted unto her most excellent majesty, the sum of three thousand pounds, to be employed, made use of and expended according to the directions of this act hereafter mentioned, and do humbly pray your excellency it may be enacted,

A house to be built, for the governor.

And be it enacted by the governor, council and burgesses, of this present general assembly, and it is hereby enacted, by the authority of the same, That an house for the residence of the governor of this colony and dominion, be with all convenient expedition erected, built, and finished upon the land bought of Henry Tyler, joyning to the City of Williamsburgh, or upon so many of the next adjacent lotts laid out for the City of Williamsburg, as to the directors of the said city shall seem most fitt and convenient, or upon either or both of them, and that the said land containing sixty-three acres, and lying on the north side of the said city, together with the forementioned lotts, and the said house, and all and singular the appurtenances, shall from time to time, and at all times hereafter, be held and enjoyed by the governor or commander in chief of this dominion, for the time being, for ever to his own proper use and behoof, and shall not be applyed to any other use whatsoever.

Land appropriated for that purpose.

Dimensions and materials.

And that the said house be built of brick, fifty-four foot in length, and forty-eight foot in breadth, from inside to inside, two story high, with convenient cellars underneath, and one vault, sash windows, of sash, glass and a covering of stone slate, and that in all other respects the said house be built and finished according to the discretion of the overseer, which shall be employed by virtue of this act to take care of the same; under the direction of the governor and councill.

Kitchen and stable.

And be it further enacted, That a kitchen and stable, suitable for such an house be likewise built upon the land before mentioned, according to the discretion of the said overseer, and by the direction aforesaid.

Directors authorised to send to England for materials.

And be it further enacted, That for the more easy and better building and finishing the aforesaid house and out houses, the said overseer have full power to send *for* England for iron work, glass, lead, stone, slate, or any other necessarys to be made use of in or about the said buildings, and that the same be imported at the risque of the country, and also on the like risque to buy such and so many slaves, horses, carts, and other materials as in his discretion he shall think fitt, for the more expeditious and cheap carrying on the said work.

Governor authorised to draw on the treasurer.

And be it further enacted, That for a supply of monys to begin, carry on and finish the aforesaid house and out houses, the said overseer shall from time to time as the occasion shall require, make application to his excellency the governor or the governor or commander in chief of this colony and dominion for the time being, who is hereby desired upon such application to issue his warrant upon the late and present treasurer of this dominion for so much money as may be wanted untill the full sum of three thousand pounds given and granted to her majesty as aforesaid, shall be fully paid out.

3000*l.* appropriated.

And be it further enacted, That the said sum of three thousand pounds shall be employed, made use of, and expended in building the house and out houses directed by this act, and the charges thereupon accruing, and to and for no other use or uses whatsoever.

Overseer, or director appointed.

Vacancy, how supplied.

And be it further enacted, That Henry Cary be appointed, and he is hereby appointed an overseer to inspect, oversee, and provide for the building aforesaid, with full power to begin, carry on, and finish the same, according to the directions of this act, and in case at any time hereafter there be a necessity of appointing a new overseer by means of the death or disability of the said Henry Cary, or any other person that shall succeed him in the said employment and trust his excellency the governor or the governor or commander in chief of this colony and dominion for the time being, is hereby desired on all such occasions to nominate and appoint such new overseer, and every person so appointed is hereby declared to have as full power to proceed and act in carrying on and finishing the said buildings, as the said Henry Cary hath by virtue of this act.

And be it further enacted, That the said Henry Cary and every other person which after him shall be appointed to be an overseer as aforesaid, shall be paid and allowed for the time of their respective service and attendance in the employment and trust aforesaid, after the rate of one hundred pounds a year. **Salary of director.**

Provided always, and be it enacted, That the said Henry Cary and every other person which after him shall be appointed to be an overseer as aforesaid, shall before his admittance into the said imployment and trust, enter into bond with one surety, of five hundred pounds sterling to our sovereign lady the queen, her heirs and successors, that he will not imbezile or convert to his own use any part of the money or materials put into his hands for carrying on the building aforesaid, but that according to the best of his skill and understanding and the trust reposed in him he will faithfully lay out all such monys in and about the uses and services for which he receives it, and also that he will lay an account of his disbursments from time to time, before the governor and councill, and before the assembly at their meeting, and make oath thereto when required. **To give bond.**

And be it further enacted, That all such charge and expence as shall or may hereafter accrue for repairing the house and out houses directed by this act, shall be defrayed out of her majesty's revenue of two shillings per hogshead. **Appropriation for repairs.**

CHAP. XIX.

An act for establishing the General Court, and for regulating and settling the proceedings therein.

I. FOR a speedy and regular determination of all controversies and differences between any persons; and for continuing, constituting, and erecting such courts as shall be competent and necessary, to hear and adjudge all such causes as shall be brought before them,

II. ***Be it enacted, by the governor, council, and burgesses of this present general assembly, and it is hereby***

General court, established.

enacted, by the authority of the same, That at some one certain place, to be lawfully appointed, and at such times as herein after directed, there shall be held one principal court of judicature, for this her majesty's colony and dominion of Virginia; which court shall be, and is hereby established, by the name of the general court of Virginia; and shall consist of her majesty's governor, or commander in chief, and the council, for the time being, any five of them to be a quorum; and they are hereby declared and appointed judges or justices, to hear and determine all suits and controversies which shall be depending in the said court.

Composed of Governor and council.

Oaths.

III. *And be it enacted,* That every person, which shall, from time to time, or at any time hereafter, enjoy the office of a judge or justice of the said general court, at and before his entring into and upon the said office, shall take the oaths appointed by act of parliament to be taken, instead of the oaths of allegiance and supremacy; and shall make and subscribe the declaration appointed by one act of parliament, made in the twenty-fifth year of the reign of the late King Charles the second, intituled, An act preventing dangers which may happen from Popish recusants, and the oath mentioned in an act of parliament, intituled, An act to declare the alteration in the oath appointed to be taken by the act, intituled, An act for the further security of her majesty's person, and the succession of the crown in the protestant line; and for extinguishing the hopes of the pretended prince of Wales, and all other pretenders, and their open and secret abettors; and for declarin the association to be determined. And if any person whatsoever shall presume to sit, judge, decree, direct, act, or do, any manner of act or acts, thing or things whatsoever, appertaining and properly belonging to the office of a judge or justise of the said general court, before he hath taken the said oaths, and every of them; every person so presuming to sit, judge, decree, direct, act, or do, as aforesaid, without taking the oaths, and making and subscribing the declaration afore-mentioned, and every of them, shall, for every such offence, be fined five hundred pounds sterling; one moiety thereof to her majesty, her heirs and successors, for and towards the better support of this government, and the contingent charges thereof; and the

Penalty for acting without.

other moiety thereof to him or them that shall inform, or sue for the same.

IV. *Provided always,* That if the said oaths, declaration, or any of them, shall be abrogated by authority of the parliament of England, or become otherwise void, the same shall also be adjudged, deemed, and taken to be abrogated, and to become void in this colony and dominion also. Proviso.

V. *And be it further enacted,* That the said general court shall take cognizance of, and are hereby declared to have full power and lawful authority and jurisdiction, to hear and determine, all causes, matters, and things whatsoever, relating to or concerning any person or persons, ecclesiastic or civil, or to any other persons or things, of what nature soever the same shall be, whether the same be brought before them by original process, or appeal from any other court, or by any other ways or means whatsoever. Jurisdiction.

VI. *Provided always,* That no person shall take original process, for the trial of any thing in the general court, of less value than ten pounds sterling, or two thousand pounds of tobacco, on penalty of having such suit dismissed, and the plaintiff being non-suited, and paying costs of suit. Limitation of jurisdiction.

VII. *Provided always,* That if the justices of any county court, or the vestry of any parish, shall become liable to prosecution for the breach of any penal law, relating to their office; in such case, it shall and may be lawful for her majesty's attorney-general, or any other person or persons thereunto permitted or impowered by law, to inform or sue in the general court, for the penalty due on the breach of such penal law, although it be of less value than ten pounds sterling, or two thousand pounds of tobacco; any thing herein contained to the contrary, notwithstanding. Proviso.

VIII. *And be it further enacted,* That the said general court shall be held two times every year; to wit, one court shall begin upon the fifteenth day of April, if not on a Sunday, and then on the Monday thereafter, and shall continue to be held eighteen natural days, Sundays exclusive; and one other court shall begin on the fifteenth day of October, if not on a Sunday, and then on Monday thereafter, and shall continue to be held eighteen natural days, Sundays exclusive. Terms.

Proviso.

IX. *Provided nevertheless,* That if all suits, and other matters depending in the said courts, shall be ended in less time than the days appointed by this act, for them to sit; in such case, it shall be lawful for the said judges or justices to adjourn until the next succeeding general court.

Other oaths.

X. *And be it further enacted,* That the said judges or justices, and every one of them, at the time of his or their entring into and upon his and their office or offices, shall take the following oaths, and every of them, for the due execution of his and their said office and offices, under the like fine, penalty, and forfeiture, as is before mentioned, for not taking the oaths appointed by act of parliament to be taken, instead of the oaths of supremacy and allegiance: To be recovered and divided in the same manner.

The Oath of a Judge of the General Court.

Oath of a Judge.

YOU shall swear, that you will well and truly serve our sovereign lady the queen, and her people, in the office of a judge or justice of the general court of Virginia; and you shall not council or assent to any thing, the which might turn to the hurt or disheriting of the queen, by any way or colour; and you shall do equal law, and execution of right, to all the queen's subjects, rich and poor, without having regard to any person: You shall not take, by yourself, or by any other person, any gift or reward, of gold, silver, or any other thing, (except meat and drink, and that but of small value:) You shall not take any fees, or other gratuity, of any person, great or small, except such salary as shall be by law appointed: You shall not maintain, by yourself, or any other, privily or openly, any plea or quarrel hanging in any of the queen's courts: You shall not delay any person of common right for the letters of the queen, her governor of this country, or of any other person, nor for any other cause: And in case any letter come to you, contrary to the law, you shall nothing do for such letter, but you shall proceed to do the law, the said letters notwithstanding: And lastly, in all things belonging to your said office, during your continuance therein, you shall faithfully, justly, and truly, according to the best of your skill and judgment, do equal and impartial justice, without fraud. *So help you God.*

The Oath of a Judge of the General Court, in Chancery.

YOU shall swear, that well and truly you will serve our sovereign lady the queen, and her people, in the office of a judge or justice of the general court of Virginia, in Chancery; and that you will do equal right to all manner of people, great and small, high and low, rich and poor, according to equity and good conscience, and the laws and usages of this colony and dominion of Virginia, without favour, affection, or partiality. *So help you God.*

Of a judge in Chancery.

XI. And for the more easy and regular prosecution and determination of all suits and actions in the general court,

XII. *Be it enacted, by the authority aforesaid,* That all original process, (either by writ, summons, or any other manner or means, to bring any person or persons whatsoever, to answer any action, suit, information, bill, or plaint, in the general court,) and all executions, and all attachments awarded by the general court, at the common law, and all manner of subpœnas, attachments, and other process in Chancery, and all and every other process whatsoever, regularly and legally belonging or appertaining to, or for, or concerning any cause, suit, matter, or thing depending, or to be depending, or prosecuted, in the general court, shall be issued from the secretary's office, signed by the clerk of the general court; and shall also be again returned into the same office and offices, whence the same were issued.

Writs, tests and return.

XIII. *And be it further enacted,* That if any action, suit, bill, plaint, information, or any other thing, shall be commenced, brought, had, or made, against any person being a member of her majesty's council of state within this colony and dominion; then, instead of any other process which might be legally taken in like case against any other person, the clerk of the general court shall issue a summons, to the sheriff of the county where such councillor usually resides, reciting the matter or cause charged against him, and summoning him to appear and answer the same, upon such a certain day of the general court as shall be therein mentioned: And if the said councillor shall not appear at the day,

Process against a councillor.

according to the said summons, then it shall be lawful for the court to issue an attachment against the estate of every such councillor so failing to appear; and thereafter, the proceedings in such cases, shall be in the same manner, as upon the sheriff's returning *non est inventus*, on any ordinary process.

Against a sheriff, directed to coroner.

XIV. And for the prosecution of any action, suit, bill, plaint, information, or any other thing of the like nature, against the sheriff of any county, the like process shall be issued by the clerk of the general court, to the coroner of the county where the sheriff resides; and thereupon the like proceedings shall be had against such sheriff, in the same manner as is before directed, concerning the members of the council.

Rules for issuing writs, &c.

XV. *And be it further enacted,* That the clerk of the general court shall not issue writs, subpœnas, or any other original process, for more than twelve suits or actions returnable to any one day of the general court; neither shall he issue such process returnable to any day, except there shall have theretofore issued process for twelve suits or actions returnable to every preceding day of that general court.

How process shall be executed and returned.

XVI. *And be it further enacted,* That all process whatsoever, returnable to the general court, shall be executed, at least ten days before the day mentioned therein for the return thereof; and if any process shall be delivered to any sheriff, or other officer, so late that he cannot execute the same ten days before the day of the return, then it shall not be lawful for such sheriff, or other officer, to execute the same, but he shall make return thereupon, according to the truth of the case: And if any person takes out any original process whilst the general court is sitting, or within ten days before the beginning of any general court, such process shall be made returnable to the next general court after that then sitting, or beginning within ten days, as aforesaid, and not otherwise: And all such process issued and made returnable, otherwise than is herein directed, shall be, to all intents and purposes, null and void.

Proviso, as to criminal cases, and breaches of the peace.

XVII. *Provided always,* That nothing herein contained, shall be construed, deemed, or taken, to extend to the disabling or incapacitating any judge or justice of the General court, or any justice of the peace, or other officer, having lawful authority for the same, to apprehend, or cause to be apprehended, any traitor, felon, pirate, rioter, breaker of the peace, or any other criminal offender: but that all and every such offender or offenders, shall and may be bound over to appear at the general court, in like manner as heretofore hath, or might have been, lawfully practised, according to the laws of England.

XVIII. *Provided also,* That nothing herein, shall be construed to invalidate or vitiate any writ, process, warrant, or other mandate or precept, which shall be issued, made, or given, by any one or more of the judges or justices of the general court, returnable to the general court. **Further proviso.**

XIX. *Provided also,* That nothing herein contained, shall be construed to prohibit the clerk of the general court from issuing process for any more than twelve actions, suits, or prosecutions, in her majesty's behalf, returnable to the fourth day of the general court; but that it shall and may be lawful to and for her majesty's attorney-general, for the time being, or any other person prosecuting, on her majesty's behalf, to take process for any treason, murder, felony, piracy, breach of the peace, misdemeanor, or contempt, returnable to the fourth day of the general court, although there shall be theretofore issued process for twelve, or more actions, suits, or prosecutions, returnable to the same day; any thing herein contained to the contrary, in any wise, notwithstanding. **Criminal prosecutions, how returnable.**

XX. And because many controversies may arise, concerning the manner of accounting any number of days, that is hereby, or in any other act of assembly hereafter shall be set, for issuing, serving, or returning of process, for filing declarations, or other matters or things of the like nature: Therefore,

XXI. *Be it enacted, by the authority aforesaid,* That in all cases, where there is, or shall be, a certain number of days appointed, either for issuing, executing, or returning of process, filing declarations or pleas, or for any other matter or thing whatsoever, such number of days shall be accounted by natural days, exclusive of the days of issuing, executing, and returning of such process; and so in like manner for all other cases. **How the number of days to be calculated.**

XXII. *And be it further enacted, by the authority aforesaid,* That upon the issuing of process to any she-

Bail, how to be returned.

riff, for attaching the body of any one or more person or persons, to answer any suit, action, complaint, or information, if such sheriff, upon the execution of the process, shall return bail by him taken, for the appearance of such person or persons so attached, and the said person or persons shall fail to appear accordingly, then judgment shall be given against such bail, for what shall appear to be justly due to the plaintiff or prosecutor, at the next court; on condition, that if such person or persons so attached as aforesaid, shall make his, her, or their personal appearance at the next court after such judgment shall be given against the bail, as aforesaid, then the bail shall be discharged; otherwise the bail shall have the same liberty of defending himself, that the principal defendant might have had, if he had appeared; and then the judgment shall be confirmed against the bail for what shall appear due to the plaintiff or prosecutor: And if the sheriff, upon the execution of the process, shall not return any bail, and the defendant shall fail to appear, then judgment shall be given against the sheriff, in the same manner, and with the same condition, that is before expressed, against the bail. And in case the person or persons attached, shall fail to appear at the next court after such judgment against the sheriff, then the sheriff shall have the same liberty, and be liable to the like judgment as is before directed, for and against the bail: And if the sheriff depart this life before such judgment be confirmed against him, in such case, it shall and may be lawful to confirm such judgment as aforesaid, against the executors and administrators of the said sheriff: And if there shall not any will be proved, or administration of his estate granted, then it shall be lawful to confirm the said judgment against the estate of the said sheriff; and accordingly a writ of *fieri facias* shall and may issue to seize and levy so much of the goods and chattels of the deceased sheriff, as will satisfy the said judgment, and every part thereof.

Liability of.

Defence by.

Liability of sheriff.

How discharged.

Executors or administrators of sheriff liable.

Proviso, as to mode of defence by bail or sheriff.

XXIII. *Provided always*, That in all cases where the defendant or tenant shall fail to appear at the first court, the sheriff or bail shall not take any advantage by imparlance, or otherwise, of the plaintiff or demandant, for his, her, or their not having filed any declaration before the day whereto the writ was returnable, but judgment shall be given in manner aforesaid, against the bail or sheriff, his executors, administrators, or estate, as if the declaration had been filed in due time.

Special bail.

XXIV. *Provided also,* That after such conditional judgment as aforesaid, against the sheriff or bail, the said sheriff or bail shall not be discharged by the appearance of the defendant or tenant only, unless, at the same time, he, she, or they shall give special bail, for the abiding by the award of the court: And in case such special bail shall not be given, the proceedings shall be had against the sheriff or bail as aforesaid, as if the defendant or tenant had never appeared.

Remedy of bail and sheriff by attachment.

XXV. *Provided always, and it is hereby enacted and declared,* That in every case, where judgment shall be confirmed as aforesaid, against the bail or sheriff, or against his executors or administrators, or against his estate, for or by reason of the non-appearance, or other failure of the defendant as aforesaid, it shall and may be lawful for the court where such judgment shall be so confirmed, upon the motion of the bail or sheriff, or of his executors or administrators, or of any other person, on behalf of them, or either of them, to order an attachment to issue, to attach so much of the estate of the defendant, as shall be of value sufficient to satisfy such judgment, and the costs, and all other costs and charges concerning the same: Which attachment shall be returnable to the next succeeding general court, and thereupon the estate shall, by the court, be condemned, for satisfaction of the judgment, costs, and charges, as aforesaid, and shall cause the same to be lawfully appraised; and accordingly, so much thereof as shall be sufficient, shall be delivered to the bail or sheriff, or his executors or administrators, against whom the judgment shall have been confirmed, as aforesaid, to his and their own proper use, and the remainder shall be returned to the person from whom the same was attached.

Rules of proceeding.—See chap. 3, 1727.

XXVI. *And be it further enacted, by the authority aforesaid,* That for the better and more regular prosecution and determination of all causes in the said general court; and for the more exact entring of the judgments of the said court; and for the preservation of the records thereof, these following rules and methods shall be observed; to wit,

Declaration.

That every plaintiff or demandant shall file his declaration three days before the day whereto the writ is returnable; and if no declaration is filed in that time, (but yet shall be filed before the day of the return,) the defendant or tenant shall have one imparlance of course, more than otherwise should have been allowed; and if no declaration be filed before the day of the return, then the plaintiff or demandant shall be nonsuit.

Nonsuit.

That if the plaintiff or demandant fails to appear and prosecute his suit, he shall be nonsuit.

Costs on nonsuit.

That where any nonsuit is awarded by the court, there shall be paid for the same, (besides the costs of suit,) in manner following, to wit; If the defendant or tenant (or where there are several defendants or tenants, if any one of them) shall dwell twenty miles, or less, distant from the place of holding the general court, one hundred and fifty pounds of tobacco, and five pounds of tobacco, for every mile above twenty.

Plea.

That the defendant or tenant shall prepare his plea in writing, to the declaration of the plaintiff or demandant.

Duty of clerks.

That the clerk of the court do carefully preserve the declarations, pleas, and all evidences, and other papers, relating to any cause; and that they be all filed together in the office.

Land causes.

That in all cases, where the title of any estate, in land, is determined, the pleadings shall be all in writing; and shall be entered at large, with the judgment thereupon, in particular books set apart for that purpose.

Suits against justices and vestries.

That in all cases, where any fine is laid on the justices of any county court, or the members of the vestry of any parish, one action may be brought against them all jointly.

Orders of each day to be drawn up.

That for prevention of errors, in entring the judgments of the court, the proceedings of every day, shall be drawn at large by the clerk, against the next sitting of the court, when the same shall be read in open court, and such corrections as are necessary, shall be made therein; and then the same shall be signed by the secretary of this dominion, for the time being, or his deputy: Which draughts of the proceedings, so signed, shall also be very carefully preserved amongst the records.

XXVII. And forasmuch as in many cases, for the trials of matters of fact, in the said general court, it may be necessary to examine several witnesses, that the truth, in such cases, may be the better known:—Therefore,

XXVIII. *Be it enacted, by the authority aforesaid,* That the following orders, rules, and methods, for the summoning, examination, and taking affidavits of witnesses, in all cases depending in the said court, and every of them, be observed, and put in practice, hereafter mentioned, to wit, Subpœnas, how to issue.

That in all cases, where witnesses are to appear at the general court, a summons shall be issued for the same, by the clerk of the general court, for the time being, expressly mentioning the time and place where the witnesses are to appear, and the names of the parties to the suit wherein they are to give evidence, and at whose request they are summoned.

That if any witness, by sickness, age, or other lawful disability, be incapable of attending, to give his or her evidence, according to such summons, then every person so incapacitated, shall procure a certificate of such disability, under the hand (at least) of one justice of the peace of the quorum, in the county where he or she resides: And in such case, the judges or justices of the court where such suit is depending, or any two of them, shall or may, by one or more commission or commissions, from time to time, as need shall require, impower such and as many persons as they shall think fit and necessary, in any county within this dominion, to take and receive all and every the affidavit and affidavits, of any person or persons so disabled, as aforesaid, and procuring a certificate in manner as is before directed. Depositions of witnesses, when to be taken.

XXIX. *Provided always.* That the party praying for and obtaining such commission or commissions, for taking or receiving any affidavit or affidavits, as aforesaid, shall make known unto the other party against whom the same are to be taken, the time and place of the execution of every such commission, at least ten days before the day appointed for such execution. And Commissions, how obtained.

all affidavits otherwise taken than is herein directed, shall be, to all intents and purposes, null and void.

Witnesses refusing to depose, to be committed.

XXX. That if any person whatsoever shall be summoned as a witness, and upon his or her appearance in the general court, or before the persons appointed to take affidavits, as aforesaid, shall refuse to give evidence upon oath, when thereto lawfully required; then such person so refusing, shall immediately thereupon be committed to the common goal, there to remain without bail or mainprise, until he or she shall be willing to give evidence, upon oath, in such manner as the law now doth, or at any time hereafter shall direct.

Affirmation of Quakers allowed.

XXXI. *Provided always*, That the people commonly called Quakers, shall have the same liberty of giving their evidence, by way of solemn affirmation and declaration, as is prescribed by one act of parliament, *Septimo & Octavo Gulielmi Tertii Regis*, intituled, *An act that the solemn affirmation and declaration of the people called Quakers, shall be accepted instead of an oath, in the usual form*; which said act of parliament, for so much thereof as relates to such affirmation and declaration, and for the time of its continuance in force, and not otherwise, shall be, to all intents and purposes, in full force within this dominion.

Popish recusants, negroes, Indians, incapable of being witnesses.

That popish recusants convict, negroes, mulattoes and Indian servants, and others, not being christians, shall be deemed and taken to be persons incapable in law, to be witnesses in any cases whatsoever.

Penalty on witnesses failing to attend.

That if any person shall be summoned to attend at the general court as a witness, and shall fail to attend, according to the summons, for every such failure, he or she who shall be guilty thereof, shall forfeit and pay to the party agrieved, one thousand pounds of good tobacco: to be recovered, with costs, by action of debt, in any court of record within this dominion.

Proviso.

XXXII. *Provided always*, That if at the time such person so summoned ought to have appeared to have given evidence, sufficient cause be shewn of his or her incapacity to attend, then no forfeiture or penalty shall be incurred by such failure; but if sufficient cause be not shewn at the next succeeding court after such failure, then, upon the motion of the party agrieved, it shall be lawful for the said court to grant judgment for the forfeiture afore-mentioned, against the person or persons so summoned, and failing to appear as aforesaid.

That upon the commitment of any person or persons, for any capital or criminal offence or offences, the magistrate or magistrates making such commitment, shall cause all the witnesses of the fact, that shall come to his or their knowledge, to enter into recognizances for their and every of their appearance, to give evidence, *viva voce*, upon the trial, of such offender or offenders, and every of them. Recognizance of witnesses in criminal cases.

That during the attendance of any person summoned as a witness at the general court, and as the said person shall be going to, and returning from the place of such attendance, (allowing one natural day for every twenty miles such person's residence shall be distant from the same, no person or persons whatsoever, shall serve or execute, or cause to be served or executed, upon any person so attending, going to, or returning from, such place of attendance as aforesaid, any writ, process, warrant, order, judgment, or decree; and if any such be served or executed, contrary to this act, the same shall be void, to all intents and purposes whatsoever. Witnesses privileged from arrest.

That for every mile any person shall travel, either in going to, or returning from, the place where he or she shall be summoned to appear as a witness, there shall be paid to him or her, by the person or persons at whose suit the summons issued, one pound of tobacco and a half per mile, together with the necessary charges of ferriage, in going and returning, and sixty pounds of tobacco, per day, for every day's attendance, from the time appointed for the appearance of such witnesses, until the time they shall be discharged. Their allowance.

That in any bill of costs, there shall not be allowed the charge of above three witnesses, to the proof of any one particular matter of fact. 3 taxed in bill of costs.

XXXIII. And to the intent that erroneous proceedings and judgments of the other her majesty's courts within this dominion, may be corrected and amended, with as much expedition, and with as little charge to the parties concerned, as may be: Therefore,

XXXIV. *Be it enacted by the authority aforesaid*, That if any person or persons, bodies politic or corporate, shall, at any time hereafter, take him, her, or themselves to be agrieved, contrary to law and justice, Appeals.

by the judgment, decree, or sentence of any other court within this dominion, of what nature or value soever the cause shall be; then, and in such case, it shall and may be lawful, to and for such person or persons, bodies politic and corporate, and every of them, so agrieved, to enter an appeal from any such judgment, decree, or sentence, to the said general court: Upon which said appeals, it shall be lawful to and for the parties appealing, to assign and shew forth the errors of the judgment and proceedings of the court from whence they appealed, in manner as is hereafter expressed, and not otherwise: That is to say,

Rules, as to assigning errors on appeals not exceeding 20l.

Upon an appeal, in any personal action, where the judgment, decree, or sentence of the court appealed from, shall be for any sum not exceeding twenty pounds sterling, or four thousand pounds of tobacco, the appellant or appellants, in his or their declaration, or bill of errors, exhibited in the general court, shall not be permitted to assign any error, to reverse the judgment, decree, or sentence of any court, other than errors in matter of right. And if, upon hearing the cause in the general court, such judgment, decree, or sentence, shall appear to be rightly and justly given, the same shall be affirmed; notwithstanding any mispleading, or other error in the form of the proceedings, whatsoever.

Between 20l. and 50l.

And, upon an appeal, in any personal action, where the judgment, decree, or sentence appealed from, shall be for any sum not under twenty pounds sterling, or four thousand pounds of tobacco, nor above fifty pounds sterling, or ten thousand pounds of tobacco, the appellant or appellants, in his or their declaration, or bill of errors, exhibited in the general court, shall not be permitted to assign any error, to reverse the judgment, decree, or sentence of any court, other than errors in matter of right, and such errors in the form or manner of the proceedings, as were insisted upon in the court from whence the appeal shall be made. And if, upon the hearing of the cause in the general court, the judgment, decree, or sentence appealed from, appears to be justly made, in point of right, and that the errors assigned in the manner of the proceedings shall not be sufficient to reverse the same, then such judgment, decree, or sentence, shall be affirmed in the general court; notwithstanding any other errors, which may be assigned, in the formality of the proceedings.

If above 50l.

And, upon appeals from any judgment, decree, or sentence, in personal actions, suits in chancery, informations, or other controversies, of greater value than fifty pounds sterling, or ten thousand pounds of tobacco, and all real actions, of what value soever, it shall and may be lawful to and for the appellant or appellants to assign errors, either of form or substance, in like manner as is permitted by the laws of England, in the prosecution upon writs of error.

Damages on affirmance.

XXXV. *And be it further enacted, by the authority aforesaid,* That upon an appeal, in any personal action, if the judgment, decree, or sentence appealed from, be affirmed in the general court, then the appellant or appellants shall pay unto the appellee or appellees (besides the principal sum and costs, expressed in such judgment, decree, or sentence) fifteen per cent. damage, upon the principal debt, or the sum recovered for damage, and upon the costs of suit in the court from whence such appeal shall be made.

In real actions.

And upon any appeal, in any real action, if the judgment, decree, or sentence appealed from, shall be affirmed in the general court, then the appellant or appellants, shall pay unto the appellee or appellees, in lieu of the fifteen per cent. aforesaid, the sum of two thousand pounds of tobacco, damage, over and above what shall be contained and expressed in the judgment, decree, or sentence, from whence such appeal shall be made.

Days, for appeals.

XXXVI. And, for the more regular hearing and determining of such appeals as shall be made, from the several county courts, unto the general court: *Be it enacted, by the authority aforesaid,* That all appeals from the county courts of Henrico, Prince George, Surry, Isle of Wight, Nansemond, Norfolk, and Princess Anne, shall be made to the sixth day of the next succeeding general court after such appeals respectively: And that all appeals from the county courts of James-City, Charles-City, New-Kent, Warwick, and Elizabeth-City, shall be made to the seventh day of the next succeeding general court after such appeals respectively: And that all appeals from the county courts of Gloucester, King William, King and Queen, Middlesex, and Essex, shall be made to the eighth day of the next succeeding general court after such appeals, respectively: And that all appeals from the county courts of Richmond, Westmoreland, Northumberland, Stafford, and Lancaster, shall be made to the ninth day of the next succeeding general court after such appeals, respectively: And that all appeals from the county courts of Accomack, and Northampton, shall be made to the tenth day of the next succeeding general court after such appeals, respectively: And that no appeals from any county courts, be admitted to any other day of the general court, than what is herein expressed and directed.

Supersedeas.

XXXVII. *And be it enacted by the authority aforesaid,* That upon supersedeas brought to the general court, to reverse any judgment, decree, or sentence given in any of the county courts of this dominion, the proceedings shall be in the same manner as before directed for appeals; and the like damages awarded, in case the judgment, decree, or sentence of the county court be affirmed.

XXXVIII. And forasmuch, as several fines and forfeitures, by this and several other acts, are, or may be directed to be recovered in any court of record in this dominion: For the better explanation thereof,

Courts of record.

XXXIX. *Be it enacted by the authority aforesaid,* That the general court of this dominion, and the courts held before the justices of the peace, in the several respective counties, commonly called the county courts, shall be deemed and taken, and are hereby declared to be the only courts of record, of or in this dominion; and that no other court or courts whatsoever, shall be construed, deemed, or taken to be such.

Repealing clause.

XL. *And be it further enacted,* That all and every other act and acts, and every clause and article thereof, heretofore made, for so much thereof as relates to establishing the general court; or to the regulating or settling the proceedings therein; or to any other matter or thing whatsoever, within the purview of this act, is, and are hereby repealed, and made void, to all intents and purposes, as if the same had never been made.

CHAP. XX.

An act for enlarging the power of the Sheriff attending the General Court, and of the Constables of Bruton Parish.

Preamble.

I. WHEREAS the City of Williamsburg is so placed, that persons may easily evade being summoned to attend the general court, as grand jurors, jurors, and evidences, or to be taken, upon any precept of the said court, unless the power of the sheriff, and his officers attending the said court, be enlarged.

Sheriff attending general court, may execute process in Williamsburg, and half a mile around.

II. *Be it therefore enacted, by the governor, council, and burgesses, of this present general assembly, and it is hereby enacted, by the authority of the same,* That the sheriff, and his deputies and bailiffs, which shall attend the general court, and every of them, be impowered, and they and every of them are hereby empowered, during the sitting of the general court, to summon grand jurors, jurors, and evidences, and to execute other the commands of the general court, in all and every part of the city of Williamsburg, and half a mile compass from the same, and to make return thereof; which return shall be sufficient for the general court to proceed thereon.

Constables of Bruton parish, may act in Williamsburg, &c.

III. *And be it further enacted by the authority aforesaid.* That it shall and may be lawful for the constables of Bruton parish, appointed or to be appointed by the courts of the counties of James City, or York, respectively, to do and execute all matters and things appertaining to the office of a constable within any part of the city of Williamsburg, and half a mile compass from the same.

Repealing clause.

IV. *And be it enacted,* That all and every other act and acts, and every clause and article thereof, heretofore made, for so much thereof as relates to any matter or thing whatsoever, within the purview of this act, is, and are hereby repealed, and made void, to all intents and purposes, as if the same had never been made.

CHAP. XXI.

Edi. 1733, and 1752.

*An Act concerning the Granting, Seating, and Planting, and for Settling the Titles and bounds of Lands; and for preventing unlawful Shooting and ranging thereupon.**

[From MS.]

Importation rights declared.

50 acres of land each.

BE it enacted, by the governor, councill and burgesses of this present general assembly, and it is hereby enacted and declared by the authority of the same, That all and every person, male or female imported and coming into this colony and dominion free, has a right to fifty acres of land; and every christian servant, male or female imported after he or she becomes free, or time of servitude is expired, has a right to fifty acres of land for his or her importation; and every person coming into this colony, and importing a wife or children under age, hath a right to fifty acres of land for himself, his wife and every such child so imported, and certificate thereof shall be granted to every such free person and master of a family demanding the same, and to every servant after such their freedom in manner and form as is by this act hereafter directed, and that no person or persons by virtue of such importation shall hereafter claim any right to land other than the persons so imported as aforesaid, or those to whom they shall assign their right in the presence of two witnesses; any law, usage or custom to the contrary in any wise notwithstanding.

Not to extend to transient persons.

Provided always, That nothing herein contained shall be construed to give a right to any factor, master of a ship or other seafaring man not setling him or themselves, and becoming tithable in the country, to claim or take up any land by colour of his or their importation, nor to any person whatsoever to claim a right for his importation more than once.

---

* The title only, of this important act, is given in the editions of 1733 and 1752, under an erroneous impression, it is presumed, that the whole law was repealed by chap. 13, of 1710.—But, by comparing the two laws together, it will at once be perceived that all of the first part of this act, which relates to the various modes of acquiring titles to lands, the forms of patents, &c. is omitted in the act of 1710;—and that act only professes to repeal so much of this, or any other, "for so much thereof, as relates to any matter or thing, within the purview" of that act.

And be it enacted by the authority aforesaid, That every person claiming, or pretending any right to take up and patent any land within this colony for the importation of any person or persons, shall make proof of such importation upon his or her corporall oath, either in the general court, or in some county court, and a certificate thereof shall be produced in the secretarys office. Whereupon, that is to say, upon proof made as aforesaid in the general court, or in some county court, and a certificate produced in the secretarys office; the clerk of the said office is hereby required to make a certificate thereof, and give the same to the party claiming the right as aforesaid, upon which certificate from the clerk of the secretarys office any sworn surveyor unto whom the same shall be exhibited lawfully may, and is hereby required within his respective precincts to survey for the party claiming and desiring the same, so much land not theretofore legally occupied or possessed by any other person as by the certificate shall appear to be due, and accordingly shall make a return thereof into the secretarys office to the end that a patent may issue thereupon.

Mode of obtaining patents for importation rights.

Surveys, how and by whom made.

And be it further enacted by the authority aforesaid, That if any person not having right to any land for importation as aforesaid, shall be willing and desirous to take up and plant any land in this colony, it shall and may be lawful to and for every such person to obtain a right thereto, in manner following: that is to say, the person desiring such right shall pay unto her majesties receiver generall of the revenues in this dominion for the time being, for and towards the better support of the government of this her majesties colony and dominion, and the contingent charges thereof, the sum of five shillings current money for every fifty acres of land he or she intends to take up and plant, and so after that rate for a lesser quantity, and thereupon the said receiver general is hereby impowered and required to make a certificate thereof under his hand, and to give the same unto the party from whom he received the money; upon which certificate any sworn surveyor unto whom the same shall be exhibited lawfully may, and is hereby required within his respective precincts to survey for the party claiming and desiring the same, so much land not theretofore legally occupied or possessed

How patents for other lands are to be obtained.

Rates of land, payable to receiver-general.

Certificates.

Surveys,

to be returned to secretary's office.

by any other person as by such certificate shall appear to be due, allowing after the rate of fifty acres for every five shillings, so paid as aforesaid, and accordingly shall make a return of such survey so made unto the secretarys office to the end, that a patent may issue thereupon; and all patents heretofore obtained, or which hereafter may be obtained for any lands in this colony upon such certificates as aforesaid from the receiver generall for the time being, shall be, and are hereby declared to be to all intents, constructions and purposes, as firm, valid and available in law, to convey and assure the lands therein granted unto the patentee and patentees, and to his, her and their heirs and assigns for ever, as if the same had been obtained upon certificate for the importation of persons into this colony.

Patents to issue.

Confirmation of former patents.

Limitation of the quantity of land, which may be taken up, by one person in a tract.

And be it enacted by the authority aforesaid, That it shall and may be lawful for any person, upon producing rights by importation, or otherwise, to claim or take up any quantity of land not exceeding five hundred acres in one tract, and that there shall not hereafter be granted to any person or persons not being owner or owners of five tithable servants or slaves at least, any greater quantity of land in one tract than five hundred acres. But if any person or persons being owner or owners of five or more tithable servants or slaves, shall be desirous to take up land upon certificate of rights obtained as aforesaid, there shall be granted unto such person or persons over and above the said five hundred acres, the quantity of two hundred acres more for every tithable servant or slave, which he or they shall prove him or themselves to be owners of.

Greatest quantity.

Proviso, as to former entries.

Provided, That no grant of land to any person whatsoever shall exceed four thousand acres in one patent, excepting always such tracts of land for which entrys are already made, and for which rights have been duly entered, with the surveyor before the making of this act; all which tracts so entered for shall be granted to the persons by whom the said entrys were made in the same manner as the same might have been granted before the making hereof.

Provided always, That nothing herein contained shall be construed or taken to enable or entitle any person or persons (having a right to land for importation or otherwise as aforesaid) to take up and patent any swamps, marshes or low grounds, lying adjacent to the high land of any person or persons theretofore patented, untill such person or persons so intending to take up and patent the same, shall in the presence of two witnesses have given notice of such his intention to the proprietor and possessor for the time being in possession of such high land, and untill one whole year shall be fully expired from and after the time of giving such notice as aforesaid; and then it shall and may be lawfull to and for such person or persons (having given notice as aforesaid) and to his, her or their heirs or assigns to take up and patent the same, in which patent shall be particularly expressed and sett down whether the lands therein granted are swamps, marshes or low grounds, and to whose high lands they are adjoining, and all and every patent and patents which shall be obtained contrary to the true intent and meaning hereof, are hereby declared to be to all intents, constructions and purposes whatsoever, null and void as if the same had never been made. Any law statute or usage to the contrary notwithstanding.

Swamps, marshes, and sunken grounds, rules concerning.

And if any controversy shall thereafter arise concerning such notice being given within five years after such person or person (having given notice as aforesaid) shall be in actuall possession of such swamps, marshes or low grounds as aforesaid, the *onus probandi* shall lye upon the person who ought to have given the notice, and if no such controversy do arise in that time, five years possession shall be held and taken as good proof that notice was given according to the true intent and meaning hereof.

Limitation as to notice.

Provided always, That nothing herein contained shall be construed, deemed or taken to give liberty to any person or persons to take up and patent any such swamps, marshes or low grounds, lying adjacent to the high lands of any *feme covert,* infant under the age of one and twenty years, or any person not being *compos mentis* on pretence, or by virtue of notice, being given as aforesaid, either to such *feme covert,* infant or person *non compos mentis,* or to the husband, guardian or other person being in possession thereof.

Saving the rights of infants, femes covert, &c.

And forasmuch as severall controversies hereafter may arise concerning the validity of patents for land in this colony formerly issued, but are not to be found amongst the records in the secretarys office, or for which no rights have been legally obtained, or have not been duly entered upon record, as they ought to have been,

For prevention of any inconveniencys that hereafter may arise thereby,

Confirmation of former patents, to those in possession.

Be it enacted by the authority aforesaid, That all such patents for any lands within this colony, heretofore granted by the governor or commander in cheif thereof, for the time being, shall be held deemed and taken, and are hereby declared to be to all intents, constructions and purposes as firm, valid and available in law, to convey and assure the lands therein granted unto such person and persons as the same shall have been granted unto respectively, and to their heirs and assigns for ever, being now in possession thereof as if the same patents had been legally entered upon the records in the secretarys office, and as if rights had been legally obtained for the same, and duly entered upon the records as they ought to have been, any law, statute or usage to the contrary thereof in any wise notwithstanding; and upon the passing of any patent for lands hereafter, the secretary of this dominion, for the time being, is hereby required to cause the same to be truly entered upon the records of his office, together with the certificate (either for rights by importation or of money paid to the receiver general as aforesaid) whereupon such patent shall have been obtained.

Duty of secretary, in future.

And be it further enacted, that the patents for lands with this colony shall for ever hereafter be granted in the several respective forms herein after expressed and set down, that is to say,

Form of patents.

For importation rights,

"ANNE, by the grace of God, of England, Scotland, France and Ireland, Queen, defender of the faith, &c. To all to whom these presents shall come greeting: know ye that for divers good causes and considerations, but more especially for and in consideration of [the importation of persons to dwell within this our colony of Virginia, whose names are A. B. &c.] or [for and in consideration of the sum of of good and lawfull money for our use, paid to our receiver general of our revenues in this our said colony and dominion of Virginia] we have given, granted and confirmed, and by these presents for us, our heirs and successors, we do give, grant and confirm unto N. R. of the county of Q. one certain tract or parcell of land containing acres, lying and being in the parish of T. in the county of S. and bounded as followeth, to wit: with all woods, underwoods, swamps, marshes, low grounds, meadows, feedings, rivers, waters, water courses, together with the priviledges of hunting, hawking, fishing and fowling, and all veins, mines and quarries, as well discovered as not discovered, and all other proffits, commoditys and hereditaments whatsoever to the same, or any part thereof belonging, or in any wise appertaining to have, hold, possess and enjoy the said tract or parcell of land, and all other the before granted premises, and every part thereof with their and every of their appurtenances unto the said N. R. and to his heirs and assigns for ever, to the only use and behoof of him the said N. R. his heirs and assigns for ever, to be held of us, our heirs and successors, as of our manor of East Greenwich, in the county of Kent, in free and common soccage, and not in capite or by knight service yeilding and paying unto us, our heirs and successors for every fifty acres of land, (and so proportionably for a lesser quantity than fifty acres) the fee rent of one shilling yearly to be paid upon the feast of Saint Michael the Arch Angell.

or composition paid to the receiver-general

Provided always, That if the said N. R. his heirs and assigns do not seat or plant upon the premises herein before granted in manner as is directed by one act of assembly, entitled, an act concerning the granting, seating and planting, and for setling the titles and bounds of lands; and for preventing unlawfull shooting and ranging thereupon, the same to be so seated or planted upon within the space of three years next coming, after the date of these presents, then the estate hereby granted shall cease and be utterly determined, and thereafter it shall and may be lawfull to and for us, our heirs and successors to grant the same lands and premises with the appurtenances unto such other person or persons, his and their heirs and assigns as shall make lawfull suit for the same. In witness whereof we have caused these our letters patents to be made. Witness, E. N. esq. our lieutenant and governor general of our said colony and dominion, &c."

The forme of a patent for land that hath been taken up and forfeited for want of seating or planting.

Form of patents, for lands forfeited, by not seating and planting.

"ANNE, by the grace of God, of England, Scotland, France and Ireland, Queen, defender of the faith, &c. to all to whom these presents shall come greeting. Whereas by one patent under the seal of this our colony and dominion of Virginia, bearing date at the day of in the year of our reign, There was granted to A. B. of the county of C. one certain tract or parcell of land containing acres, lying and being in the parish of D. in the county of E. and bounded as followeth, to witt: Which said tract or parcell of land was granted on condition of seating or planting as in the said patent expressed; and whereas the said A. B. hath failed to make such seating or planting, and F. G. of the county of H. hath made humble suit to our general court of our said colony and dominion, and hath obtained a grant of the same land; therefore, know ye, that for divers good causes and considerations, but more especially for and in consideration of [the importation of persons to dwell within this our colony of Virginia, whose names are A. B. &c.] or [for and in consideration of the sum of of good and lawfull money for our use, paid to our receiver general of our revenues in this our said colony and dominion of Virginia] we do give grant and confirm unto the said F. G. and to his heirs and assigns for ever, all and every part and parcell of the said tract or parcell of land, with all woods, underwoods, swamps, marshes, low grounds, meadows, feedings, rivers, waters, water courses, together with the priviledges of hunting, hawking, fishing and fowling, and all veins, mines and quarries, as well discovered as not discovered, and all other proffits, commoditys and hereditaments, whatsoever, to the same or any part thereof belonging, or in any wise appertaining to have, hold, possess and enjoy the said tract or parcell of land, and all other the before granted premises, and every part thereof with their and every of their appurtenances unto the said F. G. and to his heirs and assigns for ever, to the only use and behoof of him the said F. G. his heirs and assigns for ever, to be held of us, our heirs and successors as of our manor of East Greenwich, in the county of Kent, in free and common soccage, and not in capite or by knights service, yeilding and paying unto us, aur heirs and successors for every fifty acres of land, and so proportionably for a lesser quantity than fifty acres, the fee rent of one shilling yearly, to be paid upon the feast of Saint Michael the Arch Angell.

Provided always, That if the said F. G. his heirs or assigns do not seat or plant upon the premises herein before granted in manner as is directed by one act of assembly, entitled, an act concerning the granting, seating and planting, and for settling the titles and bounds of lands, and for preventing unlawfull shooting and ranging thereupon, or cause the same to be so seated or planted upon within the space of three years next coming, after the date of these presents, then the estate hereby granted shall cease and be utterly determined, and thereafter it shall and may be lawfull to and for us, our heirs and successors, to grant the same lands and premises with the appurtenances unto such other person or persons, his and their heirs and assigns as shall make lawfull suit to us for the same. In witness whereof, we have caused these our letters patents to be made. Witness, E. N. esq. our leiutenant and governor general of our said colony and dominion."

The form of a patent for escheat Lands.

Form of patents for escheated lands.

"ANNE, by the grace of God, of England, Scotland, France and Ireland, queen, defender of the faith, &c. To all, to whom these presents shall come greeting: Whereas by one inquisition, indented, taken at the day of in the year of our reign, by virtue of a warrant directed to our escheator for the county of it appears that [here is to be inserted the material of the inquisition] and whereas A. B. of the county of hath made humble suit to our general court of our said colony and dominion, and hath obtained a grant of the same land, paying the composition and other charges usuall in the cases, Therefore, know ye, that for divers good causes and considerations us thereunto moving, but more especially for and in consideration of the sum of two pounds of tobacco for every acre of the said land for our use, already paid by the said A. B. to our receiver general of our revenues in this our said colony and dominion of Virginia, we have given, granted & confirmed, and by these presents, for us, our heirs and successors, we do give, grant and confirm unto the said A. B. and to his heirs and assigns for ever, all and every part and parcell of the said of land, with houses, edifices, buildings, gardens, orchards, fields, fences, woods, underwoods, swamps, marshes, low grounds, meadows, feedings, rivers, waters, water courses, together with the priviledges of hunting, hawking, fishing and fowling, and all veins, mines and quarries, as well discovered as not discovered, and all other proffitts, comoditys and hereditaments whatsoever to the same, or any part thereof belonging, or in any wise appertaining, to have, hold, possess and enjoy the said tract or parcell of land, and all other the before granted premises, and every part thereof with their and every of their appurtenances unto the said A. B. and to his heirs and assigns for ever, to the only use and behoof of him the said A. B. his heirs and assigns for ever, to be held of us, our heirs and successors as of our manor of East Greenwich, in the county of Kent, in free and common soccage, and not in capite, or by knights service, yeilding and paying unto us, our heirs and successors for evey fifty acres of land, and so proportionably for a lesser quantity than fifty acres, the fee rent of one shilling yearly, to be paid upon the feast of Saint Michael, the Arch Angell. In witness whereof we have caused these our letters patents to be made. Witness E. N. esq. our lieutenant and governor general of our said colony and dominion, &c."

Rights of patentees.

And all and every patent and patents hereafter to be granted in manner herein before expressed and set down, shall be held deemed and taken, and are hereby declared to be to all intents, constructions and purposes, firm, valid and available in law to convey and assure the lands therein mentioned unto the severall respective persons to whom the same shall be thereby granted, and to their heirs and assigns for ever, together with the severall priviledges and royaltys therein granted.

And whereas by the said patent it is provided that the patentee or patentees shall seat and plant the land therein to him or them granted within three years from the date of the patent, for the better and more certain understanding of the said proviso.

What shall constitute a seating and planting.

Be it enacted by the authority aforesaid, That the building of one house of wood, after the usuall manner of building in this colony, being at least in length twelve foot, and in breadth, twelve foot, and clearing, planting and tending at least one acre of land, shall be, and is hereby declared to be a good and sufficient seating and planting of land pursuant to the said proviso.

Proviso, as to swamps, marshes, &c.

Provided always, That when any patent shall be granted for swamps, marshes or other unhabitable grounds, no seating or planting shall be required for the same, but all and every such patent and patents shall be, and are hereby declared to be as valid and available in law to all intents and purposes, without such seating and planting, as if the same (being high land) had been actually seated and planted as aforesaid. Anything in the said proviso, in the patent, to the contrary thereof notwithstanding.

New patents for surplus lands, how obtained.

Provided also, That if upon a new survey of any lands theretofore granted to any person or persons, there shall appear to be a greater number of acres within the bounds expressed than are mentioned and sett down in the patent, in such case it shall be lawfull for the proprietor and possessor of such lands for the time being, to sue forth a new patent for the same lands, wherein the just quantity of land shall be more exactly set down, yet nevertheless such proprietor and possessor shall not be obliged to make any new seating or planting upon the said land for or by reason of the proviso in such new patent, but the same shall enure and take effect to his benefitt and advantage as fully and absolutely to all intents and purposes as if the said proviso were not mentioned in such new patent. Any thing herein contained to the contrary thereof in any wise notwithstanding.

Double patents heretofore granted, confirmation of.

Provided also, That where any person hath heretofore taken up any tract or parcell of land adjoining to any other tract of land theretofore in the possession of such person, and shall thereupon have obtained a patent, (commonly called a double patent) wherein both tracts shall have been joyned together, in such case all patents heretofore so granted, shall be, and are hereby declared to be valid and available in law to confirm the same to the patentee and patentees, and those claiming under him, her or them being in possession thereof, and to his, her and their heirs for ever, without making any new seating and planting for or by reason of two tracts being joyned in one patent as aforesaid. Any thing in the said proviso in the patent contained to the contrary thereof in any wise notwithstanding.

No double patents hereafter to avail, without seating and planting.

Provided always, That nothing herein contained shall be construed, deemed or taken to give liberty to any person or persons hereafter to sue forth such double patents as aforesaid, and to enjoy the lands therein granted (by virtue thereof) without seating and planting that part of the land so taken up and joyned as aforesaid to the land theretofore in his, her or their possession according to the said proviso in the patent.

Lands not seated and planted within 3 years, lost, and all rights on which the patent was obtained.

And be it further enacted by the authority aforesaid, That if any person or persons shall hereafter obtain a patent for any tract of land within this colony, and shall fail to seat and plant the same within three years according as is herein before directed, such person or persons shall not only loose the land so granted and not seated and planted, but shall also forfeit and loose all benefit and advantage he might otherwise make by those rights upon which he obtained such patent.

No patent to issue for forfeited land, in less than three years;

nor without an order of the general court.

Mode of proceeding to obtain such order.

And be it further enacted, That no patent shall hereafter be granted to any person or persons for any tract or parcell of land as lost and forfeited for want of seating and planting as aforesaid, untill three years shall be expired from and after the date of the first patent granted for the same, neither shall any patent be granted by reason of such forfeiture, untill an order of the general court shall be procured for the same, which order shall be obtained in manner following, that is to say, the person petitioning for any such order, shall in his petition set forth, what county the land lyes in and to whom it was formerly granted, and in what county the grantee resides, whereupon such grantee shall by order of court be cited to appear at the next succeeding general court, upon a certain day thereof, to shew cause why such land formerly granted to him, and by him forfeited for want of seating and planting, may not be granted to the party petitioning for the same, which order shall be served upon such grantee by the sheriff or under sheriff of the respective county where he resides, and if upon the return thereof, so served, the grantee do not appear, or some other person in his behalf, and make sufficient proof that the land petitioned for hath been seated and planted according as herein is directed, then the same shall be granted in the same manner and under the same restrictions as is directed for the granting of lands not before patented, allowing always the first choice of any part of the said forfeited lands to the first petitioner, he making manifest his right (either by importation or otherwise) to take up and patent so much land as shall be proportionable to the number of tithable servants or slaves, whereof he or she is owner, and the residue of the said forfeited lands (if any be) shall be granted to such other person or persons as shall petition for the same, he, she or they producing rights, and making manifest the number of tithable servants or slaves, whereof he, she or they are owners proportionable to the quantity of land claimed.

Provided always, That if upon tryall it shall appear that such lands so petitioned for, as forfeited, shall have been seated and planted by the first patentee, or those claiming under him before the exhibiting of such petition, in that case such seating and planting, tho' not made within three years after the date of the patent shall be adjudged, and it is hereby declared to be a sufficient seating and planting to fulfill the proviso aforementioned, expressed in the patent. Any thing herein contained, or any law, statute or usage, or any other matter or thing to the contrary thereof in any wise notwithstanding.

Proviso, as to those who seat and plant before the exhibition of the petition.

Provided also, That if any patentee shall depart this life within the three years limited by his patent for seating and planting, in such case those claiming under such patentee shall have the liberty of three years from and after such departure, wherein to seat and plant as aforesaid. Any thing herein, or any law, custom or usage to the contrary thereof in any wise notwithstanding.

Further time allowed to heirs of patentee, dying before expiration of 3 years.

And whereas his most gratious majesty, Charles the second, late king of England, by his royall charter, being letters patents under the great seal of England, bearing date at Westminster, the tenth day of October, in the twenty eighth year of his reign, did declare and

Recital of Charter of 10th of October, 28th Car. II;

grant to all the subjects of himself, his heirs and successors, from time to time, inhabiting within this colony and plantation of Virginia, that all lands then possessed by the severall and respective planters or inhabitants of Virginia, were and should be thereby confirmed and established to them and their heirs for ever, where the property of any particular mans interest in any such lands should not be altered or prejudiced by reason thereof.

and of divers inquests of escheat.

And whereas divers inquests of escheat have been taken since the granting of the said charter, whereby several tracts or parcells of land have been found to escheat to her majesty and to her royall predecessors, notwithstanding the same had been peaceably and quietly possessed by the then present possessors, and those under whom they claimed, not only at the time of granting the said charter, but for many years theretofore; for the prevention whereof for the future,

Exposition of the charter.

Be it enacted by the authority aforesaid, and it is hereby enacted and declared, That the said charter is, and shall be from time to time, and at all times held, deemed and taken to all intents, constructions and purposes whatsoever, valid and available in law, to confirm and establish all the lands within this colony to the severall respective persons then in possession thereof, and to their heirs and assigns for ever against any claim, pretence, title or demand to be made against them for the same, for or in behalf of his said late majesty, his heirs and successors without any inquest or office thereupon to be found, and without any further or other grant or confirmation thereof.

No office of escheat shall operate, to divest those in possession, prior to the date of the above charter.

And be it further enacted by the authority aforesaid, That no office of escheat shall at any time hereafter be found so as to vest a right or title in her majesty, her heirs or successors, of, in or unto any tract or parcell of land within this colony, for or by reason of any loss or forfeiture, or for or by reason of any defect in the title whereby the same lands became escheatable at any time before the tenth day of October, in the twenty eighth year of the reign of his said late majesty, and every such office found contrary to the true intent and meaning thereof, is hereby declared to be to all intents and purposes, null and void as if the same had never been. Any law, custom or usage to the contrary thereof in any wise notwithstanding.

And to prevent any fraudulent or collusive practice herein, every escheator and deputy escheator is hereby prohibited and forbidden to return any office of escheat, either to the secretarys office, or to any other office or place whereupon any patent or grant may be issued, unless there shall be therein particularly set forth, the persons from whom, and the time when such land (whereon the inquiry shall be made) is alledged to have escheated, to the end that thereby it may manifestly appear that a grant may be lawfully made thereof according to the true intent and meaning of the said charter.

Rules, in taking inquests of escheats.

And be it further enacted and declared by the authority aforesaid, That all lands within this colony of Virginia which are escheated, or shall at any time hereafter be found to escheat to her majesty, her heirs and successors, shall be granted and confirmed by patent under the seal of the colony to the severall respective possessors thereof for the time being, and to their respective heirs and assigns for ever, paying two pounds of tobacco composition for every acre of land so granted and confirmed, (without any further or other composition for or by reason of any buildings or other improvements which may be thereupon) and also paying five pounds sterling for the escheators fee, with the other costs and charges thereupon lawfully ariseing.

Right of composition, to possessors of escheated lands.

And to prevent any controversy that may arise about paying the said fee to the escheator, and the other charges, it is hereby declared that the same be paid by every person who shall sue forth any writt, whereupon an inquiry shall accordingly be made.

By whom to be paid.

Provided always, That no person being tenant under any other, shall be taken to be in possession of any lands, so as to claim a grant upon the escheat thereof as aforesaid.

Who deemed a tenant in possession.

And if any tract or parcell of land shall hereafter escheat by the death of any person (leaving a widow) without lawfull heir to inherit the same, or making any disposition thereof, in every such case, except only where such escheat shall happen to be by reason of the conviction or attainder of the person from whom the same escheats, such widow shall occupy, possess and enjoy the same

Rights of widows, in escheated lands.

to her own proper use and behoof, during her naturall life, and after her death the said lands shall be granted and confirmed as aforesaid, to the next relation of the person from whom the same shall be found to escheat, such relation paying the composition ffees and other charges as aforesaid. And if there be no such relation, then the next heir of the whole bloud to the widdow, and if there be none such, her next relation shall have the grant and confirmation as aforesaid. And if any lands become escheat by the death of feme covert, in such case the said lands shall be held and enjoyed by her husband during his life, and after his death the same shall be granted and confirmed as aforesaid to the next relation of such feme covert, and if there be no such relation, then the same shall be granted and confirmed as aforesaid, to the next heir of the whole bloud of the husband, and if there be none such to his next relation, in every of which cases the person or persons obtaining such grant and confirmation, is to pay the composition fees and other charges as aforesaid.

Rules as to descent, after the deaths of widows, & femes covert.

Provided always, That if by virtue hereof, severall persons in equall degree shall claim the right of having the grant and confirmation of any lands as next relation as aforesaid, in such case the male relation shall be preferred, and if there be severall male relations in equall degree, the eldest of them and their representatives according to their severall stocks shall be preferred.*

Rule, where the claimants, by descent, are in equal degree.

And be it further enacted by the authority aforesaid, That no lands, tenements or other hereditaments shall pass, alter or change from one to another, whereby any estate of inheritance in fee simple, fee tail, generall or speciall, or any estate for life or lives, or any greater or higher estate shall be made, or take effect in any

No estate of inheritance in lands to pass, unless by deed in writing,

---

* By the act of 1710, chap. 13, intituled "An act for settling the titles and bounds of lands; and for preventing unlawful shooting and ranging thereupon," so much of this act, as came within the purview of that act, was repealed. The preceding part of this act, which relates to the mode of acquiring title to lands, by importation rights, composition money, escheats, and forfeitures, and the forms of patents, is not embraced by the act of 1710; and consequently was not repealed thereby. It is very unaccountable that so important a law should have been omitted in the revisal of 1733, and only the title printed, under an apprehension, it is presumed, that the whole law was repealed.

person or persons, or any use thereof, to be made by bargain and sale, lease and release, deed of settlement to uses of ffeoffment or other instrument, unless the same be made by writing, indented, sealed and recorded in the records of the general court of this colony, or in the records of that county court where the land mentioned to be granted or passed shall lye in manner following, that is to say, if the person or persons who shall make and seal such bargain and sale, lease and release, deed of settlement to uses of ffeoffment or other instrument at the time of such making and sealing, shall be resident within this colony, then the recording thereof as aforesaid, shall be made within eight months from the sealing and delivery, but if the person so making and sealing as aforesaid at the time thereof, shall be resident in any other place, (than within this colony) the recording as aforesaid shall be made within two years from the sealing and delivery.

and recorded.

Where to be recorded.

Within what time.

Provided always, That no such bargain and sale, lease and release, deed of settlement to uses, deed of ffeoffment or any other instrument as aforesaid, shall by the general court, or county court as aforesaid be admitted to record, unless the same be acknowledged in such court by the person or persons making and sealing the same, or by some or one of them to be his, her or their proper act and deed, or else that proof be made of such making and sealing upon oath by three witnesses at the least.

Must be acknowledged by the party, or proved by 3 witnesses.

And be it further enacted by the authority aforesaid, That the bargain and sale, lease and release, or other deed or instrument heretofore made, or hereafter to be made in writing, indented and sealed both by the husband and wife, and by them personally acknowledged in the general court, or county court as aforesaid, (the wife being, or having been first privily examined, whether she doth voluntarily assent thereto) shall be, and is hereby declared to be, to all intents and purposes, as valid and sufficient in law to convey and pass over all the estate, right, title, interest, claim and demand, which such wife may or shall have in any lands, tenements or hereditaments so to be granted, conveyed and passed over, whether the same be in right of dower in fee simple, or whatever other estate (not being fee tail) she may have therein, as if the same had been done by

Deed by husband and wife, how to pass estate of wife.

fine and recovery, or by any other ways or means whatsoever. Any law, custom or usage to the contrary thereof notwithstanding.

Estates tail, not to be barred, but by act of assembly.

And be it further enacted by the authority aforesaid, That it shall not be lawfull at any time hereafter for any person or persons whatsoever to levy any fine, or to suffer any recovery to be had, whereby to cut off or defeat any estate in fee tail, generall or speciall of or in any lands, tenements or hereditaments within this colony, neither shall any such estates tail be cut off or otherwise avoided or defeated by any ways or means whatsoever, except only by an act of the general assembly of this dominion, for the time being, in such particular case respectively, to be had and made, and all and every fine and fines, recovery and recoverys, and every other act and acts, thing and things whatsoever, which shall hereafter be levyed, suffered, made, done, performed or executed for and towards the cutting off, avoiding or defeating any estate tail whatsoever otherwise than by act of assembly as aforesaid, shall be adjudged, deemed and taken, and are hereby declared to be to all intents and purposes, null and void. Any law, custom or usage to the contrary thereof in any wise notwithstanding.

Fines and recoveries prohibited.

For prevention of controversies as to titles of lands heretofore irregularly passed.

And whereas in times past, several persons purchasing lands in this colony, have procured their deeds and conveyances for the same to be acknowledged and recorded, but not within six months after the making thereof as by law *(a)* hath heretofore been required, and some persons have procured their said deeds and conveyances to be recorded in other county courts than where the lands have layn and to be registred in the councill books, and other persons purchasing lands as aforesaid, have taken deeds and conveyances for the same, not indented nor sealed, or wherein no valuable consideration has been particularly set down and expressed, and some have taken assignments for lands only endorsed on the patents, and others have purchased lands and taken deeds for the same, but by reason of the death of the grantor or some other such like acci-

(a) In the revisal of 1733, pa. 258, a quere is made, what law this was;—it will be found in chap. 4. of December 1656, vol. 1 of Stat. at Large, pa. 417.

dent, the said deeds have not been acknowledged in court according to the strict letter of the law, in that case heretofore made, but yet have been proved in court by the oaths of two or more witnesses, and recorded, and others have purchased lands and taken deeds and conveyances for the same, without livery and seizin being made thereupon in due form of law, by reason of which severall inadvertences and omissions, many controversies may hereafter arise to the great grievance and charges of her majesty's good and lawfull subjects in this dominion: for the prevention thereof,

All deeds, &c. heretofore acknowledged, and registered in the council books, and recorded in any county court, valid.

Be it therefore enacted by the authority aforesaid, That all deeds and conveyances whatsoever, for any lands within this colony, heretofore acknowledged and recorded at any time after the expiration of the said six months, or registered in the councills books, or recorded in any other county court than where the lands therein mentioned to be conveyed have layen, shall be adjudged, deemed and taken, and are hereby declared to be, to all intents and purposes as valid and available in law, and shall enure and take effect as fully and absolutely to the benefit and advantage of all persons in possession of any lands claimed thereby, and to their heirs and assigns as if the same deeds and conveyances had been recorded within the said six months in the general court, or in that county court where the lands have layen, and not otherwise. Any law, statute, act, custome or usage to the contrary thereof in any wise notwithstanding.

All deeds not indented and sealed, or not expressing for valuable consideration, &c. if bona fide made—& all assignments on patents adjudged good.

And all deeds and conveyances whatsoever, bona fide made for lands within this colony, not indented or sealed, or wherein no valuable consideration hath been particularly set down and expressed, and all assignments endorsed on patents, shall be adjudged, deemed and taken, and are hereby declared to be to all intents, constructions and purposes as valid and available in law, and shall enure and take effect as fully and absolutely to the benefit and advantage of all, and every person and persons in possession of any lands claimed thereby to his and their own proper use and behoof, as if the same deeds and conveyances had been actually indented and sealed, and as if a valuable consideration had been therein particularly expressed and set down, and as if the said assignments had been made, and the lands therein mentioned conveyed in due form of law and not otherwise. Any law, statute, custom or usage to the contrary thereof in any wise notwithstanding.

The same, if proved by two witnesses only.

And that all deeds and conveyances heretofore bona fide made for any lands within this colony proved in court by the oaths of two or more credible witnesses to have been the acts and deeds of the persons therein mentioned to have made sealed and delivered the same, and a record thereof made, shall be judged, deemed and taken, and are hereby declared to be as firm, valid and available in law to all intents and purposes, and shall enure and take effect as fully and absolutely to the benefit and advantage of all and every person and persons in possession of any lands claimed thereby, to his and their own proper use and behoof, as if the same deeds and conveyances had been really acknowledged in court by the grantor himself in person. Any law, statute, custom or usage to the contrary thereof in any wise notwithstanding.

Also, if livery of seizin were not made.

And that all deeds and conveyances whatsoever, where livery of seizin might otherwise have been required heretofore, bona fide made by any person or persons for any lands, tenements and hereditaments within this colony, where the person or persons to whom the same have been conveyed, have actually entered thereupon, and they and those who have their rights, do still continue in possession thereof, by virtue of such deeds and conveyances, shall be adjudged, deemed and taken, and are hereby declared to be to all intents, constructions and purposes as firm and valid in law, and shall enure and take effect as fully and absolutely to the benefit and advantage of all and every person and persons in possession of any lands claimed thereby, as if livery of seizin had been thereupon made in due form of law, and not otherwise. Any law, statute or custom to the contrary thereof in any wise notwithstanding.

Not to extend to those, not in possession.

Provided always, That nothing herein contained shall be construed, deemed and taken, so as to confirm any lands, tenements or hereditaments whatsoever to any other person than those now in actuall possession thereof, and such as shall from time to time, or at any time hereafter claim by, from or under them. Any thing herein contained to the contrary, or seeming to the contrary thereof notwithstanding.

And be it further enacted by the authority aforesaid, That when any deeds or conveyances for any lands, tenements and hereditaments within this colony, shall hereafter be acknowledged or proved in any court in order to be recorded as aforesaid, the livery of seizin thereupon made (in such cases where the same by law is required) shall also in like manner be acknowledged or proved, and shall likewise be recorded together with the deed or conveyance so requiring the same, and whereupon it shall have been made.

Livery of seizin, when to be taken and recorded.

And for the better quieting and avoiding of suits,

Be it enacted by the authority aforesaid, That all writts of formedon in descender formedon in remainder and formendon in reverter of any lands, tenements or other hereditaments whatsoever, at any time hereafter to be sued or brought by occasion or means of any title or cause heretofore accrued, happened or fallen, or which hereafter may happen, shall be sued and taken within twenty years next after the title and cause of action first descended or fallen, and at no time after the said twenty years, and that no person or persons that now hath or have, or which hereafter may have any right or title of entry into any lands, tenements or hereditaments shall at any time hereafter make any entry but within twenty years next after his or their right or title hath heretofore descended or accrued, or hereafter shall descend or accrue to the same, and in default thereof, such persons so not entering, and their heirs, shall be utterly excluded and disabled from such entry after to be made.

Limitation of real actions.—[See Stat. 21, Jac. 1, s. 1, 2.]

Right of entry.

Provided nevertheless, That if any person or persons that is or shall be entituled to such writt or writts, or that hath or shall have such right or title of entry be or shall be at the time of the said right or title first descended, accrued, come or fallen within the age of one and twenty years feme covert, *non compos mentis,* imprisoned or out of this colony, that then such person and persons, and his and their heir or heirs shall or may, notwithstanding the said twenty years are expired, bring his action, or make his entry as he might have done before this act, so as such person and persons, or his or their heir and heirs shall within ten

Saving, to infants, femes covert, &c.

years next after his or their full age, discoverture coming of sound mind, inlargement out of prison or coming into this dominion, or death, take benefit of, and sue for the same, and at no time after the said ten years.

Limitation of writs of right. [See 32 Hen. 8, ch. 2, s. 1.]

And be it further enacted by the authority aforesaid, That no manner of person or persons shall, from henceforth sue, have or maintain any writt of right, or make any prescription, title or claim to or for any lands, tenements, rents, annuitys or other hereditaments of the possession of his or their ancestor or predecessor, but only of the seizin or possession of his ancestor or predecessor, which hath been, or now is, or shall be seized of the said lands, tenements, rents, annuitys or other hereditaments within thirty years next before the teste of the same writt, or next before the said prescription, title or claim, so hereafter to be sued, commenced, brought, made or had, and that no manner of person or persons shall hereafter sue, have or maintain any assise of mort dancestor cosinage ail writt of entry upon disseizin done to any of his ancestors or predecessors, or any other action, possessory upon the possession of any of his ancestors or predecessors for any lands, tenements or other hereditaments of any further seizin or possession of his or their ancestor or predecessor, but only of the seizin or possession of his or their ancestor or predecessor, which was, or hereafter shall be seized of the same lands, tenements or other hereditaments within thirty years next before the teste of the same writt hereafter to be brought, and that no person or persons shall hereafter sue, have or maintain any other action, writt or suit whatsoever, for any lands, tenements or other hereditaments of or upon his own seizin or possession therein, or of or upon the seizin and possession therein, of any other person or persons (whose right he or they shall have) above thirty years next before the teste of the same writt hereafter to be brought.

Saving, to infants, femes covert, &c.

Provided nevertheless, That if any person or persons, that is, or shall be intituled to such writt or writts of right, assise of mort dancestor cossinage ail writt of entry upon disseisin, or that hath or shall have such right to make any prescription, or to have or maintain any other action, writt or suit as aforesaid be or shall be at the time of such right or title, first descended, accrued, come or fallen within the age of one and twenty years feme covert, *non compos mentis*, imprisoned or out of this colony, that then such person or persons, and his and their heir and heirs shall or may, notwithstanding the said thirty years are expired, bring his suit or make his prescription, title or claim as he might have done if this act had not been made so as such person or persons, or his and their heir and heirs, shall within ten years next after his or their full age, discoverture comeing of sound mind, inlargement out of prison or comeing into this dominion, or death, take benefit of and sue for the same, and at no time after the said ten years.

Saving, to persons out of the colony.

Provided always, That all persons that are now out of this colony, and have any pretence of right, title or claim to any lands, tenements or hereditaments within this colony, where they or those under whom they claim have not been in actuall possession thereof within the space of twenty years last past, shall commence and prosecute their suit for the recovery thereof within five years next coming, after the last day of September, which shall be in the year of our Lord one thousand seven hundred and six, and at no time after the said five years.

And for preventing any controversys that may hereafter arise about the bounds of lands held and possessed by the inhabitants of this colony,

Processioning of lands, when and how to be made.

Be it enacted by the authority aforesaid, That once in every four years the bounds of every persons land shall be proscessioned, (or gone round) and the land marks renewed in manner following, that is to say, the court of every county at some court between the first day of June, and the first day of September, which shall be in the year of our Lord God, one thousand seven hundred and eight, and so between the first day of June and the first day of September in every fourth year thereafter, by order of court, shall direct the vestry of each parish within their county respectively, to divide their parishes into so many precincts as to them shall seem most convenient for proscessioning every particular persons land in their severall respective parishes, and to appoint the particular times between the last day of September and last day of March, then next coming, when such proscessioning shall be made in every precinct, and also to appoint at least two intelligent honest freeholders of every precinct, to see such prosscessioning performed, and take and return to the vestry an account of every persons land, they shall proscession, and of the persons present at the same, and of what lands in their precincts, they shall fail to proscession, and of the particular reasons of such failure, which order shall be signifyed in writing to the church wardens of every parish within every respective county in this colony by the clerk of the court, within ten days after the making thereof, and thereupon the church wardens shall cause a vestry to be summoned to meet within ten days after the receipt of such order, at which vestry the said order of court shall be exactly and punctually obeyed in every perticular, and thereupon notice shall be punctually given by the church wardens at the church or chappell of the parish, at least three Sundays next before the same is to be performed of the persons and times so appointed by the vestry for proscessioning in every severall precinct as aforesaid, and also the vestry shall cause the accounts of the two honest freeholders of every precinct made and returned to them as aforesaid, to be registered in particular books to be kept for that purpose by the clerk of the vestry, and to prevent any mistakes or omission that may happen in every such register, the churchwardens, in presence of the vestry of the parish, shall examine the same, and compare them with the originall returns within six months after such return shall be made, from time to time, and shall accordingly certify the same by setting their hands to an attestation thereof, in the register, so by them examined and compared, and that no person may pretend ignorance of his duty herein, the vestrys are also to direct what precinct or precincts in their parishes respectively, every perticular freeholder thereof shall attend and perform the proscessioning as aforesaid, and if any parish shall hapen to lye in severall countys, then the orders of the court of each county shall be signifyed as aforesaid to the churchwardens thereof as aforesaid, and shall also be obeyed by the vestry in manner as is before directed; and if any county court shall at any time hereafter fail to perform their duty herein, every justice of the peace in such county shall forfeit and pay the sum of one thousand pounds of tobacco, and if any vestry shall at any time hereafter fail to perform their duty herein, every perticular member of such vestry shall forfeit and pay the sum of two hundred pounds of tobacco; and if any church warden or church wardens shall at any time hereafter fail to perform his or their duty herein, every such church warden shall forfeit and pay the sum of five hundred pounds of tobacco; and if the clerk of any court shall hereafter fail to perform his duty herein, such clerk shall forfeit and pay one thousand pounds of tobacco, which said forfeitures shall be one moiety to our sovereign Lady the Queen, her heirs and successors for and towards the better support of the government, and the contingent charges thereof, the other moiety to him or them that will inform for the same, to be recovered with costs, by action of debt, bill, plaint or information in any court of record within this dominion, wherein no essoin, protection or wager of law shall be allowed.

Penalties, for failure of duty.

Provided always, That upon any information brought, or suit commenced against any justice of the peace, vestry-man, or church-warden for the breach of this act, if the defendant or defendants shall give sufficient evidence to the court where such information or suit shall be depending, that he was necessarily absent from such court or vestry, or that being there he offered to do his duty in pursuance of this act, then the information or suit shall be dismist, and if any other person shall fail to perform his duty herein, every such person shall forfeit and pay the sum of one hundred pounds of tobacco, to be recovered with costs, by the church-warden or church-wardens of the parish before any justice of the peace in that county, to be applyed for and towards the purchasing of ornaments for the church or chappell of such parish wherein the forfeiture shall be incurred.

What will excuse from the penalty.

Other penalties.

And be it further enacted, That the proscession of the bounds of any persons land at three severall times of proscessioning in manner aforesaid, shall be held, deemed and taken to be sufficient to settle the bounds so as the same may never thereafter be altered.

Bounds three times proscessioned, unalterably fixed.

Provided, That such proscessionings be made by the consent of the owners of the said lands respectively.

Proviso.

Provided always, That the proscessioning and setling the bounds of any lands belonging to any person being within the age of one and twenty years, feme covert,

Further proviso as to infants.

non compos mentis, imprisoned or out of the colony, shall not be conclusive to such person untill after the expiration of six years, from and after the said severall incapacitys shall be removed and determined.

Shooting, hunting, &c. on lands of others prohibited.

And be it further enacted and declared, That if any person or persons shall at any time hereafter shoot, hunt or range upon the lands and tenements, or fish or fowl in any creeks or waters included within the lands of any other person or persons without lycence for the same, first obtained of the owner and proprietor thereof, every such person so shooting, hunting, fishing, fowling or ranging, shall forfeit and pay for every such offence, the sum of five hundred pounds of tobacco, to be recovered with costs, by the person or persons that shall be thereby agrieved to their own proper use, by bill, plaint, information, or action of debt, in any court of record within this dominion, in which no essoin, protection, priviledge or wager of law, or any more than one imparlance shall be allowed, and moreover shall be lyable to an action at common law, wherein the party greived shall recover his damages; and if any person shall be a third time convicted of such shooting, hunting, fishing, fowling or ranging, the justices of that court (over and above giving judgment for the forfeiture as aforesaid) shall commit such person to the common goal, there to remain untill he shall find sufficient sureties, to be bound with him in the sum of ten pounds sterling for his good behaviour for one year, then next comeing, and if he shall, within that time be any more guilty of shooting, hunting, fishing, fowling or ranging as aforesaid, the same shall be, and is hereby enacted and declared to be a breach of the good behaviour.

Penalty.

When game may be pursued on the lands of others.

Provided nevertheless, That if any person being owner of six slaves, at least, shall shoot any game upon his own land, or the land of any other where he shall have leave to hunt and his game shall run off from that land upon other lands where he hath not leave to hunt, in that case it shall be lawfull for such person to follow his game upon any other persons land, and to take it and carry it away without being lyable to any penalty or forfeiture for the same.

And be it further enacted, That all and every other act and acts, and every clause and article thereof heretofore made for so much whereof as relates to any matter or thing whatsoever within the purview of this act is, and are hereby repealed and made void to all intents and purposes, as if the same had never been made.

Repealing clause.

CHAP. XXII.

An act directing the duty of Surveyors of Land, and ascertaining their Fees.

See ch. 19, 1748.

Surveyors to be sworn.

I. *BE it enacted, by the Governor, Council, and Burgesses of this present general assembly, and it is hereby enacted, by the authority of the same,* That all such as are surveyors of land, within any county of this her majesty's colony and dominion of Virginia, shall, within three months after the publication of this act, and all such as shall hereafter be made surveyors of land, within any county of this her majesty's said colony and dominion, shall, before their entrance upon the execution of such trust, or office, take a solemn oath, before the court of that county whereto they shall be appointed surveyors, for their true and faithful execution and discharge, to the best of their knowledge and power, of their said trust, office, and emploiment. And the several county courts, that now are, or hereafter shall be, within this her majesty's said colony and dominion, are hereby authorized to administer such oath and oaths, as aforesaid; and to cause a record thereof to be made.

Penalty for refusing to survey.

II. *And be it also enacted by the authority aforesaid, and it is hereby enacted,* That if any surveyor, upon reasonable notice to him given, shall refuse to survey, and lay out, any land, for any person requiring the same, in a lawful manner, and which may lawfully be done, he shall forfeit and pay four thousand pounds of tobacco; one half to the queen's majesty, her heirs and successors, for and towards the support of this government, and the contingent charges thereof, and the other half to the party grieved, if he will inform and sue for the same.

Their duty in marking and bounding lands.

III. *And be it also enacted by the authority aforesaid, and it is hereby enacted,* That each surveyor, when he makes a survey of any land, shall see that the land so by him surveyed, be plainly bounded, either by natural bounds, or by marking trees, or making other artificial boundaries: And shall, within six months after survey, give to his emploier a survey and plot of the said land so by him surveyed and laid out: For all which services, and for keeping a fair book, both of the survey and plot, bound either in vellum or leather, and made of large Dutch paper roial, each book to contain about two quires in bigness, it shall be lawful for him to demand, receive, and take, after the rates herein set down, (that is to say) for every survey, so made, plotted, and entered, if the same contain no more than one thousand acres of land, five hundred pounds of tobacco; and if above one thousand acres of land, for every hundred acres of land therein contained, over and above the said one thousand acres, and besides the said five hundred pounds of tobacco, thirty pounds of tobacco, and no more: And if any surveyor shall demand and take any greater fee for surveying, as aforesaid, than in and by this act is allowed and set down, he shall forfeit and pay, for every such offence, two thousand pounds of tobacco; one half whereof to be to her majesty, her heirs and successors, for and towards the support of this government, and the contingent charges thereof; and the other half to the informer.

When to deliver a plat.

Their fees.

Penalty for exceeding legal fees.

IV. *Provided nevertheless*, That if at any time it shall happen, that in differences concerning adjacent lands, or other claim whatsoever, the surveyor be stopped and hindred from finishing his said survey, it shall be lawful for him, notwithstanding, to demand and take two hundred and fifty pounds of tobacco for his trouble and progress so made in the survey.

Proviso.

V. And for the better enabling all surveyors to be exact in their surveys, *Be it enacted*, That no surveyor shall make any survey of land without chain carriers, sworn to measure justly and exactly, according to the best of their knowledge, and to deliver their account thereof truly to the surveyor; which oath, every surveyor in his several district, is hereby authorised and impowered to administer accordingly.

Chain-carriers to be sworn.

VI. *And be it further enacted*, That upon any entries hereafter legally made, for unpossessed land, where the surveyor cannot, at the time of entry made, attend to survey, such entry shall stand good, until such sur-

Entries to be surveyed within one month

veyor shall give notice of his being ready to go upon the survey thereof: And if such party claiming by such entry, his heirs or assigns, shall not, within one month of such notice given him, attend the surveyor, with all necessaries for making such survey, and give him timely warning thereof, every such entry shall be void, as if the same had never been made.

after notice, by surveyor, otherwise void.

VII. And for prevention of hasty and surreptitious grants upon surveys,

VIII. *Be it also enacted, by the authority aforesaid, and it is hereby enacted,* That no surveyor, within six months after survey made, give a copy of the said survey, or plot, other than to the person that first, in lawful manner, emploied him to make the said survey; upon pain of forfeiting and paying to the party injured, his executors or administrators, five hundred pounds of tobacco, for every hundred acres of land the said survey shall contain.

No plat to be delivered, other than to the person making the entry, in less than six months.

IX. And because the quiet of our estates, in a great measure, depends upon the faithfulness, understanding, and care of our surveyors, and the fair and regular keeping of their proceedings,

X. *Be it enacted, by the authority aforesaid, and it is hereby enacted,* That each surveyor that now is, shall immediately, upon the publication of this act; and every surveyor hereafter to be appointed, shall immediately, upon his entring into the said office of surveyor, apply himself to the county court (who are hereby authorized to levy the charge thereof upon the county) for such a book, as is herein before mentioned, for the entring of surveys and plots, and shall fairly enter and plot, or cause to be fairly entred and plotted, all the surveys that he shall make, during his continuance in the said office of surveyor, within two months after every such survey made, with indications in the plots of all the rivers, creeks, and branches, that he shall cross in his courses; and also of the boundaries and adjacent plantations, &c. that he shall meet with: And also shall, annually, in the month of June, return to the county court clerk's office, to be by him recorded, a true and perfect list of all surveys by him made in that county, viz. For whom, what quantity of land, and the place or parish where it lies; upon pain of forfeiting, for every default in any of the premises, two thou-

Their duty in entering plats and surveys, in books.

Penalty for failure.

sand pounds of tobacco; one half to the queen, her heirs and successors, for and towards the support of this government, and the contingent charges thereof; and the other half to the informer.

Inspectors of surveyors' books to be appointed.

XI. *And also, be it enacted by the authority aforesaid, and it is hereby enacted,* That the county court, at any time when they shall think fit, either of their own motion, or upon the complaint or suggestion of any other person, may, and hereby have full power and authority to appoint two or more understanding persons of their county, to view and examine the surveyor's book, of the county surveys or plots; and to make report thereof to them, whether it be kept, in all things, according to this act.

On the death of a surveyor, how his books to be disposed of.

XII. *And also be it enacted by the authority aforesaid, and it is hereby enacted,* That upon the death, or removal, of any surveyor, from his place and office, the said county court, by their order, shall have, and hereby have full power and authority, to retake the surveyor's said book, and either cause the same to be preserved among the county records; or, if there be much blank paper in it, let the same to the next surveyor, at their discretion, for his county book also, to enter his surveys and plots in: But where it shall so happen, that the same is let to the next surveyor, the county court shall always, before the doing thereof, take the said surveyor's oath, to preserve the said book, with the best of his care, and under his own lock and key; and not to alter, or suffer any thing to be altered therein, of what was done before his time of surveyorship.

Fees for surveying lots in towns.

XII. *Provided always, and it is hereby enacted,* That any thing herein before recited, shall not extend, nor be construed to extend, to the surveyor's fee, for lots taken up, or to be taken up, in any city, town, port, or public landing, or place, laid out, or hereafter to be laid out, for any city, town, port or public landing: But that it shall be sufficient for the surveyor, having once entred the whole plot of such city, town, port, or public landing, in the book, to keep a note of the person's name that shall take up any lot, in any such city, town, port or public landing, with the number of the lot therewith: And for so doing, and laying out one lot, or renewing the bounds of one lot, and so for each lot laid out or renewed, shall have and receive twenty pounds of tobacco, and no more; any thing before in this act contained to the contrary, in any wise, notwithstanding.

XIV. *And be it further enacted by the authority aforesaid, and it is hereby enacted,* That all penalties and forfeitures, which shall be incurred, by virtue of this act, shall and may be recovered, with costs, by action of debt, bill, plaint or information, in any court of record within this her majesty's colony and dominion; wherein no essoin, protection, or wager of law, shall be allowed. Penalties how recoverable.

XV. *And be it further enacted,* That all and every other act and acts, and every clause and article thereof, heretofore made, for so much thereof as relates to any matter or thing whatsoever, within the purview of this act, is, and are hereby repealed and made void, to all intents and purposes, as if the same had never been made. Repealing clause.

CHAP. XXIII.

An act declaring the Negro, Mulatto, and Indian slaves within this dominion, to be real estate.

See chap. 11, 1727.

I. FOR the better settling and preservation of estates within this dominion,

II. *Be it enacted, by the governor, council and burgesses of this present general assembly, and it is hereby enacted by the authority of the same,* That from and after the passing of this act, all negro, mulatto, and Indian slaves, in all courts of judicature, and other places, within this dominion, shall be held, taken, and adjudged, to be real estate (and not chattels;) and shall descend unto the heirs and widows of persons departing this life, according to the manner and custom of land of inheritance, held in fee simple. Slaves declared real estate.

III. *Provided always,* That nothing in this act contained, shall be taken to extend to any merchant or factor, bringing any slaves into this dominion, or having any consignments thereof, unto them, for sale: But that such slaves, whilst they remain unsold, in the possession of such merchant, or factor, or of their executors, administrators, or assigns, shall, to all intents and purposes, be taken, held, and adjudged, to be personal estate, in the same condition they should have been in, if this act had never been made. Proviso as to merchants and factors.

May be taken in execution.

IV. *Provided also,* That all such slaves shall be liable to the paiment of debts, and may be taken by execution, for that end, as other chattels or personal estate may be.

Not escheatable.

V. *Provided also,* That no such slaves shall be liable to be escheated, by reason of the decease of the proprietor of the same, without lawful heirs: But all such slaves shall, in that case, be accounted and go as chattels, and other estate personal.

Transfer of slaves need not be recorded.

VI. *Provided also,* That no person, selling or alienating any such slave, shall be obliged to cause such sale or alienation to be recorded, as is required by law to be done, upon the alienation of other real estate: But that the said sale or alienation may be made in the same manner as might have been done before the making of this act.

Possessor of, not to give a right to vote.

VII. *Provided also,* That this act, or any thing therein contained, shall not extend, nor be construed to extend, to give any person, being owner of any slave or slaves, and not seized of other real estate, the right or privilege as a freeholder, meant, mentioned, and intended, by one act of this present session of assembly, intituled, *An act for regulating the elections of Burgesses, for settling their privileges, and for ascertaining their allowances.*

Recoverable by personal action.

VIII. *Provided also,* That it shall and may be lawful, for any person, to sue for, and recover, any slave, or damage, for the detainer, trover, or conversion thereof, by action personal, as might have been done if this act had never been made.

Writs of partition and dower may be prosecuted for.

IX. *Provided always,* That where the nature of the case shall require it, any writ *De Partitione facienda,* or of dower, may be sued forth and prosecuted, to recover the right and possession of any such slave or slaves.

Heir at law to account with other children for their proportion of appraised value.

X. *Provided, and be it enacted,* That when any person dies intestate, leaving several children, in that case all the slaves of such person, (except the widow's dower, which is to be first set apart) shall be inventoried and appraised; and the value thereof shall be equally divided amongst all the said children; and the several proportions, according to such valuation and appraisement, shall be paid by the heir (to whom the said slaves shall descend, by virtue of this act) unto all and every the other said children. And thereupon, it shall and may be lawful for the said other children, and every of them, and their executors or administrators, as the case shall be, to commence and prosecute an action upon the case, at the common law, against such heir, his heirs, executors and administrators, for the recovery of their said several proportions, respectively. Action for.

XI. *And be it further enacted by the authority aforesaid,* That if any widow, seised of any such slave or slaves, as aforesaid, as of the dower of her husband, shall send, or voluntarily permit to be sent out of this colony and dominion, such slave or slaves, or any of their increase, without the lawful consent of him or her in reversion, such widow shall forfeit all and every such slave or slaves, and all other the dower which she holds of the endowment of her husband's estate, unto the person or persons that shall have the reversion thereof; any law, usage or custom to the contrary notwithstanding. And if any widow, seized as aforesaid, shall be married to an husband, who shall send, or voluntary permit to be sent out of this colony and dominion, any such slave or slaves, or any of their increase, without the consent of him or her in reversion; in such case, it shall be lawful for him or her in reversion, to enter into, possess and enjoy all the estate which such husband holdeth, in right of his wife's dower, for and during the life of the said husband.

Widow, sending dower slaves out of the state, forfeits her right.

So, of her husband.

CHAP. XXIV.

An act for settling the Militia.

Edi. 1733, and 1752.

[From MS.]

FOR the setling, arming and training a militia for her majestie's service, to be ready on all occasions for the defence and preservation of this her colony and dominion,

Be it enacted, by the governor, council, and burgesses, of this present general assembly, and it is hereby enacted, by the authority of the same, That from and after the publication of this act, the colonel or chief officer of the militia of every county have full power and authority to list all male persons whatsoever, from sixteen to sixty years of age within his respective county, to serve in horse or foot, as in his discretion he shall

Persons, from 16 to 60, liable to militia duty.

see cause and think reasonable, having regard to the ability of each person, he appoints to serve in the horse, and to order and place them and every of them under the command of such captain in the respective countys of their abode, as he shall think fitt.

Who exempted from.

Provided nevertheless, That nothing herein contained shall be construed to give any power or authority to any colonel or chief officer whatsoever, to list any person that shall be, or shall have been of her majesty's councill in this colony, or any person that shall be, or shall have been speaker of the house of burgesses, or any person that shall be, or shall have been her majesty's attorney general, or any person that shall be, or shall have been a justice of the peace within this colony, or any person that shall have born any military commission within this colony as high as the commission of a captain, or any minister, or the clerk of the councill for the time being, or the clerk of the general court for the time being, or any county court clerk during his being such, or any parish clerk or schoolmaster during his being such, or any overseer that hath four or more slaves under his care, or any constable during his being such, or any miller who hath a mill in keeping, or any servant by importation, or any slave, but that all and every such person or persons be exempted from serving either in horse or foot. Any thing in this act heretofore to the contrary notwithstanding.

Proviso, as to overseers.

Provided always, That if any overseer that is by this act exempted from being listed shall appear at any muster, either of horse or foot, he shall appear in arms fit for exercise, and shall perform his duty as other private soldiers do, on pain of paying the fine inflicted by this act upon such persons as do not provide troopers, arms and other accoutrements. But for as much as severall of the persons exempted as aforesaid, though they be of sufficient ability to find and keep a serviceable horse and horse arms, and such men whose personal service may not only be usefull, but necessary upon an insurrection or invasion, which God prevent, by virtue of the proviso aforesaid, will perhaps account themselves free from provideing and keep the same at the places of their abode, which is not intended:

Be it therefore enacted by the authority aforesaid, and it is hereby enacted and declared, That the persons of a councellor, of a speaker of the house of burgesses, of a justice of the peace, of an attorney-general, and of a captain or an higher officer in the militia, are exempted from being listed and serving either in horse or foot under command as the rest of the militia do, merely for the dignity of the office which they do or shall have held, and that notwithstanding the said proviso or any thing therein contained, it is the true intent and meaning of this act, that all and every such person or persons, and also the clerk of the councill, the clerk of the general court, and every county court clerk shall provide and keep, and they and every of them are hereby required and enjoyned to provide and keep at their respective places of abode a troopers horse, furniture, arms and ammunition, according to the directions of this act hereafter mentioned and expressed, and to produce or cause the same to be produced in the county where they respectively reside yearly, and every year at the generall muster appointed by this act, to the colonel or chief officer present, upon pain of forfeiting for every neglect therein, twenty shillings current money of Virginia.

Persons exempted, to provide themselves with arms, &c.

And in case of any rebellion or invasion shall also be obliged to appear when thereunto required, and serve in such stations as are suitable for gentlemen, under the direction of the colonel or chief officer of the county where he or they shall reside, under the same penaltys as any other person or persons, who by this act are injoyned to be listed in the militia, any thing herein contained to the contrary or seeming to the contrary in any wise notwithstanding.

And, on invasions or insurrections must perform duty, as gentlemen.

And be it further enacted, by the authority aforesaid, That the colonell or chief officer of the militia of every county be required, and every of them is hereby required, as soon as conveniently may be, after the publication of this act, to make or cause to be made, a new list of all the male persons in his respective county capable by this act to serve in the militia, and to order and dispose them into troops or companys, according to the directions of the governor or commander in chief of this dominion for the time being, and the respective circumstances of the ability of the persons listed, to the end each trouper or ffoot soldier may be thereby guid-

Militia to be enrolled and divided into troops or companies.

ed to provide and furnish himself with such arms and ammunition and within such time as this act hereafter directs.

Arms, &c. to be provided by each foot soldier.

And be it enacted, by the authority aforesaid, That every ffoot soldier be provided with a firelock, muskett or fusee well fixed, a good sword and cartouch box, and six charges of powder, and appear constantly with the same at time and place appointed for muster and exercise, and that besides those each foot soldier have at his place of abode two pounds of powder and eight pounds of shott, and bring the same into the field with him when thereunto specially required, and that every soldier belonging to the horse be provided with a good serviceable horse, a good saddle, holsters, brest plate and crouper, a case of good pistolls well fixed, sword and double cartouch box, and twelve charges of powder, and constantly appear with the same when and where appointed to muster and exercise, and that besides those each soldier belonging to the horse have at his usuall place of abode a well fixed carabine, with belt and swivle, two pounds of powder and eight pounds of shott, and bring the same into the ffield with him, when thereunto specially required.

By the cavalry.

Fines.

And be it further enacted, by the authority aforesaid, That whatsoever trooper or ffoot soldier shall fail to appear at time and place appointed, or appearing shall not be furnished and provided with arms and ammunition as aforesaid for muster and exercise, or shall not keep at his place of abode what by this act he is directed there to have and bring into field with him all and singular the arms and ammunition directed by this act when thereunto specially required, such trooper or ffoot soldier shall for his neglect in any of the premises, be fined one hundred pounds of tobacco, every time he is warned or appointed to appear.

Time allowed to provide arms, &c.

Provided always, and be it enacted, That eighteen months time be given and allowed to each trouper and ffoot soldier not heretofore listed to furnish and provide himself with arms and ammunition according to this act, & that no trooper or foot soldier be fined for appearing without or not having the same at his place of abode untill he hath been eighteen months listed, any thing in this act to the contrary, or seeming to the contrary notwithstanding.

And for the encouragement of every soldier in horse or ffoot to provide and furnish himself according to this act and his security to keep his horse, arms and ammunition, when provided,

Horse, arms, &c. exempted from distress, execution, &c.

Be it enacted, by the authority aforesaid, That the musket or ffuzee, the sword, cartouch box and ammunition of every ffoot soldier, and the horse, saddle and furniture, the carbine, pistolls, sword, cartouch box and ammunition of every trooper provided and kept in pursuance of this act to appear and exercise withall be free and exempted at all times from being impressed upon any account whatsoever, and likewise from being seized or taken by any manner of distress, attachment, or writt of execution, and that every distress, seizure, attachment or execution made or served upon any of the premises, be unlawfull and void, and that the officer or person that presumes to make or serve the same be lyable to the suit of the party greived, wherein double damages shall be given upon a recovery.

And to the end the militia of this her majestys colony and dominion, being settled and armed as aforesaid, may be the better fitted for service,

General muster.

Be it further enacted, by the authority aforesaid, That the colonel or chief officer of the militia of every county once every year at least, cause a generall muster and exercise of all the horse and ffoot in his county at one place and oftener if there be occasion, and that every captain both of horse and foot once in every three months, muster, train and exercise his troop or company, or oftener if occasion require.

Company musters.

Provided, That no soldier in horse or foot, be fined above five times in one year for neglect in appearing.

Punishment, for disobedience or mutiny.

And be it further enacted, by the authority aforesaid, That all soldiers in horse and ffoot during the time they are in arms, shall observe and obediently perform the commands of their officer relating to their exercise-ing according to the best of their skill, and that the chief officers upon the place shall and may imprison mutineers and such soldiers as do not their dutys as soldiers at the day of their musters and training, and shall and may inflict for punishment for every such offence, any mulct not exceeding fifty pounds of tobacco, or the penalty of imprisonment without bail or mainprise, not exceeding ten days.

Fine, for not attending alarms.

And be it further enacted by the authority aforesaid, That if any soldier either in horse or foot upon occasion of an incursion, invasion, insurrection or rebellion, or other alarm or surprise, shall be summoned to meet at a certain time and place and shall fail to appear accordingly, such soldier shall for such his offence be fined ten pounds current money, or suffer three months imprisonment, without bail or mainprise.

And forasmuch as some difficulty hath been found in procuring some soldiers to be willing to serve as serjeants, corporals, drummers or trumpeters, all of them absolutely necessary in troops and companys: For prevention of the like in time to come,

Fine, for failing to serve as non-commissioned officer, &c.

Be it enacted, by the authority aforesaid, That whatsoever soldier shall refuse to take upon him, act in and execute any of the said places and offices in the troop or company wherein he is listed, being known to be capable and thereunto appointed by his captain, shall for such his refusall be fined five hundred pounds of tobacco, which being once paid, he shall thereafter be exempted from being fined for any such refusall.

And to the end no wilfull and obstinate defaulter or offender by virtue of or against this act may escape the penalty inflicted by this act for his default or offence,

Delinquencies, how noted.

Be it enacted, by the authority aforesaid, and it is hereby enacted, That all captains of troops and foot companys within this her majestys colony and dominion be required, and every of them is hereby strictly required and injoyned, at every muster (generall or particular) to take or cause to be taken an exact account in writing of every such default or offence made or committed in his troop or company, by whom the default or offence was made or done, and at what time, and to sign the same with his own hand and deliver it, or cause it to be delivered within a month after the taking to the colonel or chief officer of the militia of the county whereunto he belongs, for such further proceeding thereupon as the persons hereafter impowered to inquire into the merit of the said defaults or offences shall judge reasonable in the pursuance of, and according to the tenor and true intent and meaning of this act.

And be it further enacted, by the authority aforesaid, That the field officers and captains of every county, or the major part of them, whereof the colonel, lieutenant colonel, or major, shall be always one, have full power and authority to meet yearly at the court-house in their respective countys on the first Thursday in October, or in case of a failure in meeting that day, on the next Thursday following, to inspect the severall lists or accounts given by the captains to the colonel or chief officer as aforesaid, and thereupon to mulct every defaulter or offender therein charged, according to the merit of his default or offence, and the directions of this act. Fines, how assessed.

Provided always, That nothing in this act contained be construed to give any power or authority to the said ffield officers and captains to meet or act as aforesaid at any other place or times then the times and place aforesaid, or to mulct any defaulter or offender for any default or offence whatsoever by or against this act, which hath been made or done above a year, any thing heretofore to the contrary notwithstanding. Proviso.

And because severall persons may happen to be charged with default or offence in their captains said list or accounts who are not wilfully guilty thereof, or may have a fair and just excuse for their not complying with this act—

For remedy in such cases,

Be it enacted, by the authority aforesaid, That whensoever any soldier charged with a default or offence as aforesaid can and doth shew forth to the said ffield officers and captains at their meeting to mulct delinquents as aforesaid, such matter and cause that he ought not to be fined for the same as they shall judge reasonable, and be convinced withall before he be actually fined, it shall be lawfull for the said ffield officers and captains, and they are hereby required to admit of such soldiers excuse and to lay no mulct or ffine upon him for such default or offence, any thing in this act to the contrary notwithstanding. Fines, how remitted.

And be it further enacted, by the authority aforesaid, That the severall fines and penaltys mentioned in this act, which the said ffield officers and captains shall at their meetings as aforesaid order and direct, be levyed by distress and sale of the goods and chattles belonging to the defaulter or offender by warrant from the colonell or chief officer of the county to the sheriff (in case the defaulter or offender refuse to pay the same in spe- Fines, how collected.

cie upon the ffield officers and captains order without further process) and that the said colonel or chief officer sign and issue a warrant in order thereunto as occasion requires.

Clerk, of court-martial.

And be it further enacted, by the authority aforesaid, That the said ffield officers and captains have full power and authority to appoint and imploy a clerk to attend them at the said meetings, and to keep a register of all their proceedings, and to allow the said clerk such sallary for his said service, and for providing necessary books and paper for their use as in their discretion they shall think fit and reasonable, and to pay the same out of the penaltys and fines accrewing by this act.

Fines, how appropriated.

And be it further enacted, by the authority aforesaid, That the said ffield officers and captains at their meetings as aforesaid, have full power and authority to order and dispose the tobaccoes which shall hereafter accrew and arise upon the ffines, penaltys and fforfeitures mentioned in this act, in such manner as in their discretions shall seem best for paying therewith a clerk as aforesaid, and for furnishing the severall troops and companys belonging to the county with necessary drums, colours, trumpets, leading staffes, partizans and halberts, and for procuring such and so many books of military dissipline as shall be thought convenient, and after all these for providing arms and ammunition for the countys use with the overplus.

Clerk, of troop or company.

And be it further enacted, by the authority aforesaid, That every captain of a troop of horse or ffoot company within this colony be permitted and allowed to take one of the soldiers under his command to be clerk to his troop or company, and that such clerk in consideration of his service in that respect be excused from carrying or appearing in arms at any muster, generall or particular, except in case of a rebellion or invasion, any thing in this act heretofore to the contrary notwithstanding.

Repealing clause.

And be it further enacted, That all and every other act and acts, and every clause and article thereof heretofore made, for setling the militia, or any other matter or thing whatsoever, within the purview of this act is and are hereby repealed and made void to all intents and purposes, as if the same had never been made.

CHAP. XXV.

An act to prevent Indians hunting and ranging upon patented lands.

Penalty for employing Indians to hunt on patented lands.

I. *BE it enacted, by the Governor, Council, and Burgesses, of this present General Assembly, and it is hereby enacted, by the authority of the same,* That if any person whatsoever, shall, after the publication of this act, entertain or employ any *Tuscarora,* or other Indian, not being a servant or slave, to hunt or kill deer; or furnish them with guns, powder, or shot, to hunt, as aforesaid, upon any lands now patented, or that shall hereafter be patented, and belong to any of her majesty's subjects within this her majesty's colony and dominion of Virginia, he, she, or they, so employing any Tuscarora, or other Indian, as aforesaid, shall forfeit and pay to the person or persons upon whose land such Indian shall be found to hunt as aforesaid, the sum of one thousand pounds of tobacco: To be recovered, with costs, by action of debt, in any court of record within this colony and dominion; any law, custom, or usage, to the contrary, notwithstanding.

Gun, &c. may be seized.

II. And moreover, when any person shall find any such Indian shooting, ranging, or hunting upon his land, contrary to this act, it shall be lawful for such person to take away the gun, powder, and shot, which he shall find upon such Indian, and to keep and convert the same to his own use: And upon any complaint made, or suit brought against any person for such taking and keeping of the gun, powder, and shot, as aforesaid, it shall be lawful for the defendant to plead the general issue, not guilty, and to give the special matter in evidence; and the defendant shall be admitted to declare the truth, upon his own oath, which shall be taken as evidence in that case; any law, usage, or custom to the contrary thereof, in any wise, notwithstanding.

Persons sued may plead the general issue, and give special matter in evidence.

Exceptions.

III. *Provided nevertheless,* That nothing in this act contained, shall be construed to extend to the Pamunkey or Chickahominy Indians, or to the Indians on the Eastern shore, hunting or ranging as heretofore they have been accustomed to do.

IV. *And be it enacted,* That all and every other act and acts, and every clause and article thereof, hereto-

Repealing clause.

fore made, for so much thereof as relates to any matter or thing whatsoever, within the purview of this act, is, and are hereby repealed, and made void, to all intents and purposes, as if the same had never been made.

CHAP. XXVI.

Edi. 1733, and 1752.

[Repealed by proclamation, June 22nd, 1708.]

An act for raising a publick revenue for the better support of the government of this her majesty colony and dominion of Virginia, and for ascertaining the sallary of the councill.

[From MS.]

Preamble.

WHEREAS there is a great and continuall charge required for the maintenance of the governor and severall other officers and persons, as also for forts and fortifications, besides many other contingent expences absolutely necessary for the support of the government of this her majestys colony and dominion,

Duty of 2s. a Hhd. on tobacco exported.

Be it therefore enacted, by the Governor, Councill and Burgesses of this present Generall Assembly, and it is hereby enacted, by the authority of the same, That for every hogshead, box, chest, case or barrell of tobacco, which shall at any time hereafter be shipped or laden on board any ship or vessell whatsoever within this colony and dominion, in order to be exported hence by water to any other port or place whatsoever, there shall be paid by the shipper or shippers thereof, the sum of two shillings current money of England, and also for every five hundred pounds of tobacco shipped or laden on board any ship or vessell in order to be exported as aforesaid in bulk to any of her majestys other plantations, and so after that rate for a less quantity.

On 500 lbs. in bulk.

And for avoiding all manner of doubts which may hereafter arise concerning the payment of the duty aforesaid for tobaccoes of the growth of another place and shipped here,

To extend to all tobacco, absolutely the growth of another place.

Be it enacted, by the authority aforesaid, and it is hereby enacted and declared, That the true intent and meaning of this act is that the aforesaid duty of two shillings shall be paid for all tobaccos whatsoever shipped or laden on board any ship or vessell within this colony and dominion in order to be exported hence, although the same were made in and imported or brought from another place.

And be it also further enacted by the authority aforesaid, and it is hereby enacted, That every ship or vessell which shall at any time hereafter be entered in this her majestys colony and dominion, or any district or port thereunto belonging, in order to unlade the goods and merchandises imported in her or in order to lade and take on board any tobaccos or other goods or merchandises whatsoever for exportation out of this colony, shall pay for every tunn which the said ship or vessell is of burthen, the sum of one shilling and three pence, current money of England for port dutys.

Tonnage duty.

Provided always, and it is hereby enacted and declared, That nothing in the aforesaid clause contained, shall be construed so as to charge any ship or vessell which at any time hereafter shall arrive into this colony and dominion and here unlade and relade with payment of the port dutys two times for the same, and that the true intent and meaning of this act is, that in such a case the aforesaid port dutys shall be paid no more than once for that voyage.

Port duties to be paid but once.

And be it further enacted and declared, That all ships and vessels lyable to the payment of the port dutys by this act imposed shall be gaged and measured in manner following, that is to say, every single decked ship or vessell shall be measured by the length of the keel, taken within board so much as she treads upon the ground, and the breadth to be taken within board by the midship beam from plank to plank, and the depth of the hold from the plank below the kelsey to the under part of the deck plank, and for a two deckt ship which carrys goods between decks, the depth of her hold to be taken from the plank below the kelsey to the under part of the upper deck plank, and the length and breadth as before, then multiply the length by the breadth and the product thereof by the depth, and divide the whole by ninety-four, and the quotient will give the true contents of the tonnage, according to which method and rule all ships and vessels shall be measured, and the said port dutys thereby be computed and collected accordingly, any custome, practice or usage, to the contrary notwithstanding.

Rules for ascertaining the tonnage of vessels.

Duty on passengers, servants & slaves, of 6d. per poll.

And be it also further enacted, by the authority aforesaid, and it is hereby enacted, That every ship or vessell which shall at any time hereafter come into any port, creek, harbour or road within this colony and dominion, and shall be there entered in order to unlade and put on shore goods, merchandises, passengers, servants or slaves, shall pay six pence per poll for every passenger, servant, slave or other person imported in her the marriners belonging to and in actuall pay of the said ship or vessell and every of them excepted.

And to the end the aforesaid imposition or duty of six pence per poll may be truly paid according to the intent of this act,

Penalty for making short entry.

Be it further enacted, by the authority aforesaid, and it is hereby enacted, That if any master of a ship or vessell shall wittingly or willingly make a short entry of the number of persons imported in his said ship or vessell for which the imposition or duty aforesaid ought to be paid, he shall forfeit and pay ten pounds current money, one moiety to our sovereign lady the queen, her heirs and successors for and towards the better support of this government and the contingent charges thereof, and the other moiety to him or them that will inform or sue for the same, in any court of record within this colony and dominion, by action of debt, bill, plaint, or information, wherein no essoin, protection or wager of law shall be allowed.

Duties to be paid to collectors.

And be it further enacted, by the authority aforesaid, and it is hereby enacted, That all and every of the impositions or dutys aforesaid, shall be paid to the respective collectors or officers which shall be appointed to receive the same, and shall be to our sovereign lady the queen, her heirs and successors for ever, to and for the better support of the government of this her majestys colony and dominion of Virginia, in such manner as is herein before exprest, and to and for no other use, intent or purpose, whatsoever.

Govr. &c. to appoint collectors, and fix their salaries.

And be it further enacted by the authority aforesaid, and it is hereby enacted, That for collecting and receiving all and every the impositions or dutys aforesaid, the governor or commander in chief of this colony and dominion for the time being, shall be, and is hereby impowered and authorised, with the advice of the councill, from time to time and at all times hereafter, to nominate, constitute and appoint such and so many collectors, receivers or other officers as shall be found necessary, and to allow them such sallarys not exceeding six per cent. as shall be thought suitable.

And for encouragement to all masters of ships and vessells, or other persons who shall hereafter be concerned in the payment of the impositions or dutys aforesaid, to give in true accounts and to pay down the whole dutys of a ship in one intire sum, either in money or good and sufficient bills of exchange, to the likeing and sattisfaction of the collector appointed to receive the same,

Be it enacted, by the authority aforesaid, and it is hereby enacted, That the governor or commander in chief of this colony and dominion for the time being, be and is hereby farther authorised and impowered, with the advice of the councill, to give and allow to every master of a ship or vessell, or other person which shall so do such reasonable allowance and abatement of the impositions or dutys aforesaid, not exceeding six per cent. as shall be judged fitting.

Abatement for prompt payment.

Provided always, and it is hereby enacted and declared, by the authority aforesaid, for encouragement to Virginia owners, that every ship or vessell wholy and solely belonging to the inhabitants of this colony and dominion, shall have the priviledge of being allowed the aforesaid dutys or impositions of two shillings, and of one shilling & three pence accrewing due upon her lading of tobacco, and for her port dutys to the proper use, benefit and advantage of her owner or owners, and every collector or receiver of the aforesaid dutys or impositions is hereby required to allow the same accordingly, unto the master of every such ship or vessell upon his clearing, any thing in this act, or any other act, law, usage or custom, to the contrary notwithstanding.

Privilege of Virginian owners.

And be it further enacted, That in all cases of fees for entering, clearing, cockets, and other matter or thing whatsoever, demandable by a navall officer or collector, all ships and vessells wholy and solely owned by the inhabitants of this country, shall be acquitted for half fees, chargeable or to be chargeable on others.

And for prevention of frauds which may be used to obtain the priviledge aforesaid,

Who shall be deemed Virginian owners.

Be it also further enacted and declared, by the authority aforesaid, That no ship or vessell whatsoever shall be accounted or taken to belong wholy and solely to the inhabitants of this her majestys colony and dominion of Virginia till proof thereof be made by the oath of one of her owners before the governor or commander in chief of this colony and dominion for the time being, and his testimonial thereupon, had under the seal of the colony or untill such proof be made before the generall court and a certificate thereupon had from the clerk of the said court under the seal of his office, and that no collector or receiver of the impositions or dutys aforesaid, or either of them shall allow to any ship or vessell whatsoever the aforesaid priviledge upon the impositions or dutys aforesaid, or either of them, unless the master of the said ship or vessell at the time he demands the same shall produce testimonial or certificate as aforesaid, and also himself make oath that he does not know that any part of the said ship or vessell doth belong to any person whatsoever, which is not inhabitant of Virginia, any thing in this act aforesaid to the contrary or seeming to the contrary notwithstanding.

Allowance to members of council to be paid according to their attendance.

And be it further enacted, That out of the money ariseing by the duty of two shillings for every hogshead, box, chest, case or barrell of tobacco exported, imposed by this act, there shall be annually paid unto such of the members of her majestys honorable councill, for the time being, as now are inhabitants, or at the time of such payment shall have been inhabitants of this colony for the space of three years then next preceeding the sum of three hundred and fifty pounds sterling, in consideration of their trouble and charge in the generall assemblys and generall courts, and that the same shall be proportioned and paid to every of the said severall members according to the time of his attendance respectively.

Repealing clause.

And be it further enacted, That all and every other act and acts, and every clause and article thereof, heretofore made, for so much thereof as relates to raising a publick revenue for the better support of the government of this her majestys colony and dominion of Virginia, or to any other matter or thing whatsoever, within the purview of this act, is, and are hereby repealed and made void, to all intents and purposes, as if the same had never been made.

CHAP. XXVII.

An act for preventing frauds in the customs, and in clearing of ships; for ascertaining collectors and naval officers fees; and to prohibit and prevent the casting of ballast, and dead bodies, into rivers and creeks.

I. FOR the better prevention of frauds and concealments, or any other ways or means which may be made use of, to evade due clearing of ships and vessels, and the paiment of the customs, duties, or impositions, laid upon tobaccos, skins, furrs, or any other goods or merchandizes whatsoever, to be exported out of this colony and dominion, Preamble.

II. *Be it enacted, by the governor, council and burgesses of this present general assembly, and it is hereby enacted by the authority of the same,* That the master of every ship or vessel, coming into this her majesty's colony and dominion, for trade, or which being here, is designed to take on board and lade any tobaccos, skins, furrs, or other goods or merchandizes whatsoever, in order to export and carry the same out of this colony and dominion, at his entry, and before he be permitted to break bulk and trade, or to lade and take on board any goods or merchandizes whatsoever, shall give bond, with one surety, to the queen's majesty, her heirs and successors, that he will not depart with his said ship or vessel from the district or port where she is entred, until paiment be made of the several customs, duties, impositions, and fees, accruing due from the said ship or vessel, or for or by reason of any tobaccos, skins, furrs, or other goods and merchandizes shipped and laden in her, nor until the said ship or vessel be duly cleared by the collector and naval officer of the said district or port. Entry of vessels, and duty bonds.

III. *And be it further enacted by the authority aforesaid, and it is hereby enacted,* That if the ship or vessel be under fifty tons, the said bond shall be for fifty pounds; if above fifty tons, and under one hundred tons, for one hundred pounds; and if one hundred tons, Penalty of bonds.

or above one hundred tons, for two hundred pounds; and shall be delivered back, upon due clearing with the officers aforesaid; but wholly forfeited, without any relief in equity, in case the condition thereof be broken.

Oaths of master.

IV. *And be it further enacted, by the authority aforesaid, and it is hereby enacted,* That the master of every ship or vessel, upon clearing, shall make oath, before the officer with whom he clears, (which oath the said officer is hereby impowered and required to administer) what tobaccos, skins, furrs, or other goods or merchandizes, are then shipped and laden on board his said ship or vessel; and that he will not afterwards lade or take on board his said ship or vessel, any more tobaccos, skins, furrs, or other goods or merchandizes whatsoever, (for which any custom, duty or imposition is to be paid, or which the law requires to be entred) without a lawful permit for his so doing, from an officer of the district or port wherein the said tobaccos, skins, furrs, goods or merchandizes, are to be so laden and taken in.

Duties to be paid before clearance granted.

V. *And be it further enacted, by the authority aforesaid, and it is hereby enacted and declared,* That the customs, duties, or impositions, accruing due for any tobaccos, skins, furrs, or other goods or merchandizes whatsoever, which shall hereafter be shipped or laden on board any ship or vessel, in order to be exported out of this colony and dominion, shall be answered and paid to the collector or receiver of the said customs, duties, or impositions, in the district or port where the said ship or vessel shall happen to ride, when the said tobaccos, skins, furrs, goods or merchandizes are laden and taken in, and to no other collector or receiver whatsoever; notwithstanding the same be brought thither from another district or port.

Mariners may be examined on oath.

VI. *And be it further enacted, by the authority aforesaid, and it is hereby enacted,* That upon any suspicion of fraud or concealment, or that the master of any ship or vessel doth make a false report of his lading, it shall and may be lawful for the naval officer and collector of the district or port, or either of them, for discovery of the said fraud or concealment, and for the better finding out the truth of the matter, to examine, upon oath, the mate, boatswain, or any other of the seamen belonging to the said ship or vessel, as also any other person or persons whatsoever, concerning the lading of the said ship or vessel, as to the said collector and naval officer, or either of them, shall seem fit and convenient.

Collectors' fees.

VII. *And be it enacted, by the authority aforesaid, and it is hereby enacted,* That the collectors fees shall be as followeth: That is to say,

	l.	*s.*	*d.*
For entring and clearing any ship or vessel, of fifty tons, or under, (all vessels transporting goods or commodities from one district to another excepted) and all fees thereunto incident,	00	10	00
For entring and clearing any ship or vessel, above fifty tons, and under one hundred tons, and all fees thereunto incident,	00	15	00
For entring and clearing any ship or vessel, of one hundred tons, or above, and all fees thereunto incident,	01	05	00
For taking a plantation bond, pursuant to the act of trade and navigation,	00	02	06
For a certificate of duties paid upon goods shipped to the plantations,	00	02	06

Naval officers' fees.

And that the naval officers fees shall be as followeth: That is to say,

	l.	*s.*	*d.*
For entring and clearing any ship or vessel, of fifty tons, or under, (excepting as is before excepted,)	00	07	06
For entring and clearing any ship or vessel, above fifty tons, and under one hundred tons,	00	10	00
For entring and clearing any ship or vessel, of one hundred tons, or above,	01	05	00
For taking a bond,	00	02	06
For a permit to trade,	00	02	06
For every loading Cocquet here,	00	00	06
When ports for import and export shall be established, and in the mean time, for a permit to load a ship or vessel for exportation,	00	02	06
For a certificate for all imported goods, that shall be removed out of one district or river into another, after they are once			

landed, until ports shall be established, to be paid to the officer of the district from whence the said goods are brought, 00 02 06

Virginian owners pay half fees.

That the naval officers and collectors, for any the services before-mentioned, shall charge no more than half of the fees aforesaid, for any ship or vessel wholly belonging to the inhabitants of this country.

Penalty for exceeding legal fees.

VIII. *And be it further enacted, by the authority aforesaid, and it is hereby enacted,* That it shall not be lawful for any collector or naval officer, within this colony and dominion, to demand and take any fee or fees for any other business, matter, or thing by him done and performed, as collector or naval officer, or as collector or receiver of any Virginia duties, than the particulars before enumerated in this act; or to demand and take any greater fee, for any of the particulars before enumerated, than the fee given and allowed by this act, for the same: And that if any collector or naval officer shall offend in either of the premises, and be thereof lawfully convicted, he shall, for the first offence, forfeit and pay one hundred pounds current money; one moiety to our sovereign lady the queen, her heirs and successors, for and towards the better support of this government, and the contingent charges thereof; and the other moiety to the party injured: To be recovered, with costs, in any court of record within this colony and dominion, by action of debt, bill, plaint, or information, wherein no essoin, protection, or wager of law, privilege, or more than one imparlance, shall be admitted or allowed. And if the said collector or naval officer shall offend a second time, and be thereof lawfully convicted, he shall be thereby disabled in law, and made utterly incapable to hold, execute, and enjoy his place and office of collector or naval officer, or any profits or advantage arising therefrom, for ever; and the said place and office shall, immediately after such conviction, be void, to all intents and purposes, as if the said collector or naval officer had been naturally dead; and moreover, shall forfeit and pay to the informer, the sum of twenty pounds current money: To be recovered with costs, as aforesaid.

1st offence.

2d offence.

IX. *And be it further enacted, by the authority aforesaid, and it is hereby enacted,* That if any person injured by any collector or naval officer, demanding and taking any fee or fees, contrary to this act, shall fail to inform against the said collector or naval officer for the said offence, within three months after the offence committed, it shall and may be thereafter lawful for any other person or persons whatsoever, to prosecute the offender, and recover; any thing in this act before contained to the contrary, or seeming to the contrary, notwithstanding.

Who may prosecute.

Provided always, and be it enacted, by the authority aforesaid, and it is hereby enacted, That no collector or naval officer whatsoever, shall, at any time hereafter, be impeached or questioned, for or concerning any offence aforesaid, unless such collector or naval officer be prosecuted within the space of one year next ensuing such offence committed.

Limitation of prosecution.

XI. *And be it further enacted, by the authority aforesaid, and it is hereby enacted,* That every collector and naval officer, within this colony and dominion, shall be, and is hereby strictly enjoined and required, within three months after the publication of this act, to set up, or cause to be set up, in his office, a fair written table or copy of his fees, according to this act, and from time to time to continue the same, by setting up a new and fresh table or copy, as the occasion requires.

Table of fees to be set up.

XII. And whereas, the casting or unlading of stones, gravel, or other ballast, into the rivers and creeks of this her majesty's colony and dominion, may, in time, prove, not only dangerous, but wholly obstructive, to the passage of ships, sloops, boats, and other vessels: For prevention thereof,

XIII. *Be it enacted, by the authority aforesaid, and it is hereby enacted,* That it shall not be lawful, for the master of any ship, sloop, boat, or other vessel, or for any other person or persons whatsoever, to cast or unlade any stones, gravel, or other ballast, into any river, creek, haven, or harbor, within this colony and dominion; but to lay the same on the land only above high water mark: And that if the master or owner of any ship, sloop, boat, or other vessel, shall actually offend herein, or shall suffer and permit any other person or persons, under him, to do it, such master, or owner, for every such offence, shall forfeit and pay the sum of ten pounds current money: one moiety to our sovereign lady the queen, her heirs and successors, for

Penalty for casting ballast into rivers, creeks, &c.

and towards the better support of this government, and the contingent charges thereof; and the other moiety to him or them that will inform, or sue for the same: To be recovered, with costs, in any court of record within this colony and dominion, by action of debt, bill, plaint, or information; wherein no essoin, protection, or wager of law, privilege, or more than one imparlance, shall be admitted, or allowed.

XIV. And, whereas it is represented to this assembly, That the commanders or masters of the ships or vessels which have imported negros into this colony and dominion, have caused such negros as died on board, to be cast into the rivers or creeks where such ships or vessels did then ride, to the great annoiance of the inhabitants adjacent: For prevention thereof, for the future,

Penalty for casting dead bodies into a river or creek.

XV. *Be it enacted, by the authority aforesaid, and it is hereby enacted,* That when any negro, or other person whatsoever, shall happen to die on board any ship or vessel, riding or being within any river or creek, within this colony and dominion, the master of such ship or vessel shall cause the negro, or other person, so dying, to be carried on shore, and there buried; upon pain of forfeiting and paying, for his neglect therein, or for suffering the said negro, or other person, to be cast into the water, the sum of ten pounds current money: one moiety thereof, to our sovereign lady the queen, her heirs and successors, for and towards the better support of the government, and the contingent charges thereof; and the other moiety to him or them that will inform, or sue for the same: To be recovered, with costs, in any court of record within this colony and dominion, by action of debt, bill, plaint, or information; wherein no essoin, protection, or wager of law, privilege, or more than one imparlance, shall be admitted or allowed.

Repealing clause.

XVI. *And be it further enacted,* That all and every other act and acts, and every clause and article thereof, heretofore made, for so much thereof as relates to any matter or thing whatsoever, within the purview of this act, is, and are hereby repealed, and made void, to all intents and purposes, as if the same had never been made.

CHAP. XXVIII.

An act for the continuing of General Assemblies, in case of the death or demise of her majesty, her heirs and successors; and for making valid all acts of the governor and council, and all judgments and proceedings at law, which shall happen between the death of any king or queen of England, and the notification thereof in this country.

Preamble.

I. WHEREAS, by reason of the great distance of this colony and dominion of Virginia from our mother kingdom of England, there may happen to be a considerable space of time between the death or demise of the king or queen, for the time being, and the proclamation of his or her successor in this colony and dominion: For preventing the many mischiefs, inconveniences, and unnecessary charges, which may happen or be occasioned, by reason of such interval;

General assemblies not to be dissolved, by demise of the crown.

II. *Be it enacted, by the governor, council, and burgesses, of this present general assembly, and it is hereby enacted, by the authority of the same,* That this present general assembly, or any other general assembly, which shall hereafter be summoned and called, under the authority of her majesty Queen Anne, her heirs and successors, by the governor, lieutenant governor, or commander in chief, by and with the advice and consent of the council of state, of this her majesty's colony and dominion, or by the president and council, for the time being, shall not determine or be dissolved, by the death or demise of her said majesty, her heirs or successors; but that such assembly shall, and is hereby enacted, to continue, and be impowered to meet, convene, and sit, according to the writs or summons, whereby the said assembly was, or shall be convened; and to act, notwithstanding such death or demise, for and during the time of six months, and no longer; unless the same shall, by such governor, lieutenant governor, commander in chief, or president, and council, be sooner prorogued or dissolved: And if the said general assembly shall be so prorogued, then it shall meet and sit, on and upon the day unto which it shall be prorogued, and continue for the residue of the said time of six months, unless sooner prorogued or dissolved, as aforesaid.

Official acts, between death of king, and proclamation of successor, valid, and

III. *And be it also enacted*, That all acts, deeds, and sentences, of the governor, lieutenant governor, commander in chief, or president and council, in this colony and dominion, for the time being, which he or they might lawfully do, sign, or pass, during the life of the king or queen, for the time being, shall be valid, to all intents and purposes in law, although the same happen to be acted, done, or signed, after the death of the said king or queen, and before the said death is by proclamation publicly notified in this country: As also, all acts of the council, judgments of all courts, acts of justices of the peace, and all other officers, civil and military, within this colony and dominion, which they might lawfully do, or pass, during the life of the king or queen, for the time being, be valid, to all intents and purposes in law, although the same happen to be acted after the death of the said king or queen, and before the notification thereof, by the government, in this colony and dominion. And that all treasons, rebellions, and all other crimes whatsoever, committed, or which shall be committed, during the said time, shall be punishable, to all intents, as if the king or queen had been actually alive at the time of the committing thereof.

crimes punishable.

Not to limit the power of the executive.

IV. *Provided always, and it is hereby declared*, That nothing in this act contained, shall extend, or be construed to extend, to alter, or abridge the power of the governor, lieutenant governor, or commander in chief, or president and council, of this colony and dominion, for the time being, here, to prorogue or dissolve this or any other general assembly, in this dominion, within the said six months, or at any other time: Nor to limit the governor, lieutenant governor, commander in chief, or president and council, for the time being, in the execution of any instructions he or they shall receive from the succeeding king or queen of England, relating to the prorogation or dissolution of assemblies.

CHAP. XXIX.

An act for laying an imposition upon skins and furrs; for the better support of the College of William and Mary, in Virginia.

I. *BE it enacted, by the Governor, Council, and Burgesses of this present general assembly, and it is hereby enacted, by the authority of the same,* That there shall be satisfied and paid, to her majesty, her heirs and successors, for and towards the better support and maintenance of the college of William and Mary, in Virginia, the following duties, customs and imposts, for the following goods, wares and merchandizes, which shall be exported and carried out of this her majesty's dominion, either by land or water: (That is to say,) Duty on skins.

For every raw hide, three pence; For every tann'd hide, six pence: For every drest buck-skin, one penny three farthings: For every undrest buck-skin, one penny: For every doe-skin drest, one penny half penny: For every undrest doe-skin, three farthings: For every pound of bever, three pence: For every otter-skin, two pence: For every wild cat-skin, one penny half penny: For every mink-skin, one penny: For every fox-skin, one penny half penny: For every dozen of racoon-skins, three pence, and so proportionably for a greater or lesser quantity: For every dozen of musk-rat-skins, two pence, and so proportionably for a greater or lesser quantity: And, for every elk-skin, four pence half penny. Specification.

II. *And be it enacted,* That the said duties, customs, and imposts, shall be paid and satisfied, by the person or persons exporting or carrying out the same, either by land or water, to the collector or collectors, which shall be appointed by the governor, or commander in chief, for the time being, with the advice of the council, to receive the said dutys, customs, and impost, before the said goods, wares, and merchandizes shall be shipped off, exported, or carried out of and from this dominion, either by land or by water; and a certificate thereof obtained from the collector or collectors of the district where such goods, wares and merchandizes shall be so exported or carried away, signifying the paiment and satisfaction of such duties, customs, and impost, as aforesaid; under the penalty of forfeiting such of the goods, wares, and merchandizes, which shall be shipped off, or loaden on board of any boat, sloop, ship, or other vessel, in order to the exportation thereof by water, or endeavoured to be carried out of this country by land: The one moiety thereof to her majesty, her heirs and successors, to and for the better support of the government, and the contingent charges How payable. Penalty, on failure.

thereof; and the other moiety to him or them that shall sue or prosecute for the same, in any court of record within this colony: To be recovered, with costs, by action of debt, bill, plaint, or information, wherein no essoin, protection, or wager of law, shall be allowed.

Commissions on collecting.

III. *And be it further enacted,* That the several collectors, or officers, appointed to collect and receive the said duties, customs, and imposts, shall, from time to time, be accountable and pay the same to the governors of the said college of William and Mary, or such other person or persons as shall be by them lawfully deputed: And that for the receiving and paying thereof, the said collector or collectors shall be allowed six per cent.

Repealing clause.

IV. *And be it further enacted,* That all and every other act and acts, and every clause and article thereof, heretofore made, for so much thereof as relates to any matter or thing whatsoever, within the purview of this act, is, and are hereby repealed, and made void, to all intents and purposes, as if the same had never been made.

CHAP. XXX.

An act for the effectual suppression of vice, and restraint and punishment of blasphemous, wicked, and dissolute persons.

Atheism, deism, and infidelity, how punishable.

I. *BE it enacted, by the Governor, Council, and Burgesses, of this present General Assembly, and it is hereby enacted, by the authority of the same,* That if any person or persons, brought up in the christian religion, shall, by writing, printing, teaching, or advised speaking, deny the being of a God, or the Holy Trinity, or shall assert or maintain there are more Gods than one, or shall deny the christian religion to be true, or the holy scriptures of the old and new testament to be of divine authority, and be thereof lawfully convicted, upon indictment or information, in the general court of this her majesty's colony and dominion; such person or persons, for the first offence, shall be adjudged uncapable, or disabled in law, to all intents and purposes whatsoever, to hold and enjoy any office or emploiment, ecclesiastical, civil, or military, or any part in

1st offence.

them, or any profit or advantage to them appertaining, or any of them: And if any person or persons, so convicted, as aforesaid, shall, at any time of his or their conviction, enjoy or possess any office, place or emploiment, such office, place or emploiment, shall be void, and is hereby declared void: And if such person or persons shall be a second time lawfully convicted, as aforesaid, of all or any of the crimes aforesaid, that then he, she, or they, shall from thenceforth be disabled to sue, prosecute, plead, or use, any action or information, in any court of law or equity, or to be guardian to any child, or to be executor or administrator of any person, or capable of any deed of gift or legacy, or to bear any office, civil or military, for ever, within this her majesty's colony and dominion; and shall also suffer, from the time of such conviction, three years imprisonment, without bail or mainprise.

2nd offence.

II. *Provided always, and be it enacted, by the authority aforesaid, and it is hereby enacted,* That no person shall be prosecuted, by virtue of this act, for any word spoken, unless information, upon oath, be given in, of the words, before one or more justice or justices of the peace, within one month after such words spoken, and the prosecution of such offence be within twelve months after such information.

Limitation.

III. *Provided also, and be it enacted, by the authority aforesaid, and it is hereby enacted,* That if any person or persons convicted the first time, of all, or any of the aforesaid crimes, in manner aforesaid, shall, within the space of six months after his, her, or their conviction, make his, her, or their public acknowledgement and renunciation of such offence, or erroneous opinions, in the same court where such person or persons was or were convicted, that then, he, she, or they, shall be thence freed and discharged from all penalties and disabilities incurred by such conviction; any thing in this act to the contrary, in any-wise, notwithstanding.

Recantation.

IV. *And be it further enacted, by the authority aforesaid, and it is hereby enacted,* That if any person or persons shall profanely swear or curse, or shall be drunk, he, she, or they so offending, for every such offence, being thereof convicted, by the oath of one or more witnesses, which oath, any justice of the peace is hereby impowered and required to administer, (or by con-

Swearing, cursing, or drunkenness, how punishable.

fession before one or more justice or justices of the peace in the county where such offence shall be committed,) shall forfeit and pay the sum of five shillings, or fifty pounds of tobacco, for every such offence; or if the offence or offences be committed in the presence and hearing of one or more justice or justices of the peace, or in any court of record in this her majesty's colony and dominion, the same shall be a sufficient conviction, without any other evidence; and the said offender shall, upon such conviction, forfeit and pay the sum of five shillings, or fifty pounds of tobacco, for every such offence: And if any person or persons shall refuse to make present paiment, or give sufficient caution for the paiment of the same, at the laying of the next parish levy after the said offence committed, then the said fines and penalties shall be levied upon the goods of such person or persons, by warrant or precept, from any justice of peace before whom the same conviction shall be; which warrant may be directed to the sheriff of the county, or to the constable in his respective precinct, to be appraised and valued, as in other distresses: And if the offender or offenders be not able to pay the said sum or sums, then he, she or they, shall have and receive ten lashes upon his or her bare back, well laid on, for every such offence.

Proof.

Fines, how collected.

Punishment.

V. *Provided always*, That every prosecution, by virtue of this act, for swearing, cursing, or for being drunk, shall be made within two months after the offence committed, and not afterwards.

Limitation.

VI. And to the end, that the Lord's Day, commonly called Sunday, may be kept holy,

VII. *Be it enacted, and it is hereby enacted, by the authority aforesaid*, That if any person, being of the age of twenty-one years, or upwards, shall wilfully absent him or herself from divine service at his or her parish church or chapel, the space of one month, (excepting as is excepted in an act of parliament passed in the first year of King William and Queen Mary, intituled, An act for exempting their majesty's protestant subjects dissenting from the church of England, from the penalties of certain laws;) and shall not, when there, in a decent and orderly manner, continue till the said service is ended; and if any person shall, on that day, be present at any disorderly meeting, gaming, or tippling,

Not attending church.

Toleration act.

or shall, on the said day, make any journey, and travel upon the road, except to and from church, (cases of necessity and charity excepted,) or shall, on the said day, be found working in their corn or tobacco, or any other labour of their ordinary calling, other than is necessary for the sustenance of man and beast; every person failing or making default in any of the premises, and being lawfully convicted, by confession, or otherwise, before one or more justice or justices of the peace of the county wherein such offence shall be committed, (so that prosecution be made within two months after such default,) shall forfeit and pay, for every such offence, the sum of five shillings, or fifty pounds of tobacco: And if any person or persons herein offending, shall refuse to make present paiment, or give sufficient caution for the paiment of the fine at the laying of the next parish levy after such offence committed, each party so offending, and not paying or giving security as aforesaid, shall, by order of such justice or justices before whom such conviction shall be, receive on his or her bare back, ten lashes, well laid on.

Working on Sunday.

Punishment.

VIII. *And be it also further enacted, by the authority aforesaid, and it is hereby enacted,* That every person, not being a servant or slave, committing adultery or fornication, and being thereof lawfully convicted, by the oaths of two or more credible witnesses, or confession of the party, shall, for every offence of adultery, forfeit and pay one thousand pounds of tobacco, and cask; and for every offence of fornication, five hundred pounds of tobacco, and cask: To be recovered by the suit or prosecution of the churchwarden or churchwardens of the parish wherein such offence shall be committed, by bill, plaint, or information, in any court of record within this her majesty's colony and dominion, wherein no essoin, protection, or wager of law, shall be allowed. And if any person or persons offending herein, shall refuse to make present paiment, or give sufficient caution for the paiment of the fine, at the laying of the next parish levy after such conviction, each party so offending, and not paying or giving security as aforesaid, shall receive on his or her bare back, at the public whipping-post, twenty-five lashes, well laid on.

Adultery and fornication, how punishable.

IX. *And be it enacted, by the authority aforesaid, and it is hereby enacted and declared,* That all the fines and

Fines appropriated.

forfeitures in this act mentioned, shall be paid to the churchwardens of that parish wherein the offence shall be committed; who shall be accountable for the same, to the vestry, for the use of the poor of the parish: Which said vestry shall annually, on Easter Tuesday, if fair, (if not, the next fair day,) at the parish church, distribute the said fines and forfeitures, according to their discretion, among the poor of their parish.

This act to be read in churches.

X. *And be it further enacted, by the authority aforesaid,* That this act shall be publicly read two several times in the year in all parish churches and chapels within this colony, by the minister, clerk, or reader of each parish, immediately after divine service; that is to say, on the first or second Sunday in April, and on the first or second Sunday in September, under the penalty of twenty shillings for every such omission and neglect; and the churchwardens of every parish are hereby required to provide a copy of this act, at the charge of the parish.

Further punishment on clergyman.

XI. *Provided always,* That nothing therein contained, shall be construed to exempt any clergyman within this colony, who shall be guilty of any of the crimes herein before-mentioned, from such further punishment as might have been inflicted on him for the same, before the making of this act; any thing herein contained to the contrary, notwithstanding.

Repealing clause.

XII. *And be it further enacted,* That all and every other act and acts, and every clause and article thereof, heretofore made, for so much thereof as relates to the suppression of vice, or restraint and punishment of blasphemous, wicked, and dissolute persons, is, and are hereby repealed and made void, to all intents and purposes, as if the same had never been made.

CHAP. XXXI.

Edi. 1733, and 1752. See chap. 5, 1727.

An act for security and defence of the country in times of danger.

[From MS.]

FOR the better security and defence of this country in times of danger,

Be it enacted, by the governor, council and burgesses of this present general assembly, and it is hereby enacted, by the authority of the same, That upon any invasion of the enemy by sea or land, or upon any insurrection, the governor or comander in chief of this colony and dominion, for the time being, have full power to levy, raise, arm and muster such a number of forces out of the militia of this colony as shall be thought requisite and needfull for repelling the invasion or suppressing the insurrection, and the same being raised, to order, direct, march, employ, continue, discharge and disband, as the occasion shall require, or the cause of danger ceases for which they were raised.

Governor authorised to call out the militia, on invasions or insurrections.

And be it further enacted, That upon raising or continuance of forces as aforesaid, it shall and may be lawfull by warrant under the hand and seal of any commander in chief, colonel, lieutenant colonel or major, commanding any part of the same, to impress and take up necessary provisions off and from any person or persons, and to impress and take up sloops and boats necessary for the transportation of forces over rivers and creeks, or the main bay of Chesapeak, together with the rigging, tackell, furniture and apparell, belonging thereunto, and also all manner of conveniencys for the land carriage of provisions, great guns, arms and ammunition, from place to place, and likewise to impress and take up any manner of utensils, tools or instruments which shall or may be wanted for digging and intrenching, or towards the mounting the great guns and making them usefull.

Power of impressment, of provisions, carriages, &c.

And further, That it shall and may be lawfull by warrant as aforesaid, to impress able and fit men to go in sloops and boats, and also to impress any smith, wheel-right, carpenter or other artificer whatsoever, which shall be thought usefull for the fixing of arms and making of carriages for great guns, or for doing any other work whatsoever, where need shall be of such artificer.

Of artificers, &c.

Provided always, and be it enacted, That it shall not be lawfull to make use of any provisions, conveniencys for land carriage, utensills, tools or instruments, impressed and taken up as aforesaid, untill appraisment hath been made thereof in tobacco by two good and lawfull men upon oath, nor of any boat or sloop untill appraisement hath been made of the same as aforesaid, with the severall appurtenances belonging thereunto and also an estimate made by the same men, of a suita-

Articles impressed, how appraised.

ble allowance in tobacco by the day for the use of the said boat or sloop and every person impressing and taking up any of the particulars aforesaid, is hereby required to take care that an appraisement and estimate be made as aforesaid, and to give a receipt to the owner for every perticular by him impressed and taken up, with an account therein how the same was appraised and how estimated, and for what use and service imprest and taken up, upon pain of being lyable to the action of the party grieved, for an unlawfull seizure.

And because it may be an advantage to discover the enemy in his approach and there may be a necessity of taking up arms before notice can be given of an alarm to the governor and his commands or orders thereupon had how to act,

Look-outs to be employed towards the sea.

Be it therefore enacted, That in each of the countys of Elizabeth City, Princess Anne and Northampton, at such times and places as the governor or commander in chief of this colony and dominion shall think fit to direct one man be appointed by the chief officer of the militia residing within the respective countys, which men shall keep a constant look out to seaward by night and by day, and if any of the said men shall happen to espy any ship or vessell upon the sea, he shall diligently observe the courses and motions of the said ship or vessell, and if upon such observation he shall suspect that the said ship or vessell doth belong to an enemy he shall imediately give notice thereof to the next field officer in his county.

Duty of officers, in giving intelligence of the approach of an enemy.

And be it further enacted, That when any notice shall be given to the chief militia officer within any ffrontier county either by sea or land of the approach of an enemy, such chief officer is hereby authorised, impowered and required, immediately to issue his warrant for the impressing of horses, boats and men, as the occasion shall require, to carry an account of the said intelligence to the governor or commander in chief of this colony and dominion for the time being to the commander in chief of the militia in the said county, and to the chief militia officer residing in the next adjacent ffrontier county, and how he designs to proceed thereon.

And be it further enacted, That any chief militia officer to whom notice of the approach of an enemy shall be given as aforesaid, shall thereupon have full power to levy and raise all or any part of the militia under his command, and with the advice of the commission officers that meet him to march the same against and engage the enemy untill notice of the alarm can be sent to the governor and orders and directions come from him how to act. Militia to be embodied.

And be it further enacted, That the officers and soldiers which shall be raised and the look-outs which shall be appointed by virtue of this act, shall be paid and allowed by the publick after the following rates, to wit: Pay of officers, soldiers and look-outs.

A colonel and commander in chief, seventy pounds of tobacco per day.

A colonel of horse, sixty pounds of tobacco per day.

A lieutenant-colonel of horse, fifty pounds of tobacco per day.

A major of horse, fifty pounds of tobacco per day.

A captain of horse or dragoons, thirty-five pounds of tobacco per day.

A lieutenant of horse or dragoons, thirty pounds of tobacco per day.

A cornet of horse or dragoons, twenty-five pounds of tobacco per day.

A horseman or dragoon, twenty pounds of tobacco per day.

A colonel of foot, fifty pounds of tobacco per day.

A lieutenant-colonel of foot, forty pounds of tobacco per day.

A major of foot, forty pounds of tobacco per day.

A captain of foot, thirty pounds of tobacco per day.

A lieutenant of foot, twenty-five pounds of tobacco per day.

An ensign of foot, twenty pounds of tobacco per day.

A foot soldier, fifteen pounds of tobacco per day.

A look-out, after the rate of two hundred pounds of tobacco per month.

Provided always, and it is the true intent and meaning of this act, That for the pay and allowance given by this act as aforesaid, every horseman and dragoon shall find and provide himself with an horse and horse furniture, arms and ammunition, and every foot soldier shall find and provide himself with a foot soldiers arms and ammunition. Soldiers to provide their own arms and accoutrements

Proviso, where the militia are not employed above 4 days.

Provided also, That whensoever any part of the militia raised by virtue of this act shall be discharged again within four days, no pay or allowance shall be given for the same, but every man shall bear his own charge, and that when any part of the militia raised as aforesaid, shall be kept in service above four days, the same shall be paid and allowed for the whole time of service according to the rates directed by this act, any thing in this act before contained to the contrary thereof in any wise notwithstanding.

Pay of artificers.

And be it further enacted, That every smith, wheel-right, carpenter or other artificer imprest by virtue of this act and employed about fixing of arms, making of carriages for great guns, or other work requiring an artificer, shall be paid and allowed by the public after the rates following, to witt: every smith fifty pounds of tobacco per day, and every carpenter, wheel-right or other artificer impressed as aforesaid, forty pounds of tobacco per day, and that every man imprest as aforesaid to go in a sloop or boat, shall be paid and allowed by the publick fifteen pounds of tobacco per day.

Of men impressed to go in boats.

Expresses.

Provided always, and it is the true intent and meaning of this act, That for any message sent according to the directions of this act, either by land or water, allowance shall be made for carrying the same as the law directs for other expresses, and not otherways, any thing in this act to the contrary notwithstanding.

Articles impressed, how paid for.

And be it further enacted, That the owner or owners of any provisions, conveniencys for land carriage, utensills, tools or instruments, impressed and taken up by virtue of this act, shall be paid and sattisfyed for the same by the publick according to the respective value thereof by the appraisement, made in pursuance of this act.

Boats, and sloops, how paid for, if lost.

And be it further enacted, That the owner or owners of any boat or sloop, imprest, taken up, and employed by virtue and according to the directions of this act, shall be allowed and paid by the publick for the use of the same according to the estimate made in pursuance of this act, and in case such sloop or boat be cast away or lost in the service, then the owner or owners thereof shall be paid for the same according to the appraisement made in pursuance of this act, and half the pay for the use.

And be it further enacted, That if any boat or sloop, impress, taken up and imployed by virtue and according to the directions of this act, be damnifyed in the service, then sattisfaction shall be made to the owner or owners thereof, according to the damage received, beside the pay for the use. If damaged.

Provided always, and it is hereby meant and intended, That all such damage shall be inquired and found by two indifferent persons upon oath, to be chosen and appointed by any justice of the peace within the county where the sloop or boat so damnifyed shall happen to be. Damage, how ascertained.

And be it further enacted, That this act continue in force till the thirtyeth day of June, which shall be in the year of our Lord, one thousand seven hundred and eight, and no longer. Limitation of this act.

And be it further enacted, That all and every other act and acts, and every clause and article thereof, heretofore made, for so much thereof as relates to any matter or thing whatsoever, within the purview of this act, is, and are hereby repealed and made void to all intents and purposes, as if the same had never been made. Repealing clause.

CHAP. XXXII.

An act concerning Juries.

I. FOR the more regular inquiry into the breaches of penal laws, and trials of matters of fact, in the several courts of judicature in this dominion, by grand juries and petit juries,

II. *Be it enacted, by the Governor, Council, and Burgesses of this present General Assembly, and it is hereby enacted, by the authority of the same,* That every county court, shall cause at least four and twenty freeholders of their county, to be summoned to appear at May court, and November court, in every year; out of which, shall be impannelled a grand jury, who shall be sworn to make inquiry into the breach of the laws, and to make presentment of the offenders: And such grand jury having made presentment of all such matters as come to their knowledge, shall be discharged at the adjournment of the same court; but if they cannot Grand juries, in county courts, when to be summoned.

How to make presentments.

agree upon all their presentments before such adjournment, then they shall have liberty to finish their presentments, and to appear, and present them at the next court; always observing, that when they make any presentment, upon the information of any other persons than themselves, that they write the names of such persons under the presentment, to the end the same may be the more effectually prosecuted: And if any freeholder, summoned to appear at May court, or November court, as aforesaid, shall fail to appear, (so as no grand jury can thereupon be impannelled,) such freeholder, so failing to appear, shall be fined by the court, in the sum of two hundred pounds of tobacco, to our sovereign lady the queen, her heirs and successors, for the use of the county: And if the court of any county shall fail to give order for the summoning four and twenty freeholders of their county, as aforesaid, to make a grand jury; or, upon the appearance of fifteen of them, shall omit to swear a grand jury, as aforesaid, every member of such court, so failing, or omitting, shall forfeit and pay four hundred pounds of tobacco, to our sovereign lady the queen, her heirs and successors, for and towards the better support of the government of this her majesty's colony and dominion, and the contingent charges thereof: To be recovered by action of debt, bill, plaint, or information, in any court of record within this dominion, in which no essoin, protection, or wager of law, shall be allowed. And if the sheriff of any county, upon order given by the court, to summon twenty-four freeholders, as aforesaid, shall fail to perform his duty therein, and to return the names of the persons summoned, he shall forfeit and pay one thousand pounds of tobacco, to our sovereign lady the queen, her heirs and successors, for and towards the better support of the government of this her majesty's colony and dominion, and the contingent charges thereof: To be recovered by action of debt, bill, plaint, or information, in any court of record, within this dominion; in which no essoin, protection, or wager of law, shall be allowed.

Fine for not appearing.

Number of grand jury.

Penalty on court failing to order a grand jury;

On sheriff failing to summon.

Grand juries in general court, may be composed of bye-standers.

III. And, for presentments to be made at the general court, it shall be lawful, for the sheriff, or other officer, attending the said court, to summon a grand jury of the by-standers, being freeholders, who shall and may, and are hereby declared to have full power, to make presentments of any offences whatsoever, committed or to be committed or done, within this colony. And, to the end that the grand juries summoned to the general court, may be constituted of the most capable persons, it shall be lawful for the said general court, upon the first or second day of their sitting, to make a rule, for the sheriff, or other officer, attending the court, to summon twenty-four persons, as aforesaid, to attend the court, for a grand jury: And if any person, so summoned, shall fail to appear, he shall forfeit and pay four hundred pounds of tobacco, to our sovereign lady the queen, her heirs and successors, for and towards the better support of the government of this her majesty's colony and dominion, and the contingent charges thereof: To be recovered, by action of debt, bill, plaint, or information, in any court of record within this dominion; in which no essoin, protection, or wager of law, shall be allowed.

Fine for not appearing.

IV. *Provided always*, That no grand jury shall make any presentments, as of their own knowledge, upon the information of less than two persons of their own number.

How to make presentments.

V. *And be it further enacted*, That for the trial of all causes, (treason and felony excepted) both in the general court, and county court, the sheriff, and other officer, attending the court, shall, every morning the court sits, summon a sufficient number of the by-standers, qualified as hereafter is directed, to attend the court, for that day; that out of them may be impannelled a sufficient jury, for the trial of any cause (except before excepted) which shall be depending in such court. And if any by-stander, being summoned, as aforesaid, shall fail to attend the court, so as a sufficient jury cannot be impannelled, every such by-stander, so failing, shall be fined by the court, four hundred pounds of tobacco, to our sovereign lady the queen, her heirs and successors, for and towards the better support of the government of this her majesty's colony and dominion, and the contingent charges thereof.

Petit jury, for trial of civil causes, their number and qualifications.

Fine for not appearing.

VI. And, for the trials of all treasons and felonies, *Be it enacted, by the authority aforesaid*, That the petit jury for the same, shall be made up in manner following: (That is to say,) When any person shall be com-

Venire, for criminal causes, how summoned.

mitted, for treason or felony, the sheriff, or other officer to whom such person shall be committed, shall signify the same to the clerk of the general court, for the time being, together with the crime for which such commitment shall be made, and the particular place wherein the same shall be alledged to be committed: Whereupon, the clerk of the general court shall issue forth a writ of *venire facias*, to the sheriff of the county where the crime shall be alledged to be committed, requiring him to summon and return the names of six discreet and honest freeholders of his county, residing as near as may be to that part of the county where the crime shall be alledged to be committed, to appear at the fourth day of the general court then next coming, to be of the jury for the trial of the same; which six freeholders, or so many of them as shall not be challenged, shall be of the jury; and as many persons more as shall be wanting to make up the pannel, shall be taken of the by-standers, being discreet and honest freeholders within this colony, and who shall, every one of them, be possessed of a visible real and personal estate, of the value of one hundred pounds, at least.

Qualifications of jurors, in criminal and civil causes.

VII. *And be it further enacted, by the authority aforesaid,* That no person shall be capable to be of a jury, for the trial of any treason, felony, breach of the peace, or of any misprision, breach of any penal law, or any other pleas of the crown, or of any estate of freehold, or any estate or title in or to any lands, tenements or hereditaments, in any court in this dominion, unless such person shall be a freeholder, and shall be possessed of a visible estate, real and personal, of at least the value of one hundred pounds sterling. And that no person shall be capable to be of a jury for the trial of any cause whatsoever, in the general court, unless he be a freeholder, and possessed of a visible estate, real and personal, of the said value of one hundred pounds sterling, at the least. And that no person shall be capable to be of a jury, for the trial of any cause whatsoever, in any county court within this dominion, unless he shall be possessed of a visible estate, real or personal, of the value of fifty pounds sterling, at the least. And that no sheriff, or other officer, shall, at any time hereafter, summon or return any person to serve as a juryman, in any court who shall not be capacitated for the same, according as is herein before directed.

VIII. *Provided always,* That the exceptions to be taken to any jury-man, on account of his estate, shall be taken before he be sworn, or else not to be allowed. Exceptions, when taken.

IX. *And be it further enacted,* That all and every other act and acts, and every clause and article thereof, heretofore made, for so much thereof as relates to the inquiry into the breaches of penal laws, and trials of matters of fact, in the several courts of judicature, in this dominion, by juries, or concerning any matters or things within the purview of this act, is, and are hereby repealed, and made void, to all intents and purposes, as if the same had never been made. Repealing clause.

CHAP. XXXIII.

An act for the distribution of intestates estates, declaring widows rights to their deceased husbands estates; and for securing orphans estates.

I. FOR the more equal distribution of the estates of persons dying intestate,

II. *Be it enacted, by the governor, council, and burgesses, of this present general assembly, and it is hereby enacted, by the authority of the same,* That after debts, funerals, and just expences of every sort, first paid and allowed, the surplusage of all and singular the goods, chattels, and personal estate of every person dying intestate, shall be distributed amongst the wife and children or childrens children, if any such be, or otherwise, to the next of kin to the dead person, in equal degree, or legally representing their stocks, *pro suo cuique jure,* according to the laws in such cases, and the rules and limitations herein after set down; that is to say, one third part of the said surplusage to the wife of the intestate, and all the residue, by equal portions, to and amongst the children of such persons dying intestate, and such persons as legally represent such children, in case any of the said children be then dead, other than such child or children (not being heir at law) who shall have any estate by the settlement of the intestate, or shall be advanced by the intestate, in his life time, by

Intestates' estates, how distributed.

Dower of wife, where there are children.

Advancements to children, how accounted for.

portion or portions, equal to the share which shall, by such distribution, be allotted to the other children, to whom such distribution is to be made: And in case any child (other than the heir at law) shall have any estate by settlement from the intestate, or shall be advanced by the said intestate in his life time, by portion, not equal to the share, which will be due to the other children, by such distribution as aforesaid, then so much of the surplusage of the estate of such intestate, to be distributed to such child or children, as shall have any lands by settlement from the intestate, or were advanced in the life time of the intestate, as shall make the estate of all the said children to be equal, as near as can be estimated: But the heir at law, notwithstanding any land he shall have by descent, or otherwise, from the intestate, is to have an equal part in the distribution with the rest of the children, without any consideration of the value of the land which he hath by descent, or otherwise, from the intestate. And if, after the death of a father, any of his children shall die intestate, without wife or children, in the life time of the mother, every brother and sister, and the representatives of them, shall have an equal share with her: And if all the children shall die intestate, without wife or children, in the life time of the mother, then the portion of the child so dying last, shall be equally divided, one moiety to the mother, and the other moiety to the next of the kindred by the father: And if there be no such kindred by the father, then the whole shall be to the mother; any law, usage, or custom to the contrary, notwithstanding.

Heir at law, not to account for land by descent.

Portions of children dying how distributed.

Dower of wife, where no children.

And in case there be no children, or any legal representatives of them, then one moiety of the said surplusage to be allotted to the wife of the intestate, and the other moiety to be distributed equally to every of the next of kindred to the intestate, who are in equal degree, and those who legally represent them; and if there be no such kindred, then all the said surplusage to be to the wife.

Collaterals, how far estimated,

III. *Provided*, That there be no representations admitted amongst collaterals, after brothers and sisters children. And in case there be no wife, then all the said surplusage to be distributed equally to and amongst the children. And in case there be no child, then to the next of kindred, in equal degree of or unto the in-

Where no wife.

testate, and their legal representatives, as aforesaid; and in no other manner whatsoever.

IV. *Provided also*, That when any person dies testate, if he leaves one or two children, and no more, he shall not have power to dispose of more than two third parts of his estate, by will, to any other person or persons than his wife; and one third part thereof, at the least, shall be given to her. And if such person shall leave more than two children, he shall not leave his wife less than a child's part, according to the number of children: But if such person leaves no child, then the wife shall have at least one equal moiety of his estate. And if any person shall leave a will, wherein a lesser part of his estate shall be given to his wife than is herein directed, such will, as to so much thereof as relates to the wife, upon her petition to the court where the same shall be proved, shall be declared null and void: And thereupon, she shall and may be impowered to sue for and recover, such part of her deceased husband's estate as is herein before directed to be given her.

Where only 2 children, what part must be bequeathed to the wife;

Where more than two children.

Wills otherwise made, void as to wife.

V. *Provided always*, That if such wife shall die, before distribution of her deceased husband's estate shall be made, according to this act, then in such case, her executors and administrators shall be impowered to sue for and recover, so much of the said estate, as shall be given to her by will, and no more; any thing herein before, to the contrary, notwithstanding.

Rights of executors of wife dying before distribution.

VI. *Provided also*, That if the widow of any person dying intestate, shall depart this life, before the estate of her deceased husband shall be appraised, then the right of such widow, to her said husband's estate, or any part thereof, shall be determined: Neither shall her executors or administrators have power to commence or prosecute any suit, for recovery thereof.

Where widow of intestate dies, before appraisement.

VII. *Provided also, and be it enacted, by the authority aforesaid*, to the end that a due regard be had to creditors, That no such distribution, as aforesaid, of the goods of any person dying intestate, be made, till after nine months be fully expired, after the intestate's death: And that such, and every one to whom any distribution and share shall be allotted, shall give bond, with sufficient sureties, in the court where such distribution shall be made, That if any debt or debts, truly owing by the intestate, shall be afterwards sued for,

When to be distributed.

Bond to indemnify.

and recovered, or otherwise duly made to appear, that then, and in every such case, he or she shall respectively refund and pay back to the administrator, his or her ratable part of that debt or debts, and of the costs of suit, and charges of the administrator by reason of such debt, out of the part and share so as aforesaid allotted to him or her, thereby to enable the said administrator to pay and satisfy the said debt or debts, so discovered after the distribution made, as aforesaid.

Dower of widows.

VIII. *And be it further enacted,* That the widow of any person dying intestate, shall be endowed of one full and equal third part of all her deceased husband's lands, tenements, and other real estate, in manner as is directed and prescribed by the laws and constitutions of the kingdom of England: And till such dower shall be assigned, it shall be lawful for her to remain and continue in the Mansion house, and the messuage or plantation thereto belonging, without being chargeable to pay the heir any rent for the same: Any law, usage, or custom, to the contrary, in any wise, notwithstanding.

Quarantine.

Jointure, when a bar to dower.

IX. *Provided always,* That if any widow shall have such a jointure settled on her, in the life-time of her husband, as by law doth barr her of her dower, she shall not hold possession of any houses or messuages of her said deceased husband, other than what shall be so settled on her.

X. And if it shall so happen, that any person dies, leaving an estate of so small value, that no one will take administration thereupon,

When estate may be committed to sheriff.

XI. *Be it enacted,* That in such case, it shall be lawful for the court, at the expiration of three months next after such person's decease, to impower and direct the sheriff of the county, to take the said estate into his possession, and make sale thereof, by way of outcry: And the buyers of such estate, shall give obligations, with security, for the paiment of what shall be due from them to the said estate; which obligations shall be made paiable to the sheriff and shall by him be assigned to such creditors of the deceased, or to such other persons as the court shall direct; always regarding the dignity of the debts: And for his trouble herein sustained, the sheriff shall be paid out of such estate, after the rate of five pounds per cent. of the value for which it shall be sold.

XII. And for the better securing the estates of all persons deceased, and of all orphans estates,

XIII. *Be it enacted and declared,* That when any person shall be chargeable, as executor or administrator, or otherwise, with the estate of any person deceased, or with any orphan's estate, and shall die so chargeable, the estate of such person so dying, shall be liable to pay and satisfy such other deceased person's, or orphan's estate, before any other debt whatsoever, any law, custom, or usage to the contrary hereof, in any-wise, notwithstanding.

Debts due as executor or administrator, or to orphans, of first dignity.

XIV. *And be it further enacted,* That every county court shall take good security of all guardians, for the estates of the orphans committed to their charge, and that they shall yearly inquire into such securities; and if any of them become defective or insufficient, shall cause new security to be given: And if it shall appear that the said estates are likely to be imbezzelled, or that the orphans are not taken care of, and educated, according to their estates; then the said court shall have power to remove the said orphans (not being of age to choose their guardians) and their estates, and to place them under the care of such other persons, as to them shall seem most proper; always taking good security for the said orphans estates, that when the same shall become paiable to the said orphans, they shall be paid without making any abatement or allowance (other than of the profits of the said estates) for diet, cloathing, or any other matter whatsoever: And if the estate of any orphan be of so small a value, that no person will maintain him for the profits thereof, then such orphan shall, by direction of the court, be bound apprentice to some handicraft trade, or mariner, until he shall attain to the age of one and twenty years. And the master of every such orphan shall be obliged to teach him to read and write: And, at the expiration of his servitude, to pay and allow him in like manner as is appointed for servants, by indenture or custom. And if it shall appear, than any such apprentice be ill used by his master, or that he fails to teach him his trade, the court shall have power to remove him,

Guardians to give good security;

which is to be annually examined.

Courts may remove orphans.

When to be bound apprentices.

Duty of their masters.

Power of courts in hearing their complaints.

and to bind him to such other person as to them shall seem most proper.

Justices, when liable, for insufficient security.

XV. *And be it further enacted, and declared,* That if any county court shall grant an administration, upon the estate of any person deceased, or shall commit an orphan's estate to the charge of any person, and shall fail to take good security for the same, in such manner as the law directs; in every such case, the justices that shall grant such administration, or commit such orphan's estate, as aforesaid, and every of them, shall be chargeable for all such loss and damage as shall accrue by reason of such failure: To be recoverable by action at the common law, at the suit of the party grieved.

Security, how relieved.

XVI. *Provided always, and be it further enacted,* That when any party, being security in any court, for any decedent's estate, or for the estate of any orphan, shall think himself in danger of suffering, by reason of being such security, and shall petition the said court for relief, either by counter security, or otherwise, then it shall and may be lawful for the said court to summon the party with whom such security was given, and to make such order and decree therein, as to them shall seem consistent with equity and good conscience, for the relief and indemnifying of such party so petitioning, as aforesaid.

Funeral expences, regulated.

XVII. *And be it further enacted,* That the county court shall have power, by their discretion, to regulate the funeral expences of any person deceased, and to make allowance for the same, according to his estate.

Repealing clause.

XVIII. *And be it further enacted,* That all and every other act and acts, and every clause and article thereof, heretofore made, for so much thereof as relates to any matter or thing whatsoever, within the purview of this act, is, and are hereby repealed, and made void, to all intents and purposes, as if the same had never been made.

CHAP. XXXIV.

An act declaring how long judgments, bonds, obligations, and accounts, shall be in force, for the assignment of bonds and obligations, directing what proof shall be sufficient in such cases; and ascertaining the damage upon protested bills of exchange.

Edi. 1733, and 1752.

Repealed by proclamation, April 15th, 1730.

[From MS.]

BE it enacted, by the Governor, Council, and Burgesses of this present general assembly, and it is hereby enacted, by the authority of the same, That no action of debt upon the case, or other action shall be commenced or prosecuted against any person or persons whatsoever, their heirs, executors, or administrators, for or in order to any recovery or obtaining of judgment for any debt due by judgment upon record, bond, bill obligatory, or other note, or upon account, unless the same action or suit be commenced and prosecuted within the several limitations and times hereinafter mentioned and expressed, that is to say, for every debt due by judgment upon record, the suit shall be commenced and prosecuted as aforesaid, within the space of seven years next after such judgment shall have been first obtained, or after the same shall have been renewed by *scire facias*; for every debt due by bond or bill obligatory wherein no certain day of payment is expressed, the suit shall be commenced and prosecuted as aforesaid, within five years next after the date of such bond or bill obligatory; and if any certain day or days of payment be expressed, then the suit shall be commenced and prosecuted within five years after the last day of payment so expressed; and upon any bond for performance of covenants the suit shall be commenced and prosecuted as aforesaid within five years next after the breach of covenants assigned shall happen; and for any debt due by note drawn on any person within this colony the suit shall be commenced and prosecuted as aforesaid (either on behalf of the person to whom the same shall be made payable, or of the person that shall accept and pay the same) against the drawer within three years after the date of such note; and if such note shall be accepted by the person on whom it shall be drawn the suit shall be commenced and prosecuted against such acceptor within three years

Limitation of action on judgment;

On bonds or bills, where no day of payment is expressed;

where a day of payment is expressed;

on bonds for performance of covenants

on notes drawn and accepted, by payee, or drawer.

On accounts, against residents, and non-residents.

after such acceptance: And for debts due by account for goods or wares delivered or for clerks, sheriffs or other officers fees, chiurgeons accounts or any other accounts whatsoever, the suit shall be commenced and prosecuted as aforesaid within three years after the same shall grow due if the person or persons to whom the same shall be due be resident within this colony and within five years after the same shall grow due if the person or persons to whom the same shall be due be not resident within this colony.

Limitation not to extend to debtors removing out of the country, not leaving visible estate.

Provided always, That if any person or persons in any wise chargeable by any judgment, bond, bill obligatory or other note or by any account shall abscond or privily remove him, her or themselves out of the county wherein he, she or they became so chargeable, and shall not leave sufficient visible estate within the same county to sattisfy and pay all such judgments, bonds, bills, notes or accounts, such person or persons shall not have or receive any benefit or advantage by the severall limitations herein before set down, or any of them, any thing herein contained to the contrary notwithstanding.

Discounts may be proved on trial.

And be it further enacted, by the authority aforesaid, That when any suit shall be commenced and prosecuted in any court within this colony for any debt due by judgment, bond, bill or otherwise, the defendant shall have liberty upon tryall thereof to make all the discount he can against such debt, and upon proof thereof the same shall be allowed in court.

Assignments on bonds, &c. permitted;

and assignee may sue in his own name,

And be it further enacted, That it shall and may be lawfull to and for any person or persons to assign or transfer any bond or bill for debt over to any other person or persons whatsoever, and that the assignee or assignees, his and their executors and administrators by virtue of such assignment shall and may have lawfull power to commence and prosecute any suit at law in his or their own name or names, for the recovery of any debt due by such bond or bill as the first obligor, his executors and administrators, might or could lawfully do.

and must allow all discounts, against himself, or first obligee.

Provided always, That in any suit commenced upon such bond or bill so assigned, the plaintiff shall be obliged to allow all discounts as aforesaid that the defendant can prove either against himself or against the first obligee.

And be it further enacted, That when any suit shall be commenced for the recovery of any debt due by account (other than for secretarys, county court clerks, sheriffs or other officers fees, public, county or parish levys, or physitians or chirurgeons accounts, and the accounts of merchants living out of this country) if the plaintiff shall not prove his account by the oaths of two witnesses or by his own and the oath of one other witness, it shall be lawfull for the defendant in open court upon his corporal oath to deny the receipt of the particulars or the performance of the services wherewith he is charged, or any part thereof, and such oath so made shall be held sufficient to discharge him of so much as shall be so denyed, and if the defendant shall not make any such oath, the plaintiffs oath to the truth and justness of the account shall be held and taken to be good proof thereof, and judgement shall accordingly be granted thereupon. And if the plaintiff be an executor or administrator who cannot be capable of making oath to the account of his testator or intestate if he can bring one evidence to prove the account of the testator or intestate, and shall himself make oath that he found the account so stated in the testators or intestates books or papers, such proof shall be accounted sufficient, but if he cannot bring such evidence besides his own oath, in such case the defendant shall be admitted to deny the same upon oath, and if the defendant shall refuse to deny the same upon oath, then the plaintiffs making oath that he found the account so stated in the testators or intestates books or papers, shall be held and taken to be good proof thereof, and judgement shall accordingly be granted thereupon, and in case of *non est inventus* returned, if the defendant do not appear the oath of the plaintiff as aforesaid shall be taken to be good and sufficient proof that the account is justly due, and judgement shall accordingly be granted thereupon.

Proof of accounts.

When defendant may deny, on oath.

Proof of accounts, by executors or administrators.

Where the defendant does not appear.

Provided always, That when any suit shall be commenced upon a physitians or chirurgeons account it shall be lawfull for the court to put such a reasonable valuation upon the medicines administred, and the visits, attendance and other services performed, as to them shall seem meet and just, any thing herein before contained, to the contrary notwithstanding.

Courts may reduce physicians' accounts.

In suits against ex'r. & adm'rs. the plaintiff not being one, must make oath.

And be it further enacted, That when any suit shall be prosecuted against the executor or administrator of any person deceased upon any judgment, bond or bill, the plaintiff not being an executor or administrator, shall declare upon oath that he hath not received any part of sattisfaction of such judgement, bond or bill, or what part he hath received.

Where plaintiff may make oath.

Provided always, and be it enacted, That in all cases where the plaintiff or creditor is obliged by this act to make oath to the truth or justness of any debt or account, it shall be lawfull for such plaintiff or creditor to appear and make such oath in the court of that county where he shall reside, and if he be out of the country before the governor or mayor of the place where he is, and to take a certificate thereof from the clerk of the same court, or the governor or mayor as the case is, and such oath so made and a certificate thereof so obtained, shall be as sufficient and available as if the same oath had been made in the court where any suit (requiring such oath to be made) shall be depending.

Where the plaintiff is unable to travel to court.

Provided also, That if the plaintiff or creditor obliged by this act to make oath as aforesaid, be not able to travail to the court of the county where he resides, it shall be lawfull for such plaintiff or creditor to make such oath before two justices of the peace whereof one shall be of the quorum in the said county, and to take a certificate from them thereof, and such oath so made and certificate thereof so obtained, shall be as sufficient and available as if the same oath had been made according to the directions of this act before mentioned and exprest. And to the end persons out of the country may have a suitable time to produce a certificate of oath made according to this act,

How long executors and administrators must retain for absent creditors.

Be it enacted, by the authority aforesaid, That if a suit be brought against the executor or administrator of a person deceased upon a judgment, bond or bill, and the plaintiff or creditor bringing such suit be out of the country, the executor or administrator shall take care to retain assets in his hands sufficient to sattisfy the said judgment, bond or bill, for the space of two years, and shall not suffer the same to be recovered out of his hands in that time by any creditor upon a debt of less dignity than what the creditor out of the county sues upon.

And to prevent any controversys that may arise thereupon, *It is hereby enacted and declared*, That all goods, wares and merchandises imported into this colony by any person whether as factor or otherwise, shall be held, deemed and taken to be the proper estate of the possessor, and accordingly shall be chargeable for all debts by him contracted.

Goods imported by factors, to be deemed the goods of the possessor.

And be it further enacted, That if any bill of exchange drawn by any person or persons in this colony to be paid in the kingdom of England, Ireland, Wales or the town of Berwick upon Tweed, shall be returned protested, in such case there shall be paid to the person or persons on whose behalf such protest shall be made, and to such other person or persons as have right to sue for the same, his, her or their executors and administrators, for his, her and their damage in that behalf sustained, after the rate of fifteen per cent for the sum expressed in the bill, and for the costs and charges of protest and no more.

Damages on protested bills of exchange.

And be it further enacted, That all and every other act and acts, and every clause and article thereof, heretofore made, for so much thereof as relates to the declaring how long judgments, bonds, obligations and accounts shall be in force, or the assignment of bonds and obligations, or directing what proof shall be sufficient in such cases, or ascertaining the damage upon protested bills of exchange, is, and are hereby repealed and made void, to all intents and purposes, as if the same had never been made.

Repealing clause.

CHAP. XXXV.

An act for limitation of actions, and avoiding of suits.

I. FOR avoiding of law suits, *Be it enacted, by the governor, council and burgesses of this present general assembly, and it is hereby enacted, by the authority of the same*, That all actions of trespass, *quare clausum fregit*, all actions of trespass, detinue, action sur trover, and replevin, for taking away of goods and cattle, all actions of account, and upon the case, other than such accounts as concern the trade of merchandize between

Limitation of actions on the case, accounts, trespass, debt, detinue, replevin.

merchant and merchant, their factors or servants, all actions of debt grounded upon any lending or contract, without specialty, all actions of debt for arrearages of rent, all actions of assault, menace, battery, wounding, and imprisonment, or any of them, which shall be sued, or brought, at any time after the end of this present session of assembly, shall be commenced and sued within the time and limitation hereafter expressed, and not after; (that is to say,) The said actions upon the case, (other than for slander;) and the said actions for account; and the said actions for trespass, debt, detinue, and replevin, for goods and cattle; and the said actions for trespass, *quare clausum fregit*, within two years next after the end of this present session of assembly, or within five years next after the cause of such actions or suits, and not after; and the said actions of trespass, of assault, battery, wounding, imprisonment or any of them, within one year next after the end of this present session of assembly, or within three years next after the cause of such actions or suits, and not after; and the said actions upon the case for words, within one year after the end of this present session of assembly, or within one year next after the words spoken, and not after.

Assault, battery, wounding and imprisonment.

Slander.

Further time allowed after revival of judgment.

II. *Provided nevertheless, and be it enacted*, That if in any of the said actions or suits, judgment be given for the plaintiff, and the same be afterwards reversed by error; or a verdict pass for the plaintiff, and upon matter alledged in arrest of judgment, the judgment be given against the plaintiff, that he take nothing by his plaint, writ, or bill; or if any of the said actions shall be brought by original, and the defendant therein, be outlawed, and shall after reverse the outlawry, that in all such cases, the party plaintiff, his heirs, executors, or administrators, as the case shall require, may commence a new action or suit, from time to time, within one year after such judgment reversed, or such judgment given against the plaintiff or outlawry reversed, and not after.

Disclaimer and tender of amends.

III. *And be it further enacted*, That in all actions of trespass, *quare clausum fregit*, hereafter to be brought, wherein the defendant or defendants shall disclaim, in his or their plea, to make any title or claim to the land, in which the trespass is, by the declaration, supposed to be done, and the trespass be by negligence, or involuntary, the defendant or defendants shall be admitted to plead a disclaimer; and that the trespass was by negligence, or involuntary, and a tender or offer of sufficient amends for such trespass, before the action brought, whereupon, or upon some of them, the plaintiff or plaintiffs shall be enforced to join issue: And if the said issue be found for the defendant or defendants, or the plaintiff or plaintiffs shall be nonsuited, the plaintiff or plaintiffs shall be clearly barred from the said action or actions; and all other suit concerning the same.

In case for slander, when no more costs than damages.

IV. *And be it further enacted, by the authority aforesaid,* That in all actions upon the case, for slanderous words, to be sued or prosecuted by any person or persons in the general court of this dominion, or in any court whatsoever, that hath power to hold plea of the same, after the end of this present session of assembly, if the jury, upon the trial of the issue in such action, or the jury that shall inquire of the damages, do find or assess the damages under forty shillings, then the plaintiff or plaintiffs in such action shall have and recover only so much costs as the damages so given or assessed amount unto, without any further increase of the same; any law, statute, custom, or usage to the contrary, in any-wise, notwithstanding.

Further time allowed for infants, femes covert, &c.

V. *Provided nevertheless, and be it further enacted,* That if any person or persons, that is or shall be entitled to any such action of trespass, detinue, action surtrover, replevin, actions of account, actions of debt, actions of trespass for assault, menace, battery, wounding, or imprisonment, be, or shall be, at the time of any such cause of action given or accrued, fallen or come, within the age of twenty-one years, feme-covert, *non compos mentis,* imprisoned, beyond the sea, or out of the country; that then such person or persons shall be at liberty to bring the same actions, so as they take the same within such times as are before limited, after their coming to or being of full age, discovert, of sane memory, at large, and returned from beyond the seas, or from without this country, as by other persons, having no such impediment, should be done.

VI. *Provided also, and be it further enacted,* That if any person or persons, defendant or defendants to any

Person removing or concealing himself.

of the aforesaid actions, shall abscond or conceal themselves, or by removal out of the country, or the county where he or they do or shall reside, when such cause of action accrued; or by any other indirect ways or means, defeat or obstruct any person or persons, who have title thereto, from bringing and maintaining all or any of the aforesaid actions within the respective times limited by this act; that then, and in such cases, such defendant or defendants are not to be admitted to plead this act in bar, to any of the aforesaid actions; any thing in this law, in any-wise to the contrary, notwithstanding.

Edi. 1733, and 1752.

CHAP. XXXVI.

See chap. 3, 1727, sect. 29.

An act for attorneys prosecuting suits on behalf of persons out of the country to give security for the payment of such costs and damages as shall be awarded against them.

[From MS.]

In suits, for non-residents, security for costs to be given.

BE it enacted, by the Governor, Council, and Burgesses, of this present General Assembly, and it is hereby enacted, by the authority of the same, That if any person or persons by virtue of any letter or warrant of attorney or letter or warrant of substitution or by virtue of any other deputation or power from any person or persons residing in other parts than within this colony shall at any time hereafter sue forth any process or commence or prosecute any suit either in law or equity against any person or persons inhabiting within this colony, such person so suing forth any process or commencing or prosecuting any suit at his or their first appearance in any court or before any judge or magistrate to prosecute, shall enter into bond with good and sufficient surety to sattisfy and pay to the party prosecuted, all such damages, costs and charges, as upon the same suit shall be awarded to him, her, or them, by the court, judge or magistrate before whom the suit shall be heard and determined, and if such person or persons so appearing to prosecute shall fail to give such bond, then the suit shall thereupon abate, and the party prosecuted shall be thence dismist without day.

CHAP. XXXVII.

Edi. 1733, and 1752. See chap. 3, 1726.

An act directing the manner of levying executions, and for relief of poor prisoners for debt.

[From MS.]

Writs of *fieri facias*, how executed.

BE it enacted, by the Governor, Council, and Burgesses of this present General Assembly, and it is hereby enacted, by the authority of the same, That when a writt of fieri facias shall at any time hereafter be delivered to the sheriff or other officer lawfully impowered to make execution thereof, such sheriff or other officer (having by virtue thereof levyed the debt, damages and costs therein mentioned, or any part thereof, upon the goods and chattles therein commanded to be levyed) shall thereupon proceed in manner following; that is to say, that the goods and chattles so levyed shall remain in the possession of the sheriff or other officer levying the same by the space of twenty-four hours, at the expiration of which time they shall be appraised, unless the party from whose custody and possession they were taken, shall give bond with good and sufficient surety, that they shall be produced for appraisement at the end of three days after such surety given, and then the appraisement shall be made (as hereafter is directed) and thereupon the property of the goods and chattles so appraised shall be vested in the sheriff or other officer levying the same, to and for the use of the person or persons at whose suit the writt shall have issued, and accordingly such sheriff or other officer shall give notice thereof to the said person or persons, that he or they may receive the said goods and chattles into his or their own possession. And for the more equal appraisment of goods and chattles so levyed as aforesaid, the sheriff or other officer levying the same shall give immediate notice thereof to the person or persons from whom they shall be taken, and also to the person or persons at whose suit the writt shall have issued, to the end that each party may nominate and elect two such appraisers as they shall think fitt to appraise and value the goods and chattles so levyed upon their corporall oath, which oath the sheriff or other officer as aforesaid, is hereby impowered and required to administer, and in case either of the partys shall refuse or neglect to nominate two appraisers as aforesaid, then the said

Goods, how appraised.

sheriff or other officer shall nominate two discreet, honest, freeholders of the vicinage, for the party so neglecting to appraise and value the said goods and chattles as aforesaid, and if it shall so happen that the said appraisers are equally divided in their judgments as to the value of any goods and chattles which shall be produced them for appraisement, then they shall choose a fifth man, who, upon his corporall oath, to be administred as aforesaid, shall declare his opinion which of the said appraisers have made the truest valuation of the said goods and chattles, which opinion of the said fifth man shall in that case be taken as the true value.

Provided always, That if the goods and chattles so appraised as aforesaid, shall amount to a greater value than will sattisfy the debt, damages and costs to be levyed, then the said sheriff or other officer shall immediately return the overplus to the party from whom it was taken, if it can be divided, if not, the value thereof.

Levari facias.

And be it further enacted, by the authority aforesaid, That when any writt of levari facias shall be at any time hereafter delivered to any sheriff or other officer as aforesaid, to levy any debt, damages, costs or other dues, upon the goods or chattles of any person or persons, the proceedings thereupon as to the said goods and chattles, shall be in like manner as is herein before directed, upon a writt of fieri facias, and after execution so done as aforesaid, upon either of the said writts, the sheriff or other officer so having made execution thereof, shall also make return thereof to such office or place from whence the same shall have issued, which return shall be entered in the records of such office.

Returns.

Capias ad satisfaciendum.

How the body may be discharged, on tendering property.

And be it further enacted, by the authority aforesaid, That when any person shall be taken and imprisoned by virtue of a capias ad satisfaciendum, for the payment of any debt, damage and costs, due in money, tobacco or other comoditys whatsoever, if such person shall, upon his corporal oath declare, before some justice of the peace of that county where he shall be imprisoned (which oath any such justice is hereby impowered and required to administer) that he hath none of that specie which is due from him, whether it be money, tobacco, or other comoditys as aforesaid, then it shall be lawfull for such person to make tender to his creditor or other person to whom the same shall be due, of so much of his estate as shall be of treble the value of the sum to be paid out, of which the said creditor or other person shall make choice of so much as upon a reasonable valuation of four or five men to be nominated and elected as aforesaid, shall be sufficient to make him sattisfaction as well for what is due to himself as for all costs concerning the same matter, and after such appraisement the person so imprisoned shall be discharged from imprisonment, and the estate so appraised shall be delivered to such creditor or other person as aforesaid, and if it shall so happen that the whole personal estate of the person imprisoned shall not amount to treble the value of the sum due, then after oath made as aforesaid, he shall exhibit upon oath to the best of his knowledge a true inventory of all his personall estate and make tender thereof to the creditor or other person as aforesaid, out of which shall be chosen and appraised as aforesaid, so much as will be sufficient to make sattisfaction as aforesaid, whereupon the person imprisoned shall be discharged, and the estate so appraised shall be delivered to the creditor or other person as aforesaid, and if it shall so happen that upon tender made as aforesaid, the creditor or other person as aforesaid, to whom such tender shall be made shall not make his choice as aforesaid within the space of three days after such tender made, then it shall be lawfull for some one justice of the peace of the county to make the choice and choose the appraisers, and thereupon proceedings shall be had in like manner as is before directed, and the person imprisoned shall also thereupon be discharged and in these cases it shall be lawfull to and for the sheriff or other officer as aforesaid, to make return of such capias ad satisfaciendum according to the truth of the case into such office from whence the same shall have issued there to be entered upon record, and if any person so imprisoned as aforesaid, shall make such tender as is afore directed, to the sheriff or other officer in whose custody he or she shall be, such sheriff or other officer shall within twenty-four hours thereafter give notice thereof to the creditor or other person as aforesaid, if he be to be found within his county, and if he be not within his county nor any known attorney for him, then notice thereof shall be given to some justice of the peace of the county, who at the end of three

Return, according to the truth of the case.

Notice to creditor.

days after such notice given, shall make choice as aforesaid, and if any sheriff or other officer shall neglect to do his duty herein, he shall be liable to an action at the common law for false imprisonment at the suit of the party grieved.

What deemed a tender.

Provided always, That nothing shall be accounted a tender of any estate within the meaning of this act, unless it shall be made in such manner that immediately upon the making choice thereof as aforesaid, the estate may and can be delivered to the sheriff or other officer as aforesaid, for the use of the creditor or other person to whom the same shall be due.

Debtor delivering up his whole estate, and lying three months in prison, to be discharged.

And be it further enacted, That if any person taken and imprisoned as aforesaid, and having delivered up to the sheriff or other officer in whose custody he shall be all his whole estate for and towards the payment and sattisfaction of the debt or other dues for which he was imprisoned, after having layen three months in prison, shall upon his corporall oath before two justices of the peace of the same county, declare that he hath no estate left either real or personal, save only one suit of clothes, not exceeding the value of fifty shillings (which oath the said justices are hereby impowered and required to administer) then the said justices shall make certificate thereof to the sheriff or other officer as aforesaid, and thereupon such person having such certificate shall be discharged.

This act not to extend to debts previously contracted; nor if the sum exceed 10l.

Provided always, That no prisoner under execution as aforesaid for any debt heretofore contracted, shall be allowed to discharge himself from the same by virtue of this act, and that no prisoner whatsoever shall be discharged or receive any benefit by his making oath as aforesaid in case the debt for which he is kept in prison exceed the sum of ten pounds current money or two thousand pounds of tobacco.

Estate real & personal of debtor discharged, forever liable.

Provided always, and be it further enacted, by the authority aforesaid, That notwithstanding the discharge of the person of such prisoner as aforesaid, upon taking the oaths aforesaid, all and every judgment and judgments had and taken against him or her alone, or with any other person or persons, shall stand and be good and effectuall in the law to all intents and purposes, against the lands, tenements, hereditaments, goods and chattles only of the said prisoner so discharged as aforesaid, and that it shall and may be lawfull to and for such creditor or creditors of such prisoner or prisoners so discharged as aforesaid, his, her, or their executors, administrators or assigns, to take out any new execution against the lands, tenements, hereditaments, goods and chattels of such prisoner or prisoners (his or her wearing apparel, beding for his or her family and tools necessary for his or her trade or occupation only excepted) for the sattisfaction of his, her, or their said debt in such sort, manner and form as he, she or they might have done, if the person or persons of such prisoner or prisoners had never been taken in execution, and that no act of limitation shall be pleadable against such judgment or judgments, any act, statute, law or custom, to the contrary in any wise notwithstanding.

Provided also, and be it enacted, That when any person in prison shall offer to tender his estate as aforesaid upon oath, or shall desire to be admitted to make oath before two justices as aforesaid, in such cases it shall be lawfull for the sheriff or other officer as aforesaid, to carry such person out of prison before such justice or justices as the case shall require, in order to the taking such oath without being lyable to any prosecution for or on pretence of an escape or on any other pretence whatsoever. **Sheriff may carry debtor out of prison, in order to take the oaths.**

Provided nevertheless, That if such person carried out of prison as aforesaid, be not discharged upon taking his oath, the sheriff or other officer shall carry him back to prison or be lyable to prosecution for an escape. **Proviso.**

And be it enacted, That all and every other act and acts, and every clause and article thereof, heretofore made, for so much thereof as relates to any matter or thing whatsoever, within the purview of this act, is, and are hereby repealed, and made void, to all intents and purposes, as if the same had never been made. **Repealing clause.**

CHAP. XXXVIII.

An act for removing criminals from the goals of the counties where they shall be apprehended, to the public goal at Williamsburg.

I. *BE it enacted, by the Governor, Council, and Burgesses of this present general assembly, and it is hereby*

Examining courts, how constituted.

enacted, by the authority of the same, That when any person shall, at any time hereafter, by precept from any justice of the peace within this dominion, be committed to the goal of the county, for any such criminal offence, as shall appear to such justice to be triable in the general court only; in such case, it shall be lawful for the same justice to issue his warrant to the sheriff of the county, requiring him to summon the justices of the same county, to meet at a certain time to be appointed in the said warrant, not less than five days, nor above ten days after the date thereof, and hold a court for examining the prisoner, and all witnesses and circumstances relating to the matter whereof he or she shall be accused; and to consider whether, as the case shall appear to them, he or she may be tried in the county, or must be removed from thence, to be tried at the general court: Which warrant the said sheriff is hereby required to obey and execute; and by virtue thereof, the said justices may lawfully meet and hold court for the intents herein mentioned: And if, upon examination before the said court, they are of opinion, that the prisoner ought to be tried for the fact whereof he or she is accused, before the general court, they shall signify the same, by entring such their opinion upon record in the said court, and shall remand the said prisoner to the county gaol; and thereupon, it shall be lawful for any two justices of the said court, (whereof one shall be of the quorum) by precept under their hands and seals, signifying the true cause of commitment, directed to the keeper of the public goal at the city of Williamsburg, to remove the said prisoner, and to commit him or her to the said public goal, there to remain until he or she shall be thence delivered by due course of law: By virtue whereof, the sheriff of the said county shall, as soon as he can conveniently, remove the prisoner to the said public goal, and shall deliver him or her, together with the said precept, to the keeper thereof; who is hereby required to give due obedience thereunto, and to receive, and in his custody safely to keep such prisoner so delivered unto him, by virtue thereof. And for the better enabling the said sheriff to perform his duty herein, it shall be lawful for the said two justices as aforesaid, by warrant under their hands and seals, to impower the said sheriff, as

Prisoners, how removed to Williamsburg.

well within his own county, as in all other counties through which he shall have occasion to pass with the said prisoner, to impress such and so many men, horses, sloops, or boats, as shall be necessary, for the safe conveying the said prisoner to the public gaol aforesaid; which warrant, the said sheriff is hereby authorised and impowered to put in execution: And all other persons are required to give due obedience thereunto, so as the said sheriff shall proceed therein, in manner as is directed by law upon such impressing in other cases.

In bailable offences, when to be removed.

II. *Provided nevertheless,* That when any prisoner shall, by the court, be remanded to the county goal, as aforesaid, if the offence be of such a nature, as the prisoner may be admitted to bail; then, and in such case, he or she shall not be removed out of the county, to the said public goal, in less than twenty days after such remanding: To the end, that in that time, bail may be procured and given in the county.

Bail after removal.

III. *Provided always,* That nothing herein contained, shall be construed so as to exclude or hinder any person from being admitted to bail, after his or her removal into the said public goal, in such case as by law he or she may be bailable.

Witnesses for prisoner, how summoned.

IV. *And be it further enacted,* That if, upon the first commitment of any prisoner to the county goal, he or she shall desire any witnesses on his or her behalf to be examined at the said county court, then the sheriff, upon his or her request, is hereby required to summons such witnesses to appear at the said court accordingly. And if, after being remanded to goal as aforesaid, the prisoner shall desire any witnesses to appear at the trial, in the general court, then the clerk of the said general court, at his or her request, or at the request of any other person, in his or her behalf, shall issue subpœnas, for the summoning such witnesses to appear accordingly.

Guards may be impressed by jailor.

V. *And be it further enacted,* That in the time of the general court, it shall be lawful for the keeper of the public goal, being thereto impowered by order of the said court, to impress such and so many persons as shall be necessary for the guarding and safe keeping of all such prisoners as shall be and remain committed to his custody.

Fees of sheriffs, for removal.

VI. *And be it further enacted,* That the fees due to the sheriff, for such removal of any prisoner, as aforesaid, from the county goal to the public goal, shall be after the rate of one hundred pounds of tobacco, for every twenty miles distance. And the fees to the said sheriff and keeper of the public goal, for keeping and dieting any prisoner in their goal, shall be five pounds of tobacco for each day, and no more.

For diet.

Repealing clause.

VII. *And be it further enacted,* That all and every other act and acts, and every clause and article thereof, heretofore made, for so much thereof as relates to any matter or thing whatsoever, within the purview of this act, is, and are hereby repealed, and made void, to all intents and purposes, as if the same had never been made.

CHAP. XXXIX.

An act for making, clearing, and repairing the highways, and for clearing the rivers and creeks.

I. FOR the more convenient travelling and carriage, by land, of tobaccos, merchandises, or other things within this dominion,

Public roads, how and where established.

II. *Be it enacted, by the governor, council, and burgesses, of this present general assembly, and it is hereby enacted, by the authority of the same,* That where the same is not already done, public roads shall be laid out by the surveyors of the highways, in their several precincts, in such places as shall be most convenient for passing to and from the City of Williamsburg, the court house of every county, the parish churches, and such public mills and ferries as now are, or hereafter shall be erected, and from one county to another; and that the highways already laid out, together with such as shall hereafter be laid out, by virtue of this act, shall, at all times hereafter, be kept well cleared from woods and bushes, and the roots well grubbed up, at least thirty foot broad: And if any person shall, at any time hereafter, fall any tree or trees into such highway, and shall not cut the same away again, within the space of forty eight hours after such falling; or shall make any fence into the highway, the person so offending, shall forfeit and pay, for every such offence, the sum of

Penalty for obstructing.

ten shillings current money, to the informer: To be recovered, with costs, upon information made to a justice of the peace of the county where the offence is committed.

May be altered.

III. *Provided nevertheless, and it is the true intent and meaning of this act,* That it shall be in the power of any county court, by their order, to direct the alteration of the public road, or the making of new roads, in such places as to them shall seem convenient. And for assistance to lay out and clear the highways, as aforesaid,

Who to work on.

IV. *Be it enacted,* That all male labouring persons that are tithable, shall, when thereunto required by the surveyors of the highways, assist the said surveyors in laying out and clearing the highways: And if any male labouring free tithable person, being so required, shall fail to go and assist therein; or if the master or owner of any labouring tithable person or persons being required to send such tithable person or persons to assist as aforesaid, shall fail to send accordingly, such free person shall, for such failure, forfeit and pay five shillings current money: And such master or owner, for every such tithable person as he fails to send, shall forfeit and pay five shillings like money, to the informer: To be recovered, with costs, as aforesaid.

Penalty for refusal.

Proviso.

V. *Provided nevertheless, and it is hereby enacted,* That any justice of the peace, to whom any information shall be made, of any such failure, shall have liberty, upon hearing the cause of the failure, to give judgment for the defendant, in case such cause appear to him to be reasonable: Which judgment shall be sufficient to acquit him from the forfeiture aforesaid.

Penalty on surveyors of roads.

VI. And, if any surveyor of the highways, shall fail to perform his duty, as the same is or shall be directed in this act, such surveyor shall forfeit and pay fifteen shillings current money, to the informer: To be recovered, with costs, as aforesaid.

Duty of surveyors.

VII. *And be it further enacted,* That every surveyor of the highways, shall have power, and be obliged, with the assistance aforesaid, to make bridges in all necessary places, within their respective precincts, which shall be at least ten foot broad, and level and passable: and also shall, from time to time, keep the same in good repair. And if it shall so happen, that there be

Bridges, how erected.

occasion for a bridge over any place, where the surveyors, with the assistance aforesaid, cannot make it, then the county court shall have power, and be obliged, to covenant with some skilful workman for the making thereof: And also, they are hereby impowered to lay a county levy upon the poll, to pay for the same. And if such a bridge shall be wanting over any place, which lies between two or more counties, then the court of each county shall join in the agreement; and shall have power to lay a county levy, for the paiment thereof, proportionable to the number of tithables in each county: And every person having a plantation, is hereby directed and required to make a convenient passage for man and horse to go to his dwelling house, and from time to time to keep it in repair; upon pain of forfeiting and paying to the informer, for his neglect in making such passage, ten shillings current money; and also ten shillings for every six months such passage shall not be made, or being made, shall continue unrepaired: To be recovered, with costs, as aforesaid.

Roads to houses.

VIII. And, for the greater conveniency of such persons as inhabit upon plantations far distant from rivers and creeks,

Public landings, what deemed.

IX. *Be it enacted,* That all such landing places, as have store-houses, commonly called rolling-houses, built at or near them, or have heretofore been commonly used for bringing tobaccos unto, and to which there are plain roads already made, shall be held and accounted public landings: And the roads to such landings, or any other public landings hereafter to be appointed by the county courts, shall be kept in repair, sufficient for carts to pass to and from the same.

Surveyors of roads, when appointed.

X. *And be it further enacted,* That at some court, between the last day of April, and first day of August, yearly, the court shall appoint surveyors of the highways; and also, such persons, as to them shall seem most proper, to clear the rivers and creeks, within their respective precincts, from all trees, roots, or other things, which may be dangerous to any boat, sloop, or other vessel, passing up or down the same. And if any court shall fail to perform their duty herein, such court shall forfeit and pay two thousand pounds of tobacco, to him or them that will inform, or sue for the same: To be recovered, with costs. And if any person, so

Penalties.

appointed to clear the rivers and creeks, shall fail to perform his duty herein, some time in the months of March and October, yearly, he shall forfeit and pay the sum of fifteen shillings current money, to the informer: To be recovered, with costs, before a justice of the peace. And if any person shall fall any tree, into any river or creek, and not immediately clear the same away again, he shall forfeit and pay, for the first offence, ten shillings current money; and for every such offence after the first, fifteen shillings, of like money, to the informer: To be recovered, with costs, before a justice of the peace.

Falling trees into rivers or creeks.

XI. *And be it further enacted,* That if any person shall set, or cause to be set, a weir, in any river or creek, such person shall cause the stakes thereof to be taken up again, as soon as the weir becomes useless: And if any person shall fail of performing his duty herein, he shall forfeit and pay fifteen shillings current money, to the informer: To be recovered, with costs, before a justice of the peace.

Weirs, when to be removed.

XII. *And be it further enacted,* That all and every other act and acts, and every clause and article thereof, heretofore made, for so much thereof as relates to clearing, making, and repairing the highways, and for clearing the rivers and creeks, or any other matter or thing whatsoever, within the purview of this act, is and are hereby repealed, and made void, to all intents and purposes, as if the same had never been made.

Repealing clause.

CHAP. XL.

An act for regulating Ordinaries, and restraint of Tippling houses.

I. FOR regulating the abuses of ordinaries, and other houses of entertainment, and restraint of tippling houses,

II. *Be it enacted, by the governor, council and burgesses of this present general assembly, and it is hereby enacted, by the authority of the same,* That all persons whatsoever, retailing liquors, shall sell the same by sealed measures, and none other; and that all licensed ordinary-keepers, or keepers of houses for public entertainment, be provided therewith, viz. with gallon,

Sealed weights and measures, alone to be used.

pottle, quart, pint, and half-pint sealed measures; on penalty of forfeiting and paying, to the informer, ten shillings current money, with costs: To be levied by distress, by virtue of a warrant from a justice of the peace of the county where the offence shall be committed.

Bottled liquors.

III. *Provided always,* That all person or persons whatsoever, who shall retail liquors in any public house or houses, shall have liberty to sell any liquors in bottles, the said bottles being sold for no more than they hold or contain.

Penalty for retailing liquors, without license.

IV. *And be it also enacted, by the authority aforesaid, and it is hereby enacted,* That whosoever shall retail liquors in their houses, without license first had and obtained, according to the directions of this act, shall forfeit and pay two thousand pounds of tobacco: And that the method of obtaining such license, be as followeth: Whoso intends to set up an ordinary, or house of public entertainment, let him petition the county court, and they, by their discretion, shall judge whether it is convenient to suffer such a house to be set up; and whether the person petitioning, be of ability sufficient to comply with the intent of the law, in providing convenient lodging and diet for travellers, and pasturage, fodder, provender, and stableage for their horses, as the season shall require, and upon security also, as therein is directed, to grant or reject the same accordingly: For the said court shall not, under pretence of keeping any poor body from the parish charge, give them any power of selling drink, as hath been some times done, and is found very prejudicial; but shall only grant license to such as seem to them to be of ability to find and provide continually, all things necessary for entertainment, and have housing fitting for the same, according to the intent of this act. And the said petition being approved, the court shall then take bond of the party petitioning, with good and sufficient security, in the sum of ten thousand pounds of tobacco, paiable to the queen, &c. with condition annexed, to find and provide constantly, good, wholsome, and cleanly lodging and diet for travellers, and stableage, fodder and provender, or pasturage, as the season shall require, for their horses; with such other conditions, as the form of the bond, set down in this act, shall specify.

Licences, how and when to be granted.

Bond and security.

Form of bond.

KNOW all men by these presents, that we A. B. and C. D. are held and firmly bound unto our sovereign lady Anne, by the grace of God, of England, Scotland, France, and Ireland, Queen, Defender of the Faith, &c. in the sum of ten thousand pounds of tobacco, convenient in the said county of E. To which paiment well and truly to be made to our said sovereign lady the queen, her heirs and successors, we bind ourselves, and every of us, our and every of our heirs, executors, and administrators, jointly and severally, firmly by these presents. In witness whereof, we have hereunto set our hands and seals, the day of

THE condition of this obligation is such, That whereas the above bound A. B. hath obtained a license to keep an ordinary at if therefore the said A. B. doth constantly find and provide in his said ordinary, good, wholesome, and cleanly lodging and diet for travellers, and stableage, fodder and provender, or pasturage and provender, as the season shall require, for their horses, for and during the term of one year, from the day of and shall not suffer or permit any unlawful gaming in his house; nor on the sabbath day suffer any person to tipple and drink more than is necessary; then this obligation to be null, void, and of none effect; otherwise to be and remain in full force, power, and virtue.

Licenses, how signed, and how long to continue.

The bond and security being thus taken, the court may grant their order; and the clerk shall thereupon prepare a license, and present it to the first justice of the peace for that county, who shall sign the same; and that license to continue and be of force for one year only, from the date of the said order, and no longer.

Governor's fee.

V. *And be it also enacted, by the authority aforesaid, and it is hereby enacted,* That there be paid, by the party obtaining such license, thirty-five shillings current money of Virginia, for the use of the governor, or commander in chief of this her majesty's colony and dominion, for the time being.

VI. *And also be it enacted, by the authority aforesaid, and it is hereby enacted,* That if any ordinary-keeper

Gaming, tippling, or sabbath breaking, at ordinaries, &c. how punishable.

shall permit in his house unlawful gaming; or shall suffer any person or persons, on the Lord's day, or any other day set a-part by public authority for religious worship, to tipple in his house, or drink more than is necessary; or shall harbour, or entertain any seamen or servants, contrary to the intent and meaning of this act, it shall and may be lawful for any two justices of the peace, (whereof one to be of the quorum,) upon their own view or knowledge, or upon proof made to them, by the oath of one credible witness, to suppress the said ordinary until the next succeeding court: And upon certificate made by the said two justices, of the said offence, and further inquiry into the same, the said county court shall either disable the offender from keeping ordinary thereafter, until they shall think fit to grant him a new license, or to restore him to keep ordinary upon the former license, as they shall see cause: And if any ordinary-keeper shall presume to sell, or retail any liquor, after he hath been so discharged by the aforesaid two justices, and before he be restored by the court, he shall be liable to all the penalties and forfeitures, as if he had never obtained a license.

Tavern rates.

VII. *And also, be it enacted by the authority aforesaid, and it is hereby enacted,* That the justices of each county, shall, annually, at their court in March, set and rate the prices that ordinaries shall entertain and sell at; that is, of liquors, according to the measures aforementioned; and of diet, lodging, fodder, provender, and pasturage; upon penalty of forfeiting and paying five thousand pounds of tobacco.

VIII. *Provided always,* That if any county court failing to set the rates aforesaid, in March, because a sufficient number of justices did not meet then, shall, at the next court held for the said county, do the same, they shall not be culpable by this law.

Penalty for exceeding legal rates.

IX. *And be it also enacted, by the authority aforesaid, and it is hereby enacted,* That if any ordinary-keeper shall ask, demand, receive, or take, greater prices for any drink, diet, lodging, fodder, provender, or pasturage, than shall be set down and rated by the justices of the county, according to this act, he or she shall, for every such offence, forfeit and pay ten shillings, to the informer: To be recovered, with costs, before a justice.

X. *And be it also enacted, by the authority aforesaid, and it is hereby enacted,* That every ordinary-keeper within this her majesty's colony and dominion, shall, within one month after the rates shall be so set by the county court where the license was granted, obtain of the clerk of the said court, a fair table of the rates and prices set by the court; which being so obtained, shall be openly set up in the common entertaining room of the said ordinary, and there continually kept during the whole year, and until the rates shall be again set by the court: And every ordinary-keeper failing herein, shall forfeit and pay two thousand pounds of tobacco; one half of all which fines and forfeitures before mentioned, and not otherwise disposed of, to be to the queen, her heirs and successors, for and towards the support of this government, and the contingent charges thereof; and the other half to him or them that will inform or sue for the same: To be recovered, with costs, by action of debt, bill, plaint, or information, in any court of record within this her majesty's colony and dominion, wherein no essoin, protection, or wager of law, shall be allowed.

Table of rates to be set up.

XI. *And also be it enacted, by the authority aforesaid, and it is hereby enacted,* That if any person, contrary to the true intent and meaning of this act, shall presume to keep a tippling house, or retail liquors, as aforesaid, without license, and being thereof lawfully convicted, shall not pay down the said fine of two thousand pounds of tobacco, or forthwith, upon such conviction, give security to pay the same at the crop, he or she so offending, shall immediately, by order of the court before whom such conviction shall be, receive at the public whipping-post, on his or her bare back, twenty-one lashes, well laid on, in lieu of paying the said fine of two thousand pounds of tobacco; and then also, the informer not to be chargeable with any fees accrued, by reason of such information.

Penalty, on conviction of keeping a tippling house, or retailing liquors, without license.

XII. And forasmuch as the unlimited credit given by ordinaries and tippling houses, within this her majesty's colony and dominion, to seamen and others, where they spend not only their ready money, but their wages and other goods, which should be for the support of themselves and families, is found prejudicial, and occasions many persons newly free, to run away to the neighbouring plantations, to the great disadvantage of this country:

Penalty for selling liquors to sailors, on credit.

XIII. *Be it therefore enacted, by the authority aforesaid, and it is hereby enacted,* That if any ordinary-keeper or master of a tippling house shall, after publication of this act, trust or sell drink to any sailor in actual pay on board any ship, for any value whatsoever, upon credit; or to any person or persons, who are not masters of two servants, or visibly worth fifty pounds sterling at least, more than the value of three hundred pounds of tobacco, such ordinary-keeper, or master of a tippling house, shall lose all such overplus tobacco and money, for which they shall give such credit: And in case any ordinary-keeper, or other master of a tippling house, shall take or get from any person trusted, as aforesaid, any obligation, bill, or other security, for any sum above three hundred pounds of tobacco spent in one year, under pretence that it is for other goods, the said ordinary-keeper shall forfeit his license; and also double the sum of such obligation so convenously taken: one half to her majesty, her heirs and successors, for and towards the support of this government, and the contingent charges thereof; the other half to him or them that shall inform or sue for the same, in any court of record in this her majesty's colony and dominion: To be recovered, with costs, by action of debt, bill, plaint, or information, wherein no essoin, protection, or wager of law, shall be allowed.

Limitation of credit, to others.

Selling to sailors or servants without leave.

XIV. *And also be it further enacted, by the authority aforesaid,* That if any ordinary-keeper whatsoever, within this colony, shall harbour, entertain, or sell any liquors to any sailor in actual pay, on board any ship, or any servant belonging to any person within this colony, without license from their respective masters, such ordinary-keeper shall, for every such offence, forfeit and pay ten shillings to the master of the ship the sailor belongs to, or master of such servant: To be recovered, with costs, upon complaint of the said master before a justice of the county where the said ordinary-keeper lives.

Proviso as to Williamsburg.

XV. *Provided,* That this act, or any thing therein contained, shall not extend to the ordinary-keepers of the City of Williamsburg, giving credit to any person whatsoever, in the time of the general court, or during the sitting of a general assembly; any thing aforesaid to the contrary, notwithstanding.

XVI. *And be it further enacted*, That all and every other act and acts, and every clause and article thereof, heretofore made, for so much thereof as relates to regulating ordinaries; and restraint of tippling houses; or to any other matter or thing whatsoever, within the purview of this act, is, and are hereby repealed, and made void, to all intents and purposes, as if the same had never been made. Repealing clause.

CHAP. XLI.

An act for encouragement of building Water-mills.

I. FOR encouragement of persons to build Water-Mills, *Be it enacted, by the governor, council and burgesses, of this present general assembly, and it is hereby enacted, by the authority of the same*, That if any person or persons, willing to build any water-mill, on some convenient run, hath land only on one side of the run, and the owner of the land on the other side shall refuse to let him have an acre of land adjoining, at a reasonable rate, for the conveniency of the same, the court of the county wherein such land shall lie, upon petition of the party so refused, are hereby impowered and required to order two commissioners, or such other credible persons as they shall think fit, to view the said land; and if it take not away housing, orchards, or other immediate conveniencies, to value the same, and put the party (who desires to build the mill) in possession thereof; which way of possession, in such case, shall be good and available to create a fee simple in the said acre of land, to the person so going about to build the mill, and his heirs. Persons owning land on one side a run, how to obtain an acre on the other. Proviso, as to houses, orchards, &c.

II. *Provided always*, That the person so being put in possession, forthwith pay down the money to the owner thereof, upon such valuation. Valuation money.

III. *And provided also*, That the said person so being put in possession, shall within one year, begin to build a water-mill, and finish the same within three years; and shall thereafter keep up the same, for the use and ease of all such as shall be customers to it; otherwise the said land shall return to the person from Proviso, as to building and keeping the mill.

whom it was taken, or to such other persons as shall have his right.

Further proviso, as to mills burnt, or belonging to infants, &c.

IV. *Provided always*, That if any water-mill belonging to any person within the age of twenty-one years, feme-covert, *non compos mentis*, or imprisoned, be let fall, burnt, or destroyed; that then such person or persons, and their heir and heirs, shall have three years to rebuild and repair such mill, after his or their full age, discoverture, coming of sound mind, enlargement out of prison, or death.

Restriction as to mill on same run.

V. And also for a further encouragement, *Be it enacted, by the authority aforesaid, and it is hereby enacted*, That when there shall be a public mill standing upon any run, there shall not be another mill or dam built upon the same run below such mill, within a mile thereof; nor upon the same run above such mill; without the particular leave of the general court, or county court, in which such mill is intended to be set.

Proviso.

VI. *Provided*, That this act, nor any thing therein contained, shall not be construed to prohibit the carrying on and finishing any mill now begun upon any run where another mill is standing; but that the same may be done, in such manner as it might have been before this act.

Remedy.

VII. *Provided also*, That where any owner or owners of a mill already built, or that shall hereafter be built on any run, shall conceive himself injured by the building of a water-mill, by any person or persons on the same run, it shall and may be lawful for the party injured, to bring his action on the case, against the owner or owners of such latter built mill, in the same manner as he might have done before the making of this act; any thing herein contained to the contrary, or seeming to the contrary in any-wise, notwithstanding.

Duty of millers.

VIII. And, for prevention of abuses, by evil-minded covetous, and exacting millers, or owners of mills, *Be it enacted, by the authority aforesaid, and it is hereby enacted*, That all millers shall grind according to turn; and shall well and sufficiently grind the grain brought to their mills; and shall take no more for toll or grinding, than one eighth part of wheat, and one sixth part of Indian corn. And every miller, or keeper of a mill, making default herein, viz. Not grinding according to turn, not well and sufficiently grinding the grain, or

Toll.

exacting more for toll, than herein is set down and allowed, shall, for every such offence, forfeit and pay fifteen shillings, to the party injured: To be recovered, with costs, before a justice of peace of the county where such offence is committed. Penalties.

IX. *Provided always*, That it shall be in the power of the owner of any mill, to grind, or cause to be grinded, his own grain, at any time he thinks fit; any thing in this act to the contrary, notwithstanding. Privilege of owners.

X. And, for the better discovery of such exacting millers, *Be it enacted, by the authority aforesaid, and it is hereby enacted*, That all millers shall keep in their mills these several measures, either of English sealed measures, or sealed by the court of the county wherein such mill shall be, viz. a bushel, half-bushel, and peck; and shall measure all by strike measure; and use no toll-dish but what shall be also sealed by the county court, (who are hereby impowered and required, at the county charge, to provide an iron brand, for the said uses.) And every owner of a mill, by himself or servant keeping such mill, and failing to provide such measures, and toll-dishes, shall, for such failure, forfeit and pay fifteen shillings, to the informer: To be recovered, with costs, before a justice of peace of the county where such failure shall happen. And if any miller, keeping a mill, shall be a servant or slave, then the master or owner shall be answerable for the defaults of such servant or slave, in the cases aforesaid: And where the master shall live out of the county, and have no known attorney in the county for that purpose, upon complaint made, for any of the abuses aforesaid, the appearance of such servant or slave before the justice, shall be deemed a sufficient appearance for the justice to proceed against the master or owner, as if the master or owner appeared in person; but if the owner shall live in the county, or have a known attorney in the county, for that purpose, then the appearance of them shall be required. Sealed measures.

XI. *Provided nevertheless*, That where a mill is kept by a slave, or imported servant, that shall refuse to grind according to turn; or that shall grind grain insufficiently; or that shall exact more for toll, than is allowed by this act, such servant or slave, for his first offence, shall have thirty lashes, and for his second, for- Punishment of servants or slaves.

ty lashes, on his bare back, well laid on, in lieu of the penalty or forfeiture given by this act: But in case such servant or slave be a third time guilty of any the said offences, then the master or owner of such servant or slave shall be liable to pay for the same, according to this act, and for every offence such servant or slave shall afterwards commit, in breach of this act.

Repealing clause.

XII. *And be it further enacted*, That all and every other act and acts, and every clause and article thereof, heretofore made, for so much thereof as relates to water-mills; or any other matter or thing whatsoever, within the purview of this act, is, and are hereby repealed, and made void, to all intents and purposes, as if the same had never been made.

Edi. 1733, and 1752.
Repealed by proclamation, July 5th, 1710.

CHAP. XLII.

An act for establishing ports and towns.

[From M. S.]

Preamble.

WHEREAS her most sacred majesty, Queen Anne, out of her princely care of this her colony and dominion of Virginia, by instructions to his excellency Edward Nott, Esq. her majestys lieutenant and governor-generall here, has been pleased to take notice that the building of towns, warehouses, wharfs and keys, for the more expeditious lading and unlading of ships at proper places in this colony, exclusive of others, will be particularly usefull and serviceable to her majesty, in bringing our people to a more regular settlement and of great advantage to trade, and has therefore caused it to be recommended by her said governor to this generall assembly to pass an act for that purpose, suitable to the interests and conveniencys of this colony,

Ports of entry, and landing.

Be it therefore enacted, by the Governor, Council, and Burgesses of this present General Assembly, and it is hereby enacted, by the authority of the same, That from and after the twenty-fifth day of December, which shall be in the year of our Lord 1708, all goods, wares and merchandises which shall be imported into this colony by water (servants, slaves and salt, excepted) shall be entered, allowed and landed at some one or other of the ports, wharfs, keys or places hereafter mentioned and appointed in this act, and at none other place whatsoever, until they shall have been first landed at one of the ports or wharfs aforesaid, and a certificate thereof obtained from the officer of the port, appointed or to be appointed by his excellency the governor or the governor and commander in chief of this colony for the time being, by advice of the councill of state here for collection of the Virginia dutys, upon pain of forfeiture and loss of all such goods, wares and merchandises.

Servants, slaves and salt when entered.

And be it also enacted, That from and after the said twenty-fifth day of December, 1708, all servants, slaves and salt, which shall be imported into this colony by water, shall be reported and entered at some one or other of the ports, wharfs, keys or places by this act appointed as aforesaid, and a certificate thereof obtained as aforesaid, before they shall be landed, bought or sold, upon pain of forfeiture and loss of every such servant and slave so landed, sold, or put to sale.

Goods exported

And be it also enacted, That from and after the said twenty-fifth day of December, 1708, all goods, wares and merchandises of what nature or kind soever, to be exported out of this colony by water, coal, corn and timber excepted, shall, before they be put on board any ship or vessell for exportation, be landed or cleared at some one or other of the ports, wharfs, keys or places, as aforesaid, upon pain of forfeiture and loss of all such goods, wares and merchandises.

And because there will be an absolute necessity of ware houses and other convenient buildings for reception of all sorts of goods and persons, at these ports,

Townships or burghs.

Be it therefore enacted, That a township or burgh be established at each of the places hereinafter appointed by this act for ports, and that from and after the said twenty-fifth day of December, 1708, all goods, wares and merchandises whatsoever, which shall be imported for sale into this colony (servants, slaves and salt, excepted) shall be bought and sold in one or other of these towns hereinafter appointed, or not within five miles of any of them water born or on the same side the great river the town shall stand upon, except such persons as are all ready inhabited, and their heirs and such other persons as having been for the space of three years inhabitants of this colony, shall reside at the time of claiming such priviledge within the said five miles, on pain of forfeiting and paying by the vendor the full value of the goods, wares, and merchandises so sold, with costs of suit, and on pain of forfeiture and loss by the purchaser of all goods, wares and merchandises bought contrary to the tenor hereof. Neither shall any ordinary keeping be licenced or allowed without the limits of these towns, unless above ten miles, from every of them, or at a public ferry or court-house.

And whereas a smugling trade (if any such be used here) may most privately be carried on by avaritious and ill-minded persons keeping store on board their sea vessells, for prevention thereof for the future,

No goods, except servants, slaves or salt, to be sold on board vessels.

Be it enacted, That from and after the said twenty-fifth day of December, 1708, no goods, wares nor merchandises whatsoever, which shall be imported into this colony (servants, slaves, and salt excepted) shall be bought or sold while they are water born in the sea vessels, they were imported in upon pain of forfeiting and paying by the vendor the full value of all such goods, wares and merchandises so sold, with costs of suit, and on pain of forfeiture and loss by the purchaser of all such goods, wares and merchandises, bought contrary to the tenor hereof, all which fines, forfeitures and penaltys before in this act mentioned, shall be one third part thereof to the governor or commander in chief of this her majesties colony and dominion for the time being, one other third to the port and town whose officer shall first make claim, and the other third to the informer.

Privilege of inhabitants of towns, in relation to duties.

And be it also enacted, That in all dutys hereafter to be laid on the trade of this colony in any sort the town inhabitants here shall be acquit for three-fourths of the dutys that all other persons shall be obliged to unless it shall be otherwise directed by act imposing the said dutys.

Further privileges.

And be it also enacted, That all persons whatsoever, comeing to live and reside in any of the ports and towns by this act to be constituted, or that at any time hereafter shall come to live and reside in any of them shall be thereafter free and acquitt from all levys that shall be laid on the poll in tobacco for the space of fifteen years next after the five and twentyeth day of December, 1708, except for their slaves only, and also except for the payment of parish levys where the church already stands, or shall hereafter be built within any of the said ports or towns respectively.

And for a further invitation of persons to cohabit in towns,

Be it enacted, That no person whatsoever inhabiting, or that shall inhabit any of the ports or towns to be constituted by virtue of this act, during his being such an inhabitant, shall be obliged to muster without the town land whereof he shall be an inhabitant, nor forced to march therefrom except when the exigency shall be such that the country shall be actually ingaged in war, neither then shall the inhabitant of any port or town to be constituted by virtue of this act, be forced to march or be removed more than fifty miles from the burgh whereof he shall be inhabitant, nor imprest to go to warr upon any other occasion.

Their priviledges as to military duty.

And be it also enacted, That as soon as and whenever a court of Hustings shall be established in any of the burghs to be constituted by virtue of this act, no inhabitant of such burghs shall thereafter be held to plead or go to court for any summons or law business, without the burgh, except in local actions, where the cause shall arise without the jurisdiction of such town, or where the value of the thing in demand shall exceed thirty pounds sterling, or in the generall court or to bear evidence in some court as the laws of this country direct, neither shall they be forced to serve on a jury in any court without such burgh, except in the generall court.

Court of Hustings.

Jurisdiction of.

And be it also enacted, That all fines and mulcts that shall hereafter be laid upon an inhabitant of any of the ports or towns appointed by this act, shall be paid to the director of such town whereto he shall belong, for the use and benefit of the town, and to no other use or purpose whatsoever.

Fines to the use of the town.

And for explanation of what shall be counted an inhabitant of a town,

Be it enacted, That any person keeping a family in town, or whose common residence shall have been in town for six months past, next before the time of claiming such privilege shall be counted an inhabitant of such town, to all intents and purposes, and within the meaning of this act.

Who deemed inhabitants

And because such a number of people as may be hoped will in process of time become inhabitants of these ports and towns cannot expect to be supported without such regulations are made and methods put in practice as are used in the towns of other countrys,

All towns, Free burghs. Market. Fairs. Merchant guilds. Community.

Be it enacted, That each town to be erected by virtue of this act, be constituted, and every of them, singly and apart, is hereby constituted and established a free burgh, shall have a market at least twice a week, and a fair once a year, at such times as hereafter is appointed, shall have a merchant guild and community with all customs and libertys belonging to a free burgh, and when there shall be thirty familys besides ordinary keepers resident in any of the burghs to be constituted by virtue of this act, and so on as fast as any of the said burghs shall come to have thirty familys besides ordinary keepers resident in them, such burghs shall have eight of the principal inhabitants who shall be called benchers of the guild hall for the better rule and governance of the town and for managing the public affairs thereof, these benchers shall be chosen by the freeholders and inhabitants of the town of twenty-one years of age and upwards, not being servants or apprentices, to be at first called together by writt from the governor or commander in chief of this colony for the time being, upon application to him made by the town, and being once chosen shall continue so long as they well behave or till death or removal from such town, which shall first happen, and if any bencher shall happen to be suspended, die, or remove out of such town, then upon proclamation made, three market days in open market between the hours of eleven and one by direction of the hustings, and day and place set by them, the freeholders and inhabitants of the town shall assemble on such day and place, and choose another bencher in the room of him so incapacitated, and so on from time to time as there shall be occasion, which elections shall be determined by the major part of the votes that shall be given, according to day and place aforesaid, and all disputes therein shall be determined by the hustings, these five benchers shall annually choose one of themselves to preside, by the name of director, and if any director shall happen to dye or remove within his year, the benchers or the major part of

Benchers. How chosen. Vacancies, how supplied. Director.

them on the next or some convenient court day afterwards, shall meet and choose another in his room, and so on as occasion shall happen to supply the year out, and in the interval of a directors dying and anothers being elected, the eldest of the benchers of such burgh then actually resident, shall preside and perform what should have been incumbent on the director of such town to perform.

And for the encouragement and bettering of the markets in the said towns,

Be it enacted, That no dead provision, either of flesh or fish, shall be sold within five miles of any of the ports or towns appointed by this act, on the same side the great river the town shall stand upon, but within the limits of the town, on pain of forfeiture and loss of all such provision by the purchaser, and the purchase money of such provision sold by the vendor, cognizable by any justice of the county, the director or one of the benchers of the next adjacent burgh, or any one of them, be the same of what value soever, saving an appeal to the county court or court of hustings, upon security given. Provisions to be sold in market only.

And be it enacted, That the director for the time being, of each of the burghs appointed by this act, or his substitute, and any three or more of the benchers of his burghs, shall be and hereby are appointed a quorum to hold court, every which court shall be held, deemed, and taken, to be a court of record within this colony, shall make to themselves one comon seal, with liberty at any time to break or change it, shall have jurisdiction of all causes of meum and tuum, bargain, traffique and trade within their town, and the road and harbour thereto belonging, or wherein any inhabitant of the town is or shall be concerned, not exceeding the value of thirty pounds sterling, and all penal statutes of this country, as also of every thing relating to the town lands, saving and reserving always a liberty to any party not content with their judgment, to have an appeal to the generall court, upon security given within four and twenty hours after any such judgment, to abide the award of the said court, and if any one shall take advantage of his liberty, and shall depart the town without sattisfying such judgment or appealing, a copy thereof, certified by the town clerk to the clerk of any Courts how constituted Common seal. Jurisdiction. Appeal.

Executions.

county court shall be sufficient for him to issue execution thereon, according to the tenor thereof, and he is hereby required to do the same accordingly.

Proviso, as to jurisdiction of county courts.

Provided always, and be it enacted, That all causes of greater value than thirty pounds sterling, ariseing within the precincts or jurisdiction of any burgh, may be tryed, heard and determined by the respective county courts, wherein the said burghs ly in the same manner as might have been done before the making of this act.

Jurisdiction of petty offences.

Moreover they the said director and benchers shall take cognisance of all petty larcenies happening within the precincts of their burgh and the road and harbour thereto belonging, and all other crimes of immorality cognisable by a justice of the peace or county court as cursing, swearing, sabbath breaking, drunkenness, fornication, bastardy and the like, when such shall happen within the precincts of their burghs respectively, or the road and harbour thereof, with power likewise to impose mulcts and fines on refractory persons, not exceeding five pounds sterling, to imprison for any time not exceeding or passing by a generall court, and to bind criminals in a greater degree over to the generall court and take recognisances that shall be necessary on such occasions, with power likewise to hold court once a week called hustings, and from time to time to make choice of and swear a town clerk, bailiff, cryer and constable, for recording, arresting, bringing before and regular proceedings in the said courts, and all other inferior officers necessary for the same, and for keeping the peace and good order within their severall and respective burghs, which officers shall have full power in the execution of their severall offices throughout their towns respectively, and the road and harbour thereto belonging, with power to the said court of hustings to administer and take oaths de fideli, and for clearing the truth in all cases happening before them, and to turn out, change and supply such officers as there shall be occasion, upon misdemeanor, death or removal.

Court to be called *Hustings.*

Town clerk, bailiff, cryer and constables.

Director and benchers, their powers.

And be it further enacted, That the director and benchers which shall be elected by virtue of this act, and every of them, singly and apart, shall take cognisance of all breaches of the peace, swearing, cursing, sabbath breaking, drunkenness and immorality, as justices of the peace usually have or ought to have within this colony, and to cause the punishments and forfeitures to be inflicted and levied upon such offenders, their goods and chattels accordingly, within their several and respective burghs, and the precincts thereof, respectively.

And be it further enacted, That the benchers aforementioned, and every of them, at the time of his entering into and upon his said office, shall take such oaths of fidelity to her majesty, her heirs and successors, as shall be from time to time appointed by law, for the other people of this colony to take, and also shall take the following oath. Oaths.

The Oath of a Bencher.

"YOU shall swear that truly and faithfully you will serve our sovereign lady the queen, and the burgh of A. in the office of bencher, and that you will do equal right to all manner of people, rich and poor, and to the said burgh without favour, affection or partiality, and that you will not directly or indirectly take any gift or reward for any thing relating to your said office. *So help you God.*" Oath of a bencher.

And be it further enacted, That the director and benchers of every burgh respectively to be chosen by virtue of this act, shall be, and they are hereby erected and constituted to be a body corporate and politick, and to have a continual succession forever, by the name of the director and benchers, with power to implead, sue and be sued, to purchase and enjoy lands, tenements, and other estate, real and personal, of whatsoever nature and quality, and to dispose off and alienate the same or any part thereof at their pleasure, with power likewise by subscription and other voluntary gifts and bequests, to raise a joynt stock or capital ffund for the use and benefit of their burgh, and the public necessary charges thereof, and to build and keep a place or tenement within their burgh, where they shall think most desent and honourable to erect a guild hall and such other usefull and necessary buildings as they, with the advice of the common councill, shall think fitt. Director and benchers, a body corporate.

And when the director and benchers shall be thus constituted in any of the burghs appointed by this act,

Feoffees of towns to transfer their rights to directors and benchers.

the ffeoffees of such burgh or town shall transfer all their right to such director and benchers, and their successors forever, who shall thereafter parcell out the land and lots in town in such manner and under such rules and limitations as is appointed by law to the ffeoffees, and that by transferr and assignments made and entered in their own books and records, without any other formality of law, reserving to themselves and their successors forever, to the use of the town, one ounce of flaxseed and two ounces of hempseed, for every lot or piece of land so parcelled out.

Tenure of lands so transferred.

And be it enacted, That thereafter the director and benchers of every such burgh as aforesaid, shall hold the lands within the precincts of their said burgh to them and their successors for ever, in free and common soccage, yielding and paying to her majesty, her heirs and successors, the annual quit rent of twelve pence for every fifty acres, and if any person having a lott in town upon the water side, will build out into the water before his own lott, for the better conveniency of landing and shipping off goods, such persons shall have the whole benefit of such building, and the land so built upon shall be reckoned as part of his own lott, and it shall intirely be his as the lott itself, without any further duty or acknowledgement.

Brethren assistants, when to be appointed.

Common seal.

Jurisdiction.

And be it also enacted, That when there shall be resident in any burgh appointed by this act sixty familys, then such burgh shall have fifteen persons who shall be called brethren assistants of the guild hall, who shall be of common council to the burgh in the making and declaring statutes and ordinances touching or concerning the good reigiment state and governance of the burgh, and from time to time shall be assistant to the director and benchers of such burgh for the time being, that then the constitution shall be held perfect, that thereafter the director and benchers or the major part of them, with the advice and consent of the common councill, or the major part of them, shall have power to raise a levy on their own inhabitants, by such ways and means as they shall think fitt for the necessitys and benefit of the burgh, and shall make, ordain and institute, and under their common seal publish and declare statutes and ordinances for the better rule and governance of the burgh, and of all things happening therein or within the precincts, road and harbour thereof, and again the same to revoke and alter, as with the advice and consent aforesaid, shall be found convenient and necessary.

Provided, always, That no statute or ordinance thus to be made, shall be contradictory to act of assembly, nor shall be binding upon any one until it shall have been published three market days in open market, between the hours of nine and eleven in the forenoon, and that the town clerk have it in keeping to give a copy thereof to any one that shall demand it for the charge of fifteen pence fee, for every such statute or ordinance.

Proviso, as to the obligation of statutes.

And be it further enacted, That the election of the comon councill or brethren assistants of the guild hall aforesaid, shall be made by the freeholders and inhabitants of each burgh respectively, being men of twenty-one years of age and upwards and not servants, who shall be called together by proclamation from the court of hustings, made three market days successively, in open market, between the hours of nine and eleven in the forenoon, and every member of the comon councill being once chosen so, shall continue so long as he well behaves, or till death or removal from such town, and as one dyes, removes or happens to be suspended, another in like manner shall be chosen in his stead.

Common council or brethren assistants, how elected.

And be it further enacted, That the brethren assistants aforementioned, and every of them, at the time of his entering into and upon his said office, shall take such oaths of fidelity to her majesty, her heirs and successors, as shall be from time to time appointed by law for the other people of this colony to take, and also shall take the following oath.

Oaths.

The oath of an Assistant.

"YOU shall swear as an assistant of the guild hall of the burgh of A. that to all things proposed, you shall deliver your opinion faithfully, justly and honestly, for the generall good and prosperity of this burgh, and every member thereof, and to do your endeavour to prosecute that without mingling therewith any particular interest of any person or persons wheresoever. *So help you God.*

Oath of an assistant.

When a burgh entitled to send a burgess to the general assembly.

And be it further enacted, That when the constitution of any of the burghs appointed by this act shall become perfect as aforesaid, then such burgh shall have one burgess to represent them in the generall assembly of this dominion with the like powers and authoritys to vote and act in the said assembly, as fully and amply as any other burgess hath or ought to have, which burgess shall be returned by the director for the time being of such burgh upon writ to him directed from the governor or commander in chief of this colony for the time being, in the form of the other writts mutatis mutandis, and shall be chosen by the freeholders and housekeepers of the town, being men of twenty-one years of age and upwards.

And for prevention of exactions in the charge of warehouse room, which will most likely happen in the beginning, while there shall be but few houses built,

Rates of storage in ware houses.

Be it enacted, That the warehouse rent for any cask containing sixty gallons or upwards, or any bail or parcel of the like or greater bulk, shall be twelve pence for the first day or for the first three months, and six pence for every month afterwards, and for any cask under sixty gallons and every bail or parcel of less bulk than a sixty gallon cask six pence, and three pence in form aforesaid, that these rates shall continue in each burgh respectively, until the director, benchers and common councill shall have been constituted one year and afterwards to be in their power to set and regulate the rates for wharfage, lighteridge and warehouse room, cartage and the like, from time to time as they shall see occasion.

Penalty for exceeding legal rates.

And if any shall exact greater prices for warehouse room than is in this act set down, or after the constitution shall be perfect, shall exact greater prices for wharfage, lighteridge, warehouse room, cartage or other labour than shall be appointed and allowed by the director, benchers and common council of such burgh respectively, he shall be lyable to pay to the party injured ten pence for every penny so exacted over and above the rates aforesaid admitted and allowed, or to be admitted and allowed with cost, cognisable by a justice of the peace of the county, until the director and benchers shall be chosen for such town, and thereafter only by the director or any of the benchers of the burgh saving appeal to the court of Hustings upon security given.

And be it enacted, That the places hereinafter named, shall be the ports meant and intended by this act, and none other place or places whatsoever, (vizt.) Towns, where established.

On James river, Hampton, James City, Flower de Hundred.

On Elizabeth river, Norfolk Town.

On Nansemond river, Nansemond Town.

On York river, York town and Tindals point one port, and West point.

On North river in Mockjack Bay, at Blackwater on Hills land.

On Rappahanoch river, Corrotomen upon the town land formerly appointed in Lancaster county.

Middlesex upon the town land formerly appointed Hobbshole.

On Wicocomoco river upon col. Coopers land in Potomack district.

On Potomack River.

Yohocomoco upon the land of Richard Tidwell in Westmoreland.

Potomack creek at the town land in Stafford.

On Easterne Shore.

The mouth of Kings creek in Northampton county, upon the land called the secretarys land.

Orancocke upon the town land formerly appointed in Accomack.

Provided always, That it shall be lawfull from time to time for any of the inhabitants of the city of Williamsburgh to land or ship off by permit from the officer of any port in York or James river any goods or commoditys in this act mentioned, at either of the publick landings belonging to that city, any thing in this or any other law to the contrary, notwithstanding. Proviso, as to inhabitants of Williamsburg.

And be it also enacted, That at each of the said ports there be forthwith laid out by the common consent of the burgesses and justices of the county wherein such port shall be fifty acres of land, which land so laid out shall be appropriated, and is by virtue hereof appropriated to a town for every such port respectively, and all the lands so laid out or to be laid out and appropriated at the ports aforesaid, and every tract thereof severally 50 acres of land, to be laid out for a town.

and the inhabitants of each of them respectively, are and shall be accounted the free burghs and burghers, meant mentioned and intended by this act, and the inhabitants thereof shall injoy the libertys, freedoms and benefits thereof accordingly, and that the said burghs be named as followeth, (vizt.)

Names of burghs and fairs. Hampton.

That at Hampton in Elizabeth City county to be called Hampton, and to have Wednesday and Saturday in each week for market days, and the tenth day of October and four following days, exclusive of Sundays, annually for their fair.

Norfolk.

That at Norfolk town to be called Norfolk, and to have Tuesday and Saturday in each week for market days, and the third day of October and four following days, exclusive of Sundays, annually their fair.

Nansemond.

That at Nansemond town to be called Nansemond, and to have Mundays and Thursdays in each week for market days, and the fifteenth day of October and four following days, exclusive of Sundays, annually their fair.

James City.

That at James City to be called James City, and to have Tuesdays and Satturdays in each week for market days, and the twentieth day of October and four following days, exclusive of Sundays, annually their fair.

Powhatan.

That at Flower de Hundred to be called Pohatan and to have Tuesdays and Satturdays in each week for market days, and the first Tuesday in November and four following days annually their fair.

York

That at York Town to be called York, and to have Wednesdays and Satturdays in each week for market days, and the first Tuesday in October and four following days annually their fair.

Queensborough.

That at Black Water to be called Queensborough, and to have Tuesdays and Thursdays in each week for market days, and the last Tuesday in November and four following days annually their fair.

Delaware.

That at West Point to be called Delaware, and to have Tuesdays and Satturdays in each week for market days, and the second Tuesday in September and four following days annually their fair.

Queens Town.

That at Corrotomen to be called Queens town, and to have Tuesdays and Satturdays in each week for market days, and the third Tuesday in October and four following days annually their fair.

That at Middlesex to be called Urbanna, and to have Tuesdays and Frydays in each week for market days, and the second Tuesday in March and four following days annually their fair. Urbanna.

That at Hobbs Hole to be called Tappahannock, and to have Tuesdays and Saturdays in each week, for market days, and the fifth day of October and four following days, exclusive of Sundays, annually their fair. Tappahannock.

That at Wicocomoco to be called New-Castle and to have Mundays and Frydays in each week for market days, and the second Tuesday in October and four following days annually their fair. New Castle.

That at Yohocomoco to be called Kingsale, and to have Tuesday and Satturday in each week for market days, and the nineteenth day of October and four following days, exclusive of Sundays, annually their fair. Kingsale.

That at Potomac Creek to be called Marlborough, and to have Munday and Fryday in each week for market days and the twenty-fifth day of September and four following days, exclusive of Sundays, annually their fair. Marlborough.

That at Kings Creek in Northampton county to be called Northampton, and to have Tuesday and Satturday in each week for market days, and the twenty-sixth day of September and four following days, exclusive of Sundays, annually their fair. Northampton.

That of Orancock to be called Orancock, and to have Munday and Fryday in each week for market days, and the second Tuesday in October and four following days annually their fair. Orancock.

And be it further enacted, That where any port is by this act appointed to be at a place that hath land already purchased and laid out for a town, such land so laid out, is hereby declared to be the land where the ports and towns appointed by this act shall be settled and built, and where a port or town is appointed by this act at any place not having land purchased for that purpose, the county court is hereby impowered and required to purchase fifty acres of land for the uses in this act mentioned, and if the proprietor of any land designed by this act for a town shall not be willing to make sale of his land or shall demand too great a consideration for it, or shall be a feme covert under the age of twenty-one years or out of the country, in all these cases it shall be lawfull, Former town land appropriated.

for the county court that is to purchase the land, to issue their precept to the sheriff of one of the adjacent countys at their discretion, requiring the said sheriff to summon five justices of the peace of his county to appear at such time and place as in the said precept shall be directed, to value the land as aforesaid and accordingly the valuation of the said five justices of the peace, or of any three of them upon their oaths (and which oath any justice of the peace of the county whereof the land lyes is hereby impowered to administer) returned under their hands and seals to the next county court and entered upon record there shall be taken as the true value of the land, and thereupon the said county court shall cause the land to be surveyed and laid out into lots or half acres, which shall also be recorded, and upon demand made by the person that hath a lawfull right to have and receive the value of the said land, shall raise the same in tobacco by a levy upon the poll in their county and the conveyance of any proprietor that is willing to make sale of his land or the valuation thereof recorded as aforesaid shall be sufficient in law to vest a firm absolute and indefeasible estate in fee simple, in such feoffees as shall be from time to time appointed by the county court to sell and dispose of the same for the uses aforesaid, and the ffeoffees until the director and benchers shall be elected for such burgh respectively, shall convey and make over unto any person requesting the same and paying the first cost and fifty per cent advance (for the reimbursement of the county) one half acre or lott of land in the said town, reserving the annual rent of one ounce of flax-seed and two ounces of hemp-seed, to be paid the tenth of October in every year to the director and benchers of such town, when they shall be elected, and with this limitation that the said grantee, his heirs or assigns, shall within twelve months next ensuing such grant, begin and without delay proceed to build and finish on the said lott one good house to contain twenty foot square at the least, otherwise such grant to be void and the said lott lyable to the choice and purchase of any other person in manner as aforesaid.

Tenure.

Conditions of building.

Surveyor's fee.

And be it enacted, That the surveyors fee for surveying the town land and laying the same out in streets and lotts and giving a fair plott thereof, shall be five hundred pounds of tobacco and cask, and as the lotts shall be sold, twenty pounds of tobacco for each lott as it shall be sold.

CHAP. XLIII.

An Act Continuing the Act directing the building the Capitol and the city of Williamsburg; *with additions.*

I. WHEREAS by an act made at a General Assembly begun at *James* City the twenty-seventh day of *April*, and in the eleventh year of his late Majesty's reign, entituled, *An Act directing the building the Capitol, and the City of* Williamsburg, it is enacted, that Whereas the state-house where the general assemblies and general courts for this his majesty's colony and dominion of *Virginia*, were kept and held, hath been unhappily burnt down; and it being of absolute necessity that another building be erected, with all the expedition possible, for the convenient sitting and holding of the general assemblies and courts, at a healthy, proper and commodious place, suitable for the reception of a considerable number and concourse of people, that of necessity must resort to the place where the general assemblies will be convened, and where the council and supreme court of justice for his majesty's colony and dominion will be held and kept: Preamble.

And forasmuch as the place commonly called and known by the name of the *Middle Plantation*, hath been found by constant experience, to be healthy, and agreeable to the constitutions of the inhabitants of this his majesty's colony and dominion, having the natural advantage of a serene and temperate air, dry and champaign land, and plentifully stored with wholesome springs, and the conveniency of two navigable and pleasant creeks, that run out of *James* and *York* rivers, necessary for the supplying the place with provisions and other things of necessity, Williamsburg to be built at Middle Plantation.

II. *Be it enacted, by the governor, council and burgesses of this present general assembly, and the authority thereof, and it is hereby enacted,* That four hundred seventy-five foot square of land, lying and being at the said *Middle Plantation*, which hath been already agreed Ground appropriated.

upon by his excellency the governor, council and burgesses, of this present general assembly,* to be taken up and surveyed, as a convenient place for such uses, be the ground appropriated to the only and sole use of a building for the general assemblies and courts to be held and kept in: And that the said building shall forever hereafter be called and known by the name of the *Capitol*, of this his majesty's colony and dominion of Virginia; and that the space of two hundred foot of ground, every way from the said capitol, shall not be built upon, planted, or occupied, forever, but shall be wholly and solely appropriated and kept for the said use, and to no other use or purpose whatsoever.

Capitol.

Form and dimensions.

III. *And be it further enacted by the authority aforesaid, and it is hereby enacted*, That the said capitol shall be erected and built in manner and form according to the rules and dimensions following, viz. That the said building shall be made in this form and figure H; that the foundation of the building shall be four bricks thick, up to or near the surface of the ground; and that the walls of the said building, from thence, shall be three bricks and a half thick, to the water table; and from the water table, to the top of the first story, three bricks thick; and from thence to the top of the second story, two bricks and a half thick; the length of each side or part of which building shall be seventy-five foot, from inside to inside; the breadth thereof, twenty-five foot from inside to inside; and the first story of each part or side, shall be fifteen foot pitch, one end of each side or part of which shall be semi-circular, and the lower rooms at the said end, fifty foot long, and shall be parted by a wall, from the rest of the building, on each side or part; which other part shall be divided into four divisions, whereof one to be for a large and handsome staircase: That the middle of the front, on each side of the said building, shall have a circular porch, with an iron balcony upon the first floor over it, and great folding gates to each porch, of six foot breadth both; and that four galleries shall be in the room below, that shall be called the general court house; the upper story of each side to be ten foot pitch, and be divided as shall be directed by the committee appointed to revise the laws: That the two parts of the building shall be joined by a cross gallery of thirty foot long, and fifteen foot wide each way, according to the figure herein before specified, raised upon piazzas, and built as high as the other parts of the building; and in the middle thereof, a cupola to surmount the rest of the building, which shall have a clock placed in it; and on the top of the said cupola shall be put a flag upon occasion: That the windows to each story of the building, shall be sash windows, and that the roof shall be a hip roof, with dormant windows; and shall be well shingled with ciprus shingles; and that the great room below, of each building, shall be laid with flag stones: One part or side of which building, shall be, and is hereby appropriated to the use of the general court, and council, for the holding and keeping of the said general court, and council therein, and the several offices thereto belonging; and the other part or side of the said building, shall be and is hereby appropriated to the use of the house of burgesses, and the officers thereof, and to no other use or uses whatsoever.

To what uses appropriated.

IV. *And be it further enacted, by the authority aforesaid, and it is hereby enacted,* That the committee appointed for the revisal of the laws, are hereby impowered and required, from time to time, to inspect and oversee the said building, until it shall be finished; and to covenant and agree with such and so many undertakers or overseers of the said building, as they shall think fit, and to give such necessary orders and directions therein, from time to time, as they shall see cause for the carrying on, furtherance and finishing of the said work, according to the aforesaid rules and dimensions; and that the said committee be likewise empowered, by virtue of this act, on the public account and risque, to send for, out of England, iron-work, glass, paint, stone and all other materials, as they shall think necessary, for and towards the carrying on and finishing the said building.

Committee appointed.

Materials

V. *And be it further enacted, by the authority aforesaid, and it is hereby enacted,* That the said committee as often as they shall have occasion for money for the uses aforesaid, shall, from time to time, apply themselves to the governor, or commander in chief, for the time being, to issue out his warrant to the treasurer of this his majesty's colony and dominion, requiring him to pay so much money as they shall have occasion for,

Money appropriated

not exceeding the sum of two thousand pounds sterling; who is hereby impowered and required to deliver and pay the same to the said committee, upon such warrant: Which said sum or sums, the said committee shall account for to the next meeting of the assembly, and also make report of their proceedings in the building of the said Capitol.

How accounted for.

Town.

VI. And for as much as the general assemblies, and general courts, of this his majesty's colony and dominion, cannot possibly be held and kept at the said capitol, unless a good town be built and settled adjacent to the said capitol, suitable for the accommodation and entertainment of a considerable number of persons, that of necessity must resort thither: And whereas, in all probability, it will prove highly advantageous and beneficial to his majesty's roial college of *William & Mary*, to have the conveniencies of a town near the same,

Land appropriated for a city.

VII. *Be it therefore enacted, by the authority aforesaid, and it is hereby enacted,* That two hundred eighty-three acres, thirty-five poles and a half of land, situate, lying and being at the Middle Plantation, in *James City* and *York* counties, bounded according to a draught, plot, or survey made, by the order of the governor, council and burgesses, of this present general assembly, and now lying in the assembly-office of his majesty's colony and dominion, shall be and is hereby reserved and appropriated for the only and sole use of a city to be there built, and erected, and to no other use, intent, or purpose whatsoever.

For building.

VIII. *And be it further enacted, by the authority aforesaid, and it is hereby enacted,* That two hundred and twenty acres of the said land, according to the bounds of the aforesaid draught or plot, shall be and is hereby appointed and set a-part for ground, on which the said city shall be built and erected, according to the form and manner laid down in the said draught or plot; which said city, in honour of our most gracious and glorious king *William*, shall be forever hereafter called and known by the name of the city of *Williamsburg*: And fifteen acres, forty-four poles and a quarter, of land, according to the aforesaid draught or plot, shall be and is hereby appointed and set a-part for a road or way from the said city, to the creek commonly called or known by the name of *Queen's* creek, running into

Williamsburg.

Queen's Road.

York river: And fourteen acres, seventy-one poles and a quarter of land, according to the aforesaid draught or plot, lying on the said Queen's creek, shall be and is hereby appointed and set a-part for a port, or landing place, for the said city of Williamsburg, on the said creek; which said port or landing place, in commemoration of the late Queen Mary, of blessed memory, shall forever hereafter be called and known by the name of Queen Mary's port; and the afore-mentioned road or way leading thereto, shall be called Queen's road: And ten acres forty two poles and a half of land, according to the aforesaid draught or plot, shall be and is hereby appointed and set a-part for a road or way, from the said city of Williamsburg, to the creek commonly called and known by the name of *Archer's Hope* creek, running into James river; which said creek, shall forever hereafter be called and known by the name of Princess creek: And twenty three acres, thirty-seven poles and a half, of land, according to the aforesaid draught or plot, lying upon the said Princess Creek, shall be and is hereby appointed and set a-part for a port or landing place, for the said city of Williamsburg, on the said creek; which said port or landing place, in honour of her roial highness the Princess *Anne* of *Denmark*, shall be called and known by the name of Princess *Anne* port forever hereafter; and the afore-mentioned road or way leading thereto, shall be called Princess road.

Queen Mary's port.

Princess Road.

Princess Ann port.

IX. *And be it further enacted, by the authority aforesaid, and it is hereby enacted*, That the ground or land, by virtue of this act, set a-part for the use of the said city of Williamsburg, shall be laid out and proportioned into half acres; every of which half acre shall be a distinct lot of ground, to build upon, in manner and form as is hereafter expressed; (that is to say,) That whosoever shall build in the main street of the said city of Williamsburg, as laid out in the aforesaid draught or plot, shall not build a house less than ten foot pitch, and the front of each house shall come within six foot of the street, and not nearer; and that the houses in the several lots in the said main street shall front alike; which said street, in honour of his highness *William* Duke of *Gloucester*, shall forever hereafter be called and known by the name of *Duke of Gloucester* street: And that the other streets and lanes shall be built in such

Size of Lots.

Streets & building.

manner, and according to such rules and orders as shall be given and made by the directors, by virtue of this act; hereafter appointed, or by the incorporation of the Mayor, Aldermen, and Commonalty of the City of Williamsburg.

X. And to the end, reasonable satisfaction may be paid, allowed, and given, for all such land and ground, as by virtue of this act is taken up, and appropriated to the use aforesaid,

Property in land, how acquired.

XI. *Be it enacted, by the authority aforesaid, and it is hereby enacted,* That his excellency the governor, or the governor or commander in chief, for the time being, is hereby impowered and desired to issue out his warrants to the several sheriffs of *James City*, *York* and *New Kent* counties commanding them respectively to impannel four of the most able and discreet freeholders in each of their bailiwicks, no ways concerned in interest in the said land, or any ways related to the owners or proprietors thereof, to meet at such time, as he shall think fit; who shall be sworn by such person or persons as he shall appoint; and upon their oaths, value and appraise the said land or ground, in so many several and distinct parts and parcels, as shall be owned and claimed therein, by several and distinct owners, proprietors, and claimers thereof: and after such valuation and appraisement so made, the said jury shall forthwith return the same under their hands and seals, to the secretary's office of this his majesty's colony and dominion: And after such valuation and return made as aforesaid, the feoffees or trustees, by virtue of this act, hereafter appointed, shall enter; and immediately upon such entry made, the said feoffees or trustees, and every of them, shall be vested with, and seized of and in, a pure, absolute, perfect, and indefeasible estate of inheritance in fee, in trust to and for the intents, uses, and purposes hereafter mentioned; and shall be binding and effectual in law, (without further or other act or acts) to all intents and purposes, against all and every the said owners, claimers and proprietors, (whether they be capable of consenting thereto, or disabled by nonage, coverture, intail, or other impediments,) and all and every their heirs, executors, administrators and assigns, forever, or any claimer or pretender thereto.

XII. *Provided always, and be it further enacted, by the authority aforesaid, and it is hereby enacted,* That the said jury, in the said valuation, shall have due regard to the respective interests and estates in the same; and shall make a valuation and estimation thereof, accordingly.

XIII. *And be it further enacted, by the authority aforesaid, and it is hereby enacted,* That *Lewis Burwell*, *Philip Ludwell*, Junior, *Benjamin Harrison*, Junior, *James Whaley*, *Hugh Norwell*, and *Mongo Ingles*, Gentlemen, shall be and are hereby nominated and appointed Feoffees or Trustees of the land appropriated to the uses aforesaid: Which said Feoffees or Trustees, in manner aforesaid, shall have, hold, and enjoy, a good, pure, absolute, and indefeasible estate in fee, of and in the aforesaid two hundred eighty-three acres, thirty-five poles and a half of land; in special trust and confidence, to and for the uses hereafter mentioned, (that is to say) to the uses, intents and purposes, that the said Feoffees and Trustees, or any two or more of them, shall, out of two hundred and twenty acres of the said land hereby appropriated for the use of the said city of *Williamsburg*, convey and assure, in fee, unto any person requesting the same, and paying the said Feoffees or Trustees, the first cost of the purchase thereof, and fifty *per cent.* advance, one or more half acre, or half acres, of the said land or ground, by such good and sufficient deed, and assurance, in the law, unto such person or persons, their heirs and assigns, for-ever, as by such person or persons, or their council learned in the law, shall be required.

Trustees.

Their interests.

Sales by them.

XIV. *Provided always, and be it further enacted, by the authority aforesaid, and it is hereby enacted,* That if such grantee, his heirs or assigns, shall not, within the space of twenty-four months, next ensuing the date of such grant, begin to build, and finish, on each half acre or lot so granted, one good dwelling house, containing twenty foot in width, and thirty foot in length, at the least (if in the main street, called *Duke of Gloucester* street, of ten foot pitch, and within six foot of the street,) if in any other place, according to the rules and directions that shall be given by the directors hereafter appointed; that then such

Condition as to building.

grant and conveyance, so made, shall be utterly void, and null in law; and the lands therein granted, liable to the choice and purchase of any other person or persons, and shall be immediately re-invested in the said Trustees or Feoffees, to the uses aforesaid, in as full and ample manner, as if the same had never been disposed of.

Proprietors of land, how paid.

XV. *And be it further enacted, by the authority aforesaid, and it is hereby enacted,* That the costs and charges of the purchase of the said two hundred eighty-three acres, thirty-five poles and a half of land, shall be paid and satisfied by the public, at the next session of assembly, to the several and respective proprietors and owners thereof, according to the valuation and appraisement made, in manner as is before expressed: And also, that the aforesaid Feoffees and Trustees shall render an account of the produce and profits of the several half acres, or lots of land, by them sold, in manner aforesaid, to the next general assembly; which shall be then allowed and disposed of, for the reimbursement of the public, in the first purchase of the said land; and until the same be fully paid and reimbursed, and to no other use, intent, or purpose whatsoever.

Trustees to account.

Vacancies in trustees, how supplied.

XVI. *Provided always, and be it further enacted, by the authority aforesaid, and it is hereby enacted,* That in case of the death, removal out of the country, or into remote parts, or other legal disability, of one or more of the said Feoffees or Trustees, his excellency the governor, or the governor or commander in chief, for the time being, is hereby impowered and desired to nominate such and so many Feoffees or Trustees, as shall, from time to time, be under the number of six: which said Feoffees or Trustees, so nominated and appointed, shall be immediately vested with equal right and title to the aforesaid land and ground, to the uses aforesaid, as the Feoffees or Trustees appointed by virtue of this act, might or could have, or as if they were by this act particularly nominated and appointed.

XVII. *Provided likewise, and be it further enacted, by the authority aforesaid, and it is hereby enacted,* That the lots at the aforementioned ports or landings shall be proportioned at the discretion of the directors hereafter mentioned: *Provided*, That each lot shall not exceed sixty foot square; which said lots shall be disposed of in manner aforesaid, and the produce thereof to be accounted for, by the said Feoffees or Trustees, in manner as is before expressed; any thing in this act to the contrary, in any wise, notwithstanding. Size of lots, at ports.

XVIII. *Provided also*, That a sufficient quantity of land at each port or landing place shall be left in common, at the discretion of the directors hereafter appointed. Common.

XIX. *And be it further enacted, by the authority aforesaid, and it is hereby enacted*, That it shall and may be lawful to and for his excellency the governor, and to and for his majesty's governor or commander in chief of this his majesty's colony and dominion, for the time being, by letters patents, under the seal of this his majesty's colony and dominion, to incorporate all and every person and persons, who, from time to time, or at any time hereafter, shall have an interest, freehold or habitation, in the said city, to be one body politic and corporate, by the name of the mayor, aldermen, and commonalty of the city of Williamsburg; and by that name, to have perpetual succession, and a common seal; and that they, and their successors, by the name aforesaid, shall be able and capable in law, to have, purchase, receive, enjoy, possess, and retain to them and their successors forever, any lands, rents, tenements, and hereditaments, of what kind, nature, or quality soever; and also to sell, grant, demise, alien, or dispose of the same: and by the same name, to sue and implead, be sued and impleaded, answer, and be answered, in all courts of record, and any other place whatsoever: and from time to time, under their common seal, to make and establish such bylaws, rules and ordinances, (not contrary to the laws and constitutions of England, and this his majesty's colony and dominion,) as shall by them be thought requisite and necessary for the good ordering and government of such persons as shall, from time to time, reside within the limits of the said city and corporation, or shall be concerned in interest therein; and by the name aforesaid, to do and execute all and singular other matters and things, that to them shall or may appertain to do. Power of incorporating inhabitants. Their capacity

XX. And that there may not be any defect in the good ordering or management of the said land appropriated by this act, for the building of the said city, and in providing for the better regulation thereof, until the next meeting of assembly,

Directors.

XXI. *Be it enacted, by the authority aforesaid, and it is hereby enacted,* That his Excellency *Francis Nicholson*, esq. his majesty's lieutenant and governor general of Virginia, *Edmund Jenings*, esq. of his majesty's honourable council, *Philip Ludwell*, esq. and *Thomas Ballard*, gentlemen, members of the right worshipful house of burgesses of this present general assembly, *Lewis Burwell*, *Philip Ludwell*, Junior, *John Page*, *Henry Tyler*, *James Whaley*, and *Benjamin Harrison*, Junior, gentlemen, or any five, or more of them, shall be and are hereby nominated, authorized, and impowered, by the name of the directors appointed for the settlement and encouragement of the city of Williamsburg, to make such rules and orders, and to give such directions in the building of the said city and ports, not already provided for by this act, as to them shall seem best and most convenient.

Markets and fairs.

XXII. *And be it further enacted, by the authority aforesaid, and it is hereby enacted,* That his excellency the governor, or the governor or commander in chief of this his majesty's colony and dominion, for the time being, is hereby impowered and desired, by letters patents, under the seal of this his majesty colony and dominion, to grant unto the said city of Williamsburg, the liberty and privilege of holding and keeping such and so many markets and fairs, at such time and times, and upon such conditions, and under such limitations, as he shall think fit.

When lots to be sold.

XXIII. *Provided always, and be it further enacted, by the authority aforesaid, and it is hereby enacted,* That no lot or lots of any half acre, or half acres of land, shall be sold or disposed of, to any person or persons whatsoever, before the twentieth day of October next ensuing the date of this act: To the end, that the whole country may have timely notice of this act, and equal liberty in the choice of the lots.

Former law confirmed.

XXIV. Now, forasmuch as several parts and clauses recited in the aforesaid act, are not executed, others necessary to remain in force, and for confirming every thing already done, by any person or persons whatsoever, by virtue of, and pursuant to, the aforesaid act, *Be it enacted, by the governor, council, and burgesses, of this present general assembly, and it is hereby enacted, by the authority of the same,* That the afore-recited act, and every part and clause thereof, be and are hereby declared to be in full force.

Encouragement for building on Duke of Gloucester street.

XXV. *And be it further enacted,* If any person shall hereafter take a grant of two lots, or half acres of land, upon the great street of the said city, commonly called *Duke of Gloucester* street, and within the space of four and twenty months next ensuing such grant, upon the said lots or half acres, or either of them, shall build and finish one house fifty foot long and twenty foot broad, or within the space aforesaid upon the said lots, or half acres, or either of them, shall build and finish one brick house, or framed house, with two stacks of brick chimnies, and cellars under the whole house, bricked, forty foot long, and twenty foot broad, either of the said performances, shall be sufficient to save the grant of both the said lots, or half acres, from becoming void, and shall be so adjudged, deemed, and taken; any law, usage, or custom heretofore, to the contrary, notwithstanding.

On other streets.

XXVI. And if any person shall hereafter take a grant of two lots, or half acres of land, upon the great street of the said city, and one or more lots, or half acres backward, and within the space of four and twenty months next ensuing such grant, upon the lots or half acres contiguous to the great street, or either of them, shall build and finish in ordinary framed work, as much dwelling housing, as will make five hundred square feet superficial measure, on the ground plat, for every lot, or half acre taken up; or within the space aforesaid, upon the said two lots, or half acres, or either of them, shall build and finish, in brick work, or framed work, with brick cellars under the whole, and brick chimnies, as much dwelling housing, as will make four hundred square feet superficial measure on the ground plat, for every lot, or half acre taken up, either of the said performances shall be sufficient to save the grant of all and every of the said lots, or half acres, from becoming void, and shall be so adjudged, deemed, and taken; any law, usage, or custom heretofore, to the contrary, notwithstanding.

XXVII. *Provided always,* That the building of one house be the dimensions thereof never so large, shall not save more than two lots, or half acres, on the great street; and that whatever lots, or half acres more, the builder is willing to take a grant of, shall be taken backwards.

Lots, when to be inclosed.

XXVIII. *And be it further enacted,* That every person having any lots, or half acres of land, contiguous to the great street, shall inclose the said lots, or half acres, with a wall, pails, or post and rails, within six months after the building, which the law requires to be erected thereupon, shall be finished, upon penalty of forfeiting and paying five shillings a month for every lot or half acre, so long as the same shall remain without a wall, pails, or rails, as aforesaid: To be recovered before any justice of the peace of *York* or *James City* county, upon the complaint of any one of the trustees or directors, and to be disposed of by the directors as they shall think fit, for the use and benefit of the said city and ports thereunto belonging.

Proviso as to lots formerly laid out.

XXIX. *And be it further enacted, by the authority aforesaid, and it is hereby enacted,* That none of the lots, or half acres of land in the city of Williamsburg, whereon any houses were standing, at the laying out of the said city, shall vest in the said feoffees and trustees of the said city, to be disposed of, as the rest of the lots, and half acres may be, by virtue of the said act, made at a general assembly begun at *James City*, the twenty-seventh day of April, one thousant six hundred ninety-nine, intitutled, *An act directing the building the capitol, and the city of* Williamsburg; but that all and every of the said lots and half acres, shall remain and continue the proper estate of the respective proprietors unaltered by the said act, and so shall be adjudged, deemed, and taken; any thing in the said act to the contrary, or seeming to the contrary, notwithstanding.

Saving to Benjamin Harrison.

XXX. *And be it also enacted,* That the four lots, or half acres, which at the first laying out of the land for the said city, were laid out and appropriated for the buildings then erected on the same, by *Benjamin Harrison, jr.* esq. shall remain and continue to the use of the said *Benjamin Harrison*, his heirs and assigns, and shall not lapse for want of other building thereon; any thing in this act to the contrary, notwithstanding.

XXXI. And whereas, by the death, removal out of the country, or into remote parts, of several of the persons nominated directors in the afore-recited act, and the refusal of others to concern themselves therein, the powers and authorities to them granted, have not been so fully executed as was intended; and it being necessary, for the better regulating and ordering the building of the said city of Williamsburg, that a competent number of directors be appointed and continued to inspect the same:

Other directors.

XXXII. *Be it therefore enacted, by the authority aforesaid, and it is hereby enacted,* That his excellency *Edward Nott*, esq. her majesty's lieutenant and governor general of Virginia, *Edmund Jennings*, *Philip Ludwell*, *William Byrd*, and *Benjamin Harrison*, jr. Esqrs. *Henry Tyler*, *David Bray*. *Frederick Jones*, *Archibald Blair*, *Chichley-Corbin Thacker*, and *William Robertson*, gentlemen, or any five, or more of them, be, and they are hereby authorised and impowered, by the name of the directors of the settlement and encouragement of the city of Williamsburg, from time to time, and at all times hereafter, until the said city shall be erected into a corporation, in manner aforementioned, to direct and order the laying out the lots and streets of the said city, where the bounds and marks thereof are worn out, to lay out a convenient space of ground for the Church-yard, to enlarge the market-place, and to alter any of the streets or lanes thereof, where the same are found inconvenient; and also to settle and establish such rules and orders for the more regular and orderly building of the houses in the said city, as to them shall seem best and most convenient.

Main or D. of Gloucester street not to be altered.

XXXIII. *Provided always*, That the main street, called Duke of Gloucester street, extending from the capitol, to the utmost limits of the city westward, 'till it joins on the land belonging to the college, shall not hereafter be altered, either in course or dimensions thereof.

Vacancies in directors, how supplied.

XXXIV. *And be it further enacted*, That in case of the death, removal out of the country, or other legal disability, of any one or more of the directors before named, it shall and may be lawful for the surviving or remaining directors, from time to time, to elect and chuse so many other persons, in the room of those so dead or removed, as shall make up the number of ten; which directors so chosen, shall be, to all intents and purposes, vested with the same power, as any other in this act particularly nominated and appointed.

CHAP. XLIV.

An act for confirming titles to town lands.

Preamble.

I. WHEREAS, an act made at a general assembly, begun at James city, the sixteenth day of April, one thousand six hundred ninety and one, intituled, *An act for ports, &c.* stands suspended: And forasmuch as, pursuant to the said act, divers tracts of land have been purchased, and laid out for ports and towns, in the respective places appointed by the said act, and vested in trustees; many of which have conveyed lots, or half acres therein, to several persons, who have built thereon, and have made considerable improvements:

Titles to town lands confirmed.

II. *Be it enacted, by the governor, council and burgesses of this present general assembly, and it is hereby enacted, by the authority of the same,* That where any county or counties have purchased, laid out, and paid for any lands, for ports or towns, pursuant to the said act, for ports, &c. or to any other act of assembly, and have vested the same in feoffees or trustees, according to the said act or acts; such feoffees or trustees so invested, are hereby declared to have a good, absolute, and indefeasible estate in fee, in such lands respectively, which have not been disposed of by the former trustees, in trust and confidence, to and for the uses in the said act for ports, &c. mentioned, and for no other use or purpose whatsoever; and the said land or lands are hereby confirmed to the said feoffees or trustees, in fee, to such use or uses; any thing in the said suspension, or any other law, statute, usage, or custom, to the contrary, in any-wise, notwithstanding.

Trustees to be appointed.

III. *And be it further enacted,* That where any county or counties, pursuant to the said act for ports, or any other act of assembly, have purchased, laid out, and paid for fifty acres of land, and the same, by the death, or refusal of the proprietor, or other accident, hath not been conveyed to trustees, according to the said law or laws; such land or lands shall be and are hereby confirmed to such feoffees or trustees, as hereafter, by virtue of this act, shall be appointed by the county courts, to and for the uses aforesaid, in as full and ample manner, as if the said land or lands, had been really and actually conveyed in law, by such proprietors to such feoffees or trustees, in manner, as by the said law for ports, is expressed.

Vacancies how supplied.

IV. *And be it further enacted, by the authority aforesaid, and it is hereby enacted,* That if in any county, the feoffees or trustees already appointed, by virtue of the said act for ports, be dead, or departed out of this country, the county court of such respective county is hereby impowered and required to appoint other feoffees or trustees, who are hereby invested and confirmed in the fee of all such land or lands (not by former trustees disposed of) to the use or uses aforementioned, and to no other use or purpose whatsoever: and all feoffees or trustees, by virtue of the said act for ports, &c. already made, or by virtue of this act hereafter to be made, are hereby impowered and required, in their respective county, to convey and make over any lot or lots, half acre or half acres of land, to such person or persons as shall desire to take up the same, according to the said act for ports, and upon the conditions therein specified, as if the said act for ports had never been suspended; any law, statute, usage, or custom, to the contrary notwithstanding.

Purchasers confirmed in their titles.

V. *And be it further enacted,* That if any person or persons have purchased and paid for any lot or lots, half acre or half acres of land, in any of the said places, of any feoffees or trustees, pursuant to the said law, and have fully complied with the conditions in the said law mentioned and set down; such person or persons are hereby declared to be invested with, and have a good, absolute, and indefeasible estate in fee, to such lot or lots, half acre or half acres of land; and the same is hereby confirmed in fee to such person and persons, and to his and their heirs forever.

CHAP. XLV.

An act for Naturalization.

Preamble, see vol. 2, tit. "Naturalization."

I. WHEREAS nothing can contribute more to the speedy settling and peopling of this her majesty's colony and dominion, than that all possible encouragement should be given to persons of different nations to transport themselves hither, with their families and stock, for to settle, plant, or reside, by investing them with all the rights and privileges of any of her majesty's natural free-born subjects within this colony:

Aliens how naturalized.

II. *Be it therefore enacted, by the governor, council, and burgesses, of this present general assembly, and it is hereby enacted, by the authority of the same,* That it shall and may be lawful for the governor, or commander in chief of this colony and dominion, for the time being, by a public instrument, or letters patents, under the broad seal thereof, to declare any alien or aliens, foreigner or foreigners, being already settled, or inhabitants in this colony, or which shall hereafter come to settle, plant, or reside therein, upon his, her or their taking, before him, the oaths appointed by act of parliament to be taken, instead of the oaths of allegiance and supremacy, the oath mentioned in an act, intituled, *An act to declare the alterations in the oath appointed to be taken by the act,* intituled, *An act for the further security of his majesty's person, and the succession of the crown in the protestant line, and for extinguishing the hopes of the pretended prince of* Wales, *and all other pretenders, and their open and secret abettors, and for declaring the association to be determined, and subscribing the test,* to be, to all intents and purposes, fully and completely naturalized; and that all persons having such public instrument, or letters patents, shall, by virtue of this act, have and enjoy to them, and their heirs, the same immunities and rights, of and unto the laws and privileges of this colony and dominion, as fully and amply as any of her majesty's natural-born subjects have or enjoy within the same, and as if they themselves had been born within any of her majesty's realms or dominions; any former act, law, ordinance, usage, or custom, to the contrary, notwithstanding.

III. And to the intent, the said public instrument,

or letters patents, under the broad seal of this colony, as aforesaid, may be obtained, without any great difficulty or charge,

IV. *Be it further enacted*, That the governor, or commander in chief of this colony and dominion, granting such public instrument or letters patents, shall have and receive for the same, forty shillings, and his clerk, for writing of it, ten shillings, and no more. Fees to governor.

V. And whereas several aliens and foreigners, that have formerly transported themselves to this her majesty's colony and dominion, and have taken up and patented, in their own name, several parcels of land, or otherwise made purchase of lands, houses, tenements, or other real interest, and have afterwards sold the same to some of her majesty's liege people, or inhabitants of this colony and dominion,

VI. *It is hereby further enacted*, That all persons which have purchased and held, under any such alien or aliens, any lands, houses, or tenements, be secured, and by virtue of this present act, for ever, be confirmed in the quiet and peaceable possession of the said purchases, unto them and their heirs for ever; any former law, usage, or custom, to the contrary, in anywise, notwithstanding. Land purchased of aliens, confirmed.

VII. *Provided*, That nothing in this act contained, shall be construed to enable or give power or privilege to any foreigner, to do or execute any matter or thing, which by any of the acts made in England, concerning her majesty's plantations, he is disabled to do or execute. Proviso, as to privileges of aliens.

CHAP. XLVI.

An act for improving the staple of Tobacco; and for regulating the size and tare of tobacco hogsheads.

I. BE *it enacted, by the governor, council, and burgesses, of this present general assembly, and it is hereby enacted, and declared, by the authority of the same*, That all tending of seconds, for tobacco, is hereby forbid: and that whosoever shall tend, or cause or suffer to be tended any seconds, shall forfeit and pay five hundred pounds of tobacco for every tithable person he Penalty for tending seconds.

shall have or employ that year, upon the plantation where the second shall grow.

On overseers.

II. *Provided*, That where any person or persons, shall entrust his or their plantation or plantations, and the servants and slaves thereon, to the management of an overseer, being a free man, the owner of such plantation, servants and slaves, shall not be liable to prosecution, for any breach of this act: But such overseer, tending, or causing or suffering to be tended, any seconds, shall incur the said penalty of five hundred pounds of tobacco, for every tithable person that shall be employed that year, upon the plantation under his charge, where such seconds shall grow, as aforesaid.

Penalties for exposing to sale, deceitfully packed.

III. *And be it also enacted, by the authority aforesaid, and it is hereby enacted*, That whosoever shall hereafter pack, or caused to be packed, any hogshead of tobacco, they pack or caused the same to be packed fairly, and without deceit, and equally good throughout, as it appears at the head. And that if any person or persons whatsoever, shall pay away, or put to sale, or offer to pay away, or put to sale, any hogshead of tobacco, which he hath deceitfully, or hath caused or suffered to be deceitfully packed, by putting thereinto any stones, or intermingling therewith any dirt, sand, tobacco-stocks, stems, seconds, ground leaves, or other trash whatsoever, shall forfeit, for every hogshead so deceitfully packed, one thousand pounds of tobacco.

Viewers.

IV. *And be it also enacted, by the authority aforesaid, and it is hereby enacted*, That when any plaint or information shall be made, or suit brought, to any court, concerning the false packing of a hogshead of tobacco, the court shall forthwith appoint two or three men, who are reputed to be skilful planters, to search and view the said hogshead of tobacco; and to make report, upon oath, to the court, how they find the same; and whether, in their opinions, it be fairly packed, as this act directs: And their report therein, shall be admitted as good evidence at the trial.

Abatement.

V. *Provided*, That five pounds weight, and no more, be allowed in one hogshead, for sand, dust, and mean tobacco, (to wit,) such tobacco as is not passable by itself, without better joined with it.

VI. *And be it also enacted, by the authority aforesaid, and it is hereby enacted,* That if any creditor shall omit to demand or receive a tobacco debt, by the last day of January, it shall be lawful for the debtor, at any time in February, to apply himself to two justices of the peace of the county, to make a tender of the tobacco he owes, according to the tenor of the specialty or bargain by which it appears due: Which said two justices shall be and are hereby impowered and required, to appoint, without delay, three honest and able men of the neighbourhood, on their oaths, to view the tobacco; and if they find it merchantable, and packed fairly, according to the direction of this act, they shall weigh and mark the same for the use of the creditor, on whose account and hazard it shall thereafter lie. And upon producing certificate from the said justices, of the said tender, to the next county court, and that, the tobacco is found good, and fairly packed, as the law directs, the said court is hereby authorised and impowered, by their order, to discharge the debtor from his said debt.

Tender of tobacco, in payment.

VII. *Provided,* The said tender was made in place according to specialty: And *Provided,* That the said debtor still endeavour to secure and preserve the said tobacco as before the tender, and as it were still his own.

Proviso.

VIII. *And be it enacted, by the authority aforesaid, and it is hereby enacted,* That the debtor making tender, as aforesaid, shall bear and defray the charge accruing thereby: And that each viewer shall be allowed twenty pounds of tobacco per day.

Allowance to viewers.

IX. *And also be it enacted, by the authority aforesaid, and it is hereby enacted,* That every tobacco hogshead, in which tobacco shall be packed, paid away, or put to sale, shall be made of dry and well seasoned timber, and which hath been hewed three months at least before the setting up; and shall be set up in strong and substantial hoops; the stave shall be in length forty-eight inches, and no more, and at least one third of an inch in thickness, on the thinnest edge thereof; the size of the head on the inside shall be thirty inches in diameter, and no more.

Size and quality of tobacco casks.

X. *And be it enacted, by the authority aforesaid, and it is hereby enacted,* That all and every cooper and

Coopers to be sworn.

coopers, or other persons intending to set up tobacco hogsheads, do go before a justice of the peace for the county where he dwells, and make oath, that he shall not willingly or wittingly set up any tobacco hogsheads of a larger size than is herein directed: And also to tare, or cause to be tared, with a marking-iron, or branding-iron, every tobacco hogshead that by him shall be set up, with the true weight thereof, on the bulge and head of the hogshead; together with the first letter of his proper name and sir-name: And shall take a certificate from the said justice, of such oath so made. And if any person or persons shall employ any negro, mulatto, or other servant, in making tobacco hogsheads, such emploier shall go before a justice of the peace for the county where he or she dwells, and make oath, That he or she so employing the said negro, mulatto, or other servant, shall not willingly nor wittingly, suffer or permit any tobacco hogsheads to be set up for them, of a larger size than is herein directed; but shall use their utmost endeavours to prevent the same: and also, that what hogsheads by such negro, mulatto or other servant, shall be made or set up for him or her, shall be tared, and the two first letters of his or her proper name and sir-name set thereon, in manner aforesaid: And shall also take a certificate from the said justice, of such oath made.

Others to take an oath.

XI. *And be it further enacted, by the authority aforesaid, and it is hereby enacted*, That if any cooper, coopers, or any other person or persons, set up tobacco cask, contrary to this act; or shall pay away, put to sale, or put, or cause to be put on board any boat, sloop, ship, or other vessel, in order to exportation, any tobacco whatsoever, packed in cask of a greater size than is herein before expressed and set down; or that is made of less seasoned timber or staves, thinner than before directed; or that is not tared with their just weight, as before in this act is enjoined; or shall presume to set the tare upon any hogshead, before oath made, and a certificate obtained, as aforesaid, such cooper or coopers, other person or persons, if free, and if not, the emploier shall, for every tobacco hogshead so made, paid away, put to sale, or shipped, forfeit and pay the sum of five hundred pounds of tobacco; one moiety of all the fines and forfeitures in this

Penalty for setting up casks, contrary to this act.

Fines appropriated.

act before mentioned, shall be to our sovereign lady the queen, her heirs and successors, for and towards the better support of this government, and the contingent charges thereof; and the other moiety to him or them that will sue or inform for the same: To be recovered, with costs, by action of debt, bill, plaint, or information, in any court of record in this her majesty's colony and dominion, wherein, no essoin, protection, or wager, of law, shall be allowed.

Allowance for moisture.

XII. *Provided always*, That every justice of the peace before whom complaint of the breach of this act shall be brought, shall be and is hereby impowered to consider what any tobacco hogshead, after it hath lain some time packed, may, by the moisture of the tobacco, or weather increase in weight; and give judgment accordingly.

Allowance for cask.

XIII. *And also be it enacted by the authority aforesaid, and it is hereby enacted*, That the buyer or receiver of tobacco in cask, shall receive and take the same at the tare thereon set, and allow thirty pounds of tobacco for each hogshead, notwithstanding any bill, bond, or contract expressing the same, to be paid with cask; on penalty of one hundred and fifty pounds of tobacco, paiable to the informer; and recoverable, with costs, upon complaint, before any justice of the peace of the county.

Proviso, as to rents.

XIV. *Provided*, That neither this act, nor any thing therein contained, shall be construed to extend to contracts, grants, rents, or reservations of cask, with the tobacco upon leases, for lands; but that the cask shall and may be paid, received, demanded, sued for, and recovered, according to the conditions, contracts, grants, and reservations of the rents, upon such leases.

And persons shipping their own tobacco.

XV. *Provided also*, That this act, nor any thing herein contained shall be construed or intended to restrain or prohibit any person or persons from freighting or shipping of their own tobacco in hogsheads of a lawful size, although the hogsheads be not tared, nor any oath made thereto, according to this act, the freighter or freighters, owner or owners of the said tobacco, neither directly nor indirectly exposing the same to sale in the country.

Allowance by public collectors.

XVI. *Provided always*, That the sheriffs and collectors of public dues, shall allow, for all public tobaccos paid in hogsheads, to the paier thereof, eight per cent. for cask, instead of the thirty pounds of tobacco per hogshead, it being so raised in the public proportions, as hath of a long time been accustomed; any thing in this act to the contrary, in any-wise, notwithstanding.

Repealing clause.

XVII. *And be it further enacted, by the authority aforesaid*, That all and every act and acts, and every clause and article thereof, heretofore made, for so much thereof as relates to improving the staple of tobacco, and regulating the size and tare of tobacco hogsheads, is and are hereby repealed, and made void, to all intents and purposes, as if the same had never been made.

This act was confirmed by the Queen, in council, Anno 1707.

CHAP. XLVII.

See chap. 2 of May 1702.

An act to prevent ships sailing in contempt of embargos.

Preamble.

I. Forasmuch, as several masters of ships and vessels in this colony and dominion, have in comtempt of embargos, sailed out of the colony; and that such practices may be of dangerous consequence, by a discovery of the state of the colony, and the trade here, in case any ship or vessel so sailing, should happen to be taken by the enemy:

Bonds to be given by masters of ships.

II. *Be it therefore enacted, by the governor, council, and burgesses, of this present general assembly, and it is hereby enacted, by the authority of the same*, That all masters of ships and vessels, when they make their entry, shall give bond to the naval officer, according to the burthen of their ships or vessels, as followeth; if the ship or vessel be under one hundred tons, the bond shall be for one hundred pounds sterling; if one hundred tons, and not two hundred tons, the bond shall be for two hundred pounds sterling; if two hundred tons, and upwards, the bond shall be for five hundred pounds sterling: To all which bonds, the condition shall be, not to depart this colony, when any embargo is laid, during the continuance of such embargo; and also to observe and follow such rules and directions as shall be thought necessary to be given by the government, for the making up of fleets.

Notice of embargoes to be given.

III. *Provided always, and it is the true intent and meaning of this act,* When any embargos are laid on ships and vessels within this dominion, that the collectors or naval officers, upon receipt of the order for such embargo, shall forthwith give notice to the several masters of ships and vessels within their respective districts, of the said embargo, and the time of the continuance thereof; and that no bond whatsoever required and given, by virtue of this act, shall be adjudged, deemed, or taken to be forfeited, unless notice hath been given, as aforesaid, and breach be made of the condition of the said bond, after such notice; any thing in this act to the contrary, or seeming to the contrary, notwithstanding.

Repealing clause.

IV. *And be it enacted,* That all and every other act and acts, and every clause and article thereof, heretofore made, for so much thereof as relates to any matter or thing whatsoever within the purview of this act, is and are hereby repealed, and made void, to all intents and purposes, as if the same had never been made.

CHAP. XLVIII.

An act concerning Marriages.

Ministers not to marry, without license or publication of banns.

I. *BE it enacted, by the Governor, Council, and Burgesses of this present general assembly, and it is hereby enacted, by the authority of the same,* That no minister or ministers shall celebrate the rights of matrimony between any persons, or join them together as man and wife, without lawful licence, or thrice publication of the banns according as the rubric in the common prayer book prescribes, which enjoins, that if the persons to be married, dwell in several parishes, the banns shall be published in both parishes; and that the curate of the one parish shall not solemnize the matrimony until he have a certificate from the curate of the other parish, that the banns have been thrice published, and no objection made against the parties joining together: And if any minister or ministers shall, contrary to the true intent and meaning of this act, celebrate the rites of matrimony between any persons, or otherwise join them

In what form.

in marriage, he or they so offending, shall, for every such offence, be imprisoned without bail or mainprize, by the space of one whole year; and also shall forfeit and pay five hundred pounds current money of Virginia: And if any minister, contrary to the true intent and meaning of this act, shall go out of this her majesty's colony and dominion, and there join together in matrimony, any person or persons belonging to this country, without such licence or publication of banns, as is herein prescribed, every minister so offending, shall incur the same penalties and forfeitures, as if the same had been done in this colony.

Penalty.

Banns, how published where no minister.

II. *Provided always, and be it enacted, by the authority aforesaid,* That where any parish or parishes have not a minister, it shall and may be lawful for the clerk or reader to publish the banns of matrimony between any persons desiring the same; and if no objection be made, to grant a certificate thereof, and such certificate shall be as sufficient for any minister to solemnize the rites of matrimony, as if the same had been signed, according to the directions herein before mentioned.

Penalty for granting a false certificate.

III. *And be it also enacted,* That if any minister, clerk or reader, shall grant a false certificate, he shall suffer one year's imprisonment, without bail or mainprize, and be fined five hundred pounds sterling, and shall also be liable to further punishment, as in case of forgery: And all such offences may be prosecuted, tried, and determined, in any court of record in this colony; which courts are hereby impowered to hold cognizance thereof, and to hear and determine the same, according to the course of common law; and upon conviction of the party accused, by confession, verdict, or otherwise, to award execution, and inflict the penalties provided by this act for the same: And in such case, the said offence may be alleged and laid in any county within this colony.

Licences, by whom issued.

IV. *And be it also enacted, by the authority aforesaid, and it is hereby enacted,* That all licences for marriage, shall be issued by the clerk of the court of that county where the feme shall have her usual residence, and by him only, and in such manner, and under such rules and directions as are herein mentioned and set down; (that is to say,) he shall take bond to our sovereign lady the Queen, her heirs and successors, with good surety, in

How obtained.

the penalty of fifty pounds current money of Virginia, under condition, that there is no lawful cause to obstruct the marriage, for which the licence shall be desired; and each clerk failing herein, shall forfeit and pay fifty pounds current money of Virginia: And if either of the persons intended to be married, shall be under the age of one and twenty years, and not theretofore married, the consent of the parent or guardian of every such person under the age of one and twenty years, shall be personally given before the said clerk, or signified under the hand and seal of the said parent or guardian, and attested by two witnesses: All which being done, the clerk shall write the licence, and shall certify specially the said bond: And if the persons, in the licence, or either of them, be under the age of one and twenty years, as aforesaid, he shall also certify the consent of the parent or guardian of such so under age, and the manner thereof, to the first justice in commission of the peace for that county, or to such other person as shall be thereto commissionated by the governor of this her majesty's colony and dominion, or commander in chief thereof, for the time being; which premises being performed, the said justice of the peace, or other person commissionated, as aforesaid, is hereby authorized, impowered, and required to sign and direct the said license: And a licence so obtained and signed, and no other whatsoever, is hereby declared to be a lawful licence, according to the true intent and meaning of this Act: And if any county court clerk shall, in any other manner, issue any licence of marriage, or contrary to this act, make certificate for any licence of marriage; and if any person whatsoever shall sign or direct a licence of marriage, in any other manner, than is by this act permitted and allowed, or without such certificate from the county court clerk as is by this act prescribed, all and every person and persons so offending, shall be imprisoned without bail or mainprise, by the space of one whole year; and moreover, shall forfeit and pay five hundred pounds current money of Virginia.

By whom signed.

Penalty on clerks, for breach of this law

V. *And be it also enacted, by the authority aforesaid, and it is hereby enacted*, That if any woman-kind, or maiden, of the age of twelve years or upwards, and under the age of sixteen years, shall contrary to the will or consent of her parent or guardian, and without

Penalty on females between 12 and 16 for marrying without consent of parents, &c. or

publication of banns.

publication of the banns, as aforesaid, consent and agree in her marriage with any person whatsoever; that then the next of kin to such woman-kind, or maiden, to whom the inheritance should descend or come, shall have right to enter upon and take possession of all the lands, tenements, hereditaments, and all other real estate whatsoever, which the said woman-kind, or maiden, at the time of her said marriage and agreement, had in possession, reversion, or remainder; and have, hold, occupy, and enjoy the same, to him, and the representatives of his stock, with all the immunities and privileges thereto belonging, during the coverture: And that after the determination thereof, the said lands, tenements, hereditaments, and other real estate, and also the possessions, reversions, and remainders thereupon, with all the rights, immunities, and privileges thereto belonging, shall then immediately vest, remain and be in the said woman so agreed and married, as aforesaid, and her heirs, or such person or persons as should have enjoied the same, if this act had never been made, other than the person with whom she shall so consent in marriage; with power to them, and every of them, to re-enter and take possession of the same; any thing herein contained, to the contrary thereof, in any-wise, notwithstanding.

Penalty on minister, for marrying servants without leave of owner.

VI. *And be it also enacted, by the authority aforesaid, and it is hereby enacted*, That if any minister or reader shall wittingly publish, or cause or suffer to be published, the banns of matrimony, between any servants, or between any free person and a servant; or if a minister shall wittingly celebrate the rites of matrimony between any such, without a certificate from the master or mistress of every such servant, that it is done by their consent, he shall forfeit and pay ten thousand pounds of tobacco: And every servant so married, without the consent of his or her master or mistress, shall, for his or her said offence, serve his or her said master or mistress, their executors, administrators, or assigns, one whole year, after the time of service, by indenture or custom, is expired: And moreover, every person being free and so marrying with a servant, shall, for his or her said offence, forfeit and pay to the master or owner of such servant, one thousand pounds of tobacco, or well and faithfully serve the said master or owner of the said servant one whole year, in actual service.

On servants.

On free person marrying with servant.

VII. *And be it also enacted, by the authority aforesaid, and it is hereby enacted,* That the clerk of each county court, annually, in October, send to the governor, or commander in chief of this her majesty's colony and dominion, for the time being, an account of the marriage licences issued by him; and also shall deliver to the sheriff, or collector for the county, the account of the governor's dues for the said licences, to be collected by the said sheriff, or collector, for the governor's use; and each clerk failing herein, to be fined one thousand pounds of tobacco.

List of marriage licences, annually to be returned to the governor

His dues, how collected.

VIII. *And be it also enacted, by the authority aforesaid, and it is hereby enacted,* That the fees upon the said marriages, be as follows, viz.

To the governor, or commander in chief, for the time being, for each licence or marriage, twenty shillings, or two hundred pounds of tobacco.

Fees to governor.

To the clerk of the county court, issuing the same, five shillings, or fifty pounds of tobacco.

To Clerk.

To the minister, if by licence, twenty shillings, or two hundred pounds of tobacco; if by banns five shillings, or fifty pounds of tobacco.

To minister.

To the minister, or reader, for publishing banns and certifying the same, if required, one shilling and sixpence, or fifteen pounds of tobacco.

For publication of banns.

And that these, and every of these said fees, if not in ready money, shall be paid, at time of year, in tobacco, of the growth of the parish where the feme lives; and upon refusal of paiment, be leviable by distress, by such officer, or person, and in such manner as directed for clerks fees.

How collected.

IX. *And be it enacted, by the authority aforesaid, and it is hereby enacted,* That if the bridegroom live out of the county where the licence is granted, or if the clerk of the county court making out such licence, shall have ground to suspect, that the person taking out such licence intends to remove out of the county, before the time of paiment of the aforesaid dues, or is insolvent, the said clerk is hereby impowered and required, in such case, to demand and take bond of every such person or persons, with good security in the county, to pay all fees accruing due, by reason of such licence, at such time, and in such manner, as is herein before directed,

Clerk may demand security for fees.

and upon refusal of paiment, the said fees shall and may be levied on the estate of the security, by distress, as aforesaid.

Penalty for exceeding legal fees.

X. *And be it also enacted, by the authority aforesaid, and it is hereby enacted,* That if any minister shall refuse to celebrate the rites of matrimony, for the fees herein set down and allowed him; or shall exact greater or other fees than are hereby allowed to the minister, he shall forfeit and pay, for every such offence, (that is to say,) four thousand pounds of tobacco, if the marriage was, or was to have been, by licence; and five hundred pounds of tobacco, if by banns: one moiety of all the fines, forfeitures, and penalties, in this act before mentioned, and not particularly appropriated, to be to her majesty, her heirs and successors, for and towards the support of this government, and the contingent charges thereof; and the other moiety to him or them that will inform, or sue for the same: And to be recovered, with costs, by action of debt, bill, plaint, or information, in any court of record in this her majesty's colony and dominion, wherein no essoin, protection, or wager of law, shall be allowed.

Penalty for refusing to publish banns, &c.

XI. *And be it also enacted, by the authority aforesaid, and it is hereby enacted,* That if the minister or reader of any parish shall refuse to publish and certify the banns, for the fees herein set down, and allowed him; or shall exact greater or other fees, than are hereby allowed for the same, he shall, for every such offence, forfeit and pay to the party grieved, one hundred and fifty pounds of tobacco: To be recovered, with costs, before a justice of the peace.

Ministers entitled to all the fees of their parish.

XII. *Provided always,* That the minister serving the cure of any parish, shall have the benefit of the perquisites for marriages and funeral sermons in the said parish, (if he do not neglect or refuse to do the service thereof) although another minister be emploied to do the same.

Repealing clause.

XIII. *And be it further enacted,* That all and every other act and acts, and every clause and article thereof, heretofore made, for so much thereof as relates to any matter or thing whatsoever, within the purview of this act, is and are hereby repealed. and made void, to all intents and purposes, as if the same had never been made.

CHAP. XLIX.

An act concerning Servants and Slaves.

I. *Be it enacted, by the governor, council, and burgesses, of this present general assembly, and it is hereby enacted, by the authority of the same,* That all servants brought into this country without indenture, if the said servants be christians, and of christian parentage, and above nineteen years of age, shall serve but five years; and if under nineteen years of age, 'till they shall become twenty-four years of age, and no longer. How long servants shall serve.

II. *Provided always,* That every such servant be carried to the county court, within six months after his or her arrival into this colony, to have his or her age adjudged by the court, otherwise shall be a servant no longer than the accustomary five years, although much under the age of nineteen years; and the age of such servant being adjudged by the court, within the limitation aforesaid, shall be entered upon the records of the said court, and be accounted, deemed, and taken, for the true age of the said servant, in relation to the time of service aforesaid. To have their age adjudged by the court.

III. *And also be it enacted, by the authority aforesaid, and it is hereby enacted,* That when any servant sold for the custom, shall pretend to have indentures, the master or owner of such servant, for discovery of the truth thereof, may bring the said servant before a justice of the peace; and if the said servant cannot produce the indenture then, but shall still pretend to have one, the said justice shall assign two months time for the doing thereof; in which time, if the said servant shall not produce his or her indenture, it shall be taken for granted that there never was one, and shall be a bar to his or her claim of making use of one afterwards, or taking any advantage by one. When to produce their indentures.

IV. *And also be it enacted, by the authority aforesaid, and it is hereby enacted,* That all servants imported and brought into this country, by sea or land, who were not christians in their native country, (except Turks and Moors in amity with her majesty, and others that can make due proof of their being free in England, or any other christian country, before they Who shall be slaves.

were shipped, in order to transportation hither) shall be accounted and be slaves, and as such be here bought and sold notwithstanding a conversion to christianity afterwards.

Penalty for importing and selling free persons as slaves.

V. *And be it enacted, by the authority aforesaid, and it is hereby enacted,* That if any person or persons shall hereafter import into this colony, and here sell as a slave, any person or persons that shall have been a freeman in any christian country, island, or plantation, such importer and seller as aforesaid, shall forfeit and pay, to the party from whom the said freeman shall recover his freedom, double the sum for which the said freeman was sold. To be recovered, in any court of record within this colony, according to the course of the common law, wherein the defendant shall not be admitted to plead in bar, any act or statute for limitation of actions.

Being in England no discharge from slavery.

VI. *Provided always,* That a slave's being in England, shall not be sufficient to discharge him of his slavery, without other proof of his being manumitted there.

Duty of masters to servants.

VII. *And also be it enacted, by the authority aforesaid, and it is hereby enacted,* That all masters and owners of servants, shall find and provide for their servants, wholesome and competent diet, clothing, and lodging, by the discretion of the county court; and shall not, at any time, give immoderate correction; neither shall, at any time, whip a christian white servant naked, without an order from a justice of the peace: And if any, notwithstanding this act, shall presume to whip a christian white servant naked, without such order, the person so offending, shall forfeit and pay for the same, forty shillings sterling, to the party injured: To be recovered, with costs, upon petition, without the formal process of an action, as in and by this act is provided for servants complaints to be heard; provided complaint be made within six months after such whipping.

Restriction as to correction.

Complaints of servants, how redressed.

VIII. *And also be it enacted, by the authority aforesaid, and it is hereby enacted,* That all servants, (not being slaves,) whether imported, or become servants of their own accord here, or bound by any court or church-wardens, shall have their complaints received by a justice of the peace, who, if he find cause, shall bind the master over to answer the complaint at court; and it shall be there determined: And all complaints of servants, shall and may, by virtue hereof, be received at any time, upon petition, in the court of the county wherein they reside, without the formal process of an action; and also full power and authority is hereby given to the said court, by their discretion, (having first summoned the masters or owners to justify themselves, if they think fit,) to adjudge, order, and appoint what shall be necessary, as to diet, lodging, clothing, and correction: And if any master or owner shall not thereupon comply with the said court's order, the said court is hereby authorised and impowered, upon a second just complaint, to order such servant to be immediately sold at an outcry, by the sheriff, and after charges deducted, the remainder of what the said servant shall be sold for, to be paid and satisfied to such owner. Remedy on second complaint.

IX. *Provided always, and be it enacted,* That if such servant be so sick or lame, or otherwise rendered so uncapable, that he or she cannot be sold for such a value, at least, as shall satisfy the fees, and other incident charges accrued, the said court shall then order the church-wardens of the parish to take care of and provide for the said servant, until such servant's time, due by law to the said master, or owner, shall be expired, or until such servant, shall be so recovered, as to be sold for defraying the said fees and charges: And further, the said court, from time to time, shall order the charges of keeping the said servant, to be levied upon the goods and chattels of the master or owner of the said servant, by distress. Sick and disabled servants, how provided for.

X. *And be it also enacted,* That all servants, whether, by importation, indenture, or hire here, as well feme coverts, as others, shall, in like manner, as is provided, upon complaints of misusage, have their petitions received in court, for their wages and freedom, without the formal process of an action; and proceedings, and judgment, shall, in like manner, also, be had thereupon. Servants wages, how recovered.

XI. And for a further christian care and usage of all christian servants, *Be it also enacted, by the authority aforesaid, and it is hereby enacted,* That no negros, mulattos, or Indians, although christians, or Jews, Moors, Negroes, &c. disabled from purchasing servants.

Mahometans, or other infidels, shall, at any time, purchase any christian servant, nor any other, except of their own complexion, or such as are declared slaves by this act: And if any negro, mulatto, or Indian, Jew, Moor, Mahometan, or other infidel, or such as are declared slaves by this act, shall, notwithstanding, purchase any christian white servant, the said servant shall, *ipso facto*, become free and acquit from any service then due, and shall be so held, deemed, and taken: And if any person, having such christian servant, shall intermarry with any such negro, mulatto, or Indian, Jew, Moor, Mahometan, or other infidel, every christian white servant of every such person so intermarrying, shall, *ipso facto*, become free and acquit from any service then due to such master or mistress so intermarrying, as aforesaid.

Intermarrying with such.

Contracts of masters with their servants void unless approved in court.

XII. *And also be it enacted, by the authority aforesaid, and it is hereby enacted,* That no master or owner of any servant shall during the time of such servant's servitude, make any bargain with his or her said servant for further service, or other matter or thing relating to liberty, or personal profit, unless the same be made in the presence, and with the approbation, of the court of that county where the master or owner resides: And if any servants shall, at any time bring in goods or money, or during the time of their service, by gift, or any other lawful ways or means, come to have any goods or money, they shall enjoy the propriety thereof, and have the sole use and benefit thereof to themselves. And if any servant shall happen to fall sick or lame, during the time of service, so that he or she becomes of little or no use to his or her master or owner, but rather a charge, the said master or owner shall not put away the said servant, but shall maintain him or her, during the whole time he or she was before obliged to serve, by indenture, custom, or order of court: And if any master or owner, shall put away any such sick or lame servant, upon pretence of freedom, and that servant shall become chargeable to the parish, the said master or owner shall forfeit and pay ten pounds current money of Virginia, to the church-wardens of the parish where such offence shall be committed, for the use of the said parish: To be recovered by action of debt, in any court of record in this her majesty's co-

Property in goods.

Sick, not to be discharged.

lony and dominion, in which no essoin, protection, or wager of law, shall be allowed.

Freedom dues.

XIII. And whereas there has been a good and laudable custom of allowing servants corn and cloaths for their present support, upon their freedom; but nothing in that nature ever made certain, *Be it also enacted, by the authority aforesaid, and it is hereby enacted,* That there shall be paid and allowed to every imported servant, not having yearly wages, at the time of service ended, by the master or owner of such servant, viz: To every male servant, ten bushels of indian corn, thirty shillings in money, or the value thereof, in goods, and one well fixed musket or fuzee, of the value of twenty shillings, at least: and to every woman servant, fifteen bushels of indian corn, and forty shillings in money, or the value thereof, in goods: Which, upon refusal, shall be ordered, with costs, upon petition to the county court, in manner as is herein before directed, for servants complaints to be heard.

Penalty on servants resisting their masters

XIV. *And also be it enacted, by the authority aforesaid, and it is hereby enacted,* That all servants shall faithfully and obediently, all the whole time of their service, do all their masters or owners just and lawful commands. And if any servant shall resist the master, or mistress, or overseer, or offer violence to any of them, the said servant shall, for every such offence, be adjudged to serve his or her said master or owner, one whole year after the time, by indenture, custom, or former order of court, shall be expired.

Penalty for dealing with servants, or slaves, without leave of their owners.

XV. *And also be it enacted, by the authority aforesaid, and it is hereby enacted,* That no person whatsoever shall buy, sell, or receive of, to, or from, any servant, or slave, any coin or commodity whatsoever, without the leave, licence, or consent of the master or owner of the said servant, or slave: And if any person shall, contrary hereunto, without the leave or licence aforesaid, deal with any servant, or slave, he or she so offending, shall be imprisoned one calender month, without bail or main-prize; and then, also continue in prison, until he or she shall find good security, in the sum of ten pounds current money of Virginia, for the good behaviour for one year following; wherein, a second offence shall be a breach of the bond; and moreover shall forfeit and pay four times the value of the things so bought, sold, or received, to the master or owner of such servant, or slave: To be recovered, with costs, by action upon the case, in any court of record in this her majesty's colony and dominion, wherein no essoin, protection, or wager of law, or other than one imparlance, shall be allowed.

Punishment by stripes.

XVI. *Provided always, and be it enacted,* That when any person or persons convict for dealing with a servant, or slave, contrary to this act, shall not immediately give good and sufficient security for his or her good behaviour, as aforesaid: then, in such case, the court shall order thirty-nine lashes, well laid on, upon the bare back of such offender, at the common whipping-post of the county, and the said offender to be thence discharged of giving such bond and security.

Servants may be whipped, in lieu of fines, for a breach of penal laws.

XVII.* *And also be it enacted, by the authority aforesaid, and it is hereby enacted, and declared,* That in all cases of penal laws, whereby persons free are punishable by fine, servants shall be punished by whipping, after the rate of twenty lashes for every five hundred pounds of tobacco, or fifty shillings current money, unless the servant so culpable, can and will procure some person or persons to pay the fine; in which case, the said servant shall be adjudged to serve such benefactor, after the time by indenture, custom, or order of court, to his or her then present master or owner, shall be expired, after the rate of one month and a half for every hundred pounds of tobacco; any thing in this act contained, to the contrary, in any-wise, notwithstanding.

Women servants having bastards.

XVIII. And if any women servant shall be delivered of a bastard child within the time of her service aforesaid, *Be it enacted, by the authority aforesaid, and it is hereby enacted,* That in recompence of the loss and trouble occasioned her master or mistress thereby, she shall for every such offence, serve her said master or owner one whole year after her time by indenture, custom, and former order of court, shall be expired; or pay her said master or owner, one thousand pounds of tobacco; and the reputed father, if free, shall give security to the church-wardens of the parish where that child shall be, to maintain the child, and keep the parish indemnified; or be compelled thereto by order of the county court, upon the said church-wardens

Duty of reputed father.

complaint: But if a servant, he shall make satisfaction to the parish, for keeping the said child, after his time by indenture, custom, or order of court, to his then present master or owner, shall be expired; or be compelled thereto, by order of the county court, upon complaint of the church-wardens of the said parish, for the time being. And if any woman servant shall be got with child by her master, neither the said master, nor his executors administrators, nor assigns, shall have any claim of service against her, for or by reason of such child; but she shall, when her time due to her said master, by indenture, custom or order of court, shall be expired, be sold by the church-wardens, for the time being, of the parish wherein such child shall be born, for one year, or pay one thousand pounds of tobacco; and the said one thousand pounds of tobacco, or whatever she shall be sold for, shall be emploied, by the vestry, to the use of the said parish. And if any woman servant shall have a bastard child by a negro, or mulatto, over and above the years service due to her master or owner, she shall immediately, upon the expiration of her time to her then present master or owner, pay down to the church-wardens of the parish wherein such child shall be born, for the use of the said parish, fifteen pounds current money of Virginia, or be by them sold for five years, to the use aforesaid: And if a free christian white woman shall have such bastard child, by a negro, or mulatto, for every such offence, she shall, within one month after her delivery of such bastard child, pay to the church-wardens for the time being, of the parish wherein such child shall be born, for the use of the said parish fifteen pounds current money of Virginia, or be by them sold for five years to the use aforesaid: And in both the said cases, the church-wardens shall bind the said child to be a servant, until it shall be of thirty one years of age.

Master getting his servant with child.

Women servants having bastards by negroes.

Or free women.

How long the child to be bound.

XIX. And for a further prevention of that abominable mixture and spurious issue, which hereafter may increase in this her majesty's colony and dominion, as well by English, and other white men and women intermarrying with negros or mulattos, as by their unlawful coition with them, *Be it enacted, by the authority aforesaid, and it is hereby enacted*, That whatsoever English, or other white man or woman, being free,

Penalty on white persons marrying with negroes.

shall intermarry with a negro or mulatto man or woman, bond or free, shall, by judgment of the county court, be committed to prison, and there remain, during the space of six months, without bail or mainprize; and shall forfeit and pay ten pounds current money of Virginia, to the use of the parish, as aforesaid.

On ministers marrying them.

XX. *And be it further enacted*, That no minister of the church of England, or other minister, or person whatsoever, within this colony and dominion, shall hereafter wittingly presume to marry a white man with a negro or mulatto woman; or to marry a white woman with a negro or mulatto man, upon pain of forfeiting and paying, for every such marriage the sum of ten thousand pounds of tobacco; one half to our sovereign lady the Queen, her heirs and successors, for and towards the support of the government, and the contingent charges thereof; and the other half to the informer: To be recovered, with costs, by action of debt, bill, plaint, or information, in any court of record within this her majesty's colony and dominion, wherein no essoin, protection, or wager of law, shall be allowed.

Freedom of servants to be recorded.

XXI. And because poor people may not be destitute of emploiment, upon suspicion of being servants, and servants also kept from running away, *Be it enacted, by the authority aforesaid, and it is hereby enacted*, That every servant, when his or her time of service shall be expired, shall repair to the court of the county where he or she served the last of his or her time, and there, upon sufficient testimony, have his or her freedom entered; and a certificate thereof from the clerk of the said court, shall be sufficient to authorise any person to entertain or hire such servant, without any danger of this law. And if it shall at any time happen, that such certificate is worn out, or lost, the said clerk shall grant a new one, and therein also recite the accident happened to the old one. And whoever shall hire such servant, shall take his or her certificate, and keep it, 'till the contracted time shall be expired. And if any person whatsoever, shall harbour or entertain any servant by importation, or by contract, or indenture made here, not having such certificate, he or she so offending, shall pay to the master or owner of such servant, sixty pounds of tobacco for every natural day he

Penalty for entertaining them without certificate.

or she shall so harbour or entertain such runaway: To be recovered, with costs, by action of debt, in any court of record within this her majesty's colony and dominion, wherein no essoin, protection, or wager of law, shall be allowed. And also, if any runaway shall make use of a forged certificate, or after the same shall be delivered to any master or mistress, upon being hired, shall steal the same away, and thereby procure entertainment, the person entertaining such servant, upon such forged or stolen certificate, shall not be culpable by this law: But the said runaway, besides making reparation for the loss of time, and charges in recovery, and other penalties by this law directed, shall, for making use of such forged or stolen certificate, or for such theft aforesaid, stand two hours in the pillory, upon a court day: And the person forging such certificate, shall forfeit and pay ten pounds current money; one half thereof to be to her majesty, her heirs and successors, for and towards the support of this government, and the contingent charges thereof; and the other half to the master or owner of such servant, if he or she will inform or sue for the same, otherwise to the informer: To be recovered, with costs, by action of debt, bill, plaint or information, in any court of record in this her majesty's colony and dominion, wherein no essoin, protection, or wager of law, shall be allowed. And if any person or persons convict of forging such certificate, shall not immediately pay the said ten pounds, and costs, or give security to do the same within six months, he or she so convict, shall receive, on his or her bare back, thirty-nine lashes, well laid on, at the common whipping post of the county; and shall be thence discharged of paying the said ten pounds, and costs, and either of them.

Runaways forging or stealing certificates.

XXII. *Provided*, That when any master or mistress shall happen to hire a runaway, upon a forged certificate, and a servant deny that he delivered any such certificate, the *Onus Probandi* shall lie upon the person hiring, who upon failure therein, shall be liable to the fines and penalties, for entertaining runaway servants, without certificate.

Runaways hired on a forged certificate.

XXIII. And for encouragement of all persons to take up runaways, *Be it enacted, by the authority aforesaid, and it is hereby enacted*, That for the taking up of

Reward for taking up runaways.

every servant, or slave, if ten miles, or above, from the house or quarter where such servant, or slave was kept, there shall be allowed by the public, as a reward to the taker-up, two hundred pounds of tobacco; and if above five miles, and under ten, one hundred pounds of tobacco: Which said several rewards of two hundred, and one hundred pounds of tobacco, shall also be paid in the county where such taker-up shall reside, and shall be again levied by the public upon the master or owner of such runaway, for re-imbursement of the same to the public. And for the greater certainty in paying the said rewards and re-imbursement of the public, every justice of the peace before whom such runaway shall be brought, upon the taking up, shall mention the proper-name and sur-name of the taker-up, and the county of his or her residence, together with the time and place of taking up the said runaway; and shall also mention the name of the said runaway, and the proper-nâme and sur-name of the master or owner of such runaway, and the county of his or her residence, together with the distance of miles, in the said justice's judgment, from the place of taking up the said runaway, to the house or quarter where such runaway was kept.

(Repealed by ch. 4, 1726.)

XXIV. *Provided*, That when any negro, or other runaway, that doth not speak English, and cannot, or through obstinacy will not, declare the name of his or her masters or owner, that then it shall be sufficient for the said justice to certify the same, instead of the name of such runaway, and the proper name and sur-name of his or her master or owner, and the county of his or her residence and distance of miles, as aforesaid; and in such case, shall, by his warrant, order the said runaway to be conveyed to the public gaol, of this country, there to be continued prisoner until the master or owner shall be known; who, upon paying the charges of the imprisonment, or giving caution to the prison-keeper for the same, together with the reward of two hundred or one hundred pounds of tobacco, as the case shall be, shall have the said runaway restored.

Runaways to be sent from constable to constable and whipt.

XXV. And further, the said justice of the peace, when such runaway shall be brought before him, shall, by his warrant commit the said runaway to the next constable, and therein also order him to give the said runaway so many lashes as the said justice shall think fit, not exceeding the number of thirty-nine; and then to be conveyed from constable to constable, until the said runaway shall be carried home, or to the country gaol, as aforesaid, every constable through whose hands the said runaway shall pass, giving a receipt at the delivery; and every constable failing to execute such warrant according to the tenor thereof, or refusing to give such receipt, shall forfeit and pay two hundred pounds of tobacco to the church-wardens of the parish wherein such failure shall be, for the use of the poor of the said parish: To be recovered, with costs, by action of debt, in any court of record in this her majesty's colony and dominion, wherein no essoin, protection or wager of law, shall be allowed. And such corporal punishment shall not deprive the master or owner of such runaway of the other satisfaction here in this act appointed to be made upon such servant's running away.

XXVI. *Provided always, and be it further enacted*, That when any servant or slave, in his or her running away, shall have crossed the great bay of Chesapeak, and shall be brought before a justice of the peace, the said justice shall, instead of committing such runaway to the constable, commit him or her to the sheriff, who is hereby required to receive every such runaway, according to such warrant, and to cause him, her, or them, to be transported again across the bay, and delivered to a constable there; and shall have, for all his trouble and charge herein, for every such servant or slave, five hundred pounds of tobacco, paid by the public; which shall be re-imbursed again by the master or owner of such runaway, as aforesaid, in manner aforesaid. How transported over the bay. Sheriff's fee.

XXVII. *Provided also*, That when any runaway servant that shall have crossed the said bay, shall get up into the country, in any county distant from the bay, that then, in such case, the said runaway shall be committed to a constable, to be conveyed from constable to constable, until he shall be brought to a sheriff of some county adjoining to the said bay of Chesapeak, which sheriff is also hereby required, upon such warrant, to receive such runaway, under the rules and conditions aforesaid; and cause him or her to be conveyed as aforesaid; and shall have the reward, as aforesaid. Runaways crossing the bay.

XXVIII. And for the better preventing of delays in returning of such runaways, *Be it enacted*, That if any Penalty on sheriff's suffering runaways to work.

sheriff, under sheriff, or other officer of, or belonging to the sheriffs, shall cause or suffer any such runaway (so committed for passage over the bay) to work, the said sheriff, to whom such runaway shall be so committed, shall forfeit and pay to the master or owner, of every such servant or slave, so put to work, one thousand pounds of tobacco; To be recovered, with costs, by action of debt, bill, plaint, or information, in any court of record within this her majesty's colony and dominion, wherein no essoin, protection, or wager of law, shall be allowed.

Suffering to escape.

XXIX. *And be it enacted, by the authority aforesaid, and it is hereby enacted*, That if any constable, or sheriff, into whose hands a runaway servant or slave shall be committed, by virtue of this act, shall suffer such runaway to escape, the said constable or sheriff shall be liable to the action of the party grieved, for recovery of his damages, at the common law with costs.

Runaways to repay all expences.

XXX. *And also be it enacted, by the authority aforesaid, and it is hereby enacted*, That every runaway servant, upon whose account, either of the rewards aforementioned shall be paid, for taking up, shall for every hundred pounds of tobacco so paid by the master or owner, serve his or her said master or owner, after his or her time by indenture, custom, or former order of court, shall be expired, one calendar month and an half, and moreover, shall serve double the time such servant shall be absent in such running away; and shall also make reparation, by service, to the said master or owner, for all necessary disbursements and charges, in pursuit and recovery of the said runaway; to be adjudged and allowed in the county court, after the rate of one year for eight hundred pounds of tobacco, and so proportionably for a greater or lesser quantity.

To be allowed by county court.

Proviso.

XXXI. *Provided*, That the masters or owners of such runaways, shall carry them to court the next court held for the said county, after the recovery of such runaway, otherwise it shall be in the breast of the court to consider the occasion of delay, and to hear, or refuse the claim, according to their discretion, without appeal, for the refusal.

Penalty for permitting slaves of others to remain on a plantation.

XXXII. *And also be it enacted, by the authority aforesaid, and it is hereby enacted*, That no master, mistress, or overseer of a family, shall knowingly permit any slave, not belonging to him or her, to be and remain upon his or her plantation, above four hours at any one time, without the leave of such slave's master, mistress, or overseer, on penalty of one hundred and fifty pounds of tobacco to the informer; cognizable by a justice of the peace of the county wherein such offence shall be committed.

Runaway servants may give security to repay expenses.

XXXIII. *Provided also,* That if any runaway servant, adjudged to serve for the charges of his or her pursuit and recovery, shall, at the time, he or she is so adjudged, repay and satisfy, or give good security before the court, for repaiment and satisfaction of the same, to his or her master or owner, within six months after, such master or owner shall be obliged to accept thereof, in lieu of the service given and allowed for such charges and disbursements.

Killing slaves, under correction, no felony.

XXXIV. And if any slave resist his master, or owner, or other person, by his or her order, correcting such slave, and shall happen to be killed in such correction, it shall not be accounted felony; but the master, owner, and every such other person so giving correction, shall be free and acquit of all punishment and accusation for the same, as if such accident had never happened: And also, if any negro, mulatto, or Indian, bond or free, shall at any time, lift his or her hand, in opposition against any christian, not being negro, mulatto, or Indian, he or she so offending, shall, for every such offence, proved by the oath of the party, receive on his or her bare back, thirty lashes, well laid on; cognizable by a justice of the peace for that county wherein such offence shall be committed.

Penalty on slave resisting a white person.

Guns, &c. found in possession of slaves.

XXXV. *And also be it enacted, by the authority aforesaid, and it is hereby enacted,* That no slave go armed with gun, sword, club, staff, or other weapon, nor go from off the plantation and seat of land where such slave shall be appointed to live, without a certificate of leave in writing, for so doing, from his or her master, mistress, or overseer: And if any slave shall be found offending herein, it shall be lawful for any person or persons to apprehend and deliver such slave to the next constable or head-borough, who is hereby enjoined and required, without further order or warrant, to give such slave twenty lashes on his or her bare back, well laid on, and so send him or her home: And all horses, cattle, and hogs, now belonging, or that hereafter shall be-

Horses, &c. belonging to slaves may be seized.

long to any slave, or of any slaves mark in this her majesty's colony and dominion, shall be seised and sold by the church-wardens of the parish, wherein such horses, cattle, or hogs shall be, and the profit thereof applied to the use of the poor of the said parish: And also, if any damage shall be hereafter committed by any slave living at a quarter where there is no christian overseer, the master or owner of such slave shall be liable to action for the trespass and damage, as if the same had been done by him or herself.

Owners of slaves, at a quarter, without an overseer liable for their trespasses.

Baptism of slaves.

Children bond, or free, according to condition of their mothers.

XXXVI. *And also it is hereby enacted and declared*, That baptism of slaves doth not exempt them from bondage; and that all children shall be bond or free, according to the condition of their mothers, and the particular directions of this act.

Outlying slaves how apprehended.

XXXVII. And whereas, many times, slaves run away and lie out, hid and lurking in swamps, woods, and other obscure places, killing hogs, and committing other injuries to the inhabitants of this her majesty's colony and dominion, *Be it therefore enacted, by the authority aforesaid, and it is hereby enacted*, That in all such cases, upon intelligence given of any slaves lying out, as aforesaid, any two justices *(Quorum unus)* of the peace of the county wherein such slave is supposed to lurk or do mischief, shall be and are impowered and required to issue proclamation against all such slaves, reciting their names, and owners names, if they are known, and thereby requiring them, and every of them, forthwith to surrender themselves; and also impowering the sheriff of the said county, to take such power with him, as he shall think fit and necessary, for the effectual apprehending such out-lying slave or slaves, and go in search of them: Which proclamation shall be published on a Sabbath day, at the door of every church and chapel, in the said county, by the parish clerk, or reader, of the church, immediately after divine worship: And in case any slave, against whom proclamation hath been thus issued, and once published at any church or chapel, as aforesaid, stay out, and do not immediately return home, it shall be lawful for any person or persons whatsoever, to kill and destroy such slaves by such ways and means as he, she, or they shall think fit, without accusation or impeachment of any crime for the same: And if any slave, that hath run a-

When they may be killed.

When may be

way and lain out as aforesaid, shall be apprehended by the sheriff, or any other person, upon the application of the owner of the said slave, it shall and may be lawful for the county court, to order such punishment to the said slave, either by dismembring, or any other way, not touching his life, as they in their discretion shall think fit, for the reclaiming any such incorrigible slave, and terrifying others from the like practices.

dismembered.

XXXVIII. *Provided always, and it is further enacted,* That for every slave killed, in pursuance of this act, or put to death by law, the master or owner of such slave shall be paid by the public:

Value of slaves killed, to be repaid by the public.

XXXIX. And to the end, the true value of every slave killed, or put to death, as aforesaid, may be the better known; and by that means, the assembly the better enabled to make a suitable allowance thereupon, *Be it enacted,* That upon application of the master or owner of any such slave, to the court appointed for proof of public claims, the said court shall value the slave in money, and the clerk of the court shall return a certificate thereof to the assembly, with the rest of the public claims.

Court of claims to certify the value.

XL. And for the better putting this act in due execution, and that no servants or slaves may have pretense of ignorance hereof, *Be it also enacted,* That the church-wardens of each parish in this her majesty's colony and dominion, at the charge of the parish, shall provide a true copy of this act, and cause entry thereof to be made in the register book of each parish respectively; and that the parish clerk, or reader of each parish, shall, on the first sermon Sundays in September and March, annually, after sermon or divine service is ended, at the door of every church and chapel in their parish, publish the same; and the sheriff of each county shall, at the next court held for the county, after the last day of February, yearly, publish this act, at the door of the court-house: And every sheriff making default herein, shall forfeit and pay six hundred pounds of tobacco; one half to her majesty, her heirs, and successors, for and towards the support of the government; and the other half to the informer. And every parish clerk, or reader, making default herein, shall, for each time so offending, forfeit and pay six hundred

This act to be registered in each parish, and read.

pounds of tobacco; one half whereof to be to the informer; and the other half to the poor of the parish, wherein such omission shall be: To be recovered, with costs, by action of debt, bill, plaint, or information, in any court of record in this her majesty's colony and dominion, wherein no essoin, protection, or wager of law, shall be allowed.

Repealing clause.

XLI. *And be it further enacted*, That all and every other act and acts, and every clause and article thereof, heretofore made, for so much thereof as relates to servants and slaves, or to any other matter or thing whatsoever, within the purview of this act, is and are hereby repealed, and made void, to all intents and purposes, as if the same had never been made.

CHAP. L.

An act to prevent killing Deer at unseasonable times.

Penalty for killing deer between certain periods.

I. FOR the prevention of killing deer at unseasonable times, *Be it enacted, by the governor, council, and burgesses, of this present general assembly, and it is hereby enacted, by the authority of the same*, That it shall not be lawful to kill or destroy any deer running wild in the woods, or unfenced grounds of this colony and dominion, by gun, or any other ways or means whatsoever, between the first day of January in each year, and last day of August succeeding; or to buy or receive of any Indian, or other person whatsoever, any deer killed or destroied within the times aforesaid: And if any person, not being a servant or slave, shall kill or destroy any deer, contrary to this act, or shall buy or receive of any Indian, or other person whatsoever, any deer killed or destroied, contrary to this act, and be thereof lawfully convicted, the said person, for every deer so killed or destroied, or bought or received, as aforesaid, shall forfeit and pay the sum of five hundred pounds of tobacco.

When servants or slaves kill deer by order of their masters.

II. *And be it further enacted, by the authority aforesaid, and it is hereby enacted*, That if any servant or slave, by order or command of his or her master, mistress, or overseer, shall kill or destroy, or buy or receive any deer, contrary to this act, the master, mistress, or overseer, giving such order or command, being thereof lawfully convicted, for every deer so killed or destroied, or bought or received, as aforesaid, shall forfeit and pay the aforesaid penalty of five hundred pounds of tobacco, as if the said master, mistress, or overseer, had actually committed the offence.

Where without order to be whipped.

III. *And be it further enacted, by the authority aforesaid, and it is hereby enacted,* That if any servant or slave, of his or her own accord, without any order or command from his or her master, mistress, or overseer, shall kill or destroy, or buy or receive any deer contrary to this act, and be thereof convicted, by the oath of one credible witness before a justice of the peace of the county wherein the offence is committed, for every deer so killed or destroied, or bought or received, as aforesaid, the said servant or slave shall have and receive, on his or her bare back, thirty lashes well laid on, to be inflicted by order of the justice, before whom the conviction shall be; unless some sufficient person will become bound to pay for the said servant or slave, the sum of five hundred pounds of tobacco, within six months, in lieu of the punishment aforesaid, to the church-wardens of the parish where the offence is committed, for the uses directed by this act.

Fines appropriated.

IV. *And be it enacted, by the authority aforesaid, and it is hereby enacted,* That one moiety of the forfeitures of this act, shall be to the church-wardens of the parish where the offence is committed, for the use of the parish; and the other moiety to the informer: To be recovered, with costs, in any court of record within this colony and dominion, by action of debt, bill, plaint, or information, wherein no essoin, protection, or wager of law, shall be allowed.

Repealing clause.

V. *And be it further enacted,* That all and every other act and acts, and every clause and article thereof, heretofore made, for so much thereof as relates to killing deer, or any other matter or thing, within the purview of this act, is and are hereby repealed, and made void, to all intents and purposes, as if the same had never been made.

CHAP. LI.

See chap. 5. 1726.

An act to explain part of an act of this present session of assembly, intituled, An act directing the manner of levying executions; and for relief of poor prisoners for debt.

[From MS.]

Preamble.

WHEREAS, by one act past at this present session of assembly, entituled an act directing the manner of levying executions, and for relief of poor prisoners for debt, it is directed that when any goods or chattels are taken in execution for any debt they shall remain a certain time in that act expressed before they shall be appraised, now for the better and more certain understanding of the said act,

If the debtor tender to the sheriff, the amount of execution, within three days, the goods so taken to be restored.

Be it enacted, by the governor, councill, and burgesses of this present generall assembly, and it is hereby enacted, and declared by the authority of the same, That when any goods or chattels shall be seized or taken in execution, either by a writ of fieri facias or levari facias, the party from whom the same shall be taken, shall have the liberty of three naturall days (Sundays exclusive) from and after the time of such seizure to make payment of what shall be due, and if in that time he or she shall offer to pay unto the sheriff or other officer in whose custody the goods and chattels shall be, the sum comanded to be levyed by the said execution (with such costs as are also to be levyed) either in money or such other specie as shall be due, then and in such case the said sheriff or other officer is hereby required to accept of such payment and thereupon to discharge the goods and chattels so taken in execution and every part thereof, as if the same had never been seized or taken; any law, custom, or usage, to the contrary in any-wise, notwithstanding.

CHAP. LII.

See vol. 1 & 2, Index, tit. INDIANS.

An act for prevention of misunderstandings between the tributary Indians, *and other her majesty's subjects of this colony and dominion; and for a free and open trade with all Indians whatsoever.*

I. FOR prevention of all manner of animosities, jealousies, fears, misunderstandings, and differences whatsoever, between the tributary Indians and other her majesty's subjects of this colony and dominion, as also the several revenges and mischiefs which may thereupon be sought after and ensue,

Tributary Indians disabled from conveying lands.

II. *Be it enacted, by the Governor, Council and Burgesses of this present general assembly, and it is hereby enacted, by the authority of the same,* That it shall not be lawful for an Indian king, or any other of the said tributary Indians whatsoever, to bargain and sell, or demise to any person or persons, other than to some of their own nation, or their posterity in fee, for life, or for years, the lands laid out and appropriated for the use of the said Indians, or any part or parcel thereof; or to bargain and sell, as aforesaid, any other land whatsoever, now actually possessed, or justly claimed and pretended to by the said Indians, or any of them, by virtue of the articles of peace made and concluded with the said Indians, the twenty-ninth day of May, one thousand six hundred and seventy-seven, or by virtue of any other right or title whatsoever; and that every bargain, sale, or demise hereafter made, contrary to this act, as aforesaid, shall be and is hereby declared to be null and void, to all intents, constructions, and purposes whatsoever.

Penalty for taking conveyances from Indians.

III. *And be it further enacted, by the authority aforesaid,* That if any person or persons, (other than the Indians, and their posterity) shall, from and after the publication of this act, presume to purchase or obtain any deed or conveyance in fee, or any lease for years, from any of the tributary Indians, of any lands, tenements, or hereditaments laid out or appropriated, or now actually possessed, or justly claimed and pretended to, by the said Indians; or shall occupy or tend any of the said lands, by permission of the said Indians, or otherwise, every person or persons so offending, and being thereof lawfully convicted, in any court of record within this colony, shall forfeit and pay the sum of ten shillings current money, for every acre of land so purchased, leased or occupied: And for every year during the continuance of the possession, or occupation of any lands, by virtue of such purchase or lease, the person or persons so offending, shall forfeit and pay the sum of ten shillings current money for every acre of land so possessed or occupied, as aforesaid; one moiety of which said forfeitures shall be to our sovereign lady the Queen, her heirs and successors, for and towards the better support of the government of this her majesty's colony and dominion, and the contingent charges thereof; and the other moiety to the informer: To be recovered by action of debt, bill, plaint, or information, wherein no essoin, protection, or wager of law, shall be allowed.

Proviso in favour of some individuals.

IV. *Provided nevertheless*, That it shall and may be lawful for the general court of this dominion, to receive and examine the several claims of George Shilling, to three hundred acres of land; of Michael Waldrop, to ninety acres of land; and of the heir of George Southerland, deceased, to two hundred acres of land: All which lands are said to be part of the lands laid out for the Pamunkey Indians; and if it shall appear to the said court, that the said persons or any of them, have as equitable pretensions to the said lands, as those persons had, who have already obtained patents for other part of the land laid out for the said Indians, then it shall be lawful for the governor, or commander in chief of this dominion, for the time being, by and with the advice and consent of the council, to grant patents to the several persons before named, (or so many of them as make the equity of their pretensions appear) for the said several quantities of land by them claimed respectively, if there shall be so much contained within their bounds, but not for any greater quantity, although their bounds contain the same.

V. And to the end, no different constructions may be made concerning the sense and meaning of a certain clause contained in the aforesaid articles of peace in these words, 'It is hereby concluded and established, 'that no English shall seat or plant, nearer than three miles of any Indian town,'

Explanation of a clause in the articles of peace.

VI. *Be it enacted, by the authority aforesaid, and it is hereby enacted and declared*, That where an Indian town is seated, on or near a navigable river, and the English have already seated and planted within three miles of the said town, on the opposite side of the river, the said clause shall not be construed, deemed, or taken, to give the said Indian town any privilege on the said opposite side: But in such a case, the privilege of the said Indian town, shall be limited by the river.

VII. *And be it further enacted, by the authority aforesaid, and it is hereby enacted,* That the Indians tributary to this government, shall be well secured and defended in their persons, goods, and properties; and that whosoever shall defraud, or take from them, their goods, or do hurt or injury to their persons, shall make satisfaction, and be punished for the same, according to law, as if the Indian sufferer had been an Englishman.

Tributary Indians, protected by the laws.

VIII. *And be it further enacted, by the authority aforesaid, and it is hereby enacted,* That the Indians tributary to this government, shall have and enjoy their wonted conveniencies of oistering and fishing, and of gathering, on the lands belonging to the English, tuckahoe, cuttenemons, wild oats, rushes, puckoon, or other things, not useful to the English, upon a licence first had from a justice of the peace of the county where they come for those purposes: And if any Englishman take from any of the said Indians, any goods, or kill, wound, or maim any one of them, as they come in, whilst they tarry, or as they return, he shall be punished, and suffer, as if he had done the same thing to an Englishman.

May be licenced to oyster, fish, &c.

IX. *Provided always, and it is hereby meant and intended,* That the said Indians shall not bring with them any guns, ammunition, or offensive weapons, but tools only for their use; that they shall not presume to oister, fish, and gather tuckahoe, or other things, as aforesaid, without a licence first had from a justice of the peace, as aforesaid; that the justice, in his licence, shall limit the time of the Indians stay; and that it shall not be lawful for the Indians to tarry beyond the time limited.

But shall not carry offensive weapons.

X. *And be it further enacted, by the authority aforesaid, and it is hereby enacted,* That all Indian kings and queens tributary to this government, having the least notice of a march of strange Indians near the English quarters or plantations, shall forthwith repair, or at least send one of their great men, to the next militia officer, to acquaint him what they know of their nation, number, and design, and which way they bend their course; and if the tributary Indians then desire any aid against the strange Indians, the colonel of the militia in those parts, shall forthwith send out a convenient party of the said militia to join with them for their better defence and security on that occasion.

Shall give notice of approach of strange Indians.

Shall march with the English.

XI. *And be it further enacted, by the authority aforesaid, and it is hereby enacted,* That all Indians tributary to, and under the protection of this government, shall march, with the English, in pursuit of foreign Indians, whensoever they are thereunto commanded, and shall continue with the English in the said pursuit as the occasion requires.

Free trade with all Indians.

XII. *And be it further enacted, by the authority aforesaid, and it is hereby enacted,* That there be a free and open trade for all persons, at all times, and at all places, with all Indians whatsoever.

Sale of rum or brandy, prohibited in Indian towns, or on their lands.

XIII. *Provided always, and be it enacted, by the authority aforesaid,* That if any person or persons shall after the publication of this act, sell, or offer to sale, any rum, or brandy, within any town of the tributary Indians, or to any Indian, upon any land belonging to any such town; every such person or persons so offending, and being thereof lawfully convicted before any justice of the peace of the county where the offence shall be committed, shall forfeit and pay ten shillings current money, for every quart of rum, or brandy sold, or offered to sale, as aforesaid, and so proportionably for a greater or lesser quantity; one moiety of which fines shall be to her majesty, her heirs and successors, for and towards the support of the government of this colony, and the contingent charges thereof: and the other moiety to the informer.

Discoveries westward of the mountains, may be encouraged by charters of incorporation.

XIV. *Provided nevertheless, and be it enacted,* That if any person or persons shall hereafter, at his or their own charge, make discovery of any town or nation of Indians, situate or inhabiting to the westward of, or between the Appalatian mountains; in such case, it shall be lawful to and for the governor, or commander in chief of this dominion, for the time being, by and with the advice and consent of her majesty's council of state, by charter or grant, under the seal of the colony, to grant, unto such person or persons so discovering, as aforesaid, and to their executors, administrators, and assigns, for the space of fourteen years then next coming, the sole liberty and right of trading to and with all and every such town or towns, nation or nations of Indians so discovered as aforesaid, with such clauses or articles of restraint or prohibition of all other

* See ante ch. IX, 1691, and notes.

persons from the said trade, and under such penalties and forfeitures as shall be thought convenient: Which said charter or grant is hereby enacted and declared to be good and valid in law, to the intents and purposes therein mentioned; and all and every clause and article thereof shall be observed, fulfilled, and obeyed, under the penalties and forfeitures therein to be contained: And if occasion shall so require, the said governor, or commander in chief, with the advice and consent of the council, as aforesaid, is hereby impowered, by such charter or grant as aforesaid, to make and constitute such discoveries and such other persons as they shall desire, to be one body corporate and politic, by such name, in such manner, and with such liberties and privileges as shall appear to be necessary, for the better enabling them to make the most benefit and advantage of the said trade exclusive of all other persons; any thing in this act contained to the contrary, or seeming to the contrary, in any-wise, notwithstanding.

XV. *And be it further enacted*, That all and every other act and acts, and every clause and article thereof, heretofore made, for so much thereof as relates to the tributary Indians; or to a free and open trade with all Indians; or any other matter or thing whatsoever, within the purview of this act, except one act made at a general assembly, held by prorogation, the eighteenth day of April, one thousand seven hundred and five, intituled, *An act concerning the* Nansiaitico, *and other* Indians, is and are hereby repealed, and made void, to all intents and purposes, as if the same had never been made. **Repealing clause.**

CHAP. LIII.

An act for the regulation and settlement of Ferries; and for the dispatch of public expresses.

I. Whereas a good regulation of ferries in this her majesty's colony and dominion will prove very useful for the dispatch of public affairs, and for the ease and benefit of travellers, and men in business, **Preamble.**

II. ***Be it therefore enacted, by the governor, council, and burgesses, of this present generall assembly, and it is hereby enacted, by the authority of the same,*** **That**

Ferries be constantly kept at the places hereafter named; and that the rates for passing the said ferries be as followeth, viz.

On James River.

Ferries established, and rates of ferriag.

In Henrico county, at Varina, the price for a man three pence three farthings, for a man and horse seven pence halfpenny.

At Bermuda hundred, the price for a man six pence, for a man and horse one shilling.

In Charles City county, at Westover, the price for a man seven pence halfpenny, for a man and horse fifteen pence.

In Appamatock river, at the usual place, near colonel Byrd's store, the price for a man three pence three farthings, for a man and horse seven pence halfpenny.

In Prince George county, at Coggan's point, and Maycock's, the price the same as at Westover.

From Powhatan town to the landing at Swineherd's, the price for man seven pence halfpenny, for a man and horse fifteen pence: And then from the Sicamore landing by Windmill point to the widow Jones's landing at Wyanoke, the same price as from Powhatan.

In Surry county, from Hog-Island to Archer's Hope, so long as the ferry-keeper will, at his own charge, keep a sufficient bridge over Hog-Island creek, and upon failure thereof, from Hog-Island main, to the end, the said bridge may never become a county charge, the price for a man fifteen pence, for a man and horse two shillings and six pence.

At the mouth of Upper Chipoake's creek, over to the Row, or Martin's Brandon, the price for a man six pence, for a man and horse one shilling.

From Swan's point to James Town, the price for a man seven pence halfpenny, for a man and horse fifteen pence.

From Crouche's creek to James Town, the price for a man one shilling, for a man and horse two shillings.

In James City county, at James Town, the price to Swan's point, for a man seven pence halfpenny, for a man and horse fifteen pence.

From James Town to Crouche's creek, for a man one shilling, for a man and horse two shillings.

At Williamsburg, from Princess Ann port to Hog-Island, for a man two shillings and six pence, for a man and horse four shillings.

At Chickahominy, at the usual place, on each side the river, the price for a man six pence, for a man and horse one shilling.

From John Goddale's to William's neck, or Drummond's neck, for a man three pence three farthings, for a man and horse seven pence halfpenny.

In Nansemond county, from Coiefield's point to Robert Peale's near Sleepyhole, the price for a man six pence, for a man and horse one shilling.

In Elizabeth City county, at Hampton Town, from the Town point to Brooke's point, the price for a man three pence, for a man and horse six pence.

From Hampton Town to Sewell's point, the price for a man three shillings, and for a man and horse six shillings.

In Norfolk county, from Norfolk Town to Sawyer's point, or Lovet's plantation, the price for a man six pence, for a man and horse one shilling.

Upon York River.

In New-Kent, from Robert Peaseley's to Philip Williams's, the price for a man six pence, for a man and horse one shilling.

From the Brick-house to West Point, the price for a man one shilling, for a man and horse eighteen pence.

From the Brick-house to Graves's the price for a man one shilling, for a man and horse two and twenty pence halfpenny.

In King William county, from Spencer's over to the usual landing place, the price for a man six pence, for a man and horse one shilling.

From Thomas Cranshaw's to the usual landing place, the price for a man three pence, for a man and horse six pence.

From Philip Williams's to Peaseley's point, the price for a man six pence, for a man and horse one shilling.

From West Point to the Brick-house, the price for a man one shilling, for a man and horse eighteen pence.

From Abbot's landing, over Mattapony river, the price for a man three pence, for a man and horse six pence.

From West Point to Graves's, the price for a man six pence, for a man and horse one shilling.

In York county, from York town to Tindal's point, the price for a man seven pence halfpenny, for a man and horse fifteen pence.

From Queen Mary's port at Williamsburg, to Claybank creek, in Gloucester county, the price for a man two shillings and six pence.

From Captain Matthews's to Capahosack, the price for a man fifteen pence, for a man and horse two shillings and six pence.

In Gloucester county, from Tindal's point to York town, the price for a man seven pence halfpenny, for a man and horse fifteen pence.

From Capahosack to Captain Matthews's landing, or Seimmino creek, the price for a man fifteen pence, for a man and horse two shillings and six pence.

From Bailey's over Peankatank, the price for a man six pence, for a man and horse one shilling.

In King and Queen county, from Graves's to West Point, the price for a man six pence, for a man and horse one shilling.

From Graves's to the Brick-house, the price for a man one shilling, for a man and horse two and twenty pence halfpenny.

From Burford's to old Talbot's, the price for a man six pence, for a man and horse one shilling.

From Captain Walker's mill landing, the price for a man three pence, for a man and horse six pence.

In Middlesex county, over Peankatank, at Turk's ferry, the usual place, the price for a man three pence, for a man and horse six pence.

On Rappahannock River.

In Middlesex county, from Shelton's to Mattrom Wright's, the price for a man two shillings, for a man and horse four shillings.

From Brandon, to Chowning's point, the price for a man two shillings, for a man and horse four shillings.

In Essex county, over Rappahannock, from the land of Daniel Henry to William Pannell's, the price for a man six pence, for a man and horse one shilling.

From Bowler's, at the usual place, to Sucket's point, the price for a man fifteen pence, for a man and horse two shillings and six pence.

From Tappahanock town, over Rappahanock river, to Webley Pavies, or to Rappahannock creek, on either side thereof, the price for a man fifteen pence, for a man and horse two shillings and six pence.

From Henry Long's over Rappahanock river, to the usual place, the price for a man six pence, for a man and horse one shilling.

In Richmond county, from William Pannel's over Rappahanock river, the price for a man six pence, for a man and horse one shilling.

From Sucket's point to Bowler's the price for a man fifteen pence, for a man and horse two shillings and six pence.

In Stafford county, from colonel William Fitzhugh's landing, in Potowmack river, over to Maryland, the price for a man two shillings and six pence, for a man and horse five shillings.

From the Port of Northampton to the port of York, the price for a man fifteen shillings, for a man and horse thirty shillings.

From the port of Northampton to the port of Hampton, the price for a man fifteen shillings, for a man and horse thirty shillings.

III. *And be it further enacted*, That where a ferry is appointed by this act, on one side of the river, and none on the other to answer the same, it shall and may be lawful for the county courts, in such a case, to appoint an opposite ferry, and to order and allow the prices directed by this act.

County Courts may appoint ferries at opposite landings.

IV. And for the more orderly and better keeping the said ferries, *Be it enacted*, That the court of each county, wherein any ferry is or shall be appointed, by virtue of this act, shall have, and hereby hath full power and authority of licensing, allowing and appointing the ferry-keeper, and of ordering and directing what boat or boats and hands shall be kept there; and also, upon neglect or omission in the good and orderly keeping thereof, of discharging and turning out that ferry-keeper, and putting another in the place.

And may license keepers.

V. *Provided always*, That the said court, upon appointing any person to keep a ferry, do take bond, with one sufficient surety, in the sum of twenty pounds sterling, paiable to her majesty, for the constant and well keeping the same with boats and hands, according to

But shall take bond and security.

the directions of the said court; and also for the giving passages without delay to such public messages and expresses, as shall be mentioned by this act, to be ferry free.

Privileges of keepers of ferries.

VI. And for encouragement of the said ferry-keepers in the better keeping of the same, and in consideration of setting over the public messages and expresses, *Be it further enacted* That all the men attending in the said ferry boats, be free of public and county levies, and from all other public services, as musters, constables, clearing highways, being impressed, and other things of the like nature; and shall have their licence without any fee or reward paid for obtaining the same, or fon the petition, bond, or other matter or thing whatsoever, relating thereto: And also, if the said county court shall find it requisite or useful, that an ordinary be kept at such ferry, then, and in such case, they are hereby authorized and impowered to licence, such ferry-keepers to keep ordinary, without any other fee either for the license or for the obtaining the same, except half of the fee allowed by law to the governor, notwithstanding there be otherwise a sufficient number of ordinaries in the same county: And moreover, that in such case, no other person be permitted to keep ordinary, within five miles of such ferry-keeper so licenced to keep ordinary, unless it shall so happen, that the place of a county court, or land laid out for a town, shall require it.

as to fees.

Ordinaries.

VII. *Provided always, and it is the true intent and meaning of this act*, That when any ferry-keeper shall be so licenced to keep ordinary, the person so licenced, shall, notwithstanding the immunities aforesaid, be liable to such like bonds, securities and penalties as other ordinary-keepers are and shall be liable unto.

Penalty for taking ferriage where not licensed.

VIII. *And be it also enacted*, That if any other person whatsoever, for reward, shall set any person or persons over any of the rivers whereon ferries are or shall be appointed by virtue of this act, (except necessity of a parish require it for going to church, he or they so offending, shall forfeit and pay for every such offence, five pounds current money of Virginia: one half thereof to be to the nearest ferryman to the place where such offence shall be committed; and the other half to the informer; and if the ferry-keeper be the informer, then he to have the whole: to be recovered, with costs, by action of debt, bill, plaint, or information, in any court of record in this her Majesty's colony and dominion, wherein no essoin, protection, or wager of law, shall be allowed.

Power of county courts, as to agreement with keepers of ferries, for transportation of militia.

IX. *Provided, nevertheless, and be it enacted*, That it shall and may be lawful for any county court within this colony and dominion to appoint a ferry over any river or creek within the county, where the same shall be thought convenient; and also to agree with the keeper of any ferry appointed, or which shall be appointed by virtue of this act, to set over the militia of the county on muster days, and to raise an allowance for the same in the county levy.

X. *Provided*, That nothing in the aforesaid proviso contained, shall be construed to give liberty to any county court to levy or raise any allowance upon the inhabitants of the county for any ferry whatsoever, over a river or creek to another county.

Public expresses, what deemed.

XI. And for explanation of what shall be accounted public messages or expresses within the meaning of this act, *Be it enacted*, That all expresses which shall be sent by the secretary, any one of the council, sheriff of a county, commander in chief, colonel, lieutenant colonel or major in the militia to his excellency the governor, or the governor or commander in chief of this colony and dominion, for the time being; or which shall be sent by such governor or commander in chief, or by the clerk of the council, to any person; or which shall be sent by any chief militia officer to the governor, or to the chief militia officer of the next county, to give intelligence of the approach of an enemy; or which shall come from beyond sea, directed to the governor or commander in chief of this colony, shall be accounted public messages and expresses, and shall be ferry free, and within the meaning of the condition of the bond aforementioned, in case such expresses be directed for her Majesty's service, and signed upon the superscription by the person or persons sending the same.

Public messengers, how paid.

XII. And for the greater ease and encouragement of all messengers carrying such messages or expresses, *Be it further enacted*, That her Majesty's receiver general of this her Majesty's colony and dominion, for the time being, shall be and is hereby obliged to pay, always at the seat of the government, out of the revenue arising by virtue of the imposition of two shillings per hogshead, head money, fort duties, fines and rights, as being a contingency of the government, to every such messenger ready money, after the rate of four pence per mile for himself and horse, for every miles going he shall be sent forward on such public messages, in full consideration of his going and returning. And if; at any time such messenger shall be kept attending, by the governor or commander in chief of this her Majesty's colony and dominion, for the time being, the said receiver general shall, over and above, pay to such messenger for every such day's attendance, five shillings per day out of the fines and revenues aforesaid.

Must produce certificates.

XIII. *Provided*, That the messengers from the several counties, bring with them from the superscriber of the express, a certificate of the name of the messenger, and the distance of miles sent, and the days attendance certified by the governor, or commander in chief, for the time being, or the clerk of the council, otherwise such messenger and attendant not to be paid or allowed.

Expresses by water, what paid.

XIV. *And be it further enacted*, That if any messages or expresses be sent by water, the same shall be paid for as aforesaid, after the rate of fifteen pence per day for the boat, and two shillings per day for each man emploied to go in her.

Made perpetual by ch. 6, 1713.

XV. *And be it further enacted*, That this act shall continue in force seven years, and thereafter to the end of the next session of assembly.

CHAP. LIV.

An act appointing a Treasurer.

Edi. 1733 and 1752. [From MS.]

Impost duties to be paid to treasurer.

BE it enacted by the governor, council, and burgesses, of this present general assembly, and it is hereby enacted, by the authority of the same, That all and every sum and sums of money to be raised by one act of assembly, passed this session, entituled an act laying impositions on liquors and slaves be constantly accounted for and paid by the collectors or receivers thereof to the treasurer of this her Majesty's colony and dominion for the time being.

And be it further enacted, by the authority aforesaid, and it is hereby enacted, That Benjamin Harrison, junr. esq. shall be, and is hereby nominated, constituted and appointed treasurer of the revenues arising by the before specifyed act, and the said treasurer is hereby authorised, impowered and required to demand, receive and take off and from every collector and collectors all and every sum and sums of money ariseing by force of the before recited act of assembly; and the said Benjamin Harrison is authorised and required to keep and retain all such money in his own custody and possession until he shall be ordered and required to dispose of the same in such manner, and by such warrant, and for such uses, intents and purposes, and no other as are limited, appointed and directed in the said act.

Benjamin Harrison, junr. appointed treasurer.

His power and duties.

And be it further enacted, by the authority aforesaid, and it is hereby enacted, That the sallary of four per cent shall be allowed and paid to the said treasurer out of all and every sum and sums of money by him received and accounted for to the general assembly according to the directions of the said act.

His salary.

And be it further enacted, That the said Benjamin Harrison, before his entry and admission into the said office of treasurer, and before his taking upon him to execute and manage the same, shall give bond in the secretary's office with good and sufficient security in the sum of five thousand pounds sterling, payable to her Majesty, her heirs and successors for the true and just performance and discharge of the aforesaid office and place of treasurer according to the true intent and meaning of the afore recited act of assembly.

Bond and security.

Provided always, That in case of the death, departure out of the country or other legall disability of the treasurer hereby appointed, that then it shall and may be lawfull to and for his excellency the governor, and the governor and commander in chief for the time being, with the advice of her Majesty's council to appoint and constitute such other person as he shall think fit to execute the said office of treasurer according to the severall rules and directions in this act expressed, who shall hold, have and enjoy the said office of treasurer, with all and singular its rights and profits untill the next session of assembly, giving such bond and se-

Vacancy in office of, how supplied.

curity as herein is before directed. Any thing in this or any other act to the contrary in any-wise notwithstanding.

Edit. 1733 and 1752.

CHAP. LV.

An act making the French Refugees, inhabiting at the Manakin Town, and the parts adjacent, a distinct Parich by themselves, and exempting them from the payment of Public and County levies, until the twenty-fifth day of December, 1708.

[From MS.]

WHEREAS a considerable number of French Protestant Refugees have been lately imported into this her Majesty's colony and dominion, severall of which refugees have seated themselves above the falls of James River, at or near a place commonly called and known by the name of the Manakin Town, for the encouragement of the said refugees to settle and remain together as near as may be to the said Manakin Town:

French inhabitants at Manakin town to constitute a distinct parish.

Be it enacted by the governor, councill and burgesses of this present general assembly, and it is hereby enacted by the authority of the same, That the said Refugees, inhabiting at the said Manakin Town, and the parts adjacent, shall be accounted and taken for inhabitants of a distinct parish by themselves, and the land which they now do or hereafter shall possess at or adjacent to the said Manakin Town, shall be, and is hereby declared to be a parish of itself, distinct from any other parish, to be called and known by the name of King William Parish, in the county of Henrico, and not lyable to the payment of parish levys in any other parish whatsoever.

King William parish.

Exempt'd from the payment of levies, till 25th Dec. 1708.

And be it further enacted, That such, and so many of the said refugees as are already settled, or shall hereafter settle themselves as inhabitants of the said parish at the Manakin Town, and the parts adjacent shall themselves, and their familys, and every of them be free and exempted from the payment of publick and county levys until the twenty-fifth day of December, which shall be in the year of our Lord one thousand seven hundred and eight. Any law or usage to the contrary in any-wise notwithstanding.

Provided always, and it is hereby enacted, and declared, That the allowance settled by law for a minister's maintenance, shall not be construed to extend to the minister of the said parish of King William, but that the inhabitants of the said parish are hereby intended to be left at their own liberty to agree with and pay their minister as their circumstances will admit. Allowance to ministers, to be at discretion of inhabitants.

CHAP. LVI.

[Not in Edition of 1733 or 1752.]

An act confirming the Naturalization of Joshua Mulder and others.

WHEREAS by former acts of assembly, Joshua Mulder, Henry Weedick, Christopher Regault, Henry Fayson Vandoevarage, John Mattoon, Dominick Theriate, Jeremy Packquett, Nicholas Cock, Henry Wagaman, Thomas Harmenson, John Peterson, Reynold Anderson, Michael Vanlandigham, Minor Doodes, Doodes Minor, Herman Kelderman, Christian Peterson, Garret Johnson, Abraham Vinckler, John Michael, Jacob Johnson, John Pimmitt and John Keeton, aliens, received grants of naturalization. [From MS.] Naturalization of foreigners confirmed.

Be it therefore enacted by the governor, council and burgesses of this present general assembly, and it is hereby enacted by the authority of the same, That the said Joshua Mulder, Henry Weedick, Christopher Regault, Henry Fayson Vandoeverage, John Mattoon, Dominick Theriate, Jeremy Packquett, Nicholas Cock, Henry Wagaman, Thomas Harmenson, John Peterson, Reynold Anderson, Michael Vanlandigham, Minor Doodes, Doodes Minor, Herman Kelderman, Christian Peterson, Garret Johnson, Abraham Vinckler, John Michaell, Jacob Johnson, John Pimmitt and John Keeton, and all other persons whatsoever having heretofore received any grant of naturalization by virtue of any former acts and their heirs for ever shall have, hold and enjoy all and singular the estates, priviledges, capacitys, rights, immunitys, libertys, propertys and advantages of the naturall born subjects of this colony and dominion in the same manner, and as fully and amply to all intents and purposes as they, or any of them might or ought to have done if they and every of them had been expressly named in this or any other particular act of assembly for that purpose made' or provided. Their privileges.

Any law, custom or usage to the contrary, or seeming to the contrary, notwithstanding.

CHAP. LVII.

[Not in Edition 1733 or 1752.]

An act for settling the dividing lines between the Counties of Prince George, Surry, Isle of Wight and Nansemond, on the South side Black Water Swamp.

[From MS.]

WHEREAS many inconveniencys attend the inhabitants of the severall countys of Prince George, Surry, Isle of Wight and Nansemond, by reason of the uncertainty of the bounds of the said countys on the south side the Black Water Swamp, for prevention whereof for the future,

Boundaries of Prince George, Surry, Isle of Wight and Nansemond, how ascertained.

Be it enacted by the governor, councill and burgesses of this present general assembly, and it is hereby enacted by the authority of the same, That the surveyors of the said countys (where the same is not already done) at some convenient time before the twenty-fifth day of December, one thousand seven hundred and six, do survey and lay out the Blackwater Swamp in their said countys, and by comparing their severall surveys together to reduce the same into one straight line, from which said line so reduced, a perpendicular shall be raised, and a line run parallel to that perpendicular from the head of the bounds of each of the said counties, formerly settled to the Blackwater Swamp, shall hereafter be the dividing line of each county backwards as farr as this government extends, and that the said lines or bounds be run out by the surveyors of the respective countys, at the charge of their said countys within three months after the said twenty-fifth day of December.

Penalty on surveyors neglecting their duty.

And be it further enacted by the authority aforesaid, and it is hereby enacted, That if the said surveyors, or any of them shall refuse or neglect to lay out the bounds of their respective countys according to the direction of this act, then such surveyor or surveyors so refusing, shall be fined ten thousand pounds of tobacco, to be recovered by action of debt, bill, plaint or information in any court of record within this colony and dominion, wherein no essoign, protection or wager of law shall be allowed, one half of which fine shall be to her Majesty, her heirs and successors for and towards the support of this government and the contingent charges thereof, the other half to the informer, and if the Courts of the said respective Countys shall refuse or omitt to levy the tobacco accruing due to such surveyor for his service and charge therein in their next County Levy, then upon application made to the next Assembly, after such refusall, the said tobacco shall be levyed upon such County for the use of the said surveyor. How paid.

CHAP. LVIII.

An act for raising a Publick Levy.

[Not in edition 1733 & 1752.]

BE it enacted, by the governor, council, and burgesses, of this present general assembly, and it is hereby enacted, by the authority of the same, That the sume of three pounds and a quarter of tobacco be paid by every tithable person within this her Majesties Colony and Dominion of Virginia, for the defraying and payment of the publick charge of the country, being the public levy from the eighteenth day of April, one thousand seven hundred and five, to the four and twentieth day of April, one thousand seven hundred and six; and that it be paid by the collectors of the severall countys to the several persons to whom it is proportioned by this generall assembly; and if it shall happen that there shall be more tythables in any county than the present levy is laid on, then such county to have credit for so much to the use of the county; and if there shall happen to be less tithables in any county, then such county shall bear the loss. Public levy or taxes.

And be it further enacted, That there shall be paid to the clerke of the house of burgesses the sum of two thousand pounds of tobacco and cask for every copy of the laws of this present session of assembly that shall be sent to the severall county courts; and that the said courts shall raise the same in their county levys, at the next levy after the receipt of the said copys respectively. Fee to clerk of house of burgesses, for copy of acts of this session.

Copy—Test,

WILLIAM RANDOLPH,
Clerke House Burgesses.

Signed by Edward Nott, Esq. *Governor.*
Benjamin Harrison, *Speaker.*

N 3

Alex. Spotswood, Esq. Governor.

AT A

General Assembly,

BEGUN AND HOLDEN AT

THE CAPITOL, IN THE CITY OF WILLIAMSBURG, THE TWENTY-FIFTH DAY OF OCTOBER: IN THE 9TH YEAR OF THE REIGN OF OUR SOVEREIGN LADY ANNE, BY THE GRACE OF GOD, OF GREAT BRITAIN, FRANCE, AND IRELAND, QUEEN, DEFENDER OF THE FAITH, &c. ANNO DOMINI, 1710.

CHAP. I.

An act for laying a Duty on Liquors and Slaves.

[This act is preserved in a MS, with which the Editor was furnished by Mr. Jefferson, late President of the United States, and was given to him by John Page, of Rosewell, whose grandfather, Mathew Page, had been employed on one of the revisals; but as the law agrees almost verbatim with the 1st chap. of the acts of 1705, it is unnecessary to repeat it. It was limited in its duration to three years.]

CHAP. II.

[From MS.]

*An act for finishing a House for the Governor of this Colony and Dominion.**

Preamble.

WHEREAS by an Act of Assembly, made at a General Assembly, begun at the Capitol the twenty-third day of October, in the fourth year of the reign of our Sovereign Lady Anne, Queen of Great-Britain, France and Ireland, and in the year of our Lord one thousand seven hundred and five, intituled an act directing the building a house for the Governor of this Colony and Dominion, a house according to the dimensions, discriptions and directions, in the said act

* The MS. used, in the acts of this session, is that referred to under chap. 1, and will be designated the "*Page MS.*"—It contains all the laws of 1710 and 1711, tho' differently arranged from the printed revisal of 1733.

mentioned and given, together with a kitchen and stable, suitable to the said house, for the residence of the Governor of this Colony and Dominion, was directed to be built and finished on the land therein mentioned; which said house, kitchen and stable not being finished according to the directions of the said act;

Wee, her Majesties most dutiful and loyal subjects, the Burgesses, now assembled, having seriously considered the necessity of finishing the said house and the great delay that hath happened in perfecting the same, have chearfully and unanimously given and granted unto her most gracious Majestie the sum of fifteen hundred and sixty pounds, to be employed, made use of and expended in finishing and compleating the said house, kitchen and stable, according to the directions in the said act given, and do humbly pray your honour it may be enacted. Appropriation for Governor's house.

And be it enacted by the Lieut. Governor, Council and Burgesses of this General Assembly, and it is hereby enacted by the authority of the same, That the said house, kitchen and stable be finished and compleated according to the directions laid down and given in the said Act of Assembly, with all convenient expedition for the uses and purposes therein mentioned.

And whereas, for rendering the said house more compleat and commodious for the reception of the Governor of this antient Colony and Dominion, severall buildings, gardens and other ornaments and things are further necessary and convenient to be made and done; therefore we, the Burgesses aforesaid, taking the same into our serious consideration, have freely and unanimously given and granted unto her most gracious Majestie the further sum of six hundred thirty-five pounds, to be employed, laid out and made use of according to the directions in this act, hereafter mentioned, and do humbly pray your honour it may be enacted. Further appropriation for other edifices.

And be it enacted by the authority aforesaid, That a Court-Yard, of dimentions proportionable to the said house, be laid out, levelled and encompassed with a brick wall four foot high, with ballustrades of wood thereupon, on the said land, and that a Garden of the length of two hundred fifty-four foot and of the breadth of one hundred forty-four foot from out to out, adjoining to the said house, be laid out and levelled and en- Court-Yard.

closed with a brick wall, four foot high, with ballustrades of wood upon the said wall, and that handsome gates be made to the said court-yard and garden, and that a convenient kitchen garden be laid out on the said land and be enclosed with pailes, and that an orchard and pasture ground be made on the said land and be enclosed with a good ditch and fence, and also that a house of wood be built and finished for houseing cattle, and that a house of wood for poultry be built and finished, with a yard thereto enclosed, on the said land.

Garden, Orchard, &c.

Furniture.

And be it further enacted, That out of the sume of six hundred thirty-five pounds, hereby given and granted to her Majestie, the sume of two hundred and fifty pounds shall be expended and laid out in buying necessary standing and ornamentall furniture for the said house, which furniture shall be provided in this country or sent for from Great-Britain by the overseer, hereinafter named, by the direction and appointment of the Lt. Governor or Commander in Chief of this Colony, for the time being, and shall forever hereafter belong to and is hereby appropriated to the said house.

Money, how drawn.

And be it further enacted, That for a supply of money to begin, carry on and finish the aforesaid house, stable, kitchen, court-yard, garden, orchard, out-houses, and all other the work herein directed to be made and done, and also to buy the furniture aforesaid, the said overseer shall, from time to time, as occasion shall require, make application to his honour the lieut. governor, or the governor, or commander in chief of this colony and dominion, for the time being, who, upon such application, is hereby desired to issue his warrant upon the admr. of the estate of the late treasurer, & upon the present treasurer of this dominion, for so much money as may be wanted untill the full sum of fifteen hundred and sixty pounds and of six hundred thirty-five pounds shall be employed, made use of and expended in finishing the said house, kitchen and stable, and in making and finishing the court-yard, garden, orchard, out-houses, aforesaid, and all the work herein before mentioned and directed to be made and done, and in buying the said furniture, and the charges thereupon accruing, and to and for no other use or uses whatsoever.

And for the more easy, expeditious and cheap carrying on the building and work aforesaid;

Be it enacted, That the said overseer have full power to send to Great Brittain for iron-work, glass, lead, or any other necessary materials to be made use of in and about the said house and work, and that the same be imported at the risque of the country, and on the like publick risque, to buy such and so many slaves, horses, carts and other necessaries for carrying on the said work as he, by and with the approbation of the Lieut. Governor or Commander in Chief of this Colony and Dominion, for the time being, and Council shall think fitt.

Materials may be imported.

And be it further enacted, That Henry Cary be appointed, and is hereby appointed overseer to inspect, oversee and provide for the building and all and singular the work and things hereby directed to be made and done, with full power to begin, carry on and finish the same, under and with the direction of the Lieut. Governor or Commander in Chief of this Colony and Dominion, for the time being and Council, and in case, at any time hereafter, there be occasion of appointing a new overseer, by means of the death or disability of the said Henry Cary or of any other person that shall or may succeed him in the said employment and trust, his honor the Lieut. Governor, or the Governor or Commander in Chief of this Colony and Dominion, for the time being, is hereby desired, on such occasions, to nominate and appoint a new overseer, and every person who shall be so appointed, is hereby declared to have as full power to proceed and act in carrying on, finishing and doing all the buildings, work and other things hereby directed by the overseer to be performed and done as the said Henry Cary hath by virtue of this act.

Overseer, or director.

And be it further enacted, That the said Henry Cary and every other person which after him shall be appointed to be overseer as aforesaid, shall be paid and allowed for the time of his respective service and attendance in the employment and trust aforesaid, after the rate of one hundred pounds a year.

His salary.

Provided always, and be it enacted, That the said Henry Cary and every other person which after him shall be appointed to be overseer as aforesaid, shall, before he be admitted into the said employment and trust, enter into bond, with one or more surety's, in the penalty of five hundred pounds sterling, to our sove-

Must give bond with surety.

reign Lady the Queen, her heirs and successors, that he will not imbezell or convert to his own use, any part of the moneys, materials or other things put into his hands or under his care for carrying on the building or other the work, aforesaid, but that according to the best of his skill and understanding and the trust reposed in him, he will faithfully lay out all such moneys in and about the uses and services for which he shall receive the same; and also that he will lay an account of his disbursements, from time to time, before the Governor and Council and before the General Assembly at their meeting, and make oath thereto when required.

Repairs, how paid for.

And be it further enacted, That all such charge and expense as shall or may hereafter accrue for repairing the house, out-houses, gardens and all other the work herein directed to be done, shall be defrayed out of her Majestie's revenue of two shillings per hogshead.

CHAP. III.

An act prohibiting Seamen being harboured or entertained on Shore.

Preamble.

I. WHEREAS many of her Majesty's ships of war, and merchant ships, trading into this colony and dominion, suffer very much by their seamen running away, and absconding from their ships: for prevention thereof,

Runaway seamen, how taken up and conveyed back.

II. *Be it enacted, by the lieutenant-governor, council and burgesses, of this present general assembly, and by the authority thereof, and it is hereby enacted,* That every seaman that shall run away, or absent himself unlawfully from the ship or vessel he belongs to, shall be and is hereby liable to be taken up or secured by any person or persons, and upon a warrant from a Justice of Peace of the County where he is taken up, conveyed from Constable to Constable, till he be put on board the ship or vessel he belongs to; and that Constable who shall deliver such seaman on board any such ship or vessel, shall take receipt for the said seaman of the master, mate, or other officer, to which such seaman belongs, and shall immediately carry and deliver the same to the naval officer of the district where such

Duty of Constable.

ship or vessel rides before she is cleared; for which service, the said Constable shall receive of the naval officer, if ten miles, or under, five shillings, and if above ten miles, ten shillings; which the naval officer shall be reimbursed by the commander of the said ship or vessel. Reward.

III. *And be it further enacted,* That every Justice of Peace within this Colony, before whom such runaway seaman shall be brought, be impowered and required to give the taker-up of the said seaman a certificate under his hand, according to this act, to entitle him to the reward hereafter given for so doing. Certificates, to taker-up.

IV. *And be it further enacted,* That the reward for taking up a runaway seaman, shall be twenty shillings, if it be done ten miles, or upwards, from the ship or vessel the seaman belongs to, and if under ten miles, ten shillings, and no more; which several sums of money, as the occasion is, shall be paid to the taker-up, upon certificate, as aforesaid, by the naval officer of the district where the ship or vessel rides, that the seaman belongs to, and the captain or master of the said ship or vessel shall reimburse the same to him, before he be cleared, or be permitted to sail from that district. Reward to taker-up.

V. *And be it further enacted,* That the Justice's certificate aforementioned, to be given to the taker-up of a runaway seaman, shall expressly declare what ship or vessel the said seaman belongs to, what place the said seaman was taken up at, and whether it be ten miles from the said ship or vessel, or under, or above, and that the taker-up made oath before him to the place of taking up. Form of Certificates.

VI. *And be it further enacted,* That if a runaway seaman, taken up by virtue of this act, shall belong to a merchant ship or vessel gone out of the country before the said seaman is taken up, or can be got on board the said ship or vessel; in such case, the said seaman shall be put on board any one of her Majesty's ships of war which shall happen to be here, if the captain thereof will receive him on board, and pay the reward for taking up; and if the commander of any of her Majesty's ships of war shall refuse to receive such seaman, and pay the said reward, then the said seaman shall be delivered to the master of any merchant ship that will receive him, on paying the said reward. Where ship has sailed, how runaway to be dealt with.

Expenses, how reimbursed.

VII. *And be it further enacted,* That in all cases where a runaway seaman belonging to any of her Majesty's ships of war, or to merchant ships, gone out of the country, shall happen to be put on board any of her Majesty's said ships, the captain or commander of such ship shall reimburse the naval officer the charge of taking up, and shall and may stop it out of the wages due, or thereafter accruing due to the said seaman.

Rewards, how paid.

VIII. *And be it further enacted,* That the naval officers of this colony and dominion, may use and take out of her Majesty's revenue of two shillings per hogshead in their hands, so much money as shall be necessary to pay off the certificates produced to them for taking up runaway seamen as aforesaid, till they can be reimbursed, as by this act is before directed; provided due care be taken to get in the same.

Penalty for suffering escapes.

IX. And for prevention of escapes which may happen, *Be it enacted,* That whatever Constable, or other officer, to whom a runaway seaman shall be committed, according to this act, shall wittingly, willingly, or negligently suffer the said seaman to make his escape, or in due time, as before directed, to deliver the receipt aforesaid to the naval officer of such district, as before in this act is directed, such constable or other officer, shall, for his said offence, forfeit and pay to the Queen's Majesty, her heirs and successors, five hundred pounds of tobacco, with costs of suit: to be recovered, by action of debt, bill, plaint, or information, in any of her Majesty's courts of record in this colony and dominion.

On ordinary-keeper, for entertaining or concealing.

X. And to prevent the entertainment, harbouring, or concealing of runaway seamen, *Be it further enacted,* That if any Ordinary-keeper, or other person, shall hereafter entertain, harbour, or conceal any seaman, except he be able to give a good account that he is about his lawful business, such ordinary-keeper, or person, shall forfeit and pay five hundred pounds of tobacco to him, her, or them, that will inform or sue for the same, in any court of record in this colony and dominion: to be recovered, with costs, by action of debt, bill, plaint, or information, wherein no essoin, protection, or wager of law, shall be allowed. And if it so happen, that such offender shall not be able to pay the said sum of five hundred pounds of tobacco, or to give security for the paiment thereof at the succeeding crop, the said offender shall have and receive on his or her bare back, twenty lashes, well laid on, for his or her offence.

XI. *Provided always*, That this act shall continue in force for two years, and from thence, to the end of the next session of Assembly. Revived and made perpetual, by chap. 7, 1713.

CHAP. IV.

An act to explain part of an act of Assembly, intituled An act for establishing the General Court, and for regulating and settling the proceedings therein.

I. WHEREAS, by an Act of Assembly, made at a General Assembly, begun at the Capitol, the twenty-third day of *October*, in the year one thousand seven hundred and five, intituled, *An act for establishing the General Court, and for regulating and settling the proceedings therein; It is, among other things, enacted*, That the General Court of this Dominion, and the Courts held before the Justices of the Peace, in the several respective Counties, commonly called the County Courts, shall be deemed and taken, and are hereby declared to be the only Courts of Record of or in this Dominion; and that no other Court or Courts whatsoever, shall be construed, deemed, or taken to be such: whereupon some doubts and questions have been made; wherefore, for the better explanation of the said act, Preamble. (See chap. 19, 1705, sec. 39.)

II. *Be it enacted and declared, by the lieutenant-governor, council and burgesses, of this general assembly, and the authority of the same*, That nothing in the said act contained, shall be construed, deemed, or taken to derogate from, lessen, or abridge the roial power, prerogative, and authority of her Majesty, her heirs and successors, of granting commission or commissions of *oier and terminer*, or of constituting and erecting such other court or courts of record, as her Majesty, her heirs or successors, by her or their commission or commissions, instruction or instructions to her or their governor or commander in chief of this colony & dominion, for the time being, shall direct, order or appoint. Royal prerogative to erect other courts of record, not abridged.

III. *And be it further enacted*, That nothing in the said act contained, shall be construed, deemed, or taken to derogate from, lessen, or abridge the roial pow- Or to receive appeals from judgments of the General Court.

er, prerogative and authority of her Majesty, Queen *Anne*, her heirs and successors, of receiving, hearing and determining any cause or causes which shall or may be brought before her Majesty, her heirs or successors, by appeal from the judgment, decree, or sentence of the said General Court; or to debar or hinder any person whatsoever, from demanding and obtaining an appeal from any judgment, decree, or sentence of the said General Court, which shall or may be given or made against him, to her Majesty, her heirs and successors; in such cases, where the same are, or at any time hereafter shall or may be allowable, by the order or instruction of her majesty, her heirs or successors, to her or their governor or commander in chief of this colony and dominion, for the time being: and that all such appeals, commissions and instructions shall be allowed, held good, valid and available; any thing in the said act of assembly to the contrary, or seeming contrary thereto, in any wise, notwithstanding.

CHAP. V.

An act for raising a Public Revenue for the better support of the Government of her Majesty's Colony and Dominion of Virginia. *(a)*

Preamble.

I. WHEREAS a great and continual charge is required for the maintenance of the governor, and several other officers and persons, as also for forts and fortifications; besides that, there are many other contingent expences, absolutely necessary for the support of the government of this her Majesty's colony and dominion:

Duty of 2s. on every hogshead, &c. of tobacco exported;

II. *Be it therefore enacted by the lieutenant-governor, council and burgesses, of this present general assembly, and it is hereby enacted by the authority of the same,* That for every hogshead, box, (*b*) chest, case, or barrel of tobacco, which shall at any time hereafter be shipped or loaden on board any ship or vessel whatsoever, within

Notes to Edition 1733.

(*a*) The act of 1680, chap. 3, with this title, having passed the Roial Assent, could not be altered by this act; and there is but little difference betwixt them, except what is here noted.

(*b*) Box, chest, case and barrel, is not in the act of 1680.

this colony and dominion, in order to be exported hence by water, *(a)* to any other port or place whatsoever, there shall be paid by the shipper or shippers thereof, the sum of two shillings, current money of *Great-Britain;* and also for every five hundred pounds of tobacco shipped or loaden on board any ship or vessel, in order to be exported, as aforesaid, in bulk, to any of her Majesty's other plantations, the like sum of two shillings; and so, after that rate, for a lesser or greater quantity. *(b)* and on every 500 pounds in bulk.

III. *(c)* And for avoiding all manner of doubts which may hereafter arise concerning the paiment of the duty aforesaid, for tobaccos of the growth of another place, and shipped here, *Be it enacted by the authority aforesaid, and it is hereby enacted and declared,* That the true intent and meaning of this act is, that the aforesaid duty of two shillings shall be paid for all tobaccos whatsoever, shipped or laden on board any ship or vessel within this colony and dominion, in order to be exported hence, although the same were made in, and imported or brought from another place. Although the tobacco was of the growth of another place.

IV. *And be it also further enacted, by the authority aforesaid, and it is hereby enacted,* That every ship or vessel, which shall at any time hereafter be entred in this her Majesty's colony and dominion, or any district or port thereunto belonging, in order to unlade the goods and merchandizes imported in her, or in order to lade and take on board any tobaccos, or other goods or merchandize whatsoever, for exportation out of this colony, shall pay, for every ton which the said ship or vessel is of burthen, the sum of one shilling and three pence, current money of *Great-Britain,* for port duties. *(d)* Duty of 1s. 3d. per ton, on shipping.

V. *Provided always, and it is hereby enacted and declared,* That nothing in the aforesaid clause contained, Ships not to pay twice for

---

Notes to Edition 1733.

(*a*) The act of 1680, lays the duty upon all tobaccos exported by land or water.

(*b*) There is a penalty in that act of 100l. and treble the duty upon the master who shall make a false entry of the number of hogsheads, the burthen of the ship, or number of persons imported.

(*c*) This clause in addition to the other act, but quære the necessity of it.

(*d*) By the other act, the master has his election pay; 1-2 pound of gun-powder and 3 pounds of shot, or 1s. 3d. per ton.

the same voyage.

shall be construed so as to charge any ship or vessel, which at any time hereafter shall arrive into this colony and dominion, and here unlade and relade, with paiment of the port duties two times for the same: and that the true intent and meaning of this act is, that in such a case, the aforesaid port duties shall be paid no more than once for that voiage.

Method of measuring ships.

VI. (a) *And be it further enacted and declared,* That all ships and vessels liable to the paiment of the port duties, by this act imposed, shall be gaged and measured in manner following; that is to say, every ship or vessel shall be measured by the length of the gun-deck, deducting three-fifths of the greatest breadth, from outside to outside, and multiplying the product by the breadth from out to out, and not within board; and that product again, by half the said breadth; and that product divided by ninety-four, which will give the true contents of the tonnage; and according to which method and rule, all ships and vessels shall be measured, and the said port duties thereby shall be computed and collected accordingly; any custom, practice, or usage to the contrary, notwithstanding.

Duty of 6d. per poll, on all passengers, servants and slaves.

VII. *And be it also further enacted, by the authority aforesaid, and it is hereby enacted,* That every ship or vessel, which shall at any time hereafter come into any port, creek, harbour, or road, within this colony and dominion, and shall be there entered, in order to unlade and put on shore goods, merchandizes, passengers, servants, or slaves, shall pay six pence per poll for every passenger, servant, slave, or other person imported in her, the mariners belonging to, and in actual pay of the said ship or vessel, and every of them, excepted.

Penalty for short entry.

VIII. And to the end, the aforesaid imposition or duty of six pence per poll may be truly paid, according to the intent of this act, *Be it further enacted, by the authority aforesaid, and it is hereby enacted,* That if any master of a ship or vessel shall wittingly or willingly make a short entry of the number of persons imported in his said ship or vessel, for which the imposition or duty aforesaid ought to be paid, he shall forfeit and

---

Notes to Edition 1733.

(a) This clause is not in the other act.

pay ten (a) pounds, current money; one moiety to our sovereign lady, the Queen, her heirs and successors, for and towards the better support of this government, and the contingent charges thereof; and the other moiety to him or them, that will inform or sue for the same, in any court of record within this colony and dominion, by action of debt, bill, plaint, or information, wherein no essoin, protection, or wager of law, shall be allowed.

Duty to be paid to collectors.

IX. *And be it further enacted, by the authority aforesaid, and it is hereby enacted,* That all and every of the impositions or duties aforesaid, shall be paid to the respective collectors or officers which shall be appointed to receive the same, and shall be to our sovereign lady, the Queen, her heirs and successors, forever, to and for the better support of the government of this her Majesty's colony and dominion of *Virginia*, in such manner as is herein before expressed, and to, and for no other use, intent, or purpose, whatsoever.

Salary to collectors.

X. *And be it further enacted by the authority aforesaid, and it is hereby enacted,* That for collecting and receiving all and every the impositions or duties aforesaid, the governor, or commander in chief of this colony and dominion, for the time being, shall be and is hereby impowered and authorized, with the advice of the council, from time to time, and at all times hereafter, to nominate, constitute, and appoint such and so many collectors, receivers, or other officers, as shall be found necessary, and to allow them such salary, (b) not exceeding ten *per cent.* as shall be thought reasonable: And for encouragement to all masters of ships and vessels, or other persons, who shall hereafter be concerned in the paiment of the impositions or duties aforesaid, to give in true accounts, and to pay down the whole duties of a ship, in one entire sum, either in money, or good and sufficient bills of exchange, to the liking and satisfaction of the collector appointed to receive the same,

Allowance to masters of ves-

XI. *Be it enacted, by the authority aforesaid, and it is hereby enacted,* That the governor, or commander in

---

Notes to Edition 1733.

(a) The master, by the of act 1680, forfeits, for this offence, 100l.

(b) The salary is not limited by the other act.

sels on payment of duties. chief of this colony and dominion, for the time being, be and is hereby further authorized and impowered, with the advice of the council, to give and allow to every master of a ship or vessel, or other person, which shall so do, such reasonable allowance and abatement of the impositions or duties aforesaid, not exceeding ten *per cent.* as shall be adjudged fitting.

Privilege of Virginia owners. XII. *Provided always, and it is hereby enacted and declared, by the authority aforesaid,* for encouragement to *Virginia* owners, That every ship or vessel wholely and solely belonging to the inhabitants of this colony and dominion, shall have the privilege of being allowed the aforesaid duties or impositions of two shillings, and of one shilling and three pence accruing due upon her lading of tobacco, and for her port duties, to the proper use, benefit, and advantage of her owner or owners; and every collector or receiver of the aforesaid duties or impositions, is hereby required to allow the same accordingly, unto the master of every such ship or vessel, upon his clearing; any thing in this act, or any other act, law, usage, or custom to the contrary, notwithstanding.

Proof of property, in ships, how made. XIII. And for prevention of frauds which may be used to obtain the privilege aforesaid, *Be it also further enacted and declared, by the authority aforesaid,* That no ship or vessel whatsoever, shall be accounted or taken to belong wholely and solely to the inhabitants of this her Majesty's colony and dominion of *Virginia*, until proof thereof be made, by the oath of one of her owners, before the governor or commander in chief of this colony and dominion, for the time being, and his testimonial thereupon had, under the seal of the colony, or until such proof be made before the general court, and a certificate thereupon had, from the clerk of the said court, under the seal of his office: And that no collector or receiver of the impositions or duties aforesaid, or either of them, shall allow to any ship or vessel whatsoever, the aforesaid privilege, upon the impositions or duties aforesaid, or either of them, unless the master of the said ship or vessel, at the

---

Notes to Edition 1733.

(a) By the 134th act, 1661, confirmed by the act of 1680, the governor is made judge of the property.

time he demands the same, shall produce testimonial or certificate, as aforesaid, and also himself make oath, that he doth not know that any part of the said ship or vessel doth belong to any person whatsoever, which is not an inhabitant of *Virginia;* any thing in this act, aforesaid, to the contrary, or seeming to the contrary, notwithstanding.

XIV. *And be it further enacted,* That all and every other act and acts, and every clause and article thereof, heretofore made, for so much thereof as relates to raising a public revenue for the better support of the government of this her Majesty's colony and dominion of *Virginia,* or to any other matter or thing whatsoever, within the purview of this act, is and are hereby repealed and made void, to all intents and purposes, as if the same had never been made. Repealing clause.

CHAP. VI.

An act appointing a Treasurer. [From MS.]

BE it enacted, by the lieut. governor, council, and burgesses, of this present general assembly, and it is hereby enacted, by the authority of the same, That all and every sume and sums of money, to be raised by one act of assembly, passed this session, entituled an act, laying a duty on liquors and slaves, be constantly accounted for and paid by the collectors or receivers thereof, to the treasurer of this her Majesties colony and dominion, for the time being. Duties to be paid to treasurer.

And be it further enacted by the authority aforesaid, and it is hereby enacted, That Peter Beverley, esq. shall be and is hereby nominated, constituted and appointed treasurer of the revenues arising by the before specified act; and the said treasurer is hereby authorized, impowered and required to demand, receive and take of and from every collector and collectors, all and every sum and sums of money arising by force of the before-recited act of assembly; and the said Peter Beverly is authorized and required to keep and retain all such money in his own custody and possession untill he shall be ordered and required to dispose of the same in Peter Beverley appointed treasurer.

such manner and by such warrant, and for such uses, intents and purposes, and no other, as are limited, appointed and directed in the said act.

His salary.

And be it further enacted, by the authority aforesaid, and it is hereby enacted, That the sallary of four per cent. shall be allowed and paid to the said treasurer, out of all and every sum and sums of money by him received and accounted for to the general assembly, according to the directions of the said act.

Must give bond and surety.

And be it further enacted, That the said Peter Beverly, before his entry and admission into the said office of treasurer, and before his takeing upon him to execute and manage the same, shall give bond in the secretary's office, with good and sufficient security, in the sum of five thousand pounds sterling, payable to her Majesty, her heirs and successors, for the true and just performance and discharge of the aforesaid office and place of treasurer, according to the true intent and meaning of the afore-recited act of assembly.

Vacancy, how supplied.

Provided always, That in case of the death, departure out of the colony, or other legal disability of the treasurer hereby appointed, that then it shall and may be lawfull to and for his honor the lieutenant-governor, and the governor and commander in chief, for the time being, with the advice of her Majesties councill, to appoint and constitute such other person as he shall think fitt to execute the said office of treasurer, according to the severall rules and directions in this act expressed, who shall hold, have and enjoy the said office of treasurer, with all and singular the rights and profitts to the said office belonging, untill the then next session of assembly, giveing such bond and security as herein before is directed, any thing in this or any other act to the contrary, in any wise, notwithstanding.

CHAP. VII.

An act for reviving and continuing an act for security and defence of the country in time of danger.

[This merely revives and continues chap. 31, of 1705, till the 10th day of December, 1712, and need not be printed.]

CHAP. VIII.

An act for prevention of abuses in Tobacco shipped on freight.

Preamble.

I. WHEREAS great abuses are frequently committed by the unfair and unwarrantable practices of masters of ships, and other vessels, whereon tobacco is freighted, by their cropping, cutting away the bulge, drawing the staves, and otherwise injuring the tobacco cask, when freight is paid them for the full size and proportion of the said cask, settled by law, at a certain size, under great penalties; and by means of the breaking and cutting the said hogsheads, great quantities of tobacco that fall out, are purloined by the sailors, and afterwards run on shore, to the great prejudice of her Majesty, in her customs, as well as of the owners and fair traders,

Masters of vessels, &c. before entry, to give bond, not to injure, &c. Tobacco, taken on freight.

II. *Be it therefore enacted, by the lieutenant-governor, council and burgesses, of this present general assembly, and it is hereby enacted, by the authority of the same,* That from and after the publication of this act, all masters of ships and vessels that shall arrive in this colony, before they be admitted to enter, trade, and load tobacco, shall give bond to her Majesty, her heirs and successors, in the sum of two hundred pounds *sterling*, with condition, that he will not crop, cut away the bulge, draw the staves, or otherwise abuse, or cause or suffer to be cropt, cut, drawn, or otherwise injured and abused, by his knowledge, privity, or procurement, any tobacco-cask freighted on board the said ship or vessel, unless it be so agreed upon between the freighters and the said master, and make oath accordingly; which bond & oath, the said naval officer is hereby authorized and required to take and administer: And if any naval officer shall grant a permit to load tobacco, before the master of the ship or vessel, desiring the same, shall have given bond, and made oath, in manner aforesaid, such naval officer so offending, shall forfeit and pay the sum of two hundred pounds *sterling;* one half to the Queen's Majesty, her heirs and successors, for and towards the better support of the government, and the contingent charges thereof; and the other half to the informer: to be recovered, with costs, by action of debt, bill, plaint, or information, in any court of re-

Penalty on naval officers, for neglect of duty.

cord within this her Majesty's colony, wherein no essoin, protection, or wager of law, shall be allowed.

On mariners injuring tobacco cask.

III. *And be it further enacted, by the authority aforesaid, and it is hereby enacted,* That if any other officer or mariner belonging to any ship or vessel on freight, shall crop, cut away the bulge, draw the staves, or otherwise abuse, or be aiding or assisting in the cropping, cutting away the bulge, drawing the staves, or other abusing of any cask wherein tobacco is freighted by any person within this colony, unless in such cases, as aforesaid, where it is so agreed between the master and freighters, every person so offending, shall forfeit and pay five pounds *sterling* to the informer: to be recovered, with costs, in any court of record within this her Majesty's colony and dominion of *Virginia*, by action of debt, bill, plaint, or information, wherein no essoin, protection, or wager of law shall be allowed; and may, moreover be held to special bail: which fact may also be laid to be done in any county where the offender shall be arrested, in manner as aforesaid, without liberty of traverse, as is aforesaid; and if there be more actors in the same fact than one, each party shall be adjudged to the whole fine separately; and that the master be moreover liable to answer damage to the party grieved.

Defendant may be held to bail.

Mariners may give evidence.

IV. And because evidences, for discovery of the truth in such cases, may most commonly be wanted, unless the mariners belonging to the said ship or vessel may be admitted, *Be it further enacted and declared, by the authority aforesaid, and it is hereby further enacted and declared,* That the summoning any of the mariners as witnesses, in a prosecution upon this act, shall, *ipso facto,* discharge them of any accusation thereafter, to be made for any thing that shall be discovered on such prosecution, and themselves thereby qualified to give evidence in the cause; and if a mariner, faulty in the premises, becomes the informer, that shall also excuse him from the said fine of five pounds, for the fact whereof he is informer.

Ship may be searched.

V. *And be it further enacted, by the authority aforesaid, and it is hereby enacted,* That it shall be lawful for the collector, or naval officer, within whose district any ship or vessel shall lie, or any searcher, or any person having tobacco on board, to go on board any such ship or vessel, during the time of her loading, and to search whether any breach has been committed against this act: And if any master, officer, or other mariner, shall hinder any such search from being made, he shall, for every such offence, forfeit and pay the sum of ten pounds *sterling*; half to her Majesty, for and towards the better support of the government, and the contingent charges thereof; and the other half to the informer: to be recovered, with costs, in any court of record within this her Majesty's colony and dominion of *Virginia*, by action of debt, bill, plaint, or information, wherein no essoin, protection, or wager of law shall be allowed.

VI. This act to continue in force, until the twenty-fifth day of *December*, which shall be in the year of our Lord, one thousand seven hundred and thirteen, and from thence, to the end of the next session of assembly.

Made perpetual, by chap. 5, 1714.

CHAP. IX.

An act for supply of certain defects found in an act prescribing the method for appointing Sheriffs.

[From MS.]

WHEREAS by one Act of Assembly, made at a General Assembly, begun at the Capitol, the twenty-third day of October, in the fourth year of the Reign of our Sovereign Lady Anne, of Great Brittain, France and Ireland, Queen, Defender of the Faith, &c. intituled, *An Act prescribing the method of appointing Sheriffs*, and for limiting the time of their continuance in their Office, and directing their duty therein, a method is laid down how Sheriffs shall be appointed, which is found to be defective and to want amendment, in regard, no provision is made by the said Act what shall or may be done, when persons appointed to be Sheriffs, refuse to accept the office, or when the County Courts neglect or refuse to recommend persons according to the directions of the said Act, or when a person happens to dye in the time of his Sheriffalty, and that by such contingences justice hath not only been obstructed, but sundry other mischiefs have accrued.

Preamble.

***Therefore be it enacted, by the Lieutenant-Governor, Council and Burgesses, of this General Assembly, and it is hereby enacted, by authority of the same,* That**

Penalty for refusing the office of Sheriff.

every person hereafter commissionated to be a Sheriff of any County within this Colony and Dominion upon a recommendation from the County Court, in pursuance of the said Act, and thereupon refusing to accept the office of Sheriff, and to perform the duty thereof, pursuant to his Commission, shall forfeit and pay five thousand pounds of Tobacco, of the produce and growth of the said County.

Court failing to nominate, the Governor may commission a Sheriff.

And be it further enacted, by the authority aforesaid, That if any County Court shall hereafter neglect or refuse to recommend three persons to be Sheriffs, according to the directions of the said Act, it shall and may be lawfull, in such a case, for the Governor or Commander in Chief of this Colony and Dominion, for the time being, and he is hereby desired to appoint and constitute by his Commission, any one person nominated a Justice in the Commission of the Peace for the said County, to be Sheriff of the County, as he shall think proper, although such person be not then sworn a Justice. And if such person shall thereupon refuse to accept the Sheriff's office and to perform the duty thereof, pursuant to his Commission, he shall forfeit and pay five thousand pounds of Tobacco, of the produce and growth of the said County.

Sheriff dying, how a successor appointed.

And be it further enacted, by the authority aforesaid, That if any person, being one of the three persons recommended by the County Court and appointed Sheriff in pursuance of the said Act, shall happen to depart this life in the time of his Sheriffalty, it shall and may be lawfull, in such a case, for the Governor or Commander in Chief of this Colony and Dominion, for the time being, and he is hereby desired to appoint and constitute one of the survivors recommended, as aforesaid, to be Sheriff, in his room. And when any Sheriff appointed, upon a neglect or refusal of the County Court to recommend three persons according to the directions of the said Act, shall happen to depart this life in the time of his Sheriffalty, it shall and may be lawfull for the Governor or Commander in Chief of this Colony and Dominion, for the time being, and he is hereby desired to appoint and constitute by his Commission, any one person nominated a Justice in the Commission of the Peace for the said County, to be Sheriff of the County, in the room of the said deceased person; although such new appointed person be not then a Justice. And whatsoever person appointed and constituted Sheriff, upon the death of another Sheriff, as aforesaid, shall refuse to accept the office of Sheriff and to perform the duty thereof, pursuant to his Commission, such person shall forfeit and pay five thousand pounds of Tobacco, of the produce and growth of the said County.

Penalty for refusing to accept.

And be it further enacted, That whatsoever person shall hereafter, by virtue of this Act, be appointed Sheriff of any County by the Governor or Commander in Chief, for the time being, upon the neglect or refusal of any County Court to recommend three persons, according to the directions of the said recited Act, or upon the death of any Sheriff, in the time of his Sheriffalty, such person so appointed by the Governor or Commander in Chief, for the time being, shall not, or may not, by any thing in this Act contained, be compelled, or have power to continue in the said office of Sheriff, or to execute the same, for any other time than by the said recited Act is directed.

Persons thus appointed, how long to continue.

And be it further enacted, by the authority aforesaid, That all the fines and forfeitures mentioned in this Act, shall be to our Sovereign Lady the Queen, her heirs and successors, for and towards the support of this Government, and the contingent charges thereof, and shall and may be recovered, with costs, by action of debt, bill, plaint or information, in any of the County Courts, or in the Generall Court of this Colony and Dominion, wherein no essoin, protection, priviledge, or wager of law, shall be allowed.

Fines, how appropriated.

Provided alwayes, That when any person refusing to execute the office of Sheriff, as aforesaid, shall have paid the said forfeiture of five thousand pounds of Tobacco, such person shall not afterwards be appointed Sheriff of the same County, for which he refuses to execute the office of Sheriff, till such time as every Justice named, or to be named, in the Commission of the Peace for such County, shall have served once in the office of Sheriff for such County, or shall have paid the said forfeiture of five thousand pounds of Tobacco, for not accepting the said office.

Where the fines have been once paid.

Provided also, That if any person, hereafter appointed to execute the office of Sheriff in any County of this Colony and Dominion, shall be willing to execute the

When the party cannot get security.

same, but cannot get sufficient security for the performance of his duty therein, as by the said act is required, shall make oath in the Court of the County for which he shall be appointed Sheriff, or if there be no Court in the said County, then before the next County Court, that he hath used his best endeavour, truely and bona fide, without any covin or collusion, to gett security for his performance thereof, and that he cannot obtain such security; which oath, the said County Courts are hereby impowered and required to administer; that then such person making oath, as aforesaid, shall not incurr or be lyable to the forfeiture of five thousand pounds of Tobacco, in this Act mentioned, nor shall any person, whatsoever, which hath actually served as Sheriff in any County of this Colony and Dominion, be lyable to any of the forfeitures mentioned in this Act, for any refusal to take upon him the office of Sheriff in the same County, if he be thereto again appointed, unless every person named in the Commission of the Peace for the said County, hath actually, after him, served in the office of Sheriff for the said County, or paid the forfeiture given by this Act for refusal, any thing in this, or any other Act, contained, to the contrary thereof, in any wise, notwithstanding.

Limitation of act. (Revived, ch. 4, 1720.)

And be it further enacted, That this Act continue in force three years, from and after the publication thereof, and from thence to the end of the next Session of Assembly, and no longer.

[From MS.]

CHAP. X.

Repealed, ch. 9, 1727, sec. 9.

An Act for settling and ascertaining the current Rates of Foreign Coins in this Dominion.

Preamble.

WHEREAS her Majestie, by her Royall Proclamation, bearing date the 18th day of June, in the third year of her Reign, has been pleased to direct, that Foreign Coins shall not pass in her Plantations in America, above a certain value, therein mentioned, and forasmuch as the said Coins have not hitherto been ascertained in this her Majesties Colony and Dominion of Virginia,

Rates of Foreign Coins.

Be it enacted, by the Lieutenant-Governor, Council and Burgesses, of this present Generall Assembly, and it is hereby enacted, by the authority of the same, That the several Species of Coin, hereafter mentioned and sett down, shall be current within this her Majesties Colony and Dominion, in all payments for the discharge of any contracts, bargains or debts, to be made or contracted after the publication of this Act, and shall pass, be accounted, and received, at the following rates, to wit:—Pieces of Eight of Mexico, Sevil and Pillar Ducatoons of Flanders, Eccus of France, or Silver Lewis and Crusados of Portugal, and all halves, quarters, and lesser pieces, of the same, shall pass at three pence three farthings the pennyweight; and all Peru pieces, Cross Dollars and old Rix Dollars of the Empire, and lesser pieces of the same, shall pass at three pence half penny the pennyweight.

Penalty for refusing to receive them.

And be it further enacted, by the authority aforesaid, and it is hereby enacted, That if any person or persons, whatsoever, deny or refuse to take & receive the aforesaid Coins or Moneys, or any of them, when offered or tendered in payment of a money debt, contracted after this Act, he, she, or they, so refusing, shall lose and forfeit to the party who offers or tenders the same, such sum or sums of money as he, she, or they so refuse and deny to take, to be recovered by action of debt, in any Court of Record within this Dominion, wherein no essoign, protection, or wager of law, shall be allowed; and in case the forfeiture be less than twenty shillings, to be recovered upon a complaint before any Justice of the Peace in the County where the refusal happens to be made.

And for the conveniency of change and small payments,

Copper Coins.

Be it further enacted, That if her Majestie, her heirs or successors, shall think fitt, at any time hereafter, to permit copper money to be brought in and pass in this Colony, the same shall pass and be current in this Colony, at the like rates it doth pass in Great Brittain.

In what proportion.

Provided, That no person shall be obliged to take above two shillings and six pence of the said copper mony in any one payment, whatsoever, above twenty shillings, or to take above one shilling of the said copper money in any one payment under twenty shillings.

Penalty for counterfeiting.

And be it further enacted, by the authority aforesaid, That if any person or persons shall hereafter presume to coin, counterfeit, falsifye, or debase any of the Coins above mentioned, or shall be aiding, consenting or councilling therein, he, she, or they, so offending, upon being thereof lawfully convicted, shall be deemed and adjudged as offenders in treason, and shall suffer such paines, penalties and forfeitures, as are mentioned in the Act of Parliament, made in the eighteenth year of the Reign of Queen Elizabeth.

To what payments not to extend.

Provided nevertheless, and it is hereby meant and intended, That nothing contained in this Act shall extend, or be construed to extend, to any money payment already due, or to her Majesties revenues arising within this Colony, or to the several Sallarys payable out of the same, or to any protested Bills of Exchange, or any other Specialty expressly limited to be sterling money, or any debt contracted in Great Brittain.

Proviso.

Provided also, and it is hereby declared, That nothing in this Act mentioned shall extend, or be construed to restrain her Majestie from regulating and setling the several rates of the said Species of Foreign Coins within this her Majesties Colony and Dominion, in such other manner, and according to such other rates and proportions, as her Majesty, by her royal instructions to her Governor or Commander in Chief of this Colony, for the time being, shall, from time to time, judge proper and necessary.

CHAP. XI.

An act for establishing County Courts, and for regulating and establishing the proceedings therein.

County Courts.

I. FOR the better and more expeditious determination of all controversies that shall or may arise, *Be it enacted by the Lieutenant Governor, Council and Burgesses of this present General Assembly, and it is hereby enacted by the authority of the same,* That in every County within this dominion, respectively, there shall be held a monthly court, according to the antient custom and usage heretofore in that behalf practised; which courts shall be called county courts, and shall be held in the several respective places already assigned for that purpose, or at such other place or places as shall be lawfully appointed for that use, and shall consist of eight or more justices for every court respectively, who shall be called justices of the peace, and shall be commissionated by the governor, or commander in chief of this dominion, for the time being, by commission, under the seal of the colony, and not otherwise; any four of which said justices (whereof one to be of the *quorum*) shall be sufficient to hear and determine all causes which shall be depending in the said county courts respectively.

Oaths, to be taken by Justices.

II. *And be it enacted, by the authority aforesaid,* That every person which shall, from time to time, or at any time hereafter, be commissionated to execute the office of a justice of the peace, at and before his entring into and upon the said office, shall take the oaths appointed by act of parliament to be taken, instead of the oaths of allegiance and supremacy, and the oath mentioned in an act, intituled, *(a) An act, to declare the alteration in the oath appointed to be taken by the act,* intituled, *(b) An act for the further security of his Majesty's person, and the succession of the Crown in the Protestant line; and for extinguishing the hopes of the pretended Prince of* Wales, *and all other pretenders, and their open and secret abettors, and for declaring the association to be determined;* and shall make and subscribe the declaration appointed by one act of parliament, made in the twenty-fifth year of the reign of the late King *Charles* the Second, intituled, *An act preventing dangers which may happen from Popish Recusants.* And if any person whatsoever shall presume to take upon him the office of a justice of the peace in any county in this dominion, before he shall have taken the said oaths, and every of them, and made and subscribed the said declaration as is afore-directed, every person so presuming to take upon him the execution of the said office, before he shall have taken the oaths, and made & subscribed the declaration afore-mentioned, and every of them, shall, for every such offence, forfeit and pay three hundred pounds *sterling;* one moiety thereof to her Majesty, her heirs and successors; and the other moiety thereof, to him, her, or them, that shall inform or sue for the same: to be recovered by action of debt, in any court of record within this dominion, wherein

---

Notes to Edition 1733.

(a) 1 *Anne*, Chap. 22.
(b) 13 *William* 3, Sec. 1, Chap 6.

no essoin, protection, privilege, wager of law, or any more than one imparlance shall be allowed.

III. *(a) Provided always*, That if the said oaths, declaration, or any of them, shall be abrogated by the authority of the Parliament of *Great-Britain*, or shall become otherwise void, the same shall also be adjudged, deemed, and taken to be abrogated, and become void, in this colony and dominion.

Court Days. IV. *And be it enacted, by the authority aforesaid*, That the said county courts shall be holden upon the several days and times hereafter mentioned, that is to say:

For the county of Henrico, the court shall be held upon the first Monday in every month.

For the county of Charles City, upon the first Wednesday in every month.

For the county of Prince George, on the second Tuesday in every month.

For the county of Surry, upon the third Wednesday in every month.

For the county of Isle of Wight, upon the fourth Monday in every month.

For the county of Nansemond, upon the fourth Wednesday in every month.

For the county of Norfolk, upon the third Friday in every month.

For the county of Princess Anne, upon the first Monday in every month.

For the county of Elizabeth City, upon the third Wednesday in every month.

For the county of Warwick, upon the first Thursday in every month.

For the county of York, upon the third Monday in every month.

For the county of James City, upon the second Monday in every month.

For the county of New-Kent, upon the second Thursday in every month.

For the county of King William, upon the third Thursday in every month.

Notes to Edition 1733.

(a) 4 *Anne*, Chap. 8, after the death of the Queen, an oath instead of the oath prescribed by 1 *Anne*, is appointed to be taken. And see the oaths appointed to be taken by the Statute 1 *Geo*. Chap. 13.

For the County of King and Queen, upon the fourth Monday in every month.

For the county of Gloucester, upon the fourth Thursday in every month.

For the county of Middlesex, upon the first Tuesday in every month.

For the county of Essex, upon the second Thursday in every month.

For the County of Richmond, upon the first Wednesday in every month.

For the county of Lancaster, upon the second Wednesday in every month.

For the county of Northumberland, upon the third Wednesday in every month.

For the county of Westmoreland, upon the last Wednesday in every month.

For the county of Stafford, upon the second Wednesday in every month.

For the county of Northampton, upon the third Tuesday in every month. And

For the county of Accomack, upon the first Tuesday in every month.

V. And that all persons may be the better ascertained when to attend any process or pleas, they shall have depending in the said county courts, or any of them, *Be it enacted by the authority aforesaid,* That the courts of the several counties shall be holden upon the respective days herein before appointed, and shall not be adjourned to any other time than the next succeeding court, which shall be in course, according to this act.

Courts to be held, as above.

VI. *Provided always,* if it should so happen, That all causes depending, or to be depending in any of the said county courts, cannot be heard and determined upon the day herein before appointed for holding the courts respectively; that then, and in such cases, it shall be lawful to and for the justices of such court to adjourn and hold the court *de die in diem,* until all causes and controversies then depending before them, shall be heard and determined, or otherwise continued, according to the due course of law.

Power of adjournment.

VII. *And be it further enacted, by the authority aforesaid,* That the justices of the said county court, or any four of them, as aforesaid, may & shall take cognizance of, and are hereby declared to have full power and lawful authority and jurisdiction to hear and determine all

Four Justices to constitute a Court.

causes whatsoever, cognizable at common law, or in chancery, within their respective counties, except such criminal causes, wherein the judgment, upon conviction, shall be for the loss of life, or member, and except the prosecution of causes to outlawry against any person or persons, and also except all causes of less value than twenty shillings *sterling*, or two hundred pounds of tobacco; all which said causes of less value than twenty shillings *sterling*, or two hundred pounds of tobacco, are hereby declared to be cognizable, and finally determinable by any one justice of the peace.

Jurisdiction.

Proviso, where the sum is reduced by discounts.

VIII. *Provided always*, That if any suit shall be commenced for twenty shillings *sterling*, or two hundred pounds of tobacco, or any greater sum, and upon settling & adjusting accounts, the ballance due, shall be less than those sums, or any one of them; yet judgment shall be granted for such lesser sum; any thing herein before contained to the contrary, notwithstanding.

Authority and jurisdiction of Justices of the Peace.

IX. *And be it further enacted, by the authority aforesaid*, That the said justices of the peace, and every of them, from time to time, and at all times, during their continuance in that office, as well out of court, as within, shall have power to maintain and keep the peace within their respective counties, in which, and in the hearing and determining all causes in court, according to the authority and power herein before mentioned to be granted to and vested in them, or which is or shall be granted to or vested in them by this or any other act, they and every of them shall proceed to do justice to all persons whatsoever, according to law: and to that intent, the said justices of the peace, and every one of them, at his or their entring into and upon the execution of the said office of a justice of the peace, are hereby required and enjoined, under the like penalties and forfeitures as is before mentioned, for not taking the oaths appointed by act of parliament to be taken, instead of the oaths of allegiance and supremacy, (to be recovered and divided in the same manner,) to take the following oaths, and every of them, for the due execution of his and their said office and offices respectively.

THE OATH OF A JUSTICE OF THE PEACE.

Oath of a Justice of the Peace.

YOU shall swear, *That as a Justice of the Peace in the County of A, in all articles in the Commission to you directed, you shall do equal right to the Poor and to the Rich, after your cunning, wit, and power, and according to Law; and you shall not be of council of any quarrel hanging before you; and the issues, fines, and amerciaments that shall happen to be made, and all forfeitures which shall fall before you, you shall cause to be entered, without any concealment or imbezzelling; you shall not let for gift, or other causes, but well and truly you shall do your office of Justice of the Peace, as well within your County Court as without; and you shall not take any fee, gift, or gratuity, for any thing to be done by virtue of your office; and you shall not direct, or cause to be directed, any warrant (by you to be made) to the parties, but you shall direct them to the Sheriff or Bailifs of the said County, or other the Queen's Officers or Ministers, or other indifferent persons, to do execution thereof.* So help you God.

THE OATH OF A JUSTICE OF THE COUNTY COURT IN CHANCERY.

In Chancery.

YOU shall swear, *That well and truly you will serve our Sovereign Lady the Queen, and her People, in the Office of a Justice of the County Court of* A, *in Chancery; and that you will do equal right to all manner of people, great and small, high and low, rich and poor, according to equity and good conscience, and the laws and usages of this colony and dominion of* Virginia, *without favour, affection, or partiality.* So help you God.

X. *And be it enacted,* That it shall and may be lawful for any Justice of the Peace, upon complaint made to him by any person, that his Debtor is removing himself out of the County privately, or hath absconded & concealed himself, so as the ordinary Process at Law cannot be served against him, to grant an Attachment against the Estate of such Debtor, or so much thereof, as shall be of value sufficient to satisfy the Debt of the Party praying such Attachment, returnable to the next County Court; which Estate being so attached, shall be repleviable by security given, and appearance at the said next Court.

Attachments against absconding debtors.

May be replevied.

XI. *Provided,* That before granting such Attachment, the said Justice shall take Bond and Security of the Person praying the same, to pay all damages that

Bonds, on granting attachments.

shall be awarded to the Defendant, in case the Plaintiff, or Person, desiring such Attachment, shall be cast in the Suit.

Rules, for issuing and returning process.

XII. And for the more easy and regular prosecution and determination of all Suits and Actions in the County Courts, *Be it enacted by the authority aforesaid,* That all original Process, either by Writ, Summons, or any other manner or means, to bring any person or persons whatsoever, to answer any action, suit, information, bill, or plaint, in any of the County Courts, and all Executions and Attachments awarded by any of the said Courts, at the Common Law, and all Subpœnas, Attachments, and other Process in Chancery, and all other Process regularly and legally belonging and appertaining to any Cause or Matter depending, or to be depending, in any of the said County Courts, shall be issued by the Clerk of the said County Courts, respectively, and shall also be again returned to the same Office whence they were issued.

Must be executed 3 days before return.

XIII. *And be it further enacted,* That all Process whatsoever, returnable to any County Court, shall be executed at least three days before the Court Day therein mentioned, for the return thereof; and if any Process shall be delivered to any Sheriff, or other Officer, so late that he cannot execute the same three days before the return, then it shall not be lawful for such Sheriff, or other Officer, to execute the same, but he shall make return thereupon, according to the truth of the case: And if any person take out any original Process within three days before a County Court Day, such Process shall be made returnable to the next Court, after the Court Day coming, within three days, as aforesaid, and not otherwise; and all such Process issued and made returnable, otherwise than is herein directed, shall be, to all intents and purposes, null and void.

Proviso, as to criminals.

XIV. *Provided always,* That notwithstanding any thing herein contained, it shall and may be lawful for any Justice or Justices of the Peace, by Warrant under their hand, to cause any Traitor, Felon, Pirate, Rioter, Breaker of the Peace, or other criminal offenders, to be apprehended and brought before the same, or some other Justice or Justices, or before the next County Court, although there shall not be three days between the execution of such Warrant and the day of the return thereof.

XV. *And be it further enacted, by the authority aforesaid,* That the issuing of Process against any Member of Her Majesty's Council, or against the Sheriff of the County, and the proceedings of the Court thereupon, shall be after the same manner in the County Court, as is directed for the General Court; and that upon the Sheriff's attaching the body of any person or persons, and upon such person or persons failing to appear thereupon, the method of process against the Sheriff, his Executors or Administrators, or against his Estate; and also an Attachment for the Bail or Sheriff, or his Executors or Administrators, against the Estate of the person failing to appear, shall be had and pursued after the same manner, as is directed for the General Court.

Process against a Member of the Council, or Sheriff.

XVI. And for the better and more regular prosecution and determination of all Causes in the said County Courts, and for the more exact entring of the Judgments of the said County Courts, and for the preservation of the Records thereof, *Be it enacted, by the authority aforesaid,* That these following Rules and Methods shall be observed, to wit:

That every Plaintiff or Demandant shall file his Declaration one day before the Court; and any person that desires the Clerk to draw his Declaration, shall give directions for the same in writing to such Clerk, at least two days before the Court.

Rules of practice.

That if the Plaintiff or Demandant fails to file his Declaration, or to appear and prosecute his Suit, he shall be Nonsuit.

That where any Nonsuit is awarded by the Court, there shall five shillings be paid for the same, besides costs of Suit.

That the Defendant or Tenant shall prepare his Plea in writing, to the Declaration of the Plaintiff or Demandant.

That the Clerk of the Court do carefully preserve the Declarations, Pleas, and all Evidences, and other Papers relating to any Cause, and that they be all filed together in the Office.

Clerk to preserve papers.

That in all Cases where the Title or Bounds of any Estate in Land is determined, the Pleadings shall be

Land Causes.

all in writing, and shall be entred at large, with the Judgment thereupon, in particular Books set apart for that purpose only.

Criminal cases.

That all Proceedings and Judgments in Pleas of the Crown, for Fines and Forfeitures, and in other matters relating to Her Majesty's Revenues, be recorded in particular Books set apart for that purpose.

Vestries, how sued.

That in all Cases, where any fine is laid upon the Members of the Vestry of any Parish, one Action may be brought against them all jointly.

Minutes, to be read and signed.

And for prevention of errors in entring the Judgments of the County Courts, the Justices, before they adjourn the Court, shall cause the Minutes of their Proceedings to be publicly read by the Clerk, and corrected as occasion shall require; and then the same shall be signed by the First Justice in Commission, present at such Reading and Correction; which Minutes so signed, shall be taken in a Book, and carefully preserved amongst the Records; and no Proceedings or Judgments of any Court shall be of force or valid, until they be so read and signed, as aforesaid.

Special bail, when liable.

XVII. *And be it further enacted,* That the person who shall become Special Bail in any Personal Action, shall be liable for satisfying the Judgment that shall be given against the Defendant, unless he shall render his body in execution in discharge of his bail; and if in any personal action, the Plaintiff shall move, that the Defendant may be obliged to give special bail for satisfying the Judgment, it shall and may be lawful for the Court where such action shall be depending, if they see cause, to commit the Defendant to the Custody of the Sheriff, until he shall give sufficient bail accordingly.

Court may rule to bail.

No special bail for breach of penal laws.

XVIII. *Provided,* That no person shall be obliged to give Special Bail in any Suit that shall be depending for the breach of a Penal Law.

Dilatory pleas.

XIX. And forasmuch, as by exceptions taken to Declarations by Delatory Pleas, Justice is often delaied, to the great vexation and unnecessary charge of Her Majesty's good Subjects, *Be it therefore enacted,* That in all personal actions where the Declaration shall plainly set forth all matters of substance required therein, to proceed upon the merits of the cause, the Suit shall not abate for want of form.

XX. *And be it further enacted*, That no Process depending in any County Court shall be discontinued, for or by reason of the Justices failing to hold Court upon the day appointed for the same by this Act; but in case of such failure, all suits, process, matters, and things depending, shall be continued, and all returns and appearances shall be made to the next succeeding Court, in the same manner as if such succeeding Court had been the same Court, whereto such suits, process, matters, and things were continued, or whereto such returns and appearances should otherwise have been made; and all recognizances, bonds, and other obligations for appearance, and all returns, shall be of the same force and validity to enjoin the appearance of any person or persons at such succeeding Court, as if the same had been expressly mentioned and set down therein: And if any one or more Justice or Justices of the Court shall be a party or parties concerned in any suit, process, matter or thing, depending in any County Court, and there shall not be Justices enow present to make a Court according to this Act, besides such Justice or Justices so concerned; then such suit, process, matter, or thing depending, shall stand continued to the next succeeding Court, as aforesaid; any law, custom, or usage to the contrary hereof, in any wise, notwithstanding. **Discontinuances, not for court failing to set.**

XXI. And for the better discovering the truth in matters of fact to be tried in the County Courts, *Be it enacted*, That the Rules and Orders hereafter set down, shall be observed, to wit:

That in all cases where witnesses are to appear in the County Court, a Summons shall be issued for the same, by the Clerk of such County Court, for the time being, expressly mentioning the time and place where the witnesses are to appear, and the names of the parties to the Suit wherein they are to give evidence, and at whose request they are summoned. **Witnesses, how summoned.**

That if any witness live in another County than where the Suit is depending, in which his evidence is required to be given, a Summons shall be issued by the Clerk, and signed by one Justice of the *quorum* in the County where the Suit is depending, directed to the Sheriff of the County where such witness resides; which Summons such Sheriff is hereby required to execute: And **Commissions to take depositions, de bene esse, when to issue.**

if thereupon, the witness shall fail to appear, he shall be fined in like manner as is hereafter directed, for witnesses living within the County. And if such witness shall attend, according to the Summons, he shall be allowed for the same, in like manner as is directed for witnesses attending the General Court. And if any such witness shall, by sickness, age, or other disability, be incapable to attend, than it shall be lawful for the Justices of the Court where such witness should have attended, or any two of them, (whereof one to be one of the *quorum,*) to issue one or more commission or commissions for taking the affidavit of such witnesses so incapable to attend in manner as is directed in the like case, for the General Court.

Penalty on witnesses, failing to appear.

That every person summoned as a witness to any County Court, and failing to appear accordingly, and attend the trial, for every such failure, shall forfeit and pay to the party grieved, three hundred and fifty pounds of Tobacco: to be recovered, with costs, by action of debt, in any Court of Record within this Dominion; and shall be further liable to an action on the case, at the suit of the party grieved, for what damages he shall sustain for want of such person's testimony: *Provided always,* That if at the time such person so summoned ought to have appeared, sufficient cause be shewn of his or her incapacity to attend, then no forfeiture or penalty shall be incurred by such failure.

Appeals.

XXII. And for the more regular granting of Appeals from the County Courts to the General Court, *Be it enacted,* That when any person or persons being Defendant or Tenant, in the County Court, shall pray an Appeal to the General Court, such person or persons (before such Appeal shall be granted) shall give Bond, with good and sufficient Security, for the prosecuting the same with effect, and to perform the Judgments of the General Court, and to pay damages, if the Judgments of the County Court shall be affirmed, in manner as is hereafter directed, to wit:

Bond and security.

Damages, in personal and mixt actions.

In all personal and mixt Actions, the damages shall be fifteen *per cent.* upon the principal sum, with all the costs and damages, ordered to be paid by the Judgment of the County Court.

In real actions.

And in every real Action, the damage shall be two thousand pounds of Tobacco, over and above all costs, and other charges and damages, ordered to be paid by the Judgment of the County Court.

And if any person or persons, being Plaintiff or Demandant in the County Court, shall appeal to the General Court, then the same Bail which shall be given for the appearance of the Defendant or Tenant at the County Court, shall also stand bound for the like appearance at the General Court, to answer the Appeal; unless, upon good reason shewn, the County Court shall think fit to direct that Special Bail be given to answer such Appeal.

Bail bond, where plaintiff appeals.

And if any Plaintiff or Demandant shall appeal to the General Court, as aforesaid, he shall give Bond, with Security, in the sum of twenty pounds, current money, that he will prosecute the same with effect; and if he do not appear to prosecute the said Appeal, then the said Bond shall be forfeited to the Defendant or Appellee; and if the Appellant do appear, and upon trial, the County Court's Judgment shall be affirmed; in such case, the Appellant shall pay to the Appellee, fifty shillings, current money, or five hundred pounds of Tobacco, besides all costs accruing on such Appeal.

Penalty of bond, where plaintiff appeals.

XXIII. *And be it further enacted,* That when a Judgment shall be obtained against any person or persons, in the County Court, in any transitory Action, and the person against whom the same is granted, shall remove himself out of that County, so as execution cannot thereupon be served on him, it shall and may be lawful for the Clerk of the Court where such Judgment was granted, to make out, and for any Justice of the Peace of the *Quorum,* in the said County, to sign an Execution against the Body of the said Defendant, and to direct the same to the Sheriff of any County within this Colony; and any Sheriff, to whom the said Execution shall be delivered, is hereby impowered and directed to serve the same upon the Body of the Defendant being within his County, in the same manner, as if the Execution had issued from the Court of the County where such Defendant shall be found.

Executions against a person removing out of his County.

XXIV. *And be it further enacted,* That all and every other Act and Acts, and every clause and article thereof, heretofore made, for so much thereof as relates to any matter or thing whatsoever, within the purview

Repealing clause.

of this Act, is and are hereby repealed, and made void to all intents and purposes, as if the same had never been made.

CHAP. XII.

[From Stat. 21 Jac. chap. 27.]

An Act to prevent the destroying and murdering of Bastard Children.

Preamble.

I. WHEREAS several leud women, that have been delivered of bastard children, to avoid their shame, and to escape punishment, do secretly bury or conceal the death of their children; and after, if the child be found dead, the said women do alledge, that the said child was born dead; whereas it falleth out sometimes, (although hardly it is to be proved) that the said child or children were murdered by the said women, their leud mothers, or by their assent or procurement: for preventing therefore of this great mischief,

Murder to conceal the death of a bastard child.

II. *Be it enacted by the Lieutenant-Governor, Council and Burgesses, of this present General Assembly, and it is hereby enacted by the authority of the same,* That if any white or other woman, not being a slave, after one month next ensuing the end of this present Session of Assembly, be delivered of any issue of her body, male or female, which being born alive, should by law be a bastard, & that she endeavour privately, either by drowning, or secret burying thereof, or any other way, either by herself, or the procuring of others, so to conceal the death thereof, as that it may not come to light, whether it were born alive, or not, but be concealed; in every such case, the mother so offending, shall suffer death, as in case of murder, except such mother can make proof, by one witness at the least, that the child (whose death was by her so intended to be concealed) was born dead.

This act to be yearly read in Churches.

III. And to the end, this Act may be made public, *Be it further enacted, by the authority aforesaid,* That the same shall be read yearly, on some Sunday in May, in all Parish Churches and Chappels within this Colony, by the Minister or Reader of each Parish, immediately after Divine Service, under the penalty of five hundred pounds of Tobacco for every omission and neglect therein: to be recovered, with costs, by the informer, in an action of case, wherein no essoin, protection, or wager of law, or more than one imparlance shall be allowed. And the Churchwardens of every Parish, are hereby required to provide a copy of this Act, at the charge of the Parish, under the penalty of five hundred pounds of Tobacco: to be recovered in manner aforesaid.

CHAP. XIII.

An act for settling the Titles and Bounds of Lands: and for preventing unlawful Shooting and Ranging thereupon.

[See chap. 21, of 1705, and notes.]

I. *BE it enacted, by the lieut. governor, council, and burgesses, of this present general assembly, and it is hereby enacted, by the authority of the same,* That no lands, tenements, or other hereditaments, shall pass, alter, or change from one to another, whereby an estate of inheritance in fee simple, fee tail, general, or special, or any estate for life or lives, or any greater or higher estate, shall be made or take effect in any person or persons, or any use thereof, to be made by bargain and sale, lease and release, deed of settlement to uses of feofment, or other instrument, unless the same be made by writing, indented, sealed and recorded in the Records of the General Court of this Colony, or in the Records of that County Court where the Land mentioned to be granted or passed, shall lie, in manner following, that is to say: If the person or persons who shall make and seal such bargain and sale, lease and release, deed of settlement to uses of feoffment, or other instrument, at the time of such making and sealing shall be resident within this Colony, then the recording thereof, as aforesaid, shall be made within eight months from the sealing and delivery: but if the person so making and sealing, as aforesaid, at the time thereof, shall be resident at any other place, (than within this Colony,) the recording, as aforesaid, shall be made within two years from the sealing and delivery.

No estate of inheritance, or for life, to pass without deed.

Deeds, when to be recorded.

II. *Provided always,* That no such bargain and sale, lease and release, deed of settlement to uses, deed of feoffment, or any other instrument, as aforesaid, shall, by the General Court, or County Court, as aforesaid,

Deeds, how proved.

be admitted to record; unless the same be acknowledged in such Court by the person or persons making or sealing the same, or by some, or one of them, to be his, her, or their proper act and deed; or else, that proof be made of such making and sealing, upon oath, by three witnesses at the least.

Deeds, by husband and wife, to pass the wife's estate.

III. *And be it further enacted, by the authority aforesaid,* That the bargain and sale, lease and release, or other deed or instrument heretofore made, or hereafter to be made, in writing, indented and sealed, both by the husband and the wife, and by them personally acknowledged in the General Court, or County Court, as aforesaid, (the wife being, or having been first privily examined, whether she doth voluntary assent thereto,) shall be, and is hereby declared to be, to all intents and purposes, as valid and sufficient in law, to convey and pass over all the estate, right, title, interest, claim, and demand, which such wife may or shall have in any lands, tenements, or hereditaments, so to be granted, conveyed, and passed over, whether the same be in right of dower, in fee simple, or whatsoever other estate (not being fee tail) she may have therein, as if the same had been done by fine and recovery, or by any other ways or means whatsoever; any law, custom, or usage, to the contrary thereof, notwithstanding.

Estates tail, only barred by act of assembly.

IV. *And be it further enacted, by the authority aforesaid,* That it shall not be lawful, at any time hereafter, for any person or persons whatsoever, to levy any fine, or to suffer any recovery to be had, whereby to cut off or defeat any estate in fee tail, general, or special, of or in any lands, tenements, or hereditaments, within this colony; neither shall any such estates tail be cut off, or otherwise avoided or defeated, by any ways or means whatsoever, except only by an Act of the General Assembly of this Dominion, for the time being, in such particular case, respectively to be had and made. And all and every fine and fines, recovery and recoveries, and every other act and acts, thing and things whatsoever, which shall hereafter be levied, suffered and made, done, performed, or executed, for and towards the cutting off, avoiding, or defeating any estate tail whatsoever, otherwise than by Act of Assembly, as aforesaid, shall be adjudged, deemed, and taken, and are hereby declared to be, to all intents and purposes, null and void; any law, custom, or usage to the contrary thereof, in any wise, notwithstanding.

For prevention of controversies.

V. And whereas, in times past, several persons purchasing Lands in this Colony, have procured their Deeds and Conveyances for the same, to be acknowledged and recorded, but not within six months after the making thereof, as by law (*a*) hath heretofore been required: And some persons have procured their said Deeds and Conveyances to be recorded in other County Courts, than where the Lands have lain, and to be registred in the Council Books; and other persons purchasing Lands, as aforesaid, have taken Deeds and Conveyances for the same, not indented or sealed, or wherein no valuable consideration has been particularly set down and expressed; and some have taken Assignments of Lands only indorsed on the Patents; and others have purchased Lands, and taken Deeds for the same: But by reason of the death of the grantor, or some other such like accident, the said Deeds have not been acknowledged in Court, according to the strict Letter of the Law in that Case heretofore made, but yet have been proved in Court by the oaths of two or more witnesses, and recorded; and others have purchased Lands, and taken Deeds and Conveyances for the same, without livery and seizin being made thereupon in due form of law; by reason of which, several inadvertencies and omissions, many controversies may hereafter arise, to the great grievance and charges of her Majesty's good and lawful subjects of this Dominion: for the prevention thereof,

Former conveyances recorded in the council books, or any county court, declared valid.

VI. *Be it therefore enacted, by the authority aforesaid,* That all Deeds and Conveyances whatsoever, for any Lands within this Colony heretofore acknowledged and recorded at any time after the expiration of the said six months, or registred in the Council Books, or recorded in any other County Court, than where the Lands therein mentioned to be conveyed, have lain, shall be adjudged, deemed, and taken, and are hereby declared to be, to all intents and purposes, as valid and available in Law, and shall enure and take effect as fully and absolutely to the benefit and advantage of all

---

Note to Edition 1733.

(*a*) Quære, by what Law this was required.—(See act 4, of 1656, vol. 1, pa. 417—also act 73, of March, 1661-2, vol. 2, pa. 98.)

persons in possession of any lands claimed thereby, and to their heirs and assigns, as if the same Deeds and Conveyances had been recorded within the said six months, in the General Court, or in that County Court where the Lands have lain, and not otherwise; any law, statute, act, custom, or usage to the contrary thereof, in any wise, notwithstanding. And all Deeds and Conveyances whatsoever, *bona fide*, made for Lands within this Colony, not indented or sealed, or wherein no valuable consideration hath been particularly set down and expressed; and all Assignments indorsed on Patents, shall be adjudged, deemed, and taken, and are hereby declared to be, to all intents, constructions, and purposes, as valid and available in Law, and shall enure and take effect as fully and absolutely to the benefit and advantage of all and every person and persons in possession of any Lands claimed thereby to his and their own proper use and behoof, as if the same Deeds and Conveyances had been actually indented and sealed, and as if a valuable consideration had been therein particularly expressed and set down, and as if the said Assignments had been made, and the Lands therein mentioned, conveyed in due form of law, and not otherwise; any law, statute, custom, or usage to the contrary thereof, in any wise, notwithstanding. And that all Deeds and Conveyances heretofore, *bona fide*, made for any Lands within this Colony, proved in Court by the oaths of two or more credible witnesses, to have been the acts and deeds of the persons therein mentioned to have made, sealed, and delivered the same, and a record thereof made, shall be adjudged, deemed, and taken, and are hereby declared to be as firm, valid, and available in law, to all intents and purposes, and shall enure and take effect as fully and absolutely to the benefit and advantage of all and every person and persons in possession of any Lands claimed thereby to his and their own proper use and behoof, as if the same Deeds and Conveyances had been really acknowledged in Court by the grantor himself in person; any law, statute, custom, or usage to the contrary thereof, in any wise, notwithstanding. And that all deeds & conveyances whatsoever, where livery of seizin might otherwise have been required, heretofore *bona fide* made, by any person or persons, for any lands, tenements, and hereditaments, within this Colony, where the person or per-

Assignments in patents, deeds, &c. confirmed.

sons to whom the same have been conveyed, have actually entred thereupon; and they and those who have their rights, do still continue in possession thereof, by virtue of such Deeds and Conveyances, shall be adjudged, deemed, and taken, and are hereby declared to be, to all intents, constructions, and purposes, as firm and valid in law, and shall enure and take effect as fully and absolutely to the benefit and advantage of all and every person and persons in possession of any Lands claimed thereby, as if livery of seizin had been thereupon made in due form of law, and not otherwise; any law, statute, or custom to the contrary thereof, in any wise, notwithstanding.

Proviso.

VII. *Provided always,* That nothing herein contained, shall be construed, deemed, and taken, so as to confirm any lands, tenements, or hereditaments whatsoever, to any other person than those now in actual possesion thereof, and such as shall, from time to time, or at any time hereafter, claim by, from, or under them; any thing herein contained to the contrary, or seeming to the contrary thereof, notwithstanding.

Livery of seizin.

VIII. *And be it further enacted, by the authority aforesaid,* That when any Deeds or Conveyances for any lands, tenements, or hereditaments, within this Colony, shall hereafter be acknowledged or proved in any Court, in order to be recorded, as aforesaid, the livery of seizin thereupon made (in such cases where the same by law is required) shall also, in like manner, be acknowledged or proved, and shall likewise be recorded, together with the Deed or Conveyance so requiring the same, and whereupon it shall have been made.

[Stat 21, Jac. 1, sec. 1, 2.]

IX. And for the better quieting and avoiding of suits, *Be it enacted, by the authority aforesaid,* That all writs of *formedon in discender, formedon in remainder,* and *formedon in reverter* of any lands, tenements, or other hereditaments whatsoever, at any time hereafter to be sued or brought, by occasion or means of any title or cause heretofore accrued, happened, or fallen, or which may hereafter happen, shall be sued and taken within twenty years next, after the title and cause of action first descended or fallen, and at no time after the said twenty years; and that no person or persons that now hath, or have, or which hereafter may have any right or title of entry into any lands, tenements, or heredi-

Limitation of writs of formedon.

Of entry.

taments, shall at any time hereafter make any entry, but within twenty years next, after his or their right or title hath heretofore descended or accrued, or hereafter shall descend or accrue to the same: and in default thereof, such person so not entring, and their heirs, shall be utterly excluded and disabled from such entry after to be made.

Saving to infants, feme coverts, &c.

X. *Provided nevertheless,* That if any person or persons that is or shall be entitled to such writ or writs, or that hath or shall have such right or title of entry, be or shall be at the time of such right or title first descended, accrued, come, or fallen, within the age of one and twenty years, feme covert, *non compos mentis,* imprisioned, or out of this Colony; that then such person and persons, and his and their heir or heirs, shall or may, notwithstanding the said twenty years are expired, bring his actions, or make his entry, as he might have done before this act, so as such person and persons, or his or their heir and heirs, shall within ten years next, after his or their full age, discoverture, coming of sound mind, enlargement out of prison, or coming into this dominion, or death, take benefit of, and sue for the same, and at no time after the said ten years.

Limitation of writs of right.

XI. *And be it further enacted, by the authority aforesaid,* That no manner of person or persons shall from henceforth, sue, have, or maintain any writ of right, or make any prescription, title, or claim, to or for any lands, tenements, rents, annuities, or other hereditaments, of the possession of his or their ancestor or predecessor, but only of the seizin or possession of his ancestor or predecessor, which hath been, or now is, or shall be seized of the said lands, tenements, rents, annuities, or other hereditaments, within thirty years next, before the teste of the same writ, or next before the said prescription, title, or claim, so hereafter to be sued, commenced, brought, made, or had: And that no manner of person or persons shall hereafter sue, have, or maintain any assize of *mort d'ancestor, cosinage, ayel,* writ of entry upon disseizin done to any of his ancestors or predecessors, or any other action possessory upon the possession of any of his ancestors or predecessors, for any Lands, tenements, or other hereditaments, of any further seizin or possession of his or their ancestors or predecessors; but only of the seizin or possession of his or their

[32 H. 8, c. 2, s. 1.]

[Ibid, s. 2.]

ancestor or predecessor, which was, or hereafter shall be seized of the same lands, tenements, or other hereditaments, within thirty years next before the teste of the same writ hereafter to be brought: And that no person or persons shall hereafter sue, have, or maintain any other action, writ, or suit whatsoever, for any lands, tenements, or other hereditaments, of or upon his own seizin or possession therein, or of or upon the seizin and possession therein, (a) of any other person or persons (whose right he or they shall have) above thirty years next before the teste of the same writ hereafter to be brought. [Ibid. s. 3.]

XII. *Provided nevertheless,* (b) That if any person or persons that is or shall be entitled to such writ or writs of right, assize of *mort d'ancestor, cosinage, ayel,* writ of entry upon disseizen; or that hath or shall have such right to make any prescription, or to have or maintain any other action, writ or suit, as aforesaid, be or shall be at the time of such right or title first descended, accrued, come or fallen, within the age of one and twenty years, feme covert, *non compos mentis,* imprisoned, or out of this Colony; that then such person or persons, and his and their heir and heirs, shall or may, notwithstanding the said thirty years are expired, bring his suit, or make his prescription, title or claim, as he might have done, if this act had not been made, so as such person or persons, or his and their heir and heirs shall, within ten years next after his or their full age, discoverture, coming of sound mind, enlargement out of prison, or coming into this Dominion, or death, take benefit of, and sue for the same, and at no time after the said ten years. Saving to infants, &c.

XIII. *Provided always,* That all persons that are now out of this Colony, and have any pretence of right, title, or claim, to any lands, tenements, or hereditaments, within this Colony, where they, or those, under whom they claim, have not been in actual possession thereof within the space of twenty years last past, shall commence and prosecute their suit for the reco- Saving to persons out of the country.

Notes to Edition 1773.

(a) The sense of this part of the clause is hard to be understood.

(b) This proviso has introduced a great difficulty, in counting in a writ of right, where the demandant is within the benefit of the saving.

very thereof within ten years next coming after the last day of *May*, which shall be in the year of our lord, one thousand seven hundred and eleven, and at no time after the said ten years.

Former patents confirmed.

XIV. And forasmuch, as the right and titles to Lands in this Colony, do originally and chiefly depend on, and are derived from patents granted for the same: For prevention of controversies which hereafter may arise concerning the validity of Patents for Land in this Colony, formerly issued, which are not to be found among the Records in the Secretary's Office, or which have not been duly entred upon Record, or for which no Rights have been obtained, in the manner prescribed by Law,

XV. (a) *Be it enacted, by the authority aforesaid,* That all such Patents for any Lands in this Colony, formerly granted by the Governor, or Commander in Chief thereof, for the time being, shall be held, deemed, and taken, and are hereby declared to be, to all intents, constructions, and purposes, as firm, valid, and available in Law, to convey and assure the Lands therein granted, unto such person and persons as the same shall have been granted unto respectively, and to their heirs and assigns forever, now being in possession thereof, as if such Patents had been legally entred upon the Records in the Secretary's Office, and as if the Rights had been in legal manner obtained for the same, and duly entred upon the Records as they ought to have been; any law, statute, or usage to the contrary thereof, in any wise, notwithstanding.

Patents, &c. to be recorded in secretary's office.

XVI. And upon the passing of any Patent for Land hereafter, the Secretary of this Colony and Dominion, for the time being, is hereby required to cause such Patent to be truly entred upon the Records of his Office, together with the Certificate for Rights, either by importation, or by money paid to the Receiver-General of this Colony, whereupon such Patent shall have been obtained.

Explanation of the proviso, in patents.

XVII. And whereas, in and by Patents granted for Land in this Colony, *It is provided,* That the Patentee or Patentees shall seat and plant the Land therein to him or them granted, within three years from the date

---

Note to Edition 1733.

(a) This clause seems to be useless.

of the Patent: For the better and more certain understanding of the said proviso,

XVIII. *Be enacted, by the authority aforesaid,* That if upon a new Survey of Lands heretofore granted to any person or persons, there shall appear to be a greater number of acres within the bounds expressed, than are mentioned and set down in the Patent; in such case, it shall be lawful for the proprietor and possessor of such Lands, for the time being, to sue forth a new Patent for the same Lands, wherein the just quantity of Land shall be more exactly set down: Yet nevertheless, such proprietor and possessor shall not be obliged to make any new Seating or Planting upon the said Land, for or by reason of the Proviso in such new Patent; but the same shall enure and take effect to his benefit and advantage, as fully and absolutely, to all intents and purposes, as if the said proviso were not mentioned in such new Patent; any thing herein contained to the contrary thereof, in any wise, notwithstanding. And that where any person hath heretofore taken up any Tract or Parcel of Land adjoining to any other Tract of Land theretofore in the possession of such person, and shall thereupon have obtained a Patent, (commonly called a Double Patent,) wherein both Tracts shall have been joined together; in such case, all Patents heretofore so granted, shall be, and are hereby declared to be valid and available in Law, to confirm the same to the Patentee and Patentees, and those claiming under him, her, or them, being in possession thereof, to his, her and their heirs forever, without making any new Seating and Planting, for or by reason of two Tracts being joined in one Patent, as aforesaid; any thing in the said Proviso in the Patent, contained to the contrary thereof, in any wise, notwithstanding.

New patents, for surplus lands.

No new seating on such.

Double patents confirmed, without new seating, &c.

XIX. *Provided always,* That nothing herein contained, shall be construed, deemed, or taken, to give liberty to any person or persons hereafter to sue forth such double Patents, as aforesaid, and to enjoy the Lands therein granted, (by virtue thereof,) without Seating and Planting that part of the Land so taken up, and joined, as aforesaid, to the Land theretofore in his, her, or their possession, according to the said Proviso in the Patent.

Persons hereafter obtaining double patents must seat, &c.

Land not seated, &c. for 3 years, lost.

XX. *And be it further enacted, by the authority aforesaid,* That if any person or persons shall hereafter obtain a Patent for any Tract of Land within this Colony, and shall fail to seat and plant the same within three years, according to the proviso thereof, or shall fail to pay the full quit-rents for the quantity of Land mentioned in his Patent, according to the condition thereof, for the space of three years; such person or persons shall not only lose the Land so granted, and not seated and planted, and for which the quit-rents shall be unpaid, during the space aforesaid, but shall also forfeit and lose all benefit and advantage he might otherwise make by those rights, upon which he obtained such Patent.

[See 7 Geo. 1, c. 2, s. 12.]

How and when patents obtained for lapsed land.

XXI. *And be it further enacted,* That no Patent shall hereafter be granted to any person or persons for any Tract or Parcel of Land, as lost and forfeited, for want of seating and planting, or for not paying the quit-rents, as aforesaid, until three years shall be expired, from and after the date of the first Patent granted for the same, or unless there shall be three years quit-rents in arrear: Neither shall any Patent be granted, by reason of such forfeiture, until Judgment and Certificate obtained from the General Court, shall be procured for the same, in manner following, that is to say: The person desiring such Grant of forfeited Lands, shall first petition the Governor, or Commander in Chief of this Colony, for the time being, and shall, in his Petition set forth, what County the Land lies in, and to whom it was formerly granted, for what cause the same is become forfeited, and in what County the Grantee resides; and the said Petitioner shall, at the same time, file a Copy of his said Petition in the Secretary's Office, whereupon it shall and may be lawful to and for the Clerk of the said Office, and he is hereby authorized and required to issue out a writ to the Sheriff of the County where the Grantee resides, to summon the said Grantee to appear at the next succeeding General Court, on a certain day thereof, to shew cause why such Land formerly granted to him, and by him forfeited, for want of seating and planting, or for nonpaiment of the quit-rents, as the case is, may not be granted to the party petitioning for the same. Which writ shall be served upon such Grantee by the Sheriff, or Under-Sheriff of the respective County where he re-

Method of obtaining patents for lapsed lands.

sides; and if, upon the return thereof so served, the Grantee do not appear, or some other person in his behalf, and make sufficient proof, that the Land petitioned for, hath been seated and planted, or that the quit-rents hath been duly paid for the same, as the case is, then the General Court shall adjudge the said Lands to be forfeited and vested again in the Crown, and shall cause an Order or Judgment to be entred accordingly, and shall certify the same to the Governor or Commander in Chief of this Dominion, for the time being; and also, that it doth appear to them, that the then prosecutor was the first Petitioner for the said Land, and hath pursued the same with effect: which Certificate shall entitle the party obtaining the same to have a Patent for the said Lands, in the same manner, and under the same restrictions and provisos, as Lands not before patented. And if there shall happen to be a greater quantity of such forfeited Land, than shall be granted to the first Petitioner, then the residue of such Land so forfeited, shall be granted to such other person or persons as shall petition for the same, under the like restrictions and provisos, and in the same manner, as Lands not before patented, shall be granted.

Proviso.

XXII. *Provided always,* That if upon trial it shall appear, that such Lands so petitioned for, as aforesaid, shall have been seated and planted by the first Patentee, or those claiming under him, before the exhibiting of such Petition; in that case, such seating and planting, though not made within three years after the date of the Patent, shall be adjudged, and is hereby declared to be a sufficient seating and planting to fulfil the Proviso aforementioned expressed in the Patent.

Saving to infants, feme coverts, &c.

XXIII. *Provided always, and it is hereby declared to be the true intent and meaning hereof,* That where any person shall obtain a Patent for Land, and shall depart this life within three years after the date of the Patent, without seating and planting, or paying the quit-rents, according to the condition and limitation in his said Patent, and the right of inheritance to the said Land, shall descend to any infant under the age of one and twenty years, feme covert, or person out of the country; in that case, the said Land shall not be adjudged to be forfeited for non-paiment of the quit-rents, or for not seating and planting thereon, until three years after the death of such patentee: And if the guardian to such

Guardian or husband, suffering land to lapse, answerable to the heir. [See 11 Anne, c. 4, s. 2, 3.]

infant under the age of one and twenty years, or the husband of the said feme covert, to whom the said Land shall descend, shall suffer the said Land to lapse and become forfeited, for want of seating and planting thereon, or for non-paiment of the quit-rents within the said three years, such guardian and husband respectively, and their heirs, executors, and administrators, shall be liable to answer the full value of the Land so forfeited, unto the heir at law, after his or her coming of age or discoverture.

XXIV. And whereas, divers persons in this Colony have entred for, and obtained patents of swamps, marshes, and sunken grounds, lying adjacent to the high grounds of persons theretofore patented, without the knowledge or privity of the owner of such adjacent high land, to the great prejudice and inconvenience of the owners of such high lands: For remedy whereof for the future,

Marshes, swamps, &c. how taken up.

XXV. *Be it enacted by the authority aforesaid,* That no person or persons whatsoever, shall take up and patent any swamps, marshes, or sunken grounds, lying contiguous to the high land of any person or persons theretofore patented, until such person or persons, intending to take up and patent the same, shall, in the presence of two witnesses, have given notice of such his intention, to the proprietor and possessor, for the time being, in possession of such high land, and until one whole year shall be fully expired from & after the time of giving such notice as aforesaid; and then it shall and may be lawful to and for such person or persons, (having given notice as aforesaid,) and to his, her, or their heirs or assigns, to take up and patent the same: In which patent, shall be particularly expressed and set down, whether the lands therein granted, are swamps, marshes, or sunken grounds, and to whose high lands they are adjoining. And all and every patent and patents which shall be obtained, contrary to the true intent and meaning hereof, are hereby declared to be, to all intents, constructions, and purposes whatsoever, null and void, as if the same had never been made; any law, statute, or usage to the contrary, notwithstanding. And if any controversy shall thereafter arise concerning such notice being given, within five years after such person or persons (having given notice as aforesaid) shall be in actual possession of such swamps.

marshes, or low grounds, as aforesaid, the *onus probandi* shall lie upon the person who ought to have given the notice; and if no such controversy do arise in that time, five years possession shall be held and taken as good proof that notice was given, according to the true intent and meaning hereof.

XXVI. *Provided always*, That nothing herein contained, shall be construed, deemed, or taken, to give liberty to any person or persons to take up and patent any such swamps, marshes, or sunken grounds, lying contiguous to the high lands of any feme covert, infant under the age of one and twenty years, or any person not being *compos mentis*, on pretence, or by virtue of notice being given, as aforesaid, either to such feme covert, infant or person *non compos mentis;* or to the husband, guardian, or other person, being in possession thereof. Saving to infants, &c.

XXVII. And whereas, through the ignorance or negligence of surveyors in former times, divers persons have taken up and held greater quantities of land than are mentioned in their patents or deeds, (and for which they pay no quit rents:) For quieting the possessions of such persons, and for preventing all controversies that may hereafter arise by any person or persons pretending to take up the said surplus land,

XXVIII. *Be it enacted, by the authority aforesaid*, That it shall not be lawful for any person to enter for any parcel of land held of the crown, for or by reason of its being surplus land, until the party intending to take up and patent the same, shall have given notice to the person holding such lands, in the like manner as is herein before directed for marshes, swamps, and sunken grounds, and until one whole year shall be fully expired, from and after the time of giving such notice: And in case the possessor of the said land shall not, within the said year, obtain rights for the said surplus lands and give an account to the sheriff of the county where the said lands lie, of the just quantity held by him, and pay all the quit-rents that shall be due for the same, from and after the publication of this Act, it shall and may be lawful to and for the person who gave the notice, as aforesaid, to survey the said lands at his own charge, and to sue forth a new patent for all the surplus land that shall be found within the bounds of the patent, deed, or other title, or conveyance, by which Surplus land how acquired.

the same is held; which lands shall be granted to him, in the same manner, and under the like restrictions, limitations, and conditions, as lands not before patented.

Proviso.

XXIX. *Provided always*, That it shall be in the power of the patentee or possessor, to assign and allot the surplusage land to the person claiming the same, in what part of the tract he pleases, in one entire piece.

Further proviso.

XXX. *Provided also*, That if upon notice given, as aforesaid, the person in possession shall, within the said year, survey his tract, and it be found that he hath no more land than he pays quit-rents for, the person giving such notice, shall be liable to pay all the charge of the said survey, for his unjust vexation, and be liable to an action on the case, for the same, at the suit of the party grieved; and that in all such new surveys, an allowance shall be made to the patentee or possessor, of five acres for every hundred, for the variation of instruments.

Processioning, how and when to be.

XXXI. And for preventing any controversies that may hereafter arise about the bounds of lands held and possessed by the inhabitants of this colony, *Be it enacted, by the authority aforesaid*, That once in every four years, the bounds of every person's land shall be processioned, (or gone round,) and the land marks renewed, in manner following, that is to say: The court of every county, at some court between the first day of June and the first day of September, which shall be in the year of our Lord God, one thousand seven hundred and eleven, and so between the first day of June and the first day of September, in every fourth year thereafter, by order of court, shall direct the vestry of each parish within their county respectively, to divide their parishes into so many precincts, as to them shall seem most convenient for processioning every particular person's land in their several respective parishes; and to appoint the particular times between the last day of September and the last day of March then next coming, when such processioning shall be made in every precinct; and also to appoint at least two intelligent honest freeholders of every precinct, to see such processioning performed, and take and return to the vestry, an account of every person's land they shall procession, and of the persons present at the same, and of what lands in their precincts they shall fail to procession, and of the particular reasons of such failure: which order shall be signified in writing to the church-wardens of every parish within every respective county within this colony, by the clerk of the court, within ten days after the making thereof; and thereupon, the church-wardens shall cause a vestry to be summoned to meet within ten days after the receipt of such order, at which vestry, the said order of court shall be exactly aud punctually obeyed in every particular; and thereupon notice shall be punctually given by the church-wardens at the church or chapel of the parish, at least three Sundays next before the same is to be performed, of the persons and times so appointed by the vestry, for processioning in every several precinct as aforesaid; and also, the vestry shall cause the accounts of the two honest freeholders of every precinct, made and returned to them, as aforesaid, to be registered in particular books, to be kept for that purpose, by the clerk of the vestry. And to prevent any mistakes or omissions that may happen in every such register, the church-wardens, in presence of the vestry of the parish, shall examine the same, and compare them with the original returns, within six months after such return shall be made, from time to time, and shall accordingly certify the same, by setting their hands to an attestation thereof in the register so by them examined and compared: And that no person may pretend ignorance of his duty herein, the vestries are also to direct what precinct or precincts in their parish respectively, every particular freeholder thereof shall attend and perform the processioning, as aforesaid: And if any parish shall happen to lie in several counties, then the orders of the court of each county shall be signified, as aforesaid, to the church-wardens thereof, as aforesaid, and shall also be obeyed by the vestry, in manner as is before directed; and if any county court shall at any time hereafter fail to perform their duty herein, every justice of the peace in such county shall forfeit and pay the sum of one thousand pounds of tobacco; and if any vestry shall at any time hereafter fail to perform their duty herein, every particular member of such vestry shall forfeit and pay the sum of two hundred pounds of tobacco; and if any church-warden or church-wardens shall at any time hereafter fail to perform his or their

Penalty on justices, &c. for breach of this law.

duty herein, every such church-warden shall forfeit and pay the sum of five hundred pounds of tobacco; and if the clerk of any court shall hereafter fail to perform his duty herein, such clerk shall forfeit and pay one thousand pounds of tobacco; which said forfeitures shall be one moiety to our sovereign lady the Queen, her heirs and successors, for and towards the better support of the government, and the contingent charges thereof; the other moiety to him or them that will inform or sue for the same: to be recovered, with costs, by action of debt, bill, plaint, or information, in any court of record within this dominion, wherein no essoin, protection, or wager of law, shall be allowed.

Absence, &c. when an excuse.

XXXII. *Provided always*, That upon any information brought, or suit commenced, against any justice of the peace, vestryman, or church-warden, for the breach of this act, if the defendant or defendants shall give sufficient evidence to the court where such information or suit shall be depending, that he was necessarily absent from such court or vestry, or that being there, he offered to do his duty in pursuance of this act, then the information or suit shall be dismissed; and if any other person, not having lawful excuse, shall fail to perform his duty herein, every such person shall forfeit and pay the sum of five hundred pounds of tobacco; to be recovered, with costs of suit, by the church-warden or church-wardens of the parish wherein such forfeiture shall be incurred, to be applied for and towards the purchasing of ornaments for the church or chapel of such parish.

Penalty for neglect of duty.

Bounds, three times processioned, unalterably fixed.

XXXIII. *And be it further enacted*, That the procession of the bounds of any person's land, at three several times of processioning, in manner aforesaid, shall be held, deemed, and taken, to be sufficient to settle the bounds, so as the same may never thereafter be altered.

XXXIV. And whereas divers persons, owners of lands in this colony, refuse to suffer their said lands to be processioned, to the great inconvenience and damage of the owners of lands thereto adjoining: For remedy whereof,

Persons refusing to have their land processioned, court shall di-

XXXV. *Be it enacted, by the authority aforesaid*, That if the owner of any lands shall refuse to suffer his lands to be processioned, pursuant to the directions in this act, given, that then, and in such case, the two freeholders appointed to procession the same, shall, within ten days after such refusal, certify the same, under their hands, to the churchwardens of the parish where the said lands shall lie, who shall carry the said certificate to the next sitting of the court, from which the order for processioning the said lands did issue; which said court shall order the surveyor of their county, with a jury, to lay out and procession the lands of the person refusing to suffer his lands to be processioned, at the charge of the person so refusing, and to return the survey thereof, with the proceedings, to the next court after the survey made; which survey and proceedings shall be recorded in the records of the said county court, and a copy thereof shall, by the clerk of the said county court, be sent within ten days after the return of the said survey and proceedings, to the churchwardens of the parish where the said lands shall lie, and shall be registred in the vestry-book of the said parish: And if the lands of the person refusing to suffer such processioning to be made, shall happen to lie in more counties than one, then a certificate shall be made to each of the courts of the said counties, in manner aforesaid; whereupon the court for the county, in which the beginning of the bounds of such lands shall lie, shall order the surveyor, with a jury of their county, to survey and procession the whole bounds of such land, and the sheriff of each of the said counties to attend such surveyor in their respective counties; which survey and surveys, in manner aforesaid made, shall be held, deemed, and taken, to be a sufficient processioning of the said lands, to all intents and purposes, as if the same had been made and done, by and with the consent of the owner of the said lands: And if any justice of the peace, churchwarden, county court clerk, or other person, shall fail to perform his or their duty herein, not having lawful excuse therefore, he and they shall forfeit and pay the like penalties, as are before in this act laid and given on such justice, churchwarden, clerk, and other person respectively, failing to do his and their duty in the due execution of this act: to be recovered in like manner, and to the uses aforesaid.

rect it, at the charge of the party.

XXXVI. *Provided always*, That the procession and settlement of the bounds of any lands belonging to any person, being only tenant for life of the said lands, shall not bar or conclude the heir in reversion or remainder

Heir may controvert bounds within 6 years.

to the said lands, but that such heir may at any time within six years after the death of the tenant for life controvert the said bounds, as if such procession and settlement had never been made.

Saving to infants, &c.

XXXVII. *Provided also*, That the processioning and settling the bounds of any lands belonging to any person, being within the age of one and twenty years, feme covert, *non compos mentis*, imprisoned, or out of the colony, shall not be conclusive to such person, until after the expiration of six years from and after the said several incapacities shall be removed and determined.

[See act of 1705, c. 21.]

XXXVIII. And whereas by an act of assembly, made at a general assembly, begun at the capitol, the twenty-third day of October, in the year one thousand seven hundred and five, intituled, *An act concerning the granting, seating, and planting, and for settling the titles and bounds of lands; and for preventing unlawful shooting and ranging thereupon, It is among other things, enacted*, That the bounds of every person's land in this colony shall be processioned, in manner therein directed: In pursuance of which said act of assembly, the lands of several persons in this colony, have at great charge and trouble been processioned,

Bounds processioned, under act of 1705 confirmed.

XXXIX. *Be it therefore enacted, by the authority aforesaid*, That all and every processioning of lands which shall have been performed and made, in pursuance of, and according to the directions of the said act, shall be held to be good, valid and effectual; and that every procession of land which shall have been made and performed, in pursuance of the said act, in manner thereby prescribed, shall be held, deemed, and taken, and is hereby declared to be one of the three times of processioning the said land, by this act, held, deemed, and taken, to be sufficient to settle the bounds of lands, so as the same may never thereafter be altered.

Hunting, &c. on others land, without licence, penalty for.

XL. *And be it further enacted, and declared*, That if any person or persons shall, at any time hereafter, shoot, hunt, or range, upon the lands and tenements, or fish or fowl in any creeks or waters included within the lands of any other person or persons, without licence for the same first obtaining of the owner and proprietor thereof, every such person so shooting, hunting, fishing, fowling, or ranging, being thereof convict, by confession, or the oath of one witness, shall forfeit and pay, for every such offence, the sum of five hundred pounds of tobacco: to be recovered, with costs, by the person or persons that shall be thereby aggrieved, to their proper use, by bill, plaint, information, or action of debt, in any court of record within this dominion, in which no essoin, protection, privilege, wager of law, or more than one imparlance, shall be allowed; and moreover shall be liable to an action at common law, wherein the party grieved, shall recover his damages. And if any person shall be a third time convicted, in manner aforesaid, of such shooting, hunting, fishing, fowling, or ranging, the justices of that court, over and above giving judgment for the forfeiture, as aforesaid, shall commit such person to the common jail, there to remain until he shall find sufficient sureties to be bound with him in the sum of ten pounds *sterling*, for his good behaviour for one year then next coming; and if he shall, within that time, be found guilty, by confession, or the oath of one witness, of shooting, hunting, fishing, fowling, or ranging, as aforesaid, the same shall be, and is hereby enacted and declared, to be a breach of the good behaviour.

XLI. *And be it further enacted*, That one act of assembly, made at a general assembly, begun at the capitol, the twenty-third day of October, in the year one thousand seven hundred and five, intituled, *An act concerning the granting, seating, and planting, and for settling the titles and bounds of lands; and for preventing unlawful shooting and ranging thereupon*, and all and every other act and acts, and every clause and article thereof, heretofore made, for so much thereof as relates to any matter or thing whatsoever, within the purview of this act, is and are hereby repealed, and made void, to all intents and purposes, as if the same had never been made.

Repealing clause.

Act of 1705, repealed, in part.

CHAP. XIV.

An act for the further restraint of tippling houses, and other disorderly places.

I. WHEREAS, by one act of assembly, made at her Majesty's roial capitol, the twenty-third day of October, in the fourth year of her Majesty's reign intituled, *An act for regulating ordinaries, and restraint of tipling houses*, *It is enacted*, That whosoever shall

Preamble.

Recital of 4 Anne, cap. 40.

retail liquors in their houses, without licence first had and obtained, according to the directions of the said act, shall forfeit and pay two thousand pounds of tobacco: notwithstanding whereof, divers loose and disorderly persons have found means to evade the intent of the said law, by keeping strong drink in their houses, and selling the same out of doors; and by setting up booths, arbours, and stalls, at court-houses, race-fields, general-musters, and other public places, where, not only the looser sort of people resort, get drunk, and commit many irregularities, but servants and negros are entertained, and encouraged to purloin their master's goods, for supporting their extravagancies: For remedy of which abuses,

Penalty for retailing liquors, in houses, booths, arbours, &c.

II. *Be it enacted by the Lieutenant-Governor, Council, and Burgesses, of this present General Assembly, and it is hereby enacted by the authority of the same*, That from and after the publication of this act, no person whatsoever shall sell by retail, any wine, beer, cider, brandy, rum, or spirits, either in houses, or booths, arbours, or stalls, or any other place whatsoever, unless such person or persons shall first obtain a licence for so doing, in the manner directed by the afore-recited act of assembly. And if any person or persons shall take upon them to retail any strong liquors, without having first obtained such licence for the same, every such person or persons so offending, shall be liable to all the penalties and forfeitures contained in the aforesaid act, for selling drink without licence.

Merchants excepted.

III. *Provided always*, That nothing herein contained, shall be construed, deemed, or taken, to prohibit or restrain any merchant, or other person, to sell, in what quantity he pleases, any of the aforementioned liquors, not intended to be tippled or drunk out at the houses, stores, or plantations, where the same are sold.

CHAP. XV.

[From MS]

An act for raising a public levy.

Public levy or taxes, from 1706 to 1710.

BE it enacted, by the Lieut. Governor, Council and Burgesses of this present General Assembly and it is hereby enacted, by the authority of the same, That the sum of nine pounds and a quarter of tobacco be paid by every tythable person within this her majesty's colony and dominion of Virginia, for the defraying and payment of the public charge of the country, being the publick's levy, from the twenty-fourth day of April, one thousand seven hundred and six, to the twenty-fifth day of October, one thousand seven hundred and ten; and that it be paid by the collectors of the several countys to the severall persons to whom it is proportioned by this general assembly: And if it shall happen that there shall be more tythables in any county than the present levy is laid on, then such county to have credit for soe much, to the use of the county; and if there shall happen to be less tythables in any county, then such county shall bear the loss.

And be it further enacted, That there shall be paid to the clerk of the house of burgesses the sume of one thousand pounds of tobacco, and cask, for every copy of the laws of this present session of assembly that shall be sent to the severall county courts; and that the said courts shall raise the same in their county levyes, at the next levy after the receipt of the said copyes respectively.

Fee of the clerk, for a copy of the laws of this session.

CHAP. XVI.

An act to set free Will, *a Negro belonging to Robert Ruffin.*

WHEREAS a Negro Slave, named *Will*, belonging to Robert Ruffin, of the county of Surry, was signally serviceable in discovering a conspiracy of diverse negros in the said county, for levying war in this colony, for a reward of his fidelity and for encouragement of such services,

A conspiracy, having been discovered by Negro *Will*,

Be it enacted, by the Lieutenant-Governor, Council and Burgesses, of this Generall Assembly, and it is hereby enacted, by the authority of the same, That the said Negro *Will*, is and shall be forever hereafter free from his slavery, and shall be esteemed, deemed and taken, and is hereby declared to be a free man, and shall enjoy and have all the liberties, priviledges and immunitys

he is emancipated, as a reward for his services.

of or to a free negro belonging, and shall inhabit, continue and be within this colony and dominion of Virginia, if he think fit to continue therein.

Owner paid. *And be it further enacted, by the authority aforesaid,* That the sume of forty pounds sterling be paid and satisfyed to the said Robert Ruffin for the price of the said negro *Will*, made free as above said, by Elizabeth Harrison, widow and administratrix of the goods and chattles, rights and credits, of Benjamin Harrison, the younger gentleman, decd. late treasurer of the public impositions of this colony, out of the public moneys in her hands.

[From MS.]

CHAP. XVII.

An act to enable Elizabeth Harrison, widow and administratrix of Benjamin Harrison, late of the county of Charles City, gentleman, decd. to sell certain Lands and Slaves, late the estate of the said Benjamin, for payment of the debts of the said Bejamin.

Preamble. WHEREAS Elizabeth Harrison, widow and administratrix of the goods and chattles, rights and credits of Benjamin Harrison, the younger, late of the county of Charles City, gentleman, deceased, hath alledged that the said Benjamin Harrison, her late husband, was seized in fee simple of and in diverse lands and tenements, situate, lying and being in the countys of Charles City, James City, Prince George and Surry, in this colony and dominion of Virginia; as also of and in diverse Negro Slaves to the said Lands appertaining, and did in his last sickness desire certain of his lands and plantations lying on the south side of the river Nottoway, in the said county of Surry, as also twenty of his Slaves to the said plantations appertaining, should be sold, and that the money therefrom ariseing, should be applyed for and towards satisfaction of his just debts; and did direct his will to be made in writing, thereby appointing the same to be performed; and the said Elizabeth Harrison praying to be enabled to sell and dispose of the said plantations and twenty slaves, according to the desire and appointment of her said husband; all which said allegations, being sufficiently proved to be true to the satisfaction of this house of burgesses, as also that the said Benjamin Harrison, at the time of his death, was seized in fee simple of twenty thousand acres of land and of above eighty slaves, and that Nathaniel Harrison, gentleman, next brother to the said Benjamin Harrison, is freely consenting to the passing this act.

Certain lands and slaves of Benj. Harrison, dec. vested in Elizabeth Harrison, his adm'x, with power to sell, &c.

Be it therefore enacted, by the lieutenant-governor, council and burgesses, of this general assembly, and it is hereby enacted, by the authority of the same, That all that plantation, seat, or tract of land, commonly called and know by the name of Rattle hill, situate, lying and being on the south side of the river Nottoway, in the said county of Surry, containing by estimation, two thousand one hundred acres, more or less, and all that the plantation, seat or tract of land, commonly called and known by the name of Hunting quarter, situate, lying and being on the south side the said river Nottoway, in the said county of Surry, containing by estimation, one thousand six hundred acres, more or less, and also all that plantation, seat, or tract of land, commonly called or known by the name of Goodriche's Quarter, situate, lying and being on the south side the said river Nottoway, in the said county of Surry, containing according to estimation, one thousand seven hundred acres, be the same more or less, together with all and singular the edifices, buildings and houses, to the said plantations and seats of land belonging, with the appurtenances; and also twenty negro and mulatto slaves, named as followeth: Cæsar, Ned, Stephen, New England Jack, Michael, Sambo, Cæsar, Dick, Simon, James, Kea, Wasa, Sarah, Betty, Adam, Ben, Roger, Giles, Prue and Phœbe, to the said plantations or tracts of land, or to one of them belonging and appertaining, be and are hereby vested and settled in the said Elizabeth Harrison, and her heirs, as fully and absolutely to all intents and purposes whatsoever, as the said lands and negros and mulattos were vested in the said Benjamin Harrison, at the time of his death, to the uses and purposes hereafter mentioned, that is to say: That the said Elizabeth Harrison, shall and may, as soon as conveniently may be, sell and dispose of all and singular the lands, plantations, slaves and premises hereby vested in her, to the best purchaser and for the best price that may be gott for the same; and that the moneys ariseing by the sale thereof shall by the said Elizabeth Harrison be applyed and disposed of for the paying and satisfying such debts as the said Benjamin Harrison justly owed at the time of his death, and that the surplus of the moneys ariseing by such sale, after the debts aforesaid shall be truly paid, shall remain and be in the hands and possession of the said Elizabeth Harrison, for the use and benefitt of Benjamin Harrison, only son of the said Benjamin Harrison, decd. by the said Elizabeth Harrison, and of his heires to be paid to him when he shall attain to the age of twenty-one yeares.

Surplus, how disposed of.

Proviso.

And if the said Benjamin Harrison, the son, shall depart this life before he attain to the age of twenty-one yeares, aforesaid, or without issue, that then the said surplus shall be paid to Elizabeth Harrison, only daughler of the said Benjamin Harrison, decd. by the said Elizabeth Harrison, his said wife, and to no other use or purpose whatsoever.

And for the better security and satisfaction of the purchasers of all or any of the said lands or slaves,

Purchasers assured of their titles:

Be it enacted, by the authority aforesaid, That all and every person or persons, their heires and assigns, who shall become purchaser or purchasers of any of the said lands or slaves, mentioned or intended to be vested in or conveyed by these presents, to the said Elizabeth Harrison, shall quietly hold and enjoy the same according to their severall and respective purchases, in as full, ample and beneficial manner as the said Benjamin Harrison, decd. could by any conveyance, deed, or writeing, executed in his life time, with the consent of the said Elizabeth Harrison, late his wife, have conveyed the same.

Profits, how appropriated till sale.

Provided always, and it is the true intent and meaning of these presents, That until sale shall be made of the said several lands and tenements, hereby vested in the said Elizabeth Harrison, that the rents, issues and profitts ariseing and accruing by or out of the said lands and slaves, shall accrue and be to the use, benefitt and advantage of such person and persons as the same would have done if this act had not been made.

HISTORICAL DOCUMENTS.

FROM 1682 TO 1710.

[THE troubles produced by Bacon's rebellion, in 1676, had scarcely subsided, when new commotions arose. By an act of 1680, "*for cohabitation and encouragemen of trade and manufacture*," the assembly endeavoured to carry into effect what had long been a favourite project with many of the colonists, that of establishing *towns*. To these TOWNS, *upon paper*, all vessels arriving in the colony were restricted, both in the delivery of their merchandize, and in the receipt of return cargoes; and the planters were compelled to carry all their tobacco and other produce, for exportation, to the same places. While strong inducements were held out to comply with the law, severe penalties were imposed for its infraction: (See the act, vol. 2, p. 471.) The want of accommodation, and proper houses for deposit, added to the difficulty of transporting produce to those places, rendered the execution of the law highly inconvenient, if not wholly impracticable. Masters of vessels, instead of being permitted to coast along our navigable rivers, as formerly, and dispose of their goods, and receive on board the produce of the country, as might be most convenient to their customers, were confined to certain ports, where there was neither shelter for themselves, nor their merchandize. Some absolutely refused to comply with the act, and traded as usual, others abandoned the voyage. Such was the effect, upon the revenue in England, that the law was suspended, by the king in council, in 1681: (See vol. 2, p. 508.) But violations of the law, in Virginia, had led to *prosecutions* for the penalties. *These* were chiefly carried on by interested persons. The low price of tobacco, consequent on this stagnation of trade, the privations of the colonists, and the vexatious prosecutions commenced under the act for establishing towns, excited a general spirit of disaffection. To enhance the price of tobacco, a suspension of its cultivation, then called a *cessation*, was deemed the best expedient. Petitions to the governor, from several counties, to call an assembly, for that purpose, were circulated, and obtained many signatures. An assembly was summoned by the governor, without advice of council, to meet in April 1682. It met accordingly, and after some time spent in fruitless debates, it was dissolved, and another resumoned. Disappointed in their hopes of relief from the assembly, a number of the inhabitants of Gloucester, New-Kent, and Middlesex, which were the petitioning counties, for the call of an assembly, riotously proceeded to cutting up all tobacco plants; to prevent which, several proclamations were issued by the deputy governor. But the principal actors being obscure persons, no prosecutions were instituted, hoping that time would discover the authors and abettors of these outrages: (*See the report of the council on the state of the country*, vol. 2, p. 561.) This *plant-cutting*, gave rise to the act of April 1684, by wihch such offences are declared high treason: (See ante p. 10.)

We have already seen that the immediate actors in the plant-cutting scene escaped prosecution. The vengeance of the government was reserved for some distinguished individual. This was Major *Robert Beverley*, clerk of the house of burgesses. He had incurred the displeasure of the governor and council, by refusing to deliver to them copies of the journal, without the permission of the house: (*See Burk's Hist. Vir.* vol. 2, p. 240.) Notwithstanding the important services rendered by Major Beverley, in suppressing Bacon's rebellion, and which had secured him the confidence and friendship of Sir William Berkeley, the then governor,* yet this conscientous discharge of his duty was construed into a contempt, and drew down upon him the resentment of those in power, who did not fail to add to the catalogue of his offences, every accusation, which the malignity of his enemies could invent.

In the first edition of this work, the editor collected and published, in chronological order, every paper which

* Mr. Burk, in his History of Virginia, vol. 2, p. 240, speaking of the persecutions of Major Beverly, says " This man, *possibly* the same, who acted during the late rebellion, with so much activity and success in the restoration of Sir William Berkeley," &c. The papers now published, at the end of this volume, prove most conclusively that he was the indentical person.

he could find, either in MS. or in the public offices, in relation to the case of Robert Beverley. Since that period, he has received from Robert Beverley, esqr. of Blandfield, in Essex county, the *remnant of a very ancient manuscript*, which seems to have been written by Major Robert Beverley himself, or compiled under his immediate inspection; as it contains as far as the MS. had been preserved, an account of the charges and proccedings against him, with his explanations or defence, opposite each distinct head, in his own words. Unfortunately, the MS., as far as page 18, has been torn off; but sufficient remains to show its correctness, on comparing the part preserved with other papers, collected from the public offices. This MS. is indorsed "*Major Robert Beverley's Testimonies of his Services in the Rebellion*, 1676." Beside these testimonies, consisting of letters from Sir William Berkeley, and other documents, which are preserved entire, it contains, as already noticed, the proceedings against Major Beverley, with his remarks. In the present edition, both the matter comprised in the first edition and in the MS. will be published.]

Extracts from the Records of the General Court, &c.

Robert Beverley committed a prisoner on board the Duke of York.

May the 9th, 1682.—It is the opinion of the board, that Robert Beverley hath been eminently instrumental, in the late commotions, by stirring up informations upon the act of cohabitation, also by setting on foot petitions for an assembly, and from thence giving assurances of a cessation, by which and other practices the inhabitants have been provoked to the present disorder; therefore, he is ordered to be committed a prisoner, by the Sheriff of Middlesex, under safe custody, on board the Duke of York, there to remain, till further order.—[*Bland MS. pa.* 493.]

By his Maj'ties Dep'y Gov'r, &c.

GLOCESTER SCT.

Warrant for Beverley's imprisonment.

You are hereby in his Maj'ties name willed, required and commanded to receive and safely deteine on board your ship Duke of York, the person of Majr. Robert Beverley, committed prisoner on board yo'r ship, by Col. Cuthbert Potter, by warrant from Majr. Genl. Robert Smith, the said Majr. Robert Beverley, according to the said commitment, you are to deteine and safely to secure, until my further order, and for the better performance hereof, and security of the person of Majr. Robert Beverley, most notoriously instrumental in our present distractions, if you have occasion for a guard, upon yo'r application therein to Majr. Genl. Robert Smith, a guard will be ordered; herein you are not to fail, and for your so doeing this shall be yo'r warrant.

Given under my hand, May y'e 12th, 1682.

HEN: CHICHELEY.

To Capt. John Purvis Commander of y'e Ship Duke of York.

[From a book in the office of the General Court, labelled "Depositions, &c." No. 25, pa. 106.]

Smith's order to Purvis to receive him.

These are to will and require you in his Maj'ties name to receive into your custody the body of Majr. Robert Beverley, and him to deteine in safe custody until the Govern'rs pleasure be further known—hereof you are not to faile, as you will answer the contrary, it being by the govern'rs command.

Given under my hand, this 11th day of May, 1682.

ROBERT SMITH.

To Capt. John Purvis, Commander of the Ship Duke of York, or in his absence to the chiefe officer on board y'e said ship.

May y'e 13th, 1682.

Capt. John Purvis,

Smith's letter to Purvis.

I am by command from the govern'r to require you not to permit Majr. Robert Beverley to have any communication with any person, but in your heareing (or some other trusty person whom you shall appoint) nor suffer him either to send or receive any letters but such as I shall first peruse, and for so doing, this shall be yo'r sufficient warrant.

Given under my hand, this 13th of May 1682.

ROBERT SMITH.

To Capt. John Purvis.

I would desire you to shew this order to Majr. Beverley that he may prevent my looking into any of his letters, which I desire not to doe.

May 13*th*, 1682.

Capt. John Purvis,

I have been by you deteined prisoner on board yo'r ship Duke of York, in Rappa. river, from Thirsday night the eleventh day of this instant, May 1682, to this time, being Saturday evening the thirteenth of the said month. I should be wanting to my selfe if I did not demand of you whether you hold me on board your ship, still prisoner, or not, and why you doe it, for I know noe crime I have committed worthy confinement, nor is any to my knowledge laid to my charge, and as I am a free borne subject of England, I ought not to be committed prisoner without deserved crime. Pray lett me have your answere and resolutions in writing, that I may know how to demean, for as I resolve to submitt to due authority, I am also unwilling to suffer wrong. Beverley's letter to Purvis.

Your friend to serve you,

ROBERT BEVERLEY.

To Capt. John Purvis, Commander of the ship Duke of York, in Rappa. River.

May 26*th*, 1682.—Ralph Wormley, esq. Matthew Kemp, and Christopher Wormley ordered to seize the Assembly papers, in the possession of Robert Beverley, and to break open doors, if they are refused.—[*Bland MS. p.* 494.] Certain persons ordered to seize the assembly's papers in Beverley's possession.

Robert Beverley ordered to be delivered, by capt. Purvis, upon Purvis's petition, commander of the Duke of York, to capt. Jefferies, commander of the Concord; and a guard appointed to keep him till further order.—[*Ibid.*] Beverley transferred from the Duke of York to the Concord,

I doe acknowledge that Major Robert Beverley was brought on board my ship Concord by capt. John Purvis, and by an order from the Governor and Councell, without soldiers on the 31st day of May 1682, as witness my hand. Jeffrey's receipt for Beverley.

WILLIAM JEFFREYS.

[From a book in the office of the General Court, labelled "Depositions, &c. No. 25, pa. 107.]

Is ordered to be sent to the Eastern Shore.

June 15th, 1682.—Robert Beverley ordered to be sent prisoner to the Eastern Shoar, and to be conveyed by a guard and the Sheriff of York, on board Col. Custis's sloop, and delivered to the Sheriff of Northampton, and the sheriff of York to return with the guard, and press any sloop.—[*Bland MS. pa.* 494.]

Escapes, and is retaken, and ordered before governor and council.

June the 19*th*, 1682.—Robert Beverley having escaped out of the custody of the Sheriff of York, from on board Col. Custis's sloop, where he was kept in order to be sent over to Northampton, and being again taken at his house in Middlesex, he is ordered to be safely conveyed to James City, and to be brought before the Governor and Council, to receive such further order, as shall be found expedient.

Again ordered to Northampton.

June 25th.—He is again ordered on board Col. Custis's sloop, and to be transported to Northampton, and the master ordered to receive him.—[*Bland MS. pa.* 494.]

Petitions for a *habeas corpus*, which is denied.

September 25th, 1682.—Robert Beverley petitions for a *habeas corpus*, to be directed to the Sheriff of Northampton, which was denied, the whole proceeding being transmitted to his majesty, and his pleasure not yet known.—[*Bland MS. pa.* 495.]

Decision on Robert Beverley's case, suspended till the king's pleasure known.

November the 11*th*, 1682.—Maj. Robert Beverley, being under vehement suspicion of being instrumental in stirring up the late outrages of plant-cutting, and having been committed to the Sheriff of Northampton, till the king's pleasure known, and the board having represented the matter to the king, and the arrival of the lord Culpeper being daily expected, with the signification of the king's pleasure, therefore to procede upon the charge against him would speak want of duty to his majesty, and respect to his excellency. And the board being informed that the said Beverley was at that juncture, at large, which might prove inconvenient, they order him to be taken in custody of the Sheriff of James City, who was ordered to transport him back to the Sheriff of Northampton, by him to he kept until he shall be remanded thence by order of the board.—[*Ibid.*]

Beverley, being at large, is ordered to be committed to the Sheriff of James City, and transported to Northampton.

November 16*th*, 1682.—Robert Beverley, being detained on this side the bay, by contrary winds, is ordered to be committed to the sheriff of York, by him to be kept in such place as he should think fit, till he should be thence remanded.

Being detained by contrary winds, is ordered to be committed to the Sheriff of York.

The following is the order refusing the writ of *habeas corpus:*

Whereas Maj. Robert Beverly, by his attorney Mr. William Fitzhugh, moved that a writ of habeas corpus might be granted him, directed to the Sherriffe of York County, for the removal of his body to James City, to the end he might have a legal tryal, and acquitted, bailed, or remanded to confinement, as in law his cause should merrit, which being granted, the aforesaid Sherriffe, according to the warrant directed to him, brought the body of the above named Robert Beverley into Court, where it was ordered, y't in regard that the said Beverley's offences and misdemeanors were of soe high a nature, y't the same were transmitted to his Majesty for England, whose Royal will and pleasure not being y't signified, but daily expected. It's therefore ordered that the aforesaid Sherriffe of York County take into his custody the body of the aforesaid Majr. Robert Beverley, and to-morrow morning convey him into York county in the custody of which Sherriffe he is to remaine untill he give good and sufficient security to the value of two thousand pounds sterling for his good behaviour, with condition not to stir out of the bounds of Middlesex county (where he is forthwith to repair) and Glouster county untill the second day of the next general court, or sooner, as this court shall think fit to order, att which time he is to make his appearance, and y't in the mean time he be suspended from all offices both civil and military, as well as that of a surveyor as the practice of an attorney.

[Extract from the orders of the General Court of November 28th, 1682, Order Book, No. 5, pa. 55.]

January 10*th*, 1682-3.—Consideration was had about Robert Beverley, and found it could be proved against him,

New charges against Robert Beverley.

That he had broken up public letters directed to the secretary's office, with writs inclosed for the calling the Assembly in April 1682, and took upon him the exercise of that part of the government which belongs to the secretary, but contrary to his;—Sir H. Chicheley affirming that the same was done without his privity, order or consent.

That he had made up the Journal, and inserted his majesty's letter therein, being first communicated to the house of burgesses at their prorogation, after their said prorogation.

That he refused to deliver copies of the journal of the house of burgesses, 1682, to the lieut. governor and council; saying he might not do it, without leave of his masters.—[*Bland MS. pa.* 496–497.]

His conviction, concessions, and pardon.

May 9th 1684.—Robert Beverley being found guilty of high misdemeanors, upon an information of the attorney general, his judgment being respited, and now asking pardon, on his bended knees, his crime is remitted, giving security for his good behaviour.—[*Bland MS. pa.* 501.]

The following is a literal transcript of Robert Beverley's petition, as recorded in a book in the office of the General Court, labelled "Deeds, &c." No. 3, pa. 130.

To his Excellencie Ffrancis Lord Howard Barron of Effingham, his Majesties Lieut. and governor General of Virginia, and to the honourable Councell of State.

Robert Beverley most humbly presenting sheweth,

That the true sence of his misfortunate offenses hath brought him to that degree of compunction, that hee is under an unexpressible sorrow for the same, which is much augmented by the consideration that hee should soe inconsiderately forfeited that esteem from the government that he had with the often hazard of his life endeavoured to purchase, and which had been gratiously laid upon him beyond his deserts, the weight of which consideration is enough to smite him into an abysse of despair; but that the hope hee hath, that hee shall not miss that mercy which is most obviously inherent and an inseparable concomitant in your lordshipps noble breast and those of the honourable his majesties councell of state, here not only buoys him up and withholds him from perishing in that gulph, but also gives him confidence most humbly to address himselfe to your excellency and the honorable court to looke upon him with an indulgent eye, lying at the foote of your justice and most humbly imploring your mercy; this my lord is the only way he hath to approach your lordship by the free confession of his offences and true repentance his heart is filled with, not without almost an assured hope that it will meete with a benigne reception in your lordship's merciful heart, because the King of kings and Lord of lords is well pleased that the prayers, teares and true repentance of every sinner should reach his blessed throne, even to the expiation of their sins and re-establishment in grace.

Your lordship hath been gratiously pleased to assign councell for this your sorrowful petitioner to make his defence in law; but he is resolved not to make use of any meanes either to vindicate himself or to extenuate his crimes, but most humbly to throw himselfe upon the mercy of your lordship and the court, which if your lordship shall be pleased to extend towards him all the days of his life shall be spent in the study to expiate his guilt and truly and faithfully to serve his most gratious soveraigne in a ready and most willing obedience to your lordships and the councells commands with the last drop of his blood and shall most heartily pray for a long and happy raigne to his most excellent majestie and health honor and prosperity for your lordshipp and the councell.

ROBERT BEVERLEY.

May 3d, 1684.

Presented to his Excellencie and Councell in Court by Maj. Robert Beverley upon his bended kness, and was then ordered to be recorded.

E. Chilton, Cl. Gen. Ct.

Death of Beverley.

April 1687.—Robert Beverley, being lately dead, his widow is ordered to deliver the assembly papers, and records, to Ralph Wormley and Christopher Wormley.—[*Bland MS. pa.* 506.]

Clerk of the house of burgesses to be appointed by the governor.

☞ The case of Robert Beverley furnished a pretext to king *James* II, to deprive the house of burgesses of the privilege of appointing their own clerk. Accordingly by a letter addressed to lord Howard, then governor, dated the 1st of August, 1686, reciting the disturbances in Virginia, and the rebellious spirit of the house of burgesses, in doubting the king's prerogative, in the negative power vested in his governor, he expressly orders him "on the convening of assem-"blies, to appoint a fit person to execute the office of "clerk of the house of burgesses, and not to permit "any other person whatsoever, upon any pretence whatsoever to execute that office, and requires the "assembly to make them the usual allowance."—[*Bland MS. pa.* 483, 484.]

Francis Page appointed clk. of the house of burgesses.

April 25th, 1688.—Francis Page appointed [by the governor] clerk of the house of burgesses.—[*Bland MS. pa.* 507.]

April 15*th*, 1691.—Peter Beverley appointed [in like manner] clerk of the house of burgesses.—[*Bland MS. pa.* 512.]

Appeals to the Assembly abolished, by instructions from king Jas. II.

Appeals to the king, in council, limited.

May 23*d*, 1683.—Lord Culpeper communicated to the board, an instruction from his majesty, which directed and appointed that no appeal should be permitted from any order of the governor and council to the assembly as formerly and usually; nor to his majesty in council [a rule formerly to be observed] under the value of one hundred pounds sterling. The council thereupon unanimously return his majesty most humble thanks for his care therein, and withall most humbly propose, having duly considered what great inconveniencies appeals have and may produce, by constraining several honest and indigent persons to be deprived of their just rights and dues, until the appeal be determined, which in all probability cannot be expected, in less time, than a year, that his majesty would be pleased to order, that no appeal be suffered or allowed from an order of the governor and council, under the value of 200*l.* sterling; and that immediately execution may issue on the aforesaid order of the governor and council, if desired, before his majesty's determination; and that the appellant give bond with good security, for payment of the judgment, with double damages, if his majesty should confirm the judgment. And it is further proposed, that his majesty should order proclamation to issue, signifying his will and pleasure, that all appeals from the General Court, depending before the Assembly, should be heard before the Governor and Council.—[*Bland MS. pa.* 199, 500.]

[For the following papers, in relation to the persecutions of Majr. Robert Beverley, the editor is indebted to Robert Beverley, Esqr. of Blandfield, in Essex, who politely favoured him with the fragment of a *very ancient* MS. from which they are printed.]

Major Robert Beverley's Testimonies of his Services in the Rebellion, 1676.

he can pass from James Citty to the place of confinement, appointed by the said order, and to be remanded back in due time, in order to his tryall this ensueing Generall Court, and, missing that, the next succeeding General Court, by appointment of Law, not being to be held, vntill the fifteenth day of Aprill next, and that such confinement soe remote from his dwelling, and the whole and only passage, through rugged and dangerous seas, dureing the whole winter season, will not only be ruinous to his family and creditts, and other estate, but will in all likelyhood, not only returne and bring upon him his late long and dangerous distemper, soe much reigning in y'e county, with which from the last day of July last past, to the twenty-ninth day of the passed October, he hath been constantly afflicted, and is as yet but weakly recouered, but probably, indanger the loss of his life; That, therefore, your honours will please to accept and take such sufficient bayle, as the Law requires for his forth coming and appearance, whensoeuer he shall be called to tryall; which, (if will be accepted, he hath ready now in towne to giue; or, if your honours refuse him that, (as he humbly hopes you will not, for that the Laws allow it,) That then he may be confined in y'e countie

Note, if this petition had been readily granted, then Beuerley had been continued clerk of the assembly, and not impouerished, as, by putting him by that imployment, was effected, not only by the loss of the place, but by keeping from him 14,000*lb.* of tobaccoes, his just due, and soe voted by the burgesses, but stoped from him by the councell.

where he liues, at his owne house, or that being denied, as neer to the same as your, honours shall thinke fitt.

And as in duety bound he shall euer pray.

No. Z. *Att a Councell held at James Citty, Nov. 18th*, 1682.

Note, the Assembly had now chosen and sworn a new clerk, and Beuerley quite displaced there. Note, alsoe, the comittee of the councell, appointed to inspect the matters about plant-cutting, viz. Col. Bacon, Col. Ludwell, Col. Cole, and Col. Page, are now tampering with one Sackler, to haue euidence against Beuerley, and Sackler to saue himselfe, cuningly insinuates into favour, by perswadeing them into a beliefe he can euidence great matters against Beuerley, which makes them keep him neer, to be ready for triall as they see occation.

Whereas, Major Robert Beuerley was by order of this board, comitted prisoner to the sherrife of James Citty county, in order to be transported in either sloop or shallop, to the Eastern shore, and there to be continued 'till order from this board. And whereas, the Right Honorable the Lieutenant-Governor and Councell, are informed, that the aforesaid Major Robert Beuerley, is yett on this side the bay, being hitherto obstructed by the winds; And seeing, that the Generall Court is now neer at hand, this board haue, therefore, thought fitt, and doe hereby accordingly order, that Mr. Richard Moore, under sherrife of York countie, doe take the person of Major Robert Beuerley in his custodie, out of the charge of y'e sherrife of James Citty, where he is now continued, and is hereby ordered to deliuer him, the said Major Robert Beuerley, to the aforesaid Mr. Richard Moore, who is hereby required to continue him in such place, as he shall think most fitt and convenient, while he shall be remanded from him by order of this board.

Copia vera. Test. ED. CHILTON, Cl. Coun.

No. A A. *Att a Generall Court, held at James Citty, November the 29th*, 1682.

Note, that Beuerley though brought into court by the sherrife, was immediately returned into his custodie, without one word said to Beuerley, or his being any

Whereas, Major Robert Beuerley, by his attorney Mr. William Ffitzhugh, moued that a Writt of Habeas Corpus might be granted him, directed to the sherrife of York county for y'e remouvall of his body to James Citty, to the end he might haue a legall tryall, and acquitted, bayled, or remanded to confinement, as in law his cause should merritt; which being granted, the aforesaid sherrife, according to the Writt directed to him, brought the body of y'e aboue named Robert Beuerley into Court, where it was ordered, That in regard the said Major Robert Beuerley's offences and misdemeanors, were of soe high a nature, that the same were transmitted, to his Majesty for England, whose Royall will and pleasure not being yett signified but daily expected. I'ts therefore ordered, that the said sherrife of York countie, take into his custodie, the bodie of the aforesaid Major Robert Beuerley, and to-morrow morning convey him into York countie, in the custodie of which sherrife, he is to remain vntill he give good and sufficient securitie, to the value of two thousand pounds sterl., for his future good behauiour, with bond payable to his Majesty, with condition not to stirre out of the bounds of Middlesex countie, where he is forthwith to repaire, and Glos'tr countie, vntill the second day of the Gen'rall Court, or sooner as this Court shall think fitt to order, at which time he is to make his appearance. And that in the meantime he be suspended from all offices, both millitary and ciuill, as well that of a surveyor, as the practice of an attorney.

Test. ED. CHILTON, Cl. Consl.

waies charged, and this order made, in his absence, and without his knowledge or answer to any thing objected against him.

Note, they haue now found Sacklers cuning, and that he indeed knowes nothing against Beuerley, nor will not be brought to swear against him.

Note, Beuerley is still denied tryall; is confined for five moneths longer, and bound in 2,000*l.* & bond, with able securities for y'e behauiour, and to keep him poor, put by geting his vsual liuelihood, by which he most subsisted, and bound in bond, to desist from geting his lawfull liuelihood, though nothing of crime can be laid to his charge.

No. BB.

Copie of y'e bond.

Know all men by these presents, that Wee, Robert Beuerley, Abraham Weeks, Christopher Robinson of Middlesex countie, gentl'm., Henry Whiteing and John Buckner of Gloster countie, gentl'm., are hereby firmly bound and obliged, to our Soueraigne Lord the King, and his heires and successors, in the penall sume of two thousand pounds sterling. To the true and just payment whereof upon demand, wee binde ourselues, our heires, executors and administrators, joyntly and seuerally firmly by these presents, to our said Soueraigne Lord the King, his heires and successors. As witness our hands and seales, this second day of December, 1682.

The condition of this obligacion is such, that if the aboue bounden Robert Beuerley, shall well and truely futurely demean himselfe, towards his Majesty and all his leig people, presume not to exercise any office, either ciuill or military, nor the profession of an attorney, forthwith repaire into the countie of Middlesex, depart not out of the bounds of the said Middlesex and

Gloecester counties, without liberty of the right honourable the Gouernor and Councell, and appeare on the second day of the next Generall Court, or sooner, as the Governor and Councell shall think fitt, then to answer to all such things as shall be objected against him in the behalfe of his Majestie. That then this obligacion to be void, and of none effict, or elce to stand and be in full force and vertue.

Signed, sealed and deliuered in presence of	R. B. (l. s.)
Arthur Smith,	A. W.
Arthur Allen,	C. R.
Ed. Chilton.	H. W.
	I. B.

To the Right Honourable Henry Chicheley, Knt., his Majestys Lieutenant-Gouernor of Virginia. And to the Honourable Councell of State.

No. C C. Robert Beuerley, humbly sheweth,

Beuerley's petition for inlargement from confinement, preferred to the gouernor and councell, the 30th day of November, 1682, and rejected.

That yesterday afternoone being the 29th of this instant, November, yo'r petitioner, being brought before your Honours sitting in Court, by the sherrife of York countie, by vertue of a writt of habeas corpus, bearing date the 25th day of the said November, in order for tryall, yo'r honours were pleased not to enter vpon such tryall, but to direct, that in regard the offences and misdemeanors (of which your petitioner stands only suspected) were of soe high a nature, that the same were transmitted to his Majesty for England, whose Royall will and pleasure not yett being signified but dayly expected in: that the sherrife of York countie, take into his custody the body of yo'r petitioner, and forthwith to convey him into York countie, there to remaine vntill he giue good and sufficient securitie, to the value of two thousand pounds sterling, for his future good behauiour, with bond payable to his Majesty, with condition not to stirre out of the bounds of Middlesex countie, vntill the second day of the next Generall Court or sooner as yo'r Honours should direct, and then to make his appearance, and that in the meantime, he be suspended from all offices both military and ciuill. In obedience to which order, your petitioner hath endeavoured to gett such securitie here in town, as is thereby required, but findes the same verry difficult to be obtained, on other tearms than for yo'r petitioners ready appearance before your hono'rs, at any time prefix't as your hono'rs shall direct, and in the meantime well to behaue and demean himselfe, and stand suspended, from all offices as the said order directs. Which securitie your petitioner is now ready to produce for your honours acceptance.

And humbly prayes, your honours will order they may be taken now in town, by entering into recognizance as the law directs, and that your petitioner be therevpon at large, soe as he may prosecute his needfull occations, in order to his liuelyhood, and more especially in Gloster and other adjacent counties, where great part of it is well known to lye. For your petitioner most humbly hopes, that this securitie and confinement, (as now orderred) is design'd by your honours, for the securitie and quiett of this gouernment, which, such securitie will binde him to endeavour, and not to doe any perticuler prejudice to your petitioner in his estate and liuelyhood.

And as in duety bound he shall euer pray.

Note, that this petition is rejected, and Beuerley must either enter into the before written bond, of two thousand pounds sterling, to stand confined to two counties, (when 'tis well known he had considerable buisiness in most parts of the countrie; and that he will desist from pursueing the best part of his liuelihood, which noe waies secures his Majesties peace) or he must lie confined in close prisson, as he had soe long time before done.

To his Excellencie, Thomas, Lord Culpeper, Baron of Thorsway, his Majesties Lieftenant and Gouernor General of Virginia.

No. D D.

Robert Beuerley, Most humbly sheweth,

That your petitioner, hath been vnder strict confinement vpwards of seaven months, and at present is rebound to his good behauiour, and limitted to certain bounds with good and sufficient securitie, vnder the high penaltie of two thousand pounds sterling, which your petitioner (being well assured of his owne inocency) thinks very hard, and therefore now humbly implores' your Excellencie will please to call your petitioner to spedy tryall, at which he doubts not to manifest his inocence; or if your lordships more weighty occations, will not suddenly admitt of such tryall, then your petitioner humbly prayes, your Excellencie will please to take of his confinement in the two counties of Gloster and Middlesex, and grant him the libertie of this whole countrey,

Beuerley's petition to his excellencie the lord Culpeper, rejected; presented in December, 1682; soon after his excellencies arriuall in Virginia, by the hand of Mr. Ed Chilton; for that Beuerly could not obtain the fauor of presenting a petition by his owne hand. Soe heinous is he rendered, although inocent of crime, and soe often and soe long denied tryall.

whereby he will be enabled to prosecute the needfull affaires of his liuelihood.

And as in duety bound he shall euer pray.

No. E E.

Beuerley's appearance in Aprill court, and nothing then laid to his charge.

In obedience to the order of the Generall Court, made the 29th of November, 1682, and numbered (AA.) Beuerley keeps within y'e bounds of confinement, and vpon the second day of the next Generall Court, being the 17th day of Aprill, 1683, appeares at the barre before his Excellencie and the Councell, when he is only told, and order is made, that he must attend the Munday following, being the 23d day of y'e said moneth. On the Satterday before the Munday appointed, (in Beuerley's absence,) his day is prolonged to the Wedensday following, being the 25th day of Aprill, and the eighth day of the Generall Court, when vpon his appearance, nothing is laid to his charge, he is told he shall haue the old bond vp, as being an hard and seuere bond, and must enter into another bond, with securities of two thousand pounds sterling for y'e behauiour, and for his appearance when thereto required. See the seuerall orders and bonds hereafter recited.

Att a Generall Court held at James Citty, Aprill the 17th, 1683.

No. F F.

Present his Excellencie and y'e Councell.

Note, Beuerley makes humble promiss of attendance.

Major Robert Beuerley, according to the tenor of his bond, this day made his appearance in open Court, which bond being read, it was ordered that he should attend on Munday next, in order for further proceeding therein.

Copia vera. test. Ed. Chilton, Cl. Consl.

Att a Generall Court held at James Citty, Aprill the 21st, 1683.

Note, this order is made in Beuerley's absence, probably in hopes by delaying time to finde something of euidence against him.

Present his Excellencie and the Councell.

The appearance of Major Robert Beuerley, is referred 'till Wedensday next.

Att a Generall Court held at James Citty, Aprill the 25th, 1683.

No. G G.

Note, that Beuerley findeing by his excellencies words, that the court intended not to bring him to tryall, moued to be heard speak for himselfe, and takeing a paper in his hand, in which he had written down, (to help his memory in,) what he purposed to insist upon, was in friendlywise admonished by his excellency to accept of the tearms offered him, to enter into a more easy bond, on which, he forbore to speak, and submitted to what the court offered; on which submission, this record was made.

Quere, What crime doth Beuerley yet stand charged with, and why if ill behaued, not admitted triall, except because nothing can be made out against him.

PRESENT.

His Excellencie, Tho. Lord Culpeper, Gouernor, &c.

Mr. Secretary Spencer,	Col. William Cole,
Mr. Auditor Bacon,	Ralph Wormley, Esq.
Maj. Gen. Smith,	Col. Richard Lee.
Col. Joseph Bridger,	Col. John Page.
Col. Phillip Ludwell,	Col. William Bird.

Major Robert Beuerley being called into court, according to a former order of this court, was by his Excellencie admonished of his ill behauiour, and what ill apprehensions he lay under. Wherefore it was ordered, that the bond, which he had alreādy entered into should be forthwith discharged, giueing bond, with good and sufficient securitie for his future good abearance towards his Majesty, and all his leig people, for and during the tearm of one yeare and a day, after the date hereof. And for his personall appearance before the Gouernor and Councell when required.

Copia vera. Test. Rowld. Dauis,
Ed. Chilton, Cl. Gen. Ct.

My Lord,

No. H H.

What Beuerley intended to haue said for himselfe in open court, but was prevented.

It pleased yo'r excellencie on Tuesday last was Senitt, being the second day of this court, to command my appearance here at this barre, and then to call for and comand the reading my bond, bearing date the second day of December, 1682; wherein I stood bound with fowre sufficient securities to his Majestie, in the penall sum of two thousand pounds sterling, for the performance of seuerall conditions, therevnto anexed.

Your Excellencie was pleased then to say, that the condition thereof, consisted of diuers parts, the last of which was, that I should make my personall appearance that day in this place, (and the words of the condition are, then to answer to all such things as shall be objected against me on behalfe of his Majesty.) And your excellencie, was pleased to accept, that my appearance, for compliance in that part of y'e condition, but withall to direct and comand my further appearance at this barre, on the Munday following, rendering for reason, that for as much as the condition of the said bond, consisted of diuers parts, and that it was not known, whether they were all complied with, that, therefore, necessary time must be taken to enquire thereof, and then told me that both myselfe and securities stood, therefore, obliged by the said bond, for such appearance on the said Munday.

Your Lordshipp was then alsoe pleased to signifie, in some part his Majesties resentments in Councell, of informations there exhibited, relating to plant cutting, and of his Majesties order therevpon made in Councell, on which your Excellencie was pleased to hint, that proclamacions would shortly be sent to all parts of this, his Majesties countrey, as I should finde. That part of the order of his Majestie in Councell, (for soe in all humillity I apprehend it to be,) which perticulerly relates to me, your Excellencie was pleased to read in Court, and therevpon to prohibite, and comand, that for the time to come, I should not presume to exercise any office of trust vnder his Majestie, in this his countrey, (with perticuler intimation,) noe not that of a notary publique.

My Lord, I receiued the comand with great humillity and cheerfull resolution, to continue in all dutifull obedience thereto, and at that time, (because your lordship had already appointed the Munday following for further examinacion of my compliance with the other parts of the condition of my bond,) I said nothing, to trouble your Excellencie, or spend the Courts time, but humbly submitted, and promised obedience to your Lordships comands. And now I most humbly begg your Excellencie will permitt, my speaking for myselfe, soe farre as I shall keep within the bounds of duety and good maners.

My lord, I belieue it lyes heavy on euery loyall minde, to apprehend himselfe vnder his Majesties disfavour, I am sure 'tis to me soe great a burthen as would sinke me to the ground, had I not the prop of an inocent conscience.

How my heart hath been filled from my youth vp, with loyalty to my king and duety to his ministers, and still continues soe to be, the All-knowing God I call to witness, and appeale to.

My abode in this countrey, hath now been twenty years, in all which I haue not 'till of late, (and that I begg leave to say by mistake,) been accused of the least unduetifulness or misdemeanor, to authority or my neighbour.

From the yeare 1668, to the yeare 1676, I served his Majesty in military and ciuill offices of trust, with fidellity and approbation.

That yeare, (when was more than ordinary tryalls of Loyalty,) how I behaued myselfe, in hazardous service, and with what success, I appeale to the knowledg and relation of his Majesties Councell, here sitting, the magistrates, millitary officers, and euery loyall subject in this his Majesties countrey.

This will be generally testified by great and small, and is soe palpable that the worst and most of all malitious enemies, dare not offer one word in derogation.

What I haue since done or said, or of what I stand accused to his majesty, that hath occasioned, the first and later comands of your Excellencie for incapacitateing me from further services in offices of trust, I am altogether vnknowing of. What informations or euidence hath been taken against me here, before my confinement or since, that hath occationed its soe long continuance, (if any such there be) 'tis not only taken in my absence, but wholly kept from my knowledg, against which I canot, therefore, possibly make any defence, and must consequently lye continued vnder vnavoidable censure.

God knows my inocence; my inocencie giues my minde quiett, and if I may be favoured with your excellencies comands and order, that I may, (at my owne charge,) haue copies from Mr. Secretaries office, authentiquely attested, of such informations or euidence, as hath been giuen and lyes there against me; which I now most humbly sue to your excellencie for; I humbly hope, soe to acquitt myselfe, as that it will appeare to his most Sacred Majesty, to his Ministers and Councell of State in England, to your Excellency and the Councell here, and to all other his Majesties good and loyal subjects, that I haue not been disloyall, tumultuous, or disobedient. And I am sure, (as much as man can be of himselfe,) my resolutions are, in all humillity and due obedience, quietly to submit myselfe to authority, and the remainder of my life, on all occations, to serue my King as a loyall subject, and your Excellencie his Lieftenant, and

Beuerley is still denied the knowledge of informations or euidence made against him.

and all other his magistrates, with due obedience and humble submission.

And as in duety bound euer pray.

May his Majesty long and happily reigne, his laws runn in their due course, and his subjects flourish in their obedience.

No. I I.

Copie of bond for y'e behauiour.

Know all men by these presents, That Wee Robert Beuerley and Cr. Robinson, of Middlesex countie, gentlemen, and John Armisteed and John Smith, of Glocester countie, gentlemen, are hereby firmly bound and obliged, to our Sovereign Lord the King, his heirs and successors, in the penall sume of two thousand pounds sterling, to be paid vpon demand; to the true and just payment whereof, wee binde ourselues, our heires, executors, and administrators, to our said Souereign Lord the King, his heirs, and successors, joyntly and seuerally, firmly by these presents. As witness our hands and seals, this twenty-sixth day of Aprill, 1683.

Quere, if once being called before the gouernor and councell and complying therewith, doe not compleat and fulfill this condition, as to that part. Or is Beuerley bound by the same, times innumerable, and time without limit, to attend whensoeuer called; if soe, he is imprissoned in Virginia dureing life.

The condition of the aboue recognizance is such, that if the aboue bounden Robert Beuerley, shall personally appeare before the Gouernor and Councell, when thereto required, to doe and receiue that, which by the said Gouernor and Councell shall be enjoyned him, and that for and during the full tearm of one yeare and a day after the date hereof, he be of good behauiour, (and doe keep the peace, of our Souereign Lord the King) towards his Majesty and all his leig people. That then this obligacion be void and of none effect, or else to be in full force and vertue.

Signed, sealed and deliuered
in presence of
Ed. Jenings,
Geo. Ludlow,
Ed. Chilton.

R. B. (*l. s.*)
C. R.
J. A.
J. S.

Beuerley, being returned home, thus long put of from tryall, notwithstanding a whole yeare is passed from his first confinement, and three Generall Courts or Goale deliueries passed, to all which he made suite and petition to be tryed, is, the twenty-second day of May following, called before y'e Gouernor and Councell, fifty miles from his dwelling house, by vertue of this following warrant.

By his Excellencie. No. K K.

The Gouernors warrant for Beuerley.

These are in his Majesties name, by and with the advice of the Councell, to will, and require you to sumons Mr. Robert Beuerley, to make his personall appearance before me, and the Councell, on the 22d day of this instant, May, at Green Spring. Herein you may not fayle, as you will answer the contrary at your vtmost perrill. Giuen vnder my hand and the seale of the colonie, this tenth day of May, 1683. Anoq. R. R. Caroli, 2d, y'e 35th.

THO. CULPEPER.

To the Sherrife of Middlesex Countie.

Beuerley appears vpon the warrant, and is demanded these following questions by his Excellencie.

Question.

Why did you break open a pacquett, sent by Sir Henry Chicheley, directed to Mr. Ed. Chilton, clerk of Mr. Secretaries office, wherein were inclosed seuerall writts for electing Burgesses to the Assembly, held in Aprill, 1682.

No. L L.

Answer.

I did it in pure and simple obedience to his honours comands, sent me by Mr. Farmer, his clerk, and (before that,) giuen me himselfe at his owne house, which pacquett was sent open to be delivered me at my house, by his honours said clerk, and by him there sealed and sent me to Glocester Court, with directions to open the same, and to take out and convey such writts as I could with expeditious safety, and to send the rest to Mr. Ed. Chilton at Mr. Secretaries office; but finding none I could safely send forward, I imediately inclosed them in the same couer, and sent them to Mr. Chilton, (as directed,) biding y'e messinger acquaint him, why the pacquett was opened, which was accordingly by him performed, and all the Writts inclosed in that couer went speedily and safely to Mr. Chiltons hand, as the packett was directed and y'e Gouernor comanded me.

This is rendered a comon breaker up of publique pacquetts, and a takeing vpon him the secretaries offices: which God knows was done in pure obedience, as is sufficiently manifested by sending all the Writts to the office, and acquainting the clerk vpon deliuery for what reason the couer was vnsealed.

No. M M.

Mr. Farmer's affidavid about y'e Gouernors pacquett.

Richard Farmer, aged thirty-eight years or thereabouts, deposeth and saith, viz:

That some time in the moneth of February, Ano Domini, 1681-2, this deponent, at the comand of the Right Honourable Sir Henry Chicheley, Knt. his Majesties then Deputie Gouernor of Virginia, with whom this deponent then liued and serued as his clerk, did draw out a forme or rough draught of the Writt for calling the Assembly, the 18th of Aprill, 1682. Which forme or rough draught being well approved of, Sir Henry Chicheley comanded this deponent to engross out faire in writeing one of the said Writts, for euery respectiue countie in this Colonie, and a particular Writt for James Citty, which this deponent haueing done, Sir Henry comanded him to make vp in a pacquett those Writts for y'e Southern counties, viz:

James Citty countie, James Citty, Eliz. Citty countie, Warwick Countie, Henrico County, Charles Citty countie, Surry countie, Isle of Wight countie, Nantzemond Countie, and Lower Norfolke countie.

Note, none of the Writts were taken out by Beuerley, but all sent safe to Mr. Chilton, for that Beuerley could giue none of them a sure and spedie conveyance, according as he was ordered by the Gouernor, and did therefore send them all in the same couer to Mr. Chilton, who had them all delivered to him the next day, and yet Beuerley, (because nothing elce can be found against him) is threatened with a premvnire for this act of obedience; and stands excepted by name in a proclamation of pardon.

And direct the pacquett to Mr. Ed. Chilton, at James Citty, for the more spedy conveyance of them to the sherrifs of the respectiue counties, as they were directed, which this deponent accordingly did. Sir Henry comanding this deponent to carry the said pacquett (unsealed) to Major Robert Beuerley's house, to be by him, (if he thought fitt) perused, sealed and conveyed to Mr. Chilton, from Gloster Court, (which to this deponents best remembrance, was to be the day following) but this deponent being informed at Major Beuerley's house, that he was (the day before,) gone ouer into Gloster, in order to his going to Court, and findeing at Major Beuerley's house, Mr. Tho. Rabley, of James Citty, he, this deponent did, then and there, (according to Sir Henry's comand) seale the said pacquett, and desired Mr. Rabley to deliver it to Major Beuerley, at Gloster Court, (whither he then was going,) together with directions, as well by word of mouth, as by a note or letter, from Sir Henry to Major Beuerley, in case he should be gone before this deponent brought the pacquett to his house, to break open the same, and if he thought fitt, to disperse any of the said Writts, that he would doe it accordingly, if not, that he should forthwith send the pacquett to Mr. Chilton, which (as this deponent hath since been informed,) Major Beuerley then did, and sent the same to Mr. Chilton by Mr. Rabley: All which this deponent, is and shall be ready to averre, justifie and proue vpon oath, if occation shall require.

RICHARD FARMER.

VIRGINIA.

Proclamation, (l. s.)

By his Excellencie. A Proclamtion.

No. N N.

Note, Beuerley was at James town at the Assembly and General Court, from the 18th day of Aprill to the 8th day of May, and the 11th of May made prissoner on board the shipp Duke of York, and kept prissoner on board, and at Accomack vntill the 3d day of November following, which renders it impossible, that he should be assembled or combineing with the plant cutters or plant destroyers, the treuth of which all the Councell well know, and cannot disowne, for that he was dayly in their sight and companie all the whole time.

Whereas, many euill and ill-disposed persons, inhabitants of this colonie, contrary to their duety and allegiance to our Souereigne Lord the King, on the first day of May, in the 34th yeare of the reign of our Soueraigne Lord the King, and since, tumultuously and mutinously assembled and gathered together, combineing, and presumeing to reform this his Majesties Gouerment, by cvting vp and destroying all tobacco plants, and to perpetrate the same, in a traiterous and rebellious maner, with force and arms, entered the plantations of many his Majesties good subjects of this colonie, resolving by open force a generall and totall destruction of all tobacco plants in this his Majesties dominion, to the hazarding the subverssion of the whole Gouernment, and ruin and destruction of these his Majesties good subjects, if by Gods assistance, and the prudent care and conduct of the then Lieftenant-Gouernor and Councell, the mutineers had not been timely suppressed, for which treasons and rebellions against his Majesty, and this his goverment, some notorious actors haue been indicted, convicted, and condemned, and suffered such pains and punishments as for their treason and rebellion they justly deserued. And whereas, I and the Councell are well satisfied, that many of his Majesties good subjects, were preuailed with, and seduced from their allegiance, by the specious (though false) pretences, of the designers and contrivers of those crimes, misdeeds, treasons, and rebellions: And haueing, since, by their dutifull demeanor, manifested themselues sencible of the notoriousness of their crimes, and how lyeable they are to answer for the same according to Law, and those apprehensions lyeing heavie on the spirrits of many his Majesties seduced subjects, which being taken into serious consideration,

I therefore, Tho. Lord Culpeper, Barron of Thorsway, his Majesties Lieftenant and Gouernor Generall of Virginia, out of pitty and compassion to his Majesties seduced subjects, and for the setling and composeing their disturbed minds, haue thought fitt, and in his Majesties name, by and with the advice of the Councell, by this proclamation, doe publish and declare, that all and every person and persons, whatsoeuer, his Majesties subjects of this colonie, who haue ingaged with, or adhered to the said traiterous and rebellious plant cutters and plant destroyers, in the yeare of our Lord 1682, first taking the oath of obedience mentioned in the act of Parliament, made in England, in the third yeare of the reign of his Majesties Royall Grand Father, before two of his Majesties justices of the peace, whereof one to be of the quorum; or in open Court; shall be and hereby are pardoned and forgiuen, all the treasons, rebellions, crimes, and misdeeds, by him or them, acted, done, comitted, or concealed in relation to the said plant destroying and disturbance of his Majesties Gouernment as aforesaid, and shall be free from all punishments, and forfeitures for, or by reason of the same.

Except Richard Bayley, late convicted and condemned for the same; John Hayley, Henry Ismon, and John Wise, who are fled, not dareing to abide their legall tryalls. *As alsoe Robert Beuerley, John Sackler and Thomas Amies.

And to the end all his Majesties subjects, in this dominion, may haue notice thereof, I doe in his Majesties name require and comand, all sherrifs in their respectiue counties, to publish and make known this proclamation, at the Court house, and in all other publique places of the said counties: As likewise all ministers, in their respectiue parishes, to the intent none may pretend ignorance thereof. Giuen vnder my hand and the seale of the colonie, this 22d day of May, 1683. Anoq. R. R. Caroli. 2d, Angliæ, y'e. 35th.

God saue the King.

THO. CULPEPER.

To the Sherrife of —— County, or his Deputie.

* Quere. Doth not the words, (as alsoe Robert Beuerley) as they are placed in this proclamation, declare him to the world to be fledd from justice, not dareing to abide his tryall; and if soe, what great wrong is done him, since he hath all along petitioned for a legall tryall, and hath been three Generall Courts or Goale deliueries, denied and kept from tryall, and still is, vnder pretence of staying to know his Majesties pleasure; but truly because nothing of crime, or couler thereof appears against him.

Beuerley being thus by name excepted in the Proclamation, is not only wronged in his good name, credit, and reputation, but still to keep him poore and vnder the hatches, he is thereby rendered, by those in authority, vnfitt and vncapable to exercise any imployment of profitt, and put by getting his liuelihood, (as formerly he did to a considerable anuall value, not less then three hundred pounds sterling per an.) by pleading as an attorney and practizeing the mistery of a surveyor, besides the loss of his clerks place in the Assembly, worth (to him) about one hundred pounds sterling per an., and that of Deputie vnder the Auditor Generall, for which he had yearly paid him twenty-five pounds sterling, and all grounded on vntrue, and indeed, vncoulerable suggestions.

See the following passages concerning his pleading, offered lately at Gloster Court.

Gloster Countie. Att a Court, held July the 16*th*, 1683.

No. P P.

Passages in Gloster Court, about Beuerley's pleading.

PRESENT.

Col. Lawrence Smith, Capt. Thomas Ramsey,
Lt. Col. Jon. Armisteed, Lt. Col. Tho. Walker,
Lt. Lol. Phill. Lightfoot, Capt. John Smith.

Major Robert Peyton, arresting Edward Bayley to this Court, in an action of trespas, the defendant appeared and offered to answer to the said suite by his attorney, Major Robert Beuerley, vpon which the court put it to the vote.

Whether Major Beuerley may plead at this barre or noe.

And the Justices, thereto, seuerally made answer as followeth.

Captain John Smith, Saith he never did see any thing, that did forbid Major Robert Beuerley from pleading as an attorney, and therefore sees noe reason but why he may plead here.

Lt. Col. Jon. Armisteed, Saith, that although Major Robert Beuerley be excepted in my Lords proclamacion of pardon, yett in his opinion, he ought to vse all honest means for a liuelyhood, and therefore ought to plead any honest cause at this barr.

Lt. Col. Lightfoot, Is of opinion, that Major Robt. Beuerley ought not to plead at this barre.

Lt. Col. Tho. Walker, Saith, I am of Col. Lightfoots opinion.

Capt. Tho. Ramsey, Saith, that he knows nothing to the contrary, why Major Robert Beuerley may not plead in this Court.

Col. Law. Smith's opinion is, That Major Rober Beuerley, being excepted in my Lords pardon, and put by bearing all offices, both millitary and ciuill, ought not to plead in this Court.

* And further saith that if Major Robert Beuerley pleads here, he will not sitt in Court, vntill he hath cleered himselfe of those things he is taxed withall.

Vera Copia, Test. Jon. Buckner, Cl. Consl.

* Note, the rancour of y'e judge against Beuerley, and how like a judge 'tis spoken to the other, his fellow justices, and on the next day he posted to Mr. President of the Councell, with complaint against Beuerley and his fellow justices, who returned this letter to the Court.

To the Worshipfull his Majesties Justices of the Peace in Gloster Countie.

August the 13th, 1683.

Worthy Genttlemen,

I vnderstand at the last Court held for yo'r countie of Gloster, Mr. Robert Peyton, brought his action against Edward Bayley for plant-cutting, and that Major Robert Beuerley, not rightly considering the circumstances he lyes vnder, presumed to appeare attorney at Law for Edward Bayley, in your Court of Gloster, in which I offer to your consideration, Whether it can either be fitt or just to admitt a person to appeare at the seat of justice, an open advocate for another person, when he himselfe is rendered soe obnoxious to gouernment, by proclamation to be excepted from pardon; i'ts such an incongruitie, that it needs not words to sett it forth, especially to Gentlemen of your worth, vnderstanding and loyaltie, and as I canot thinke Major Beuerley will presume to offer at the like practice, whilst as at present circumstanced, soe neither can I doubt your judgments or resolutions to maintain his Majesties authoritie in his Courts, with vnited hearts and mindes, which is intirely wished by,

Gentl'm. yo'r humble servant,

Nicholas Spencer.

As not being enough to hurt Beuerley in his reputation, by wrongfully useing his name in y'e pardon, who they canot finde the least fault in: but he must by that artifice be ruined in estate, by being put by the getting his liuelihood. Note, Virginia allows noe certain attorneys, nor is any fee for pleading allow'd of in y'e bill of costs, but euery man pleads for himselfe or friend according to his abillities: soe that to denie any man to plead for another, is to denie them both euery subjects right.

Quere, What is meant here, by maintaining his Majesties authoritie in Courts with vnited hearts and mindes, except, that all the justices on the bench, must [though against their consciences and better judgments] giue there votes, as they finde the president would have the cause to goe.

Some few Testimonies of Beuerley's Loyaltie and Services, in time of the Rebellion and Generall defection, Anno. 1676.

Virginia.

By the Gouernor and Capt. Generall of Virginia.

Whereas by many frequent, and succesfull services to his Sacred Majesty, this Countrey, and me, his Majesties Gouernor of it; Major Robert Beuerley hath approved himselfe to be most loyall, circumspect, and couragious in his Majesties service for the good of his countrey, and the suppressing this late horrid Rebellion, begun by Bacon, and continued since his death by Ingram, Lawrence, Hansford and others, the last of which he, the said Robert Beuerley, with courage and admirable conduct, neuer to be forgotten, this day brought to me to receiue his sentence, of a traitor and a rebell. For these and many other experiments, of the loyalty, faith, wisdome, care and conduct, of the said Major Robert Beuerley, I doe appoint him to doe and act all things that he shall finde necessary, for his Majesties and the countries service to be done. Willing, requireing, and comanding, all and euery Captain and comander of shipp or shipps, now rideing in this colonie of Virginia, and likewise all and euery planter, that either continues in, or returns to his loyalty, to his most Sacred Majesty, to be aiding and assisting to the said Major Robert Beuerley, and to obey his comands in all things, that may, or shall tend to his Majesties service, and the peace and welfare of this his Colonie. Giuen vnder my hand, in Northampton countie, this 13th of November, 1676. And in the 28th yeare of his Most Sacred Majestie's Raigne.

William Berkeley.
Gouernor of Virginia.

Copie of comission all written by Sir William Berkeley, his owne hand writeing. Note, in those times Beuerley, with a small party of forty, or less, were the only persons that pursued the rebells, and tooke seuerall of their garrisons and chiefe comanders, bringing them prissoners to Accomack to the Gouernor, more perticulerly Tho. Hansford comander in chiefe of four counties, and president of the Court of Sequestrations; Harris, comander in chief of Gloster countie, and Tho. Wilsford, on whom the rebells had great dependence, trusting in his skill to conduct them amongst the remote Indians, in case they should be driven to retreat thither.

By the Gouernor and Capt. Generall of Virginia.

Gentlemen,

The bearer, Major Robert Beuerley, is one of my trusty soldiers and servants, I therefore desire and require you to giue him all creditt and observance due to a faithfull and principall soldier, and to furnish and de-

Note, Beuerley at this time was constantly passing in sloops from place to

place, to pursue and seize the rebells in their guards, the which he effectually performed.

liuer to him, (for his Majesties especiall service,) whatsoeuer armes, amunition, provissions, or other vtensills or necessaries for land or water service, he shall have occation for, and his receipt shall be your sufficient warrant for payment. Giuen vnder my hand this 3d day of November, 1676.

WILLIAM BERKELEY.

To Capt. Saml. Groom, and euery comander, master, merchant, or supercargoe belonging to any shipp, already arrived, or which shall arrive into Virginia.

Letter from Sir Wm. Berkeley to Major Robert Beuerley, then before Wests Pointe, the rebells chiefe garrison, all written by Sir William Berkeley, his owne hand writeing, on receipt whereof Beuerley imediately went down to the Gouernor, then on board Capt. Martins shipp; and was sent one of foure, on board Captain Granthams shipp to discourse Ingram, who without any conditions (other than bare hopes of mercy) gaue vp himselfe and y'e garrison, and armes at Wests Point. Walklase alsoe, and the party of horse with him, submitted themselues, and declared for y'e gouernor.

My Dearest, Most Honoured Major Beuerley,

It is most certain, that Ingram is come down to treat of a peace, but in my opinion it is impossible for him to propose any equall conditions; for one, he offers to bring in Lawrence and Drumer with others, as I heare, for his owne pardon, but this I think is almost impossible for him to effect. I should esteem myselfe the basest ingratefull person aliue, if I concluded any thing without your present approbation and advice, who haue done soe much for me and the countrey: but, for all this treaty, I desire you to doe all things that may turn to the destruction of the enemie, for all this treaty, which, I say againe, I beliue will haue noe effect; 'tis now Friday morning, and I expect Ingram on board Capt. Grantham this day; but I will not speak with him 'till Saterday, in hope you will be downe this Friday night; but leaue such orders that Col. Ludwell and Capt. Potter, and Capt. Laramore, and Capt. Allen, may doe the enemie all the mischiefe they can. I was soe sick yesterday of my feavour, that I could not write to you, but now, God be praised, am pretty well: Pray come down if it be possible, if not send your Counsell and advice. Pray present my service to Col. Ludwell, to whom I would haue you comunicate this letter.

My worthy friend I am, Yours,

WILLIAM BERKELEY.

Friday morning, 29*th November*, 1676.

Major Beuerley,

Yesterday came on board to me, Boodle, and submitted himselfe, and promissed that, this day, his soldiers should lay downe their armes, vpon which I gaue him his pardon, and promissed his soldiers the like provided they deliuered vp their armes: if you finde nothing to doe in Middlesex, you may goe forward and settle what parts you hear is not settled. I am this day intended for Green Spring. I am,

Note, Beuerley, was now sent to settle Middlesex, and the adjacent northern counties, who on his approach, did readily submitt themselues.

Your affectionate friend and servant,
WILLIAM BERKELEY.

January the 18th, 1676.

Deare Major Beuerley,

God Almighty hath been inexpressibly mercifull to this poore countrey, Crows being taken, and Drumer, with the rogueish Monsieur, yesterday executed, and I hope a few dayes will bring in Lawrence, Haley, and Arnold, the chiefe remaining villians; I here finde the people cheerfully come in to my service, and am disarming the rogues, and would haue you take the same course where you are, and secure those magistrate's tobaccoes, who were swearers of the people to Bacon's execrable and treasonable oathes; I am now at Mr. Brayes, just going to Major Page's, where I shall rest this night, and to-morrow intend to Green Spring; I shall be glad to see you soe soone as your business is effected, and would haue those gallant men, who haue, vnder your comand, soe brauely and signally serued his majesty, and me his gouernor, to be my guard, for whom I shall alwaies haue a verry high esteem, and assure you that I am,

Your most affectionate and
Hearty friend and servant,
WM. BERKELEY.

January the 21st, 1676—7.

The northern counties being setled in quiet, Beuerley with the partie vnder him, marches directly to Green Spring, and were imediately made the guard there, dureing the whole sesion of Assembly, and then discharged and ordered pay, and the countrey fully settled in peace and quiet. Note, that Beuerley did not make any seizure vpon this letter, of any mans goods, or tobaccoes, in Middlesex countie or elcewhere; by reason none withstood, but all submitted to the Gouernor.

To his Excellencie, Thomas, Lord Culpeper, Barren of Thorsway, his Majesties Lieftenant and Gouernor Generall of Virginia.

The house of Burgesses, Most humbly present,

That for many years past, they haue been well knowing, and sencibly experienced of the great faithfulness and ready abillities of Robert Beuerley, their clerk, in the due execution of his part of the service of the house and to the great dispatch thereof; for which reason, together with the most signall demonstrations of his loyalty to his Majesty, and good services to this his colonie, this house doe most humbly pray your Excellencies approbation and allowance, that he may be continued therein, it being their vnanimous choice, and that your Excellencie will comand his being forthwith sworn to the execution of that office, by those most worthy gentlemen of the Councell, now appointed to sweare the respectiue burgesses.

And as in duety bound they shall pray.

Signed by order of the House of Burgesses.

THO. BOLLARD, Speaker.

From the house of Burgesses convened at James Citty, the 9th of June, 1680.

Col. Francis Morrison haueing misrepresented Beuerley to his Majesty: his Excellencie, the Lord Culpeper, was by instructions, comanded to disable him from bearing any office of trust, which occasioned this certificate and petition to his Excellencie; on which he was continued in his former offices; and if it will be admitted, nineteen in twenty will yet testifie Beuerley's loyaltie and great services, in the quieting Bacon's rebellion.

Att a Councell held at James Citty. June the 9th 1680.

PRESENT.

Sir. Henry Chicheley, Knight, Lieft. Gouernor.

Col. Nicholas Spencer, Sec.	Col. Joseph Bridger,
Col. Nathaniel Bacon, Aud.	Ralph Wormley, Esq.
Major Gen. Robert Smith,	Col. John Custis,
Col. William Cole,	Major Richard Lee,
Col. Augustin Warner,	Thomas Swanne, Esq.

Vpon the address of the house of Burgesses to his Excellencie, dessireing Major Robert Beuerley to be continued their clerk; the whole Councell by his Majesty appointed for this colonie, doe declare, That vpon their well knowing of Major Beuerley, they are all fully satisfied his integritie, abillity, and loyalty, deserves the character y'e house of burgesses haue represented him vnder; And are of opinion, it will be for his Majestie's, and this colonies service, that he be, by his Excellencie, accordingly admitted to the execution of that place.

Vera Copia. Test. HEN. HEARTWELL, Cl. Con.

END OF THE FOURTH VOLUME.

INDEX

TO THE

THIRD VOLUME

OF THE

Statutes at Large.

ELECTIONS.

EMANCIPATION.

EMBARGO.

ENTRY

LICENCE.

LIMITATION,

LINNEN.

LIQUORS.

LIVERY OF SEIZIN.

LOOK-OUTS,

LORD'S DAY.

LOWER NORFOLK

MANAKIN TOWN.

MANUFACTURES,

MARKETS

MARRIAGES

MARSHES

MARYLAND.

MASTERS OF VESSELS,

TOLERATION.